PENGUIN REFERENCE

The Penguin Dictionary of the Bible

John M. Court was Senior Lecturer and Cl............
University of Kent at Canterbury, where he ....ary
Senior Research Fellow in Biblical Studies a.......................... ..... rreelance
teacher, researcher and consultant. Among his ....al Interpretation:
The Meanings of Scripture, Past and Present (Co............... ...ne Book of Revelation
and the Johannine Apocalyptic Tradition (Sheffie........ ....ress, 2000).

Kathleen M. Court is his wife, who was a teacher for thirty-four years at the Simon Langton
Grammar School for Girls in Canterbury, and latterly Head of the Department of Religious
Education.

The Penguin Dictionary of
THE BIBLE

John M. Court
with Kathleen M. Court

PENGUIN BOOKS

PENGUIN BOOKS

Published by the Penguin Group
Penguin Books Ltd, 80 Strand, London WC2R 0RL, England
Penguin Group (USA) Inc., 375 Hudson Street, New York, New York 10014, USA
Penguin Group (Canada), 90 Eglinton Avenue East, Suite 700, Toronto, Ontario, Canada M4P 2Y3
(a division of Pearson Penguin Canada Inc.)
Penguin Ireland, 25 St Stephen's Green, Dublin 2, Ireland (a division of Penguin Books Ltd)
Penguin Group (Australia), 250 Camberwell Road, Camberwell, Victoria 3124, Australia
(a division of Pearson Australia Group Pty Ltd)
Penguin Books India Pvt Ltd, 11 Community Centre, Panchsheel Park, New Delhi – 110 017, India
Penguin Group (NZ), 67 Apollo Drive, Rosedale, North Shore 0632, New Zealand
(a division of Pearson New Zealand Ltd)
Penguin Books (South Africa) (Pty) Ltd, 24 Sturdee Avenue, Rosebank, Johannesburg 2196, South Africa

Penguin Books Ltd, Registered Offices: 80 Strand, London WC2R 0RL, England

www.penguin.com

First published 2007
1

Set in ITC Stone Sans and ITC Stone Serif
Typeset by Data Standards Ltd, Frome, Somerset
Printed in England by Clays Ltd, St Ives plc

ISBN 978-0-141-01533-0

For Silver

Contents

List of Maps · ix

List of Tables · xi

Introduction · xiii

Acknowledgements · xvi

Abbreviations · xvii

The Hebrew Scriptures · xviii

Old Testament Canon · xix

Old Testament Apocrypha/Deuterocanonical Books · xx

New Testament Canon · xxi

Historical Time Chart for Old and New Testaments · xxii

Maps · xxvi

The Penguin Dictionary of the Bible · 1

Old Testament Texts Quoted in the New Testament · 395

Old Testament Sources of Quotations in the New Testament · 408

List of Maps

The Ancient Near East — xxvi

David's Empire c.1000 BCE — xxviii

The Divided Monarchy c.928 BCE — xxix

Judah after the Exile – post-538 BCE — xxx

Israel/Palestine in Jesus' Time — xxxi

The Mediterranean World – 1st Century CE — xxxii

Egypt and Sinai at the Time of the Exodus — 96

List of Tables

Acts of the Apostles	4
The Hebrew and Gregorian calendars	45
Daniel	70
Ezekiel	99
Hebrews	133
Isaiah	157
Jeremiah	163
Job	173
Gospel according to John	175
Kings of Israel (the United Kingdom)	194
Kings of Judah (the Divided Kingdom)	195
Kings of the Northern (Divided) Kingdom of Israel	195
Gospel according to Luke	210
Gospel according to Mark	218
Gospel according to Matthew	225
Dating Paul's life and times	267
Pentateuch	269
Revelation	304
Romans	307
Old Testament Texts Quoted in the New Testament	395
Old Testament Sources of Quotations in the New Testament	408

Introduction

The most significant point to make at the outset concerns the nature of a Bible dictionary and the expectations of its potential readership. Almost all Bible dictionaries published in the past, and still on the market, seem to me to be essentially Church-based reference works, presupposing a Christian Church tradition of Bible reading, and the desire for some companion volume to provide resources for the Christian reader. Although the Christian Churches are still strong and growing, especially in parts of North America and Africa, outside of these Churches the perspective on the Bible has changed radically in the last decade or so.

The end of the 20th century witnessed an unprecedented and bewildering availability of new translations of the Bible which have 'broken the mould' represented by the King James (or Authorised) Version in the minds of many of the older generation. But the new expressions tend not to be memorable in the same way, do not reverberate within our world, even by comparison with overworked media soundbites. This has created new problems of access to the Bible, such as being sure what is being talked about; the difficulty is no longer in the obscurity of the older language, but rather in the ordinariness of common words, both in scripture and also then in liturgy, which have the task of conveying much deeper meanings than represented by their regular usages. In fact such difficulty resembles the problem faced by the early Christians who wrote the New Testament texts using the common Hellenistic Greek language of their day (admittedly hybridized with echoes of the Old Testament).

Even for those who operate within the tradition of the Christian Churches, recent history has complicated what it means to read the Bible. During the last two centuries the academic approach to the Bible and, as a derivative of this, the approach of many Churches, has been dominated by the scientific approaches of Biblical criticism, with a preponderant interest in the historical setting of the text, as well as an historical investigation of the ways in which the text originated. But in recent years the emphasis of even the historical approach has shifted; as a result of modern pressures, both religious and secular, there is a new interest in the variety of ways in which the Bible has been handled and understood over the centuries since its origins, and the various ways in which it can now be studied. New resources have become available, including both the ancient but sectarian rival to the Jewish traditions found in the Dead Sea Scrolls and the gospels and other early Christian texts alternative to the Biblical canon, and from more or less Gnostic sources, some of which are still coming to light.

Today there is also a fresh and widespread literary interest in the Bible. By this can be meant any interest, whether popular or intellectual, both in the Bible as a written text and also in how such ideas might be disseminated, reprocessed, or indeed criticized, in the whole variety of today's media, including that of popular culture. The focus is on the way any reader might respond to the text, rather than on what the original author might have intended to say. There is, in addition, a more specialist and academic interest in the way that the Bible's traditions have informed, for example, English literature in the past. The complaint of the modern teacher of English literature concerns the lack of resource information about this Biblical basis. A specialized reference work which was designed to meet this need was that of David Lyle Jeffrey, *A Dictionary of Biblical Tradition in English Literature* (Eerdmans, 1992). Equally there is a new interest within the history of art about the vast (and often puzzling) use, and reapplication, of religious images from the Bible, all of which require interpretation and understanding.

To give one example of this shift of attitude from historical to broadly literary questions, the priest poet David Scott wrote:

> Getting back behind the very strong influence of 'scientific' criticism … and entering the pre-Enlightenment world of commentators like Augustine, John Chrysostom and Bede, helped me have a more soul-orientated or poetic approach to reading and using the Bible. Words and phrases roam around both their minds and the Bible itself.
>
> (*Moments of Prayer*, SPCK, 1997)

Many student courses on Biblical texts in schools, colleges and universities are now beginning to reflect this wider, effectively less Church-dominated perspective; such approaches are increasingly popular, particularly in comparative literary studies. The provision of textbooks has begun: for example the series I proposed and then edited for Routledge, New Testament Readings, and its successor series for Ashgate, Testament Studies. These are not so much the traditional commentary (with its theological questions) but rather examples of a way of 'reading' the text which identifies for the student a range of primary issues for attention and discussion, namely the first things one might need to consider when opening the text. I have envisaged this dictionary of the Bible as a complementary work in this situation, providing a kind of safety-net of essential information on the Biblical and other closely related texts, including characters in the stories, key events and concepts, with adequate attention being given to the perspectives and methods of study, and the contribution which other disciplines (archaeological, historical, psychological, sociological, for example) can make to clarify the background and therefore the understanding of the text.

I believe that there is a real need and a wide market for such a dictionary. It can of course benefit existing Church memberships, where knowledge of the Bible may fall short of the comprehensive, but it will also be of much wider general usefulness, granted the more open attitudes to these texts as influenced by the current climate of study. It is important, to this end, that the dictionary reflects in its articles an inclusive and stimulating outlook, raising questions and pointing to the availability of more detailed resources. I have tried to achieve this, though inevitably my own perspectives are reflected in the range and style of the articles that follow.

I have welcomed the challenge to produce such a volume as an (almost) single-handed compiler. The subject area is obviously vast, and needs specific definition and limitation. The text limits would be those of the Biblical canon, but with due recognition of the small body of texts which came close to being included. In this way there is dramatic illustration of diversity of viewpoint within and concerning the texts, then as now. There would be no room for the whole history of Biblical interpretation. The focus would be on the Biblical origins and the present-day use and study of the texts. (One might have to make an exception for the striking detail, such as the influence of Paul's letter to the Romans on key figures such as Augustine, Luther and Wesley.) Inevitably my process of compilation reflects the subjectivity of my personal approach. Because of this I would welcome constructive suggestions towards a revised edition, as well as the identification of errors. I have drawn upon the opinions of several Biblical specialists and gratefully acknowledge their contributions here.

I qualified my role as compiler in the preceding paragraph. At this point I need to record several particular acknowledgements of the substantial assistance I have received. Firstly I must thank my wife Kathleen; I have included her name on the title page because of her invaluable assistance in the latter stages of the preparation of this volume, helping with some articles and a wealth of practical suggestions and constructive ideas, as well as with the checking of Biblical references and other copy-editing tasks.

Secondly I want to express my gratitude for the provision of the invaluable maps in this volume to Dr Geoffery Meaden, who is Principal Lecturer in the Department of Geographical and Life Sciences at Canterbury Christ Church University, and to his technical assistant Mr John Hills. They have responded, with alacrity and attention to detail, to every fluctuating request in the endeavour to ensure that the maps best complement the text.

Thirdly, for the illustrations, I particularly want to thank the artist Peter Clare. Initially I consulted him for help and advice because of his work in religious art, especially the project to illustrate and interpret verse-by-verse the Gospel of Matthew. But subsequently he rose to the challenge of producing this range of drawings to depict both Old and New Testament stories and themes. I am enormously grateful both for his enthusiasm for the project, and also for the rapid delivery of what was needed. Dover Electronic Clip Art (Dover Publications of Mineola, New York) supplied ten more of the illustrations from their collection of *Christian Symbols*, and these are gratefully acknowledged here.

Finally, and certainly not least, I want to record my thanks to the editors at Penguin Group (UK), and especially to Nigel Wilcockson, who issued the initial invitation to undertake this dictionary, clearly shared my optimism for the project, and provided guidance and encouragement at several stages in the process; and to Kristen Harrison, who took over the task in the final stages but brought to it an especially welcome and fresh enthusiasm. Her skills in the preparations for publication, and in the suggestions for mapping and illustrations, as well as for the layout of the volume, were very much appreciated.

John M. Court
Canterbury
January 2007

Acknowledgements

Quotations from the Bible, where used, are taken regularly from the *New Revised Standard Version, with Apocrypha*, copyright © 1989 by the Division of Christian Education of the National Council of the Churches of Christ in the USA. These quotations are used with permission, within the prescribed limits. All rights reserved.

A few other quotations (as indicated in the text) are taken from alternative versions, where a special comparative point is being made. Occasionally the author has used his own translation.

Strenuous efforts have been made by author and publisher to secure any other copyright permissions required from appropriate copyright holders. The author will be grateful to hear from such copyright holders, not so far identified or contacted, so that due acknowledgement may be made in any subsequent edition.

Abbreviations

The names of Biblical books and other texts have been given in full, to avoid the potential confusion which different abbreviations may cause.

Bible references are given in the form '1 Kings 8.27', which means 'the first book of Kings, chapter eight, verse twenty-seven'.

This volume uses the abbreviations BCE (Before the Common/Christian Era) and CE (Common/Christian Era) for dating, as is increasingly the practice in scholarly literature. These are alternative designations for the older BC (Before Christ) and AD (*Anno Domini* = in the year of the Lord).

For reasons of clarity, non-canonical works have been italicized where referred to in the articles, for example '*Romans*' with reference to the letter of Ignatius of Antioch but 'Romans' for Paul's New Testament epistle.

The Hebrew Scriptures

The Law	The Prophets		The Writings
	Former Prophets (i.e. the historical writings)	*Latter Prophets* (i.e. prophetic writings)	
Genesis	Joshua	Isaiah	Psalms
Exodus	Judges	Jeremiah	Job
Leviticus	Ruth	Ezekiel	Proverbs
Numbers	Samuel	*The Twelve:*	Ruth
Deuteronomy	Kings	Hosea	Song of Songs
		Joel	Ecclesiastes
		Amos	Lamentations
		Obadiah	Esther
		Jonah	Daniel
		Micah	Ezra-Nehemiah
		Nahum	Chronicles
		Habakkuk	
		Zephaniah	
		Haggai	
		Zechariah	
		Malachi	

Old Testament Canon

Genesis	2 Chronicles	Daniel
Exodus	Ezra	Hosea
Leviticus	Nehemiah	Joel
Numbers	Esther	Amos
Deuteronomy	Job	Obadiah
Joshua	Psalms	Jonah
Judges	Proverbs	Micah
Ruth	Ecclesiastes	Nahum
1 Samuel	Song of Solomon	Habakkuk
2 Samuel	Isaiah	Zephaniah
1 Kings	Jeremiah	Haggai
2 Kings	Lamentations	Zechariah
1 Chronicles	Ezekiel	Malachi

Old Testament Apocrypha / Deuterocanonical Books

*Books in Roman Catholic
and Greek Bibles*

*Books in Greek but not
Roman Catholic Bibles*

Other Books

Tobit
Judith
Esther (additions)
Wisdom of Solomon
Ecclesiasticus / ben Sirach
Baruch
Letter of Jeremiah (Baruch 6)
Daniel Additions:
  Prayer of Azariah
  Song of Three Jews/
    Children
  Susanna
  Bel and the Dragon
1 Maccabees
2 Maccabees

1 Esdras

Prayer of Manasseh

Psalm 151
(after Psalm 150 in Greek)
3 Maccabees

Slavonic 2 Esdras
  (= 1 Esdras)
Vulgate Appendix
  3 Esdras (= 1 Esdras)
Slavonic 3 Esdras
  (= 2 Esdras)
Vulgate Appendix
  4 Esdras (= 2 Esdras)*
Prayer of Manasseh
  (Vulgate Appendix)

4 Maccabees

* The original 2 Esdras is an apocalyptic work of the 1st century CE, 4 Ezra, with Christian supplementation. It was not part of the Jewish canon. In the Latin Vulgate, Ezra-Nehemiah are counted as 1 and 2 Esdras, hence the subsequent renumbering here.

New Testament Canon

Matthew	Ephesians	Hebrews
Mark	Philippians	James
Luke	Colossians	1 Peter
John	1 Thessalonians	2 Peter
Acts	2 Thessalonians	1 John
Romans	1 Timothy	2 John
1 Corinthians	2 Timothy	3 John
2 Corinthians	Titus	Jude
Galatians	Philemon	Revelation

Historical Time Chart for Old and New Testaments

Dates	Main Empires of the Ancient Near East	Israelite Rulers, Patriarchs, Judges and Kings	Main Events	Important Religious Figures
Old Testament (BCE)				
c.1750–1550	Egypt, Babylon and the Hittites	Abraham, Isaac and Jacob	Nomadic peoples move eastwards from Babylon to Canaan	
		Jacob's 12 sons	Famine drives them to Egypt	
c.1250?			The Exodus and wilderness wanderings	Moses, Aaron the priest
1220–1020	Assyria	Joshua	Conquest and Settlement of Canaan	
		Judges such as Gideon, Deborah, and lastly Samuel		Samuel as prophet/priest
1020–1004		Saul, first king	Monarchy installed by Samuel, to fight against Philistine incursions; Saul's disobedience leads to David being anointed	

	Israel has mini-empire in the absence of a strong external power	Israel	Judah		
1004–965		David		Philistia subdued, capital moved to Jerusalem	Nathan the prophet, Abiathar the priest
965–928		Solomon		Temple built in Jerusalem; many trading opportunities opened up	Zadok the priest
928		Jeroboam	Rehoboam	Kingdom splits N/S, Israel and Judah	
882–871		Omri		Israel dominates Judah and Moab (it is mentioned on the Moabite stone); Omri moved the capital to Samaria	
871–852		Ahab		Joined anti-Assyrian alliance at the battle of Qarqar 853 Pro-Ba'al policies supported	Micaiah the prophet Elijah the prophet Elisha the prophet
842–814	Assyria	Jehu		Elisha engineers Jehu's revolution; Jehu shown paying tribute to Assyria on the black obelisk of Shalmaneser III	
784–748		Jeroboam II	Uzziah 769–743	National revival	Amos, Hosea — prophets in Israel Isaiah – prophet in Judah
733–722	Assyria	Hoshea		Fall of Samaria to Assyria 722 Dispersal of Northern tribes	Micah – prophet in Judah
701			Hezekiah 727–698	Assyria invades Judah – this is also recorded on Sennacherib's prism; Judah was punished for joining Babylon against Assyria	
698–642	Assyria, but Egyptian revival		Manasseh	Much idolatry in Judah	
639–609	Babylon		Josiah	Religious reforms based on rediscovered Torah Fall of Assyrian capital Nineveh, 612, to Babylon	Zephaniah, Jeremiah, Habakkuk — prophets in Judah

Dates	Main Empires of the Ancient Near East	Israelite Rulers Patriarchs, Judges And Kings	Main Events	Important Religious Figures
		Judah		
609–605	Egypt		King Josiah killed in battle of Megiddo by Pharaoh Necho	
598–597	Babylon	Jehoiachin	First fall of Jerusalem 597; king and the cream of educated society are exiled to Babylon; the Temple is largely despoiled	Ezekiel – prophet in exile
596–586		Zedekiah	Second fall of Jerusalem and exile to Babylon; Temple further destroyed; Jeremiah forcibly taken to Egypt by the assassins of Governor Gedaliah *The Exile* Formation of the Pentateuch	Second Isaiah – prophet in exile
540	Persia		Fall of Babylon to Cyrus Jews' return from exile encouraged; policy typical from evidence of Cyrus cylinder	Haggai, Zechariah, Malachi – prophets in Judah Third Isaiah – prophet in Judah
445 onwards			Rebuilding of the Temple Religious reforms in Judah based on the Torah	Nehemiah as governor of Jerusalem, Ezra the scribe 'Jonah'? 'Ruth'?
333	Macedonia/Greece		Alexander the Great's defeat of Persia at Issus; prevalent culture is Hellenism	
	Ptolemies from Egypt rule Judah			

Date		Events	
198	Seleucids from Syria rule Judah	Hellenism aggressively imposed by Antiochus IV Epiphanes; Judaism is persecuted	
167		Jerusalem Temple defiled; result is Maccabean Revolt	'Daniel'?
165–161	Judas Maccabeus	Judah ruled by Hasmonean dynasty	
63	Rome	Pompey enters Jerusalem	
37–34	Herod the Great	Roman client-king appointed	
		Many elaborate building projects including a new Temple in Jerusalem	
New Testament			
6–4 BCE		Birth of Jesus	
	Herod's sons rule parts of his kingdom		
	Philip 4 BCE to 34 CE		
	Antipas 4 BCE to 39 CE		
	Agrippa 4 BCE to 44 CE		
	Archelaus 4 BCE to 6 CE, in Judaea was replaced by procurators including Pontius Pilate		
26–36 CE			Jesus
28–30		Ministry of Jesus	
		Jesus' crucifixion and resurrection	
		Start of the Church	
33		Conversion of S/Paul	Paul
46–47		Church spreads	
		Council of Jerusalem?	
52–60	Antonius Felix	Imprisonment of Paul	
60–62	Porcius Festus	Paul sent to Rome and ?	
64–66	Gessius Florus	First Jewish Revolt	
70		Destruction of Jerusalem	
73		Fall of Masada	

The Ancient Near East

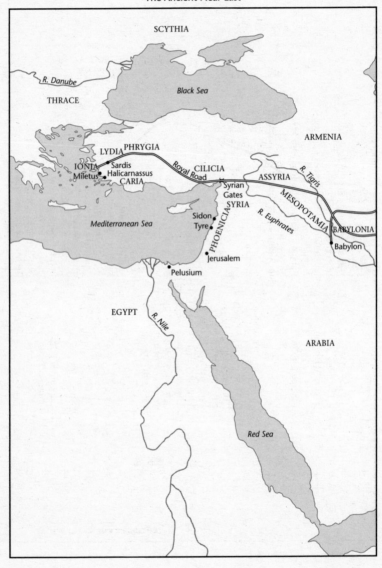

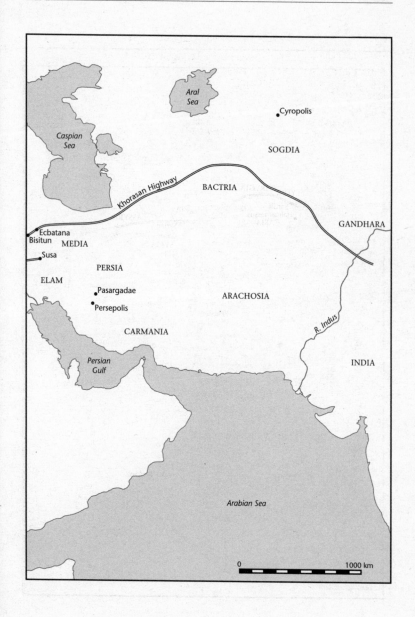

David's Empire c.1000 BCE

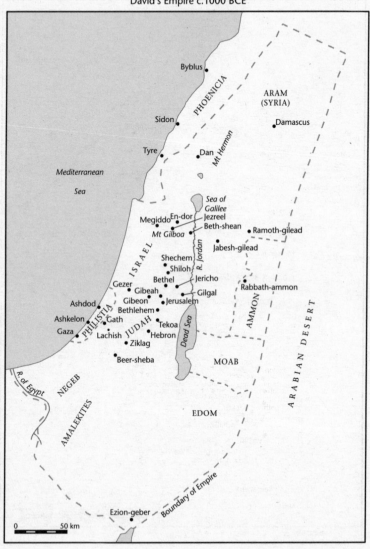

The Divided Monarchy c.928 BCE

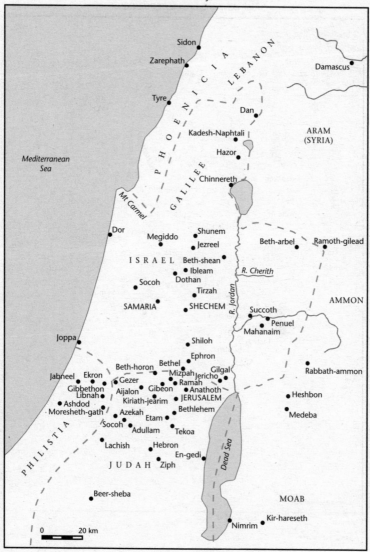

Sidon
Zarephath
Damascus
Tyre
PHOENICIA
LEBANON
Dan
ARAM
(SYRIA)
Kadesh-Naphtali
Hazor
Mediterranean
Sea
GALILEE
Chinnereth
Mt Carmel
Dor
Shunem
Megiddo
Jezreel
Beth-arbel
Ramoth-gilead
ISRAEL
Beth-shean
Ibleam
R. Cherith
Socoh
Dothan
Tirzah
AMMON
SAMARIA
SHECHEM
Succoth
R. Jordan
Penuel
Mahanaim
Joppa
Shiloh
Ephron
Beth-horon
Bethel
Jabneel
Ekron
Mizpah
Jericho
Gilgal
Rabbath-ammon
Gezer
Ramah
Gibbethon
Aijalon
Gibeon
Anathoth
Heshbon
Libnah
Kiriath-jearim
JERUSALEM
Ashdod
Azekah
Bethlehem
Medeba
Moresheth-gath
Etam
Socoh
Adullam
Tekoa
Lachish
Hebron
En-gedi
Dead Sea
PHILISTIA
JUDAH
Ziph
Beer-sheba
MOAB
Kir-hareseth
0   20 km
Nimrim

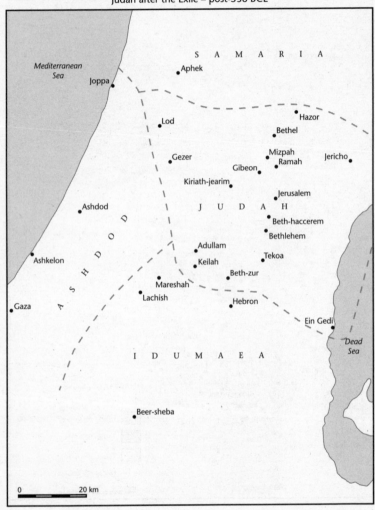

Judah after the Exile – post-538 BCE

Israel/Palestine in Jesus' Time

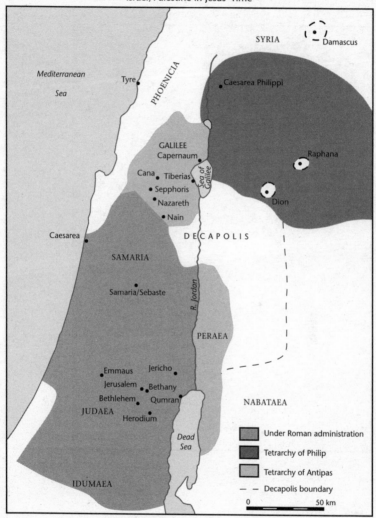

The Mediterranean World – 1st Century CE

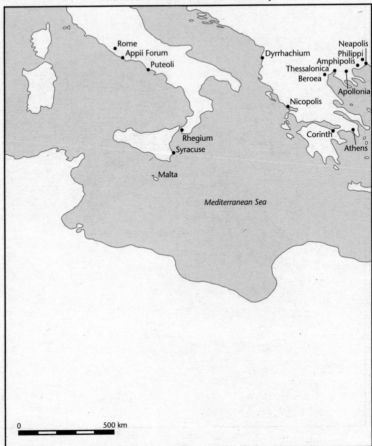

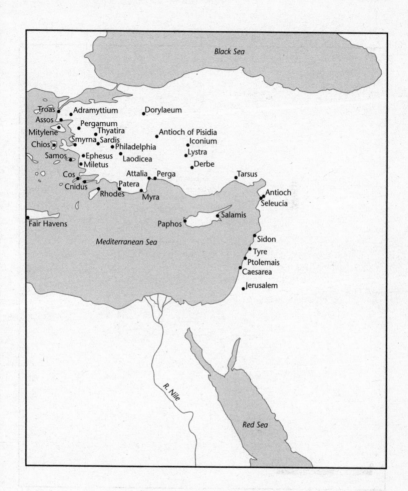

A

Aaron Aaron was the older brother of MOSES, and MIRIAM was their sister (Exodus 6.20; 2.4, 7; 15.20). He was chosen as Moses' spokesman to Pharaoh and to Israel, apparently because of his superior eloquence (Exodus 4.14). Armed with his rod he competed with the magicians of Egypt and instituted several of the PLAGUES on Egypt (see Exodus 7). When Moses went up on Mount SINAI to receive the DECALOGUE (the Ten Commandments), Aaron was far less in control and he yielded to popular pressure to manufacture an idol of a GOLDEN CALF (Exodus 32). Near the traditional site of Sinai to the north-east lies a mound now called Gebel Harun; this is believed to be the location of the Hebrews' camp, and an ancient tomb here is regarded by Christians and Muslims – but not by the Bedouin – as the burial site of Aaron. An alternative site for Aaron's grave, more consistent with Biblical references, is a hill to the north-east of KADESH BARNEA.

According to LEVITICUS (chapter 8) Aaron is anointed as High Priest. His sons also are priests and there is a distinctive tradition of the inherited priesthood of Aaron; there is a distinctive dress of the ephod (Exodus 28.6; 39.2–7), with its accommodation for the sacred lot URIM AND THUMMIM.

Abba *See* FATHER.

Abednego *See* SHADRACH, MESHACH, AND ABEDNEGO.

Abel *See* CAIN AND ABEL.

Abiathar Abiathar was the son of Ahimelech the priest; he escaped and joined DAVID's outlaw band, when his father and the other priests of Nob were slaughtered at the command of King SAUL (see 1 Samuel 22.18–21). David seems to have used him as his private chaplain (1 Samuel 23.6–12) to provide advice from God, by means of the priestly ephod. When David became king he appointed Abiathar and ZADOK together as priests. Abiathar seems to have been the senior and remained loyal to David during ABSALOM's revolt. But in the conflicts about a successor to David, Abiathar backed the wrong candidate, Adonijah, and King SOLOMON banished Abiathar for supporting his rival (see 1 Kings 2.26–27), effectively terminating the priestly line of Eli. It was Abiathar's father, Ahimelech, who provided David with the SHOWBREAD (1 Samuel 21.1–6). This action is cited as the precedent by Jesus when the PHARISEES accuse his DISCIPLES of plucking grain on the SABBATH; Mark 2.26 incorrectly names Abiathar, but the name is omitted in Matthew 12.3–4 and Luke 6.3–4.

Abraham, or Abram Abraham the Old Testament patriarch is traditionally regarded as the 'Father of the Jews' (see Psalm 105.5; Isaiah 41.8); he also has a special significance for Christians and Muslims, all of whom may be described as 'children of Abraham'. The story of Abraham is told in GENESIS chapters 11–25; he was named Abram by his father, but received the new name Abraham (which incorporated a form of the divine name), and his wife Sarai became SARAH, as a sign of the COVENANT with YAHWEH.

Abraham was the recipient of a unique promise combining territory and heirs, to form a new nation (Genesis 12.1–2). The story suggests that his family were already on the move from UR (modern Iraq) and had reached HARAN in Syria (Genesis 11.31). Such migrations were common in the ancient Near East. Abraham's acceptance of the challenge to leave behind his home (and probably the ancestral worship of other deities – speculatively Sin the moon god) and set off for CANAAN would be seen as the response of faith to an all-powerful God (see Hebrews 11.8). His founding of a dynasty, through a previously impossible birth of a son, would enable nationhood to take place, particularly through the 12 sons (the eponymous tribal heroes) of his grandson JACOB.

The child ISAAC, regarded as the bearer of the covenant (Genesis 17), was the subject of a test by God: would Abraham who had obeyed God's call, and left his homeland for the unknown, be ready to go all the way and sacrifice his God-given son? God took him to the brink of violence. But the Jews see this test, which they call the AKEDAH, as simply a trial in which God never had any intention to let Isaac be sacrificed (because it would frustrate the divine plan for the future); implicitly the story could be a condemnation of the practice of child sacrifice in the surrounding nations.

In the New Testament Abraham is the father of Israel and the ancestor of Jesus (Matthew 1). He is central to PAUL's argument about justification by faith (Romans 4 and Galatians 3.6–7): 'his faith was reckoned to him as righteousness'. In Hebrews 11 Abraham is cited for several reasons as one of the key examples of faith. The parallel between the sacrifice of Isaac on the altar and the sacrifice of Christ on the cross is hinted at in the New Testament, while developed in some later Christian thought. In Islam, Abraham's willingness to sacrifice his son is a token of the Muslim's total submission to God, and it is commemorated in the Feast of Sacrifice at the climax of the *Hajj*. But the son in question there is not Isaac but Ishmael, the elder child who was banished with his mother Hagar (at Sarah's insistence – Genesis 21; see Galatians 4.22–30) and came to Mecca.

Abram *See* ABRAHAM.

Absalom Absalom was the third son of King DAVID, with Maacah, daughter of the king of Geshur. The graphic narrative of his life, his rebellion against his father, and his death (2 SAMUEL 13–18) is a masterpiece of Old Testament writing. The failings and feuds within the royal family, with the consequent difficulty of ensuring a succession to David (and the establishment of a dynasty), are clearly regarded as punishment for David's sin with BATHSHEBA (2 Samuel 11–12) and a fulfilment of NATHAN's judgemental prophecy that the sword would never be lifted from David's house (2 Samuel 12.10–11).

Absalom's sister TAMAR was raped by Amnon, David's firstborn (see Dan Jacobson's novel *The Rape of Tamar*). Consequently Absalom contrived Amnon's death, and fled into exile. When David accepted him back, Absalom repaid him by plotting against him and usurping the throne. With the help of Hushai and Joab, David was able to defeat Absalom in battle. Absalom died ignominiously, having been caught by his hair in a tree and left vulnerable to Joab's revenge. David's grief at Absalom's death is one of the most poignant passages in literature: 'O my son Absalom, my son, my son Absalom! Would I had died instead of you, O Absalom, my son, my son!' (2 Samuel 18.33).

Acco, Acre, Akko, or Ptolemais Acco, on the eastern shore of the Mediterranean, was one of the great port cities of antiquity. In modern times its importance has been superseded by Haifa, directly to the south. Following the EXODUS from Egypt and the conquest of CANAAN, Acco was one of the coastal towns under PHILISTINE control which the Hebrews were unable to capture (see Judges 1.31). Much later, as a result of Alexander the Great's progress down this coast, the settlement was moved even closer to the sea, becoming a Hellenistic city, and renamed Ptolemais. Conflicts ensued between the Greeks and the MACCABEANS (see 1 Maccabees 5.14–15, 20–23; 12.45, 48). The Romans transformed it into a major naval base. Early Christian believers at Ptolemais were visited by PAUL, according to Acts 21.7. The citadel at Acre, once used as a prison, is now a museum devoted to the memory of the Jews who lost their lives during the period of the British Mandate.

Acre *See* ACCO.

Acts of the Apostles The book of Acts in the New Testament is usually regarded as a companion volume written by the same author as the Gospel of LUKE. There are numerous other early texts, entitled 'The Acts of [a named apostle]' which were not included in the New Testament – for these, *see* APOCRYPHA. Scholars have argued that Luke-Acts was written towards the end of the 1st century CE; it represents a meeting-point between Jewish history writing, influenced by Biblical models in the SEPTUAGINT (Greek translation of the Old Testament), and a popular cultural movement of secular Greek which blended the writing of history and the literary forms of the novel and travel writing.

The emphasis of the Acts of the Apostles is upon the message of the RESURRECTION of Jesus who had been crucified, the narrative of the missionary travels of the first messengers of the Gospel (*see* MISSION), and the confirmation of the truth of the Gospel of Luke. It is unlikely that Acts was selected, rather than other volumes of 'Acts', for the New Testament canon in order to establish the historical proof of the origins of Christianity. This did not need to be established for those within the Christian movement. But the stories of STEPHEN and PHILIP, PETER and PAUL belonged within the traditions of particular Christian Churches which influenced the selection of the canon. They wished to preserve and to celebrate the memory of their origins, as a direct result of the prophetic ministry of Jesus himself. 'Luke's Acts was written in the 80s or 90s, several decades after Paul's time, and Luke gives him an overall interpretation from within his own geographical situation, historical understanding, and theological vision. In the Acts, Paul becomes a Christian not of his own time and place, but of Luke's' (Dominic Crossan).

So Acts can be read as a kind of religious history; as a sequel to Luke's history of SALVATION in the Gospel, showing how salvation history is working in the early Church; and as a theological exposition of the resurrection and the mission to the GENTILES, with associated ideas about BAPTISM. It may also be read as a 'good read', an exciting novel and piece of narrative of its time. There is a political agenda in defending Christianity to the Roman Empire, and possibly also in defending Rome to the Christians. But with its major stakeholder Paul, and the other missionary leaders in centre stage, it offers a kind of collective and sacred biography: hagiography of the best kind.

TABULATION OF ACTS

Early days of the Church – mostly in Jerusalem 1.1–12.25

1.1–11	Ascension of Jesus
1.12–26	A replacement apostle is chosen
2.1–47	Pentecost, Peter's first sermon and life of the converts
3.1–4.4	Peter cures a beggar and preaches effectively in the Temple
4.5–31	Peter and John arraigned before the Council
4.32–5.11	Believers share goods, but deceit is punished
5.12–42	The apostles are forbidden to speak about Jesus
6.1–7	Choice of the seven servers
6.8–8.3	Trial and execution of Stephen, persecution of the Church
8.4–40	Philip's work with Samaritans and an Ethiopian eunuch
9.1–30	Saul is converted and makes a stir
9.31–10.48	Peter's work with Cornelius and others
11.1–18	Peter justifies his work with Gentiles
11.19–30	Barnabas joins forces with Saul at the mixed Church in Antioch
12.1–19	Peter's escape from prison
12.20–25	Death of Herod

Paul's first missionary journey 13.1–14.28

13.1–3	Barnabas and Saul chosen in Antioch
13.4–12	In Cyprus – Saul becomes Paul
13.13–14.28	Visits in SE Asia Minor and return to Antioch

The Council of Jerusalem and afterwards 15.1–41

| 15.1–35 | The meeting and the letter to Antioch |
| 15.36–41 | Paul and Barnabas go their separate ways |

Paul's second missionary journey 16.1–18.23

16.1–40	Paul visits Macedonia and is imprisoned in Philippi
17.1–15	Paul visits synagogues in Thessalonica and Beroea
17.16–34	Paul's address on the Areopagus in Athens

| 18.1–23 | Paul's work in Corinth and trip to Jerusalem |

Paul's third missionary journey 18.24–21.16

18.24–28	Work of Apollos
19.1–41	Paul's work in Ephesus ends in a riot
20.1–38	Paul's farewell to Ephesus and trip to Jerusalem
21.1–16	Paul's journey to Jerusalem

Paul's imprisonment 21.17–28.31

21.17–26	Paul visits the Temple, urged by the Jerusalem Church
21.27–23.11	Paul is arrested and his defence
23.12–35	Paul's transfer to Caesarea to avoid assassination
24.1–26.32	Paul's defence before two Roman governors and King Agrippa
27.1–28.31	Paul's voyage to Rome

Adam Adam is the first man, in the early chapters of GENESIS, who is together with EVE in the story of the Garden of EDEN. But the name does not actually occur for certain, as a proper noun, until Genesis 4.25, after the couple are expelled and the Eden story is over. Throughout that story he is referred to simply as 'man', which of course is how the name Adam is defined. The Hebrew text of Genesis 2.7 suggests that the name is related to the word for 'ground, soil', but this etymology may only be a pun. There are several other explanations of the name, none conclusive. The story of Adam in Eden invites comparison with the epic of GILGAMESH.

Adam appears at the start of the genealogy in 1 CHRONICLES; the genealogy of Jesus in LUKE 3 is traced to Adam, while Matthew begins with ABRAHAM. In the writings of PAUL (Romans 5 and 1 Corinthians 15) there is a significant correspondence (a TYPOLOGY) drawn between the 'first Adam' and the 'last Adam' who is Christ. The Adam described in Genesis 1 and 2 is an obviously negative example. Through the first Adam came sin and death; through the second or last Adam came RESURRECTION and God's grace. Transgression is contrasted with RIGHTEOUSNESS in Romans 5.12–21.

Adam figures extensively in apocryphal and later literature; see for example the *Life of Adam and Eve* in which SATAN blames Adam for the fact that he was banished from heaven. In traditional embellishments of the original Genesis story a rivalry between the existing ANGELS and the upstart human is common.

adultery Adultery was forbidden as part of the divinely revealed code of social relationships in the DECALOGUE (Ten Commandments): see Exodus 20.14, where it is sandwiched between murder and theft. Numbers 15.11–31 prescribes trial by ordeal when there is suspicion that the wife has committed adultery. Marital fidelity was highly prized by the Hebrews (*see* MARRIAGE), in part at least to ensure that the paternity of children raised as heirs should not be in doubt. The faithful commitment of partners to each other was seen by various prophets as symbolizing the relationship of God to Israel; but Israel was accused of breaking faith (see for example Ezekiel 23.37). Thus, metaphorically speaking, Israel's APOSTASY with alien deities was likened to adultery. HOSEA pre-eminently developed these ideas, even apparently marrying a prostitute (GOMER) and grieving that she had resumed her former ways (see Hosea 2.2). There would also be a link between apostasy, IDOLATRY, and adultery, in fact as well as in metaphor, because in Old Testament times the worship of the 'false gods' of the fertility cults, BA'AL and Anath/Astarte involved using prostitutes at their shrines.

In the New Testament, Jesus' apparent restatement of the Law in the Ten Commandments involved drastic measures to deal with the lust underlying the adultery (see Matthew 5.27–30). Further, any man divorcing his wife was guilty of forcing her into adultery (because remarriage would be essential for her economic survival; *see* DIVORCE). The ancient punishment in the TORAH for adultery had been stoning to death. Jesus' adversaries wanted to trick him into opposing this legislation, by presuming he would not go this far in an actual case. Jesus outwitted them, but notably told the woman: 'Neither do I condemn you. Go your way, and from now on do not sin again' (John 8.11). Various epistles are explicit in forbidding adultery for Christians. The book of REVELATION returns to the metaphorical/symbolic use of adultery for apostasy and idolatry (see for example 2.20–22).

advent *See* PAROUSIA.

advocate *See* PARACLETE.

aedicule An aedicule is a small niche-like shrine (in Latin *aedicula*), which is sometimes found adorned with columns on both sides, and a pediment above. The name is particularly applied to the structure covering the site of the traditional tomb of Jesus, and of his RESURRECTION, within the Church of the Holy Sepulchre in Jerusalem. It is also used of the Martyr's Chapel, thought to be that of PETER himself, found in the 1940s below the Basilica of St Peter's in Rome.

afterlife *See* LIFE AFTER DEATH.

Agabus Agabus was a Christian prophet (*see* PROPHECY) from Jerusalem who appears twice in the ACTS OF THE APOSTLES. According to Acts 11.27–28, he predicted a widespread famine in the time of Emperor Claudius, which did indeed take place. Then in Acts 21.10–11 he prophesied that PAUL would be arrested in Jerusalem and imprisoned by the GENTILES, as indeed the narrative confirms.

agony in the Garden, or agony of Christ Jesus' time of prayer, and preparation for his imminent death, in the Garden of GETHSEMANE on the slopes of the Mount of Olives in Jerusalem (see Matthew 26; Mark 14; Luke 22; but see also John 18) is often referred to as the 'agony'. It was part of the time of suffering, recorded in the concluding chapters of the Gospels, and known as the Passion Narrative. It is said that during the time of prayer an ANGEL came and strengthened him ('the angel of the agony') and that he sweated blood. But the underlying meaning of the English word 'agony' is from the Greek word *agon*, meaning a 'conflict' or 'struggle', not unrelated to the much earlier TEMPTATIONS or testing of Christ.

agrapha This is the scholarly term (in Greek meaning 'things not written') used for sayings attributed to Jesus which are not to be found in the GOSPELS within the New Testament CANON. The German scholar Joachim Jeremias discussed 21 such sayings which might have a claim to authenticity in *Unknown Sayings of Jesus* (1957). These and other sayings are to be found quoted by Church Fathers, or in marginal additions to manuscripts, in fragments of PAPYRI, in the APOCRYPHAL Gospels, and especially in GNOSTIC texts with collections of sayings. The best example of such a collection of sayings (*logia*) is the *Gospel of Thomas* (*see* THOMAS).

Ahab Ahab was the son and successor of Omri and reigned as the eighth king of the divided Northern Kingdom of Israel from c.871 until 852 BCE. His reign, building on his father's strengths, was (to judge from archaeological evidence) a time of prosperity and expansion, with elaborate construction programmes, and a military might, measured for example in numbers of chariots, to rival, if not exceed, that of SOLOMON. According to ASSYRIAN accounts Ahab fielded 2000 chariots and 10,000 soldiers against Shalmaneser III in 853 BCE. By contrast the record of the Hebrew Bible focuses on Ahab's foreign alliances, especially through his queen JEZEBEL, resulting in pagan practices including human sacrifice, and describes a tyrannical regime (*see also* NABOTH) and conflicts with the prophets of Yahweh, especially ELIJAH and MICAIAH. The king's fate, as recorded in 1 Kings 22, is seen as a divine judgement.

Ahimelech *See* ABIATHAR.

Ai, or Hai Ai was an ancient CANAANITE city-state east of BETHEL. Most scholars identify the site with et-Tell ('the mound') about a mile south-east of Bethel, but other sites have been suggested. The name in Hebrew means 'ruin' and there is a distinct possibility that the Israelites took over the name from the Canaanites and that it was already a ruin. JOSHUA sent spies to Ai after the conquest of JERICHO (Joshua 7.2); subsequently Joshua 8.1–29 describes how Joshua burnt Ai and left it a 'desolation'. According to Ezra 2.28 and Nehemiah 7.32, men numbering 123 originally from Ai and Bethel returned from the EXILE in Babylon with ZERUBBABEL in 538 BCE.

akedah The Hebrew word *akedah* means 'binding' and refers to the story in Genesis 22.1–19 of the binding of ISAAC by his father ABRAHAM for the purposes of sacrifice. The child Isaac, regarded as the bearer of the covenant (Genesis 17), was the subject of a test by God: would Abraham who had obeyed God's call, and left his homeland for the unknown, be ready to go all the way and sacrifice his God-given son? God took him to the brink of violence. But the Jews see this test as summing up a selfless devotion to God on the part of Abraham, and as a prototype of the Jewish ideal of submission to the divine will. It could be said that it was simply a trial of obedience, in which God never had any intention to let Isaac be sacrificed (because it would frustrate the divine plan for the future); implicitly the story could also be a condemnation of the practice of child sacrifice as practised in the surrounding nations (see Leviticus 20.2–5). There are frequent echoes of the akedah story in Hebrew literature, but a surprising dearth of other references to it in the Bible. It has been compared with the Christian tradition of Christ's crucifixion, and some scholars detect allusions to the theme of the akedah in the letter to the HEBREWS.

Akkadian Akkadian was a Semitic language, named after Akkad (north of Babylon – see Genesis 10.10), which was the city of Sargon I. The Akkadian language was widely used in the texts of the classical period in Mesopotamia. Speakers of Semitic languages had supplanted the SUMERIANS there in the last quarter of the 3rd millennium BCE. The name covers a group of dialects of which the most prominent are BABYLONIAN and ASSYRIAN. These became imperial languages as the political and military control exercised by Babylonia and Assyria expanded in turn.

Akko *See* ACCO.

Alalakh Alalakh is an ancient site in northern Syria, excavated in the 1930s and 40s by C. L. Woolley. It yielded important information as a major site – one of the most fertile – in the FERTILE CRESCENT, and because it was a junction of roads between northern Syria, Asia Minor and Mesopotamia (*see* HITTITES). It developed a harbour for trade on the coast to the west in the 12th century BCE; from here (known to the Greeks as Poseidon) there was a lively trade with Greece and the Mediterranean islands.

Alexander the Great *See* ALEXANDRIA; HELLENISTIC PERIOD.

Alexander Jannaeus *See* HASMONEANS.

Alexandria The Egyptian city of Alexandria was founded by (and named after) Alexander the Great in 332–331 BCE, following his conquest of the country. On the western side of one arm of the river Nile, it was connected to the island of Pharos (with its world-famous lighthouse) by means of a mole that helped to form an excellent double harbour. In the 1st century BCE the city was reckoned to house 300,000 inhabitants. It was a Greek city, although substantial numbers of Egyptians lived there, and it had a large and prosperous Jewish quarter. Alexandria became a renowned centre of science and the arts. Its cosmopolitan character provided a focus for liberal scholarship by Jews (*see* PHILO) and later by Christians (*see* ALLEGORY). The translation by Jewish scholars of the Hebrew Bible into Greek (known as the SEPTUAGINT) was undertaken here. Alexandria's great library was burnt down during the Roman civil war between the forces of Julius Caesar and Mark Antony in 47 BCE. Alexander had been buried here by Ptolemy I, although the location of the tomb is now unknown. The evangelist MARK was commemorated here by a basilica, but his body was smuggled out of the city in 828 CE and taken to Venice. Recent developments in underwater archaeology at Alexandria have revealed the royal palaces, the harbour, and, further out, the remains of the cities of Herakleion and Canopus, probably destroyed by an earthquake.

aliyah This is a Hebrew term meaning literally 'to go up' or 'to ascend'. In the history of modern Israel it has developed a technical meaning for the return or immigration of Jewish people to Israel (an organized process of immigration from the DIASPORA which began in the early 1880s). Of course ever since the Diaspora came into being, Jews have aspired to return to Israel, although at times they have been prevented from doing so, or have been disappointed when they have returned. Proof texts from the Hebrew Bible, such as Jeremiah 32.41–44 and Isaiah 49.22, are frequently used as prophecies of this climactic return and the fulfilment of God's promises. In the book of PSALMS there are 'Songs of Ascent', or songs of PILGRIMAGE (Psalms 121–135), which originally seem to have been designed for the occasion of 'going up' to the Jerusalem Temple at FESTIVAL times. The word *aliyah* can also be used for the honour of being 'called up' for the reading of the prescribed passage of the TORAH during the Jewish synagogue service.

allegory The Greek root of the word 'allegory' suggests 'alternative' meanings, as in figurative speech, or 'speaking one thing and signifying something other than what is said'. There may be practically no continuity between the original words and the meaning that is extracted from them. So Augustine of Hippo offered a dramatic reinterpretation of the pastoral image in SONG OF SONGS 4.2; 6.6 ('Your teeth are like a flock of shorn ewes that have come up from the washing') in terms of the aggressive MISSION of the Church and BAPTISM. One obvious virtue of this literary method of allegory – a long-standing way of interpreting texts – is that of problem-solving with a difficult Biblical text.

Rather than in the external application of foreign meanings to a Biblical text, it is possible to see allegory being consciously used internally within a Biblical text. Examples in the Hebrew Bible would be the prophet NATHAN's story (told to King DAVID, in 2 Samuel 12) of the poor man's ewe lamb, and the song of the vineyard, representing Israel, in Isaiah 5. PAUL used the story of Hagar and SARAH to present a mirror-image of Jewish tradition in Galatians 4.21–31. And the ancient Jewish rabbis employed allegory, especially when interpreting the Song of Songs, not as a simple love lyric about a man and a girl, but as a dialogue between GOD (the Lover) and Israel (the beloved). Among the parables of Jesus there is an explicit allegory in the parable of the Vineyard Tenants (as in Mark 12.1–12) and a possible early allegory, identifying Jesus with the Samaritan, in the story of the GOOD SAMARITAN (in Luke 10.29–37).

aloe *See* HERBS.

alpha and omega These are the first and last letters of the GREEK alphabet of 24 letters. The two are used in REVELATION 1.8 as a self-designation of GOD, represented also as the Almighty Lord of past, present and future. The divine control relates to alpha as the beginning of the world and its CREATION, and equally to omega as the end of all things and the universal judgement. A similar idea is expressed in terms of 'first and last' in the Old Testament prophets, such as Isaiah 41.4; 44.6 (from aleph to taw – the first and last letters of the HEBREW alphabet). An extension of such highly significant and symbolic use of Greek letters can be found in the exploitation of their numerical equivalents (Greek letters were used as numerals) in a technique known as gematria. This probably lies behind the 'number of the beast' (666) in Revelation 13.18; efforts to break the code are not conclusive, but it may stand for the Greek letters of the name 'Nero Caesar' (*see* NUMBER SYMBOLISM).

The Alpha Course is the name of a successful programme of Church education from first principles, launched at Holy Trinity Church, Brompton during the Decade of Evangelism in 1992.

amen 'Amen' is an affirmative response, used in spontaneous worship and in liturgies, which means 'so be it'. In origin it is a Hebrew noun meaning certainty or truthfulness. Revelation 1.7 gives an example of the liturgical kind of response; here it is notable that the Hebrew word is paralleled by a Greek affirmative equivalent (is this an indication of a bilingual LITURGY?). In the Gospels the teaching of Jesus is quite frequently prefaced by an introductory 'amen', usually translated as 'truly'. In JOHN'S GOSPEL this occurs in a redoubled form (see for example John 3.11).

Ammonites The Ammonites settled the land east of the river Jordan and to the north of the territories of EDOM and MOAB from the 13th century BCE. They are mentioned in Genesis 19.38 as the descendants of LOT; they should probably be associated with the AMORITES from northern Syria and Mesopotamia. Through much of the Old Testament period there was intermittent warfare between Israel and the Ammonites over territory (see Judges 11; 1 Samuel 11). DAVID took refuge with Nahash the Ammonite king, but subsequently there was a long war in which Ammon was defeated (2 Samuel 11.1). In the time of SOLOMON peaceful relations were cemented by his marriage with Naamah the Ammonite (1 Kings 14.21, 31). After the return from the Babylonian EXILE, NEHEMIAH (13.23ff.) banned mixed marriages with Ammonites and Edomites. Many Jews settled in the area in Persian times; under the Ptolemies it became a Jewish political entity called Ammanitis. By the end of the Seleucid period it had become an exclusively Jewish area known as PERAEA.

Amnon *See* ABSALOM; TAMAR (2).

Amorites The Amorites, together with the Canaanites and the HITTITES, are regarded as the original inhabitants of the land of CANAAN before the coming of Israel (see Genesis 15.16; Ezekiel 16.3). They can be traced at an early date in northern Syria and Mesopotamia, and are subsequently associated particularly with Transjordan. They were Semitic-speaking and seem to have been a settled population in Canaan by 1900 BCE. It is unclear whether their arrival should be associated with social changes within either the Early Bronze or Middle Bronze ages.

Amos, book of The book of Amos is the third in the collection known as the Minor Prophets. Amos was a prophet of the 8th century BCE (not to be confused with Amoz the father of Isaiah). His name means 'bearer of a burden', presumably bad news. He was born in the Judaean hills at Tekoa near Bethlehem, but was called to prophesy at BETHEL in the Northern Kingdom around 760 BCE, in the reign of Jeroboam II. According to his version of events, he was simply a shepherd and had not been trained in the prophetic schools ('I am no prophet, nor a prophet's son, but I am a herdsman, and a dresser of sycamore trees': 7.14–15). His message was one of judgement, describing the Day of the Lord not as the expected light and triumph, but as darkness and doom and a total national disaster (5.18). This lack of hope was related to a social analysis of the power of the rich and their oppression of the poor. The religious practices of Israel will not save the nation (5.21–24). Amos is the first to point out that God's choice of Israel is not unique (9.7–8) while their special relationship with God may actually be the reason for their punishment (3.2).

Amos is the earliest Biblical prophet whose oracles were collected in writing, although other prophets were active before him. Presumably, like HOSEA, his prophecies were preserved in the south after Israel fell. There are some indications of later editing and of additions (such as the oracle against Judah in 2.4–5, and the concluding hopefulness of a surviving remnant in 9.8–15). Nothing is known of the actual fate of the prophet, after the priest Amaziah tried to have him exiled (7.12).

Ananias *See* HIGH PRIEST.

anastasis, or descent into hell Anastasis is the name in the Eastern Church for what is called in the West the descent into hell. Defined otherwise as the Harrowing of Hell, this refers to the risen Christ's descent into hell in order to rescue ADAM and EVE. In artistic representations Christ is shown breaking down the fortified gates of the city stronghold of hell, trampling on the broken gates, bars, chains and locks, and plunging his cross through the figure of Hades. His central action is to pull Adam, as the symbol of humanity, from his grave. The explicit idea is found in patristic texts and Biblical tradition from the 2nd century onwards. It is mentioned in the works of St John Chrysostom and St Ephrem the Syrian among others. The story is told, from the standpoint of two witnesses, in the apocryphal Gospel of NICODEMUS, dated around 600 CE. If there is a scriptural basis for this story it is in Old Testament prophecies such as Isaiah 9.2; Daniel 12.1–3; Psalms 16.10; 23.4; 82.8; 107.13–20 and a New Testament text such as 1 Peter 3.18–20 ('He went and preached to the spirits in prison…' – see also Acts 2.23–28; Romans 10.7; Ephesians 4.8–10; 1 Thessalonians 4.13–18; Hebrews 2.14; 2 Peter 2.4; and Revelation 20.1–3, 10–15).

anathema This Greek term was widely used in Christian tradition as a slogan (compare MARANATHA) and a curse. Its original meaning was of something 'placed on high', that is set aside as consecrated, or set apart as destined for destruction. The affirmative sense is found in Judith 16.19 ('dedicated … votive offering') and Luke 21.5 ('dedicated gifts'); but the negative sense of the curse is more fierce and more frequent (see Deuteronomy 7.26; Joshua 7.11–12; Zechariah 14.11; Romans 9.3; Galatians 1.9; 1 Corinthians 16.22). Among the Church Fathers and the early Councils of the Church the term was widely employed to denounce heresy: 'If any one says … let him be anathema' (see the codicil to the Creed of Nicaea, and the Athanasian Creed).

Anathoth *See* JEREMIAH.

Andrew Andrew was a fisherman, the brother of Simon PETER (Mark 1.16; 3.18). Unlike his brother he was outside the inner circle of three DISCIPLES of Jesus, but he is mentioned several times in the Gospels, particularly the Gospel of John (see chapters 1, 6 and 12). He was originally a disciple of JOHN THE BAPTIST (John 1.35–40). Andrew is a Greek name, meaning 'manly'; like 'Peter', it may be a Christian epithet. According to the apocryphal *Acts of Andrew* he subsequently journeyed through Asia Minor and Thrace to Macedonia and Greece. He is associated as patron saint with Patras on the western coast of Greece, where tradition says he was eventually martyred. He has long been regarded as the patron saint of Scotland.

angel An angel has been defined as 'a heavenly intermediary being, who is in the service of God and functions as a messenger or servant'. 'Messenger' is a root meaning of the Greek word *angelos*. Depending on the context, angels are not necessarily regarded as beneficial. Angelic 'powers' were referred to frequently (*see also* SATAN and BEELZEBUL). They were part of an understanding of the world, and the powerful influences upon it, that might now be regarded by many as the 'archaic relics of a superstitious past, unspeakable because modern secularism simply has no categories, no vocabulary, no presuppositions by which to discern what it was in the actual experience of people that brought these words to speech' (Walter Wink).

The seven chief angels (archangels) in the Judaeo-Christian tradition are named as Gabriel, MICHAEL, Raguel, Raphael, Remiel, Saraquel, and Uriel. Gabriel appears to DANIEL, ZACHARIAS and MARY, MOTHER OF JESUS; Michael is the prince of Israel who leads the good angels in the war in heaven (Revelation 12) and contends with Satan for the body of MOSES (Jude 9); Raphael accompanies Tobias in the story of TOBIT; and Uriel ('the fire of God') is named in 2 Esdras 4.1.

animism Animism is a term developed from the Latin word *anima*, meaning 'soul'. It was introduced by the British anthropologist E. B. Tylor in 1871, but is now regarded as rather old-fashioned if not obsolete. Animism was defined as 'a belief in spiritual beings' and used of the religious ideas of traditional (or 'primitive') peoples, wherever it is believed that any natural phenomena will possess spirits or souls. This idea can embrace both the souls of individuals as well as the supernatural spirits, up to and including powerful deities. The term is now seen in the academic world as a rather incautious way of making comparisons across cultures, or charting the EVOLUTION of religion. It may be found used loosely of the earliest religious ideas which are detected in the Old Testament.

Anna, or Hannah Anna is the name of the aged daughter of Phanuel, a prophetess who prayed in the Temple in Jerusalem. According to Luke 2.36–38, she spoke 'about the child [Jesus] to all who were looking for the redemption of Jerusalem'. It is possible that the newly discovered site in central Israel of a convent of the 5th to 8th century CE was dedicated to her rather than to Anne, the traditional mother of the Virgin Mary.

Annas *See* CAIAPHAS.

annunciation This term principally refers to the announcement to MARY, MOTHER OF JESUS of the forthcoming birth of Jesus. According to the narrative in LUKE'S Gospel (1.26–38) the ANGEL Gabriel tells Mary that she will conceive, and that the birth will be through the agency of the Holy SPIRIT. This announcement is preceded in Luke's account by a parallel announcement of the birth of JOHN THE BAPTIST. Within the Roman Catholic tradition of Christianity the annunciation is celebrated now (on 25 March – Lady Day) as one of five feast days devoted to Mary. The words of the angel to Mary ('Greetings, favoured one!'), in the Latin translation of the VULGATE, form the basis of a prayer, the Ave Maria.

anointing, anointing the sick *See* UNCTION.

Antichrist In the Bible this exact term is found only in the LETTERS OF JOHN (1 John 2.18; 4.3; 2 John 7); it is also used in the plural of the author's opponents, the false teachers who are claimed to deny Christ (1 John 2.18–22). But APOCALYPTIC texts elsewhere in the New Testament employ a variety of other terms for the 'opponent of Christ' (see 2 Thessalonians 2.3–4; Revelation 11.7; 13.11–18; Mark 13.6–8, 21–22). There is a deliberate juxtaposition in Revelation, chapters 11–13, to emphasize a continuity between these hostile powers, from SATAN and the old serpent in the Garden of EDEN, to the great red dragon and other varieties of beast. For practical purposes they can be regarded as synonyms.

Antioch The city of Antioch was founded by Seleucus I in 300 BCE; situated on the Orontes river in the north-west corner of the Roman province of SYRIA, it became the third-ranking city in the Mediterranean world behind ROME and ALEXANDRIA. The Christian MISSION came to Antioch from Jerusalem, preaching to both Jews and GENTILES. PAUL and BARNABAS worked there together for about a year. And traditionally the designation 'Christian' originated in Antioch (see Acts 11.19–26; also CHRISTIANITY). The opening chapters of GALATIANS indicate a disagreement between Paul and PETER over the relationships there (especially in table fellowship) between Jewish and Gentile Christians. Later, in the 4th century CE, an important school of Biblical interpretation was active in Antioch, in controversy with another school in Alexandria; Antioch tended towards the more literal, and Alexandria towards the more allegorical interpretation (*see* ALLEGORY).

Antiochus IV Epiphanes *See* MACCABEES.

anti-Semitism The term 'anti-Semitism', referring strictly to racist attitudes against Jews, was coined in the late 19th century by a German journalist, Wilhelm Marr. It is an equivalent of 'Jew-hate' or 'Judeophobia'.

There is a popular claim that such attitudes are inspired or justified by Biblical texts. When the Hebrew Bible indicates a development of monotheistic beliefs, such that the God of Israel is the only GOD, then such claims might seem suspect to, and be resisted by, polytheistic societies in the Middle East, such as the Egyptians, Greeks, or Romans. The Roman governor Flaccus ordered the first 'pogrom' against Jews in ALEXANDRIA in Egypt in 38 CE.

Christian texts in the New Testament naturally focus on the crucifixion of Jesus, and may imply, or make explicit, the claim that the ultimate responsibility for Jesus' death rested with the Jews (see 1 Thessalonians 2.15 and the references to 'the Jews' in the Gospel of John), although it must be remembered that Jesus himself was a Jew. Crucifixion was a Roman punishment, but some Christian apologists would tend to divert attention from Roman responsibility in order to prove that Christianity presented no threat to the Roman Empire. At the same time there was increasing friction between Jews and Christians, and Christians defined themselves more and more as different from Jews. The expression 'synagogue of SATAN' to be found in the book of REVELATION is not a literal description of Judaism in general, but a metaphorical transfer within an essentially Jewish style of writing to apply to a local group of adversaries.

It is important to remember the particular historical contexts of the Biblical statements, and not simply to merge them into a single attitude of resentment towards the Jews throughout history. Modern situations, in particular the Holocaust (Shoah) in Nazi Germany, have generated new awareness and polemic (*see* HOLOCAUST). But there is no unbroken continuum of anti-Semitism which can be traced back to Biblical texts; rather there are varieties of social, economic and political as well as religious factors which have influenced popular attitudes at different times and places.

Apocalypse of John *See* REVELATION, BOOK OF.

apocalyptic *Apocalypse* is a Greek word, meaning 'that which is uncovered or revealed'. It is now used as a technical term by Biblical scholars to classify a genre of ancient writings; this includes DANIEL in the Old Testament and REVELATION in the New Testament, and some parts of other books of a similar kind. The majority of the genre is to be found among the APOCRYPHAL texts of late Judaism and early Christianity. A scholarly definition states: 'Apocalypse is a genre of revelatory literature with a narrative framework, in which a revelation is mediated by an otherworldly being to a human recipient, disclosing a transcendent reality which is both temporal, insofar as it envisages eschatological salvation, and spatial, insofar as it involves another, supernatural world.'

Much of Jewish apocalyptic literature was inspired by three major crises that befell Jerusalem and its TEMPLE. The first was the destruction of city and Temple in the Babylonian era. While the literature of this period is prophetic rather than apocalyptic, it develops already many of the themes and motifs that appear again in the apocalyptic literature of the Hellenistic and Roman periods. The second was the crisis of the MACCABEAN era, when the Temple was defiled, first by the Hellenizing High Priests and then by the Syrian soldiers of Antiochus IV Epiphanes. This upheaval was the occasion for the first great outpouring of apocalyptic literature in the books of Daniel and ENOCH, and also initiated the course of events that led to the formation of the sect that we know from the DEAD SEA SCROLLS. The third was the destruction of Jerusalem by the Romans in 70 CE. This too was the occasion of several apocalyptic visions, including the New Testament book of Revelation. The Jewish apocalypses of 4 Ezra, 2 Baruch and 3 Baruch were all written near the end of the 1st century CE, and expressed reactions to the great disaster that had befallen the Jewish people.

Apocrypha The term Apocrypha is used to denote those books, or parts of books, that are not in the Jewish CANON of the Hebrew Scriptures, but are to be found in some early Christian versions of the Old Testament. Most were not included in Jerome's VULGATE translation. They were not originally grouped together, but rather are dispersed and inserted in various places. Their collection into a separate section, following the Old Testament, and therefore set aside, was the work of Protestants at the time of the Reformation. The word 'apocrypha' literally means 'the things hidden away'. Given the variations between Christian versions of scripture, this category is by no means definitive, nor are the books in a standard order. The following are regularly included: 1 and 2 ESDRAS, TOBIT, JUDITH, ESTHER (additions), WISDOM OF SOLOMON, ECCLESIASTICUS (Sirach), BARUCH, letter of JEREMIAH, Prayer of Azariah, Song of the Three Young Men, SUSANNA, BEL AND THE DRAGON, Prayer of MANASSEH (KING OF JUDAH), 1 and 2 MACCABEES.

Apollos Apollos appears to have been a chief rival of PAUL, along with PETER, in the early mission field, according to the first chapters of 1 Corinthians (see 1.12; 3.5–6); for Paul the difficulties focused on matters of WISDOM and BAPTISM. Apollos was a Hellenistic Jew from ALEXANDRIA, according to Acts 18 and 19, 'an eloquent man, well-versed in the scriptures … he spoke with burning enthusiasm and taught accurately the things concerning Jesus'. Apparently his understanding of baptism was restricted to that of JOHN THE BAPTIST. He is also mentioned briefly in Titus 3.13. Since the time of Luther, Apollos has been suggested as a possible author of HEBREWS, but the only evidence for this is circumstantial.

apostasy Apostasy is defined as the act of rebellion against one's faith, or the abandonment of one's religion. Biblical examples reveal, in the Hebrew Bible, Israel's unfaithfulness to YAHWEH, particularly the experience of betraying God in the pursuit of alternative deities. See for examples Joshua 22.22 (the political defence by the tribes of Reuben and Gad) or the denunciation of Manasseh in 2 Chronicles 33.19. Also, 'Your apostasies will convict you. Know and see that it is evil and bitter for you to forsake the Lord your God' (Jeremiah 2.19). In the New Testament the primary references are to the abandonment of the Christian faith and the betrayal of fellow-Christians. Paul refers in Galatians 1.6 to those who are 'so quickly … turning to a different Gospel'. Hebrews 6.4–6 contains the fiercest of condemnations of apostasy: 'it is impossible to restore again to repentance those who have once been enlightened … and then have fallen away, since on their own they are crucifying again the Son of God and are holding him up to contempt'. This amounts to the unforgivable sin.

Apostles The Greek word *apostolos* simply means 'someone who is sent'. The title is applied much more specifically in the Gospels, and subsequently, to the 12 principal DISCIPLES of Jesus. After the suicide of Judas Iscariot, he was replaced as one of the 12 by MATTHIAS (Acts 1.26). The criterion indicated at Acts 1.21–22 is for someone who has been with Jesus from the beginning, and the primary task of an apostle is to bear witness to the RESURRECTION of Christ. Narrowly applied, the criterion indicates that PAUL would not qualify, although the title is sometimes accorded to him and also to BARNABAS. Paul's own self-reference in 1 CORINTHIANS 15.8–11 suggests that he has his own reasons for almost agreeing with the Lucan criteria.

Among the second generation of Christians it is likely that the term was applied more broadly to other Church officials, and in the 2nd century CE key Church writers were known as the Apostolic Fathers. Subsequently the originator of a MISSION to a particular country might well be called the 'apostle' to that place. But in a Church where traditional authority is still regarded as vital, the doctrine of apostolic succession is maintained, whereby the original 12 apostles, appointed by Christ, in turn appoint their successors in a strict and lawful continuity. The Apostles' Creed is a liturgical formula of faith; it is only known, in a form close to the modern version, in local baptismal creeds from the 4th century CE onwards, but there is a legend suggesting that it was composed, article by article, in a committee of the original Apostles. There are several documents of ecclesiastical law, liturgy and practice that have 'Apostolic' in their title, but are also later texts claiming traditional authority.

Apostolic Council *See* GALATIANS.

Apphia *See* PHILEMON.

apple Contrary to popular tradition, the 'forbidden fruit' of the tree of the knowledge of good and evil (Genesis 2.17) is not actually named in the text, and certainly not identified as an apple. The confusion arises because in the Latin version (the VULGATE) the word for apple, *malum*, is the same as the neuter of the word for evil (*malus, -um*). There is also a deceptive fruit said to grow near the Dead Sea (according to WISDOM OF SOLOMON 10.7 and JOSEPHUS, *Jewish War* 4.8.4) which is called 'apples of SODOM'.

The KING JAMES, OR AUTHORISED, VERSION originated the use of the word 'apple' for the Hebrew *tappuah* in PROVERBS 25.11 and SONG OF SONGS 2.5; 7.8. But it is debatable whether this is accurate, for the apple is not regularly associated with the Biblical lands. A better translation could be 'apricot' or 'quince'. However, the association of the apple with love and sexuality is found widely in world mythology and folklore. These ideas colour a reading of the Song of Songs, and in turn influence the understanding of the tree in Genesis.

Aquila *See* PRISCILLA.

Arad Tel Arad was an important city in the Negev, on the eastern borders of Judah, and on the main road towards EDOM. According to Numbers 21, the Israelites invading the land from KADESH BARNEA were initially repulsed by its king, Arad the CANAANITE. Subsequently, according to Judges 1.16, the Negev of Arad was settled by the KENITES (a people related to the family of MOSES). Arad was later rebuilt as a border fortress, to be defended by a Judahite garrison. The entrance courtyard of the garrison contained a temple with a sacrificial altar; this was obliterated on the orders of HEZEKIAH at the end of the 8th century BCE. Excavations have revealed not only OSTRACA from the garrison, but also in the temple area two incense altars and two standing stones (*massebot*); there may be evidence for the joint worship of YAHWEH and ASHERAH. It is clear that the garrison was maintained after Hezekiah, while the temple was dismantled and buried (perhaps indicating a lingering respect for the worship officially abandoned).

Aram *See* SYRIA.

Aramaean The term Aramaean is used to cover a range of migrating tribes in the 2nd and 1st millennia BCE. Where they originated is obscure: it may have been from the Arabian desert or from the north (a city named Aram is known in the upper Tigris area c.2000 BCE). The Hebrew Bible refers to Aram as a descendant of Shem (Genesis 10.22–23). Among the PATRIARCHS, the wives of ISAAC and JACOB were both Aramaean, and so the later Israelite confession of descent from 'a wandering Aramaean' (Deuteronomy 26.5) is justifiable. Aramaeans are mentioned in ASSYRIAN sources from the end of the 2nd millennium, and then they are referred to as desert invaders. By the 8th century BCE they are defeated by the Assyrians, and their kingdoms in SYRIA turned into imperial satrapies. The Hebrew Bible refers to several Aramaean kingdoms beyond the northern borders of Israel. Their language, ARAMAIC, survived the Aramaeans by many centuries.

Aramaic Aramaic is a language related to Hebrew and using the same script. Particular passages of the Old Testament (especially chapters in DANIEL and EZRA) were originally written in Aramaic, not Hebrew. For centuries Aramaic was the language of commerce and diplomacy, especially in the PERSIAN Empire. In all probability it was the language Jesus himself spoke. With the aim of greater realism Mel Gibson made his characters speak Aramaic or Latin (with English subtitles) in his 2004 film *The Passion of the Christ. See also* TARGUMS.

archaeology of the Bible Biblical archaeology has always tended to be a subject of controversy. Either the Bible *is* History, or archaeological research seems to run counter to, and possibly demolish the very foundations of the Bible. Two points of view from opposing sides:

> The people of Israel were unique in having preserved in the Bible a written history of their origins and early development. Yet even in the history of Biblical times the background has been supplied by archaeological research; besides, people known only by name in the Bible, such as HITTITES, and others not mentioned at all in the Scriptures, such as the SUMERIANS, have become vividly clear through archaeology (Michael Avi-Yonah).
>
> A century of Biblical archaeology has been a great embarrassment to modern research. Traditions such as the Bible's, which provided ancient society with a memory and a past to be shared, are very different from the critical histories that play a central role in modern intellectual life. The Bible's theology does not allow us to read this book as if it were history (Thomas L. Thompson).

And from J. A. MacGillivray:

> Finding proof in the dirt is the final stage of a process of wish-fulfilment.

Nowadays in fact most scholarship no longer seeks to use archaeology to prove or disprove the validity of the Bible as an historical document. Biblical archaeology has been defined as a dialogue between archaeologists and Biblical scholars. Recent scientific advances allow the circumstances of the Biblical world to be investigated in astonishing detail, in particular the social contexts in which people lived, worked and worshipped.

archangel *See* ANGEL.

Archippus *See* PHILEMON, LETTER OF PAUL TO.

Aretas Aretas IV (9 BCE–40 CE) was a king of the NABATEANS with expansionist intentions. It was his governor in DAMASCUS who attempted to seize PAUL (see 2 Corinthians 11.32).

Ariel The Hebrew name *'ari'el* appears to mean 'lion of God', although it could derive from an AKKADIAN root and mean 'mountain/altar of God'. The lion-like characteristics might apply to the description of two bold Moabites in the context of 2 Samuel 23.20 and 1 Chronicles 11.22 (*see* MOAB). In Ezekiel 43.15–16 the reference is probably to the altar; while in Isaiah 29.1–2 Ariel is a poetic synonym for JERUSALEM (as the site of God's altar). The rabbis used the name to refer to the whole TEMPLE complex. However, the GNOSTICS saw it differently as the name of an angelic figure (Yaldabaoth) who participated in the creation of the world. The idea of an angel is also found in the Testament of Solomon, later magical texts, and in the KABBALAH. So Ariel appears in Milton's *Paradise Lost* as a rebel angel excluded from heaven, and as a sprite in Shakespeare's *The Tempest*. Ariel is the first name of the former Israeli Prime Minister Sharon, but it has now been included in a list compiled by Israeli rabbis of names that should not be given to Jewish children, for fear that uttering the name could incur the wrath of that angel.

Ark of the Covenant According to the narrative of Exodus 25, the tablets of the Ten Commandments (DECALOGUE) were to be stored in a specially built chest or ark, made out of acacia wood and elaborately decorated. It was to be kept within the TABERNACLE and transported with the people on their travels. Eventually King DAVID brought it to Jerusalem, and SOLOMON built the TEMPLE there to provide more permanent housing for the central text of the COVENANT in the Holy of Holies. However, all traces of the Ark were lost five centuries after the Temple was built, presumably at the point when the Temple was looted and substantially destroyed at the start of the Babylonian EXILE. This disappearance has generated great speculation about, and expeditions in search of, the Ark's present whereabouts. One highly favoured tradition looks to an Ethiopian location. In a fictional context it became a goal for the quest of Indiana Jones.

Ark of the Covenant

Armageddon, or Megiddo 'Then they gathered the kings together to the place that in Hebrew is called Armageddon' (REVELATION 16.16). Armageddon is the symbolic site of the battle at the End of the World (see Joel 3.14: 'the valley of decision'). So the regular dictionary definition will be in terms of the final battle at the end of the world between the forces of good and evil. The name Armageddon does not actually appear in any source before the New Testament; it is a corrupted combination of the Hebrew word for mountain (*har*) and the place name Megiddo (Tel el-Mutesellim). The archaeological site of Megiddo, 18 miles south of Haifa, overlooks the Jezreel valley from a height of more than 30 metres; its strategic importance, guarding a gap in the CARMEL range, lay in the fact that it controlled the great trunk road leading from Egypt in the south to Syria and Mesopotamia in the north, the road that the Romans knew as the 'WAY OF THE SEA' (Via Maris).

Through the centuries Megiddo has been the site of major battles: in the 15th century BCE between the forces of Pharaoh Thutmose III and a coalition of CANAANITE kings (the first reference to Megiddo in a written source); of the clashes between the Israelites and the Canaanites, recounted in the Bible in the Song of DEBORAH (Judges 5.19) and in Joshua 12.21; of the confrontation with Pharaoh Necho II, in which the celebrated reforming king JOSIAH was killed in 609 BCE (2 Kings 23.29); and of the defeat of the Turks in 1917 towards the end of the First World War by General Edmund Allenby, later to become Lord Allenby of Megiddo. It is scarcely surprising then that in the prophecy of the book of Revelation it marks the site of the world's ultimate battlefield. The bus bombing by Islamic Jihad at Megiddo Junction in June 2002, which claimed the lives of 17 people, was clearly in the tradition of this area. Horrifying though such suicide bombing is, however, it still falls short of that ultimate conflict which is prophesied. There is a modern tendency to use 'Armageddon' more generally of a catastrophic and extremely destructive conflict, such as the First World War.

One of the oldest archaeological finds on the site was a huge round altar, approached by seven steps, which dates to around 3000 BCE. There is a splendid hoard of 382 ivories which date between the 14th and 12th centuries BCE. Megiddo was conquered by JOSHUA, but it is the city at the time of King SOLOMON and later under King AHAB that is of the greatest interest in relation to the Bible. Megiddo was chosen by Solomon, together with GEZER and HAZOR, to be his main fortified cities (1 Kings 9.15). They all had similar defensive gateways, built to a common pattern. Not all the structures once associated with Solomon's building operations here (e.g. 'Solomon's Stables') are now regarded as belonging to his time, but rather are assigned to Ahab. But at this period Megiddo was certainly twice the size of Jerusalem. This site was abandoned, for no known reason, by 400–350 BCE. The remains of a Christian church (early but of uncertain date, perhaps 3rd or 4th century CE) have recently been discovered, within the grounds of the Israeli Detention Centre at Megiddo. The church contains a well-preserved mosaic with references to Christ and the Christian symbol of the FISH. Megiddo and Hazor have both been named as World Heritage Sites by UNESCO.

Armenian The Bible was first translated into Armenian within the Christian Church in the 5th century CE. Textual critics are particularly interested in the Armenian version of the Old Testament because of the SYRIAC version from which it was translated.

Asaph *See* PSALMS.

ascension The ascension of Christ was very important to the early Church, but it is described in only two texts in the New Testament, both in the writings of Luke (Luke 24.50–52 and Acts 1.9). The later addition (the Longer Ending) to Mark's Gospel states that, after ascending, Jesus 'sat down at the right hand of God' (16.19). The ascension and enthronement in glory conveyed two somewhat different ideas, depending on the context of thought about Jesus. As the earthly Messiah, who died an ignominious death, his ascension represents his full vindication; he is ready to return to earth (see Acts 7.55) at the PAROUSIA for the final judgement and the justification of his followers. But the ascension is also a vital part of the pattern described in John 3.13: Christ as the divine redeemer/revealer has come down from heaven and so in due course will ascend and return to heaven.

In working out their ideas about Christ's ascension, the early Christians made a creative combination of two Old Testament texts, Psalms 110.1 and 8.6. Ascension is a rarity in Jewish tradition, but the Old Testament does refer to the ascension of two figures: ENOCH (Genesis 5.24) and ELIJAH (2 Kings 2.11). Other writings outside the canon record the ascensions of Abraham, Moses, Isaiah and Ezra. Christians who follow totally the example of Christ will also follow him in ascending to heaven, if the two witnesses of Revelation 11.12 are understood as prototype Christians (*see* MARTYR); alternatively they may stand for Old Testament figures like Enoch and Elijah.

The location where Jesus is said to have ascended into heaven (Luke 24.50–52) is traditionally marked by the Chapel of the Ascension on the Mount of Olives (et-Tur) in Jerusalem. Pilgrims are there shown a footprint of Jesus in the stone of the marble floor. A similar footprint in stone is attributed to Mohammed at the Dome of the Rock (Haram al-Sharif).

Ashdod Ashdod was one of the main PHILISTINE cities, situated in the Judaean plain, and mentioned in JOSHUA 13.3 (see 11.22) and 1 SAMUEL 5.1. In Joshua's tribal allocation Ashdod was allotted to Judah, but the Israelites failed to annex it; according to 2 CHRONICLES 26.6 King UZZIAH destroyed its walls. The site is identified as the mound Tel Ashdod that was extensively excavated in the 1960s. Recently the remains of a different kind of building (of square mud-bricks) have been discovered nearby by Israeli archaeologists; this is thought to be the administrative centre and palace of the satrap (governor) appointed by the ASSYRIAN king Sargon II, after Ashdod had revolted in 714 BCE.

Asher Asher is the second son of JACOB by Zilpah, the handmaiden of LEAH (see Genesis 30.12–13; 49.20; *see also* GAD). He was the ancestor of the tribe that bears his name which held fertile territory in the western highlands of Galilee. The Hebrew word *asher* means 'happy', but the name may derive from a deity's name, perhaps the male version of the Canaanite goddess ASHERAH.

Asherah In the religion of CANAAN Asherah was a figure of 'mother nature', frequently represented as a tree of life. Her sacred tree was also called an Asherah; this could be a living tree, representing her creative power, or a wooden pole as a sacred symbol. Biblical writers fiercely opposed these ideas, which suggests that they were regarded as possessing actual potency in Israelite agricultural life: *see* DEUTERONOMY 16.21 – 'You shall not plant any tree as a sacred pole beside the altar that you make for the Lord your God.' Pillar figurines of Asherah have been commonly discovered in Judah after the destruction of the Northern Kingdom in 722 BCE. These are unlikely to have been symbols of sexual debauchery, but more likely employed as talismens for women's needs, such as pregnancy and childbirth.

Ashkelon Ashkelon is one of the oldest, largest and most significant cities in the Holy Land, situated right on the Mediterranean coast. For that reason it was an important trading centre, a staging post on the great trade route linking Egypt and Mesopotamia (the WAY OF THE SEA), but equally also open to invasion. Evidence of the port was discovered by chance in 1997, during the construction of a marina, with antiquities rescued from sunken vessels on the seabed. During the period of the Judges, Ashkelon had been one of the five cities of the PHILISTINES (Joshua 13.3) and it features in the story of SAMSON (Judges 14.19). The population has been calculated as up to 12,000. In 604 BCE the city was utterly destroyed by NEBUCHADNEZZAR of Babylon. But the destructive conflagration preserved a wealth of materials on site for archaeology. Recent excavations have been directed by Lawrence E. Stager. Subsequently a new Ashkelon flourished under Greek and Roman rule. During a period of Roman intervention in Egypt, Cleopatra was supported by Ashkelon and coins were minted there bearing her portrait. It was also reputedly the birthplace of HEROD THE GREAT. Fresh interest (and notoriety) have been aroused by the discovery of 100 skeletons of babies in the sewers beneath the Roman city. The city was partly destroyed by Saladin in the 12th century and levelled by the Mameluke sultan Baybars in 1270. Modern Ashkelon is a sprawling city, well known for its national park and beaches.

Ashtoreth Female consort of Canaanite deity El, corresponding to ASHERAH as consort to BA'AL.

Ashurbanipal *See* ASSYRIANS; NINEVEH.

Assyrians In the 9th century BCE Assyria was a rising power, extending westwards to the Mediterranean. It was checked temporarily in 853 BCE at the battle of Qarqar by a coalition of states including Israel led by King AHAB. The Assyrian king Shalmaneser III claimed it as a victory, though in fact he was unable to press any further forward. But he returned in 841 BCE, capturing DAMASCUS and then Israel. On the Black Obelisk of Shalmaneser (in the British Museum) the Israelite king JEHU is shown paying tribute to the Assyrian king.

Assyrian pressure on Israel was relaxed during the first half of the 8th century, but thereafter Tiglath-Pileser III (744–727 BCE) and his successors extended Assyrian control into Syria and Palestine. The Northern Kingdom of Israel came to an end in 722 BCE with the capture of SAMARIA and the deportation of part of its population in a strategic kind of ethnic cleansing. The Southern Kingdom of Judah under HEZEKIAH (715–687/6 BCE) rebelled against the Assyrian king SENNACHERIB in 701 BCE, but this attempt was disastrous. JERUSALEM itself was spared but the great city of LACHISH was besieged and fell to the Assyrians. The siege is illustrated on limestone reliefs that were in Sennacherib's palace at NINEVEH. After the reign of Sennacherib Assyria largely lost control of its empire to the BABYLONIANS. The last of the great Assyrian kings, Ashurbanipal, succeeded his father Esarhaddon in 669 BCE. His reign ends obscurely c.627 BCE, but he is now well known for his library of AKKADIAN literature. This palace library was discovered in 1853 by Hormuzd Rassam, a Chaldean Christian who was working with the explorer Henry Layard. CUNEIFORM texts from this library were later translated by the British Museum cataloguer George Smith, revealing among other things the existence of a non-Biblical parallel to the story of NOAH (*see also* GILGAMESH).

Astarte *See* BA'AL.

atonement Atonement is the reconciliation (or 'at-one-ment') brought about between God and human beings, after the COVENANT relationship has been broken by human sins and disobedience. In JUDAISM reconciliation was achieved by the ritual and sacrifices of an annual Day of Atonement (*see* YOM KIPPUR). Within Christianity it is argued that atonement is effected by the DEATH OF CHRIST on the cross.

Augustus, Emperor *See* COINAGE; EPHESUS; PERGAMON.

Authorised Version of the Bible *See* KING JAMES VERSION.

authority The definition of authority can be a highly contentious issue, not least in religious matters. In general theory much depends upon the temperament and assumptions of those attempting the definition (for example liberal or FUNDAMEN-TALIST tendencies). In relation to scripture and questions of INSPIRATION, it is import-ant to concentrate in the first place on the attitudes prevailing in the ancient world.

There is a fundamental distinction between the point of composition of a text and its subsequent publication (the moment when it escapes the control of the author or group who produced it). A further distinction – more problematic to evaluate in the ancient world – is that between the publication of a text and its authority. The difference may not be easy to appreciate, for the authority of a text is initially derived from the reputation of those regarded as being responsible for it.

The Jewish *Letter of Aristeas* provides a good example of these realities. It sets out to show that the SEPTUAGINT Greek translation of the PENTATEUCH is not a private whim; on the contrary, it was ordered by the founder of the library of ALEXANDRIA and carried out by representatives of the twelve tribes of Israel who were appointed for this purpose by the High Priest in Jerusalem. Thus not only does the translation have all the religious and legal authority one could wish, but also its publication is super-vised by official copyists in the setting of the best library at the time.

This is an exceptional case. For the Biblical writings, publication and canonization are obviously two distinct phases, which in turn are quite distinct from the process of composition. On the other hand, further alteration and reworking cannot be totally excluded after publication, not even after canonization. (The text of the Hebrew Bible continued to evolve long after its translation into Greek.)

What is needed in this context is not so much a discussion of the literary origins of the books of the New Testament but rather a study of the use which the early Christians made of them. *See also* CANON.

autograph The technical sense of this term is that of the original author's manu-script, written in his own handwriting. It needs to be clearly stated that such original manuscripts are irrecoverable in the case of all books of the Bible. Readers must rely on a variety of later copies and versions.

B

Ba'al The name Ba'al means 'master' or 'lord' and was originally associated with several deities, e.g. Baal-Peor (Numbers 25.3, 5). More importantly, Ba'al was the most active of the CANAANITE deities, otherwise Hadad, the god of storms and of fertility. He was the son of the supreme god, El. In the Canaanite epics from UGARIT, he is involved in huge conflicts with Yam (the sea) and his ally Lotan (LEVIATHAN), and with Mot (Drought and Death), who was also the god of the underworld, to whom Ba'al succumbed every seven years (causing a period of famine). Ba'al was ultimately victorious and succeeded to the throne of his father El. He is depicted in military armour with the horns of a bull. His consort was ASHERAH or Ashtoreth (plural form Ashtaroth – see Judges 2.13; 10.6), in Greek script Astarte, and identified with Mesopotamian Ishtar and Sumerian Inanna. AHAB and his queen JEZEBEL are said to have promoted the cult of Ba'al in Israel (1 Kings 16.31). The prophet ELIJAH challenged the prophets of Ba'al in a contest on Mount CARMEL (1 Kings 18.20–40).

Babel Babel is the Hebrew name for BABYLON. The allegorical story of Babel in the tradition from Genesis 11.1–9 seems to have two etiological purposes: one is to provide a negative interpretation of a power base hostile to Israel (compare the APOCALYPTIC imagery of Zechariah 12); the other is to explain the origin of a plurality of languages, given that the descendants of NOAH will have spoken a single language. These descendants wished to make a name for themselves in a new territory and so built a tower (*see* ZIGGURAT) and a city in the plain of Shinar. They were spurred on by a vision resembling world empire, wanting to create a central headquarters, from which other peoples might be controlled by a despotic authority. God's reaction to their arrogance was to confound their language and scatter them over the earth. The Hebrew word *balal* means 'to confuse' and is used in Genesis 11.9 as a punning explanation of the name Babel. The story of PENTECOST in Acts 2 represents, with the coming of the Holy SPIRIT, a kind of reversal of Babel and a solution to the language problem.

The original allegory of the Tower of Babel seductively offers a variety of modern applications, including individual identifications with the dreams of Hitler or Saddam Hussein, or institutional targets such as the United Nations, or international terrorism. A reapplication of these ideas within the Bible can be found in the book of REVELATION with the threat posed by Babylon, the Beast (ANTICHRIST) and the False

Exile to Babylon 2 Kings 25.1–21

Prophet. Ultimately it is claimed that these powers will be destroyed and God will reign from the NEW JERUSALEM.

Babylon   Historically, in the Hebrew Bible, Babylon is the city-state on the Euphrates that is magnificent, pagan and full of pride. Traditionally Babylon, or BABEL, was founded by Nimrod (Genesis 10.8–10). NEBUCHADNEZZAR of Babylon waged war on Israel (2 Kings 24–25), first subduing Jerusalem and exiling its leaders to Babylon, and then ultimately destroying it. In the New Testament Babylon is a symbolic name for Rome, as in REVELATION and 1 PETER. Babylon and Rome are analogous, because both were the centres of world empire and both captured Jerusalem and destroyed the TEMPLE. Babylon as a codename for Rome also appears in Jewish apocalyptic writings. These references, like those in the New Testament, occur after the capture of Jerusalem by the Roman general TITUS in 70 CE.

Babylonians   The role of the Babylonians is particularly important in Biblical history. They and their predecessors the SUMERIANS established the philosophical and social infrastructure for most of western Asia for nearly two millennia. The key names are HAMMURABI, whose famous 'law code' needs to be studied in relation to Babylonian society, and in comparison with Israelite law; Merodach-baladan, a mysterious figure whose emissaries to Jerusalem were upsetting to the prophet ISAIAH in the days of HEZEKIAH (see Isaiah 39); NEBUCHADNEZZAR, whose name is associated with the destruction of Solomon's TEMPLE in Jerusalem; and BELSHAZZAR, during whose reign Babylonia fell to the PERSIANS.

ASSYRIA lost control of its empire after the reign of SENNACHERIB. The Babylonians captured the Assyrian capital NINEVEH in 612 BCE, and defeated the Egyptians at Carchemish in 605 BCE. JOSIAH, king of Judah (641–609 BCE), had expanded his kingdom, but Judah then fell first to the Egyptians and then to the Babylonian king Nebuchadnezzar II. After rebellion broke out, Nebuchadnezzar returned and destroyed Jerusalem, tearing down the Temple and bringing the kingdom of Judah to an end. Large-scale deportation followed, marking the beginning of the Babylonian EXILE.

Balaam Balaam is the name of the non-Israelite prophet, referred to in Numbers 22–24, who was hired by the king of MOAB to curse the Israelites (see also Micah 6.5), but ended up blessing them instead. An inscription, written in ink on plaster, was found at Deir 'Alla (Biblical Succoth) in Jordan, which reads, 'The sayings of Balaam, son of Beor, the man who was a seer of the gods'. Later references to Balaam in the Hebrew Bible and Jewish tradition take a negative view of him and denounce him for sorcery and seduction. In the same way the New Testament regards him as a proto-type of heresy, with his advocacy of permissive morality (see 2 Peter 2.15–16 and Jude 11; also Revelation 2.14). But Balaam's oracle of the star which will arise from JACOB (Numbers 24.17) is regarded as a prophecy of Christ, being illustrated in the Roman catacombs and discussed by Christian commentators.

balsam, balm Balsam was a treasured preparation for medical and cosmetic pur-poses. It is mentioned in the Hebrew Bible at Genesis 37.25 and Jeremiah 8.22 and 51.8 (Hebrew *tsori*). JOSEPHUS calls it the most precious ointment of all (*Antiquities* 14.4.1) and says that it was produced near JERICHO from the time of Solomon. HEROD THE GREAT is said to have owned the balsam plantations in the Jericho plain and at Ein Gedi; it was a major source of his wealth as the perfume was worth its weight in gold. The production processes were kept so secret that the special desert plant may eventually have become extinct. It is identified, but not without dispute, as *Com-miphora opobalsamum*; alternatively it may be the more common 'Jericho balsam', *Balanites aegyptiaca*. The fruits of the latter contain a healing oil. According to Josephus the more expensive plant yielded a resinous sap when its branches were cut (*War* 1.6.138); either an ointment was manufactured directly from the sap, or the branches were boiled in water and an aromatic oil produced from the juices with the addition of olive oil.

Balthasar *See* BELSHAZZAR.

Banyas *See* CAESAREA PHILIPPI.

baptism The initiation rite of baptism defines the membership of the new COV-ENANT community for Christian believers, corresponding to the rite of CIRCUMCISION defining the people of the old covenant. A modern Christian baptism, with the application of water to raise the initiate to a new existence, still resembles in its basic outline the rites of the early Christians, and also the baptism of Jesus himself by JOHN THE BAPTIST (see Matthew 3.13–17). But when one seeks to reconstruct the details of practice and its deepest significance a number of ambiguities emerge.

Jewish rituals of lustration, such as those practised by the Dead Sea Covenanters at QUMRAN, or the baptism with a call to repentance that was the mission of John the Baptist, are concerned with cleansing and purification. When Christian baptism went beyond this, could it be said that the washing symbolized God's ultimate forgiveness, or was it a pledge that such forgiveness could be on offer to the faithful member of the new community? (See 1 Corinthians 6.9–11.)

The Baptism of Jesus Matthew 3.13–17

The narratives of the ACTS OF THE APOSTLES show that the early converts were baptized (see Acts 2.38–41; 8.12–38; 10.48; 16.15, 33). But it is by no means clear what was the relationship between the baptismal rite and the gift of the SPIRIT: were the two experiences synchronized, or consecutive, or did it depend on the persons and circumstances? (See Acts 1.5; 2.38; 8.14–17.) Acts 9.18 relates how PAUL was baptized, but *after* receiving the Spirit; Paul himself does not mention his own baptism in his letters, and he shows in 1 Corinthians 1.12–17 that it is important to concentrate on the meaning of baptism rather than on the identity of the person who performs the rite.

The Greek word *baptizo* means to dip or submerge. It would then be natural for baptismal candidates to undergo total immersion, having removed their old clothes and perhaps putting on a new baptismal garment (this makes sense of a passage like Colossians 3.9–10). In his most detailed theological interpretation of baptism (in Romans 6) Paul shows how converts share symbolically in the DEATH OF CHRIST, and will ultimately share in Christ's RESURRECTION. The language used here, while theo-logically Christian, also owes something to the contemporary experience of the MYSTERIES in the Greco-Roman world. Initiation into the Mystery Cult was an adult experience; of course most of Paul's first converts would have been baptized as adults, whereas in the modern world the majority of Christian baptisms are probably still of infants (with the consequence that most are unable to recall the actual experience).

baptistery A baptistery is a room that is part of, or adjacent to, a church; it contains the font, used for the liturgical rite of the sacrament of BAPTISM.

Bar Kokhba 'Bar Kokhba' is the name given to the leader of a second Jewish revolt against Rome, 132–135 CE. His original name was probably Shimon bar Kosibah (son of Kosibah); he was nicknamed Bar Kozibah (Son of the Lie) by those who disap-proved of the revolt. His supporters called him Bar Kokhba (Son of the Star), asso-ciating him with the messianic prophecy of Numbers 24.17. The rebels used caves, such as those above Ein Gedi, west of the Dead Sea, as bases and hideouts (from which archaeologists have recovered evidence about them). The emperor Hadrian put down the revolt and carried out his plan to rebuild Jerusalem as a Roman colony (Aelia Capitolina), from which Jews were banned.

Barabbas John's Gospel refers explicitly (18.39), and Mark's and Matthew's impli-citly, to a custom attached to the feast of PASSOVER when a prisoner chosen by the Jewish crowds would be released. It is unclear whether this custom originated with PILATE the governor, or with the Jews. There is no evidence for the custom outside of the Gospels. Following the TRIAL OF JESUS Pilate sees this as a way of releasing Jesus, whom he regards as innocent; but the Jews call instead for the release of Barabbas, a notorious prisoner. Mark 15.7 suggests he was a terrorist, presumably a ZEALOT, while John 18.40 calls him a bandit. The name Barabbas is a patronymic ('son of' a named father) and his personal name is not given, although some traditions suggest it was also 'Jesus'. Barabbas could mean son of someone called Abba, or son of an honoured teacher ('Rabban'), or enigmatically 'son of a father'.

Barak *See* DEBORAH.

Barnabas 1 Barnabas was a missionary companion of PAUL, sent with him and JOHN MARK to Cyprus by the Church of ANTIOCH (Acts 13.2–4). Barnabas was a native of Cyprus; he had been sent by the Jerusalem Church to Antioch, where he met up with Paul (Saul). The partnership of Paul and Barnabas broke up with differences of opinion over the reliability of John Mark and over the status of GENTILES in the early Church.

2 The *Epistle of Barnabas* is a text from the 2nd century CE, with a highly critical approach to traditional Jewish concepts (going significantly further than the letter to the HEBREWS). According to its author, Judaism always has been a false religion; the law was not meant to be interpreted literally, but is a symbolic pointer to Christ (when interpreted by the methods of ALLEGORY and TYPOLOGY. See for example the reference to the crimson wool of the SCAPEGOAT ritual in *Barnabas* 7.11.) Although the text is actually anonymous, it became attributed to Barnabas. But it is improbable that the author was the same Barnabas who was Paul's companion.

Bartholomew One of the 12 DISCIPLES of Jesus, referred to in Mark 3.18 (also in Matthew 10.3; Luke 6.14; Acts 1.13). It is probable that he will have had another, personal, name because Bartholomew is a patronymic, meaning 'son of Tolmai' (Ptolemy). Because he is listed in the Gospels alongside PHILIP, it has been suggested that he is Philip's friend Nathanael (as mentioned in John 1) but there can be no proof of this. Traditionally Bartholomew is said to have been flayed alive in Armenia.

Bartimaeus Jesus, on his way to Jerusalem from JERICHO, heals a blind beggar named Bartimaeus (Mark 10.46–52). This is not only a healing but also a call to discipleship (10.52; see DISCIPLE). Bartimaeus may have become a significant person in the early Church, but MARK also seems to contrast his straightforward response with that of the rich man (10.17–22), and with the ambitions of JAMES and JOHN, SONS OF ZEBEDEE (10.35–45).

Baruch Baruch was the friend and secretary of JEREMIAH; he was known as a 'scribe' or royal clerk (see Jeremiah 36.32), a status confirmed by a seal discovered bearing his name, family and title. The text of the book of Jeremiah records the prophet's dictations to Baruch (Jeremiah 36; 45), as well as Baruch's involvement in preserving the documents relating to the purchase of the field at Anathoth (Jeremiah 32.12–16). According to Jeremiah 43.1–7, both Jeremiah and Baruch are taken from Jerusalem to Egypt, although a later tradition assumes that Baruch went to Babylon, from where he writes the APOCRYPHAL book of Baruch. This should be regarded as an edifying expansion of the Biblical tradition, to be dated late in the Second Temple period (between 200 and 60 BCE). The book consists of a narrative introduction, cast as a letter (1.1–14), followed by a prose prayer (1.15–3.8), a WISDOM poem (3.9–4.4), and a further consolatory poem (4.5–5.9) echoing Second ISAIAH. It was probably written in Hebrew, although it now exists only in translations.

Bashan, or Batanea The Bashan is the region north-east of the river Jordan, a well-watered fertile plain between Mount Hermon and Gilead. It was famous as a pasture for herds of cattle (see the metaphorical references in Amos 4.1; Psalm 22.12). Before the coming of the Israelites its king was Og, celebrated as a giant with his iron bedstead, in size about 4 x 5 metres (see Deuteronomy 3.1–13; Joshua 9.10; Numbers 21.33–35). MOSES and the Israelites fought a battle against Og, and his captured lands were first allotted to the sons of MANASSEH (SON OF JOSEPH). When the kingdoms of Israel and Judah were divided, Ramoth-gilead with the Bashan fell to the kings of SYRIA (1 Kings 22.3; 2 Kings 8.28). Subsequently it was returned to Israel, only to be conquered and its population deported by the ASSYRIANS in 732 BCE. Batanea was the name given to the area as an administrative unit in the HELLENISTIC PERIOD. It was conquered in part by JUDAS MACCABEUS (1 Maccabees 5.17–45), but annexed by the Romans under Pompey in 63 BCE and given to the Ituraeans and then to HEROD THE GREAT.

basilica Originally a basilica was a large rectangular Roman building, used for civic assemblies, and located within the forum. Very much later the term became used for Christian churches built on a similar pattern: there would be a central nave with a colonnade on either side, and a semi-circular apse at the eastern end (*see* CHURCHES, CHRISTIAN). The earliest Christian assemblies would be in the open air, or in the house of a patron or sponsor; the first purpose-built churches were likely to be of the house-church pattern, imitating the patron's house, and only became like assembly halls when the congregations had grown considerably in size.

Batanea *See* BASHAN.

Bathsheba Bathsheba is included, although not by name, in the genealogy of Matthew 1.6 as 'the wife of Uriah', the mother of SOLOMON. The story is told in 2 Samuel 11 of the seduction of Bathsheba, the wife of Uriah the Hittite, by King DAVID, leaving her pregnant. Uriah was away at war and refused the king's summons to return home (so as to conceal the adultery); David then arranged that Uriah should be killed in the siege of Rabbah. Bathsheba became David's wife, but the prophet NATHAN denounced the king's sin, prophesying the early death of the child. Solomon was her second child by David; Bathsheba organized his succession to the throne of Israel, with the help of Nathan, according to 1 Kings 1. Her other sons are listed in 1 Chronicles 3.5.

There was an ancient pool in Jerusalem, known locally as Bathsheba's pool, and believed to be the site where she was bathing when seen by David. The pool became an underground cistern for the Grand New Hotel built in 1885 near the Jaffa Gate.

bear There are 13 references to bears in the Hebrew Bible, suggesting that they were relatively common. In the New Testament there is a single reference at Revelation 13.2. The Syrian brown bear (*Ursus syriacus*) was a quite shy, but feared, animal which probably became extinct in Israel as a result both of hunting and of the clearance of the woodland which provided an ideal habitat. Similar bears do survive in Syria, Turkey and Iran.

Four references speak of the ferocity of the female bear (see Proverbs 17.12; 2 Samuel 17.8; 2 Kings 2.24; see also Hosea 13.8, illustrating divine punishment: 'I will fall upon them like a bear robbed of her cubs'). Bears as well as lions used to be found in the area of BETHLEHEM, as DAVID told SAUL: 'Whenever a lion or a bear came, and took a lamb from the flock, I went after it and struck it down, rescuing the lamb from its mouth' (1 Samuel 17.34–35). AMOS used his experience as a herdsman to describe the Day of the Lord 'as though a man fled from a lion only to meet a bear' (Amos 5.19). ISAIAH hopes for the day when 'the cow and the bear shall graze, their young shall lie down together' (Isaiah 11.7).

Beatitudes The statements of blessing in Jesus' SERMON ON THE MOUNT (in Matthew 5.3–10, 11–12) and in the Sermon in the Plain (Luke 6.20–22) are known as the Beatitudes (the Latin word *beatitudo* is found in the VULGATE translation of Romans 4.6–9). They are declarations of the present happiness and/or future blessedness of certain categories of people. They have also been called 'makarisms' (from the Greek word *makarios*, meaning 'happy', which introduces each of the sayings. The most striking feature of both the Matthean and Lucan versions is that they represent a reversal of worldly values.

Scholars argue that the makarism formula is eschatological in meaning, that is, it relates particularly to the future in the last days (*see* ESCHATON). The formula has its basis in Old Testament prophecy (see Isaiah 61.1–7), but with key modifications. The suggestion is that Jesus' teaching originally used the three blessings (on the poor, the mourners, and the hungry) and these have been expanded (in Matthew's version) by the use of the parallelism characteristic of Hebrew poetry (*see* PSALMS). The reference to persecution in Matthew 5.10 would be added when early Christians experienced such persecution (see 1 Peter 3.14). There is a telescoped version attributed to Polycarp: 'Blessed are the poor, and those persecuted for righteousness' sake, for theirs is the kingdom of heaven.' And the Gospel of THOMAS (69) has a GNOSTIC reformulation: 'Blessed are they which are persecuted in their hearts. It is they who have truly known the FATHER.' *See also* POVERTY.

Beelzebul Beelzebul (alternatively Beelzebub) is given as the name of the ruler of demons, when Jesus is accused of performing MIRACLES as a sorcerer empowered by demon possession (see Mark 3.22; Matthew 12.24, 27; Luke 11.15, 18). This is a comparatively obscure name for SATAN; its Hebrew origins are debated. The first syllable is the same as the name of the Canaanite deity BA'AL, meaning 'lord of …'. The second part means either 'of the dwelling/temple' or 'of excrement/dung heap', hence 'Lord of the flies' (see the novel by William Golding). See 2 Kings 1.2 for a possible reference to a specific pagan deity. Later references (as in the Gospels) may be neutral/factual or more likely contemptuous and so scatological.

Beer-sheba Biblical Beer-sheba is identified as Tel Sheva, three miles to the east of the modern city of Beer Sheba, in the south of the country (the Negev), although some ancient remains have also been found in the modern city. The town was important in the time of the PATRIARCHS and its name (Beer-sheba means 'well of the oath') relates to the story of ABRAHAM's well in Genesis 21.19–33. ISAAC lived there and dug a well there (Genesis 26.13–33). JACOB offered sacrifice there (Genesis 46.1–4).

Beer-sheba was captured by JOSHUA and was allocated as the territory of SIMEON (1) within the land of JUDAH (Joshua 19.2). In the time of the Judges Beer-sheba was a city, probably the centre of a district (1 Samuel 8.2). The expression 'from DAN to Beer-sheba' (the length of the country from north to south) reflects its importance, both administratively and religiously (see Judges 20.1; 1 Samuel 3.20; 2 Samuel 3.10). It must have remained a religious centre in the later days of the kingdom, because it is reproached along with Dan and BETHEL for its rivalry with Jerusalem (Amos 5.5; 8.14). In the course of JOSIAH's reform all the high places, including Beer-sheba, were defiled (2 Kings 23.8). To illustrate this, archaeologists have discovered an altar that had been dismantled and built into a wall (its essence remained, despite its removal). Beer-sheba is named as being resettled after the Babylonian EXILE (see Nehemiah 11.27). Later it was probably the southern boundary of Idumaea.

Beit El *See* BETHEL.

Bel and the Dragon These stories are found in an additional chapter in the Greek version of DANIEL. They underline the folly of worshipping idols. There are similarities with Daniel 6 in the means of punishment (being thrown into a lions' den); on the one hand this story is a heightened fantasy, but on the other hand it is more historical than Daniel on the royal succession.

belief *See* FAITH.

Beloved Disciple This enigmatic figure appears four times in JOHN'S GOSPEL: sitting next to Jesus at the Last Supper (*see* EUCHARIST) (John 13.23), where he queries the identity of the traitor; standing at the foot of the cross, beside Jesus' mother; running with PETER to the tomb on the day of RESURRECTION, in response to MARY MAGDALENE'S announcement (John 20.2–10); and in the Galilean resurrection narrative of John 21. Some would further identify him with the disciple whose acquaintance with the HIGH PRIEST gains access for himself and Peter to the courtyard during the TRIAL; but this identification is nowhere claimed in the text of 18.15–16.

His position at the Last Supper would suggest he was a particularly trusted friend, given the seating etiquette at formal meals, but who among the 12 DISCIPLES was he? Traditionally he has been thought to be JOHN, SON OF ZEBEDEE the Galilean fisherman. If this is so we have a special reason for respecting the authenticity of his reflections on the life of Christ within the Gospel (which has been attributed to him until modern times). On the other hand we have a further reason not to identify the Beloved Disciple with the one known to the High Priest, since such a relationship, across the social divide, would be rather unlikely. Some would therefore prefer to identify him with JOHN MARK, an enthusiastic young disciple whose mother's house may well have hosted the Last Supper as well as later meetings of Christians (see Acts 12.12). This John worked with PAUL, BARNABAS, and later Peter, in the MISSION field.

A position of real trust is offered to the Beloved Disciple with the care of Jesus' mother, which he takes over from the time of the crucifixion (19.26–27). Some have interpreted this symbolically, with Mary standing in for the Church and representing the future Christians; it has been taken more literally within Church traditions, and the stories of Mary living with the apostle John in EPHESUS are well documented. Indeed her house can be visited by tourists.

There are various other theories, for instance that he was LAZARUS, whom Jesus had raised from the dead (John 11) – although there is no other evidence that Lazarus occupied so central a position among the disciples – or that the Beloved Disciple ultimately represents the ideal of discipleship as a role model, rather than being any named individual. Evidence from chapters 13 and 21 does seem to suggest that the person in the frame was someone identifiable by the community for whom this Gospel is written. An ideal figure does not conduct *sotto voce* conversations, as a real person does. Jesus has been having a conversation with Peter in John 21 to challenge and restore him; whereupon Peter is said to turn attention to their patient follower. Their discussion about the future of the Beloved Disciple would suggest that his unexpected death had presented a real problem for the later Church community, as a crucial eyewitness had died before the PAROUSIA; they needed reassurance as to their own future, as well as to confirm that this Gospel book was indeed teaching stemming from this source (see 21.23–24). It remains possible that an actual revered leader of the community, and the channel for its inspired teaching, should in due time be regarded as a role model of discipleship for others; this would explain such a strangely allusive way of referring to an historic figure of such influence.

Belshazzar, or Balthasar Belshazzar was the son and also the co-regent of the Babylonian king Nabonidus who reigned from c.556 to 539 BCE. During his reign Babylonia fell to the Persian conqueror Cyrus in 539 BCE. Belshazzar is famous for the great feast which he held (according to Daniel 5) during which doom-laden words were written on the palace wall (*see* MENE, MENE ...). According to Daniel, Belshazzar not only lost the empire, but also died himself that night (but this is not corroborated in Assyrian sources). The dramatic series of events is celebrated in later poetry (for example by Heinrich Heine) and music (by William Walton).

Benjamin Benjamin is the last son of JACOB, by his second wife RACHEL, who died giving birth. This happened after the return from Mesopotamia (see Genesis 35.16–18). The name Rachel gave her son (*Ben-oni*) means 'son of my suffering/sorrow'; the name Jacob preferred (*Ben-jamin*) means 'son of the right hand/south', with connotations of good fortune. Benjamin is the ancestor of the tribe bearing his name which occupied the central ridge between Jerusalem and BETHEL (Joshua 18.11–20). Originally associated with the northern tribes, it was incorporated in the Southern Kingdom after the time of SOLOMON. Israel's first king, SAUL, had come from the tribe of Benjamin.

Beth El *See* BETHEL.

Beth Hanania *See* BETHANY.

Beth Page *See* BETHPHAGE.

Bethabara Given the variety of locations proposed for the baptismal activity of JOHN THE BAPTIST, commemorated by pilgrimage sites on both sides of the river JORDAN, it is interesting that the 6th-century mosaic map at Madaba in Jordan marks John's activity as on the west side of the river at a place called Bethabara. The reference is not, as in John's Gospel to 'Bethany beyond Jordan' (1.26–28). The Church Father Origen in the 3rd century, unable to locate this Bethany, suggested changing the text to 'Bethabara across the Jordan', a proposal that was widely influential. Bethabara means literally 'house of the crossing' and would most naturally refer to a ford in the river. Such a reference occurs at Joshua 2.7 and Judges 7.24, marking the place where JOSHUA and the Israelites crossed into the Promised Land. It could also be where ELIJAH is taken up to heaven in a fiery chariot (2 Kings 2.4–14); Elijah's Hill (Tel Mar Elias) is nearby. Christian pilgrim tradition welcomed the synchronization of Old and New Testament events, whereby Jesus leads the New Israel to heavenly salvation. The view from John's Gospel would most naturally be for a baptism site in Jordan, while conversely the map maker in Jordan would think of the west bank. A ford on the river is more than just a compromise.

Bethany, or Beth Hanania Bethany is a village on the eastern slope of the Mount of Olives outside Jerusalem (see Mark 11.1). It is suggested by some that it is identical with Ananiah, mentioned in Nehemiah 11.32. The village of Bethany plays a prominent role in the New Testament, being the home of Jesus' friends MARTHA, MARY and LAZARUS (see Luke 10.38–42; John 12.1–8; Matthew 21.17; Mark 11.11). It was here that Jesus spent the night following his triumphal entry into Jerusalem. Pilgrims to Jerusalem from Jericho would make their last halt here before entering the city. Bethany was also the location of the house of Simon the Leper, where Jesus was anointed (see Matthew 26.6–13; Mark 14.3–9; compare Luke 7.36–50). According to Luke 24.50–51 it was also the place of the ASCENSION.

The Arab village is now known as el-Azariyeh; this is a version of the name Lazarion by which it was known in early Christian tradition. This denotes a sanctuary and church that were built over the traditional site of the tomb of Lazarus.

There may have been another village called Bethany on the east side of the river JORDAN, but its actual location is unknown. It is referred to in John 1.28 as 'Bethany beyond Jordan', the site of the activity of JOHN THE BAPTIST. But in some manuscripts it is referred to as BETHABARA.

Bethel, Beth El or Beit El Bethel was a town on the border of the territory of EPHRAIM, according to Joshua 16.1–4. This was the site of JACOB's dream, as described in Genesis 28.10–22, after which he called the place 'House of God' (Beth El in Hebrew). The tribe of JOSEPH took control of Bethel from the Canaanites (Judges 1.22–26). Subsequently, according to Judges 20.26, there was a place of worship at Bethel, and SAMUEL visited it to judge the people (1 Samuel 7.16). With the pressure to centralize worship in Jerusalem, the importance of the sanctuary at Bethel was diminished; but it was then restored, following the division of the kingdom, when JEROBOAM I, king of Israel (the Northern Kingdom), built temples at DAN on the northern border and Bethel on the southern frontier. The prophet AMOS prophesied against Israel at Bethel (see Amos 7). Bethel was captured by Judah, but then retaken by Israel (2 Chronicles 13.19). It was partly destroyed by the ASSYRIANS in 721 BCE and laid waste by the BABYLONIANS in 587 BCE, but resettled following the Babylonian EXILE (Nehemiah 11.31).

The site has been excavated on several occasions by American archaeologists. Since the 1970s it has been a Jewish settlement in the occupied West Bank, the House of God symbolically reclaimed (the Jewish pioneers would say) for the modern state of Israel.

Bethesda, or Bethzatha This is the pool (or twin pools) that is the scene for the MIRACLE of healing, in JOHN'S GOSPEL 5.2–9, of the man who has been ill for 38 years. The pools which are just north of the Temple were rediscovered in 1871 and identified by the five porticoes or porches of the building beside the pool. There is evidence that the premises continued in use as a healing sanctuary after the New Testament period. The name Bethesda, used in the KING JAMES VERSION means 'house of mercy', while Bethzatha, possibly the original reading, means 'house of olives/oil'; some other versions of John 5.2 read BETHSAIDA or 'house of the fisherman/nobility' (which causes confusion with the site in Galilee). The Copper Scroll at QUMRAN (written in ARAMAIC, possibly c.100 CE) lists places where treasure is to be found, including 'Bethesdatain' – a plural word which probably denotes the twin pools on this site in Jerusalem. JOSEPHUS writing at the end of the 1st century CE puts this Aramaic name into Greek as Bezetha (the name preserved as this district of Jerusalem). Bethzatha could be an attempt to make this Greek word mean something.

Bethlehem The name in Hebrew means 'house of bread'; Bethlehem is also called 'Ephratha' (see Micah 5.2), meaning 'the fruitful'. Situated just six miles south of Jerusalem, but over the border in the Palestinian Authority, the town is revered by Jews, Christians and Muslims. It is the burial place of RACHEL, the wife of JACOB (Genesis 35.19). The Grotto of the Nativity in the basilica founded by Helena and Constantine in the 4th century marks the birthplace of Jesus Christ. Traditionally, because Bethlehem was part of the kingdom of DAVID, and JOSEPH and MARY were both of Davidic descent, they journeyed from NAZARETH to register the birth. For the massacre of the innocent children of Bethlehem, see Matthew 2.16–18 and HEROD THE GREAT. Today Bethlehem is a built-up town of 35,000 inhabitants, mostly Palestinian Arabs with a once-strong Christian denomination, and it is the location of a Palestinian Catholic University.

Bethphage, or Beth Page Bethphage is a village on the Mount of Olives, near Jerusalem. It lies close to BETHANY (see Matthew 21.1; Mark 11.1; Luke 19.29). This is where Jesus requisitioned an ass for the triumphal entry into Jerusalem. The Hebrew name for the village apparently means 'the house of unripe figs'. Its exact location is unknown.

Bethsaida 1 Three of Jesus' disciples (PETER, ANDREW and PHILIP) came from Bethsaida (John 1.44). The site of 22 acres, on the eastern bank of the JORDAN just north of the Sea of GALILEE, was identified in 1987 by Rami Arav (the shoreline of Galilee had retreated since ancient times). According to Luke 9.10–17 Jesus fed the multitude here; and in Mark 8.22–26 he restored sight to a blind man. Beneath the Hellenistic and Roman-era residential quarter of Bethsaida that Jesus knew, which was destroyed by the Romans in the JEWISH WAR (66–70 CE), was also found subsequently an Iron Age city with an elaborate city gateway (10th century BCE), likely to have been the capital of the kingdom of Geshur. It has been claimed that in the time of DAVID Bethsaida housed a larger Hebrew community than Jerusalem.

A large courtyard house from Jesus' time, built of grey basalt rocks, is thought, from the anchors and fish-hooks found there, to belong to a family with a fishing business, suggesting that fishing was not the trade of the poor (see FISH). The population of Bethsaida was predominantly middle-class. Another building which the excavators named SALOME's House, contained a wine cellar, an oven, and two basalt slabs for grinding grain. According to Mark 1.21, 29, Peter and Andrew moved to CAPERNAUM on the lakeside, presumably rather than pay tax to transport the fish and have it smoked at Magdala. Some excavators believe they have found the remains of a 1st-century temple to the cult of the Roman emperor; this could be linked to the renaming of the city as Bethsaida-Julias (in honour of Emperor Augustus' wife Livia Julia) by the Tetrarch Philip in 30 CE (*see* HERODIAN DYNASTY).

2 *See* BETHESDA.

Beth-shean, or Scythopolis Beth-shean is one of the cities of the Roman DECAPOLIS, the only one situated to the west of the river JORDAN. The centre of the Hellenistic and Roman city lies to the south-west of Tel el-Husn, the mound of the ancient city of Beth-shean (which is listed in Joshua 17.11 and Judges 1.27 as one of the cities which the Israelites were unable to conquer). Both sites have been extensively excavated by modern archaeologists, with striking results. The Roman city reveals colonnaded streets, a theatre, temple and bath houses. One inscription indicates a temple dedicated to 'Zeus Akraios' – the god of mountain tops and fortresses.

Bethzatha *See* BETHESDA.

Bible The earliest form of writing material in the New Testament period was PAPYRUS, made of strips from the inner bark of the papyrus plant which was abundant along the Nile. Documents survived well in the dry climate of Egypt, but elsewhere (by the 3rd century CE) there was a change to parchment or vellum. Parchment is the dried and treated skin of sheep or goats, and is named after PERGAMON in Asia Minor, noted for book manufacture and a famous library. Vellum is more expensive, made from the skin of calf or antelope, and used for superior quality manuscripts, such as Codex Vaticanus.

The 'codex' is a block of folded pages, sewn together between covers of wooden boards. This radically new form of book appeared gradually in secular Greek and Latin literature, from the 2nd to the 5th centuries; but it seems to have been part of a Christian-inspired revolution, as even the earliest Christian Biblical texts, copied in the 2nd century, are in codex form.

It is not unusual for ancient manuscripts to be defective and damaged, with whole sections missing. Awareness of the practical size and features of a sheep skin, or of the number of pages in a standard codex, can assist in estimating how much is missing. In the 9th century Nicephorus, Patriarch of Constantinople, used stichometry (studying the number of lines) to produce a catalogue of the book lengths of scripture – OLD TESTAMENT, NEW TESTAMENT and APOCRYPHA – which is still used today.

The Jewish scriptures (known to Christians as the Old Testament) are in three sections. The most important is the Law (Torah) – the first five books of Moses – and the other two sections are the Prophets and the Writings (or Hagiographa; see table p. xviii). The whole collection is referred to as 'Tanak' which is an acronym of the names in Hebrew – Torah, Nebiim (Prophets) and Ketubim (Writings). For more than two millennia the Jewish people have read the Torah formally in the central part of the SABBATH service in SYNAGOGUE; they read a particular portion (the *parsha*) each week, so as to complete the five Mosaic books annually. As the Chief Rabbi of England and Wales, Jonathan Sacks, says, 'Jews don't "read" the Bible. We sing it, argue with it, wrestle with it, listen to it, and turn it inside out to find a new insight we had missed before … The Bible isn't a book to be read and put down. It is God's invitation to join the conversation between Heaven and Earth that began at Mount Sinai and has never since ceased.' According to 1 Maccabees 12.9: 'we have, as encouragement, the holy books that are in our hands'. As to what constituted these holy books, see the prologue to ECCLESIASTICUS which refers to 'the Law, the Prophecies, and the rest of the books', and also 2 Maccabees 2.13–14.

Instead of reading the whole of scripture in its entirety, the Jewish poet Yehuda Amichai suggests that some might prefer a more selective process, in these words:

> I've filtered out of the book of Esther the residue
> of vulgar joy, and out of the book of Jeremiah
> the howl of pain in the guts. And out of the
> Song of Songs the endless search for love ...
> And from what was left over I pasted for myself a new Bible.

The Bible speaks with many voices, and, from the time of its emergence as an authoritative sacred text, readers and interpreters have noted its many repetitions, inconsistencies, and contradictions, as well as those parts which seem less palatable or problematic. Since the Enlightenment especially, BIBLICAL CRITICISM – that is a critical study of the Bible as far as possible without presuppositions – has irreversibly affected what may be called the 'precritical' understanding of the Bible, as simply a unified text – God's eternal, infallible and complete word.

If the idea of completeness may present difficulties, there is still a strong case in the realm of history for the idea of impressive continuity. The sequence Old Testament–New Testament–early Christian literature is closely knit, both chronologically and thematically. The Old Testament with the Apocrypha extends into New Testament times, and the New Testament with the Apostolic Fathers verges on the patristic age.

Bible*Lands* The society now known as Bible*Lands*, with its headquarters in High Wycombe in Buckinghamshire, has been in existence for more than 150 years. It is dedicated to work in a range of humanitarian projects, in partnership with local Christians in the lands of the Bible (Israel, Palestine, and Egypt), aiming to show the compassion of Jesus in tending, treating and teaching the young and the needy, regardless of their faith or nationality.

Biblical criticism Since the Enlightenment, from the 18th century CE onwards, scholarship has seen a new era of scientific criticism of the Bible, alongside and paralleled by that of other literary texts. It should not be assumed that prior to this the Christian tradition was uncritical; this would be a disservice to the intellectual wealth of studies in the periods of the Church Fathers, the Middle Ages, and the Reformation. Within the Christian traditions a prime mover for the approach of scientific criticism has been in Protestant scholarship; Roman Catholic scholarship only really accepted these methods in the 20th century. Within modern Judaism such methods created major tensions and were significantly responsible for divisions especially between the ultra-Orthodox and Reformed streams of Judaism (as are well illustrated in the novels of Chaim Potok).

It has been conventional, although not particularly helpful, to differentiate within Biblical criticism between higher and lower criticism. The image is one of a river, and the higher criticism is a movement towards the source of the river. Lower criticism would then concern itself with the Biblical text as it stands, while the higher criticisms are looking at earlier stages behind the existing text. For some detail see the articles on FORM CRITICISM, HISTORICAL CRITICISM, the varieties of LITERARY CRITICISM, and TEXTUAL CRITICISM.

Biblical Theology The first recorded use of the expression 'Biblical Theology' is found in 1629, where it is concerned with the 'relationship of theology to its Biblical bases'. Apart from this important but general sense, there is a highly technical sense, a movement of Biblical Theology which was very significant during the course of the 20th century in modern Biblical scholarship. This produced a radical shift in the meaning of the term, from the prescriptive sense ('theology that does and should accord with the Bible') to the descriptive meaning ('theology contained in the Bible'). It could also be used as a campaigning slogan in an anti-academic sense, of rescuing the Bible from the abstractions and liberal attitudes of academic scholarship.

A powerful symbol of 20th-century Biblical Theology, as of a new theological orthodoxy, was found in the commentary by Karl Barth on Paul's letter to the ROMANS (1919). This was translated into English by the Cambridge scholar Edwyn Hoskyns, whose work had a powerful influence among his students. Hoskyns himself was also influenced by a major project beginning in Germany under the guidance of Gerhard Kittel to produce a *Theological Dictionary of the New Testament* (1933–73). A theological word-book is a typical deposit of Biblical Theology, with its assumptions that 'Biblical' concepts in general are naturally distinctive and that they have an intrinsic directedness towards a full and normative exposition in the pages of the New Testament. The effect is to obscure the real distinctiveness of individual texts and particular expressions, in the interests of harmonization, and to risk suggesting that Old Testament words and meanings arrive at their fullest expression only in the New Testament. Hebrew and Greek influences make a contribution to meaning, but Christianity offers the creative perspective. This attitude can appear supersessionist, or even carry implications of ANTI-SEMITISM.

The Biblical Theology movement, in the excitement of its explorations, often failed to recognize how alien the Biblical world was from the modern one, and how difficult the process of translation could be. More recent theology has been critical of this movement. It is recognized that, while one can and should do Biblical Theology in the general sense, there is no prospect of writing any unitary Biblical Theology, much less *the* definitive Biblical Theology. But there can still be experiments and overtures to investigate particular topics and themes.

birth of Jesus *See* CHRISTMAS; INCARNATION; NATIVITY; and particularly the opening chapters of the Gospels of MATTHEW and LUKE.

birth of Moses Egypt's Pharaoh had condemned the Hebrew race to extinction, by ordering their male children killed at birth. Pharaoh's daughter saw a basket floating down the Nile and rescued it. She deduced that a Hebrew slave had given birth, wrapped the child in a blanket and, placing it in a basket, set it loose on the river in the hope that it would circumnavigate the decree of death. The Egyptian princess decided to adopt the child as her own, naming it 'Moses' (an Egyptian name probably meaning 'child', as in the name Ra-mses – 'child of the sun god'). A Jewish midrash comments: 'this is the reward for kindness, that even G*d himself called Moses by the name Pharaoh's daughter gave him'. 1 Chronicles 4.18 refers to 'a daughter of Pharaoh' named 'Bithiah' ('daughter of God') which Jewish tradition links with this princess: 'Moses was not your son, but you called him your son. You are not My daughter, but henceforth I shall call you My daughter.' According to the Jewish rabbis, Moses was born (and died) on the seventh day of the Hebrew month Adar (*see* CALENDAR); he lived as the righteous should, for 120 years.

blasphemy Blasphemy is in origin a Greek word meaning 'to damage someone's reputation'; in Classical Greek it related to what we call slander or libel. In the New Testament the secular sense of damaging anyone's reputation still persists, but the Biblical Greek of the New Testament is also coloured by the traditions of Israelite law directed against any speech or action showing contempt for God (see Mark 14.64). So in most New Testament instances the word means 'blasphemy'.

Throughout the centuries the Christian tradition has been strongly opposed to blasphemy, in order to protect religion or faith from assaults on God, the Church or the saints. It is classified as a mortal sin. Just as blasphemy was punished in the Old Testament by stoning, so also medieval canon law prescribed the severest punishments, including the death penalty. But since the Enlightenment secular legislators have regarded blasphemy not so much as a crime against God, but rather as a narrowly defined offence against society. For this reason there have been great pressures to broaden the legislation to apply, for example, to Muslim society.

blessing In the older traditions of the Hebrew Bible, blessings are simply given and shared; those who do so are those honoured by God, but not necessarily as PRIESTS. For example NOAH, who 'walked with God', was blessed ('God blessed Noah and his sons' – Genesis 9.1; 6.9), and in turn called down a blessing on Shem and those who lived in his tents (Genesis 9.26–27). A broadly similar kind of mutual blessing can be found in the New Testament, when Paul writes, 'God consoles us in all our afflictions, so that we may be able to console those who are in any affliction with the consolation with which we ourselves are consoled by God' (2 Corinthians 1.4). ABRAHAM is blessed by God after he has shown himself willing to sacrifice his only son, ISAAC, and as a result the nations of the earth are enabled to use his name as an exemplary formula by which they themselves may receive blessing (see Genesis 22.15–18).

There is another, more specific and proscribed view of blessing to be found in the Hebrew Bible. Abraham was earlier the recipient of a blessing through MELCHIZEDEK, king/priest of Salem (see Genesis 14.18–20). In this tradition only those with the appropriate ritual PURITY, or who belong to the appropriate priestly caste, are able to deliver a blessing. AARON, for example, receives his authority to bless Israel from MOSES (see Numbers 6.22–27). It is clearly a function of the priesthood to bless the worshipping community. But in JUDAISM both mother and father can have a function of blessing within the family for the SABBATH and for the PASSOVER meal. In the New Testament Gospels Jesus exercises a new authority to bless, blessing the children, blessing the bread and wine at the Last Supper (*see* EUCHARIST), blessing Simon PETER (Matthew 16.17), and as a final act blessing his disciples (in the act of blessing he withdrew from them, according to Luke 24.51). Rarely in the Gospels does anyone other than Jesus give a blessing; but SIMEON (2) blesses JOSEPH and MARY when they come to the TEMPLE in Luke 2.34. Jesus in his teaching radically redefines those who are to receive a blessing (see the BEATITUDES in Matthew 5 and Luke 6).

Boaz *See* JACHIN; RUTH.

body of Christ The overriding message of the New Testament concerns the physical death of Jesus Christ on the cross and his subsequent RESURRECTION; this makes possible, according to the New Testament writers, the bodily resurrection of humanity (see, for example, Romans 6.5; 1 Corinthians 15; 1 Peter 2.24). Because Christ died for all, and all participate in his act of dying, the crucifixion and shared resurrection has the effect of creating a new terminology, in which the 'body of Christ' comes to mean the CHURCH. This is the *corpus Christi* into which men and women are integrated by FAITH. A classic study on these themes, J. A. T. Robinson's *The Body* (SCM Press, 1952), may encourage the merging and fusing together of concepts which, however closely related, are not strictly identical: namely the physical body of Christ, his resurrection body, and the body which is the Church.

An interesting study of a section of the 'body of Christ', that is the particular Church seen in the correspondence of PAUL with the Corinthian Church in 1 and 2 CORINTHIANS, suggests some more general issues about physicality that are implicit in this terminology. 1 Corinthians 12.12 emphasizes the singleness of the body, with its corollary of the close interrelationship of the multiple members of the body (see also Romans 12.1–8). But the presence of women in the community, for example, might have raised particular issues of pollution, if Paul, or those who followed him, shared Jewish attitudes about PURITY, where pollution is avoided by carefully defining the boundaries for the human body. Invasion of the body from without is the underlying fear reflected in topics treated in 1 Corinthians 5–11. This could seem to be most acute in the question of the veiling of women in 11.2–16. When women are praying and prophesying the Church is protected from invasive pollutions because the women remain veiled. Modern society may find such issues abstruse and repugnant because we do not share such presuppositions about the body.

Bozrah Bozrah is the chief city of northern EDOM, one of the significant places on the HIGHWAY OF THE KING. This association with the royal highway helps to explain the prophetic texts of Isaiah 63.1–3. In the prophecy the appearance of splendidly crimson robes of royalty is actually explained by the red of the grape juice, resulting from the act of treading the winepress (seen as a symbol of judgement). Judgement on Edom is expressed with particular reference to Bozrah elsewhere at Isaiah 34.6; Jeremiah 49.13, 22; and Amos 1.12.

bread Bread has been made from early times, and the cultivation of grain marked the departure from the nomadic hunter-gatherer existence to a settled agrarian life. In Biblical times daily food consisted of small amounts of egg, goats' cheese or fish (rarely meat), consumed with proportionately large amounts of bread and some fruit and vegetables. The heavy reliance on bread as the bulk of the diet is marked by its name as a 'staff', i.e. 'the staff of bread' (Leviticus 26.26). The importance of this staple, which was made from a variety of grains including wheat, barley, spelt and other grindable constituents, is shown by the use of grain as currency (see Hosea 3.2), and also its indispensability in times of famine (2 Kings 7.1). Because bread was important it was offered to God in the TEMPLE. Jesus commented on DAVID's men eating the weekly offering of the Bread of the Presence in the Sanctuary in an emergency – usually only the priests ate these loaves (see Mark 2.26 and Leviticus 24.9). Bread came to mean all food, and in this broader sense may have inspired the name of Jesus' birthplace – BETHLEHEM = 'house of bread'.

Women made the bread at home, first grinding the flour, adding the necessary salt, water and a lump of old dough to raise it. Oil and honey could be included. When risen and ready it could be cooked on hot stones or an iron griddle, or even in an oven. It was a major time-consuming daily task. The round leavened cakes thus made differed from the thin biscuits of unleavened bread. The latter were also part of the normal diet, but had especial symbolic importance attached to the PASSOVER season, when they alone could be eaten (Exodus 12.15). Bread burnt as an offering in the Temple also had to be unleavened (see Leviticus 2.11).

Bread has an important role in many stories. ABRAHAM instructed SARAH his wife to make bread cakes for the heavenly visitors in Genesis 18.6. The haste of the Passover departure meant that unleavened bread figured on the menu, and the MANNA in the wilderness was regarded as heavenly bread (Exodus 16.4). Jesus was well aware of the vital role bread played in the individual's life and economy; Christians were instructed to pray 'Give us this day our daily bread' (Matthew 6.11), which may mean 'our bread for tomorrow' according to recent research into the use of the Greek (*see also* LORD'S PRAYER).

At the Last Supper (*see* EUCHARIST) Jesus chose the Passover bread as an explanation to his disciples for his coming execution. He took it, blessed it, snapped it and said, 'Take; this is my body' (Mark 14.22). John's Eucharistic Discourse (in John 6.48) develops from this the idea of Jesus as the Bread of Life, in one of his SEVEN 'I AM' SAYINGS; this happens in the related context of the Great Feeding. Christians were to recognize the presence of the risen Jesus in the repetition of what he did at the Last Supper, and to know him in the 'breaking of bread' (Luke 24.35 – *see also* EMMAUS). Paul urged the importance of respect for what was done at the early Church communion services in Corinth. Linking it to the proclamation of the Gospel he reminded them: 'For as often you eat this bread and drink the cup, you proclaim the Lord's death until he comes' (1 Corinthians 11.26). For many Christians the bread thus transcends its origins as a staple and acquires importance as a SACRAMENT in the EUCHARIST or in other religious contexts. In the tradition of the Greek Orthodox Church, for example, the 'holy bread' is that which, previously prepared, is distributed to the members of the congregation as they come to receive the final blessing.

See also SHOWBREAD, OR BREAD OF THE PRESENCE.

bridegroom The metaphor of the bridegroom is used as a title of Jesus Christ in the New Testament, as the MESSIAH in the context of the eschatological WEDDING FEAST. See, for example, John 3.29, where JOHN THE BAPTIST describes himself as 'the friend of the bridegroom'.

burning bush *See* EXODUS; IMAGES; MOSES.

C

Caesarea (Maritima) Caesarea (Arabic Qaisariyeh), on the coast of Israel halfway between Tel Aviv and Haifa, was founded by King HEROD THE GREAT between 22 and 10 BCE (on the site of a Sidonian fort known as Strato's Tower) and named in honour of Caesar. There are few natural harbours on the coast of Israel, so Herod decided to build a magnificent one to rival ALEXANDRIA, in honour of Emperor Augustus. (There is a fine temple dedicated to Rome and Augustus.) This deep sea harbour even had a sluice to flush out the sand and prevent its silting up. Caesarea served as the main port and administrative capital for Herod's kingdom, and after his death it became the headquarters of the Roman administration of Judaea. Its grandeur is described by JOSEPHUS. This was where Pontius PILATE governed, the Roman centurion Cornelius was stationed (Acts 10–11), PAUL was tried before Felix and imprisoned (c.58 CE) until he appealed to Caesar (Acts 23–26), and where the great Jewish revolts began in 66 and 132 CE (*see* JEWISH WAR). The site has been excavated since the 1950s with land and sea surveys. These have revealed harbour and streets, private and public buildings, an elaborate villa with swimming pool that may well have been Herod's palace, an aqueduct more than 10 miles long bringing water from the CARMEL mountain range, baths, circus, stadium, religious shrines, and a theatre (the Pontius Pilate inscription on a shrine dedicated to Emperor Tiberius was found nearby). Caesarea is now an Israeli Archaeological Park.

The Church Father Origen taught in Caesarea, with its famous library, and there produced the famous parallel texts and translation of the Bible known as the Hexapla. Caesarea flourished in the Byzantine period, when a large octagonal church replaced the temple. The Crusaders defended the town, but it was conquered in 1265 CE.

Caesarea Philippi, or Banyas In this area, nearly 30 miles north from CAPERNAUM and the Sea of GALILEE, is one of the sources of the river JORDAN. There, on a plateau to the south of Mount Hermon, is a large cave which was a sanctuary to the nature deity Pan, and particularly celebrated as such during the Hellenistic and Roman periods. The Greek name for the cave sanctuary was Paneion, and for the surrounding verdant area with its streams, Panias, which gives the modern Arabic name Banyas. HEROD THE GREAT enlarged the sanctuary, building a temple in front of it, dedicated to Augustus (the Augusteion). Later, in 2 BCE, his son Philip elaborated the complex further and built a city to the south of the springs, calling it Caesarea Philippi, to distinguish it from Herod the Great's foundation of CAESAREA (MARITIMA), although it was often known as Caesarea Paneas (see Pliny, *Natural History* 5.16.74). In this region is the traditional location where Jesus promised to PETER that he would become the rock on which the Church would be built (see Matthew 16.18).

Caiaphas, the High Priest Joseph Caiaphas is mentioned by name in Matthew 26 and in John 18 as the Jewish High Priest who was directly involved in the TRIAL and CRUCIFIXION of Jesus (*see* JOSEPHUS, *Antiquities* 20.9.1). His father-in-law Annas may have been the real power behind the scene; the family of Annas had achieved notoriety for corruption, and is cursed in the Talmud. One ornately decorated OSSUARY (a box for the reburial of a deceased's bones), which was found by construction workers within a family tomb at Abu Tor in Jerusalem in November 1990, carries the crude inscription in Aramaic 'Joseph called Caiaphas'. This ossuary is now in the Israel Museum and is likely to be that of the High Priest Caiaphas of the Gospels. The age of the bones and the provenance of the family tomb make this a likely identification. Inscriptions were usually roughly scratched on the casket, not carved like a tombstone, which of course would make imitation relatively easy.

Cain and Abel The story of Cain and Abel in Genesis 4.1–17 is a story of sibling rivalry: Cain is an agriculturalist while Abel, his younger brother, is a shepherd. When Abel's sacrificial offering is accepted by God, while Cain's is apparently spurned, Cain butchers his brother. Following the murder Cain disavows responsibility for his brother ('Am I my brother's keeper?' 4.9). Just as Adam and Eve were banished from the Garden of Eden (Genesis 3.24), so now Cain is both cursed and expelled (4.11) from working the land, destined to become a fugitive and vagabond. Cain is a man in basic contention with God, and his crime of fratricide is the ultimate in social unacceptability. The curious outcome is that Cain (or his descendant), far from wandering for eternity, becomes the builder of the world's first city. It is naturally tempting to read these narratives in terms of social judgement on degeneration, against agriculture and the urban life, but such a harking back to pastoral simplicity may be a naive conclusion. In the only explicit reference to the Old Testament in the first letter of John, Cain is linked with SATAN (1 JOHN 3.12); and JUDE 11 presents him as an evil example. *See also* KENITES.

calendar The Biblical calendar is lunar (based on the phases of the moon) which means, on average, that a month has $29\frac{1}{2}$ days. Although the English word 'month' is related to the word 'moon', the modern Western calendar is solar not lunar in basis. Therefore the Biblical months overlap the traditional Western months of the Gregorian calendar as well as having different names. It also meant that the lunar year would drift apart from the annual cycle of seasons; so in Judaism, as with the Babylonians, it was necessary to intercalate an additional month (a 'second Adar') every two or three years (in seven years out of 19). A similar problem was experienced in the Roman world, leading to the calendrical reforms instituted by Julius Caesar.

The Biblical year is traditionally reckoned from the beginning of CREATION (Genesis 1). At different times in their history the Hebrews operated with alternative dates for the New Year, either in the autumn equinox (as is also found in the 10th-century BCE GEZER calendar) or more usually with the spring equinox. Modern Judaism here differs from the more usual Biblical practice, with its New Year (Rosh Hashanah – not an Old Testament festival) located in the autumn.

The Hebrew word for 'week' literally means 'a seven'. In fact ancient Israel seems to have been the first society to operate with a seven-day week (see Genesis 1.1–2.3). Only the seventh day has a distinctive name, as the day of 'rest', or SABBATH. The Biblical day begins in the evening, at sunset, which again reflects the preferences of a lunar calendar.

THE HEBREW AND GREGORIAN CALENDARS

Hebrew month	English equivalent	Festival
Nisan (Abib)	March/April	PASSOVER
Iyyar (Ziv)	April/May	
Siwan	May/June	Weeks (PENTECOST)
Tammuz	June/July	
Ab	July/August	9th Ab (see LAMENTATIONS)
Elul	August/September	
Tishri (Ethanim)	September/October	YOM KIPPUR, TABERNACLES
Marcheswan (Bul)	October/November	
Kislev	November/December	HANUKKAH
Tebeth	December/January	
Shebat	January/February	
Adar	February/March	PURIM (see ESTHER)

The headmaster of a Jewish state school in England today observes: 'The rhythm of the Jewish week, culminating with the Sabbath, and the Jewish year, with its festivals, cannot punctuate the timetable and calendar if a significant proportion of the student body do not live their lives by the same cycle. The unique character of a Jewish school will … be lost.'

Caligula See references at GAIUS.

Calvary The traditional site of the CRUCIFIXION of Jesus, known as Calvary, is now to be found incorporated within the Church of the Holy Sepulchre in the Christian quarter of Jerusalem (see CHURCHES, CHRISTIAN). The rock of Calvary is visible both surrounding and beneath the altar of the Greek Orthodox chapel; upstairs the floor level of the Latin and Greek chapels corresponds to the top of the rocky outcrop on which the crucifixion of Jesus is believed to have taken place. (See also GOLGOTHA and STATIONS OF THE CROSS.)

camels The Hebrew word *gamal* refers equally to camels with one or two humps, and both kinds are found illustrated on ancient Near Eastern monuments. Camels are animals with a remarkable ability for endurance; they can survive in the desert without water for weeks on end (while a human being cannot survive beyond 36 hours). In the ancient Near East the camel was a valuable and respected animal, which would be eaten on only very rare occasions by the desert Bedouin (but regarded as 'unclean' – see Leviticus 11.4 and FOOD LAWS). It has been argued that a reference to camels, as in domesticated use, is one of the anachronistic details which help to date a literary text (see, e.g., Genesis 12.16; 24.10; Job 1.3); others say that limited use of the camel would have been possible even in the PATRIARCHAL period. In early Christian art the camel was seen as a symbol of temperance. It was occasionally regarded as symbolizing JOHN THE BAPTIST, because of its hair (see Mark 1.6).

Cana There are three possible claimants to be the site of Cana, where Jesus changed water into wine at a wedding feast (John 2); all three are near SEPPHORIS in Lower Galilee. A strong possibility is a small peasant village, Khirbet Qana, where excavations have discovered a likely Jewish synagogue with Beth Midrash, as well as a Byzantine veneration cave (where, according to pilgrimage accounts, the setting of the wedding miracle was portrayed). John's Gospel seems to depict Cana as a major centre of Jesus' ministry, comparable with CAPERNAUM. (In the 1st century CE both of them were small peasant villages, close to major centres in Galilee.) This may reflect the importance of a later Christian community here, living in close proximity with a Jewish community. All of which illustrates the problem of what constitutes evidence for a Biblical site: is it a strong tradition among earlier Christians that it was the place, or is it an archaeological discovery of storage jars and a context of Jewish purification rites (which can never establish absolutely that here and nowhere else was the site of the wedding miracle)?

Canaan The territory occupied by the Canaanites, and subsequently invaded by Israel (at least according to the story of the EXODUS), was a relatively narrow bridge of land between Africa and Asia Minor (*see also* FERTILE CRESCENT). Sometimes it is seen as the whole of PALESTINE and SYRIA; otherwise it is the land between the Mediterranean and the river JORDAN. Canaan's existence and its culture were largely dominated by either Mesopotamia or Egypt, depending on which had the superiority. The territory was strategic, controlled by whoever held the three roads running north to south: the royal road along the coast (the WAY OF THE SEA); the way through the rift valley of the Jordan (the HIGHWAY OF THE KING); and the mountain route through Judaea and Samaria. *See also* GEOGRAPHY OF THE BIBLE.

There is an alternative theory to the Biblical account of the Exodus from Egypt and the subsequent conquest of Canaan by the Israelites under JOSHUA; this suggests that the cultural shift between the original inhabitants and the tribes of ISRAEL was in whole, or in part, the result of internal and complex revolutionary movements within Canaanite society, rather than an act of invasion and conquest. But it has to be remembered that semi-nomadic activities and frequent migrations of population had been a regular feature in this region for centuries, even affecting the inhabitants of established cities.

Evidence about the Canaanites, apart from the critical viewpoints expressed in the Old Testament, comes from the letters found at Tel EL-AMARNA in Egypt, the texts excavated at UGARIT (Ras Shamra) in the north, and inscriptions relating to the PHOENICIANS.

canon of scripture 'Canon' is a Greek word which literally means a 'measuring rod'. The term is used in the Christian tradition, and elsewhere by analogy (see below), to denote a list of books which have the AUTHORITY and status of scripture. The Muratorian Canon is a catalogue (of the books of the New Testament) written in bad Latin probably in Rome at the end of the 2nd century CE. This list interestingly/ surprisingly includes the *Apocalypse of Peter*. It provides some of the earliest evidence for the Christian process towards classifying and authorizing texts. Such an important fragment survived in an 8th-century manuscript which was discovered and published in the 18th century by L. A. Muratori. The reference in 2 Peter 3.15–16 to the letters of PAUL seems to suggest a collection of his letters, seen in relationship to 'other scriptures', which again might be an early step in the process of creating a canon.

This process of determining what should be the authoritative texts extended over at least the first five centuries of the Christian era, with significant differences of viewpoint between councils of Christians in East and West. There were several pressures towards fixing the limits of authoritative Christian writings, pressures that were not unconnected with the need to define the identity of the Christian institution, the CHURCH. Among these external pressures were the various movements known generically as the Gnostics. These separatist groups with exclusive tendencies claimed to possess esoteric sources of revelation; if these GNOSTIC GOSPELS had achieved widespread acceptance within Christian communities, the nature of Christianity would have been altered drastically. So there was pressure on Christian groups, who felt themselves to be more representative of the Church, to state more clearly in text and creed the basis of their belief.

Another pressure was the activity of Marcion, son of the bishop of Sinope, who was expelled from the Church at Rome around 144 CE. His policy was to reject all religious writings that disagreed with his own theories. Hence he rejected the entire OLD TESTAMENT as unacceptable because of what he saw as its internal contradictions and its opposition to Christian revelation; he also added to the list of rejections those parts of the NEW TESTAMENT which echoed the Old Testament (for example a text like the birth stories in LUKE'S GOSPEL). This ideological discrimination and censorship left Marcion with a truncated form of Luke and the letters of Paul (as in his view representing a stand against the Jews). Marcion wrote his own prefaces to the preferred texts; his opponents produced a series of anti-Marcionite prologues to the Gospels, written in Greek but preserved in some editions of the VULGATE; these prologues date to the end of the 2nd century CE or later.

The third pressure came from a 2nd-century CE movement called MONTANISM, which emphasized Christian prophecy and the continuity of inspiration within the Church (*see* PROPHECY). The Gospels from the 1st century could not be regarded as the last word, or any final form of revelation. Montanus and his two female acolytes, operating from the mountain village of Pepuza in Phrygia, claimed to be receiving messages with ultimate authority in the names of the TRINITY in person. Montanism illustrated, for the Christian communities at large, the danger of leaving revelation as an open-ended phenomenon, without circumscribing it in some way. The earliest Church possessed as its scripture the Hebrew Bible, in its Greek translation, the SEPTUAGINT. To this was added the accumulated experience of the authoritative sayings of Jesus. The enlarged canon of scripture needed to follow up what was implicit in the Church's proclamation; the eventual result was that of the community subordinating itself to a closed body of apostolic tradition (*see* APOSTLES). The earliest exact witness to the canon of the New Testament as now regularly defined is to be found in the text of the Festal Letter of Athanasius, dated 367 CE; and the combined canon of Old and New Testament appears in the Council of Rome in 382 CE under Pope Damasus (sometimes referred to as the 'Gelasian Decree', as quoted by Gelasius in 495 CE).

The Hebrew Bible (Old Testament) has already been referred to as a 'canon' of scripture. This term should be used here with care, as only in part analogous to the formation of the Christian canon. JOSEPHUS defines the status of the scriptures (contra *Apionem* 1.38–43) on the basis of divine authority, fixity of number of books, a limited period during which they were composed, and a text that is unaltered and unalterable. The final delimitation of the Jewish canon of scripture is traditionally associated with the work of Rabbi Yohannan ben Zakkai and the Sanhedrin at Yabneh (Jamnia) after the fall of Jerusalem in 70 CE. But the main outline of the canon was widely accepted prior to the start of the Christian era (see the Greek preface to ECCLESIASTICUS which refers to 'the Law, the prophets, and the other books'). At least the first two sections had been in existence for several centuries, the result of stages of development. Whatever other disputes are recorded in the Gospels between Jesus and the Jewish leaders, the question of the limits of scripture is not one of them. Nor were the results of the Yabneh Sanhedrin the work of innovators. But debate did remain about some of the documents within the third grouping, such as ECCLESIASTES, ESTHER, and SONG OF SONGS. It has been suggested that the SADDUCEES held a different canon to that agreed, substantially by PHARISEES, at Yabneh. But this is probably a misunderstanding of Josephus' statement: the Sadducees' contrast to which he refers is between the first five books (TORAH) and the Oral Law (as taught by the Pharisees), not between Torah and Prophets, even if the Sadducees rejected the book of DANIEL.

Canticles *See* SONG OF SOLOMON.

Capernaum Capernaum (Hebrew Kefar Nahum) in the 1st century CE was a border town of possibly 1000 inhabitants on the fertile north-western shore of the Sea of GALILEE. The frequency with which it is mentioned in the Gospels suggests that Capernaum came closest to being the base Jesus used during the ministry in Galilee. Archaeologists have uncovered much of the town that he would have known, including a primitive house that became a house church and later an octagonal building. The famous synagogue has been partially restored but in its later form. The main housing in Capernaum in Jesus' day was in the form of small buildings grouped around irregular courtyards (as can be seen on the site in the area known as Insula II).

The walls were of basalt supporting a light roof (*see* MARK 2.1–12). Since the 1st century CE one room was singled out and its walls plastered; it seems to have been put to public use and venerated by association as the house of PETER the apostle, as early PILGRIMAGE descriptions attest. Later the room was enclosed within an octagonal church. The synagogue is a striking building in brilliant white against the black basalt houses. Its elaborate decoration may be dated to the 3rd century CE. But there are strong indications that it was built over a plainer, much earlier building on a slightly different axis.

carbon-14 dating Carbon-14 or radiocarbon dating is one of the main scientific techniques for dating organic remains, and thus has been used extensively in Biblical ARCHAEOLOGY. Anything organic (olive stones, wood, bone, grain) produces and therefore contains the particular isotope of carbon, carbon-14. When an organism dies, carbon is no longer absorbed and so the carbon-14 present in the material begins to decay. This rate of decay is known as regular and measurable. So by examining the carbon-14 which remains in a substance, scientists can date the point at which the carbon-14 began to decay. Matching radiocarbon years to calendar years can still be problematic, except where the precise age of an artefact is known, as in the case of a tree where its exact age can be deduced from the rings in its trunk (dendrochronology). The amount of carbon present in the atmosphere varies at different times and in different areas, so the radiocarbon calibration may need some adjustment to take account of this.

Carmel, Mount Carmel is a mountain range abutting the Mediterranean, with a very narrow coastal plain (Jeremiah 46.18), near the port of Haifa. It is the continuation in a north-westerly direction of the hills of Samaria. According to Song of Songs 7.5 it is noted as a symbol of beauty (see also Isaiah 33.9). On the mountain top an altar to BA'AL was established; here the prophet ELIJAH challenged the prophets of Ba'al to a contest (see 1 Kings 18.17–46).

carob *See* CROPS.

celibacy The Hebrew Bible uses two words which are frequently translated as 'virgin': *betulah*, meaning a woman who has never had sexual intercourse, and *almah*, referring to a young woman who is mature sexually, marriageable, or newly married. This latter word is used in Isaiah 7.14; since early Christian times it has been understood as a prophecy of the VIRGIN BIRTH, supported by the SEPTUAGINT translation with the Greek word *parthenos*, 'virgin'. In Hebrew thought a permanent state of virginity was not regarded as desirable, because to deny the possibility of MARRIAGE was to reject the responsibilities of humanity made in the image of God (see Genesis 1.27–28; *see also* IMAGO DEI). In preparation for marriage, chastity was encouraged in a young man as part of the ideal of PURITY (see Proverbs 5–7); virginity was required of a young woman, for the marriage to be valid.

In the New Testament the Greek word *parthenos* can be used of both sexes, but more usually of women (it is a feminine noun in Classical Greek). Possibly Paul uses it of male and female in 1 Corinthians 7.25–27, in a context where he states a preference for the unmarried state, and metaphorically of the whole Church in 2 Corinthians 11.2. But the striking instance is Revelation 14.4, where the word is indisputably masculine. This usage leads on to *parthenos* as an epithet of Christian figures such as JOHN THE APOSTLE.

What does *parthenos* imply in Revelation 14.4? Is it physical asceticism (celibacy) or moral purity in a metaphorical sense of abstention from sins? Does the use of marriage as a metaphor for the relationship of Christ and the Church (see Revelation 21; but compare Ephesians 5.22–27) have the effect of commending marriage, or removing it to a spiritual plane? Is the reference to those who are spiritually pure because they do not worship the Beast (see Revelation 13), or to those who observe the purity regulations required of participants in a holy war (see Deuteronomy 23.9–10 and at QUMRAN 1QM7.3–7)? Whatever the particular implications at this early date, clearly many later Christians have adopted celibacy as an ideal for priests and believers.

census A major census is recorded at the start of the book of NUMBERS: 'Take a census of all the congregation of the people of Israel, by clans, by fathers' houses, according to the number of names, every male, head by head' (1.1–2). Exodus 30.11–12 reports the belief that a military census could cause a plague, and so a tax was to be paid to the sanctuary as a 'ransom' for the lives of those counted. According to 2 Samuel 24.1–9 DAVID arranges for a census of Israel and Judah, and in doing so incurs the anger of God.

In New Testament times, within the Roman Empire, periodic censuses were common. The best known is that connected with the birth of Jesus (*see* CHRISTMAS), as recorded in LUKE 2.1–5. Some questions arise with regard to this story, particularly the association with Quirinius, who is known to have held a census as governor of Syria in 6 CE (see Acts 5.37), while scholars usually place the birth of Jesus some 10 or 11 years earlier. In addition Luke's story seems to presuppose a Jewish rather than a Roman census procedure, in that Joseph has to return to the home of his ancestors in BETHLEHEM.

charismatic A charismatic is an individual who is impressive and influential to others as a result of a spiritual power believed to be God-given. The term comes from the Greek word *charisma*, basically meaning a 'gift', and originally from the root *charis* meaning 'GRACE'. In 1 Corinthians 12 Paul enumerates the variety of spiritual gifts (*charismata*), including the specific gifts for leadership given to APOSTLES, prophets and teachers. One gift, perhaps disproportionately celebrated among charismatic movements even today, is that of 'speaking with tongues' (glossolalia); Paul is clear that such a gift needs to be accompanied by another gift, that of the interpretation of tongues. As a result particularly of the use of sociological and psychological models in Biblical interpretation, in the latter part of the 20th century there was a growing tendency to refer to JESUS himself, and other early Christian teachers, as 'wandering charismatics'. There are various backgrounds to this kind of thinking: in the Greek world the idea is of a celebrated teacher who is regarded as a divine (or divinely inspired) man; in the context of Galilean Judaism the thought is of someone who works MIRACLES in nature; and the technical sense, dependent upon Max

Weber, is of the charism of PROPHECY, which is given a revolutionary form by virtue of divine sponsorship. Charismatic leadership is essentially interactive – it must relate to others – and it can attract, or provoke, hatred; its revolutionary aspect may be random and unpredictable.

chastity *See* CELIBACY.

cherubim and seraphim The Bible refers to a diversity of heavenly and angelic figures (*see* ANGEL). The cherubim here are totally different from the chubby children shown as cherubs in Western religious art. They are frequently mentioned in the Old Testament as winged guardian figures associated with God, whether in connection with the wilderness sanctuary (or TABERNACLE), or in the TEMPLE of Solomon. As golden images they face one another on the 'mercy seat' above the sacred ARK OF THE COVENANT, and also on the curtains of the tabernacle and the veil of the Temple. They are also seen in the visions of the chariot of God (the Merkabah of Jewish mysticism) in EZEKIEL chapters 1 and 10.

The word 'seraph' comes from a Hebrew root meaning 'fiery'. The seraphim are only mentioned (with their multiple – six – wings) specifically in Isaiah 6 during the Temple vision, when they sing the TRISAGION (6.3). They function as divine attendants, rather than angelic messengers.

chiasmus Chiasmus, or chiasm, is a literary device in which the text material is structured symmetrically, but with an inversion in order following its mid-point. The name is derived from the Greek letter chi ('x'), the shape of which resembles this literary structure. Scholars debate the extent to which it is to be found in Hebrew or Greek writing within the Bible.

The classic statement of chiasmus was by Nils Lund. The essence of the laws he formulated is: the centre of the text is always its turning point, pivot and thematic focus; the relationship of the two parts is a parallelism which has the effect of heightening and developing the themes; the structure is spiral or concentric, with a helical movement that draws the reader towards the central theme; passages which frame the chiasmus, but stand outside it, function as an inclusion around the chiasmus.

A good example of a chiastic analysis, in the form of a conic spiral, is Elisabeth Schüssler Fiorenza's approach in *The Book of Revelation: Justice and Judgment* (Fortress, 1985).

chiliasm *See* MILLENNIUM.

chi-rho The Greek letters X and P (chi and rho) are the first two letters of the Greek name Christos (= CHRIST). They are frequently used as a sacred monogram (the rho superimposed over the crossing of the chi) and figure widely in the symbolism of Christian art and architecture.

Chorazin Chorazin is a Jewish town in the Upper Galilee, about three miles from CAPERNAUM. It is reproached by Jesus, together with BETHSAIDA and Capernaum, for the lack of response to the powerful deeds done there (see Matthew 11.20–24; Luke

10.13–16). It is also mentioned in Jewish literature concerning the supply of grain for ritual use in the Jerusalem TEMPLE.

Archaeologists discovered the synagogue at Chorazin in the 19th century. It is built from the local black basalt, with three main entrance doors facing Jerusalem. The walls were quite elaborately decorated, although much was damaged in antiquity by Jewish iconoclasts (*see* IMAGES). There is a basalt throne, decorated with a rosette, known as the 'Throne of Moses' which was used during the reading of the TORAH.

Christ *Christos* is the Greek word for 'anointed' (*see* UNCTION) and the translation of the Hebrew word for MESSIAH (*see also* TITLES OF JESUS). In some parts of the New Testament it is used absolutely as a title, while in other contexts it has become more like a surname for the personal name 'JESUS'.

Christianity The term *Christianismos*, or Christianity, did not exist when the bulk of the New Testament was written. It first appears in the letters of Ignatius written at the beginning of the 2nd century CE (*Romans* 3.3; *Magnesians* 10.1, 3; *Philadelphians* 6.1; see also *The Martyrdom of Polycarp* 10.1). Ignatius is asking the Romans to pray that 'he may not only be called a Christian, but may also be found to be one'. The adjective *Christianos* is used by Luke in the New Testament; but it is used rarely ('It was in ANTIOCH that the DISCIPLES were first called Christians' – Acts 11.26; see also Acts 26.28; 1 Peter 4.16) referring to individuals rather than a movement. Earlier PAUL preferred to speak of believers as being 'in Christ' or Christ being 'in them'. Subsequently in early Christian texts, during the persecutions, the martyrs are said to confess, 'I am a Christian', as in *The Martyrdom of Polycarp*. But what this confession actually meant, and how early Christian identity was constructed within the Jewish and Greco-Roman worlds, is not a straightforward matter. Often such names are applied by secular outsiders, before they become adopted within the communities themselves, when they recognize what others are calling them. An important context is that of the self-definition of Jews within the Mediterranean world of the first centuries CE (*see* JUDAISM), so as to establish what elements made early Christianity distinctive, in order to have a name of its own. The Greek suffix *-ianos* in the word *Christianos* would have been widely recognized as meaning a 'partisan/follower' of CHRIST (the MESSIAH). *See* HERODIAN DYNASTY for a similar formulation.

Christmas Christmas is the feast of the birth of Christ (the NATIVITY). The Biblical texts that are primarily relevant are the stories of the birth in the opening chapters of MATTHEW'S and LUKE'S GOSPELS (Matthew 1.18–2.23; Luke 1.26–38; 2.1–20). The Nativity plays and the Christmas cribs that are familiar in the popular Christmas of Western culture in fact owe more to St Francis of Assisi than to these Gospel texts. Elements that rarely figure in such popular presentations are the situations of POVERTY, political occupation and extreme violence against the innocent, all of which feature in the Gospels. And the birth stories in the Gospels, with significant differences between the two (such as Matthew's focus on JOSEPH and the MAGI, and Luke's on MARY and on JOHN THE BAPTIST), are both designed to present profound theological ideas with their narratives. They ask the question: What kind of a God is this? Jane

Williams (2005) wrote: 'At Christmas I believe that God, who made the whole world [see CREATION], comes to live in just one small part of it, as a tiny human baby. The whole, huge, mysterious "outsideness" of God, so much more than we can imagine or domesticate, comes "inside", into our ordinary human lives.'

The date of Christmas on 25 December is known only from the 4th century CE. A Roman Church calendar of 336 CE records this date, which was probably chosen to oppose the pagan feast of the Unconquerable Sun (Natalis Solis Invicti). Previously there had been speculation, at least in the 3rd century, and the date of May 20th was suggested by Clement of Alexandria. The Eastern Churches celebrated the Feast of the Epiphany (the coming of the Magi) on 6 January, together with a commemoration of the BAPTISM of Christ, and some connected this formally with the Nativity, while others from the 5th century onwards adopted the date of 25 December. In modern Israel, the schoolchildren have a week's holiday to celebrate HANUKKAH, but Christmas Day is a normal working day for businesses and places of education.

Chronicles, first and second books   In the Christian Bible the two books of Chronicles follow those of SAMUEL and KINGS, whose events they largely parallel, whereas in the Jewish Bible they are found at the end of the third section (the Writings), which at this point functions as a kind of appendix. The Hebrew Bible entitles them 'The Events of the Days', while the Greek translation calls them 'The Things Omitted' (*paralipomena*), indicating a desire not to omit anything from the sacred traditions.

Chronicles is, however, much more interesting than an appendix or supplement. Much of its material is to be found in Samuel–Kings as well as in Genesis (the genealogies), but its purpose is to correct, comment upon and explain what has gone before. It also assists with the textual problems encountered in 1 and 2 Samuel. The selection of the Chronicler's source material largely ignores the Northern Kingdom, although those willing to return to the Jerusalem sanctuary are to be welcomed (2 Chronicles 30.7–8). His main interest is in the continuity of scripture, focused on ADAM, DAVID, and SOLOMON, and the first and second TEMPLES at Jerusalem. The LEVITES are important: a special feature is the Temple music and its performance, for sacred song is seen as part of the sacrificial ritual.

The final verses of Chronicles (2 Chronicles 36.22–23) are repeated at the start of the book of EZRA. This has encouraged scholars to view Chronicles with Ezra-NEHEMIAH as a single work. There are similarities, such as the concern for the Jerusalem Temple; but there are also differences, since the Chronicler is much more open to those outside Jerusalem than is Ezra-Nehemiah. Chronicles was probably written in the 4th century BCE, in Jerusalem after the EXILE.

Church and images of the Church   The English word 'Church' comes from a Greek word *kuriakon*, meaning 'something belonging to the Lord'. But in the New Testament the significant word translated as 'Church' is one that means a 'calling out', an 'assembly' or 'gathering', as in the summoning by a herald of the citizens of a Greek city-state. This Greek word *ekklesia* is widely used, together with another word for a gathering (*sunagoge* – *see* SYNAGOGUE). Such expressions for communities of Christians (*see* CHRISTIANITY) correspond closely to the language of the Hebrew Bible for 'the people of God', the 'congregation of Israel', members of the COVENANT community. The closest Hebrew word is *qahal*, but at QUMRAN a favoured alternative was *yahad*, emphasizing the 'oneness' or 'union' of the 'community'. PHILO OF ALEXANDRIA referred to MOSES' meeting with God on Mount SINAI as the *ekklesia* (assembly) of God.

The actual word 'Church' (*ekklesia*) is not to be found in the Gospels on the lips of Jesus, except for two passages in Matthew (16.18 and 18.17) concerned with the status of PETER and an issue of Church discipline. It is possible, given the subject matter, that these two uses are a later clarification within the Christian community. It is a matter of controversy among scholars as to the exact sense in which it could be said that Jesus intended to found a Church. But there is no doubt that Jesus called together a specific group of DISCIPLES for the immediate MISSION, that could form the nucleus of a new 'people of God', if time allowed.

There is a wide variety of word pictures used in the New Testament as images of the Church. There are graphic descriptions of Churches as groups of believers gathered in a particular city or house, or of all Christians throughout the known world. The references are not to buildings or denominations (as the modern world thinks of churches). Among the more pictorial expressions are the following: the BODY OF CHRIST, the Bride, the Wife of the Lamb, the Flock (the Little Flock), the Household of Faith, the Family of God, God's Building, God's Foundation, the Olive Tree, the Temple of the Holy Spirit, the Church of the First-Born whose Names are Written in Heaven, the Royal Priesthood, the Chosen Generation, the Special People, the Purchased Possession, the Habitation of God, the Light of the World, the Salt, and the Wheat of the Earth (*see* the parable of the SOWER).

churches, Christian In the earliest years the Christian communities did not worship in purpose-built structures, but used what was available in towns, or even worshipped in the open air. A wealthier member of the congregation might invite others to use his villa, and function as a patron of the Christian community. In the Roman catacombs it is probable that Christians, like PAGANS, might hold a worship meal (*refrigerium*) by the grave of a departed member of their community (*see* EUCHARIST). The earliest purpose-built churches were probably house churches, functioning like the patron's villa. There is evidence for such a house church at DURA EUROPOS in Syria. One of the earliest references to a Christian church is found in the Chronicle of Edessa, which records the destruction of a 'Christian temple' by flooding at Edessa in 201 CE. Later churches were built to a similar pattern to the secular BASILICA (assembly hall) as the congregations grew in size.

Emperor Constantine established four churches in Palestine in the 4th century CE:

the Church of the Nativity at BETHLEHEM
the Church of ABRAHAM's Oak at Mamre (Ramat el-Khalil) – see Genesis 18, and HEBRON
the Eleona Church at the Mount of OLIVES (built over the cave associated with Jesus'

teaching about the destruction of Jerusalem, and near the site of the ASCENSION) –
also known as the Pater Noster Church

the Church of the Holy Sepulchre in Jerusalem.

Such state-sponsored sites, associated with Biblical events, attracted growing numbers of Christian pilgrims and settlers.

circumcision Circumcision, literally the removal in a ritual of the foreskin of the male penis, is a widespread socio-religious practice, perhaps as a rite of passage. It has long been known in the ancient world (from as early as the 23rd century BCE in Egypt) although its origin and purpose are unclear. West Semitic peoples, including CANAANITES, AMMONITES, EDOMITES, MOABITES, PHOENICIANS and ARAMAEANS, practised circumcision (see Jeremiah 9.25). But there is no evidence that Mesopotamian peoples such as the AKKADIANS, ASSYRIANS and BABYLONIANS, or the PHILISTINES were circumcised. The distinctive aspect in the Jewish tradition is that males are usually circumcised at eight days old, according to the Biblical commandments (see Leviticus 12.3 and Genesis 17.9–14: 'Every male among you shall be circumcised. You shall circumcise the flesh of your foreskin and it shall be a sign of the covenant between me and you'). Male PROSELYTES were to be circumcised before admission to the Hebrew/Jewish community. So circumcision is regarded as the symbol of membership of the Chosen People and acceptance of the COVENANT. The attempt to suppress circumcision by the Seleucids, and the response of Hellenized Jews seeking to restore their foreskins, became one of the factors leading to the revolt of the MACCABEES against Antiochus IV Epiphanes (see 1 Maccabees 1.48, 60). During the Roman period, Emperor Hadrian's edict against circumcision was one of the provocations of BAR KOKHBA's revolt (132–135 CE).

As a Jew, Jesus was circumcised and named when eight days old (see Luke 2.21). In Christian liturgical tradition the Feast of the Circumcision is celebrated on 1 January. The earliest Christians were in disagreement over whether to continue with the Jewish practice of physical circumcision (see examples in Acts at 11.2–3; 15.1–2; 16.3) while feeling their way to a distinctive identity with GENTILE members. Eventually circumcision is to be reinterpreted spiritually and metaphorically: in Paul's words, 'for in Christ Jesus neither circumcision nor uncircumcision counts for anything; the only thing that counts is faith working through love' (Galatians 5.6; see also Romans 2.28–29; 3.29–30). COPTIC Christians, however, maintained the actual practice of circumcision.

cities of the plain, five *See* ZOAR.

Claudius, Emperor *See* PRISCILLA.

cleansing of the Temple The SYNOPTIC Gospels (MATTHEW, MARK and LUKE) prepare the way for Jesus' arrest and TRIAL by the Jewish authorities when they record incidents provoking hostility and criticism throughout his ministry. The final match which then lights the fire is the episode of the cleansing during the Monday of Holy Week. 'When the chief priests and scribes heard it, they kept looking for a way to kill him' (Mark 11.18). On this occasion their determination to eradicate him resulted in the CRUCIFIXION four days later.

JOHN'S GOSPEL pursues a radically different timetable. It also is at PASSOVER time, but the cleansing is at the start of Jesus' MINISTRY, on his first trip to JERUSALEM in John 2, and is the initiation rather than the culmination of the authorities' opposition to him. Even so it brings up dark matters of death and destruction, with Jesus' coded references to his execution and RESURRECTION being misunderstood as referring to the TEMPLE building (2.18–22).

Timing apart, what is at issue is the proper use of the central shrine for JUDAISM and its use in the WORSHIP of God. All four Gospels agree that it was the resemblance of the holy place to an animal market, and the commercial aspects of the operation, which offended Jesus so much. He expelled the animals and scattered the money. Mark adds the detail that he stopped people using the precincts as a short cut (Mark 11.16); John tells us that he used force (John 2.15). Jesus' motivation seems entirely focused on the misuse of the place which he regarded as a house of prayer ('for all the nations' in Mark), quoting ISAIAH 56.7 and JEREMIAH 7.11 as he acted; he also accused the authorities of making the Temple into a robbers' den (Mark 11.17). It would seem that the noise, squalor and perhaps dishonest trading aroused Jesus to make the only act recorded of him that it is possible to call violent. John notes that the DISCIPLES later interpreted Jesus' actions in the light of PSALM 69.9: 'Zeal for your house will consume me.'

What Jesus did was extremely provocative for the Temple authorities. He performed a prophetic sign that the Temple was not 'fit for purpose', and it was 'on their watch'. Reaction was inevitable, particularly as he must have said something about the destruction of the Temple, apart from John 2.18–22 (see above). Some curious, and unprovable, hearsay evidence comes out in the Synoptic versions of his trial (see Mark 14.55–60). Toleration of this strange teacher would no longer seem possible.

coinage The use of coins in Palestine probably began in the Persian period, after the capture of BABYLON by the PERSIANS in 539 BCE, and the beginnings of the return from EXILE. Croesus, the 7th century king of Lydia, conquered by the Persians, was probably the first to mint weighed coinage as legal tender. There would be a range of foreign currency in Palestine, particularly in the trading ports and markets. In the period between the Old and New Testaments, and subsequent to that, money as coinage will have become the standard of exchange. Previously in the Old Testament money would have taken many different forms, including metals, goods, and livestock, as land and other commodities were valued.

A variety of currency is mentioned in the Bible. In the New Testament the smallest (copper) coin is a 'mite' (or 'pruta') – see Mark 12.42; this would buy a bunch of grapes or a pomegranate. It was the equivalent of the Roman quadrans and remained in wide circulation until the 4th century CE. 192 prutot were equal to 1 dinar.

The silver dinar (in Latin *denarius* or in Greek *drachma*) in the time of Jesus would probably have carried the image and name of Emperor Tiberius and his titles, since Emperor Augustus had made the use of the emperor's image universal on Roman coinage. Such a coin would have suggested the question about the tribute money (see Mark 12.14–17; Luke 20.24–25; see also Luke 10.35; 15.8). One dinar would have purchased an amphora of olive oil. It was the usual salary paid to a labourer for a day's work (see Matthew 20.2).

Shekel is a Hebrew word frequent in the Bible from Genesis 24.22 onwards. One shekel in New Testament times is the equivalent of two dinars.

There was also the Tyrian shekel, a coin minted between 126 BCE and 56 CE which had a weight in silver of 14.2 grams. It was double the value of the ordinary shekel, so equal to four dinars. As it was considered of dependable value it was used for payment of the TEMPLE tax. Moneychangers were needed to change other currencies into Tyrian shekels for the payment of the tax (John 2.13–16; Mark 11.15; Matthew 17.24). Not all Tyrian shekels were minted in Tyre.

After the time of Augustus minting ceased in Tyre, but HEROD, since pure silver coins were still needed for the Temple tax, began to mint his own. Herod Agrippa I, who was relatively popular with the Jewish nationalists, and regarded as religiously observant, was the only Jewish ruler actually to circulate coins bearing his own image. There was remarkable tolerance of his practice among the majority of Jewish groups, considering the religious reaction against IMAGES. During the Jewish Revolt from Rome (from 66 CE), the revolutionaries signalled their independence by minting their own shekel coins which were the first exclusively Jewish silver coins in history.

See also POVERTY and WEALTH.

collection The collection, or contribution for the SAINTS in Jerusalem, is discussed by PAUL in 1 Corinthians 16.1–2 and Romans 15.25–28. It is intended as an offering by GENTILE Christians for the support of the JEWISH-CHRISTIANS, and is therefore planned not just as an act of charity, but as a symbol of the unity of all believers in Christ. Paul and BARNABAS had previously brought a Jewish relief fund to Jerusalem from the Christians in ANTIOCH (see Acts 11.27–30). It is likely that the new plan was intended as a continuation of this, as well as being part of an agreement reached with the leaders of the Jerusalem Church (see Galatians 2.10). Paul also believed strongly in the idea of a universal PILGRIMAGE to Jerusalem, fulfilling the prophecies of the Old Testament (see Isaiah 60.4–7) and celebrating the ultimate unity of the Gospel at the end of time.

Contributions for the collection had been forthcoming, particularly from Macedonia (2 Corinthians 8.3–5). But the Corinthian Church appears to have been slow to transform its pledges into gifts (see 2 Corinthians 8.6; 9.1–5).

Colossae Colossae was a city of Asia Minor (modern Turkey), lying about 110 miles east of EPHESUS and 10 miles east of LAODIKEIA, in the upper valley of the river Lycus, and on the southern bank. This fertile valley yielded large crops of figs and olives. Earlier Colossae had been a wealthy commercial centre, based on the wool industry, specializing in a dark red wool cloth. But in Roman times it had declined to the status of a small town, being surpassed by the neighbouring cities of Laodikeia and HIERAPOLIS. Colossae was a cosmopolitan place, inhabited by native Phrygians, Greek settlers, and a significant number of Jewish families who were settled there in the

2nd century BCE. The Christian Church in Colossae was perhaps founded by EPAPH-RAS (see Colossians 1.7–8) and was the recipient of the letter to the COLOSSIANS, now included in the New Testament, and written either by PAUL himself or by one of his followers.

Colossians, a letter to the The letter to the GENTILE Church at COLOSSAE in Asia Minor is attributed to PAUL, but may actually be written by a follower (perhaps TIMOTHY) after Paul's death. The closest comparison in style, vocabulary and ideas is with EPHESIANS. Certainly the literary relationship between the letters deserves attention, whether Paul wrote both, or only one (Colossians), or neither. If Paul wrote Colossians, it is likely that his style was influenced by the particular controversy then active in the Church. The letter to PHILEMON also needs to be studied alongside Colossians, particularly because of the parallel greetings in the two letters (see Philemon 2.23–24; Colossians 4.10, 12, 14, 17).

The Colossian Church had not been founded by Paul, but probably by Epaphras (*see* COLOSSAE). The theological crisis now facing the Church may well be the result of other missionary endeavour, similar to that which affected GALATIANS. The 'philosophy' mentioned in 2.8 refers to alternative religious ideas in a cultic context ('Do not handle, Do not taste, Do not touch' – 2.21), not Classical Greek philosophy. The so-called Colossian 'heresy' seems to have been a developed speculation about the cosmic powers ('elemental spirits of the universe') which control individual destiny. There are possible links here with the later systems of GNOSTICISM.

This doctrine is firmly opposed, especially in the hymn which occurs in 1.15–20, by an affirmation that it is Christ who is lord of the universe, and the totality of divinity rests in him. The literary pattern of the hymn (which is a CHIASMUS) draws out the essential relationship between the Creator and the Redeemer. Christ is the image of GOD, the firstborn of CREATION; he is supreme; he is the head of the Church; by his death and resurrection he represents the new creation. This kind of presentation recalls some of the ideas of WISDOM in the Old Testament, and invites comparison with the prologue of the Gospel of JOHN. Jesus Christ is placed within the monotheistic description of God. As in Ephesians, the developed concept of the Church of Christ has a central position in the argument (*see* CHURCH).

Comforter *See* PARACLETE and SPIRIT. In the older translations the word 'comforter' should be understood in the sense of the Latin root as 'strengthener'.

Commagene This small kingdom with its capital Samosata, near the Euphrates in eastern Turkey, was ruled by a Seleucid dynasty during the Hellenistic and New Testament periods, although for 20 years (17–38 CE) it became part of the Roman province of SYRIA. It shows the importance of client kingdoms under the Roman Empire, and the significance of the Hellenistic ruler cult, where the kings took their place in a pantheon of Greek and Persian ancestors and deities.

concordance, Biblical *See* CRUDEN, ALEXANDER.

confirmation Among the Christian SACRAMENTS confirmation can be distinguished from BAPTISM as the rite which fully confers the gift of the Holy SPIRIT.

There are examples in the narratives of the Acts of the Apostles, where the Spirit is specially conferred by the 'laying on of hands' (see Acts 8.14–17; 19.1–7). But the Biblical texts do raise problems of consistency, because it is not possible always to compartmentalize the gift of the Spirit separately from the rite of baptism (see Acts 10.44–48). The fullest experience of initiation might involve washing, anointing with oil (*see* UNCTION), and the laying on of hands. In early Christianity the majority of converts will have been initiated as adults, whereas in modern Church practice infant baptism is still most common. When someone is baptized as a child, and cannot recall the event, there is a case for a second rite of renewal and confirmation of vows. But there is currently a theological debate among many Christians as to whether a distinct sacramental rite (a kind of entry into adolescence, like the Jewish Bar Mitzvah) is necessary. By contrast Eastern Orthodox Christians emphasize its importance as the culminating sacrament of the Holy Spirit (Chrismation).

contribution *See* COLLECTION.

Coptic Coptic was the last stage in the development of the language of ancient Egypt, transcribed in an alphabet adapted from the Greek, with additional letters derived from the cursive style of demotic. It first appeared in the 2nd century BCE, was stabilized in the 1st century CE, and then flourished between the 3rd and 10th centuries, before giving way to Arabic. Coptic and SYRIAC are the earliest and most significant of the oriental Christian versions of the Bible. Jews in ALEXANDRIA had used Greek to translate their scriptures from the 3rd century BCE (*see* SEPTUAGINT). Christians in Egypt in the 1st century CE also used Greek, but then Coptic was adopted, as Christianity spread more widely, particularly among the poor. Biblical manuscripts exist in different Coptic dialects: Sahidic (south or Upper Egypt); Bohairic (north or Nile Delta); and Fayyumic (Middle Egypt). Bohairic survives today in the liturgy of the Coptic Orthodox Church.

Corinthians, first and second letters to the It is probable that PAUL left Athens and arrived in Corinth in the spring of 50 CE (*see* ACTS 18.1). He stayed in close touch with the city, by visits and by correspondence, for the next four years. The young Christian community which he founded provided Paul with much food for thought. Sadly we only have Paul's account of his visits; the New Testament preserves his correspondence in the form of two letters, but scholars suggest that these incorporate more than two original letters. Some may be only fragmentary, but 2 Corinthians may actually comprise at least two letters, the earlier one being preserved in the later chapters.

Because he is dealing with their problems, Paul's letters indirectly offer glimpses of the social situation of Christians in Corinth. As well as their different groupings, and differences in religious practice and belief, there are indications of class differences which affect behaviour at the Christian meal of the Lord's Supper (*see* EUCHARIST) (1 Corinthians 11) and help to explain conflicts over pagan cultic meals (1 Corinthians 8; 10). More affluent Christians may have indulged themselves at the Christian meals, while the poorer Christians went hungry. The diet of the poor was predominantly vegetarian, other than for festivals and birthdays. Fresh meat, purchased in the *macellum* (market) by the master of the house, may well have been slaughtered in a pagan temple, and thus be problematic from a purist point of view.

Corinth was an important and prosperous trading centre which dominated the Corinthian isthmus (the land route which connected mainland Greece with the Peloponnese). Before the days of the Corinthian Canal, there was profit to be made by unloading, transferring and reloading cargoes across the isthmus between the north-western harbour of Lechaion on the Corinthian Gulf and the south-eastern harbour of Cenchreae on the Saronic Gulf. In later years a road – remains of which still exist – was built across the isthmus, so that entire ships, mounted on carts, could be towed from one sea channel to the other. Corinth had been founded by Julius Caesar in 46 BCE as a Roman colony where Latin was the official language. There was a famous temple dedicated to Aphrodite that was a centre of prostitution. This, and the large number of sailors in the port, contributed to the city's widespread reputation for immorality (in Frederic Raphael's words: 'right down into Roman times, Corinth was notorious for fancy erotic facilities').

Paul is critical of Corinthian Christians who claim to possess special 'WISDOM' or knowledge (1 Corinthians 1) and spiritual gifts of a superior kind (1 Corinthians 12–14); as they claim to possess already a spiritual maturity, they have little interest in what lies beyond this life (1 Corinthians 15). Paul defends his own ministry, over against other 'false' apostles, and is provoked to boast about his sufferings and his own spiritual experience, and he warns the Corinthians again of the judgement which is coming (2 Corinthians 10–13; *see also* LAST JUDGEMENT).

Cornelius (Roman centurion) *See* PETER.

covenant A central theme of the theology of the Hebrew Bible, and subsequently of the New Testament, is that of covenant. The basic covenant is the unconditional calling of Abraham in GENESIS 12.1–3; there are three elements in this covenant – a land, the creation of a nation/people, and a blessing through Abraham to benefit all the people of the earth. This covenant is renewed with successive PATRIARCHS: ISAAC (Genesis 26.1–5, 23–24) and JACOB (Genesis 35.9–13).

The covenant with MOSES at SINAI, related to the giving of the DECALOGUE (the Ten Commandments), is by comparison a conditional covenant, a contract between two parties that depends upon the maintenance of the relationship, essentially then Israel's obedience to the Commandments (Exodus 20.1–17; Deuteronomy 5.7–21, 28). This religion of obedience (known as 'covenantal nomism') is still a basic axiom of JUDAISM. The ARK OF THE COVENANT contained the stone tablets on which were written the Ten Commandments. It was a wooden chest used by the Israelites during their wilderness wanderings; it stood in the desert TABERNACLE, or could be carried on their journeys. Subsequently it was transferred to the Holy of Holies in the TEMPLE at Jerusalem. After the fall of Jerusalem in 70 CE its whereabouts are the subject of Ethiopian tradition or the film exploits of Harrison Ford.

Subsequently the Mosaic covenant is renewed with King DAVID (2 Samuel 7.10–16; 23.5; 1 Chronicles 17.11–14). Given the political casualties of some of David's descendants, the Davidic covenant is translated into a relationship with God's people through his Messiah.

In the prophecy of JEREMIAH a distinctively new covenant is promised (31.31–34; 32.37–41), 'not like the covenant which I made with their forefathers ... because they broke my covenant ... I will put my law in their minds and write it in their hearts.' The New Testament continues this theme of the new covenant, both as established in Jesus' Last Supper with his disciples (*see* EUCHARIST) (1 Corinthians 11.23–26; Luke 22.19–20) and as identified in the sacrifice of Jesus' death (see Hebrews 13.20, and earlier chapters 8–10).

creation One of the oldest MYTHs in the world is the Babylonian creation story (the Enuma Elish) from around 1250 BCE. Walter Wink has retold this as the 'Myth of Redemptive Violence'.

The first Christian proposition about GOD is that he is the creator of heaven and earth, and therefore a theology of nature is necessary, and of humanity in relation to God and nature (*see* IMAGO DEI). Christian belief holds God to be active in all areas of the whole of creation; and through Jesus Christ he is recreating and redeeming all that was made. 'All things were created by him and for him ... and in him all things hold together ... God was pleased ... through him to reconcile to himself all things, whether things on earth or things in heaven, by making peace through his blood, shed on the cross' (Colossians 1.16–20).

The poet Thomas Hardy wrote in pessimistic mood about God's routine process of creation and annual recreation; God does not ask the human question as to why he does it.

'I have finished another year,' said God,
'In grey, green, white and brown;
I have strewn the leaf upon the sod,
Sealed up the worm within the clod,
And let the last sun down.'

W. A. Whitehouse, asked why God created the world, provoked a storm by answering, 'For fun.' What he meant was an act for the joy of creating, particularly the joy of creating the absurd and lovable creatures who go about on two legs or four, and he saw this as serious theology.

The original creation from the hand of God comes to be regarded as corrupted and spoiled by the inadequate response of humanity (*see* FALL). Over the last few centuries of the period covered by the Old Testament and in the time of the New Testament, for many there was a growing sense of an ending to the created order, as expressed in 4 Ezra 14.10: 'For the world has lost its youth, the times begin to wax old.' The End Time (*see* ESCHATON) is characterized as including the partial or complete destruction of the existing order, and its reformation or total recreation in a new age of human history. What is notable is that the idealized descriptions of this new age are frequently expressed in the language of the original story of creation. So the picture of the Garden of EDEN is replayed (with enhancement) as the new heaven and earth, and the NEW JERUSALEM are described (see Revelation 21–22).

The original stories of creation, in the opening chapters of GENESIS, became a centre of controversy during the 19th-century debate between science and religion, focused in the work of Charles Darwin on EVOLUTION. The controversial debate continues to the present day, particularly between the more liberal and the more fundamentalist interpreters of the Biblical text. In America and now in Britain there is debate over whether and in what ways the Biblical views on creation should be taught in schools. There are strong feelings about whether the scientific and the Biblical views should be presented in parallel, as if they were straight alternatives. In some more fundamentalist circles it is argued that creationism (often referred to now as intelligent design) should be taught directly, to the neglect of the evolutionary views of scientific theories. In contrast the Archbishop of Canterbury, Rowan Williams, has recently made an emphatic criticism of the teaching of creationism: 'I think creationism is, in a sense, a kind of category mistake, as if the Bible were a theory like other theories. Whatever the Biblical account of creation is, it's not a theory alongside other theories. It's not as if the writer of Genesis or whatever sat down and said, "Well, how am I going to explain all this? I know: In the beginning God created the heavens and the earth." So if creationism is presented as a stark alternative theory alongside other theories, I think there's just been a jarring of categories. It's not what it's about. My worry is creationism can end up reducing the doctrine of creation rather than enhancing it.'

crops Only luxury goods could be imported in normal times, and farming had to make Israel self-sufficient, with the sole addition of fish – fresh and dried. Beyond grain, regular diet and usage depended on the production of olives, figs, dates, grapes (*see* VINE), and carob. There is mention of pomegranates (Deuteronomy 8.8), and of walnuts and almonds in the Song of Solomon 6.11. Field crops were commonly grain (wheat for the rich, and barley for the poor), leeks, onions, flax, and the lentils for which Esau famously sold his birthright in Genesis 25.29–34. Wild gourds were definitely not a recommended addition! (See 2 Kings 4.40.)

OLIVES (*Olea europaea*)   The olive is a Mediterranean tree, thriving on dry stony soil (see Deuteronomy 32.13). Its crop was vitally important. The yield of the orchard was assessed for quality as fruit for eating, or of a standard to press for oil. Oil presses from Biblical times survive (as do the olive stones spat out by bored guards in city gateways, rediscovered millennia later by archaeologists). The oil of the first pressing, then as now, was the top-grade virgin olive oils used in luxury cuisine; second and third pressings produced variously cheaper oil for cooking and lighting (Matthew 25.3). Olive oil was used to anoint kings, priests and prophets (see 1 Kings 1.45); ordinary people used it as a skin softener, and for first aid (see Luke 10.34; James 5.14). A ploughman's lunch was a handful of olives in flat bread.

Olive trees also play a highly symbolic role too. In ZECHARIAH's vision (Zechariah 4.1–14), the two trees probably stand for JOSHUA and ZERUBBABEL, the community leaders responsible for the rebuilding of the Jerusalem TEMPLE. This imagery is updated in REVELATION 11 with probable reference to the key Christian leaders, PETER and PAUL. In a complex metaphor on the relationship of Jews and Gentiles within the ministry of salvation in Romans 11.17–24, the GENTILES, as wild olive shoots, are grafted into the cultivated olive – the true Israel. An olive orchard, then as now, might be destroyed in punishment or revenge (*see* SAMSON's act against the PHILISTINES in Judges 15.5).

FIGS   Figs were commonly grown near houses for shade, so to feel really at home and peaceful was to be under your fig tree (Micah 4.4). Its fruit were invaluable for food, and its leaves provided modest clothing for ADAM and EVE in Genesis 3.7. JERICHO's various types of fig trees flourished in its really warm climate, and ZAC-CHAEUS climbed one to view Jesus passing by in Luke 19.3.

The fig tree was often used as a symbol of Israel or Judah; see Jeremiah 8.13, where it is used in the context of judgement and rejection. Jesus' curse of the unfruitful fig tree in Mark 11.13–14 may be seen in this context, but there is also the suggestion that this is an acting out of the (original and gentler) parable of Luke 13.6–9, where the tree's change will bring a reprieve.

CAROB   The carob pod, harvested from trees, contains seeds of such consistent weight that to this day we measure gold by the standard they set – the carat. But as diet they ranked rather poorly. They may well have been eaten by the ascetic JOHN THE BAPTIST in the desert in Matthew 3.4 ('locust' beans), but they were also the despised food of the pigs tended by the PRODIGAL SON in Luke 15.16.

crown of thorns   This item from Christ's pre-crucifixion torture has been so fre-quently depicted in art and as a motif that it is easy to forget the grim reality behind it. Jesus was crucified as the KING OF THE JEWS and it was natural therefore for the Roman soldiers to base their cruel mockery around this theme, apart from what we know of a game that was played in the fortress Antonia in Jerusalem, called the king's game. In Mark, Matthew, and John, Jesus is mocked by the Roman soldiers who give him a royal robe, sceptre (Matthew only) and crown as part of the process of soft-ening up a prisoner prior to execution. Luke has Herod and his soldiers, and not the Romans, mock Jesus; although Jesus is robed before being sent to PILATE, there is no mention of a crown at all.

For Christians there is a deep irony in these coronation events, as they regard Jesus as a king, from his royal birth of DAVID's line in BETHLEHEM onwards. John makes the moment of crucifixion that of an enthronement and exaltation in glory.

Which plant was employed to make the crown of thorns has been debated; there are a number of possibilities, including the 'Christ-thorn' *Paliurus spina-christi*, and the thorns of *Phoenix dactylifera*, which would have mimicked the sunray crown of a god.

crucifixion   In a Jewish context crucifixion was regarded as an accursed death, on the basis of Old Testament tradition such as DEUTERONOMY 21.23 ('anyone hung on a tree is under God's curse'). The nature of crucifixion and the manner in which it was carried out in the time of Jesus was illustrated by the discovery in 1968 of a right heel bone (calcenaeum) in an OSSUARY within a family tomb north-east of Jerusalem at Givat Hamivtar. The ossuary revealed the man's name as Yehochanan (John); he was 5 feet 5 inches tall and in his mid-twenties; the evidence of this 'crucified man' is now on display at the Rockefeller Center in Jerusalem.

The Crucifixion Luke 23.48

The heel had been pierced by a $4\frac{1}{2}$ inch nail and a small board fixed to the outside of his heel to prevent him from tearing his leg away because the nail had only a small head. However, the nail had bent as it was driven into the olive-wood upright of the cross, and so it could not easily be removed after death; board and nail were still attached to the body when it was taken off the cross, and the upright post cut away. The man's arms had been bound, not nailed, to the crossbar, because there were no nail marks there, and his legs were not broken as could be customary. Exceptionally, his body had been released from the cross for family burial.

There are indications of variations in practice, depending on how many nails were used, whether nails went through the bone, and whether there was a supporting foot-rest. Artistic representations of Christ crucified show even greater variations, not all of them authentic. The cause of death was often asphyxiation, because the weight of the hanging body prevented the muscles that control breathing from functioning properly. In the Roman Empire crucifixion was regularly preceded by a severe flogging; the loss of blood weakened the victim, and may have rendered him unable to carry the crossbeam to the place of execution, and brought about a relatively speedy death.

See also DEATH OF CHRIST.

Cruden, Alexander Alexander Cruden was born in Aberdeen in 1699. Educated at Marischal College, he was caught up in a scandal as a result of which he was imprisoned in the Tolbooth, an asylum. This ruined his plans to enter the Church, so he fled to London in 1719 where he worked as a private tutor and a corrector of proofs. In 1737 he was appointed bookseller by Royal Warrant to Queen Caroline (the wife of King George II). For years he had set himself the task of producing a concordance to the KING JAMES VERSION of the Bible. In his words: 'a concordance is a Dictionary, or an Index to the Bible, wherein all the words used throughout the Inspired Writings are arranged alphabetically, and the various places where they occur are referred to, to assist us in finding out passages, and comparing the several significations of the same word'. This work was a monumental achievement; two and a half million words in length, it is four times the length of the Bible. When he died in London in 1770 *Cruden's Concordance* had already run to three editions, all of which he had edited. Since that date it has never been out of print. In 1999 it was published in America as part of the *Bible of the Millennium*. Although computers can now perform similar tasks with incomparable speed, this only emphasizes the scale of his achievement. It is widely believed that the task of the *Concordance* drove him mad, but the story may well be a garbled version of his earlier imprisonment in an asylum.

cubit The cubit was the standard measure of length in the ancient Near East. It is reckoned as the length of the forearm in an adult male, that is the distance from the elbow to the tip of the middle finger. The Hebrew word *'ammah* translated as cubit originally meant 'elbow'. The unit is about 17.5 inches or 45 cm.

cuneiform Cuneiform is writing in wedge-shaped letters, produced by a stylus, usually on tablets made of mud brick which are impressed and then baked. Cuneiform was used by several Middle Eastern cultures (AKKADIANS, BABYLONIANS, ELAMITES, HITTITES and ASSYRIANS as well as SUMERIANS) to write letters, record their taxes and remember their myths. There are approximately half a million ancient Mesopotamian tablets in cuneiform which are in the possession of the world's museums (the largest collection is to be found in the British Museum in London). Many of the tablets have so far not been studied or published.

Cyrus Cyrus the Great was the founder of the PERSIAN Empire, becoming king around 557 BCE. As in the Babylonian text known as the Cyrus Cylinder (a cigar-shaped cylinder of baked clay, now in the British Museum) Cyrus himself declares, 'I am the son of Cambyses, the great king, king of Anshan'. Around 550 BCE Cyrus and his army conquered Ecbatana and the kingdom of the Medes, then four years later SARDIS and the kingdom of Lydia and Asia Minor. In 539 Cyrus defeated Nabonidus, the BABYLONIAN king, and entered Babylon. Following these conquests, the kings and rulers of the FERTILE CRESCENT came to prostrate themselves before their new overlord. At this time Cyrus, according to the cylinder, authorized the Jewish community, in EXILE in Babylon since 587 BCE, to return to Jerusalem and rebuild the TEMPLE to YAHWEH. This was part of a wider policy of tolerance towards his subject peoples and their religions; in return he may have hoped for favour from a range of

Cyrus Cylinder

deities. Cyrus is named in several books of the Bible: Daniel, Ezra, 1 and 2 Chronicles, as well as Isaiah 44.28–45.5, where Cyrus is named as God's 'anointed' (*see* MESSIAH) – the only non-Israelite so designated in the Old Testament – and his 'shepherd', as king and agent of God's saving plan for Israel. Cyrus seems to have died in battle in 530 BCE and was buried in a golden coffin at Pasargadae.

D

Dagon *See* EBLA; GOLIATH; SAMSON.

Damascus Damascus, the present capital of Syria, competes with JERICHO among others in claiming to be the oldest city in the world. It stands at the crossroads of two international roads of the ancient Near East, the WAY OF THE SEA and the HIGHWAY OF THE KING, at an oasis well supplied with water (2 Kings 5.12). It is mentioned in ancient texts, even before the frequent references in Egyptian lists of the 15th century BCE to Dimashqa. According to 2 Samuel 8.5–6, it was the centre of an ARAMAEAN state conquered by DAVID, but it was independent and hostile again by the time of SOLOMON (1 Kings 11.23–25). It was successively part of the ASSYRIAN, PERSIAN, Macedonian and Seleucid empires; after some 20 years of NABATEAN rule, it was annexed by Pompey as part of the Roman province of SYRIA. It became a member of the DECAPOLIS group.

There was a large Jewish population in Damascus. JOSEPHUS (*War* 2.561) describes a persecution in which 10,000 Jews were killed. The Damascus Document, discovered in 1896 among ancient texts in the synagogue in Cairo, provided evidence for a community in Damascus associated with QUMRAN and the DEAD SEA SCROLLS. Acts 9 refers to several Jewish synagogues in Damascus and narrates the mission of Saul of Tarsus to the city to crush the beginnings of the Christian religion there. It was before the gates of Damascus that Saul received a religious experience that radically changed his direction and purpose, so that he became PAUL the Christian apostle. Acts 9.11 refers to a 'street called Straight' in Damascus, which is the major east–west thoroughfare of the Roman city.

Dan 1 Dan is one of the 12 sons of JACOB, the first born to Bilhah, the handmaid of Jacob's second wife RACHEL (see Genesis 30.1–6; 49.16–17). The tribe of Dan, named after their ancestor, were originally allocated land to the west of the area of BENJAMIN, but they subsequently migrated northwards (see Joshua 19.40–48; Judges 18).

2 The city of Dan has a significant position on the very northern frontier of Israel, five miles east of Kiryat Shemona, looking towards Mount Hermon, and was formerly called Laish. Particular interest was aroused by the recent discovery of an inscription at Dan, which includes the words 'King of Israel' and 'House of DAVID'. Its importance rests in the fact that it offers a complementary side of the story to that of 2 Kings 8–9 about Hazael and Jehu's *coup d'état*; the inscription is a victory statement, set up in Dan, by Hazael, king of Damascus, claiming that Jehu succeeded with his support and assistance.

Tel Dan (Tell el-Qadi) has been excavated since 1966, revealing a Canaanite mud-brick gate from the Middle Bronze Age and a further complex set of gateways of the 9th century BCE, incorporating a paved piazza used for official audience, local assemblies and the settlement of legal disputes, as well as cultic items dating from the time of JEROBOAM I. The narrative of 1 Kings 12.26–30 claims that Jeroboam set up a cult place with a GOLDEN CALF at Dan, just as at BETHEL, in order that the Northern Kingdom should have its own sanctuaries, independent of Jerusalem. A large cultic area has been excavated at Dan, with a sacrificial altar comparable to that which stood in front of the Temple at Jerusalem. This clearly suggests the desire to maintain the same concept of worship, while establishing separate traditions. The altar has a horn in stone at each of the four corners. Groupings of five standing stones (*massebot*) have been found in several places on the site, including the gateway; their significance is debated and they may represent great kings or foreign deities. (PHOENICIAN deities were thought to reside on Mount Hermon.)

When the buildings outside the city gate at Dan were excavated, the director of the expedition, Avraham Biran, related them to the 'market areas' mentioned in 1 Kings 20.34 ('I will return the cities my father took from your father,' offered Ben-Hadad, the king of Aram (Syria). 'You may set up your own market areas in Damascus, as my father did in Samaria,' AHAB said. 'On the basis of a treaty I will set you free.' So he made a treaty with him, and let him go.) The Hebrew word translated here as 'market areas' is *hussot*; it comes from the same root *huts* as the word translated 'out' or 'outside', implying that the reference is to something outside rather than inside, such as the wall of a house, or in this case a 'market area' or 'street' (KJV). The buildings at Dan were just outside the city gate, and thus Biran felt that this word very suitably described them. The verse in I Kings 20.34 by its comparison with Damascus and Samaria provides very good support for this archaeological identification.

dance In the Hebrew Bible dancing is mentioned dozens of times in a variety of situations (e.g. MIRIAM in Exodus 15.20; Jephthah's daughter in Judges 11.34; the women who greeted the victorious DAVID in 1 Samuel 18.6; King David himself, escorting the ARK to Jerusalem in 1 Chronicles 15.29; and the woman in the SONG OF SONGS, 6.13, who dances in the camps of soldiers or shepherds). Two different Hebrew words are used, one for female dancing (*hwl*) and another for male dancing (*rqd*); it is likely that the genders danced separately and there was no mixed dancing. But in many cases dancing would be done intentionally for the opposite sex to see.

By contrast, in the New Testament, dance is a much more restricted activity. The striking instance is that of SALOME, the daughter of Herodias, who danced for the entertainment of King Herod, and was rewarded with the head of JOHN THE BAPTIST. Traditionally this is seen as a depraved, as well as an ill-motivated, activity; for this reason, perhaps, dance did not figure in the original Christian cult, and subsequently could often be regarded as sinful. In the APOCRYPHAL *Acts of John*, reflecting GNOSTIC attitudes of the 2nd or 3rd century CE, Christ is represented as dancing with his disciples.

The Fiery Furnace Daniel 3

Daniel, book of In Christian Bibles the book of Daniel is to be found immediately after the prophetic book of Ezekiel, and before the 12 Minor Prophets, where it was placed in the order of the Greek canon of the SEPTUAGINT. This is probably because Daniel appears to be a Jewish exile in BABYLON in the 6th century BCE. However, in the Hebrew Bible it comes among the later Writings, not the Prophets, and is placed between ESTHER and EZRA. What might appear to be future prophecy, for example in Daniel 11, is in fact a detailed reference to history that has already happened, particularly with the persecution of Jews and the desecration of the TEMPLE in Jerusalem by Antiochus IV Epiphanes, the Seleucid ruler in 167 BCE (see 1 Maccabees 1). This much later date is appropriate for the final form of this book, written by an unknown author; the actual date is determined by the point at which the historical projection goes wrong. These later events, such as the experience of the martyrs among the MACCABEES, help to explain why it is in this book that RESURRECTION is predicted for the first time unambiguously in the Hebrew Bible. The pseudonymous use of a name from the past ('Daniel' is also found in Ezekiel 14 and 28) enhances the traditional authority of the book.

The English Protestant Bible has the short text, based on the Hebrew. The APOCRYPHA (as well as the Catholic Bible) has additional chapters, based on the Greek: the Prayer of Azariah; and the Song of the Three Children/Jews (both inserted between 3.24 and 3.25); the story of SUSANNA (inserted as chapter 13); and BEL AND THE DRAGON (inserted as chapter 14). Other texts associated with Daniel are found among the QUMRAN scrolls: the Prayer of Nabonidus (4Q242); and the Apocalypse of Pseudo-Daniel (4Q245 and 246). Traditional Jewish commentators read Daniel as the future which God has planned for Israel.

However, according to modern Biblical scholarship, the book of Daniel should be regarded as an APOCALYPTIC text, the only complete apocalypse in the Old Testament, and in many ways representing the birth of Apocalyptic. As is customary with apocalyptic texts, many of its themes become recycled in the later apocalypses. Reinterpretation of Daniel, notably of the four beasts who stand for world empires, can be found in 4 EZRA (2 Esdras) and the book of REVELATION. Daniel, like other apocalypses, has a mixture of literary genres, with six chapters of narratives (stories such as the Burning Fiery Furnace and BELSHAZZAR's Feast, that may well have originally existed separately) followed by the content of four visions. Several references to 'the wise' indicate a possible link to the WISDOM BOOKS. The main message, as with other apocalyptic texts, is to encourage stability and endurance in the face of apparently superhuman threats.

TABULATION OF DANIEL

Stories about Daniel set in the exilic period (but written mid-2nd century BCE) 1.1–6.28

1.1–21	Daniel and others in training at Nebuchadnezzar's court
2.1–49	Daniel promoted after interpreting Nebuchadnezzar's dream
3.1–30	Daniel and friends survive execution in a furnace
4.1–37	Daniel interprets Nebuchadnezzar's second dream
5.1–31	Belshazzar's feast – Daniel interprets the writing on the wall
6.1–28	Daniel prospers under King Darius of Persia, having survived the lions' den

Daniel's visions 7.1–12.13

7.1–28	Vision of the four beasts
8.1–27	Vision of a ram and a goat
9.1–27	Daniel's intercession for his people is answered
10.1–12.4	Daniel's vision of international conflict
	the End Time and the resurrection, which are all to be kept secret
12.5–13	The question is – 'how long before all this happens?'

Darius I (the Great or Hystaspis) *See* HAGGAI; ZECHARIAH; ZERUBBABEL.

David 'The Biblical story of King David has everything: a mad king, ghosts and soothsayers, a fight with a giant, an heroic leader of a guerrilla band who becomes king, adultery, murder, incest, palace coups, civil war, the tragic death of a beloved son, restoration, the pangs of old age, death. No wonder artists down the centuries have plundered it for details' (Gabriel Josipovici). The basic source for David's life is in the books of 1 AND 2 SAMUEL and 1 KINGS: 1 Samuel 16.1 to 2 Samuel 2.11 covers David's first 30 years; 2 Samuel 2.12 to 1 Kings 2.11 relates the highlights of his 40-year reign.

An inscription discovered at Tel DAN in the 1990s mentions the 'House [Dynasty] of David'. This inscribed stone slab has been dated to the 9th century BCE, no more than 150 years after the king's death. It is the first known historical reference to the Israelite king and a potential corroboration of the Biblical account of David's foundation of the United Kingdom of Israel and Judah. However, some critics doubt the inscription's authenticity, or question the interpretation of 'House/Dynasty'. Current debate on the Biblical evidence also tends to question whether the accounts of David and his successor SOLOMON were about legendary rather than historical figures, or at least asks to what extent the story of David is coloured by theological or ideological motives, ideas that have been given a fresh importance in the political situation of the modern state of Israel.

Within the Bible tradition the highly important, and enduring, nature of the dynasty of David, based upon the faithfulness of God, is celebrated for example in Psalm 89. God established a COVENANT with David, which was proof of divine kingship over all CREATION (89.9–18). David's line is seen as the vice-regent of God over his people. The dynasty endures like the sun and moon as witnesses in the sky. Human failings within the dynasty will be met by God's judgement and mercy. David's kingship becomes the great Jewish ideal, which leads eventually to the concept of MESSIAH.

David is the youngest son of JESSE, first appearing as the shepherd of his father's flock. He is appointed secretly by SAMUEL as the successor to SAUL, Israel's first king. David comes to court to cure the king's melancholia with his musical talents; he becomes Saul's armour-bearer, the intimate friend of the king's son JONATHAN, and the husband of Saul's second daughter MICHAL (following a military trial of strength – see 1 Samuel 18.25). He also confronts GOLIATH, the PHILISTINES' champion, and David's success makes him a popular hero. Saul's jealousy is aroused and he sees David as a threat as well as a support, being aware in some sense that divine favour has been transferred from himself to David. David is forced to leave the court and live as an outlaw, taking refuge with the king of GATH.

Saul and Jonathan are killed in battle, and David responds with an eloquent lament (2 Samuel 1). He settles in HEBRON and is crowned king. Saul's son Eshbaal at first disputes the succession but is then murdered. David moves to capture JERUSALEM from the Jebusites and establishes it as his capital, consolidating the original Israelite tribes into a single nation. The power of the Philistines is broken, and the kingdom is greatly enlarged through victory over EDOM, the AMMONITES, MOAB, and the ARAMAEANS. Jerusalem as David's capital is the centre of religious as well as political life; accordingly he brings in the ARK OF THE COVENANT from Baale-judah (earlier name of Kiriath-jearim) – see 2 Samuel 6.1–19. Arrangements for a dynastic succession to David become increasingly important, with the role of BATHSHEBA and the birth of SOLOMON. David's eldest son Amnon rapes his own half-sister TAMAR, and is killed for his crime by his brother ABSALOM. Absalom is angry at David's failure to intervene on Tamar's behalf, and plots an ambitious rebellion against the king. The civil war is suppressed and Absalom is killed by Joab, David's military commander. The struggle for succession recurs in David's last years, with an attempted coup by another son, Adonijah, backed by Joab and the priest Abiathar. Bathsheba and the prophet NATHAN pressure David to honour his promise to Solomon; as a result Solomon is anointed and proclaimed king.

There is little doubt that King David had a royal palace in Jerusalem, even though it was left to his successor to build the TEMPLE there. According to 2 Samuel 5.11, 'Hiram of Tyre sent envoys to David, with cedar logs, carpenters and stonemasons; and they built a palace for David.' Recent excavations by the archaeologist Eilat Mazar have uncovered a large stone structure south of the Temple Mount, and adjacent to the stepped-stone structure. It is an impressive Iron Age public building dating to the 10th century BCE, which may well have been the palace of King David.

See also STAR OF DAVID.

Dead Sea The Dead Sea is the name of the lake into which the river JORDAN flows in the south. In the Bible the lake is known alternatively as the Salt Sea, the Sea of the Arabah, the Eastern Sea, and the Sea of SODOM. Geologically the Dead Sea is part of the Great Rift valley, as is the Jordan valley to the north and the Arabah to the south. It separates the hill country of Judaea to the west from the mountains of AMMON and MOAB to the east. The Dead Sea is the lowest point on the surface of the earth. It measures 50 miles in length and 10 miles in width, in area about 400 square miles, with its surface about 400 metres below sea level. The water level is dropping constantly, and the area of the sea is contracting, partly because of the dry climate, but principally due to the use of its main feeder the Jordan for national irrigation schemes. The salt and mineral content of the water is extremely high (up to 33%, compared with 4–6% in the Mediterranean) which assists humans who want to float, but effectively prevents the existence of any creatures, apart from bacteria, in its waters.

Dead Sea Scrolls The story of the discovery of the numerous scrolls and fragments in the caves in the vicinity of Khirbet QUMRAN since 1947 is one of the most romantic (and politically complicated) tales in modern Biblical ARCHAEOLOGY, and perhaps the most significant. Major scrolls acquired by Israeli scholars are now on public display in the Shrine of the Book at the Israel Museum in Jerusalem. Other texts were sought by an elaborate process of hide and seek and bargaining, and yet more have been painstakingly reconstructed from fragments. The writings are usually on animal skin (leather) or papyrus, but sometimes on OSTRACA, and in one case on sheets of copper. Around a quarter of the 800 manuscripts discovered at Qumran are manuscripts of Biblical books; the remainder are APOCRYPHAL texts, or previously unknown Jewish writings, or texts of commentaries or books of community rules belonging to a

Jewish sectarian group. These last have provided much information about the multiplicity of Jewish practice and belief in, and before, the New Testament period; there is an important emphasis on APOCALYPTIC ideas associated with the ESCHATON, especially in the *Scroll of the War of the Sons of Light against the Sons of Darkness*. Among the Biblical manuscripts, the majority of which were discovered in Cave 4, the largest number of copies are of the book of PSALMS, followed by DEUTERONOMY and ISAIAH. This presumably indicates the greatest frequency of use for these books. Significant numbers of copies are also found of Exodus, Genesis and Leviticus. The only text not discovered so far is the book of ESTHER.

death of Christ Jesus Christ died by CRUCIFIXION, between two thieves, as described in all four of the Gospel accounts (Matthew 27; Mark 15; Luke 23; John 19). The sour wine, or vinegar, that he was offered before he died was either an act of compassion (to alleviate the pain) or an act of torture. The hyssop which is mentioned in John's Gospel was a herb used for purification rites in connection with PASSOVER; it may be intended as part of the Gospel symbolism of Christ's death corresponding to the Passover sacrifice. A spear would have been more practical than a floppy plant to raise a sponge of vinegar to Jesus' lips. But see hyssop under HERBS.

Such a death by crucifixion would be scandalous, if Jesus was to be hailed as MESSIAH and Lord by the early Christians (see Deuteronomy 21.23). It would also be a scandal for GENTILE Christians, amounting to a state execution of a lowly criminal (who was not even invited to open his veins!). PAUL recognized and confronted the problem (see 1 Corinthians 1.18–25). Christian theology developed a complex of explanations for such a horrifying death; some of these ideas are found in basic form already within the New Testament. Jesus' death was seen as an act of reconciliation, an ATONEMENT, a sacrifice to deal with the sin of humanity. Paul develops this way of thinking (as in Romans 3.25) and formulates it into a theology of the cross.

Because crucifixion is seen as a curse in Jewish eyes, Christ's death could be seen to mark an end-point for Jewish TORAH (see Galatians 3.13). If Christians are initiated, through BAPTISM, in some mysterious way into the experience of the death of Christ, they are thereby regarded as dead to sin (see Romans 6.6). When, in Greek eyes, such a criminal death demonstrates weakness, the consequence, as Paul sees it, is that worldly wisdom finds itself judged, and divine strength is paradoxically revealed in such weakness (see 1 Corinthians as above). In John's Gospel the death of Christ is seen as the ultimate exaltation in divine glory; here it demonstrates the lasting effect of obedience and love (John 3.14–15; see also Philippians 2.5–11).

These four aspects (curse; death to sin; strength in weakness; divine glory) – as four arms of the cross – could be taken to symbolize the death of Christ from the theological point of view. Again there are four parts of the pattern from the human perspective of practical consequences, equally reflected in the New Testament. For the beneficiary, the death is an effective blood SACRIFICE (whose benefits are reflected in the EUCHARIST – see 1 Corinthians 11.23–26). Then it is a redemptive act, literally a 'buying-back' in which the ransom price is paid for many (see Mark 10.45).

It is an act of forgiveness of sin (see Luke 23.34; Acts 13.38–39; 1 John 4.10; also Hebrews 1.3). And finally it is that act of love which serves as an example to Christ's followers (see John 15.13).

Deborah 1 Deborah is a prophetess who is also named among the Judges of Israel (*see* JUDGES chapters 4 and 5). She was consulted in local disputes, but she also exercised a military leadership. Together with Barak, the recognized military commander, she led a successful campaign against Jabin, the Canaanite king of HAZOR, and his commander Sisera. When Sisera fled from the battle he encountered an encampment of semi-nomadic KENITES, where he met his fate at the hands of another woman, Jael, the wife of Heber the Kenite. The story is told both in the prose version of Judges 4 and in the early poetry (c.1125 BCE) of Judges 5. The poem is striking for its juxtaposition of two apparently domestic scenes: Jael's assassination of Sisera with a tent-peg, and Sisera's mother waiting for news of her son. Deborah is an ambiguous figure in tradition, but both she and Jael are naturally championed in feminist writing.

2 Deborah is also the name of REBEKAH's nurse (Genesis 35.8).

Decalogue (the Ten Commandments) The Decalogue is to be found in EXODUS 20.2–17 and in DEUTERONOMY 5.6–21. In its basic form this represents a distinctive kind of law code (known as apodictic) with short clauses, expressed in the second person ('you'), as commands or mostly negative prohibitions. This unconditional form of law is often seen as unique to Israel and characteristic of religion focused on a deity with an implacable will. Some comparisons were made with the practice of the HITTITES in formulating treaties with their vassal subjects, but these are only general comparisons illustrating a relationship established in an historical context with strongly religious sanctions. It is likely that in Israel such a law code was used on an annual religious occasion of covenant renewal, such as is illustrated in Psalm 81.

The Ten Commandments

On other occasions in Israel a structure of social law was required, for more secular purposes. This can be illustrated by the wealth of case law (casuistic formulations in the third person) to be found in the Hebrew Bible; see, for a particular example on the treatment of a slave, Exodus 21.20–21. There are numerous parallels to this kind of legislation in the ancient Near East. It is likely that it was adopted by Israel from the CANAANITE cities after the Settlement, and reflects the local jurisdiction by tribunals of elders meeting in the city gate. Later Jewish tradition speaks of 613 commandments transmitted through Moses, 249 affirmative and 365 negative. The rabbis debated about the arithmetic!

A suggested reconstruction of the original form of the Decalogue is as follows:

I, YAHWEH am your GOD.
You shall have no other God beside me.
You shall not make yourself an image.
You shall not worship them (god and image).
You shall not misuse my name.
You shall not do any work on the SABBATH.
You shall not curse your father and your mother. (See Exodus 21.17.)
You shall not kill a man in his person.
You shall not commit ADULTERY with the wife of your neighbour.
You shall not steal a man or a woman.
You shall not be a false witness against your neighbour.
You shall not covet the property of your neighbour.

It is noteworthy that in this version there are no longer 10 clauses. (*See* SAMARITANS for their Ten Commandments, with a distinctive tenth clause.) There is no Biblical authentication of the old joke about Moses coming down from Sinai and saying: 'The good news is that I got Him down to 10, the bad news is that adultery is still in.'

Decapolis The name given to the region, mostly to the east of the JORDAN and south of GALILEE, comprising 10 cities which, about the time of Christ's birth, formed an alliance for mutual trade, sustaining a Greek lifestyle and culture in an area that was substantially Semitic. In the context of Jesus' ministry, the Decapolis is mentioned in Matthew 4.25 and Mark 7.31. This HELLENISTIC confederation, of which the population was pagan and largely Greek-speaking, had been established by Greek colonists soon after the time of Alexander the Great. Apart from BETH-SHEAN (Scythopolis), these cities were located to the east of the river Jordan and the Sea of Galilee, and GADARA was for a time their capital. Among other cities were Abila, Canatha (now Kanawat in Syria) Philadelphia (modern Amman), SUSSITA (or Hippos) and Gerasa (Jerash; *see* GADARA). Another of the 10 cities, Pella, was traditionally the place of refuge for Jerusalem Christians before the end of the JEWISH WAR (Revelation 12.6, 14 may refer to this).

Delilah In the narrative of JUDGES 16, Delilah is the latest in a sequence of women with whom SAMSON falls in love. The Philistine lords put pressure on her to discover the source of Samson's abnormal strength. Three times he deceives Delilah, but finally he admits that the secret is in his hair, uncut because of his NAZIRITE VOW. Delilah, bribed by the Philistines, lulls her lover to sleep in her lap, and has a man shave off Samson's hair. His strength is gone, and so the Philistines succeed in capturing and blinding him ('eyeless in Gaza').

Demetrius *See* JOHN, LETTERS OF.

deposition As a technical term, deposition is used to refer to the act of taking down the body of the crucified Jesus from the cross, in preparation for his burial (see Mark 15.46; John 19.38). Two secret disciples of Jesus, JOSEPH OF ARIMATHEA and NICODEMUS, feature in this event, which has been the subject of artistic representation through the centuries. Often the awkwardness of the process in removing the body carefully is shown by the artist. The pincers used to extract the nails (*see* CRUCIFIXION), together with the nails themselves and the hammer used to insert them, are referred to as the Instruments of the Passion. Strictly, deposition should be distinguished from the later act of burial, referred to as entombment.

descent into hell *See* ANASTASIS.

desert *See* WILDERNESS.

Deuteronomistic History *See* PENTATEUCHAL CRITICISM.

Deuteronomy, book of Deuteronomy is the Greek name for the fifth book of the Old Testament; strictly it means a 'second' or 'repeated law', which is a misleading translation of a phrase in Deuteronomy 17.18 ('copy of the law' – referring to the copy of the law made for the future king by the priests). The original Hebrew title for the book is 'These are the words' – an effective opening for what is clearly represented as a speech by MOSES to the people of Israel. 'Words' are powerful instructions originating from God. They are put in the mouth of Moses, as his legacy of guidance to the people, when it is realized that he will not be able to lead them personally into the Promised Land of Canaan. (Moses' death is described in Deuteronomy 34.) The book contains a retrospective and prospective theological interpretation of God's plan for the nation, together with religious and moral exhortation, all of which gains added authority as the testament from a primary leader of the past. A similar device was employed again in sectarian Judaism with the *Temple* (or *Torah*) *Scroll* at QUMRAN, couched as the ultimate and definitive theological interpretation and instruction for religious experience. Scholars have established a context for Deuteronomy from the language and phonology of the book, which are said to date between the 8th and 7th centuries BCE; it is widely regarded as the book which defined King JOSIAH's reform in 621 BCE (see 2 Kings 22.3–13). A central lesson of Deuteronomy, and the programme for the reform, is the centralization of worship to a single sanctuary (in the interests of purifying the cult). This central sanctuary is not named explicitly, but the Jerusalem Temple must be meant by 'the place that the Lord your God will choose'. Such a phrase would sound more appropriate in the context of an anticipatory speech by Moses.

Diaspora *Diaspora* is a Greek word meaning 'dispersion'. It refers to Jewish settlement outside of the land of Israel. From the 6th century BCE onwards there were significant Jewish settlements in Babylonia and in Egypt. The Hebrew Bible reflects the alternatives: to yearn for a return to Jerusalem, as Psalm 137; or to think positively about a settlement in the Diaspora, as Jeremiah 29.5–7. On the one hand, Jews embraced their traditions and preserved their identity; on the other, they simultaneously accommodated to the realities, and accepted the benefits, of life outside the Jewish homeland. During the Greco-Roman periods Jews spread to many other places, throughout the Roman Empire. *See* PHILO, *In Flaccum* 46: 'For so populous are the Jews that no one country can hold them, and therefore they settle in very many of the most prosperous countries in Europe and Asia, both in the islands and on the mainland, and while they hold the Holy City where stands the sacred Temple of the most high God to be their mother-city, yet those which are theirs by inheritance from their fathers, grandfathers and ancestors even farther back, are in each case accounted by them to be their fatherland in which they were born and reared, while to some of them they have come at the time of their foundation as immigrants to the satisfaction of the founders.'

There remained an obligation on Jews outside Israel to make a PILGRIMAGE to Israel especially at a FESTIVAL time. After the destruction of the TEMPLE in 70 CE, the numbers of Jews living in Palestine were much reduced, and eventually almost all Jews lived outside the Holy Land. This state of exile was then very widely regarded by Jews as an evil, with the hope that they might one day return (see ALIYAH). Although immigration to Israel has become extensive in modern times, it is by no means universally regarded by Jews as the place to live.

Didache The *Didache* (or the Teaching of the Twelve Apostles) is significant as one of the early Christian writings to have survived outside the New Testament. It is puzzling as to where it belongs, both in Christian history (any time between 40 and 150 CE) and in its geographical place (possibly a backwater in Syria). It is a curious mixture of texts about Church liturgy and worship-practice, and of ethics and APOCALYPTIC. The ethos is Jewish, and Christian practice, such as prophecy, is seen in Old Testament terms (either as continuity of thought or as supersessionist metaphor). There seems to be a special relationship with the tradition of MATTHEW'S GOSPEL; it has even been argued that the text contains a Gospel of Jesus' sayings which could predate Matthew. In matters of Church order and theology it may be a very primitive document, an archaic survival, or it may be a more artificial compilation, a romantic idealization or even a forgery.

Dimashqa *See* DAMASCUS.

Diotrephes *See* JOHN, LETTERS OF.

disciples of Jesus Jesus called his first disciples at the beginning of his ministry in Galilee (see Mark 1.16–20; Matthew 4.18–22; Luke 5.1–11). Traditionally the group was 12 in number, a symbolic total corresponding to that of the twelve tribes of Israel (the family of JACOB) in the Old Testament. The term 'disciples' is a deliberate indicator of their role, as 'learners' with Jesus as their master/teacher. Subsequent tradition refers to them as APOSTLES (those sent out as missionaries).

In the society of his day, Jesus would from birth have lived within two sets of relationship: his extended family and the social grouping within the society of the land of Israel that would be his place as a consequence of family origins. But Jesus seems to have chosen deliberately to set up another grouping, outside of these relationships of blood or social status, in which to live and to conduct his ministry. He decided not to be defined by his family setting, and to ignore the patterns of honour which prevailed in his social group. And so he called a group of 12, including a range of people, some of whom would be regarded as undesirable in society, and so challenge the accepted privileges of his day.

Assuming that Jesus spoke ARAMAIC, the names by which he referred to his disciples are probably preserved most accurately in the Peshitta – the scriptures in SYRIAC (an Aramaic dialect). Mark 3.16–19 gives the names of the twelve as:

Shemun, called Cepha (Simon PETER)
Yaqub, son of Zabdai (JAMES, SON OF ZEBEDEE)
Yohanan (JOHN, SON OF ZEBEDEE)
Andraeios (ANDREW)
Philipos (PHILIP)
Bar-tolmai (BARTHOLOMEW, son of Ptolemy)
Matthai (MATTHEW)
Toma (THOMAS)
Yaqub, son of Halpai (JAMES THE LESSER, the son of Alphaeus)
Thaddai (THADDAEUS or JUDE)
Shemun (SIMON THE CANANAEAN)
Yihudah Secaryuta (JUDAS ISCARIOT)

For the references in JOHN'S GOSPEL to the 'disciple whom Jesus loved' *see* BELOVED DISCIPLE.

Dives *See* WEALTH.

divorce The Torah permits husbands to divorce their wives (see Deuteronomy 24.1–4), a law which has remained in force for orthodox Judaism to this day. (Remarriage for the wife was not countenanced if she had been defiled by a subsequent union.) All that was required was for the husband to write a dismissive note. The wife has no mutual possibility of divorcing her spouse. It is possible that a late prophetic protest against the injustice of this situation may be seen in Malachi 2.14–16 ('I hate divorce, says the Lord, the God of Israel'). Certainly such unilateral treatment of the wife is resisted in liberal Judaism and in the reactions of feminist movements.

Eminent rabbis at the time of Jesus discussed what were the proper grounds for divorce; they supplied a wide range of answers, more lenient or stricter, from infidelity (Beth Shammai) to the burning of a dinner (Beth Hillel)! Jesus' own views on divorce have been examined ever since by the Christian Churches, in an exhaustive quest for guidelines. He seems to have held the following views, more or less:

- The Gospels indicate that Jesus taught the ideal of MARRIAGE as a lifelong union, brought about by God. This would therefore exclude divorce as an option (see Matthew 19.4–6).
- In olden times, as reflected in the Law of Moses, God permitted divorce because the people were stubborn and resisted his ways (see Matthew 19.7–9: there is an interesting variation in tone of translations here, between 'because you were so hardhearted' (NRSV) and 'because you were so unteachable' (NEB), and 'because you knew so little of the meaning of love' (J. B. Phillips)).
- Divorce was cruel, as it forced a woman to remarry in order to survive economically. This remarriage, and any made by the original husband, was deemed adulterous (see Matthew 5.32).
- Divorce may be permitted on the grounds of ADULTERY. This point is highly dis-

puted; the clause 'except for unchastity' in Matthew 19.9 and 5.32 is often referred to as the 'Matthaean exception' because it is unique to Matthew's Gospel and may reflect the views of the contemporary school of Shammai rather than of Jesus himself. One might compare the compassionate attitude reflected in John 8.7: 'Let anyone among you who is without sin be the first to throw a stone'.

It is interesting that Mark's Gospel, probably written from the context of a GENTILE or non-Jewish community, allows for the possibility that a woman may divorce her husband; but the first three strictures listed above still apply for the followers of Jesus. *See* PAUL in 1 Corinthians 7.10–11, a context which also presumes Roman rather than Jewish law.

The later epistles all give advice on husbands and wives remaining faithful to each other (see Hebrews 13.4). It is not clear whether the ruling for early Church leaders and helpers to have only one wife (see 1 Timothy 3.2, 12) is a restriction of polygamy, or a forbidding of remarriage after divorce (or widowhood).

dogs Dogs mostly receive a bad press in the Bible. The Israelites and the Jews did not tend to keep pets, probably because of a combination of poverty, and scruples about the laws of PURITY and the food laws. In consequence the pariah dogs who patrolled the city rubbish dumps are mentioned only as a sign of the desolation of the scene – licking the blood of King AHAB (1 Kings 22.38) or the wounds of LAZARUS (Luke 16.21). Individuals could refer to themselves and others disparagingly as 'dogs' (see 2 Samuel 16.9). The one notable exception is the GENTILE woman (Canaanite or Syrophoenician (*see* SYRIA) – Matthew 15.22; Mark 7.26) who is desperately seeking a cure for her sick daughter. Just as her pet dogs functioned to hoover up leftover crumbs, so Gentiles could have the leftovers from Jewish salvation. Jesus cured her daughter. Note that the reference to 'dog' in Deuteronomy 23.18 in the KING JAMES VERSION should not be taken literally, as this is a slang term for a male prostitute (active in Canaanite fertility cults).

Domitian, Emperor *See* PATMOS; PERSECUTION OF CHRISTIANS; REVELATION.

Dor Dor was an ancient city on the Mediterranean coast (15 miles south of Haifa); its history dates back to the 20th century BCE when the CANAANITES founded it. Pottery from Cyprus and Mycenae indicates that it was an important trading site throughout the Bronze Age. In 960 BCE King SOLOMON made it his primary port on the Mediterranean and one of his 12 district capitals ('Solomon also had 12 district governors over all Israel, who supplied provisions for the king and the royal household. Each one had to provide supplies for one month in the year. These are their names: … Ben-Abinadab in the heights of Dor (he was married to Taphath, daughter of Solomon)' – 1 Kings 4.7–8, 11). The city remained prosperous until the 1st century BCE, when CAESAREA (MARITIMA) was established by King Herod eight miles to the south. Dor retained some importance as the seat of a bishopric from the 5th to the 7th century CE. There are archaeological remains from nearly every period, including a Hellenistic-Persian palace complex, recently discovered underneath a Roman wine press and bath.

doxology This technical term comes from the Greek word *doxa* (meaning 'GLORY'). It can refer more generally to expressions of praise (as 'Blessed be the Lord' for example in Genesis 24.27). It is used in Christian LITURGY to refer to a triple ascription of glory, including that to the three persons of the TRINITY (Father, Son and Holy Spirit). An example can be found as the conclusion of later versions of the LORD'S PRAYER ('yours is the kingdom, the power and the glory'), perhaps first known from the DIDACHE. Trinitarian doxologies are scarce in the New Testament (see, for examples of a two person/binitarian formula, Hebrews 13.20–21 and Jude 25), but much more common in later liturgical formulae.

Dura Europos One of the cities guarding the Syro-Mesopotamian frontier, Dura Europos (Qalat es-Salihiya) was built on a bend of the river Euphrates, being founded by the Macedonians c.312 BCE not long after the conquest of SYRIA by Alexander the Great. The ancient city of Palmyra maintained a trading centre at Dura Europos, while operating a desert trade-route between the Mediterranean, Mesopotamia and the Persian Gulf. Near the city wall, among the houses, was a Jewish community house, adapted for use as a SYNAGOGUE c.200 CE and rebuilt in 245; nearby was a Christian community house, remodelled for use in worship in 231. Both were destroyed in 257 when the wall was reinforced against the threat of Parthian attack. There was also a Mithraeum (*see* MITHRAISM), originally part of a house and gradually expanded over a period of 70 years. The archaeological remains (now in DAMASCUS) from these buildings are particularly interesting because of their date and the internal decoration: the synagogue had elaborate wall paintings, and the Christian BAPTISTERY a representation of Christ as the Good SHEPHERD. A striking feature of the synagogue is a fresco of a Mount of Olives RESURRECTION scene based on themes from Ezekiel 37 and Zechariah 14.4.

Easter Easter is the festival of the RESURRECTION of Jesus Christ, the most significant and probably the oldest festival in the Christian Church. The festival is prepared for liturgically by the season of Lent, Passiontide and Holy Week. It is not completely clear how the name originated. The Venerable Bede linked the name with that of the Anglo-Saxon spring goddess Eostre. If so this would suggest that Easter, like CHRIST-MAS, represents a Christian take-over of an existing pagan festival. The dating of Easter is influenced by its association with the Jewish PASSOVER and the lunar CAL-ENDAR used in the Old Testament period for the Paschal Full Moon.

Eastern Sea *See* DEAD SEA.

Ebionites *See* JEWISH-CHRISTIANS.

Ebla Ebla is an archaeological site in Syria, known today as Tell Mardikh, which lies some 42 miles to the south of Aleppo. Excavations have been conducted since 1964 by the Italians under the direction of Paolo Matthiae. Among the significant discoveries are a vast hoard of CUNEIFORM tablets, dating from the middle of the 3rd millennium BCE, written in SUMERIAN and another unknown Semitic language (often referred to as Eblaite). The tablets comprise palace records, texts for scribal training, literary and religious texts, and commercial treaties. There is clear evidence of widespread contacts with Mesopotamia and Egypt, and a variety of references to Sumerian, Hurrian, and CANAANITE deities, especially Dagon. What is not so clear is whether the initial publicity about the finds, which claimed references to Biblical names of people and places, can actually be substantiated.

Ecbatana *See* CYRUS.

Ecclesiastes This is often regarded as the most pessimistic of the WISDOM BOOKS of the Old Testament, which seek to establish facts and order experience in relation to faith in God. The author is unknown, but is referred to as Qoheleth (the Preacher or Teacher), and is clearly a teacher trained in the Wisdom traditions of Israel. While part of the book is in the traditional form of proverbs, much is set out as personal reflections. His views may be unorthodox, but they draw out logical conclusions and show the gaps in earlier theories. He observes that life is a riddle full of anomalies, so that people do not get what they expect or deserve (e.g. 9.11). It has been observed that there are two principal voices in the book: one that is pessimistic, associated with vanity (*hevel*); the other more optimistic, in a search for what is profitable (*yitron*). The world has injustice built into it, and oppression is rampant (4.1). But his response to the anomalies and 'meaningless emptiness' (of things that do not make sense) is to accept life and live it to the full (2.24), and face up to the fact of death (contrast Dylan Thomas' poem '*Do Not Go Gentle into that Good Night*'). Qoheleth wrestles with his questions but has no intention of abandoning the inherited traditions. H. Wheeler Robinson held that 'the book has the smell of the tomb about it', but Qoheleth is not obsessed by death; rather for him it is the ultimate uncertainty, the boundary within which we learn to live our God-given life to the full.

The book is written in a late form of Biblical Hebrew, including some Persian loan words. It is probably to be dated in the 3rd century BCE.

Ecclesiasticus, or the Wisdom of Jesus ben Sirach   Ecclesiasticus (or 'Churchly') is the preferred Christian title in the Vulgate of this book of the Old Testament APOCRYPHA, while in Greek manuscripts it is called 'The Wisdom of Jesus son of Sirach'. The New Revised Standard translation has shortened this to just 'Sirach'. Jewish tradition refers to it as 'The Instruction of Ben Sira'. The name of this author (Jesus is the relatively common Hebrew name Yeshu'a) is found in the signature at 50.27 and in the prologue which his grandson wrote when translating the book from Hebrew into Greek. About two thirds of the book still exists in Hebrew, including some texts found at MASADA and QUMRAN; for the rest one relies principally on the SEPTUAGINT Greek translation.

Ben Sirach wrote in Jerusalem sometime between 200 and 180 BCE, when the Seleucid successors of Alexander the Great were taking over control of Judaea from their rivals the Ptolemies. The book is an instruction in the traditions of Jewish life, with an awareness of the threats which the alien culture of Hellenism might pose. He combines the LAW of Moses with the traditions of WISDOM in an ethical piety that embraces the whole of life for the individual and society (see especially chapter 24 on Wisdom and Law). He makes reference to many of the books of the Hebrew Bible, with the exception of some of the third section (The Writings).

Eden, Garden of   Eden is a garden traditionally planted by God for the benefit of humanity (Genesis 2.8, 10, 15), otherwise known as the 'Garden of God/of the Lord' (Ezekiel 28.13; Isaiah 51.3); in the process of translation it becomes 'the PARADISE of delight' (VULGATE of Genesis 2.15). Among the planting of the garden was the tree of life and the tree of the knowledge of good and evil. There were also animals in the garden, brought to ADAM for him to name. The story of the expulsion from Eden is at a cultural level a folk memory of the beginnings of agriculture and the cultivation of the land, when humanity would no longer be hunter-gatherers in an idyllic parkland.

Genesis 2.10–14 refers to the four rivers that flow out of Eden: Pishon, Gihon, Tigris and Euphrates. Only the last two are readily identifiable on the map of Mesopotamia. Some theories identify Eden with an actual rather than an ideal place, and locate it in southern Iraq, the Iranian Gulf, or even in Armenia near Tabriz. But in Judaism rabbinic interpretation linked Eden with the TEMPLE Mount in Jerusalem. In this context the name of the spring Gihon, on the east side of the City of David – the primary source of water for the city – is an obvious link (*see* SILOAM). Similarly post-

Biblical Christian tradition has associated the hill of GOLGOTHA, site of the CRUCI-FIXION of Jesus, with the Garden of Eden, and the cross with the 'Tree of Life' (Genesis 2.9).

Edom, Edomites Recent archaeological excavations have uncovered evidence of large-scale copper production between the 12th and 9th centuries BCE at Khirbat en-Nahas in modern Jordan. Buildings and artefacts reveal a complex society, identifiable with the Edomite monarchy, which owed its wealth at least partly to copper. This would show that an Edomite society existed at the time of DAVID and SOLOMON, kings of Israel. The Biblical account suggests interaction between Israel and Edom at Genesis 36.31; 2 Samuel 8.13–14; 1 Kings 11.15–16 and 1 Chronicles 1.43. Edom is also mentioned in Egyptian records at the times of the Pharaohs Seti I and Rameses III. They were a Semitic people who occupied an area bounded by Ammon on the north, the DEAD SEA on the west, and desert on the south and east. Edom was conquered by the BABYLONIANS in the 6th century BCE. Their territory became the kingdom of the NABATEANS in the 2nd century BCE.

Eglon *See* PETRIE, SIR FLINDERS.

Egypt Ancient Egypt features in the Bible particularly in the stories of JOSEPH and of MOSES in the Old Testament, and in the birth story of JESUS in the New. Our knowledge of ancient Egypt derives both from ancient traditions, and from archaeological explorations, following the initiative of Napoleon. Interpretation of the many inscriptions in hieroglyphics became possible after the decoding of the Rosetta Stone, found by the French expedition, because it had parallel inscriptions in Egyptian hieroglyphics, in later cursive Egyptian (COPTIC), and in Greek. An Egyptian priest of the 3rd century BCE called Manetho compiled a list of all the Egyptian kings arranged in 30 dynasties, with the lengths of their reigns. From this and other information it was established that Egyptian civilization began c.3000 BCE, and that it could be divided into three main periods, now known as the Old, Middle and New Kingdoms (of which the respective, and approximate, dates are 2635–2155 BCE, 2060–1700 BCE, and 1554–1080 BCE. Life in Egypt depended on the regular and controlled inundation of the river Nile. Because the king of Egypt (the Pharaoh) was seen as controller of the river, giver of fertility to the land, and a person of divine power, the unification of the country and a centralized government was widely accepted.

Ekron *See* PHILISTINES.

El *See* BA'AL.

el-Amarna Tel el-Amarna lies on the Nile about 220 miles south of Cairo. It was founded by the 'heretic' Pharaoh Akhenaten about 1363 BCE when he moved his capital city here from Thebes (Luxor) in the south. But the city was abandoned after 30 years, which makes it an important archaeological site, focused on a single period, with impressive temples and palaces. Akhenaten was a controversial figure, renouncing the multiplicity of Egyptian gods in favour of the single solar deity, Aten. He is sometimes regarded as a great reformer and the precursor of Christian monotheism. But on his death Akhenaten's name was excised from the records, and his successor Tutankhamen moved the court back to Thebes.

An important archive of diplomatic correspondence was discovered here, shedding light on international relations within the Egyptian Empire in the 14th century BCE and the threat from the HITTITES. The clay tablets in AKKADIAN CUNEIFORM were exchanged between three Egyptian pharaohs and local rulers in CANAAN. Six of the letters are addressed to Abdi-Heba, ruler of JERUSALEM (called Urusalim in the tablets), and speak of the 'land of Jerusalem' and its 'towns', suggesting that Jerusalem was the capital of an Egyptian vassal-state during this period. Many of the texts refer to groups known as the Hapiru; they appear to be dispossessed and somewhat lawless peoples, living on the fringes of urban society. They are not to be equated directly with the Biblical Hebrews. It is clear from other sources that the Hapiru also existed outside of Canaan. They were not one single group of people, but the Hebrews are likely to have been among them.

Elamites Elam was a hilly country to the east of the river Tigris, between Assyria to the north and the Persian Gulf to the south. Its capital was Shushan, which became Susa, the winter capital during the PERSIAN Empire (see Nehemiah 1.1; Daniel 8.2; Esther 1.2). Early pictograms and inscribed Elamite seals depict the region's activities of hunting, fishing, herding, and agriculture. Elam figures in Genesis 14 in the context of a coalition involving its king Chedorlaomer. The coalition moved against the rulers of the DEAD SEA region and captured LOT, who was subsequently rescued by ABRAHAM. Elam is seen as a warlike nation that sometimes preserved its independence and at other times assisted, for example, the ASSYRIANS against Judah (see Isaiah 11.11; 21.2; 22.6; Ezekiel 32.24; Jeremiah 49.35–39). Jews from Elam are listed among those who returned from the EXILE (Ezra 2.7, 31; 8.7; see also Nehemiah 10.14; 12.42). Elamites are mentioned among those present in Jerusalem at PENTECOST in Acts 2.9.

elders The Greek word for 'presbyter' is in form a comparative adjective ('older') usually translated as 'elder', but with this single equivalent concealing a variety of meanings. The English word 'priest' is in fact derived from 'presbyter', but this should not be taken to mean that New Testament references to presbyters were by definition PRIESTS. The original word 'elder' can simply designate an age band – 'old man' (see 1 Timothy 5.1) – or a member of an eminent social class (as the senators of Rome) or a highly respected dignitary (this may well be the case in 2 John 1 and 3 John 1). But in line with the intention of Israelite elders (see for example Exodus 24.9; Numbers 11.16) and the later Jewish practice of the SYNAGOGUE and the SANHEDRIN, as well as at QUMRAN (1QS 6.8), early Christians may also have adopted the office of elders within the local Churches (see Acts 14.23; 15.4). Certainly in the post-apostolic period elders assumed a role in running the Churches (1 Timothy 3.5). It was vital that such people were seen to be worthy of the job by their personal and family behaviour, and that they had a good grasp on doctrine before teaching it (see Titus 1.9).

There are 24 elders (*see* NUMBER SYMBOLISM) who are seated around God's throne in the vision of REVELATION 4.4 and worship him; there has been much debate as to who they represent, perhaps originally astral deities, but now a generally accepted theory is that they were glorified human beings, symbolizing the total of the twelve tribes of Israel and the twelve APOSTLES.

elephant Elephants are mentioned in the Bible only in the first, second and third books of MACCABEES, where they play a significant part. The Seleucid monarch Antiochus IV Epiphanes goes to war with elephants as well as chariots, cavalry and a large fleet (see 1 Maccabees 1.17). In a context of war the elephant was the ancient equivalent of a tank, with a wooden tower constructed on the animal's back, to offer protection for the warriors. Apparently fermented grape-juice and mulberries were used to intoxicate them and arouse them for battle. See 1 Maccabees 6.34–37. Compare the use of elephants in warfare by Hannibal the Carthaginian general in the Punic Wars against Rome.

Elephantine Elephantine (ancient Yeb) is an island in the Nile at Aswan (ancient Syene), named after the Greek for elephant, perhaps because of the smooth black rocks that surround the island. Here an important collection of PAPYRUS documents in ARAMAIC was discovered, and published in 1911. The papyri come from a Jewish military colony (of mercenaries in the pay of the Egyptians and later the Persians) in Egypt of the 6th and 5th centuries BCE. Most concern domestic matters, such as the sale of property, loans, marriage or adoption. But some relate to religious activities, such as the observance of PASSOVER, and invite comparison with texts in EZRA-NEHEMIAH and ESTHER. The Jews had built a temple to YAHWEH (under the variant name Yaho), but their Egyptian neighbours destroyed it in 410 BCE. Accordingly these Jews appeal to Jerusalem and to the ruling Persian authorities for support to rebuild the temple. But the Elephantine temple finally disappears from record about 398 BCE. Recent archaeological evidence, together with the papyrus reference to a 'shrine', suggest that it resembled the Wilderness TABERNACLE in EXODUS. It used to be thought that the Deuteronomic law of the single sanctuary (identified as Jerusalem), which was instituted by JOSIAH in 621 BCE, was universally valid, but it is now clear that there could be local, traditional or practical reasons for alternative (substitute) sanctuaries, such as here in Egypt, and also at Maqqedah (thought to be Khirbet el-Kôm, near Hebron in the West Bank), mentioned on Aramaic OSTRACA of the 4th century BCE. In addition to the papyri, the French excavations in 1906 discovered some 250 ostraca, the contents of which have apparently still not been published.

eleven, the eleventh hour The expression 'at the eleventh hour' indicates the latest possible moment. Its origin is in Jesus' PARABLE of the Labourers in the Vineyard (see Matthew 20.1–16). In the story the householder hires five groups of labourers (in a practice which can still be observed today outside the Damascus Gate in Jerusalem) – they are employed at the first, third, sixth, ninth and eleventh hours of a 12-hour working day. In a vineyard the last group of labourers might well be hired at the eleventh hour (around 5 p.m.) in order to finish the scheduled work for the day on time. The understandable grievance of the earlier groups of workers is caused when the latest group receive the same wages, even though the wage was as originally agreed at one denarius (*see* COINAGE). The moral of the story, in God's inclusive attitude to all comers, appears slightly at odds with the concluding words ('the last will be first and the first last' – see Matthew 20.16; also 19.30; Mark 10.31; Luke 13.30). Some in the early Church understood the parable as an allegory of Biblical history, the hours standing for Adam, Noah, Abraham, Moses, and Jesus. For the expectation of Jesus' return at the end of time *see* ESCHATON and PAROUSIA.

Eli Eli was a judge and the priest in charge of the sanctuary at SHILOH in the period before the institution of the monarchy in Israel. The ARK was kept there during the period of the JUDGES. When HANNAH visited the sanctuary, Eli observed her praying (1 Samuel 1.12–17); after her child SAMUEL was born, she brought him to Shiloh and left him there, dedicated to God and with a NAZIRITE vow, as she had promised. Eli's sons, Hophni and Phinehas, were wicked men who corrupted the sacrificial cult and brought a prophecy of judgement upon themselves and upon Eli's priestly line (1 Samuel 2.11–36). Samuel succeeds Eli as priest, when Eli dies. The oracle against Eli's priestly dynasty can be seen as favouring not Samuel but the parallel priestly line of ZADOK; this prophecy was fulfilled when ABIATHAR was banished to Anathoth by King SOLOMON (1 Kings 2.26).

Eli, Eli (or Eloi, Eloi), lama sabachthani? These are the ARAMAIC words for 'My God, my God, why have you forsaken me?' in the cry of Jesus from the cross (see Matthew 27.46; longer form in Mark 15.34). *See* PASSION NARRATIVE.

Elihu *See* JOB.

Elijah The prophet Elijah came from Tishbe in the Gilead region of Transjordan (1 Kings 17.1). He and his successor ELISHA are probably the most important figures in Israel's prophetic tradition before the main 'writing' prophets (more accurately, those who have books of their prophecies named after them, e.g. Isaiah). *See also* PROPHECY. The stories told about Elijah and Elisha in 1 and 2 Kings make them stand out as individualists, even if, as has sometimes been suggested, they represent the more general protest movement of prophets and preachers against the religious failings of the monarchy.

Elijah appears with dramatic suddenness, announcing the drought to King AHAB; he revives the widow's son at Zarephath; he holds a contest with the prophets of BA'AL on Mount CARMEL; he has a protracted battle with Ahab and with his queen JEZEBEL, especially over the matter of NABOTH's vineyard. He is a figure of hyperactivity (1 Kings 18.46) and of dejection (19.4); in modern terms he might be analysed as bipolar; he is protected by ravens and an angel, and hears the voice of God in the sound of silence.

There is a persistent expectation that Elijah will return one day, since he was taken into heaven by a whirlwind and a fiery chariot (2 Kings 2; *see also* ASCENSION). He might come to take the place and the cup set for him each year at the PASSOVER meal. In his role as forerunner of the MESSIAH (Malachi 4.5) he was widely identified by the early Christians as JOHN THE BAPTIST.

Elisha Elisha is the successor of the prophet ELIJAH; at 2 Kings 2.13 he picks up the mantle of Elijah after Elijah had been taken up in the whirlwind. Stories about his own prophetic activity are contained in the subsequent chapters, up to 2 Kings 13, most famously in the resurrecting of the son of the Shunammite woman (2 Kings 4). Before Elijah departed, Elisha had asked for a double portion of Elijah's spirit. It is debatable whether the request was granted, or if Elisha should be seen as twice as great a prophet. Although these appear in the narrative to be the prophetic careers of individuals, it is notable that Elisha sometimes works from within a company of prophets (e.g. 2 Kings 6.1–7). *See also* PROPHECY.

Elizabeth Mother of JOHN THE BAPTIST (*see* ZACHARIAS) and cousin of MARY, MOTHER OF JESUS.

Elymas *See* PAUL.

Emmaus Emmaus is the destination of two disciples of Jesus, walking from Jerusalem, who encounter a stranger on their journey, and come to a realization that he is the risen Jesus when they invite him to take supper with them. The story occurs only in LUKE'S GOSPEL (24.13–35; the reference in Mark 16.12–13 is secondary), but has become an important example of Christian religious experience, and particularly a symbolic narrative of the EUCHARIST. The *Supper at Emmaus* is a favoured subject for artists; probably the most striking are those painted by Caravaggio between 1595 and 1606; two contrasted examples are to be found in the National Gallery in London and the Pinacoteca di Brera in Milan. Another echo of the story is in the question by T. S. Eliot in *The Waste Land*, 'Who is the third who walks always beside you?' See also the exploration of the Emmaus theme in Salley Vickers' novel *The Other Side of You* (Fourth Estate, 2006).

The location of Emmaus is debated, or declared unidentifiable, not helped by the variation in the distance from Jerusalem quoted in different texts. Possible sites are Abu Ghosh (Qaryet el-Enab or Kiriath-jearim – see 1 Samuel 7), favoured by the Crusaders; Latrun (Imwas, now Aijalon Park); Qubeiba (where a Franciscan church shows the 'house of Cleopas'); and most recently Qaloniyeh (four miles west of Jerusalem), identified by the late Carsten Thiede in *The Emmaus Mystery* (Continuum, 2005): 'a leafy suburb of Jerusalem, close enough to the Temple for its Jewish inhabitants to perform the necessary observances, but pleasantly close to fresh water and blessed with the fresh air of the Sorek valley'. Qaloniyeh is also equated with Emmaus by JOSEPHUS in his *Jewish War*.

Enoch Although the name Enoch occurs at Genesis 4.17–18 as the son of CAIN, the important figure of that name is the son of Jared, described in Genesis 5.18–24. This text says that Enoch 'walked with God', an expression otherwise only used of NOAH (Genesis 6.9); as a result Jewish tradition speaks of God walking with Enoch and Noah in PARADISE (see Genesis 3.8). Genesis does not mention Enoch's death; instead 'God took him', meaning an ASCENSION into heaven as is the case with ELIJAH. Because Enoch does not die, an enormous APOCALYPTIC literature built up concerning his adventures in the heavenly world.

Epaphras Epaphras is named as a fellow-worker with PAUL and his companion in prison (see Colossians 1.7–8; 4.12–13; Philemon 23). What is said about him suggests that he may well have been a native of the Lycus valley in Asia Minor, and a Christian evangelist in COLOSSAE, LAODIKEIA and HIERAPOLIS, which were towns in that area. He was highly regarded by Paul, although the order in which the names are mentioned in Philemon may not so much indicate rank as the fact that he was closest at hand. It is sometimes suggested that Epaphras should be identified with EPAPHRODITUS, who communicated with Paul in prison on behalf of the PHILIPPIAN Church (see Philippians 2.25–30; 4.18). Epaphras could be a shortened form of the name, but there is no proof of the suggestion; it may be less likely because of their different geographical regions.

Epaphroditus Epaphroditus visited Paul in prison on behalf of the PHILIPPIAN Church. *See also* EPAPHRAS.

Ephesians, letter to the Nils Dahl described Ephesians as a 'sublime, yet elusive document' containing 'almost no references to specific times, places, or persons, or to events after the baptism of the addressees'. Who these intended recipients were is even less clear because several manuscripts even lack the words 'in Ephesus' in the first verse. It may therefore have been written as a general letter. But it is probably best to regard the work as a theological essay, summing up more systematically, with the benefit of hindsight, the larger themes of PAUL's theology. It may well not have been written by Paul himself, but by a later follower after Paul's death; the style of writing with its complex sentence structure and new terminology would support this view. Nevertheless the work sums up much of the theological legacy which Paul left to the early Church.

Ephesians is written on a broad canvas, primarily for GENTILE readers, using universal and cosmic terms. In the perspective of God's plan (1.3–23) the Church has a universal role, with Christ as its head; so Church membership must reflect God's larger purpose in Christ. A key theme is that of unity and the breaking down of the historic barriers which divide (2.14). This unity is communicated through three particular images: the BODY OF CHRIST (1.23); the building which grows into a holy temple (2.20–22), of which Christ is either the cornerstone or the keystone, or perhaps both, if Christ is both the foundation and the completion of the building; and thirdly the unity of the bride with Christ (5.25–32), in the context of which the marriage unity of husband and wife is to be interpreted.

Paul's language of justification by faith (*see* ROMANS) has been transformed into the language of salvation (2.8–10). Ephesians offers the paradox of a military metaphor (drawn from a Roman soldier's armour) in the context of a Gospel of peace. The soldier (6.10–20) wears the armour, given by God, in a largely defensive role; he is no crusader in a holy war, but rather a saint who holds his ground even in defeat. God alone is ultimately victorious. Theology and ethics are closely bound together. Ephesians lists a catalogue of vices (4.17–24) and virtues (4.2–3, 25–32) and has developed, on theological grounds, a formal code for the Christian household (5.21–6.9) which applies to husbands and wives, parents and children, masters and slaves. A comparison with COLOSSIANS 3.18–4.1 shows how these guidelines are developed from Hellenistic moral teaching. The Christian is not yet arguing for the abolition of slavery, although PHILEMON shows that a special case can be made for an individual slave.

Ephesus The site of Ephesus has been excavated by the Austrian Institute of Archaeology for over 100 years and is now one of the most visited archaeological sites in the world, a showpiece on the west coast of Turkey. The first city was founded in the 6th century BCE by King Croesus around the huge temple of Artemis – Diana of the Ephesians (which was recognized as one of the seven wonders of the world). But the site of the city had to be moved because of problems with drainage and the silting of the harbour at the mouth of the river Cayster (there is a possible allusion to this change of site when REVELATION 2.4–5 speaks of removing the lampstand). The city, founded by Lysimachos in 300 BCE, was bequeathed to Rome with the rest of the empire of PERGAMON in 133 BCE. It was made the capital of the Roman province of Asia Minor, and the normal residence of the governor, by Augustus in 29 BCE. The city grew to be the fourth largest in the eastern Roman Empire with a quarter of a million inhabitants.

Lavishly decorated Roman houses, with frescoes and mosaics, were built in the early 1st century CE over the remains of earlier Hellenistic houses. Excavations revealed a Roman gymnasium, stadium, theatre, streets paved with marble, the Hall of the Muses (which became the site of the Church of the Virgin Mary – where the Ecumenical Council was held in 431 CE), the Library of Celsus, a brothel, a concert hall and the market place. Among many inscriptions found is one on the base of a statue erected by the Sacred College of Silversmiths, to which Demetrius belonged (*see* ACTS 19.24). This is the city which PAUL and John, the author of REVELATION, would have known. The temple of Artemis remained a pilgrim site, and this oriental mother-goddess the symbol of Ephesus, but other temples were also built, to the worship of the Roman emperor, and to the Egyptian cults of Serapis and Isis. Because of the receding coastline, the port was eventually abandoned; Ephesus is now at least three miles from the sea. There was difficulty in rediscovering the Artemis temple because that area was so low lying; in the end an English engineer, J. T. Wood, located it in the 1870s by retracing the route of the processional way from the theatre. The Church of St John was moved to higher ground near Seljuk sometime after 500 CE. The traditional House of the Virgin MARY (Panaya Kapulu) is outside the city to the south; it was identified as a result of visions experienced by a German invalid, Anne Catherine Emmerich, who had never been to Ephesus.

ephphatha Ephphatha is a contraction of an ARAMAIC word meaning 'let it be opened', transliterated in the Gospel at the point where Jesus uses it as a command, while applying saliva, in the course of a cure of a deaf-mute (see Mark 7.34). In the Christian tradition, the word and action were used in Milan and in Rome as part of the rite of BAPTISM.

Ephraim Ephraim is the younger son of JOSEPH, born in Egypt by Asenath (Genesis 41.50–52; his name is said to mean 'fruitful'). According to the narrative of Genesis 48, Ephraim was blessed by his grandfather JACOB ahead of his elder brother MANASSEH. In part this echoes what happened with ISAAC's blessing of Jacob and ESAU, but it is also taken as prophetic of the future ascendancy of Ephraim as a tribe (named after their ancestor). Joshua 16–17 describes the division of Joseph's territory into two, of which Ephraim's share was more favourable than Manasseh's. Later, SHECHEM from the territory of Manasseh was also included in the expanded 'hill country of Ephraim'. BETHEL and SHILOH were also significant religious centres, located in Ephraim. By the time of the 8th century BCE prophets, one could apparently use Ephraim to designate the whole Northern Kingdom of Israel.

Ephratha *See* BETHLEHEM.

epistles, or letters Just as one asks for a definition of the literary type of a 'GOSPEL', so it is desirable to define the form of an epistle (or letter), as these occupy a significant part of the New Testament. The authentic letters of PAUL, for example, are the primary source for knowledge of his life, theology and MISSION strategy.

In the ancient world there could be two different types of letter. One is the genuine letter, the item of essentially private correspondence between individuals, or between an individual and a group. Such correspondence is heart to heart. It substitutes for the writer's presence in providing at least approximately what the writer's conversation would have been had s/he been present. There is a writing technique known as the philophronetic element which seeks to overcome the physical separation of writer and recipient, and provide a framework for the exhortation (parenesis) often found in the latter part of such letters (*see* COLOSSIANS 3–4 and EPHESIANS 4–6).

But it is also possible to identify a second type of letter in the ancient world, a more formal and literary kind of epistle, intended originally for publication, rather like the 'open letter' sometimes found in a modern newspaper. They are often closer to the form of an essay, or philosophical discussion. The Roman author Seneca was a contemporary of Paul and wrote more than 100 *Epistulae morales* ('moral epistles'), formally addressed to his friend Lucilius, but which are in fact his moral and philosophical reflections on life. Some Church Fathers constructed, as a kind of apologetic, an imaginary correspondence between Paul and Seneca.

Esau The story of Esau in Genesis 25–28 interlocks with that of JACOB, his twin brother, and the account of how Esau was deprived both of his birthright and of the blessing of his father ISAAC. Tradition has developed the clues about Esau's personality: he was a hunter (25.27) who may have also been a murderer; and he was red and hairy (25.25; 27.11) and so may be regarded as the ancestor of the EDOMITES (called the 'red' people by Semitic word-play – Genesis 36.1) who symbolize the enemies of Israel (Isaiah 34–35; 63). The story offered an explanation for Israel's dominance over Edom in the days of DAVID and SOLOMON.

eschaton The Greek word *eschaton*, meaning 'the last/furthest thing', is the basis of the term eschatology (or 'study of the last things') used in Christian doctrine to refer to anything which the Bible or subsequent traditions have to say about the End Time. At different periods, even within the Bible itself, these expectations have been more (or less) imminent. They may entail a total cosmic disruption, or a more phased renewal of the created order (*see* CREATION). They are likely to involve a divine stocktaking on a collective or individual basis (*see* LAST JUDGEMENT). The language of eschatological description and revelation is often full of traditional mythology and colourful reapplication of Biblical language (*see* APOCALYPTIC). What in the Hebrew Bible is often termed the 'Day of the Lord' (see Amos 5.18), in the New Testament is frequently associated with teaching on RESURRECTION (see particularly Paul's writing in 1 Corinthians 15.20–57, which brings together a range of apocalyptic expectations in a discussion of resurrection).

Esdras, 1, 2, 3, and 4 Esdras is the Greek form of the Hebrew name Ezra. For these books see the article on EZRA.

Essenes The Essenes were a sectarian group within JUDAISM active in Palestine from the 2nd century BCE until the end of the 1st century CE. They seem to have been a largely celibate community, holding property in common, and with a strict practice of ritual. There is no mention of them within the New Testament, but detailed information about them is known from classical sources, in the writings of PHILO, the Elder Pliny, and especially JOSEPHUS, when he described the 'philosophies' within Judaism. Pliny's *Natural History* locates them on the western shore of the DEAD SEA. Since the discovery of the DEAD SEA SCROLLS many scholars have identified the community at QUMRAN with the Essenes, but this cannot be regarded as proved.

Esther, book of One of the latest books in the Hebrew Bible, Esther tells the story of the villain Haman and the salvation of the Jews. It begins with the theme of the removal of the disobedient Queen Vashti and her replacement by a virtual 'nobody' from an orphan background. Such a story of intrigue at a foreign court resembles the accounts of JOSEPH (Genesis 39–41) and DANIEL (Daniel 1–6); it is unusual in having a woman as central character, given the circumscribed attitudes to women in post-Exilic Judaism (but compare JUDITH). The queen elect, Esther, does not disclose her Jewish identity, obeying her wise counsellor Mordecai (Esther 2.10); in her behaviour she follows the advice of Hegai, the king's eunuch, and 'the king loved Esther more than all the other women' (2.15, 17).

The real significance of Esther's appointment rests in its timing: she is called upon to confront the planned, systematic destruction (pogrom) of her own people, the Jews (as is also documented in the Persian annals of the time of Xerxes). The outcome of Jewish deliverance is still celebrated in the Jewish festival of PURIM; the book of Esther is set as the text for that day, to be read publicly from a special scroll. (This is one of the Five Scrolls or Megilloth – books in the Hebrew Bible prescribed for FESTIVALS.) The popular celebration is also referred to as 'Mordecai's Day' in 2 Maccabees 15.36. The Hebrew text, as in Protestant Bibles, is shorter than the Greek version. The Greek additions found in the APOCRYPHA make the story more overtly religious and heighten the court intrigue as a cosmic battle between Jew and GENTILE. It is at first a surprising fact that Esther has not been found among the DEAD SEA SCROLLS, but it may reflect a disquiet similar to the rabbis' as to whether the text belonged within scripture.

See also HADASSAH.

eternal life *See* LIFE AFTER DEATH.

Ethiopic The old Ethiopic language, known as Ge'ez, was used for versions of the Bible, but the details are far from clear. The Jewish scriptures were translated from the Greek for use by the Falashas (Ethiopian Jews who claim ancient Jewish lineage, but may be descended from later Jewish converts. Their traditions link them with dignitaries from Jerusalem who accompanied the Queen of SHEBA on her return from visiting SOLOMON – see 1 Kings 10.) Christian origins in Ethiopia are the material of legend. According to Rufinus, Christianity was introduced to Ethiopia in the 4th century CE by two missionaries, Frumentius and Edesius, who had been taken prisoner but then released by the emperor. It is possible that the oldest Christian translations into Ge'ez, probably from the Greek, date to the 5th century CE. The Ethiopic Church has a wider canon of scriptures, including texts such as JUBILEES and 1 ENOCH.

Eucharist; the Last or Lord's Supper The last meal taken by Jesus with his disciples before his betrayal and crucifixion is referred to by Paul in 1 Corinthians 11.23–26, and is described in all four Gospels. The timing of the event in Matthew, Mark and Luke suggests that it was a celebration of the Jewish PASSOVER; in contrast the Gospel of John places the meal before the official Passover (John 18.28), although it remains possible that Jesus' meal (as in John) was actually an earlier celebration, perhaps in accordance with the alternative calendar of QUMRAN. John's account also shifts the emphasis from the elements of the meal (perhaps because the significance of the bread has already been discussed in John 6) and focuses instead on the way Jesus washed his disciples' feet (John 13).

The language of the accounts by Paul and the three Gospels reflects that of Exodus 24.7–8. The bread and the cup become symbols of Christ's body and blood. His death is regarded as a SACRIFICE on behalf of others, and the shedding of his blood as the inauguration of a new COVENANT relationship. The wording of 1 Corinthians 11.26 anticipates the idea that this meal should become the model for a Christian proclamation of the Lord's death, in an observance of the Lord's Supper. It is inevitable therefore that the accounts of the meal should become shaped by the growing practice of LITURGY within the Church. This may help to explain some variation in the wording and practice between the SYNOPTIC Gospels and 1 Corinthians. Luke's account (in 22.15–20), for example, in a shorter version which lacks verse 20, has reversed the order of wine and bread; the fuller version, adding in verse 20, has the order cup/bread/cup, where the second cup would then have the fuller significance as containing the blood of the covenant.

Early Christian practice with regard to the Eucharist is difficult to reconstruct in detail. The ACTS OF THE APOSTLES relates that believers met regularly for the breaking of bread; it is possible that different kinds of events (both SACRAMENTS and community meals) are covered by this expression. Paul's first letter to Corinth does provide a unique glimpse into the social situation of an early Christian community in a Greco-Roman environment, but the letter is also coloured by controversy with Paul's opponents, as well as reflecting the social dilemmas of the Supper observance and the not unrelated issues of food sacrificed to idols and of dining in a pagan temple. Early Christian art in the Roman catacombs, illustrating the feeding miracles as well as the Last Supper, may also reveal a practice of anniversary meals at the grave of a

Church member. A scratched inscription in the Catacomb of Priscilla, dated 374 CE, states: 'We, Florentinus, Fortunatus and Felix came for the cup'. Although ambiguity remains, it could well refer to the Eucharist.

Eutychus *See* TROAS.

Evangelist *See* GOSPEL.

Eve According to GENESIS 2.20–22, Eve is created by God from one of ADAM's ribs. She is not named, but referred to as 'woman'; subsequently the man calls her by name, 'Eve, because she was the mother of all living' (3.20: in Hebrew the name resembles the word for 'living'). These texts are highly controversial in modern discussion: it might be suggested that they emphasize the priority of man and the subordination of woman, or that Adam was the rough draft and Eve the perfect specimen of humanity. Probably both are fallacious deductions from the text, just like the characterization of Eve's role, in the FALL of humanity, as the temptress of Adam, herself being uniquely vulnerable to the serpent's cunning. Instead of reading the text in the light of such prejudices, the opening chapters of Genesis need to be seen in the context of ancient Near Eastern thought, thereby offering a critique of the views of Israel's neighbours, for example of the idea of the Mother Goddess. In Biblical terms, the positive view of Eve is reflected in the vision of the woman clothed with the sun in REVELATION 12, and in the Christian tradition focused on the Virgin MARY.

evolution and creation Evolution is usually taken to mean that animals, including man, did not come into being fully formed at some time past, and then remain as unchanging species to this day, but are the result of long-term development. The mechanism by which evolution – the process of change and development from microscopic beginnings to complex organisms – could happen, is Darwin's great discovery of natural selection. From his observations of animal life he concluded that life was a great battle for survival. That some species succeeded, bred and continued the line was because of some evolutionary advantage they had, which others lacked and did not therefore survive to breed, but died out. Factors involved in coping could include the right kind of coat to suit the environment, or the means to eat the food that was available.

This difference that Darwin made to the perception of CREATION was quite shattering to many Christians, being at total variance with the GENESIS account of six days in which fully fashioned recognizable species were made. The apparent anti-religious impact of this is still felt to this day, despite the radical reassessment of the Genesis text as a theological, pre-scientific text, wrongly perceived as in conflict with modern intellectual ideas, but needing to be appreciated in its rightful context. Various eager neo-Darwinians (e.g. Richard Dawkins and Steve Jones) promulgate an atheist view, tending to regard any opposition as either liberal hypocritical ('You can be a Christian and accept Darwin's evolution'), or fundamentalist cant ('The Bible is the inspired word of God, and therefore things happened as in Genesis 1–2, and not according to Darwin').

The Biblically derived view was that the creation of man was the culmination of the six days of creation. As man was the pinnacle of God's achievement on earth, he had a soul and stood in a very special relationship to the Almighty, conversing with Him. Man derived benefit from all else that was created for his use. But if man is the latest development by natural selection in a long line of changes by chance, set against a huge geological timescale, there is no real reason for him to have a soul that other creatures totally lack. What did it mean to say moreover that he was made in the image of God (IMAGO DEI), when his nearest relations, resembling his ancestors, were residing in London Zoo? This question really worried Victorian society. The implications were all too obvious for doctrine too – how could there be a FALL by a primitive ancestor of ours which involved mankind permanently in a taint of original SIN? Original sin and the Fall had been used by the Church to account for the need for the INCARNATION and REDEMPTION; now what was to be Christ's role, and was he now an out-of-date Redeemer 2000 years of human development later?

Confusion between natural and moral or spiritual development led to further questioning. The Bible had underwritten the morality which was seen to be the cohesive force in society, protecting property, marital and family relations, truth and life itself. Suddenly the Bible's account in Genesis 1–3 being at variance with the views of modern science meant that the whole Bible would be brought into disrepute. Further, the Church's authority to enforce that Biblical morality or its own doctrine was undermined and compromised, because it had promulgated a spurious text of a six-day creation, now shown to be false.

It is interesting that what lost Darwin his own personal faith was none of these points above, but the death of his favourite daughter and the role that blind Chance now played in a universe, where previously Providence, Design and a Divine Purpose had been seen to reign supreme.

Darwin's theory could be taken to upset the Bible and Christianity and lead to total rejection of religion, or it could itself be totally rejected, and the text of Genesis 1–3 be elevated to the level of scientific statement from God. The third option was to change the way in which the Bible was viewed (a process that was already underway), and to accept scientific findings, yet still to revere and seek to interpret the text, while refusing to force it to fit the scientific needs of a new era. How all three of these options have happened in the last century and a half is another story, outside of this dictionary's remit.

Exile In the Biblical tradition 'the Exile' relates most directly to the period of captivity in Babylonia (*see* BABYLON). Previously there had been an exchange of population between inhabitants of the Northern Kingdom of Israel and the subject areas of the ASSYRIAN Empire, resulting from the fall of SAMARIA in 722 BCE; this was the origin of Jewish suspicion about the SAMARITANS in terms of religious purity. Then subsequently came the turn of the Southern Kingdom, Judaea, when key parts of the population were deported to Babylonia. The Hebrew terms referring to this are *gola* (captivity) and *galut* (deportation). There were two main deportations: in 597 BCE under NEBUCHADNEZZAR (2 Kings 24.14); and then in 587/6 BCE those remaining, apart from the poorest inhabitants (2 Kings 25.11–12). But in terms of Israel's faith all was not lost. The prophet JEREMIAH predicted the people's return from the Babylonian captivity in terms which suggested a rewriting of the ancient creed relating to the EXODUS (see Jeremiah 23.7–8). The 'new Exodus' became a major theme in the oracles of Second ISAIAH (see 43.15–21 and 51.9–11). And the historical restoration is featured, for example, in the books of EZRA and NEHEMIAH and in the prophecies of HAGGAI and ZECHARIAH. Such Biblical themes are reinterpreted in modern Judaism in relation to the DIASPORA and the ALIYAH.

The language of exile (and subsequent restoration) also appears as a political metaphor in the New Testament. See, for examples from PAUL, Philippians 3.20 ('Our citizenship is in heaven, and it is from there that we are expecting a Saviour') and Galatians 4.26 ('the Jerusalem above is free'). See also Hebrews 11.8–10, 13–16; 12.22–23 ('they are seeking a homeland... God has prepared a city for them') and 1 Peter 1.1, 17; 2.11 ('exiles of the dispersion; the time of your exile; as aliens and exiles').

The theme of return from exile has assumed a new importance in some recent Christian theology. Instead of the literal reference to the return of the Jews to their land (historically, as indicated above), it comes to signify the political deliverance and liberation from foreign domination (as in the days of the Roman occupation), and the awaited spiritual return of YAHWEH to the TEMPLE and to ZION. In the interpretation of the New Testament this clearly offers a fresh analogy (TYPOLOGY) between an Old Testament fact and an early Christian expectation.

Exodus Exodus is a Greek word meaning 'way out' or 'exit'. Its primary application in the Biblical traditions is to the departure of the Israelite tribes under the leadership of MOSES from conditions of SLAVERY in Egypt. The narrative of these events is contained in the Biblical book of EXODUS. In terms of the faith of Israel this was regarded as a formative event, an historical turning point; and so it is often found summarized in confessions of faith: 'we were Pharaoh's slaves in Egypt, but the Lord brought us out of Egypt with a mighty hand' (Deuteronomy 6.21; see also, for example, Exodus 19.4; Jeremiah 23.7; Hosea 11.1).

The Exodus as a theological paradigm develops its significance within the Bible and beyond; it is a pattern for the continuing deliverance of God's people. The New Testament will draw creative comparisons with this formative Old Testament experience. So, for example, Matthew 2.15 uses the Hosea text just mentioned as a proof text in the narrative of Jesus' birth (Jesus and his parents go to, and return from, Egypt as analogy with Israel of old); and Luke uses the actual word *exodos* of Jesus' departure, that is his death in Jerusalem, at Luke 9.31 (Jesus' death will be at least as significant a turning point for Christian faith as the Exodus was for Israelite faith).

In modern theology the Exodus has become a powerful image of liberation from oppression, applied in numerous situations across the world, where a nationalist movement rebels against foreign domination, or in a class struggle of the poor and dispossessed against their overlords. A characteristic theme of liberation theology, that of 'bias to the poor', finds a ready identification with the Hebrews enslaved in Egypt. So Archbishop Desmond Tutu preached in 1984, when awarded the Nobel Peace Prize for his work during the apartheid period in South Africa: 'We know that you are the God of the Exodus; we know you are the God of freedom; we know that

Egypt and Sinai

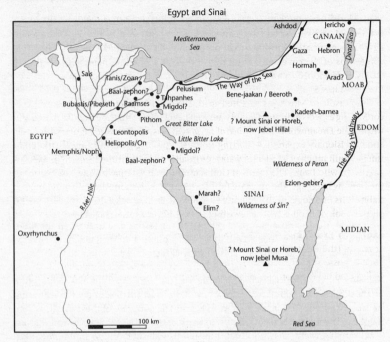

Map of the Exodus

you will lead us out of oppression and injustice; we know that you will lead us out of our Egypt and into the promised land of your freedom.'

Exodus, book of The book of Exodus is the empowerment of Israel, the account of the long march of these tribes from a slavery in EGYPT to the Promised Land and a confirmation of national identity. A strongly political text with obvious echoes to the present day in the Middle East, it has been used as a paradigm for such an experience of freedom and new beginnings, applied for example to the Pilgrim Fathers in America, to the proletariat in Marxism, to the historical situation of slavery in the southern states of the USA, as reflected in the Negro spirituals, and as the charter for liberation theology in Southern America, Southern Africa, India, Korea, Palestine and elsewhere in the modern world. The historical setting of the original Biblical event has been much debated; its timing is related to the changing dynasties of Pharaohs in Egypt and the geographical details of particular PLAGUES brought upon the Egyptians. Many place it in the late 13th century BCE. The precise route taken is debatable.

The EXODUS refers to this liberation and its outcome (see Exodus 19.1 and the preceding narratives), but the second, equally important part of the book of Exodus concerns the establishment of a COVENANT relationship between God and Israel at

Mount SINAI (chapters 19–24). This binding relationship, with MOSES as go-between, is initiated in a ritual ceremony involving blood (24), just as the departure from Egypt was associated with the ritual of the nomadic festival of PASSOVER. Then the conditions of the covenant are set out in the Ten Commandments or DECALOGUE (20) and developed in a whole sequence of laws and ritual instructions in the following chapters.

The person of Moses, as revealed in this book, is complex and powerful. The conflicting aspects of his personality are well developed from the evidence of Exodus within the Dreamworks film *Prince of Egypt*. On Moses' direct dialogues with GOD, and his visionary experience (starting from the episode of the burning bush), Judaism has built much of its theology and spirituality. God identifies himself, in Exodus 3.14: 'I am who I am.' The name of God is unique, bound up with the expression of the Hebrew language, the absolute foundation of Jewish monotheism, and impenetrable in its ontology. In the 2nd or 1st century BCE there was a dramatization based on the book of Exodus by the Jewish playwright Ezekiel the Tragedian.

exorcism Exorcism is the act of driving out evil spirits by certain prayers, formulae or rituals (the underlying Greek word means to 'put under an oath'). The idea of demon possession (which today might be termed a psychological illness) was a widespread belief among both Jews and pagans, and was readily adopted by Christians. The Gospels record examples of such MIRACLES in expelling demons, performed by Jesus (see Mark 5, and also GADARA), and by Jesus' DISCIPLES (see Matthew 10.1); the ACTS OF THE APOSTLES continues the theme (see Acts 16.18; 19.13). These narratives use a word meaning 'expel' or 'cast out' rather than the technical term involving an oath. In early Christianity candidates for BAPTISM might also have a routine exorcism, as a renunciation of evil.

Ezekiel, book of The third major book of prophecy, after Isaiah and Jeremiah, bears the name of Ezekiel, son of Buzi, a priest who had been deported to BABYLON in 597 BCE, and was then called to prophesy around 593 BCE. Among striking aspects of the book are the fact that he was both priest and prophet (these are thought to be opposing roles in Israel – perhaps Ezekiel was more a prophetic priest, and custodian of the LAW, than a priestly prophet), his APOCALYPTIC style of visionary experience (see chapter 1), and his extensive use of enacted prophetic symbolism (see, for example, chapter 4). In chapters 2 and 3 the prophet eats the scroll of his prophetic message from God; although written with 'lamentations, mourning and woe', once it is consumed it is 'as honey for sweetness'. The prophet was understandably regarded with suspicion as perhaps a psychiatric case; maybe his book should not be part of scripture, or at least (as Jewish rabbis suggested) be restricted to readers older than 30. On the other hand Ezekiel was used extensively in the DEAD SEA SCROLLS, probably because of his priestly interest and his focus on Jerusalem. The QUMRAN community could identify with those righteous early exiles who accompanied Ezekiel to Babylon.

As well as the chariot vision of chapter 1 (which became the foundation of Merkabah mysticism) Ezekiel's book records other highly charged dramatic scenes. These visions include the army of dry bones (Ezekiel 37); the great battle of chapters

Ezekiel's Vision Ezekiel 1–3

38–39 (which invites comparison with ARMAGEDDON in Revelation 16.16; the rebuild-ing of the TEMPLE (Ezekiel 40); and the millennial capital of Israel, in chapters 45 and 48, which resembles the Holy City of Revelation 21.

There are several important themes contained within the prophetic message. The traditional proverb quoted in Ezekiel 18.2 – 'the fathers have eaten sour grapes and the children's teeth are set on edge' – is reinterpreted by Ezekiel in terms of individual responsibility before God rather than the earlier perspective of communal inherit-ance. The restoration of the Temple (destroyed in 587 BCE) is described in detailed visions as the dwelling of God in what is very much a spiritualized relationship: 'It is no accident that in the erection of the new sanctuary on a very high mountain no word is said of any human participation in the construction; what is said concerns the coming of the glory of God to a dwelling in the midst of his people'(W. Zimmerli). The cultic activity in the new Temple is seen as a mechanism for the preservation of holiness, and to prevent contamination, so that God's intention to give life may never again be frustrated by the unacceptable condition of his people.

TABULATION OF EZEKIEL

The call of Ezekiel 1.1–3.27

1.1–28	Ezekiel in Babylonian exile sees God enthroned
2.1–3.27	God's command to deliver his message

The fall of Jerusalem 4.1–24.27

4.1–5.17	Ezekiel is to enact the terrible siege that will be God's punishment
6.1–14	The punishment is for idolatry
7.1–27	Poem about the disaster to come
8.1–11.25	Ezekiel's vision of contemporary idolatry back home in the Jerusalem Temple, which is followed by execution and the departure of God's glory
12.1–12.28	Ezekiel acts out being a refugee and explains relevance
13.1–14.23	Ezekiel prophesies punishment for false prophets
15.1–17.24	Jerusalem is variously condemned and its fate shown in an allegory
18.1–32	Everyone should repent or be punished for his own sins
19.1–14	A funeral lament for the Davidic dynasty
20.1–24.14	Ezekiel predicts a terrible fate for Jerusalem and explains that her conduct (and Samaria's) have brought about their own misfortune
24.15–27	Ezekiel demonstrates the people's shocked inability to mourn for Jerusalem, by his own reaction to the loss of his wife

The fate of other nations 25.1–32.32

25.1–17	Prophecies against Ammon, Moab, Edom and Philistia
26.1–28.24	Prophecies against Tyre and Sidon
28.25–26	Future restoration of the house of Israel
29.1–32.32	Prophecies against Egypt

The future for God's people 33.1–39.29

33.1–20	Repentance brings life
33.21–33	The fall of Jerusalem and its aftermath
34.1–10	A diatribe against false shepherds
34.11–31	God is the good shepherd and will restore his flock
35.1–36.38	Oracle against Edom, but blessing and restoration for Israel
37.1–14	The dry bones will live!
37.15–28	The dry sticks will reunite
38.1–39.29	God deals with the enemy Gog and then restores Israel

The vision of the new Temple 40.1–48.35

40.1–42.20	Buildings in the new Temple complex
43.1–12	The Lord in glory returns to the holy Temple
43.13–44.31	Rules concerning ritual at the altar and Temple
45.1–46.24	Rules and arrangements to run the Temple
47.1–12	The life-giving stream from the Temple
47.13–48.35	The land divided between twelve tribes

Ezion-geber The name Ezion-geber appears in passing at Numbers 33.35 and Deuteronomy 2.8. In the age of King SOLOMON it re-emerges as Israel's southern gateway and the seaport for the ships of Tarshish (see 1 Kings 10.11, 22). It is mentioned subsequently in the times of Rehoboam and Jehoshaphat. The site has not been conclusively identified. Obviously it is in the region of Eilat (referred to as Elath in the Bible). Suggested identifications are with Tel el-Kheleifeh, a mound near the centre of the north shore of the Gulf of Eilat (F. Frank and N. Glueck); alternatively with the nearby island of Jezivat Fara'um, where A. Flinder found fortifications and a harbour, with anchorages between the island and the mainland. The difficulty remains of linking either site with Solomon, or of understanding traces of what was enthusiastically identified as a smelting refinery, nearby in the Arabah.

Ezra, book of Ezra was a priest and also a leader of the Jewish community in the early period after the EXILE in BABYLON, in the middle of the 5th century BCE. The PERSIAN emperor CYRUS had conquered the Babylonian Empire in 539; subsequently he issued a decree permitting various exiles in Babylon to return to their homelands (see Ezra 1.2–4, and the Cyrus Cylinder, excavated in Babylon in the 19th century and now in the British Museum). Among them Jews were permitted to return and rebuild the Temple in Jerusalem; repairs were slow, only really beginning under ZERUBBABEL and being completed in 515 (see Ezra 6.15).

The dates of Ezra's activity are debated, but may well be around 458 BCE. King Artaxerxes I commissioned Ezra to establish the laws of the PENTATEUCH as state law in Israel. Ezra the priest read the law to the people at the Feast of TABERNACLES and set up a commission to investigate mixed marriages with non-Jews (see Nehemiah 8; Ezra 9–10).

In Judaism Ezra is regarded as especially significant for several reasons, which may or may not be historical: his role in shaping the religious community; his collecting of the holy books of the fathers of the faith; his founding of the 'Great SYNAGOGUE', whereby holy traditions were handed on to the later rabbis; his introduction from ARAMAIC of the square script (which replaced the earlier cursive), in which HEBREW is still written today.

The literary relationship between the books of Ezra, NEHEMIAH, and 1 AND 2 CHRON-ICLES is complex. The books of Ezra and Nehemiah are a direct sequel to Chronicles, continuing the story. Some argue that all the books are the final work of a single author; others emphasize the differences in authorship but say that they were designed to belong together. Ezra 4.8–6.18 is written in Aramaic, while the rest of the book is in Hebrew; this may well be due to the use of an original source of official

Persian documents at this point. Other sources, including a memoir by Ezra in Ezra 7–10 and Nehemiah 8–9, are possible.

The Hebrew name Ezra has a Greek form ESDRAS. 1 Esdras (in the Protestant APOC-RYPHA) largely overlaps with the narrative from 2 Chronicles 35 to Nehemiah 8 and is therefore concerned with Ezra only in the last two chapters. 2 Esdras is another apocryphal book, containing a set of apocalypses attributed to the historical Ezra, including, in chapters 3–14, the work known as 4 Ezra (written after 70 CE, which initially refers to Ezra as Salathiel in 3.1). 3 Esdras is the version of 2 Esdras in the Slavonic Bible. 4 Esdras is the designation of 2 Esdras in the appendix to the Latin VULGATE.

F

faith Biblical faith/belief is primarily 'faith (or trust) *in*' God or Jesus, but it also reflects the beginnings of a later meaning – a confession of faith in certain facts or opinions asserted as being true ('faith *that*').

Actual instances of the word 'faith' in the Hebrew Bible are comparatively rare (see for example Psalm 112.7: 'their hearts are firm, secure in the Lord'). But, as HEBREWS chapter 11 demonstrates, in the comprehensive survey of those who have been victorious by faith, the pattern of trust and belief in God, governing their actions, was there from the earliest stories. So it was that ABRAHAM (Hebrews 11.8) began through faith his momentous journey to the Promised Land, and it was faith that caused the walls of JERICHO to collapse (Hebrews 11.30).

During Jesus' ministry he apparently performed some (but not all) healing MIRACLES in response to a personal trust and faith in him and his abilities. See, for example, Mark 2.5, where it is the friends of the paralysed man who have faith; and Mark 5.34, where it is the sick woman's faith which brought about her cure. In contrast with these examples Mark seems to suggest that a lack of faith hindered Jesus' ability; this was strikingly evident in his home town (Mark 6.5). Jesus challenged the father of the epileptic boy with the notion that everything was possible to the person who had faith, until the tormented man cried, 'I believe; help my unbelief!' (Mark 9.24). The added interest in this story is that the DISCIPLES' failure to effect the EXORCISM, before Jesus' arrival on the scene, is linked to the need for PRAYER, and not apparently their faith.

Paul's use of the word 'faith' is frequent in ROMANS and GALATIANS. He taught that people could be put right ('justified') through faith in Jesus (see Romans 1.17; 3.22), and this is the only way that sinners can be put right. In his teaching faith is clearly and closely linked with this idea of the RIGHTEOUSNESS that cannot be achieved by human striving.

JAMES' LETTER apparently sought to correct a perceived imbalance in emphasis here, by stressing that faith *and* actions are both essential for the Christian believer, and that faith not expressed through deeds is useless and dead (James 2.26).

In preaching attributed to the early apostles in ACTS, and in formulae that have been detected elsewhere in the New Testament Gospels and epistles, there are early indications of what was later to be summarized and codified in the creeds of the Church. This was the content of faith – that Jesus had been crucified and was now resurrected, that he had been made Lord and MESSIAH (*see also* TITLES OF JESUS), and that personal salvation depended upon believing this. The sequel to this confession of faith was to accept BAPTISM, for the forgiveness of SINS, and to receive the Holy SPIRIT (see Acts 2.32–38).

The combination of these two meanings of 'faith' – the personal trust in, and dependence upon, a living God (Jesus), and the substance of what is believed – is to be seen in 1 John 5.4–5: 'This is the victory that conquers the world, our faith. Who is it that conquers the world but the one who believes that Jesus is the SON OF GOD?'

Fall Christian theology uses 'the Fall' to denote the SIN of ADAM which resulted in the expulsion of Adam and EVE from the Garden of EDEN (Genesis 3.23–24). Before this original sin, HUMAN NATURE was regarded as being in an ideal state of bliss; but humanity, lulled into a sense of security, overreached itself and sought equality of knowledge and status with the divine (Genesis 3.5). The consequence of such rash action was the experience of harsher conditions and the reality of suffering outside PARADISE; there is a bleaker version of Christian theology which sees humanity as thereby degraded and totally damned; only through Christ can the original state of blessing be restored (see Romans 5.12–19).

Jewish interpretation of GENESIS places the emphasis differently, seeing this and other narratives as illustrating an underlying tension between the good and bad inclinations of humanity. Here the ultimate sin is focused on the creation of the GOLDEN CALF at just the critical point when MOSES is receiving the LAW on Mount SINAI.

families and family relationships While the fifth of the Ten Commandments (DECALOGUE) – 'Honour your father and your mother' (Exodus 20.12) – might seem to reflect today's situation, concentrating on the nuclear family, Bible teaching should mostly be seen in the context of the extended family.

Within the Hebrew Bible in PATRIARCHAL times the family functioned as a large polygamously based economic unit, and loyalties had to be strongly reinforced for the clan to survive; inheritance was important, as was the possession of heirs. The need for wives who were good breeding stock is underlined (Genesis 28.1–3), and in stories of women who found child-bearing hard to achieve (such as SARAH – Genesis 21.1–2; RACHEL – Genesis 30.22; HANNAH – 1 Samuel 1.19) divine intervention was felt to have brought about what was humanly impossible. Inevitably in such a society there was sibling rivalry (JACOB and ESAU – Genesis 27; JOSEPH – Genesis 37.4). The group's collective protection meant care for the elderly and vulnerable within the unit (Genesis 44.30–31; 47.12). On the darker side it also meant that revenge killings happened (Genesis 34.25–29). The tracing of Israel's tribal origins to the quarrelsome brood of Jacob's 12 sons (Genesis 49) shows the importance attached to the family. By the period of the monarchy polygamy was usual for the king (for political purposes – see 1 Kings 11.1–3), but was much less so for the common man. Gradually monogamy became the norm.

The rest of the Hebrew Bible largely mirrors the view pursued by Orthodox Judaism to this day, that the man has the religious responsibilities and leadership of the family. The woman's role, beyond that of simple home-maker, was to keep the laws of PURITY and dietary hygiene (*see also* FOOD LAWS), and to bring up the children to practise the rules in their turn. Her failure as a wife could be punished by her husband's initiation of DIVORCE (see Deuteronomy 24.1). No one said child-rearing was an easy task, and PROVERBS has numerous passages discussing approaches to successful discipline. Children are admonished to listen to their parents (Proverbs 1.8). Correction and punishment were to be used as necessary by caring parents (13.24). Wise sons responded to their parents (15.20). Grandparents could be proud of them too (17.6). There are warnings against the dangers of ADULTERY and the folly of begetting illegitimate children (5.3, 16; 6.24–31; 'he who commits adultery has no sense; he who does it destroys himself' – 6.32). Proverbs advocates fidelity in marriage (5.15–20) and there is a wonderfully lyrical passage in praise of a good wife (31.10–31). Note that this paragon is contributing economically to her well-run household as well as being charitable. A sensible wife is a blessing (19.14).

Jesus was himself (humanly speaking) a member of a substantial family unit (see Mark 6.3), even if they found his behaviour strange (Mark 3.21). There is an ambivalent attitude towards Jesus, both of closeness and of concern. His mother 'treasured all these things in her heart' (Luke 2.51); traditionally she is regarded as the link person/informant for Luke's version of Jesus' birth. MARY came to faith in her son; according to John 19.25 she was present at his crucifixion. Jesus' brother/half-brother JAMES emerged as leader of the Jerusalem Church (Acts 12.17; Galatians 1.19).

Jesus' concern for family relationships, and the responsibility of care for the vulnerable, may be seen when he told the BELOVED DISCIPLE to care for his mother (John 19.27), as well as when he restored the breadwinner son to his widowed mother in Nain (Luke 7.11–17). On the other hand Jesus valued the community around him as his family (Mark 3.33–35) over and beyond blood ties. Actual teaching on family relationships (beyond what is covered in marriage and divorce) does not, however, come from Jesus. A case could indeed be made for his advocating the leaving behind of family ties in the service of the KINGDOM OF GOD – particularly under the pressure of the impending End Time (*see* ESCHATON). This the APOSTLES did (see Mark 1.18; 10.29–30). It was also recognized that family divisions and antagonisms could arise from following or rejecting Jesus, even leading to betrayal of close relatives in times of persecution (Mark 13.12; Luke 21.16).

Such potential disruption of family life is not generally reflected in the later Pauline and PASTORAL EPISTLES. There families are based on a stable monogamous union: husbands were to love their wives; wives to respect their husbands (Ephesians 5.21–33; Colossians 3.18–19; see also 1 Peter 3.1–7). Parents were not to be overbearing with their children, who in turn were to obey their parents (Ephesians 6.1–4; Colossians 3.20–21). These household codes in Ephesians and Colossians next include slaves; obedience was expected of them, as of wife and children. Slaves counted as part of the household and extended family in many of the richer GENTILE households which had been converted. It is probable, for instance, that LYDIA brought her servants and slaves from her PURPLE business into the Christian faith, together with her own relatives and dependants (Acts 16.15). Sharing of faith across the status divide was not seen as a problem (1 Timothy 6.1–2), but rather should increase the bonding.

The model Christian family is that of the Church leader (bishop) in 1 Timothy 3.1–7. The man should be monogamous (or never remarry – the wording of 3.2 is ambiguous) and control his own family and household well, and his children should obey him. The families of Church helpers are similar, with the additional warning to wives not to gossip (1 Timothy 3.8–13). Christians also had an obligation to care for the extended family, especially those in the real poverty of widowhood (1 Timothy 5.4, 8), or they were regarded as being apostate. Young widows were encouraged to remarry (1 Timothy 5.14); older pious widows might need to be cared for by the Church, if genuinely childless and alone (1 Timothy 5.9–10). However, this was second best: 'If any believing woman has relatives who are really widows, let her assist them; let the Church not be burdened, so that it can assist those who are real widows' (5.16).

The pattern of the Christian nuclear family, albeit with wider obligations, was being set for 2000 years. *See also* MARRIAGE.

fasting Fasting should strictly be defined as the entire abstinence from food for all or part of a day. The practice of fasting for set periods was rigorously observed by the pious in JUDAISM, with regular weekly fasts on Mondays and Thursdays. The whole community should fast from sunset to sunset on two major days in the year: the Day of Atonement (YOM KIPPUR – which is the only fast in the Mosaic TORAH, see Leviticus 23.27); and the ninth day of the month Ab (the day commemorating the destruction of the Jerusalem TEMPLE by the Babylonians). In addition there were three minor fast-days, to be observed from sunrise to sunset, all linked to the fate of Jerusalem and the Temple in past history. According to ZECHARIAH 8.19, in the future these fasts would be transformed into days of gladness and joy.

The earliest Christian practice of fasting was carried forward from Judaism. There is evidence from the DIDACHE, chapter 8, of a pious practice of fasting on Wednesdays and Fridays – the same idea as, but deliberately on different days from, the Jews. Jesus had recommended fasting, both in his teaching and by example (see Matthew 6.16–18; Mark 9.29, reading 'prayer and fasting'). Mark 2.18–20 raises a comparison between the practice of the PHARISEES, the disciples of JOHN THE BAPTIST, and Jesus' DISCIPLES. There is evidence elsewhere in the New Testament for the observance of fasting by the APOSTLES (see Acts 13.2; 14.23; 2 Corinthians 11.27 – here hardship rather than penance?). In the first Christian centuries the period of fasting, known as Lent, in preparation for the festival of Easter, seems to have lasted for two days, rather than the later period of 40 days (perhaps modelled on Christ's period in the wilderness, see Mark 1.13 and further on TEMPTATIONS OF CHRIST).

Father Whereas the Hebrew Bible has a rich collection of metaphors and striking images to help the understanding of God, as King, Shepherd, Warrior, Rock, the use of Father is very sparse, considering the patriarchal nature of society at the time (see Psalm 89.26; Malachi 2.10: 'Have we not all one father? Has not one God created us?').

The widespread use of the title Father for God in Christianity is usually attributed to Jesus' insights in his unique relationship as Son. So Jesus prayed 'Abba' – the intimate ARAMAIC title – in his anguish at GETHSEMANE (Mark 14.36). Jesus also prefaced the LORD'S PRAYER, his guideline to prayer, with the words 'Our Father' (Matthew 6; Luke 11). In his classic study Joachim Jeremias compared the versions and reconstructed an Aramaic original, making this a very personal prayer: 'Dear Father, Hallowed be thy name, Thy Kingdom come, Our bread for tomorrow give us today, And forgive us our debts as we also herewith forgive our debtors, And let us not succumb to temptation.'

That the title Father became commonplace in Christianity is clear from the number of references in the epistles (see for example Romans 1.7; 1 Corinthians 8.6; Philippians 1.2). Some uses sound like formulae: see 1 Timothy 1.2 – 'Grace, mercy and peace from God the Father and Christ Jesus our Lord' – and 1 Corinthians 1.3. These probably reflect early patterns of WORSHIP.

The Gospel of John pre-eminently develops the ideas inherent in the loving relationship of Father and Son (see John 3.35: 'The Father loves the Son and has placed all things in his hands'; John 11.41: 'Father I thank you for having heard me'). The Gospel relates this to Jesus' mission (see John 20.21: 'As the Father has sent me, so I send you'; see also 1 John 4.14: 'And we have seen and do testify that the Father has sent his Son as the Saviour of the world'). In the SYNOPTIC Gospels the Father is mentioned in connection with the concepts of forgiveness and mercy (see Mark 11.25).

References across the New Testament connect together the Father, the Son and the Holy SPIRIT (see Matthew 28.19) in a manner that grew to resemble a liturgical formula. But initially this linkage will have signalled the Father's gift of the Spirit (see John 14.16–17). The Spirit was to enable Christians in their turn to cry 'Abba' (Father) – see Galatians 4.6: 'God has sent the Spirit of his Son into our hearts, crying "Abba! Father!"'

Felix (Roman procurator) *See* PROCURATORS, ROMAN.

Fertile Crescent The Fertile Crescent is not a Biblical term, but one coined by a modern scholar (J. H. Breasted) to describe the area in which a high proportion of events described in the Bible take place. Strictly it denotes the crescent-shaped area of more fertile land which sweeps round from the Mesopotamian rivers of the Tigris and Euphrates, westwards through Syria to the Mediterranean, then southwards through PALESTINE, and also includes the Nile valley in Egypt. This area was the scene of mass migrations, of conquest and settlement, by tribes and nations obviously attracted to the better-quality land.

festivals, Jewish According to the PENTATEUCH it was a religious duty for a male Israelite to visit the Jerusalem TEMPLE on three occasions in the year, for the festivals of PASSOVER (Pesach), Weeks (Shavuot or in Greek PENTECOST), and TABERNACLES (Succoth – Deuteronomy 16.16). These three festivals of PILGRIMAGE structured the seasons of the religious year and originated in farming and agriculture. Two other festivals are named in the Bible: the beginning of the New Year (Rosh Hashanah), which introduces 10 days of penitence (at which the *shofar* or ram's horn is sounded at all prayers); and the Day of Atonement (YOM KIPPUR). There are two other festivals, later than the Torah, namely HANUKKAH (the commemoration of the rededication of the TEMPLE by JUDAS MACCABEUS); and PURIM (commemorating the story of ESTHER).

After the fall of the Jerusalem Temple, the Jewish holy days are commemorated in the SYNAGOGUE and the home. Often they are recollected by means of the symbols associated with each festival; these can be found represented in the mosaic pavements of ancient synagogues, and in a splendid example of a 'gold-glass' dish from the 4th-century CE Jewish catacombs in Rome. Such symbols include the MENORAH (seven-branched candelabrum) as a symbol of light; the *ethrog* or citrus fruit and the *lulab* or palm branch, both associated with Tabernacles; and the ram's horn. Another frequent feature, sometimes as a stone carving, is a representation of the facade of a building like the Jerusalem Temple, perhaps symbolizing the shrine for the TORAH, or ARK containing the scrolls of the LAW (the focus of a traditional synagogue).

figs *See* CROPS.

fish The fish is frequently encountered, as early as the 2nd century CE, as a Christian symbol. The letters of the Greek word for 'fish' (*ichthus*) are taken as a shorthand for the declaration of faith *Iesous Christos Theou Huios Soter* ('Jesus Christ Son of God Saviour'). The symbol is found in Christian iconography, and in a literary form, for example in Book 8 of *Sibylline Oracles*. A further reason for its popularity as a Christian symbol may be the number of references to fish in the New Testament: in Christ's miraculous feeding of the multitude; in the disciples as fishermen, especially with the miraculous catches of fish (see also John 21.11 and NUMBER SYMBOLISM); and in the coin for the tribute money found by Peter in the fish's mouth (Matthew 17.27).

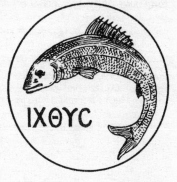

The Fish Rebus

According to Genesis 1.21 fishes were created on the fifth day of CREATION; they constitute a distinct category of living creatures over which humanity has stewardship. Later commentators speculated over whether fish, in common with other creatures, fell under the curse of the FLOOD. In Mosaic dietary laws fish with fins and scales are declared clean, while those without are unclean.

Flood The Biblical story of the Flood (Genesis 6–7), with NOAH and the Ark, has parallels in the mythology of other neighbouring civilizations (*see* MYTH). The Mesopotamian version came to light when George Smith discovered fragments of an epic poem on 7th-century BCE Assyrian tablets from NINEVEH. This epic of GILGAMESH derived from earlier SUMERIAN and BABYLONIAN stories and was widely circulated. In this epic Utnapishtim is warned by his god to build a ship, and gather together his family, treasures and living creatures of every kind. He thus escapes a terrible flood which destroys all the rest of mankind. Gilgamesh, king of Uruk, who in the story visits Utnapishtim as part of a personal quest for immortality, is thought to have ruled in Mesopotamia c.2700 BCE. Evidence of severe floods of that period exists at several sites in southern Iraq; the Babylonian story probably represents a folk-memory of various localized disasters.

A recent theory, based on seismological studies, suggested that when the sea levels rose in the Mediterranean following the last Ice Age they flooded over the Bosphorus Strait and into the lowlands of what is now the Black Sea. Many towns and villages would have been flooded by the cataclysmic event that created the Black Sea; this will have left as a legacy the legend of a vast deluge. The evidence was collected by Walter Pitman and William Ryan of Columbia University.

There is also a Greek parallel in which the upright Deucalion and his wife are spared the divine punishment of the evil world. The story is related in Ovid's *Metamorphoses*. In the New Testament the flood and Noah's Ark are taken as examples of divine judgement and salvation (see Matthew 24.37–39). The Christian tradition relished the one-to-one correspondence of TYPOLOGY which compared the Old Testament Flood and Ark with the Christian waters of BAPTISM (1 Peter 3.20–21).

flowers *See* PLANTS.

food laws The Hebrew Bible contains a range of dietary regulations, whereby the Jew is forbidden to eat certain foods. In modern Judaism observance of these rules is called kashrut; permitted food is kosher (originally meaning 'right' or 'fit' – see Esther 8.5), and forbidden food is tref (an abbreviation of *terefah* originally meaning 'torn' – translated as 'mangled' in Exodus 22.31).

The key texts relating to animals, birds and fishes are found in Leviticus 11 and Deuteronomy 14.3–21. Animals are kosher if they have cloven hooves and also chew the cud. The pig is forbidden because it does not chew the cud. There is a list of birds (game birds and birds of prey) that are forbidden, while domestic fowl such as chickens, ducks, geese and pigeons are presumed to be kosher. If a bird is forbidden, so also are its eggs; but QUAIL and quails' eggs are kosher (see Numbers 11.31–32). Only fish that have fins and scales are kosher. Worms, frogs, eels and all shellfish are not kosher; LOCUSTS are more complicated, and some species may be eaten.

The Bible forbids the eating of any part of an animal 'torn' by wild beasts, or the carcase of an animal that has died naturally. This leads to rabbinic stipulations about the necessity of ritual slaughter, and the rejection of any animal or bird with defects. Leviticus 7.26–27 and 17.10–14 had prohibited any consumption of blood; Deuteronomy 12.23 explained this: 'for the blood is the life'. The references in Exodus (23.19; 34.26) and Deuteronomy (14.21) which prohibit 'seething a kid in its mother's milk' are taken by the rabbis to prohibit the cooking, eating, or any mixing together of meat and milk in the same meal. The thigh muscle must be removed from any animal before it is eaten (Genesis 32.32), in recollection of the wound JACOB sustained when he wrestled with the angel (Genesis 32.25).

It is a matter of some debate how far the earliest Christians, particularly JEWISH-CHRISTIANS, subscribed to these dietary regulations, and applied them to GENTILE Christians. In the so-called 'Apostolic Decree' described in Acts 15.20, Gentiles should abstain 'from whatever has been strangled [not ritually slaughtered] and from blood'. This could mean an application by James of the regulations from Leviticus 17.10–18.30 (which governed outsiders in Israel as well as Israelites) to

Gentiles, so that they keep Mosaic law, but without requiring CIRCUMCISION. The ban on eating meat from sacrifices offered in a pagan temple is a different matter again (see Exodus 34.15). This was clearly a problem in a cosmopolitan society; see the laxity attacked in the book of REVELATION 2.14–15, 20. PAUL tackles the same issue in 1 Corinthians 8, but without referring to any Apostolic Decree from Jerusalem. Christians, he says, may exercise freedom in these matters, but do so in love and consideration for the weaker members of the community whose consciences might be troubled. (See also Romans 14.)

foot-washing In the ancient Near East the provision of facilities for the washing of feet is a practical aspect of hospitality, when greeting travellers and rinsing away the dust and dirt of their journey. So ABRAHAM washes the feet of the three angelic figures (Genesis 18; but compare LOT in Genesis 19) and Abigail offers to wash the feet of David's servants at CARMEL (1 Samuel 25.41 – but this may only be an expression of humility).

But there is another dimension to foot-washing in the ritual acts of cleansing. Water might be stored for such purposes of purification in stone vessels (not susceptible to contamination), as in the water pots at CANA in John 2.6. In Exodus 30.19 AARON and his sons are required as part of a ritual to wash feet and hands in a copper basin between the Tent of Meeting and the Altar of God. The general principle of ritual cleansing is shown in the Prophets (see Ezekiel 36.25: 'I will sprinkle clean water upon you, and you shall be clean from all your uncleannesses'). A celebrated instance of cleansing from leprosy is shown by the action of ELISHA to Naaman at the river JORDAN (2 Kings 5.10–14). Within JUDAISM there was provision for regular cleansing using a ritual bath (*miqweh*) in the SYNAGOGUE, or in the home, if there was room. The Essenes at QUMRAN were well provided with such baths or *miqwa'ot*, with separate steps for access and egress, to preserve the special PURITY of members of the community.

The foot-washing performed by Jesus for the DISCIPLES in John 13 is of a somewhat different order; it has in turn given rise to Christian rituals performed in imitation on Maundy Thursday. Jesus' action takes place after the meal, not before, so cannot be part of what was thought to be appropriate cleansing before eating (but see Mark 7.2–3, 5; Luke 11.38). It is a highly symbolic action of role reversal, with Jesus as master performing the act of a servant (see Mark 10.45). In later Christian thought it was regarded as a process of purification for the future, a washing away by the second Adam (Christ) of the nature of the first ADAM (Adam = 'man of dust'). *See also* REDEMPTION.

form criticism In Biblical studies 'form criticism' has a quite particular sense. It is the usual rendering in English of the term *Formgeschichte*, literally 'form history', coined by German critics. The presuppositions of this critical method are, firstly, that in the earliest days of the Biblical traditions these were oral in form (*see* ORALITY); secondly, that during this period of oral transmission the traditions became substantially shaped rather than remaining totally fluid; and, thirdly, that interaction with some religious community played a significant role in that shaping.

Form criticism as applied to the study of the written texts of the GOSPELS was developed independently by several German scholars (Rudolf Bultmann, Martin Dibelius, Karl Ludwig Schmidt) in the years following the First World War. They analysed the different types of material found in the written Gospels, especially the small paragraphs most visible in the Gospel of MARK. These units were thought to be particularly helpful in such situations as the impromptu preaching of the Gospel message, and could therefore have been shaped and designed with such purposes in view. Further, a close examination of such units can assist in determining the concerns and priorities of the early Christian communities. What began as a pre-literary analysis carried with it the likelihood of historical conclusions.

Such New Testament scholars had developed their methods under the influence of earlier examples of work of a similar kind in the study of the Old Testament. The main figure here was Hermann Gunkel, working around the year 1900 in a process which he called *Gattungsforschung* or the analysis of genres. The main foci of Gunkel's interest were the book of PSALMS and the sagas and legends of GENESIS. He classified the Psalms into five main types: hymns, communal laments, royal psalms, individual laments, individual thanksgivings. In Gunkel's commentary on Genesis, for example, he analysed the story of JACOB and ESAU in chapters 25–28: in origin this was a popular tale contrasting the two different occupations of shepherd and hunter, preferring the former; later the tale was recast and applied to the named heroes, reflecting the historical competition between Israel and EDOM (the supposed descendants of Esau).

Despite the rise in the importance of orality in the study of the Biblical tradition, some of the working assumptions of form criticism have been called into question. It is interesting that such methods, which appeared to be very radical when proposed in Germany, were only accepted very gradually and not universally in Britain. New Testament scholars in Britain began to accept form criticism's ideas in the 1930s. But they were the bridgehead for an energetic use of such methods in American scholarship.

frankincense *See* PLANTS (RESINOUS); SHOWBREAD.

friendship A modern study of friendship claims that today 'more and more is being asked of this voluntary, informal, personal relationship. It is commonplace for sociologists to note that institutions like MARRIAGE, kinship, class unions and corporations are losing their stickiness. As their power to hold society together moderates, so, they say, people are turning to friendship to support them and secure their sense of place in the world' (Mark Vernon). Among earlier definitions of friendship, Ralph Waldo Emerson wrote: 'When they are real, they are not glass threads of frostwork, but the solidest things we know.' Aristotle in *Nicomachean Ethics* said that, 'it is those who desire the good of their friends for the friends' sake that are most truly friends, because each loves the other for what he is and not for any incidental quality'. Jean Vanier, who founded the L'Arche community for the learning disabled, said, 'When we enter into a friendship we become vulnerable, fragile to each other. If I listen to you and you to me, we can come together, bridging the gap. Jesus gave us a new power to transform ourselves. This is the whole mystery of the INCARNATION, that God bent down, became our brother, walked with us, said, "I love you".'

In Greek and Roman culture special relationships such as friendship and patronage were highly valued and regularly practised. By contrast, the idea of friendship lacks much profound consideration in the Hebrew Bible; the special relationship between DAVID and JONATHAN (see 1 Samuel 18.3) is highlighted as out of the ordinary, perhaps because they might have been expected to be rivals. According to Proverbs 17.17, 'a friend loves at all times'; but the teacher of WISDOM is aware that friendship can be nominal when affected by circumstances (see Proverbs 19.4, 6–7). In the book of JOB his friends who come to help are more influenced by their own religious beliefs than by sympathy for his plight.

Biblical language of friendship (of good and evil friends) comes to a climax in statements about Christ as friend. See John 11.35–36 for the intensity of Jesus' feelings for LAZARUS. The modern theologian Jürgen Moltmann singled out two verses with specific reference to friendship: Luke 7.34 and John 15.13. In the former Jesus is denounced for keeping bad company; 'as a friend Jesus offers the unlovable the friendship of God'. In the latter, 'through the death of their friend, the disciples become his friends for ever'.

fundamentalism Fundamentalism has been defined by Dr Jonathan Sacks, the Chief Rabbi of England and Wales, as 'the attempt to impose a single truth on a plural world. What really lies behind it is a fear and profound insecurity. Aggression is always a sign of insecurity, and insecurity is always, at bottom, a lack of FAITH.' It is a word that has been applied very broadly, and usually critically, to certain strands of dogmatism within a range of world religions.

Fundamentalism is 'In Christianity, a varied movement usually affirming a set of basic beliefs by reference to the AUTHORITY of a literally interpreted, inerrant Bible,' according to David Ford. The term is commonly applied to conservative Protestants, largely in North America. Historically this is an accurate label, insofar as the origins of the word derive from a series of tracts called *The Fundamentals*, written between 1909 and 1915 as a restatement of central Christian doctrines from a conservative Protestant perspective. It is also true that the Roman Catholic Church, under Pope Pius X, especially in an encyclical of 1907, reacted strongly against liberal and modernist attitudes.

These early 20th-century reactions covered a broad span of Christian doctrines. But the word 'fundamentalism' has tended to become narrowed subsequently in an application to questions of Biblical authority and INSPIRATION, which were only a part of the original manifesto. The Bible is viewed literally; or, specifically, the text is regarded as absolutely inerrant, such that it is to be interpreted exactly as it stands, and in opposition to the approaches of modern BIBLICAL CRITICISM. Obviously this may generate conflict on a range of historical, theological and scientific issues (see, for example, EVOLUTION). Another characteristic of Protestant fundamentalism is found in the literal understanding of the PAROUSIA or second coming of Christ. Biblical prophecies of a 1000-year reign of the MESSIAH over a restored Jewish nation are expected to be fulfilled imminently. This hope for the ESCHATON often accompanies an extreme pessimism about the current state of the world.

G

Gad 1 The son of JACOB by Zilpah, the handmaid of his first wife LEAH (see Genesis 30.9–13). The use of Zilpah as a surrogate mother for both Gad and ASHER is surprising, because Leah was not childless, but had already given Jacob four sons; it might have been an act of retaliation against the childless second wife RACHEL whose handmaid Bilhah was the mother of DAN and NAPHTALI. Gad was the ancestor of the tribe that bears his name; their territory, shared with REUBEN, lay between the Jabbok and Arnon rivers (see also Genesis 49.19).

2 A prophet-seer in the time of DAVID (2 Samuel 24.11).

3 A Canaanite deity of fortune (Isaiah 65.11). The Hebrew word *gad* means 'luck'.

Gadara Gadara was a capital of the Hellenistic confederation of 10 cities, known as the DECAPOLIS, where the population was pagan and largely GREEK-speaking. Apart from Beth-shean (Scythopolis), these cities were located to the east of the river JORDAN and the Sea of GALILEE. Gadara (Um Qeia), which is five miles south-east of the lake, is the likely site of Jesus' encounter with a possessed man, from whom Jesus exorcizes demons, and sends them into a nearby herd of pigs, who rush into the lake and are drowned (see Mark 5.1–20; Matthew 8.28–34; Luke 8.26–39). There is textual confusion between the manuscripts of these accounts, and the place is variously named as Gadara, Gerasa, and Gergesa. Gerasa is the modern Jerash, which is too far away for the story, being 30 miles distant from the lake. Gergesa was an identification by the Church Father Origen who found a suitable place with precipitous cliffs opposite CAPERNAUM; he gave it the name, meaning 'Habitation of those who drove away', based on an echo of Joshua 3.10. As a result of his identification, the largest Byzantine monastery in the Holy Land was built at what is now called Kursi – a major Christian pilgrimage site on the north-east of the lake. (The name Kursi is a result of a mistaken identification by St Jerome of the site as CHORAZIN; *see* GERGESA.) Gadara, at the south-east, had its own harbour at Tel Samra, and was more directly opposite Capernaum across the lake (Mark 4.35). The confusion in Gospel manuscripts came about because Gadara was unknown to the copyists a few centuries on, while Gerasa was still a thriving cultural centre.

Gaius, Emperor (Caligula) *See* PHILO OF ALEXANDRIA; PILATE, PONTIUS.

Galatians, Paul's letter to the The letter to the Galatians may well be one of PAUL's earlier writings; a careful comparison with some themes which are developed in the letter to the ROMANS reveals Galatians as an earlier expression of these ideas, perhaps even a prototype. The treatment in Galatians is also more emotional and impassioned, while Romans is more considered and reflective. The actual dating of Galatians depends on a decision as to who were its recipients: Galatia is in Asia Minor (modern Turkey), but were the addressees in the coastal south of the area, the Roman province of Galatia, which Paul visited earlier (Acts 14), or the Celtic people living further north, whom Paul visited later (brief references in Acts 16.6 and 18.23)?

Associated with this is a key question about the Apostolic Council which is described in the ACTS OF THE APOSTLES, chapter 15. Paul also mentions, in Galatians 2.1–10, an important meeting which took place in Jerusalem, but there are significant differences, compared with Acts, in Paul's version of events. Should one trust the historical framework of Acts as being accurate in detail, or should one prefer Paul's more personal account? Another solution to the difficulty, if it can be assumed that Paul is writing to the earlier group in south Galatia, would be to suggest that the Jerusalem meeting, to which he refers, is actually an earlier visit for the purposes of 'famine relief' as recorded in Acts 11.27–30. Then he is not mentioning the Jerusalem Council meeting to the Galatians simply because it has not yet happened.

Paul had founded the Churches of Galatia, but he now writes this angry letter to them, because he has discovered that his work is being challenged by other teachers with a more directly JEWISH-CHRISTIAN agenda (whether or not sponsored by the Jerusalem Church). The relationship of early Christianity to the laws and traditions of JUDAISM was obviously a red-hot issue. Paul wants to insist on the radical character and universal scope of God's GRACE. Paul's GENTILE converts are the focus of the dispute; should the marks of Jewish identity be imposed upon them? Paul argues for a liberation from any kind of bondage, whether to the Jewish law or to the powers or conventions of the present age. He summarizes his argument (Galatians 4.21–31) by referring to the story of ABRAHAM and the two women who produced his sons. This becomes a complicated ALLEGORY (strictly a TYPOLOGY) which has mystified many church congregations when read on Mothering Sunday. Old and New Testaments are compared, and the new Christians identified as the children 'of promise', like ISAAC who came from Abraham and SARAH.

Galatians 6.11 offers an interesting glimpse into the ancient practice of letter-writing. It seems that Paul has dictated the letter to a secretary, but adds a postscript in his own hand. *See also* EPISTLES.

Galilee, Sea or Lake of The Sea of Galilee is a lake (or inland sea) in northern Israel, lying over 200 metres below sea level. It is roughly heart-shaped and measures 12 miles long by 7 miles wide. The lake is encircled by hills, leaving little space for a track along the shore; the greatest space is in the north-west at the little plain of Gennesaret. Over the centuries it has been given several names, of which Kinneret (Chinnereth) is probably the oldest, called after the town Kinnarot. By the 3rd century CE it was more often called by the names of newer towns on its shore: the Sea of Tiberias or the Waters of Ginosar. The most common names in the New Testament are the Sea of Galilee and the Sea of Gennesaret. The lake itself is relatively recent, created in the past 20,000 years. In the Old Testament it seems to be mentioned only as a border (see Numbers 34.11; Joshua 11.2). By Roman times it had become the centre of a fishing industry and supplied salted or pickled fish to the Empire, as well as exporting grain grown on the plateau to the east. Since the 1960s it has been a vital part of the Israeli National Water Carrier, supplying irrigation to the agriculture of the Negev.

'There are two seas in Israel: the DEAD SEA and the Sea of Galilee. The latter is full of life; fish, birds, vegetation. The former contains no life at all. Yet they are both fed by the same river, the JORDAN. The difference is that the Sea of Galilee receives water at one end and gives out water at the other. The Dead Sea receives but does not give. The Jordan ends there. To receive without reciprocating is a kind of death. To live is to give' (The Chief Rabbi of England and Wales, Dr Jonathan Sacks in *To Heal a Fractured World: The Ethics of Responsibility*, Continuum, 2005).

Galilee boat *See* JESUS BOAT.

Gallio, proconsul of Achaea *See* PAUL.

Gamaliel According to Acts 5.34–39 Gamaliel was a PHARISEE, a teacher of the Jewish LAW and a member of the SANHEDRIN (or Jewish Council). Citing the examples of the rebellions of Theudas and Judas the Galilean, Gamaliel advised the Council that they should release the APOSTLES from prison and wait to see the outcome: 'if this plan ... is of human origin, it will fail; but if it is of God, you will not be able to overthrow them – in that case you may even be found fighting against God'. In Acts 22.3 PAUL refers to Gamaliel as his teacher, saying that he had been brought up in Jerusalem 'at the feet of Gamaliel, educated strictly according to our ancestral law'. In rabbinic writings he is known as Gamaliel I or the Elder, and listed after Hillel as a prince of Judaism.

Gath Gath was one of the five major cities of the PHILISTINES and home to the Philistine champion GOLIATH; its ruler was King Achish. It was to Gath that the ARK OF THE COVENANT was taken when it was seized by the Philistines (see 1 Samuel 5.8–9). This is also where DAVID fled when he escaped from SAUL (see 1 Samuel 27). The site has been identified at Tel es-Shafi and recent excavation has uncovered finds from the Bronze and Iron Ages. There are Philistine remains from Iron Ages I and II and several destruction levels. One of these, from the late 9th century BCE, relates to King Hazael of Aram's conquest of Gath (see 2 Kings 12.17). Connected with this is a unique and monumental dry siege moat surrounding the site, dating from the 9th century BCE. One of the latest finds is a very early Philistine inscription, which may shed new light on the origins of the Philistine language.

Gaza *See* PHILISTINES; TRADE.

Gedaliah *See* JEREMIAH; LAMENTATIONS.

gematria *See* NUMBER SYMBOLISM.

genealogies A genealogy is a list of ancestors related to an individual, or to a family or larger group, such as a clan or a nation. The purpose is to indicate descent and therefore to establish an identity. Such genealogical lists are found in both the

Hebrew Bible and the New Testament. They may be tendentious, economical with the facts, or embellished in order to assert a theological point. The preoccupation with genealogies belongs within a tradition of learned exegesis of scripture, comparable to that of the teacher of the law in Ecclesiasticus 39.3: 'he seeks out the hidden meanings of proverbs and is at home with the obscurities of parables'.

Several examples of genealogies are to be found in GENESIS, such as the descent from ADAM to NOAH in Genesis 5.1–32, the generations from Shem to ABRAHAM in Genesis 11.10–26, and the descendants of JACOB (Genesis 46.8–27). Later the story of the book of RUTH shows how God directs even domestic human affairs in the choice of an ancestor for the royal line (see the genealogy of DAVID in Ruth 4.18–22). The longest Biblical genealogy is found in 1 CHRONICLES between chapters 1 and 9.

In the New Testament genealogies of Jesus are found in the Gospels of MATTHEW (1.1–17) and LUKE (3.23–38). Both evangelists are concerned to relate Jesus to David, while Matthew establishes the link to Abraham, and Luke right back to Adam. For Matthew the sequence from Abraham to David to Jesus, emphasized at 1.1 and 17, demonstrates the logical outcome of God's history and the fulfilment of divine promises (working through women such as Ruth and BATHSHEBA who are not matriarchs of Israel but aliens inviting suspicion). The deliberate pattern is of three sequences of 14 generations, and Matthew uses this number symbolically to reinforce the Davidic theme, for the three letters of the Hebrew name 'David' have a numerical value of 14, while Jesus himself is the starting point of a seventh group of sevens. Luke has a similar concern for structure, since his genealogy contains 11 units of 7. Such structures underline the theological points: Matthew's focus has an essentially Jewish/messianic basis, while Luke's concern is for salvation relevant to all mankind.

Genesis, book of Genesis is the first book of the Hebrew Bible (Old Testament): its first word in Hebrew is 'beginning' and its Greek title, from which our name Genesis comes, means 'origin' or 'beginning'. So Genesis is the 'beginning of beginnings' and its subject-matter covers a wide variety of issues about how things are thought to have begun (that is, philosophy and religion rather than natural science, as we understand it). The effect of such a beginning to the Hebrew Bible is to transform a local story into an account of the universe and human nature.

Historically its material needs to be compared with other mythologies of creation in the Middle East (such as the *Enuma Elish*) and also the epic of GILGAMESH. What the editors of Genesis did, however, was to reshape the material to tell the story of the dealings of their Hebrew god in the language of the symbolism of the day. Nowhere is this more true than in the stories of the CREATION and of NOAH. The stories are shaped and retold to show that the deity the Israelites experienced in their daily lives and worship was the one responsible for the world as they saw it.

A controversial issue of interpretation in Genesis 1–3 is the role of humankind in relation to God's creation: is it stewardship or mastery? Evangelical Christians often hold that man has absolute mastery and dominion over nature, based on Genesis 1.28, while more liberal and Catholic Christians advocate a stewardship in which

God intends that humankind, once banished from Eden, should serve and tend God's creation.

Other puzzling questions raised in Genesis are: why does God prefer Abel to CAIN (Genesis 4)? What was wrong with building the Tower of BABEL (Genesis 11)? Why should God command ABRAHAM to sacrifice his only son ISAAC, on whom the promise of the future depended (Genesis 22)? This story – known as the AKEDAH – is often linked in Jewish minds with the HOLOCAUST of Nazi Germany. And again what is the reason for the preference of the maverick JACOB over the elder son ESAU (Genesis 27)?

There are four sections to the book: the primordial history (chapters 1–11); the story of Abraham and the establishment of the people of the promise (chapters 12.1–25.18); the story of Jacob (chapters 25.19–36.43); and the story of JOSEPH and his brothers, who become the founders of the twelve tribes of ISRAEL (chapters 37–50). The sequence progresses in ever sharper focus, to conclude with the situation in which those who are to be Israel find themselves in EGYPT.

Gennesaret, Sea of *See* GALILEE, SEA OR LAKE OF.

Gentile The word Gentile comes from the Latin *gens*, meaning 'nation', and is used to denote non-Jews (Hebrew *goyim*). This is one of two classic definitions of 'the Other' in the ancient world: the Gentile who is not Jewish, comparable with the barbarian who is not Greek. The Hebraic distinction probably originates from the fact that, following the conquest of CANAAN, there were seven nations not driven completely from the land (Joshua 24.11). The Israelites were commanded to maintain a strict separation from them in all matters of religion, MARRIAGE and politics. There existed an ideological tension in Israel between a more open universalism, reflected in the prophecies of ISAIAH, and a particularism, especially after the EXILE. So EZRA and NEHEMIAH go to the lengths of requiring Israelites to DIVORCE their non-Jewish wives, while the books of RUTH and JONAH represent a protest against this attitude, in the interests of a more universal understanding of creation.

The mission that became CHRISTIANITY began in the context of JUDAISM. Understandably the missionary endeavours of PAUL and others among the Gentiles (non-Jews) created a problem, especially for the leadership of the Church in Jerusalem. The Council of Jerusalem in 49 CE, according to the various accounts in Acts 15 and Galatians 2.1–10, concluded that Gentile converts to the Church were not obliged to go through a preliminary stage of becoming Jewish proselytes. They could play a full part in the new emerging religion, rather than remaining in the wings as a subordinate category of 'God-fearers'.

geography of the Bible There are three main reasons for applying a scientific study of geography to the Bible. One is to set the scene for Biblical narratives and appreciate them more deeply. Another is to seek explanations for such questions as 'Why did the Israelites choose to settle the central highlands, rather than the valleys and plains, when they colonized CANAAN?' A third reason is to understand the complex geopolitical situation of the region by noting the historical changes in the land. Thus a practical course on the 'Land, Nature and Society of the Bible' could be particularly enriching for any student.

The geography of Israel had a profound impact on its historical development across the millennia. The axis of its geography was north–south. Israel was, until the advent of 20th-century transport, inaccessible other than from the north and to a lesser extent the south. Mount CARMEL, like a thumb gesticulating to the sea, ends the central hills, providing a further barrier to transport. Merchants and armies alike were squeezed through narrow passes to continue their journeys; the chief pass was guarded in the monarchical period by the fort at Megiddo, which naturally became the site of battles (*see* ARMAGEDDON).

The western boundary represented by the Mediterranean offered no obvious natural harbours for trade or invasion (although the PHILISTINES proved an exception to this). The Hebrews largely mistrusted the sea. The eastern border, beyond the river Jordan, that is the Syro-Arabian desert, was impassable even to camels. So empires from the east (ASSYRIANS, BABYLONIANS, PERSIANS) arrived by a roundabout route and entered from the north.

The north–south valley of the river JORDAN linked the freshwater Sea of GALILEE to the literally dead, dense, and salty DEAD SEA and formed the natural internal route for safe travel, rather than over the difficult hills which formed the spine of the country from north to south. The Jordan valley is claimed to be the deepest valley in the world, and the Dead Sea is at its surface 392 metres below sea level, and at the bottom of its northern basin a further 400 metres below that. Southward beyond the shores of the Dead Sea stretches the depression of the Arabah, down towards the Gulf of Aqaba and the Red Sea. The Jordan valley forms the more northerly section of the Great Rift valley which runs from southern Turkey in a south-westerly direction into Africa.

Another north–south route was provided for trade along the flatter lands of the coastal plain. This road, the WAY OF THE SEA, was also used by the attacking armies of imperial powers. Armies from Egypt, Assyria, Babylon, Persia, Greece and Rome moved this way, and in times of their strength would move inland to suppress Israel as well.

Apart from channelling cultural influences north–south, Israel's land area did not offer much opportunity for amassing surplus wealth. Minerals and good timber had to be imported. There was only a limited amount of really good agricultural land available, after subtracting the desert in the south (the Negev), the Anti-Lebanon mountains in the north (Mount Hermon is 2888 metres high), and all of the hill country in between. The hills bordering the coastal plain (the Shephelah) joined the coastal plain in supporting agriculture, but the higher and more rugged hills (for example around SAMARIA at 900 metres) and also encircling Galilee offered varying and limited opportunities. Even the coastal plain is at best 12 miles wide.

The geography of Israel meant that it was never destined to become one of the really great geopolitical players.

Gerasa *See* GADARA.

Gergesa, or Kursi *See* GADARA, for the story of the stampeding Gadarene swine.

The name Kursi probably derives from a mistaken identification by St Jerome of the site as CHORAZIN rather than from the name Gergesa (called after the land of the

Gergesenes). Khirbet el-Kursi is located on the eastern shore of the Sea of GALILEE. There are remains of a Christian monastery and church, built in stages between the 5th and 7th centuries CE. One of the rooms contains an unusually large natural boulder, but its significance is uncertain.

Gethsemane After they had eaten the Last Supper together, Jesus and his disciples withdrew from the city of Jerusalem across the Kidron valley to a quiet place 'called Gethsemane' (Hebrew *gath shemanim*, 'oil presses') on the west side of the Mount of OLIVES (see Matthew 26.36; Mark 14.26, 32; John 18.1 identifies it as 'a garden'). JUDAS ISCARIOT would have known the place, because Jesus regularly used it – John 18.2. On this evening Jesus' intention was for a time of quiet prayer for his disciples and himself, so that he might prepare himself for the suffering and death which was expected soon. The episode is often referred to as the 'Agony in the Garden'.

Today the site of Gethsemane contains very ancient olive trees which may or may not be as old as the time of Jesus. The present church on the site, the Church of All Nations, was built in 1924. There is a rock in the nave (a traditional site of Jesus' prayer) which is the central feature of this church, and of the earlier churches on this site.

Gethsemani is also the name of the Cistercian monastery in Kentucky, which was the home of the spiritual writer Thomas Merton.

Gezer The great mound of Tel Gezer is situated on the final ridge of the Judaean foothills, as they slope towards the northern plain of Shephelah. Gezer had a strategic position, guarding the crossroads of the Via Maris (the WAY OF THE SEA) and the road that crosses the plain of Aijalon towards Jerusalem and Jericho. This is near where JOSHUA commanded the moon to stand still (Joshua 10.12–13). The site was excavated by R. A. S. Macalister for the Palestine Exploration Fund early in the 20th century; he found monumental architecture, no fewer than four city walls, and a water tunnel to access the local spring (similar to the ones at HAZOR and Megiddo – *see* ARMAGEDDON). The area was first occupied c.3500 BCE; it was an important CANAANITE site, not captured by the Israelites. The Egyptian Pharaoh Thutmose III had captured it c.1482 BCE (as is recorded in the Temple of Karnak). The EL-AMARNA archives contain 10 letters from kings of Gezer written to Egyptian pharaohs. The Israel stele of Pharaoh Merneptah (c.1210 BCE) records the capture of Gezer, ASHKE-LON, and other major cities of Palestine. King SOLOMON received Gezer as a dowry when he married the daughter of the Pharaoh (1 Kings 9.15–17). A major city gate and one of the city walls bears witness to Solomon's programme of fortification.

The Gezer Calendar (now in the Istanbul Archaeological Museum) dates to the time of Solomon (mid 10th century BCE) and is one of the oldest HEBREW inscriptions from Israel. It is a limestone tablet, 10 cm tall, which describes the months of the agricultural cycle; some erasing suggests a use for scribal practice.

The city of Gezer was destroyed by the ASSYRIANS c.734 BCE and again by the BABYLONIANS c.587 BCE. In the period of the MACCABEES in the 2nd century BCE Gezer was fortified again as the residence of Simon Maccabeus (see 1 Maccabees 13.43–48, where the reference is to Gezer, not Gaza), and was subsequently the headquarters of John Hyrcanus (*see* HASMONEANS).

Christ in Gethsemane Mark 14.32–42

Gibeon The site of Gibeon lies eight miles north of Jerusalem, and south-west of AI, at el-Jib. It is one of the most ancient of Canaanite cities, and was an important centre at the time of JOSHUA ('it was greater than Ai, and all its men were warriors' – Joshua 10.2). According to Joshua 9, the Gibeonites were condemned to perpetual slavery, but Joshua also made an alliance with the city. Joshua 10 relates a victory achieved by Joshua at Gibeon over the king of Jerusalem and his allies – an occasion when it is claimed Joshua made the sun stand still (Joshua 10.12–13). There was a high place (sanctuary) at Gibeon where SOLOMON had a dream that he should build the TEMPLE in Jerusalem (1 Kings 3.4ff.).

One of the major features of the site today is a circular rock-cut pool, 11 metres in diameter and 25 metres deep, with a spiral stairway of 79 steps leading down to the bottom and nearby a large spring and two water tunnels; the water system is thought to date to the 10th century BCE, and the spring is still used today. The pool may be the one referred to in 2 Samuel 2.12–17 and Jeremiah 41.12.

Gideon Gideon was a hero of Israel whose story is told in JUDGES 6–8. He was called by God to lead resistance against the Midianite raiders and became the fifth of Israel's judges (leaders). Initially Gideon sought reassurance that his call really was from God by means of a number of miraculous tests (including a lamb's fleece that was wet or dry overnight when the surrounding earth was dry or wet). He cut down a grove of trees, dedicated to the pagan deity BA'AL. This action may be the origin of his name, Gideon, which in Hebrew means 'woodcutter', and also of his alternative name, Jerubbaal ('Let Ba'al contend' – Judges 6.32; 8.35). Gideon assembled his forces for battle, but their numbers were scaled down by divine command to a crack force of 300 men; the selection process worked by rejecting those who knelt down to drink at the spring, in favour of those who scooped up water with one hand, because they were more alert for danger. The enemy were routed, partly by psychological warfare. Gideon is included in the list of heroes of the faith in HEBREWS 11.

Gideons International is a missionary organization, founded in 1899, dedicated to distributing copies of the Bible throughout the world, for example in hotel bedrooms. Their logo recalls the empty jars, with torches placed inside (Judges 7.16), as used in the assault on the Midianite camp.

Gihon *See* EDEN, GARDEN OF; HEZEKIAH; JERUSALEM; SILOAM.

Gilgamesh, epic of The epic of Gilgamesh is the oldest recorded story about human life after death in the West, and it provides the foundations of the quest narrative as we know it; the earlier versions probably date back to 3000 BCE with the SUMERIANS. For over 2000 years other clay tablets recording this ancient epic in AKKADIAN lay buried in the ruins of NINEVEH; a century and a half of excavation has still not pieced together the whole story of Gilgamesh, king of Uruk, and his quest for immortality. Gilgamesh is two-thirds divine and one-third human, and the action of the story takes place on earth, midway between the world of the gods and the underworld. A significant element for comparison is the story of Utnapishtim (the Babylonian NOAH) and the FLOOD, and how this relates to the Biblical story. A fragment of the epic was found in Israel at Megiddo (*see* ARMAGEDDON). Not only are the tablets in fragments, but parts of the epic also survive as distinct versions in different languages. The effect is strange: for example one version speaks of 'the felled cedars' and this becomes 'sleeping camp-followers' in another. (See the translator's comments in the Penguin Classics edition.) New interest in the epic of Gilgamesh was revived in a performance at the Cheltenham Literature Festival in 2006 by the storyteller Ben Haggarty and the Greek percussionist and reed flute player Manya Maratou.

glory The prophet ISAIAH records a vision in the TEMPLE of Jerusalem, in which he sees God enthroned in majesty, towering over the Temple building (see Isaiah 6). The seraphim (*see* CHERUBIM AND SERAPHIM) call to one another, saying: 'Holy, holy, holy is the Lord of hosts; the whole earth is full of his glory' (6.3; *see also* HOLINESS). The Hebrew word *kabod* is translated as 'glory'. Its basic meaning includes the ideas of force and weightiness; these may be seen in storms and earthquakes. The earth feels the impact of the divine personality which also now radiates inner splendour and overpowering beauty. So more than an aura or a halo is involved in this description of divine glory. The localized presence of God is referred to in later JUDAISM as the SHEKINAH ('that which dwells'). The aura, symbolized by the cloud and the fire which accompanied the Israelites in their wilderness wandering, and which localized itself in the TABERNACLE (a temporary and tented dwelling), and on Mount SINAI (Exodus 24.17), becomes in later theological reflection almost an independent divine entity.

The Greek word *doxa* ('glory'/'honour'; *see also* DOXOLOGY) is used to translate the Hebrew *kabod* in the SEPTUAGINT. The New Testament use of 'glory' builds on this foundation (see Romans 9.4 for the glory that belongs to the people Israel). But PAUL argues that 'all have sinned and fall short of the glory of God' (3.23). In the teaching of Jesus the glory of the last days (*see* ESCHATON) is frequently associated with the heavenly figure of the SON OF MAN. JOHN'S GOSPEL places particular emphasis on the theme of glory as a theological fact revealed in Jesus Christ and communicated to the believers through him. 'The Word became flesh and lived among us, and we have seen his glory, the glory as of the Father's only son, full of grace and truth' (John 1.14; *see also* INCARNATION). Notice the sustained use of the noun and verb 'glory'/'glorify' in John 17, at verses 1, 4–5, 10, 22, and 24; compare also 2 Corinthians 4.3–6, which relates this glory to that of the Sinai experience.

glossolalia Glossolalia is originally a Greek word meaning 'speaking with tongues'. *See* CHARISMATIC.

Gnostic gospels These are a diverse collection of documents, written by a variety of early Christian sectarian groups, now conveniently referred to as 'Gnostics' ('those who possess [secret] knowledge'). Most of these writings bear little resemblance to the canonical GOSPELS of the New Testament, since they have little or no narrative and do not seek to present anything like a biography of the HISTORICAL JESUS. Their focus tends to be on esoteric wisdom, claimed to be communicated to certain named disciples by the risen Jesus after EASTER. Such texts offer various insights into the arcane world of Gnostic Christianity, which appears as a diverse movement largely centred in Egypt between the 2nd and 4th centuries CE. *See also* for particular text examples JUDAS ISCARIOT and THOMAS.

Many Gnostics regarded the physical world as the creation of a malevolent deity, and believed that the secret knowledge revealed to them could provide an escape route from the prison of their human bodies, into an elevated spiritual existence in heaven.

God The original terms in Hebrew and Greek that are translated by the English word 'God' were essentially general terms for any deity or deities, but most of the use in the Old and New Testaments is theologically specific to the Jewish or Christian God. In the Hebrew Bible there is a variety of proper names for the deity, ranging from El (an ancient Semitic word or name for a deity, but used of God in particular in JOB and other poetic texts), the plural form Elohim (it might be thought that the plural is a survival from earlier polytheism, but applied to Israel's God it is more likely to be a plural of majesty), more local names such as El Shaddai ('God of the mountain'), El Elyon ('God most high' – associated with Jerusalem, see Genesis 14.18–20), and El Berith ('God of the covenant', see Judges 9.46), as well as the ultimately favoured name of YAHWEH.

The faith of Israel seems to have emerged from the essentially polytheistic environment of the ancient Near East; its special emphasis was as a henotheism, that is the worship of a single god while acknowledging that in the neighbouring peoples there is a plurality of deities. Out of this henotheism there is a complex evolution which results in monotheism, that is the theological claim that there is only one God. The God of Israel is seen as the Creator (*see* CREATION), and the sustainer of the created world; he is in a COVENANT relationship with humanity, and seen as active in historical events. The metaphorical images used to portray God in the Bible are predominantly masculine concepts, such as king, judge, father, shepherd, and mighty warrior.

It has been conventional to contrast the God of the Old Testament with the God of the New Testament, for example as the God of Wrath or of Law, compared with the God of Love or of Grace. But these contrasts are simplistic, when there exist real continuities of theme about power and caring concern. In the New Testament the earlier image of 'father' is even more prominent, enhanced by the intimate relationship suggested by the term ABBA. In no way is the climax of Israel's faith in monotheism abandoned in the New Testament, although it became necessary to clarify the identities of Father, Son and Holy Spirit within the Godhead which Christian theology came to describe as a TRINITY. See, for example, the discussion of the relations between Father and Son, and the role of the SPIRIT/PARACLETE in relation to both of them in the Gospel of JOHN. In essence these theological developments are a reflection of the actual experience of early Christians, who glorified God in the various ways in which they saw him.

Gog and Magog According to EZEKIEL's vision of the last days (chapters 38–39) Gog of the land of Magog, chief prince of Meshech and Tubal (see also Genesis 10.2), is the enemy of Israel, against whom God will rain fire and brimstone. A similar APOCA-LYPTIC scenario is presented in Revelation 20.7–8 when Satan leads Gog and Magog from the four corners of the earth against the NEW JERUSALEM. The names probably denoted in origin some leaders of historical enemies of Israel from the north, but the eschatological theme is developed repeatedly in early Jewish literature (see, for example, 1QM11.15–17 among the DEAD SEA SCROLLS).

golden calf *See* AARON; BA'AL; FALL; IDOLATRY.

While the narrative of JEROBOAM's action in 1 Kings 12.28–33 is usually interpreted

as the rejection of faith in Israel's GOD (the rejection of monotheism) and the favouring of a fertility religion (such as the worship of Ba'al among the surrounding
nations), the story of Aaron in Exodus 32 is sometimes construed instead as the
worship of affluence, with the Israelite tribes during the wilderness wandering
becoming impatient for better conditions. This idea is echoed by an allusion to
the 'golden calf' by Sir Epicure Mammon in Ben Jonson's *The Alchemist* and in Mr
Pecksniff's comments on 'profit' in Charles Dickens' *Martin Chuzzlewit*.

golden rule The term 'golden rule' is not Biblical, but is used as a modern name
(since the 18th century) for the saying of Jesus in the SERMON ON THE MOUNT: 'in
everything do to others as you would have them do to you' (Matthew 7.12; also Luke
6.31). Jesus adds, 'for this is the law and the prophets', effectively a guideline to
conduct in accord with the tradition, that is the love commandment as a summary
of the law towards the neighbour.

The negative form of the rule is found in one text of Acts 15.20, 29 and in the early
Christian text the DIDACHE at 1.2. The Jewish teaching of Rabbi Hillel is somewhat
similar: 'That which displeases you, do not do to another. This is the whole law; the
rest is commentary' (*b.Sabb*.31a). In ethical terms there is an important distinction
between the love commandment, which is action for the sake of another, and other
formulations which are closer to self-interest. In the novel *The Water Babies* (1863)
the Anglican clergyman Charles Kingsley introduced the character of 'Mrs Doasyou-
wouldbedoneby' which is ironically closer to the Jewish than the Christian pattern
of the rule.

Golgotha The place of the crucifixion of Jesus is named as Golgotha in the Gospels
of Matthew, Mark and John; this name is interpreted as meaning 'the place of a
skull'. In Luke's Gospel it is simply 'the place called The Skull'. It should be noted
that the word 'skull' is singular, not plural. The reference is likely to be to the shape
of the rocky hill, rather than to any function as a charnel house. Certainly it was the
skull-like appearance which encouraged General Gordon in 1883 to identify the hill
near the Damascus Gate, behind what is now known as the Garden Tomb, as Golgotha. Locating the actual site is problematic; not only has the line of JERUSALEM's
city wall (see John 19.17, 20; Hebrews 13.12) changed at different periods in antiquity,
but the whole area has been so built over as to obliterate any physical shape such as
Golgotha might have possessed. The traditional site of the crucifixion, CALVARY, is
incorporated within the Church of the Holy Sepulchre (*see* CHURCHES, CHRISTIAN). A
connection with ADAM is made here, according to the Christian tradition, mentioned by the Church Father Origen, whereby the site of the crucifixion is also
the site of the burial of Adam's skull; such a link between Adam and Christ is celebrated theologically in texts such as Romans 5.12–19 and 1 Corinthians 15.21–22,
45–49.

Goliath Goliath was a man of giant physique who came from GATH and was the
PHILISTINE champion, defeated by the boy DAVID, according to the narrative of 1
Samuel 17.4–54. The heavily armed and experienced warrior is felled by a sling stone.
'David put his hand in his bag, took out a stone, slung it, and struck the Philistine on

David and Goliath 1 Samuel 17.4–54

his forehead; the stone sank into his forehead, and he fell face down on the ground' (17.49). If a CUBIT is reckoned as 45 cm, Goliath would have been nearly 3 metres (almost 9 feet) tall. A variant reading gives his height as four rather than six cubits, so 6 ft 9 in tall. Some Jewish commentary suggests that Goliath was related to SAMSON and wore the emblem of the CANAANITE deity Dagon, whose temple was at Gaza. The name Goliath becomes proverbial for great size and strength. But Aren Maeir from Bar-Ilan University has recently produced evidence for the real-life existence of Goliath. This is in the form of a pottery shard from c.900 BCE, with a Philistine version of the name in early Semitic script ('Alwat' or 'Wlt'), found at Tel es-Shafi, the site of Gath, Goliath's home town.

Gomer 1 Gomer is the name of the prostitute whom the prophet HOSEA is commanded to marry (1.3). Given that the marriage is used as an extended allegory for God's relation to his chosen people (chapters 1–3), it cannot be certain whether she actually was a prostitute, or a prophetic symbol for the nation's unfaithfulness to

Yahweh and preoccupation with the fertility rites associated with the Canaanite storm god Ba'al (*see* ADULTERY).

2 Gomer is also the name of a land appearing as an ally of GOG AND MAGOG in EZEKIEL 38.6.

Good Friday Good Friday (or the Great Friday in the Greek Orthodox Church) is the name given to the Friday before Easter, the Friday in Holy Week, on which the CRUCIFIXION and death of Jesus is commemorated (*see also* TRIAL OF JESUS). It is kept as a day of FASTING, without even a celebration of the EUCHARIST. A special liturgy for Good Friday, the Three Hours Service, is often observed between noon and 3 p.m. See also the STATIONS OF THE CROSS.

Good Samaritan The Good Samaritan is one of the best known PARABLES of Jesus, but it is found only in the Gospel of Luke at 10.30–35. Here the story is seen to be provoked by a lawyer's request for a definition of the word 'neighbour' in the second of the two great commandments or summary of the law (*see* TORAH). The story has special force and is indeed shocking because the neighbour in this illustration turns out to be a Samaritan. The SAMARITANS were neighbours in a geographical sense for the Jews, but for historical reasons were distrusted and certainly would not be seen as friendly contacts. The antipathy was mutual, as sometimes seems to be the case between Israelis and Palestinians today.

Gospel Gospel comes from an Old English word meaning 'good news' (Godspel); it is an accurate translation of the Greek word *euangelion*, from which comes the English word 'evangelist' (meaning 'bearer of the good news', or narrowly 'the author of a Gospel', and subsequently a missioner who preaches the good news). The Greek word does occur in the text of the New Testament (as well as in the later titles given to the books) – see Mark 1.1 and 1 Corinthians 15.1 – where it has a more flexible meaning of good news or a message handed on, rather than being a literary term for the genre of Gospel (as it later became). It was found a few times in this oral sense in the SEPTUAGINT Greek of the Old Testament; there is a Classical inscription of 9 BCE which uses the word to refer to the birthday of the Roman Emperor Augustus ('Happy Birthday!').

In the New Testament there are four examples of the literary genre of Gospel, those attributed to Matthew, Mark, Luke, and John. Whether there is significance in the number four is debatable; one Church Father regarded it as appropriate for the four winds, to communicate with the four corners of the earth. The first three Gospels, according to most scholars, have some kind of literary relationship, probably depending upon Mark as the primary source (*see* SYNOPTIC PROBLEM). The fourth Gospel, attributed to John, is rather different in style, content and organization; it is hotly debated whether it is an independent production or possibly relates in some way to the material of Mark or Luke.

See further in the articles on each Gospel under the author's name.

grace The word 'grace' denotes a gift that is strictly undeserved, but also denotes the larger relationship between the giver and the recipient, the psychology of those involved, and the will that drives the relationship. There is a problem of translation involved in English renderings of the range of relevant Hebrew and Greek words in different contexts; the result is the use of a wide variety of English words, such as 'favour', 'mercy', 'compassion', 'kindness', 'love', 'graciousness' and 'generosity'.

Grace is frequently linked in the Bible with 'MERCY' (see Exodus 33.19), and with the addition of 'PEACE' as a greeting in the New Testament epistles (see Romans 1.7). In the Old Testament it is used in relationship to the term for God's everlasting love and loyalty. This is a gift and favour which God gives to humankind, which it has done nothing to deserve; this is especially true of divine forgiveness (see Nehemiah 9.17). Within humanity it can denote an action of generosity by the more rich and powerful towards the poor and powerless (see Proverbs 22.9).

In the blessing prescribed for Aaron in the Old Testament, this indicates God's kindness to human beings ('The Lord bless you and keep you; the Lord make his face to shine upon you, and be *gracious* to you; the Lord lift up his countenance upon you, and give you peace' – Numbers 6.24–26). According to JOHN'S GOSPEL the ultimate expression of this is in the INCARNATION (see John 1.14, 17). In PAUL this is linked to Jesus and focuses on the particular act of salvation (see 1 Corinthians 1.4). This grace is a gift and not something which can be earned beforehand, although the recipients should live appropriately afterwards. Paul worked a great deal with the term grace. He linked the amount of grace on offer to the amount of sin it must offset (Romans 5.20); he juxtaposed it to the previous regime of TORAH (Law) – see Romans 6.14–15 – and saw its effect in salvation as putting people right with God (*see* RIGHTEOUSNESS). Previously, as a consequence of ADAM's sin, mortality had prevailed as humankind suffered the appropriate death sentence for sin; now, according to Paul, God's grace rules by righteousness, because Jesus' death means that humanity is pronounced 'not guilty' (see Romans 5.12–21, especially verse 16).

After much theological debate down the centuries, the mystery of grace – both why God should give it and how it works – appears impenetrable.

grail, Holy Grail The Holy Grail is an expression associated with the almost unattainable goal of a religious (or quasi-religious) quest, such as that of the knights of King Arthur; it is not a term that occurs in the Bible. This symbol actually seems to originate in the 12th century with Chrétien de Troyes, who imagined a golden vessel encrusted with jewels. The Knights Templar, who captured Jerusalem during the Crusades, were known as 'keepers of the Holy Grail'.

The New Testament basis for any Grail concept is with the cup or chalice used by Jesus Christ at the Last Supper (*see* EUCHARIST) (Mark 14); in all probability this would have been an earthenware bowl, such as those found in quantity at QUMRAN. The Christian theological concepts associated with this cup are themselves complex, from the cup of suffering and sacrifice (Mark 10.38; 14.36), and the cup of fellowship and communion (in accordance with Jewish table practice), to the sacramental cup of Christ's death, where the wine of the Christian fellowship meal is transformed (physically or symbolically) into the blood of Christ. Another understanding of the Grail, which would link with this, is as the receptacle traditionally used by JOSEPH OF ARIMATHEA to catch the blood of Christ as he bled on the cross. In the experience of the Christian community, they share in, or are baptized into, Christ's death, in the way that Paul described in Romans 6.

Greek Taking the whole history of the Greek language, from ancient to modern Greek, spanning nearly three millennia, it has been said that 'Greek has one of the longest known histories of any language, perhaps only comparable to Indian and Chinese'.

In the New Testament, and in translations of the Old Testament such as the SEPTUAGINT, we encounter a version of popular Greek language of the HELLENISTIC PERIOD, often referred to as 'Koine' (meaning 'the common language'). Following the conquests of Alexander the Great, Greek had become the language of trade and commerce throughout the Mediterranean world and the Near and Middle East. In the heyday of Classical Greece, the cultural language of the educated Hellenes had been formed from the Attic or Ionic dialects. But now Hellenistic Greek developed through contacts with other cultures; it looked different in many respects of vocabulary, pronunciation and grammar. Its life span was approximately from 300 BCE to 300 CE. The New Testament was one of the best known and most widely influential of collections of literary documents from this period.

'All the New Testament books were written within a period of one hundred years from the death of Jesus Christ, and they were all written in Greek, for Greek-speaking readers, by men who for the most part themselves lived in a Greek-speaking society. There can, then, be no accurate reconstruction of primitive Christian thought which does not rest upon an accurate study of the grammar and syntax of the Greek language during the 1st century AD [CE], and upon an accurate knowledge of the meaning which the Greek words used by the Christian writers had for their readers. Philology and lexicography form the essential groundwork of the interpretation of the New Testament' (Edwyn Hoskyns and Noel Davey, *The Riddle of the New Testament*, 1947, p. 16).

H

Habakkuk, book of This book is the eighth in the collection known as the Minor Prophets. The prophecy is usually dated to the final years of the 7th century and the first decade of the 6th century BCE, because of the reference to the Chaldeans (BABYLONIANS) in 1.6–17. After the Egyptians were defeated at Carchemish in 605 BCE, the 'Chaldeans' marched against King Jehoiakim of Judah (see 2 Kings 23.36–24.4). The prophet Habakkuk is also mentioned in the apocryphal BEL AND THE DRAGON (verses 33ff.).

This has been described as one of the most puzzling books of the Old Testament. It also illustrates the rich divergence of interpretation that is possible in efforts to solve the puzzles. Jewish tradition has adopted the third chapter, the liturgical Prayer of Habakkuk, and linked it with the giving of the TORAH on Mount SINAI. Christian doctrine has seized on Habakkuk 2.4 (as quoted in ROMANS 1.17) and turned it from the claim that 'the just man, through his faithfulness, shall live' into a proof text for the concept of 'justification by faith'. Among the DEAD SEA SCROLLS is a Commentary on Habakkuk (1QpHab): this is a typical QUMRAN *pesher* type of commentary, not explaining the original, but applying it to the circumstances of the present-day community. The reference to the Chaldeans in Habakkuk 1.6 can be emended to the *Kittim* (the Seleucid Greek rulers, or even the Romans), which has the effect of moving the whole context forward to the aftermath of Alexander the Great's conquests, and beyond. Finally, in the modern day, at the time of the first Gulf War, the Bible Society of Egypt announced a special edition of the book of Habakkuk, because they believed that the disturbing questions of the original prophecy were particularly relevant in their own day.

Habiru 'Habiru' was used by ASSYRIANS and BABYLONIANS in the 2nd millennium BCE to refer to certain nomadic groups; it is found in documents from UGARIT and MARI. They are also mentioned frequently in the EL-AMARNA letters. When these nomadic groups settled they often fulfilled the function of mercenaries or labourers and were not regarded as the social equals of the local inhabitants. The name Habiru would appear to be very close to the name of the Hebrews. A number of scholars have made this identification, concluding that the Habiru became the later (13th century BCE) Hebrew conquerors of CANAAN; but this connection has so far not been proved.

Hadassah Hadassah is an alternative name for ESTHER (see Esther 2.7). It was probably her given Hebrew name, while 'Esther' is a name with Babylonian or Persian origins (comparable with the goddess Ishtar, meaning 'star') that would have been given to her in the royal court (see Esther 2.8–9) to suit the Persian ambience. Hadassah was then much later the name given to the Women's Zionist Organization of America, founded in 1912, which raised money for health programmes. The well-known Hadassah Hospital in Jerusalem, incorporating a medical school, was built at Ein Kerem while the original hospital on Mount Scopus was inaccessible during the period 1948–67.

Hadrian, Emperor *See* BAR KOKHBA; JERUSALEM.

Hagar *See* ABRAHAM; ALLEGORY; SARAH; GALATIANS.

Haggai, book of Haggai is the tenth book in the collection of 12 known as the Minor Prophets. Other than the book itself, nothing is known about the prophet apart from the references in EZRA 5.1 and 6.14 which link together Haggai and ZECHARIAH. The works of these two post-Exilic prophets provide an important complement to the narratives of Ezra and NEHEMIAH. Haggai's oracles are dated quite precisely in their introductions to the second half of the year 520 BCE, early in the reign of Emperor Darius I (the Great) of Persia. The edict of CYRUS had permitted the Jews to return from Babylon and rebuild the TEMPLE in Jerusalem. If this work had started after 539 BCE it may well have faltered, as Haggai suggests. The prophet awaits the coming of God's kingdom, which he believed to be heralded by the historical confusions of the time of Darius. In view of impending events it was imperative that the rebuilding of the Temple should now be completed.

It is notable that Haggai, unlike earlier prophets of the 7th and 8th centuries, works with a cultic concept of the presence of God, defined by the holy place. It may be that, like EZEKIEL, Haggai stands with Zechariah in a 'theocratic' line of those concerned to re-establish the power of the Zadokite priesthood (*see* ZADOK, PRIEST). The present efforts at rebuilding the Temple may seem inadequate, but the true significance of this event will ultimately be realized. 'The latter splendour of this house shall be greater than the former [the Temple of Solomon] and in this place I will give prosperity, says the Lord of hosts' (Haggai 2.9). Interestingly, this was the text of the sermon preached by Archbishop Michael Ramsey at the dedication of Coventry Cathedral.

Hallelujah 'Hallelujah' is a Hebrew word (strictly two words) meaning 'praise the Lord' or 'let us praise the Lord'. In the Hebrew Bible it is found only in the book of PSALMS, in Psalms 104–150, where it occurs as an introduction, or as a conclusion, on a number of occasions; as a title it denotes a song of praise. Within Psalm 135.3 it is found as a grammatical part of the text. One of this group of Hallel Psalms, as they are entitled, and perhaps Psalm 136, could have been used by Jesus and his disciples after the Last Supper (*see* EUCHARIST) (Matthew 26.30). 'Hallelujah' introduces the praise of God by the ANGELS in Revelation 19.1–8.

Hammurabi, or Hammurapi Hammurabi is the best known of the early AMORITE dynasty who ruled as kings of BABYLON. He reigned for 43 years between c.1792 and 1750 BCE and is credited with unifying the country under the rule of Babylon. A highly significant AKKADIAN law code is known as the 'Code of Hammurabi'. The 282 paragraphs of LAW which it contains are expressed in the casuistic form (case law). But the whole document is not simply a legal code; written in traditional form but in the most elegant style towards the end of Hammurabi's reign, it is rather a celebration of the king's achievements, as a model for future generations. The code was inscribed on a stele, set up as a boundary stone, over two metres high, and was discovered in 1901–2 at Susa in Iran. (It is now displayed in the Louvre in Paris.) An abbreviated version on a clay tablet was found at NIPPUR and is thought to date from c.1790 BCE (now in the Istanbul Archaeological Museum).

Hannah 1 According to the narrative of 1 SAMUEL, chapters 1 and 2, Elkanah had two wives, Hannah and Peninnah. Every year they visited the sanctuary at SHILOH, where Hannah (who was barren and mocked for it by Peninnah) prayed for a son and promised to dedicate him to the Lord God. The priest Eli understood her prayer and vow, seeing her lips move although hearing no words, and gave her a blessing. Some medieval Christian interpreters saw this as an example of 'praying in the Spirit', while Jewish tradition in the Targum identified Hannah as a prophetess and saw her action as a model of Jewish prayer (the 'Amidah). Hannah gave birth to a son, SAMUEL, and then had other children. Hannah's song, celebrating her answered prayer, has similarities with the song of MARY, THE MOTHER OF JESUS (the Magnificat) in Luke 1.46–55.

2 *See* ANNA.

Hanukkah The Jewish festival of lights or feast of 'Dedication' is celebrated for eight days, starting on 25 Kislev, to commemorate the purification and restoration of the Jerusalem Temple and its furniture by JUDAS MACCABEUS in 164 BCE (1 Maccabees 4.36–59). Lights are kindled in the Jewish home, one more on each evening (the Hanukkah lamp has eight branches). This 'festival of lights' is referred to as the setting in the Gospel of JOHN 10.22. In Judaism there is a traditional game for Hanukkah, the spinning of a dreidel or top.

Haran Haran was a commercial centre, founded c.2000 BCE, on an ancient caravan route from Mesopotamia to Cappadocia, Syria and Palestine. The site is identified at Sultan Tepe. The name Haran-U means 'caravan-journey' or 'crossroad' in SUMERIAN. Terah, the father of ABRAHAM, settled here according to Genesis 11.31. Despite the distance between UR and Haran, it is plausible that they should have made this journey from one side of Mesopotamia to the other, and settled at Haran as a trading outpost of Ur.

Haran is mentioned, in the archives at MARI, as a religious centre for the worship of the moon deity Sin. Much later, in the Roman period, this site was known as Carrhae, and was notorious for two disastrous defeats experienced by the Roman army, first when Crassus was defeated by the Parthians in 53 BCE, and later again when Emperor Galerius was defeated by the Persian king Narses in 297 CE.

Hasidim The origins and details of this group of the 'pious ones' are somewhat obscure. They were a Jewish sect, strictly faithful to the LAW, who can possibly be identified with 'the wise' referred to in Daniel 11.33f. They shared the same 'zeal for the law' as did the MACCABEES and many of them supported the initial Maccabean Revolt against the Seleucid Greek rulers, in order to safeguard the essentials of their faith. But they parted company with the Maccabees after the revolt had succeeded, when plans for a HASMONEAN dynasty of Jewish high-priest/kings were evolving. They were entirely suspicious of such political ambitions. The Hasidim in turn are probably important in the preliminary stages of the movements of the ESSENES and the PHARISEES.

Hasmoneans The Hasmoneans are the 'descendants of Hashmon', a Jewish family that included the MACCABEES, and that after the Maccabean Revolt formed a dynasty of HIGH PRIESTS and kings. They ruled Judaea from 152 BCE until Pompey arrived in the eastern Mediterranean with his Roman forces in 63 BCE. Perhaps most significant among the Hasmoneans were John Hyrcanus and Alexander Jannaeus.

These are the dates of the members of the dynasty:

Jonathan	152–142 BCE
Simeon	142–134 BCE
John Hyrcanus	134–104 BCE
Aristobulus	104–103 BCE
Alexander Jannaeus	103–76 BCE
Salome Alexandra	76–67 BCE
Aristobulus II	67–63 BCE
Hyrcanus II	63–40 BCE
Matthias Antigonus	40–37 BCE

Hazor Hazor is 20 miles north of the Sea of GALILEE, and was an important city of the CANAANITES from the Middle Bronze Age, with some 20,000 inhabitants ('the head of the Canaanite kingdoms' according to Joshua 11.10). Archaeology at the royal palace of that period is beginning to reveal evidence of royal archives and an inscription which confirms the name of the city. Hazor covers a vast site of 200 acres, the largest archaeological site of the Biblical era in Israel. Its importance is indicated by references in documents elsewhere: Hazor is cursed as an enemy of EGYPT in the 19th/18th century BCE Egyptian Execration Texts; a Babylonian tablet mentions that HAMMURABI had ambassadors residing in the city; MARI on the Euphrates traded tin, silver, gold, and precious stones with Hazor. The king of Hazor, Jabin, organized resistance against the invading Israelites (Joshua 11.1–11), but he was defeated, and Hazor was burnt and destroyed at the end of the 13th century BCE (Joshua 11.13). The Israelites resettled a smaller part of the site in the 10th century BCE as a demonstration of power, and in order to guard the through route to the north; the remains of SOLOMON's city (1 Kings 9.15) were excavated in the 1950s and 1960s by Yigael Yadin. There is an impressive six-chamber city gate, usually attributed to the time of Solomon, which resembles those at Megiddo (*see* ARMAGEDDON)and GEZER. Hazor was further extended by AHAB in the 9th century BCE. The city disappears from the Biblical record after it was conquered by the ASSYRIAN ruler Tiglath-Pileser III in 732 BCE (2 Kings 15.29). There is some evidence of an Assyrian citadel on the site, as well as a few remains from PERSIAN and HELLENISTIC times.

heaven Heaven was recently defined as a place of 'restful happiness' which is a temporary prelude to the 'real New Testament hope' of bodily RESURRECTION within God's new creation (Tom Wright, *For All the Saints?*, SPCK, 2003). There are few actual descriptions of heaven in the New Testament. REVELATION chapters 4 and 5 are outstanding as visions of the presence of God. It is likely that such human language, to describe the divine, was derived either from the early Christian experience of meeting for WORSHIP, or from the political reality of being in the presence of the Roman emperor (or his representative); in the eastern half of the Empire the Romans fostered the oriental instincts of ruler worship as a way of keeping their subjects in awe. Subsequent Christian depiction of heaven is equally dependent on contemporary and earthly realities. A striking example is the late medieval altarpiece at Ghent Cathedral, painted by the Flemish Primitive artists, the brothers van Eyck, which realizes the vision of Revelation 5. Christ as the central figure of the slain lamb is worshipped by the local inhabitants, in status both high and low.

Hebrew Biblical Hebrew is the original language of almost all of the Old Testament (Hebrew Bible), with the exception of a few short sections in ARAMAIC. Hebrew was the language spoken by the ancient Israelites, but it derives from the Canaanite group of languages (*see* CANAAN, the EL-AMARNA tablets, and UGARIT). Hebrew continued to be used in the Greek and Roman periods for scriptural and other religious purposes, although since the EXILE many Jews will have used Aramaic in public communication, simply because it was the language of the PERSIAN Empire.

The first reference to the name 'Hebrew' for the language is found in ECCLESIAS-TICUS. Subsequent references in the APOCRYPHA and the New Testament (see 4 Maccabees 12.7; 16.15; and Acts 21.40; 22.2; 26.14) may not always mean Hebrew, but rather Aramaic. However, the DEAD SEA SCROLLS (*see also* QUMRAN) and the letters of BAR KOKHBA (135 CE) show that Hebrew would still be used generally in such a society for ideological reasons. Hebrew is used extensively in the religious discussions of the RABBIS: the Mishnah (at the end of the 2nd century CE) codifies the opinions of the rabbis in later Hebrew. Thereafter the Jewish Talmud commentaries (Babylonian and Palestinian) are a combination of Hebrew and Aramaic (referred to as Rabbinic Hebrew). Throughout Jewish history changing circumstances required adaptations and supplementations of Biblical Hebrew, because it lacked the necessary terms, such as for medieval philosophy. Most recently, by extension of the same principle, Modern Hebrew (Ivrit) was developed for use in the Jewish world and then in the state of Israel.

The Hebrew language is written from right to left. The first and last letters of the alphabet are aleph and taw; these may be used to denote the whole of something, or GOD as first and last (see Isaiah 41.4). There are no capital letters, but some letters have distinctive forms which are used only at the end of a word. Hebrew is usually written only in consonants, and semi-consonantal long vowels, without indicating the other vowels which are of course needed for purposes of pronunciation. But in printed texts of scripture the required vowels are usually signified by a system of marks found over, under, or between the consonantal text; these systems are known as pointing (*see* MASSORETES).

On the principles of Hebrew poetry, known as parallelism, *see* PSALMS. Psalm 119 is a good example of an acrostic poem, where each section of the poem is marked by a letter of the alphabet.

Hebrews, letter to the The author of this letter is unknown, although some have suggested it was APOLLOS or BARNABAS. Within a generation of its composition (probably around 70 CE), echoes of its phrasing are to be found in *1 Clement* (the letter of Clement of Rome to the Church at CORINTH). Subsequently it was associated traditionally with the apostle PAUL and regarded as his letter to the Jews. This is erroneous, as any comparison with Paul's authentic letters reveals, and as Church Fathers such as Origen (185–254 CE) recognized. Hebrews belongs in a JEWISH-CHRISTIAN context (as does *1 Clement* and the *Epistle of Barnabas*) which certainly does not preclude echoes of Greek philosophical expression, sophisticated language-use and rhetoric, or a polarization of the differences between Judaism and Christianity. The Old Testament, in its Greek form (the SEPTUAGINT), is quoted widely and substantially, showing its importance in the author's argument.

It may be better to regard Hebrews not as a letter but rather as a theological essay or sermon, with theology at a profound level. It ends like a letter, but does not begin like one. The conclusion, at 13.22, well indicates the purpose of writing as encouragement and a 'word of exhortation'. Hebrews 6.6 reveals the author's warning against the serious danger of APOSTASY. The faithful Christians are urged to trust in their covenant relationship with God, and to follow the example of Christ, who is their true HIGH PRIEST, living with faith, hope, and love, facing persecution patiently. The author develops profound thought on the person of Christ, to undergird his exhortation. Themes are developed on the basis of the Old Testament, but showing how far Christ moves beyond the Hebrew prototypes. He is the supreme mediator of JEREMIAH'S 'new COVENANT', superior to the Jewish priesthood (*see* PRIEST) and their animal SACRIFICES. As the perfect High Priest he offers a single sacrifice, of himself. This priesthood is defined distinctively by comparison with the figure of MELCHIZE-DEK, mentioned in Genesis 14 and Psalm 110. Christ is also the forerunner, who has gone ahead into the heavenly Jerusalem.

TABULATION OF HEBREWS

Note: all argument in this epistle is to encourage Christians to stand firm (in persecution?) and not to waver in their faith

1.1–3	Introduction: a summary of who Jesus is and what he has achieved
1.4–3.6	Arguments from scripture to show that Jesus is far greater than the angels by status and by bringing salvation
3.7–4.13	Christians must beware of forfeiting their reward from God by rebelling against him
4.14–8.6	Argument to show Jesus as the great High Priest following on Melchizedek (6.11–7.18): encouragement to readers to advance in their faith and not to renounce it

8.7–10.18	Arguments to show that Jesus has brought a new covenant, and how it has changed the worship of God. Jesus offered his life once and for all as an atonement sacrifice for sin
10.19–39	So Christians are encouraged to take part in the benefits Jesus has achieved, and not to draw back – to have faith and to be saved
11.1–40	The role of faith in the lives of OT heroes such as Abraham
12.1–29	Application of these examples to the readers to persevere – with eyes fixed on Jesus
13.1–19	Final reminders to live a good Christian life
13.20–21	Closing prayer

Hebron Hebron, to the south of Jerusalem, is one of the oldest continuously inhabited cities in the world. (For Muslims it is the fourth most holy city, after Mecca, Medina and Jerusalem.) When modern tourists visit Hebron, the focus of interest is usually a building that is now an uneasy combination of mosque and SYNAGOGUE. Inside is the massive Tomb of the PATRIARCHS, built 2000 years ago during the Herodian period, over the traditional site of the Cave of Machpelah, where (according to the Bible) the Patriarchs ABRAHAM, ISAAC, and JACOB, and the Matriarchs SARAH, REBEKAH, and LEAH are all buried. A thousand metres to the west lies the mound, Jebel er-Rumeide in Arabic, which was the site of the ancient Biblical city of Hebron. According to local tradition here are the tombs of DAVID's ancestor RUTH and his father JESSE. The excavation of the site has been hampered by the political situation following the Six-Day War in 1967, when the area ceased to be part of Jordan.

Abraham settled at the oaks of Mamre, which is 'at Hebron' – Genesis 13.18. (Abraham's Oak, where he offered hospitality to passing strangers, is still shown to visitors near the mosque.) Much later in Israelite history, after the EXODUS from Egypt, the tribes defeated a CANAANITE–AMORITE coalition, including the army of Hoham, king of Hebron. Under JOSHUA they conquered Hebron itself (Joshua 10) and the clan of Caleb settled there (Joshua 14). Later again, David ruled from Hebron for the first seven and a half years of his reign (2 Samuel 2.11), until he moved his capital to Jerusalem. The last reference in the Bible to Hebron is in the context of ABSALOM's revolt against David (2 Samuel 15.7–10).

heifer, red The red heifer denotes the particular animal whose ashes were used in a purification rite, as described in NUMBERS 19.1–22. The cow is to be killed outside the Israelite camp and its blood sprinkled in the direction of the HOLY OF HOLIES (either in the TABERNACLE or at a later time in the TEMPLE). The carcase is then burned whole, together with cedar wood, a crimson thread, and hyssop (see HERBS). The resulting ashes, blended with spring water, were to be sprinkled as a rite of purification upon someone who had become contaminated through contact with a corpse. The Numbers text was read as a warning of the need of PURITY in readiness for the offering of the Paschal lamb at the PASSOVER festival. Paradoxically this rite, while purifying the defiled, also defiled the priests who performed the rite. Rabbi Yohannan ben Zakkai (in the 1st century CE) commented: 'the corpse does not have the power by itself to defile, nor does the mixture of ash and water have the power by itself to cleanse. It is a decree of the Holy One.' See also the use made of this ritual of SACRIFICE for Christian TYPOLOGY in HEBREWS 9.13, 19 and in the *Epistle of* BARNABAS 8.1–7.

Hellenistic period Greek culture and institutions spread rapidly following Alexander the Great's conquests. When Alexander died in 323 BCE Palestine came under the control of the Ptolemies, who were his heirs in Egypt. Then in 200 BCE the Seleucids of Syria took control of Judah. The ruling classes in Judah were divided; many of them were excited by Hellenistic ideas, while others preferred the old Hebraic traditions. This eventually led to civil war, with Jerusalem the centre of revolutionary activity. The Seleucid ruler Antiochus IV Epiphanes attacked the city and looted the TEMPLE in 167 BCE. He left behind commissioners to govern the country. The consequence was the revolt of the MACCABEES, and a troubled period of independence (c.142–63 BCE) when Judah was ruled by Jewish 'kings' (the HASMONEAN dynasty) for the first time since the Temple had been destroyed in 586 BCE.

The term 'Hellenization' is used for this widespread imposition of Greek culture. The city-states of Classical Greece had collapsed and been replaced by a 'cosmopolis' (city of the world). The traditional Greek religions had broken down, such that elements of them were incorporated in religious forms and cults capable of universalization (*see also* MYSTERY RELIGIONS). There was a large groundswell, a rising tide in the view of human destiny, made possible by a universalized vision of humanity and a spread of populations.

herbs The herbs mentioned in the Bible, both for culinary and medicinal purposes, are still familiar names today. For example Jesus famously criticized the PHARISEES' excessive approach to TITHES in terms of the inclusion of the small herbs – 'mint, dill and cummin' (Matthew 23.23) – among their staple crops. We know that these were grown in Old Testament times too (see Isaiah 28.25, 27).

Hyssop's dried aromatic leaves are still in use in the Middle East as a condiment. The extent of SOLOMON's wisdom was measured as to cover all knowledge from the mighty cedar of Lebanon to the little hyssop growing from a crack in the wall. Dipped in fluid its tiny leaves could be used as a paintbrush, to daub the blood of the Paschal lamb on the doorposts and lintel in the PASSOVER story (Exodus 12.22), and to sprinkle bird's blood on a leper (Leviticus 14.4–7). It was used in ritual purification after uncleanness or pollution by corpses (see Numbers 19.6, also red HEIFER). It was associated by the Psalmist with cleansing from sin: 'Purge me with hyssop' (Psalm 51.7). John identified the wine-soaked sponge offered to the dying Christ as being lifted on a 'branch of hyssop' (John 19.29). This would tie in with his Passover symbolism, although the small herb might seem too insubstantial for the task. Modern botanists, however, would suggest that a one-metre branch of the larger version of the herb would be eminently suitable.

Mustard (*brassica nigra*) was grown in the fields and widely used for savoury and medicinal purposes. Its seed was proverbially the tiniest measure available in Jesus' day (Matthew 17.20), and Jesus also compared the amazing growth from its seed to the mature plant with the spread of the KINGDOM OF GOD (Mark 4.30–32). It has been said that mustard cannot grow to tree size for birds to roost in, but others have contradicted this, observing strong tall shrubby growth in neglected fields.

Wormwood (gen. *artemesia*) is still known as the basis of absinthe. The bitter juices of its leaves were known in ancient times – in small doses as a medicine, and in greater amounts as a poison; the latter applies to Revelation 8.11. Wormwood can also be used to symbolize God's punishment, or suffering and sorrow, as in Jeremiah 9.15, Lamentations 3.15; this would then supply an interpretation of the CRUCIFIXION for Matthew in 27.34, when Jesus is offered wine 'mixed with gall'.

The aromatic juice extracted from the leaves of the aloe was used medicinally, but also prized by the ancient Egyptians for embalming the dead. Like MYRRH it was an expensive import in Biblical times, and NICODEMUS provided lavishly for Jesus' burial in John 19.39 with about 100 pounds weight of aloe-myrrh mixture.

Bitter herbs (Exodus 12.8) are annually associated with Passover ritual; what exactly these are/were may vary (for example chicory and endives). These bitter herbs (*maror*) are eaten twice during the Passover meal, both with the unleavened bread, and then dipped into the sweetened fruit mixture. They stand as a reminder of how bitter the Egyptian slave masters made the Israelites' lives in captivity (see Exodus 1.14).

Other herbs and relevant plants discussed are BALSAM and SPIKENARD. *See also* PLANTS and TREES.

hermeneutics Hermeneutics is an impressive term derived from the Greek word for 'communication', related to Hermes, the messenger of the gods. It means 'interpretation' and has a wide application as well as referring specifically to Biblical interpretation, both historical and contemporary (see, for examples, John M. Court, *Biblical Interpretation*, T&T Clark International, 2003). Sometimes it involves a complex of philosophical theories and analysis (see *The Two Horizons* and *New Horizons in Hermeneutics* by Anthony C. Thiselton, Paternoster Press, 1980, and HarperCollins, 1992), or it asks the basic question, 'How does understanding work?'

Within BIBLICAL CRITICISM it is important to acknowledge the variety of possibilities for the interpretation of Biblical texts, both academic and popular, either within the religious communities of synagogue and church or as part of literary and popular culture in the secular world (see, for examples, John M. Court, *Reading the New Testament*, Routledge, 1997). Hermeneutics applies to the CANON of scripture, in whole or in part, and asks about the means and methods by which it has been, and can be, communicated. In any individual instance the understanding of a text is a complex process, involving both author and reader, both literal text and its content and allusiveness. Meaning can come from behind a text (in the historical sources of a text and the author's purpose), from within a text (in the interaction between the elements and structures that exist in the text), or in front of a text (in the way a reader responds to, or interacts with, a text).

Herod Antipas *See* HERODIAN DYNASTY; JOHN THE BAPTIST; NAZARETH; SALOME; SEPPHORIS; TIBERIAS.

Herod the Great Herod was born c.73 BCE, of Idumaean descent; he was appointed king of Judaea by the Roman Senate in 40 BCE. After reclaiming his kingdom from the Parthians, he consolidated his authority over against the HASMONEANS, also gaining Galilee and Ituraea in 31 BCE. He embarked on a massive building programme in Jerusalem, Judaea, and Samaria. Notable are the city of Sebaste (SAMARIA), the harbour and city at CAESAREA (MARITIMA) and palaces at Herodium, Machaerus, JERICHO and MASADA. He dedicated three temples to Augustus in the imperial cult, at Caesarea, Sebaste, and probably at Omrit, not Panias, in the north. His ambitious plans for the Jewish TEMPLE in Jerusalem were not completed until over half a century after his death in 4 BCE. He enlarged the Temple Mount with an enormous platform, much of which still survives. JOSEPHUS describes the buildings on this platform (porticos, a royal stoa, courtyards and sanctuary) of which virtually nothing remains following the Roman destruction in 70 CE (*Jewish War* 5.184–227). According to Josephus, Herodium was Herod's final resting place; a building there has been identified as a possible mausoleum, but his tomb has not been found. It is now being suggested that Herod observed Jewish law from personal conviction, not merely political convenience.

Herod's relations with his own family had been characterized by internal strife; he imprisoned some and executed others (including his principal wife, the Hasmonean Mariamne, and their sons). There was a black joke in Greek that it was safer to be Herod's pig than his son. The birth of Jesus occurred, perhaps c.6 BCE, when Herod was still king, according to Matthew 2.1–18. Herod's ruthlessness in defending himself against any threat could well explain his decision to massacre Bethlehem's children (Matthew 2.16–17): 'there is not a single solid scholarly reason to doubt the infanticide at Bethlehem' (Carsten Thiede).

Herodian dynasty Largely as a result of seven marriages, HEROD THE GREAT was the founder of a dynastic family of more than 100 members. At his death in 4 BCE he left his kingdom in his will to three of his sons, with the emperor's approval: Judaea and Samaria to Archelaus; Galilee and Peraea (Jewish area east of the Jordan) to Antipas; and the area north-east of Galilee, including the Golan, to Philip.

Archelaus (Herod the Ethnarch) was an oppressive ruler, deposed by Augustus in 6 CE. Judaea became a Roman province, administered by imperial prefects/procurators (of whom Pontius PILATE was one).

Antipas (Herod the Tetrarch) ruled until 39 CE, when he was denounced by Agrippa, deposed and exiled. He ordered the imprisonment at Machaerus and the execution of JOHN THE BAPTIST (Mark 6.14–28); according to Luke 23.7–12, Jesus was referred to him for judgement by Pilate.

Philip's primary city was Panias, which he renamed CAESAREA PHILIPPI in honour of the emperor and himself. He later married Salome, the daughter of Herodias and another Herod (Mark 6.17 and Matthew 14.3 are incorrect in saying that Philip was her father). Philip was a just ruler and reigned until 33/34 CE. He successfully made representations against Pontius Pilate when he tried to display votive shields with offensive emblems in the governor's palace at Jerusalem.

Herod Agrippa, grandson of Herod the Great, was brought up in Rome, with close connections to the imperial family. Granted the title of 'king' by Emperor Gaius (Caligula), and with further grants of territory, including Judaea and Samaria, from Emperor Claudius, he ruled an area equivalent to his grandfather's from 37 CE until his sudden death in 44 CE (see Acts 12.20–23; Josephus, *Antiquities* 19.343–344).

Herod Agrippa II, the son of Herod Agrippa, was born in 27 CE. Although too young to inherit from his father, he was granted territory to the east of Galilee, ruling from 53 CE until his death around 100 CE. He renamed Caesarea Philippi as Neronias in honour of Emperor Nero. His encounter with PAUL is described in Acts 25–26; during Paul's trial by the Roman governor Festus, Agrippa listened and replied with sympathetic irony that Paul had nearly talked him into becoming a Christian. Loyal to Rome, he tried to prevent the outbreak of the JEWISH WAR in 66 CE.

Herodians Briefly mentioned as opponents of Jesus (Mark 3.6; 12.13; Matthew 22.16), they are associated with the PHARISEES. They are probably a Jewish political party, favouring the HERODIAN DYNASTY, or in Judaea lobbying for a king from the Herod family, in place of direct Roman rule by procurator.

Hezekiah Hezekiah, the son of Ahaz, was king of Judah c.727–698 BCE during the time of the prophet ISAIAH (see chapters 36–39). The judgement of the book of Kings commends his incomparable loyalty to God (2 Kings 18.3–6); this is largely because of his reforms in matters of ritual (affecting the use of sacred pillars and trees – the ASHERAH – and the worship of the brazen serpent from the time of Moses) and the closure of cultic sites in the countryside. Hezekiah was rewarded for his piety by a longer life (the sundial symbolically turned back by 10 degrees) when it seemed as though he was ill to the point of death. Hezekiah's policies were reversed under his son MANASSEH.

Hezekiah was a vassal king under the ASSYRIANS. But at the death of Sargon in 705 Judah rebelled against his successor SENNACHERIB. Hezekiah had prepared against a possible siege of Jerusalem by the construction of the SILOAM tunnel to ensure a water supply from the spring Gihon. But Sennacherib's forces proved superior; Hezekiah was imprisoned in Jerusalem 'like a bird in a cage'. Hezekiah paid a heavy indemnity (2 Kings 18.14–16), but the departure of the Assyrian forces was celebrated as the divine intervention prophesied by Isaiah (Isaiah 37.33–35; 2 Kings 19.35).

Hierapolis Hierapolis was a city of Asia Minor (modern Turkey) situated in the upper valley of the river Lycus, and close to the celebrated hot springs of Pamukkale ('cotton castle' named from the white cliffs formed by cascades encrusted with lime). One hundred miles east of EPHESUS, it lies 12 miles from its neighbour COLOSSAE and 6 miles from LAODIKEIA. Its name suggests that Hierapolis was the village centre of a temple estate, dedicated to the Phrygian mother-goddess. Early in the 2nd century BCE the king of PERGAMON granted it the status of a city, and in 133 BCE it became part of the Roman province of Asia. Its prosperity was based on the textile industry. There are extensive remains of the Roman city. Inscriptions and literary evidence reveal a strong Jewish presence in the area. It became a significant Christian centre, but the only New Testament reference is in Colossians 4.13 which may indicate that EPAPHRAS founded a Church there.

High Priest AARON's family supplied the High Priests; they were usually appointed for life, although in later periods the interference of political masters sometimes changed that assumption. It is unclear at which point in history the office emerged, probably not until the restoration after the EXILE; certainly the leading Zadokite priests (*see* ZADOK) at the earlier royal shrine in Jerusalem were not known by this term. In the era of the second Temple the position is there, and JOSHUA is named as the High Priest, even before the Temple was rebuilt (*see* HAGGAI 1.1).

The role was primarily a religious one; as leader of the Jerusalem cultic worship the High Priest officiated at important occasions at the sanctuary, and his alone was the task to enter the HOLY OF HOLIES on the Day of Atonement (YOM KIPPUR), to achieve pardon for Israel's sins in the past 12 months. The High Priest's role as representative for God's people was symbolized by the breastplate that he wore. This contained the 12 precious gems for the twelve tribes of ISRAEL. The importance of this breastplate did not escape the scrutiny of pagan overlords, who increasingly saw fit not only to bestow the office of High Priest, but also to withhold the breastplate except for special occasions.

It will be clear that the religious role was not the only one, but that the position carried considerable political responsibilities towards the end of the period. The High Priest represented his people not only to God but to his masters, except at quiet periods after the MACCABAEAN revolt, when the HASMONEANS governed both as High Priests and secular rulers.

In the New Testament the four evangelists were familiar with the role the High Priest played, politically unwilling to upset the Romans by risking uprisings, and happy to sacrifice Jesus in this cause (see especially John 11.49–53). The High Priest of the day was the Roman puppet CAIAPHAS, although his dethroned father-in-law Annas may still have been the ultimate authority. In the TRIAL OF JESUS he dominated the SANHEDRIN, acted out shock at the apparent BLASPHEMY and ensured that the death sentence was pronounced by the council, and executed by the Roman authorities, by a skilful manoeuvring of the charge. After Jesus' RESURRECTION the activities of his APOSTLES awoke censure from the same quarter (see Acts 4.18–21), and imprisonment (see Acts 5.17–18). STEPHEN's trial was conducted by the High Priest (Acts 7.1), who also issued Saul/Paul's authorization to arrest Christians in Damascus (Acts 9.1–2). Later the High Priest Ananias struck PAUL during his own trial (Acts 23.2).

For the Jews the need for a High Priest came to an end with the destruction of the Jerusalem TEMPLE in 70 CE. For Christians the role of High Priest was now attributed to Christ, who acted as mediator between God and men, taking into the Holy of Holies not animals' blood, but his own blood, pleading his own sacrificial death upon the cross (see Hebrews 7.26–27; 9.12–14).

Highway of the King, or Royal Road The King's Highway is regarded as the proper name for a major international route for travel through Transjordan, from Damascus to the Gulf of Aqaba. The itinerary indicated in Genesis 14.5–6 shows that it was indeed an ancient route. According to Numbers 20 and 21 MOSES endeavoured to bring the Hebrews, following their EXODUS from Egypt, along this route (in Hebrew Derek Hammelek) through EDOM and MOAB.

In terms of communications through the area of the FERTILE CRESCENT and particularly PALESTINE, it is important to note that sea routes up and down the eastern end of the Mediterranean were not widely used in Old Testament times. The lack of an ideal natural harbour on the Mediterranean coast (until HEROD THE GREAT created CAESAREA (MARITIMA)) was a partial explanation for the preference for overland routes north–south. When the ancient empires of ASSYRIA, BABYLON, or EGYPT were most active politically, they would use the major highways in a quest for imperial expansion. The two main routes were the King's Highway through Transjordan, or the coastal Via Maris or WAY OF THE SEA. Israel stood the best chance for independent development when the empires were inactive.

Early in the 2nd century CE the Roman Emperor Trajan had ordered the construction of a new road, the Via Nova, along the line of the ancient King's Highway. It is also followed by one of Jordan's modern highways today.

Hilkiah *See* SHAPHAN.

Hillel *See* GAMALIEL; GOLDEN RULE.

Hippos *See* SUSSITA.

historical criticism The historical method may well be the most long-standing of critical approaches, since it depends upon a process of scrutiny, in testing the evidence of documents as well as individuals, which goes back to the law courts and political councils of ancient Greece. As applied to the Biblical text there are basically three stages to the process: firstly, the reports of events preserved in the text are tested for accuracy, both in terms of internal consistency and in comparison with material from external (non-Biblical) sources, and also with Biblical ARCHAEOLOGY; secondly, the reports assessed as reliable are used, together with any other evidence, to reconstruct the historical sequence of events; and thirdly, this reconstruction is used both to date and to assist in the interpretation of other parts of the Biblical text.

In the first stage of critical scrutiny of the document, there are several guidelines in assessing reliability. Details in a narrative may indicate the final form of that narrative (as the reference to DAN in Genesis 14.14 suggests a post-Settlement version). Exact word-for-word agreements in parallel narratives may be grounds for suspicion, while disagreements between versions should be explicable. Internal contradictions indicate an unreliable or a composite narrative. The bias of a storyteller can be detected, and should be allowed for. Biblical literature belongs to a variety of genres: annals may be historically more reliable than poetry. And a modern reader may raise questions about the presence of fanciful or miraculous elements within a narrative (*see also* MYTH).

A classic statement of the historical critical approach was given by Ernst Troeltsch early in the 20th century. There are three principles: the principle of criticism, whereby all evidence must be weighed and all conclusions remain open to revision with fresh evidence; of analogy, whereby events investigated in history are expected to be essentially similar to those in modern direct experience; and of correlation, whereby every event is seen as connected with others in a network of interrelations, and there should be no breaks such as require divine intervention. This is a materialist philosophy which rejects the concept of any absolute and universal validity for events regarded as of a wholly different kind. But events may still be individual and seemingly unique, and could therefore possess some normative character for those who subscribe to a particular point of view.

Historical Jesus, the Quest for the In 1866 Sir John Seeley published an important Victorian work of religious controversy in which he attempted to present the life of Christ in a simple and undogmatic form (*Ecce Homo: A Survey of the Life and Work of Jesus Christ*). He provoked a storm involving Gladstone, Newman, Stanley and others who accused him of effectively denying those doctrines which he had deliberately tried to avoid discussing. Lord Shaftesbury called it 'the most pestilential volume ever vomited from the jaws of hell'.

Writing at the start of the 20th century, in an historical survey of *The Quest of the Historical Jesus* (repr. Fortress, 2001), Albert Schweitzer declared: 'There is nothing more negative than the result of the critical study of the Life of Jesus.' Two of the greatest theologians of the 20th century, Rudolf Bultmann and Karl Barth, agreed, at least in their preference for understanding Christ in terms of faith rather than the objective facts of history. But the quest was not dead, and has been revived several times since, most dramatically by Bultmann's own students. Old and New versions of the Quest, from the 18th to the 21st centuries, tend to differ only in the precise focus of the Jesus they are seeking, and the kind of evidence (such as Jesus' essential Jewishness) which is seen as positive rather than negative from the latest point of view.

Today the quest for the Jesus of history, as compared with belief in the Christ of faith, might be examined in relation to the Patristic debates, and the decisions of the early Church councils, about the 'two natures' of Christ, although it is certainly not identical with these. The intellectual climate of the 4th century CE was very different from the post-Enlightenment attitudes of the 19th and 20th centuries. For the Church Fathers the two natures were the divine and the human natures of Christ. If they insisted on the ultimate reality of both, did they end up with two persons rather than one? If the range of one of the natures was restricted (for example by suggesting that Christ was driven by a divine but not by a human 'will') in order to provide a means whereby the two natures might interlock, would this not impair the reality of Christ's identification with human nature, and therefore limit his capacity to redeem humanity? Would it be possible to suggest that what one wanted to say about the Christ both as divine and as human was in reality interchangeable, or does this merely blur those distinctions which theology requires one to make?

Modern scientific historians, engaged in the quest for Jesus, tend to be sceptical about supernatural matters (*see* MIRACLES and MYTH). But according to the principles of an empirical search for evidence, there is no reason *a priori* why the historian should not include data that are literally extraordinary, provided that there is some degree of internal consistency, and such things (even if they appear miraculous) are potentially open to repetition. Over the years of various quests for the Jesus of history, there has been investigative concern for three distinct matters: the facts about Jesus' life; the nature of the evidence; and the social contexts within which he lived and died. Decisions on the value of such evidence, and more particularly the implications for the body of believers of the existence of this evidence, are matters for the admittedly subjective response of the individual historian, and the equally subjective attitudes of those who read the historian's conclusions. It would at the least be possible then for a person of faith to make theological statements about the rediscovered Jesus of history, without either compromising that person's faith or confusing the categories of talk. At the heart of the Christian faith, as understood in the modern world, is a conviction that divine actions are to be associated with the actual life's work of Jesus the Jew. This may mean that Jesus is worshipped as divine, or that we glimpse some understanding of the divine through his character and what he did, or that we regard this human being as the supreme (or particularly notable) agent of the divine in word and deed. We do not seem to be preoccupied with those concerns of the Church Fathers in calculating the wholeness of persons, or with any merging of the categories of human and divine.

Hittites Hittite is the oldest Indo-European language, written in cuneiform. A number of Hittite archives were discovered in Turkey in the 1920s, including the royal archive at Boğazköy. The site reputed as the oldest city in the world, Çatal Höyük, was a Stone Age settlement on two hills some 30 miles south-east of Konya (Iconium) which was excavated by James Mellaart in the 1960s. In fact the name Hittite covers several different peoples, whose heartland was central Asia Minor, and who were linked culturally by the arrival of an Indo-European element in the late 3rd millennium BCE. In religion they were polytheistic, claiming a pantheon of a thousand gods.

Their kingdom controlled virtually all of Asia Minor between the 17th and 12th centuries BCE. The Old Kingdom spread to penetrate Mesopotamia and northern Syria; after the assassination of the conqueror of Babylon, Mursilis I, a Hurrian dynasty took over to become the Hittite Empire or New Kingdom. In the 14th century BCE the Hittites, under the leadership of Suppiluliumas I, became the supreme political and military power in the Near East. The EL-AMARNA letters document the later struggle between the Egyptians and the Hittites for the control of Syria-Palestine. A treaty between the two powers was concluded after a battle at Kadesh-on-the-Orontes c.1285 BCE, when Rameses II was nearly killed in a Hittite ambush. The Hittite Empire declined with the invasion of the Sea Peoples c.1180 BCE (*see* PHILISTINES). Many of the Hittite cities were assimilated eventually into Assyria.

Much of the original knowledge of Hittite and the Hittites is due to the decipherment and research of Oliver Gurney. But there is ongoing research and many new discoveries since the last years of the 20th century both in Hattusa and in the regional centres of the Hittite kingdom.

holiness Research by Mary Douglas (*Purity and Danger*, Routledge & Kegan Paul, 1965) into the Biblical laws, focusing particularly on key passages in DEUTERONOMY and on the treatment of abominations in LEVITICUS, led her to suggest that the LAWS are actually concerned with order, and that holiness is exemplified by wholeness and completeness. The range of laws, covering all aspects of life from war to sexual behaviour, from social conduct to dietary rules, derives from the basic principle of holiness as order, and confusion as SIN. Holiness therefore requires completeness in a social context, and the separating out of classes and types. The key terms for 'holy' (*qadosh* in Hebrew and *hagios* in Greek) can indicate something 'set apart', as of someone who enjoys a COVENANT relationship with God.

The prophet's vision in ISAIAH 6 is a powerfully emotional text for the understanding of the intensity of holiness as a definition of GOD. God's throne here towers above the Jerusalem TEMPLE building. God towers into the heaven where sacred beings wait to serve him (*see* CHERUBIM). The form of God remains unutterable, indescribable for the prophet, and he can only describe the servants and their WORSHIP liturgy. God is holy to the highest power of holiness and transcendence. But Isaiah also experiences the impact of God upon this world in the present. The 'glory' (Hebrew *kabod*) of God is the force, the weightiness which impresses upon this world and consequently radiates inner splendour and overpowering beauty. Isaiah is deeply affected and spontaneously expresses his sense of impurity as a human being. This is the fundamental polarity in the Old Testament cult between holiness and impurity, the holy and wholly-other nature of God, which inspires awe and burns up the impurity which it encounters.

holocaust This is a technical term for a type of sacrificial offering in ancient Israel in which the offering is 'entirely burnt' on the altar; see the cult legend concerning Gideon in Judges 6.11–24. In modern history the term, often with an initial capital letter, became applied to the deaths of 6 million Jews in the death camps of Nazi Germany. Strictly then it is a religious interpretation which sees these deaths as SACRIFICES. For modern Jewish theology, and its implications for Jewish-Christian dialogue, this major 20th-century example of 'ethnic cleansing' represents a crisis of understanding. Holocaust Remembrance Day (Yom ha Shoah) was established in Israel in 1959 by the prime minister David Ben-Gurion: at 10 a.m. Israeli time on the 27th day of the month Nisan the air-raid sirens sound for several minutes and people observe a moment of silence, vowing 'Never Again' to allow this kind of tragedy to occur. The Jewish word *shoah* means 'chaos' or 'annihilation'; the Yad Vashem Holocaust Museum in Jerusalem represents an interpretation of the Shoah by those who survived the 1930s and settled in Israel. The European nations now observe a Holocaust Memorial Day on 27 January, the anniversary of the liberation of the camp at Auschwitz.

Holofernes *See* JUDITH, BOOK OF.

Holy Grail *See* GRAIL.

Holy of Holies This term is used to denote the innermost room of the TEMPLE at Jerusalem, known in Hebrew as the *debir* (literally the 'back room'). It was the sanctuary reserved for YAHWEH, where the ARK OF THE COVENANT stood. On only one day in the year, the Day of Atonement (YOM KIPPUR), was the HIGH PRIEST allowed to enter this innermost room, going behind the veil which curtained it off (see Hebrews 9.3, 7). This arrangement of the Holy of Holies behind the veil goes back, it is believed, to the desert sanctuary of Israel's wilderness wanderings, as described in the priestly traditions (see Exodus 26.33–34).

Holy Land In the Hebrew Bible the 'promised' and acquired land of Israel is frequently referred to as the Holy Land. While this relates to the general sense of HOLINESS, it expresses the particular view that the land experiences the divine presence in a unique manner. It is understood to have been gifted by God to the Israelite tribes. And the land is holy or pure in the belief that God himself resided in it (*see* NUMBERS 35.34: 'You shall not defile the land in which you live, in the midst of which I reside.' *See also* JOSHUA 22.19.) In 1 SAMUEL 26.19–20 DAVID, who is about to become a fugitive, complains to Saul that he is in effect being driven outside of his 'share in the heritage of the Lord', because he will have to go beyond the borders of Israel.

A later, more sophisticated view in the priestly texts can be described as a 'graded holiness' as one moves out from the sanctuary, through the Holy Land, and beyond to the outside world. This is well illustrated by the *Temple* or *Torah Scroll* from QUMRAN (11QT), where the movement is from the innermost 'HOLY OF HOLIES', to the outer sanctuary, and thence to the holy city, and the Holy Land. This then becomes a springboard for a range of metaphorical and symbolic ideas.

The following are among the current options for Christian interpretation of the symbolic value of Israel, based on (or reacting against) the concept of the Holy Land. (Acknowledgement is due, with thanks, for this summary of interpretation to Professor Simon Schoon of the University of Kampen in the Netherlands.)

1. Israel is in heaven, because 70 CE was the final *earthly* presence of Israel
2. Israel is in the Church; this is a theory of substitution, where the Church replaces Israel
3. Israel as SACRAMENT, as in Eastern Orthodox views of holy place and pilgrimage
4. Land of Israel as Idea, in the utopian 'Pursuit of justice'; the corollary is of Israel still in exile – the idea of the 'wandering Jew'
5. Land of Israel as an experiment in TORAH: this is a view in the Dutch Reformed Church, seeing it as the 'garden of Torah'
6. Land of Israel as focus for the end of times (*see* ESCHATON): the Six-Day War in 1967 is seen as the beginning of End Time, and the ANTICHRIST is identified with Islam
7. Land of Israel as sign of God's faithfulness, seen as a motif in the history of salvation (expressed in the 1980 declaration of the Church of the Rhineland)
8. Land of Israel as a place for learning and dialogue – the centre for the study of religious origins. It shows particularity, but is open to universalist development; it shows universality, as the centre for all nations; and it shows centrality, as the birthplace of faith. This offers a concreteness in hope, to provide a location for dreams of PEACE (as in the name JERUSALEM)

A final Christian reflection from Janet Morley:

Is this place holy because you [Jesus] walked here, died here, were raised right here to bring us life – or because, in this time, in this world of trouble and longing and hope you are alive?

Is this a holy place because several true Churches have come to fight and worship here, each hanging separate lamps to burn for your divided glory? Or is this land, like all lands, holy, where people pray, and work, raise babies and seek justice, and expect a future?

Holy Spirit *See* SPIRIT.

Holy Trinity *See* TRINITY.

holy war *See* WAR, HOLY WAR.

homosexuality LEVITICUS 20.13 is uncompromising in its prohibition of sexual relationships between men; they are an 'abomination' and the participants will be put to death (see also Leviticus 18.22). In such a legal situation there is no allowance for mitigating circumstances such as consent, coercion, or unequal relationships. Everyone involved is regarded as equally corrupted.

In PAUL's references to the idea of homosexuality, he tends to use the language, and reflect the widespread censure, of Leviticus; see 1 Corinthians 6.9–10 where 'sodomites' are included in the list of those, none of whom 'will inherit the KINGDOM OF GOD' (see also 1 Timothy 1.10). Romans 1.24–32 refers to sexual relations between males as 'impurity' and extends this to cover relations between women, as do other writings within JUDAISM. There is a tendency to define the sin of SODOM and Gomorrah as 'sexual immorality' – see Jude 7; 2 Peter 2.6; PHILO, *De Abrahamo* 26.134–36 – whereas the narrative of Genesis 19.1–29 rather resembles a case of intended gang-rape.

There is a difference in attitudes towards homosexuality between Greeks and Romans in the New Testament world. While many among the nobility of Greek cities celebrated it, Roman senators were discreet, to avoid ridicule. The dislike of homosexuality appears to have been fairly widespread in most social classes in Rome, and it was regarded as something of a weakness in the male character. It had been a capital offence in the army since the 2nd century BCE. Writers expressed the view that any same-sex relationships amounted to a transgression of traditional gender boundaries; if women are seen as passive and subordinate, then a man who plays the woman's role has descended to the woman's level.

Biblical references and the stipulations of Roman law have been widely influential in subsequent centuries, up until quite modern times. The word 'homosexuality' is actually a 19th-century coinage, but recent decades have witnessed a major shift of attitudes in some sections of society, with some redefinition of what constitutes a proper loving relationship between human beings. For example, Canon Trevor Dennis (the Vice-Dean of Chester Cathedral) wrote about a day school he was running on homosexuality:

We will not spend much time poring over Leviticus or Romans 1 (let alone Genesis 19), though we will face any questions that are raised about them. We will concentrate instead on the stories of DAVID and JONATHAN, of RUTH and Naomi; on the book of JOB and the light it sheds on the use of scripture; on the many stories in the Gospels illustrating the inclusive nature of Jesus' circle and his preoccupation with the mercy of God. We will try to reclaim the Bible as a means of liberation and mission; rediscover it as a hot-air balloon in whose wonderfully made, but creaking, basket we can take exhilarating journeys and see many things more clearly.

See also FRIENDSHIP.

Horeb *See* SINAI.

horse and rider Figurines of a horse and rider, with a significant star on the forehead of the horse, have been found by archaeologists in Israel. They are interpreted as symbols of ASSYRIAN astral religion. Of course there are a variety of alternative reasons for depicting a rider with a horse, so the star is clearly important in this case.

For mounted cavalry see references in Exodus 15.21 (the Song of MIRIAM); 2 Samuel 1.6; 15.1; 1 Kings 10.28–29; 20.20; and Jeremiah 50.42. War chariots were used by the CANAANITES and PHILISTINES against the Israelites. They had first been introduced in northern Mesopotamia, and adopted by the HITTITES. Chariots were used by the EGYPTIANS and the Assyrians, variously with up to four men on board. The major introduction of chariots as a military fighting force in Israel is credited to SOLOMON and was developed by AHAB.

In the last book of the New Testament, in chapter 6 of REVELATION, four different horses and riders appear when the scroll with seven seals is opened. The horses are white, red, black, and bilious yellow (perhaps skewbald), and the Four Horsemen of the Apocalypse are traditionally interpreted as symbols of conquest, slaughter, famine, and death. The main source for this symbolic imagery is to be found in two visions in the book of ZECHARIAH (1.8–17 and 6.1–8), although not all the horses are explicitly said to have riders, and their colour range is not so great in the original Hebrew. Here four chariots may be linked to the imagery of the four winds.

hosanna Greek and English have written as a single word what was originally a Hebrew expression of two words meaning 'Save, we pray' or 'Save now'. It can be seen in Psalm 118.25–26, a text that was recited daily during the TABERNACLES feast, and seven times on the seventh day as the four species were waved. These particular verses (25–26) became linked to the expectation of the MESSIAH, and so the acclamation is found in JOHN'S GOSPEL 12.13 as Jesus enters Jerusalem. (Compare Matthew 21.9, 15; Mark 11.9–10; Luke 19.38.)

Hosea, book of Hosea is the first of 12 prophetic books known collectively as the Minor Prophets. Its setting is the Northern Kingdom of Israel before it fell to the ASSYRIANS in 721 BCE (see 2 Kings 14–17). SAMARIA, Gilgal and BETHEL are mentioned, where presumably Hosea prophesied. But the book will have been preserved (and interpreted) in the Southern Kingdom of Judah (notice Hosea 1.1).

The personality of the prophet is important, but little is known about him. His marriage to GOMER is used as an extended ALLEGORY for God's relation to his chosen people (chapters 1–3). Either Gomer was actually a prostitute, or she symbolizes the nation's corruption and preoccupation with fertility rites associated with the Canaanite storm god BA'AL. The ultimate theme is of God's steadfast LOVE (Hebrew *hesed*: Hosea 6.6) and compassionate forgiveness of repeated SIN within the COVEN-

ANT relationship. The tradition of the EXODUS from Egypt is recalled in Hosea 11, as is the wrestling with JACOB in Hosea 12 (see Genesis 32). It is debatable whether the original northern prophecy was exclusively one of doom, while the southern inter- preters argued for the positive outcome.

Hosea 11.1 is applied as a proof text in MATTHEW'S GOSPEL (2.15) to the flight into Egypt and subsequent return of Jesus as an infant. Similarly the reference to 'the third day' in Hosea 6.2 can prefigure Jesus' RESURRECTION (1 Corinthians 15.4).

hospitality The actions involved in a friendly reception of a visitor are natural and informal in many modern societies. It was a much more complicated and rigidly enforced matter in ancient societies (as in the Near East and in Classical Greece). Essentially the process was that of changing the status of the (otherwise threatening) stranger (*ger*, or *xenos*) and outsider to that of guest and virtual friend (see Genesis 19.1–10; Matthew 25.38). The example of Simon the Pharisee in Luke 7.36–50 is a paradigm of how this system can break down: he fails to provide the initial reception of foot-washing (see Genesis 18.4); there is no greeting kiss or anointing; and he does not exclude the sinful woman who is disturbing his guests. The duties are reciprocal in the way the guest should behave towards the host and to fellow guests (*see* PAUL's problems at the Lord's Supper (*see* EUCHARIST) in 1 Corinthians 11.17–34). Christian missionaries might experience a difficult reception (see Matthew 10.11–14). Expect- ations of hospitality also applied to Christian communities receiving travelling believers (see Romans 12.13; Hebrews 13.2; 1 Peter 4.9; DIDACHE 12).

household deities There is some evidence of ancient practices – a kind of folk religion – within Israel, alongside the official worship of YAHWEH with its prohibition of images (Exodus 20.4–5). The household deities (Hebrew *teraphim*) seem to be in this category. In the time of the PATRIARCHS, Jacob's wife RACHEL steals the images from her father Laban (Genesis 31.19). During the period of JUDGES there is the case of a man Micah who had a household shrine with his son as a priest (Judges 17.5). In 1 Samuel 19.13 there is the curious episode when Michal, DAVID's wife, places the *teraphim* in David's bed, like a bolster, to deceive King SAUL. Equally a practice from folk religion is the use of a brazen serpent on a pole to cure snake bites (see Numbers 21.8–9); apparently this persisted until the 7th century BCE.

houses and homes The four-room house seems to have been the typical dwelling in the southern Levant during the Iron Age. Usually the three front rooms are not totally enclosed but separated by pillars. The central space was probably of beaten earth and may have been an open courtyard. The two side rooms had stone flooring, and might well be used for stabling. The fourth or back room of the typical house is what the Bible refers to as the 'inner room'. Such houses appear to have been the characteristic dwelling in Israelite society, at various social levels with only slight modifications. Archaeological investigation has revealed some examples with more substantial external walls and traces of an outdoor staircase, which makes it likely that the house was developed on two storeys and the main living area moved upstairs. Much interest is focused not only on how houses were built, but also on the different functions of spaces within the house, and on the residents' attitudes with their social, psychological, and religious implications. The recently reconstructed NAZARETH Village offers excellent illustration of the variations in the basic theme of housing in New Testament times.

An even more basic village house, essentially with only one room, is described by James Neil: 'In ordinary Eastern houses there are no chimneys; the fireplace is on the stone floor, in the middle of their one room. Wood is used for heating purposes, but they cook their food with dried cowdung. The sole provision made for carrying away the smoke is a number of holes over the door, and the tiny windows which are generally unglazed, though in the cold weather they are closed with rude shutters.' The effect of smoke is illustrated in Proverbs 10.26 and Isaiah 65.5.

The Hebrew term for 'house' (*bayit*) was commonly used by the ancient Israelites to refer also to buildings that were not private homes. These could include the palace or 'house' of the king and the TEMPLE or 'house' of God (YAHWEH) in Jerusalem. This strongly suggests that in such a pre-modern society the domains of public and private could easily overlap. In texts which offer theological judgements on contemporary practice, we find in the Temple sermon of Jeremiah 7.18 references to women making bread for the Queen of Heaven, and in 2 Kings 23.7 to women weaving garments for the goddess ASHERAH in 'houses' within the Temple complex.

human nature The modern interest in the psychological analysis of the individual or of the social group presents a different intellectual perspective from the ideas of the Hebrew Bible or of the New Testament world, although modern techniques can of course be applied to the ancient documents, just as in the work of C. G. Jung and his study of JOB, or in Freud's work on *Moses and Monotheism* (Hogarth, 1939).

The Hebrew Bible shows a strongly collective understanding of the social grouping, whether clan, tribe, nation, or religious community, such that it can be expressed as a singularity. But some scholars' emphasis on the universal dominance of an idea of 'corporate personality' is at least an exaggeration, based on 19th-century CE understanding of collective legal responsibility. The individual person and his/her make-up is also understood, as can be seen in Johannes Pedersen's classic four-volume work on *Israel: Its Life and Culture* (1926–47). It can be demonstrated from the earlier traditions of CREATION in Genesis 2.7: the 'living being' (Hebrew *nephesh*) is made alive by being animated by breath, and ceases to live when the breath is extinguished. The breath can be regarded as a distinctive prototype of an idea such as the soul. For the ancient Israelite there is no independent existence of the soul after death, for the dead go to the shadows of SHEOL. Flesh (Hebrew *basar*) is a vital, though weak, ingredient in the make-up of humanity, and the life of the person also exists through the blood.

In the New Testament PAUL provides a more detailed scrutiny (if not a systematic analysis) of human nature; while in dialogue with Greek ideas, he is indebted to some of the Hebrew presuppositions, by virtue of his Jewish upbringing. Are the roots of SIN connected to any particular element of human nature? Paul uses a variety of psychological terms in his letters. The 'heart' (Greek *kardia*) is the seat of thought and will, as well as affection, in substantial continuity with the use of the Hebrew Bible; it is not good or bad in itself. The 'mind' (Greek *nous*) is for Paul a faculty of reason, open to external pressures, but not in itself good or bad. This is in contrast to the HELLENISTIC or GNOSTIC attitude which sees this as a higher feature of human nature. The understanding of Paul's use of the word SPIRIT (Greek *pneuma*) depends upon whether the reference is to the human spirit or the Spirit of God; it seems not to be a significant psychological term for Paul, but almost always refers to an influence from God. The word 'soul' (Greek *psyche*) is seen by Paul as closely parallel to the Hebrew 'breath' as the vital life principle; sometimes, in contrast to a divine influence, it refers to human persons as they really are. There is what sounds like a threefold division of human nature as body, soul, and spirit in 1 Thessalonians 5.23; a complete subdivision is unlikely, for the soul animates the body, rather than being distinct from it. The 'body' (Greek *soma*) is the essential vessel of the human personality, in itself neutral (not materialist in a dualist system), but capable of being pulled in good or bad directions. Clearly Paul's teaching on sexual matters is critical here, for sexual abuses are a denial of the true purpose of the body (as a member of the BODY OF CHRIST). The final term 'flesh' (Greek *sarx*) can be used by Paul in an Hebraic and morally neutral sense of the physical constituent of the body. But much more often in Paul's letters it seems to bear sinister overtones, pointing away from God and towards the selfishness of humanity. According to Romans 8.3, Jesus was exposed to the reality of human-centred existence, but succeeded in living in a God-centred way. To concentrate on the matters of the flesh, human-orientated thinking (see Romans 8.6), provides a point of attack for sin. The superficial attitude of human self-centredness can affect both body and mind. 'Flesh' is by no means an ideal modern translation for this element, because its modern associations are misleading. The translation 'human nature' (as used in the Good News Bible) will work, if it is understood in a disparaging sense ('It's only human nature ...'). Otherwise for Paul the nature of humanity was not essentially evil. It is the dominance of the factor of sin from which humanity needs to be delivered.

humility This was not widely regarded as an admirable virtue in the Greco-Roman world; indeed it was denigrated as weakness. In contrast scripture celebrates humility: the Old Testament declares that God pledges to exalt the humble, and to humble those who exalt themselves (see Proverbs 3.34; also 2 Kings 19 – HEZEKIAH's prayer about SENNACHERIB of ASSYRIA). The Christian ethic approved of meekness and self-abasement, within the context of the example Christ had set. In his teaching Jesus had also illustrated the principle in the PARABLE of the PHARISEE and the PUBLICAN (see Luke 18.14). PAUL, possibly using an existing hymn to make his point, writes to the PHILIPPIANS: 'Let the same mind be in you that was in Christ Jesus ... who ... emptied himself, taking the form of a slave [*see* SLAVERY], being born in human likeness. And being found in human form, he humbled himself and became obedient to the point of death – even death on a cross. Therefore God also highly exalted him ...' John Bunyan, in *The Pilgrim's Progress*, develops this implication of Christ's death on the cross: 'He had stripped himself of his glory that he might do this for the poor; and they heard him say and affirm that he would not dwell in the Mountain of Sion alone ... He had made many pilgrims princes, though by nature they were beggars born, and their original had been the dunghill.'

Hurrians *See* NUZI; RACHEL.

Hymn of Jesus This text was set to music by Gustav Holst (1874–1934) as a major choral work first performed in 1920. It is taken from the APOCRYPHAL *Acts of John* which reflects Gnostic attitudes of the 2nd and 3rd centuries CE. Here a mystical use of DANCE is regarded as a proper part of religious worship, unusually in the earlier Christian tradition, and Jesus himself is represented as dancing with his disciples. This explains the exuberant central dance in Holst's work.

Hyrcanus, John *See* HASMONEANS.

hyssop *See* HERBS.

idolatry Idols are IMAGES or representations of deities, used in their worship. The terms in their Biblical use are hostile, because such practices were prohibited in the Hebrew Bible (see Exodus 20.4–5), although (or because) they were widespread in the ancient Near East, among Israel's neighbours. RACHEL's theft of the HOUSEHOLD DEITIES, and the use of the GOLDEN CALF by AARON (Exodus 32) and then by JEROBOAM I (1 Kings 12.28–33) should probably be considered in this context. There are various ways of referring to idolatry in the Bible; one favourite metaphor is that of sexual immorality, lusting after false deities. Such immorality was actual as well as metaphorical, in the institution of cultic prostitution (see 1 Kings 11.1–11, and also ADULTERY). This had its effect on political history (see 2 Chronicles 25.14–16; 28.1–4; 2 Kings 23.7 – JOSIAH's reform sweeps away the prostitutes' houses from the TEMPLE). Notice also the extended use of this metaphor in the book of REVELATION, with reference to the cult of the Roman emperor (coded as the 'great whore', 'Babylon' in Revelation 17). It is possible that the 'desolating sacrilege' referred to in Mark 13.14 may also indicate the intentions towards worship of Emperor Gaius (Caligula), by the desire to install a statue in the HOLY OF HOLIES of the Jerusalem Temple.

Idumaea *See* HEROD THE GREAT; OBADIAH.

image and symbol in the Bible 'A word-image is material and concrete, but at the same time it creates a surplus of meaning … Images should be taken literally. However, they also point to something more' (L. Thompson). Images can be understood literally, as descriptive, but also figuratively, as metaphor. So the reader can identify the named object, but also, with the aid of a disciplined imagination, fill the empty space that the image opens up. 'Images require two activities from us as readers of the Bible. The first is to experience the image as literally and in as full a sensory way as possible. The second is to be sensitive to the connotations or overtones of the image' (*Dictionary of Biblical Imagery*, IVP, 1998).

A symbol is defined as 'an image that stands for something in addition to its literal meaning'. Most importantly, the primary meaning will then rest in what the image symbolizes, as a metaphor, simile or analogy, rather than simply in its literalness or concreteness. So in 1 Corinthians 3.6 ('I planted, APOLLOS watered, but God gave the growth'), PAUL is speaking figuratively of Gospel preaching and Christian nurture, and not of a literal plant. 'The correct understanding of a symbol requires that the distinction between the symbol and the thing symbolized should be drawn clearly and always maintained in interpretation. Endless confusion results from disregarding this simple rule' (Nils Lund).

See also NUMBER SYMBOLISM.

images The religion of the Hebrew Bible and the early Jewish tradition is primarily a religion of will and obedience – of the will of God and of human obedience to him. A faith expressed in PROPHECY makes moral demands. A religion of this kind has little need of visual images (see Exodus 20.2–5; Deuteronomy 17.17), although it may have nonetheless a richness in verbal IMAGE AND SYMBOL. The LAW of Israel constituted the central religious tradition; in times of tension there would be a tightening of the prohibition on visual images, in defence of the law. Earliest Christianity maintained this emphasis, until there was a development of Christian art, for example in the catacombs.

While the law of MOSES maintains this official line, there are frequent divergences of practice against which the prophets utter condemnations. These may be lapses into the idolatrous practices of the CANAANITES, and they are well-illustrated by the conduct of the Northern Kingdom for which it was denounced (see for examples 1 Kings 12.28–33; 16.31–33; Hosea 8.4–6). *See also* HOUSEHOLD DEITIES; IDOLATRY.

Later Judaism developed a tradition of representational art, probably under HELLENISTIC influence. Biblical scenes are depicted, for example, in the 3rd-century CE synagogue frescoes at DURA EUROPOS (including Moses and the burning bush; EZEKIEL's vision of the valley of dry bones) and in the floor mosaics of the 6th-century CE SYNAGOGUE at Beth-Alpha (combining the sacrifice of ISAAC with the 12 signs of the zodiac). Jewish holy days can be found represented in the mosaic pavements of ancient synagogues. Symbols include the MENORAH (seven-branched candelabrum), the citron, and the ram's horn. Another frequent feature, sometimes as a stone-carving, is a representation of the facade of a building like the TEMPLE, perhaps symbolizing a shrine for the TORAH. For images of the Church *see* CHURCH.

imago Dei (image of God) According to Genesis 1.26–27, humanity (male and female) was created in the 'image of God'. Some theologians regard this as a basic definition of humanity, while others say that the image was obscured by the subsequent FALL and the departure of ADAM from the Garden of EDEN (*see also* HUMAN NATURE). What precisely the expression meant in the original context of GENESIS is highly debated among scholars. It could refer to outward form (even an upright posture) or an inward, spiritual capacity. Most likely the reference is to relationship, that is of humanity corresponding to GOD, or humanity in relation to CREATION, in a MARRIAGE relationship (*see* CELIBACY), or humanity as divine agent or representative. The idea is carried forward in what seems to be an early code of LAW, namely the COVENANT with NOAH (the precursor of the SINAI covenant), in Genesis 9.6, where the use of capital punishment for murder is justified because 'in his own image God made humankind'.

Incarnation The literal meaning of the word incarnation is 'taking flesh' and therefore refers to the involvement of the divine within human physical existence. The basic belief in the Incarnation within Christianity concerns a once-for-all event in which Jesus Christ, being divine, also became man. The essential idea is expressed in various ways within the New Testament, but the fullest form of the Christian doctrine entailed a series of controversies in the 4th and 5th centuries CE before its final evolution.

The experience of the first DISCIPLES, accompanying Jesus from Galilee to Jerusalem in his earthly life, was that here was no ordinary human teacher. His contemporaries struggled to find an existing label which fitted him (*see* MESSIAH and TITLES OF JESUS). After his death they became convinced that in some way Jesus lived on (expressed in the Jewish form of the idea of RESURRECTION) and that he could still be experienced as a guide in their present lives. Reflection on his actions and words brought about the conviction, expressed particularly in the stories of his BAPTISM and TRANSFIGURATION (see Mark 1.11; 9.7), that Jesus had been acknowledged by God himself as his son.

If Jesus was no semi-divine hero, but fully SON OF GOD, then it also followed that he was really human as well. It was no ghostly spirit that had shared meals with his friends, become tired, and crucially had suffered death on the cross. Jesus was fully human too, and that was the meaning of the Incarnation. An early exploration which led to this doctrinal conclusion can be glimpsed in the stories of Jesus' birth in Matthew 1–2 and Luke 1.26–56; 2.1–40. The Son of God had a human birth to a human mother. PAUL explored the meaning of the Incarnation (possibly quoting an early Christian hymn) in terms of humility: Jesus 'emptied himself, taking the form of a slave, being born in human likeness' (Philippians 2.7). Paul then traces the route Jesus took, to enact this humility by means of the cross (2.8), finally to receive his glory from the FATHER and acclamation from all heavenly and earthly beings ('and every tongue should confess that Jesus Christ is Lord' – 2.11).

JOHN'S GOSPEL probably goes further than any other New Testament writing in exploring what really happens in the CHRISTMAS story of the Incarnation. 'And the Word became flesh and lived among us' (John 1.14, *see also* WORD, GRACE, and GLORY). Notice the temporary limits that are implied in the word used here for 'lived', meaning the 'pitching of a tent' (*see* TABERNACLE). But see also the climactic stress on the uniqueness of Christ's revelation through the Incarnation: 'It is God the only Son, who is close to the Father's heart, who has made him known' (John 1.18).

INRI *See* KING OF THE JEWS; SUPERSCRIPTION.

inspiration The idea of inspiration (of a text inspired by the SPIRIT of God), when this is applied to the whole Bible, can generate great controversy, largely as a result of the presuppositions of modern readers, whose attitudes may range from liberalism to FUNDAMENTALISM. A text may be seen as deserving of special respect, endowed with a degree of proven AUTHORITY, or it may be regarded as a special (unique) revelation which gives it inerrancy or infallibility.

One may speak of an inspired prophet, or an inspired oracle or utterance of PROPHECY. The earliest prophets may well have the characteristics of ecstatic behaviour, acting under the influence of the spirit of YAHWEH. Later the prophet spoke of a divine summons: 'the Lord took me from following the flock, and the Lord said to me, "Go, prophesy to my people Israel" ' (Amos 7.15). What the prophets spoke could be termed a 'word of the Lord'. But given the range of prophetic activity, the authenticity of a particular utterance might only be verified by subsequent events. And the possibility remained of false or misleading prophecy.

The classic passage which expresses the concept of the inspiration of scripture is 2 Timothy 3.16–17: 'all scripture is inspired by God and profitable for teaching, for reproof, for correction, and for training in righteousness'. The word translated as 'inspired' is *theopneustos*, meaning 'God-breathed'. Although the early Church Fathers expanded this idea to relate to the writings of the New Testament as well, 2 Timothy can only have referred originally to the scriptures of the Hebrew Bible. It is also possible that Jewish interpreters of the time would have regarded some texts as more and some as less inspired (*see also* CANON OF SCRIPTURE).

The reference in 2 Timothy is exceptional in that it attributes inspiration to the text rather than to the authors of the text. A more usual view would be that expressed in 2 Peter 1.20–21: 'no prophecy ever came by the impulse of man, but men moved by the Holy Spirit spoke from God'. In this sense it is not the text itself but the human being who is the communicator and agent for divine revelation; however convinced (and convincing) he/she may be, the question of authenticity remains for subsequent verification. The fact that it took a considerable period of time for the Biblical canon of inspired scripture to become established acknowledges this process of experiential testing within the Christian (just as within the Jewish) communities.

'The doctrine of inspiration was certainly not given the same weight at all times and in all places – for example there was a dispute within (Christian) Reformed orthodoxy over the extent of inspiration: whether it was confined to the HEBREW consonants or also extended to the vowels supplied later by the MASSORETES' (Fritz Stolz).

irony Irony is a literary technique often used in drama, but not always easy to recognize. In a classic study in 1969, D. C. Muecke wrote: 'Getting to grips with irony seems to have something in common with gathering mist; there is plenty to take hold of, if only one could.' The simplest of definitions was actually proposed by the Roman orator Cicero: 'Irony is saying one thing and meaning another.' In drama irony is used to exploit the divide between how the characters involved in the story understand matters, and how the audience can understand with the benefit of hindsight.

JOHN'S GOSPEL provides numerous examples of this technique; indeed it is often referred to as 'Johannine irony'. A good example is found in John 11.50, when CAIAPHAS the HIGH PRIEST declares, 'it is better for you to have one man die for the people than to have the whole nation destroyed'. The reader sees that Caiaphas is wrong, both morally (because the end does not justify the means), and historically (because the death of Jesus did not save the Jewish people from the consequences of the JEWISH WAR with Rome in 66–70 CE). The Gospel writer, however, sees a deeper truth in what is said, what could be called the 'God's eye view', and underlines the irony for the reader to recognize: Caiaphas 'prophesied that Jesus was about to die for the nation, and not for the nation only, but to gather into one the dispersed children

Abraham and Isaac Genesis 22.3–13

of God' (11.51–52). Jesus dies on their behalf, like the Good SHEPHERD who gives his life for the sheep (John 10.11).

Isaac Isaac, the Old Testament patriarch, was the son of ABRAHAM and SARAH in their old age. His name is related to the Hebrew word for 'laughter' (see Genesis 17.17; 18.12–15; 21.6). According to Genesis 22, Abraham is tested by God to see if he is prepared to SACRIFICE his son Isaac, even though he is the sole means, lately achieved, of the fulfilment of God's promises (Genesis 12.1–3). Abraham is obedient, but God provides an alternative sacrifice to Isaac. If God's promise is to succeed further, special provision then needs to be made for a wife for Isaac, not from among the CANAANITES, but from the land of HARAN, from which Abraham came originally.

And so Abraham's servant is sent to secure REBEKAH, the daughter of Abraham's nephew Bethuel, as Genesis 24 tells the story. Following the marriage, Rebekah cannot have children for some 20 years; then Isaac entreats God and the result is two children, JACOB and ESAU, who have been struggling in Rebekah's womb (Genesis 25.22–26).

Isaiah, book of This collection of prophecy has 66 chapters which makes it one of the longest books in the Bible. Its history is complicated, but it is probably right to see it as a cumulative collection, including oracles which range from the 8th to the 5th centuries BCE. The literary analysis usually divides the book into three parts: chapters 1–39 (First Isaiah – a prophet from the 8th century); chapters 40–55 (Second, or Deutero-, Isaiah – a prophet from the Babylonian Exile in the 6th century); and chapters 56–66 (Third Isaiah – a prophet or prophets working after the return from Exile). But it is also important to notice other distinctive groupings of material: chapters 36–39 which are largely narrative rather than oracles and are parallel to 2 Kings 18.13–20.19; and the 'Servant Songs' (42.1–9; 49.1–7; 50.4–11; 52.13–53.12) linked by their descriptions of the figure of God's servant. But one should still think of the book as a unity, in a special sense. There are several themes which can be seen to develop throughout the corpus. And the whole book is thus a living entity, where the later prophecies augment the earlier, and reinterpret and apply the ideas to the later situations.

The book of Isaiah was a test case for the older LITERARY CRITICISM, based on distinctions of literary style, historical setting and theological ideas. It was tempting to check these findings when computer programs began to be used to test authorship, and the results substantially supported critical scholarship. But the larger view of the unifying features of the book has contributed greatly to an understanding of the phenomenon of PROPHECY in Israel, showing the growth from individual oracles, delivered orally, and subjected by scholars to analysis of form as 'messenger speech', to the encompassing, more literary, processes of the prophetic schools in anthologizing and interpretation over these centuries. As an example of the larger shape, defining the whole book of Isaiah, look at the ZION theme in 2.1–4 and 66.18–24.

There is a decidedly political aspect to the book in the consideration of oppression by a foreign power; it is to be expected that only a remnant will survive, but the eventual hope of a return from EXILE enlarges and defines this concept. The kingship of DAVID and the focus of Mount Zion are important aspects of the divine plan and purpose, but God's plan is seen to embrace all nations. While Jewish exegesis sees Israel as the vital agent and 'servant' of God, Christian interpretation has focused on the prophecies of the MESSIAH (chapters 9 and 11), combined with the sufferings detailed in the Servant Songs, as prefiguring the work of Jesus Christ.

TABULATION OF ISAIAH

3 books sharing the perception that God is active in history

1st Isaiah: mostly 8th century BCE set in Jerusalem, chs 1–39

1.1–10.34	Isaiah warns of disaster from superpower Assyria unless Judah repents, God acts through politics and war. Ch. 6 is Isaiah's vision of the heavenly court and his call to be a prophet
11.1–12.6	*Later:* hope for the future – Davidic monarchy, restored peaceful conditions and the return of the exiles singing God's praise
13.1–19.25	Messages of judgement against cruel and unjust nations. Isaiah says: God is the God of all nations and will punish them
20.1–6	Isaiah acts out the fate of many people – led away naked as captives
21.1–23.18	Vision of the fall of Babylon, with oracles about other nations and the failure of Judah to repent – her officials particularly blamed
24.1–27.13	*Later:* apocalyptic visions of the future
28.1–33.24	Judgement against Judah and Israel, especially against political leaders
34.1–17	*Later:* judgement themes
35.1–10	*Later:* the return from exile – belongs with chs 40–55
36.1–39.8	*Later:* duplicate account of Sennacherib's invasion, also in 2 Kings and 2 Chronicles

2nd Isaiah: mostly 6th century BCE, set in Babylon, chs 40–55

40.1–41.29	The Creator and sovereign Lord of history promises a safe passage home to his people. Earthly rulers and foreign gods count for nothing
42.1–9	1st Servant Song; the servant is quiet and gentle, but will bring justice
42.10–44.27	Return to themes of 40.1–41.25
44.28–48.22	God has appointed Cyrus, king of Persia, to overthrow idolatrous Babylon, and thus free his people to return home
49.1–7	2nd Servant Song: here the servant is clearly Israel
49.8–50.3	God's care for his people involves their rescue from exile
50.4–11	3rd Servant Song: the servant speaks of obedience and suffering
51.1–52.12	God will free Jerusalem
52.13–53.12	4th Servant Song: God will honour the servant, and the people will acknowledge their role in and benefit from his suffering
54.1–55.13	Judah will leave Babylon with joy because of God's love for her

3rd Isaiah: mostly late 5th century BCE, set in Palestine, chs 56–66

56.1–59.21	Oracles addressing various problems within the returned community, and God's call for justice among men to match his own
60.1–62.12	The glorious future of Jerusalem foretold
63.1–6	The arrival of the warrior-judge who has trampled the winepress
63.7–66.24	The debate of why God's great acts of the past are not repeated for today. The answers given include a lack of prayer, but there is also a promise of a new creation and a new Jerusalem

Ishmael *See* ABRAHAM; SARAH.

Ishmaelites *See* JOSEPH (FAVOURITE SON OF JACOB); POTIPHAR; SLAVERY.

Ishtar *See* BA'AL; NEBUCHADNEZZAR.

Israel, the land of *See* GEOGRAPHY OF THE BIBLE and HOLY LAND. For rulers, *see* KINGS OF ISRAEL *and* KINGS OF JUDAH.

Israel, the name of The nation of Israel traces its origins to the 12 sons of JACOB, the ancestors of the twelve tribes (see Genesis 49). Jacob was given a new name after his night of wrestling with an unnamed man at Peniel, as described in Genesis 32.24–32. The new name is 'Israel', in Hebrew *yisra'el*, meaning 'the one who strives with God' or 'God strives': see the etymological explanation at Genesis 32.28. Although the Hebrew Bible clearly seems to explain this name as having to do with struggle, other ancient Jewish and early Christian writings preferred to interpret the circumstances of the name-giving with reference to seeing God, being victorious, having angelic qualities as a heavenly champion, or simply being upright.

Issachar Issachar is the ninth son of JACOB and his fifth by his first wife LEAH (see Genesis 30.14–18; 49.14–15). The blessing suggests that the tribe, named after its ancestor, would find itself hired out to bear burdens in forced labour (*see* SLAVERY), but it may simply be a play on the name (Hebrew *sakar* means 'hire'). According to Joshua 19.17–23 its allotted territory was the fertile heights between the valleys of Jezreel and JORDAN, including the towns of Jezreel and what is now Jenin. Issachar is mentioned as important to DEBORAH in Judges 5.15.

J

J, The Book of This is the title of a work by the eminent literary critic Harold Bloom, who interprets that strand of traditional material from the PENTATEUCH which was labelled 'J' in the scholarly results of PENTATEUCHAL CRITICISM. The text was freshly translated from the Hebrew by David Rosenberg and published in 1990/1.

Jabin *See* DEBORAH; HAZOR; KEDESH.

Jachin and Boaz These are the names of the two decorated bronze pillars which stood either side of the entrance to Solomon's TEMPLE in Jerusalem (see 1 Kings 7.15–22 and 2 Chronicles 3.15–17). They do not seem to have performed any structural function, but rather were symbolic markers of the Temple enclosure. There was fire in the capitals of the pillars that was visible throughout Jerusalem, as a reminder of God's presence. All that is known of the significance of their names is that *Jachin* in Hebrew means 'he establishes'. When Jerusalem was captured in 586 BCE, they were broken up and taken to Babylon as part of the Temple spoils (2 Kings 25.13).

Jacob, or Israel The Old Testament patriarch Jacob (Genesis 25.19–49.33) was the son of ISAAC and the grandson of ABRAHAM. After Jacob had deprived his twin brother ESAU of his birthright and his father's blessing, he fled with his mother REBEKAH'S assistance to his Aramaean kinsman Laban. Laban had two daughters, LEAH and RACHEL; Jacob undertook a contractual arrangement to marry Rachel, but Laban deceived him, insisting that he must first marry Leah. These two wives together (and their maids Bilhah and Zilpah, deputizing for them) were the mothers of 12 sons, who were the ancestors of the twelve tribes of Israel. Jacob and his 12 sons are depicted in spectacular larger-than-life canvases by Francisco Zurbaran which still hang in the palace of the Bishop of Durham at Auckland Castle.

The story of Jacob in GENESIS contains two significant episodes of religious experience. On his escape northwards, away from Esau, Jacob experiences a dream at BETHEL, in which he sees a ladder set up between earth and heaven, and receives a promise of divine blessing (Genesis 28). (There is a tradition, but no firm evidence, that Jacob's pillow from Bethel travelled to Ireland via Egypt, Sicily and Spain, arriving in 700 BCE and becoming known as the Stone of Tara. In 840 CE it was taken to Scotland as the Stone of Scone, for the coronation of Scottish kings; the English king Edward I then took the stone to Westminster Abbey in 1296, where it was placed under the coronation throne of British sovereigns. In 1996 this Stone of

Jacob and the Angel Genesis 32.23–29

Destiny was returned to Scotland.) The second experience came at a ford of the river Jabbok at a place which became known as Peni-el – 'the face of God' (Genesis 32.24–30). Here Jacob wrestles through the night with a mysterious (divine) stranger, suffers a dislocated hip, and receives the new name Israel (meaning 'one who strives with God'). Jacob settles in the area of HEBRON after Isaac's death and is eventually buried in the family tomb at Machpelah (Genesis 50.13).

Jacob's well *See* SHECHEM; SYCHAR.

Jael *See* DEBORAH; KENITES; SISERA.

James, brother of Jesus James, together with his brothers, Joseph, Simon, and Judas, is named at Matthew 13.55 as one of 'the brothers of Jesus'. The word 'brother' has been interpreted in various ways, as meaning stepbrother or cousin, but it may well denote a natural sibling relationship with Jesus. Certainly James became a leader of the Jerusalem Church (see Acts 12.17; 15.13; 21.18; Galatians 1.19; 2.9) and apparently presided at the first Council of Jerusalem. According to JOSEPHUS he was martyred by stoning in 61 CE. Traditionally he was known as James the Just on account of his piety. The ascription to him of the Letter of James (see below) is by no means conclusive.

James, the lesser James the son of Alphaeus is listed as one of the 12 DISCIPLES of Jesus (e.g. in Mark 3.18). It is by no means certain that he should be identified with the James 'the younger' mentioned in Mark 15.40 as the son of Mary, whether or not this is the same Mary who is the mother of Jesus.

James, letter of The letter of James is labelled as one of the Catholic Letters, in the sense that it is a general letter addressed to the whole Christian Church ('the twelve tribes in the dispersion' – 1.1), rather than a letter to a named Church concerning local issues. The evidence for its origins and early use is obscure; it is not contained in any official canon list until the late 4th century. The attribution to JAMES, BROTHER OF JESUS is debated, on the grounds that the Greek is better than would be expected from a JEWISH-CHRISTIAN. The letter contains some 20 echoes of the sayings of Jesus, and other ethical maxims, in the context of a Hellenistic discourse ('a moral exhortation of rare passion'). The aphorisms of the first chapter are developed in the essays in chapters 2–5. The date and place of composition are uncertain, and may perhaps be around 100 CE, because of some points of contact with 1 PETER and the Apostolic Fathers (1 Clement and Shepherd of Hermas).

Recent scholarship has countered the Reformation's lack of enthusiasm for this letter, when Martin LUTHER (in the preface to his German Bible of 1522) called James 'an epistle of straw' when compared to the writings that 'show thee Christ'. 'In the reading of many Christians James has been valued for its very demanding advice on practical Christian living, and associated more with the ethical teaching of Jesus than with the theological vision of PAUL [see 2.14–26] ... This practical and ethical thrust is certainly true ... but also it flows from a profoundly theological vision of human life in the intention of God' (Richard Bauckham, James, Routledge, 1999). The Christianity of James is neither Pauline nor anti-Pauline. The law (TORAH) is appropriated through the words of Jesus as the 'law of liberty'. The author wants Christians to live by the measure of faith ('friendship with God' rather than 'friendship with the world').

James, Protevangelium of The Proto-Gospel of James was a text of the late 2nd century CE, dedicated to the task of filling the gap represented by Jesus' early years in the four canonical Gospels (apart from Luke 2.41–52). The contents are legendary stories about MARY's parents, Joachim and Anna, Mary's own miraculous birth, details of the journey to BETHLEHEM, the birth of Jesus in a cave, the explanation that Jesus' brothers and sisters were actually half-brothers and half-sisters from a previous marriage of the widower JOSEPH, and the consequent reaffirmation of Mary's perpetual virginity. The clear motive is the praise of Mary; many of these themes were taken up in the later doctrines of the Roman Catholic Church.

James, son of Zebedee James, together with his brother JOHN, were fishermen, sons of Zebedee, and members of the inner group of the DISCIPLES of Jesus, being called at an early point, according to Mark 1.19–20. They were present at the raising of Jairus' daughter (Mark 5.37), the TRANSFIGURATION (Mark 9.2), and at the AGONY IN THE GARDEN of Gethsemane (Mark 14.33). They were nicknamed 'Sons of Thunder' (Boanerges) according to Mark 3.17. The precise meaning of this is uncertain, but may be related to their zeal and hot temper (perhaps illustrated in Luke 9.54). They requested an advantageous place in the coming KINGDOM OF GOD, according to

Mark 10.35–40. James was the first of the APOSTLES to suffer martyrdom, as he was beheaded by Herod Agrippa I in 44 CE (Acts 12.2; *see* HERODIAN DYNASTY). Spanish tradition claims that his body was translated to Santiago de Compostela, where it is still the focus of pilgrimage.

Jebusites *See* DAVID; ZION.

Jehoash King of Judah (835–801 BCE) and son of King Ahaziah, Jehoash (or Joash) was proclaimed king at the age of seven, having been hidden in the Temple for six years. He was later responsible for a rebuilding of the Temple (2 Kings 12 and 2 Chronicles 24). In 2003 a black sandstone plaque with a 15-line inscription came to light, purporting to describe these renovations to the Solomonic Temple in terms recalling the Biblical narratives. If authentic this would be the first royal Israelite inscription ever found. But experts are divided as to whether this is a highly significant artefact or a skilled fake. Jehoash tried to forestall a Syrian invasion by bribing Hazael with Temple treasure. He was killed in a coup by his officers.

Jehoiachin *See* KINGS (FIRST AND SECOND BOOKS OF).

Jehovah, name of God *See* YAHWEH.

Jehu Jehu became the eleventh KING OF THE NORTHERN (DIVIDED) KINGDOM OF ISRAEL as a result of a coup in c.842 BCE. He established a new dynasty that endured for five generations and 90 years. From the perspective of the Hebrew Bible's narrative (1 Kings 19.16–18; 2 Kings 9–10) Jehu's rebellion was a crusade against the worship of BA'AL. The bloodiness of his coup, involving the killings of Jehoram king of Israel and Ahaziah king of Judah, AHAB's wife JEZEBEL, 70 sons of Ahab and other associates, Ahaziah's brothers, and numerous worshippers of Ba'al, was recalled a century later in Hosea 1.4. The inscription erected at Tel DAN by Hazael puts the actions of Jehu in a somewhat different political light. A year later, in 841 BCE, Jehu made himself the vassal of ASSYRIA, in a political move to counter the ARAMAEANS – an episode which is depicted on the Black Obelisk of Shalmaneser III. A vivid detail in the narrative of the earlier coup is the description of Jehu's imminent approach as recounted by Ahaziah's watchman: 'It looks like the driving of Jehu son of Nimshi; for he drives like a maniac' (2 Kings 9.20).

Jephthah *See* VOWS.

Jerash *See* GADARA.

Jeremiah, book of The personality of the prophet and the conditions of his life appear more prominently in this book than in other prophetic books of the Old Testament. But in some modern scholarship the quest for the historical Jeremiah has seemed as frustrating as that of the quest for Jesus (*see* HISTORICAL JESUS). Jeremiah came from Anathoth in Benjamin (see 32.7) and was a descendant of Abiathar, a chief priest of King DAVID. The prophet's sufferings feature prominently, sufferings both as a result of his calling and inner compulsion ('fire within my bones'), and as experienced in the punishments (stocks and muddy cistern, for example) which were imposed as a result of his work, and because of suspicion that he was a collaborator with the BABYLONIANS. But his last days, after Gedaliah was assassinated, are lost in obscurity. Perhaps the biographical details can become something of a distraction when seeking the message of the book. Certainly the English derivative of his name (Jeremiad) is greatly misleading.

The message of Jeremiah is of hope, despite the threat posed by the Babylonian campaigns and the destruction of Jerusalem in 587 BCE; these events were predicted as a punishment for national APOSTASY, but the ultimate promise is of restoration. The book has four sections: chapters 1–25, a collection of mostly poetic prophecies; then chapters 26–29, 32, 34–45, a narrative sequence; thirdly, inserted as chapters 30–31 and 33, prophecies of the nation's restoration ('the little book of consolation'); and fourthly in chapters 46–51, prophecies directed against foreign nations, concluded by a narrative epilogue in chapter 52. Of special note are the TEMPLE sermons (chapters 7, 26), attacking the false basis of the religion of king and Temple, and chapter 31, which defines the terms of the new COVENANT. This latter text was especially influential in Christian understanding of the Last Supper (*see* EUCHARIST) and the New Testament, and 31.31–34 is quoted extensively in HEBREWS 8.8–12 and 10.16–17. Prophecies first applied to the fall of Jerusalem to the Babylonians in 587 BCE took on a new lease of life after the fall of Jerusalem to the Romans in 70 CE. (See also the pseudepigraphical text *Paraleipomena of Jeremiah*.) The character of BARUCH, and the APOCRYPHAL texts associated with him, find their roots in the relationship of Jeremiah and Baruch in the narratives of the second section of the book of Jeremiah.

Evidence for an older collection of Jeremiah's prophecies, shorter and differently arranged, is found in the QUMRAN manuscripts, and also in the Greek translation of the SEPTUAGINT.

TABULATION OF JEREMIAH

The prophet of judgement and his teaching, chs 1–25 (mostly 627–583 BCE)

1.1–19	Jeremiah's call to be a prophet
2.1–36	Idolatry is the worst crime
3.1–25	Idolatry is seen as sexual misconduct
4.1–6.30	God's punishment is threatened, an invasion force will come from the north, i.e. from Babylon
7.1–15	Jeremiah's Temple sermon challenges hearers to live by Covenant standards
7.16–12.17	Jeremiah's involvement in prophesying doom for idolatry
13.1–14	Acted out prophecies of destruction
13.15–15.9	Doom is threatened for the people of Judah who have rejected God
15.10–17.18	Jeremiah's personal unhappiness and sacrifice in his work for God
17.19–27	*Later:* post-Exilic sermon focused on keeping the Sabbath
18.1–12	God as the divine potter shapes futures
18.13–23	Judah's rejection of God for idolatry involves their rejection of his prophet
19.1–15	Acted out prophecy of destruction
20.1–18	Jeremiah complains after punishment by a priest

21.1–22.30	Jeremiah's oracles about royalty and the destruction of Jerusalem
23.1–8	The return from exile foretold
23.9–40	False prophets
24.1–10	The good figs (i.e. the first exiles to Babylon in 597 BCE) and the bad figs (those left behind in Jerusalem) are contrasted
25.1–14	Jeremiah's early prophecies in a nutshell
25.15–38	Judgement on the nations is pronounced

Stories about Jeremiah's life and work, chs 26–45

26.1–29.32	Jeremiah's attempts to get God's word a hearing
30.1–31.40	*Later:* 'The Book of Consolation'; oracles about the later redemption of Israel and Judah, and their return home; various dates and authors
32.1–33.26	This relates to the time when Jeremiah was held prisoner, accused of desertion during the Babylonian siege of Jerusalem 588 BCE
32.1–44	As a prophetic sign of an eventual return to normality, Jeremiah buys a field during the siege
33.1–26	Promise of restoration and the righteous branch
34.1–22	Disaster foretold for Zedekiah and his people
35.1–19	The obedience of the Rechabites (in an earlier story relating to King Jehoiachin) is contrasted to the current lack of obedience in Jerusalem
36.1–32	Jeremiah replaces a scroll of his oracles which had been destroyed by King Jehoiachin
37.1–38.28	An attempt to kill the prophet for demoralizing the people under siege is thwarted
39.1–18	The Babylonians capture Jerusalem, its king and its people in 587 BCE
40.1–43.7	Jeremiah is released by the Babylonians and goes to Gedaliah, who is acting governor until assassinated; Jeremiah is forcibly resettled in Egypt with the survivors
43.8–44.30	Jeremiah prophesies the Babylonian conquest of Egypt too, and condemns the idolatry of his countrymen 583 BCE
45.1–5	Jeremiah's oracle to his scribe Baruch in 605 BCE

Concluding additions, chs 46–52

46.1–51.58	*Later:* oracles against Israel and Judah's neighbours and Babylon (the authorship by Jeremiah of some or all of them is disputed)
51.59–64	Oracles against Babylon
52.1–34	*Later:* this chapter comes from 2 Kings, and it explains how the exile came about, what happened to the Temple furnishings and to the Temple itself, concluding with Jehoiachin's later release from prison in 560 BCE

Jericho Ancient Jericho, or Tell es-Sultan, is one of the oldest fortified cities in the Near East, if not in the world, being first occupied towards the end of the last Ice Age, about 12,000 years ago. The British archaeologist Kathleen Kenyon revealed a sequence of occupation phases in the Neolithic period between 8000 and 4500

BCE. Jericho changed from being a substantial town, with massive walls, to a simple unwalled village. According to the Biblical account (in Joshua 6) the walls of the city fell, at the sound of trumpets, after a seven-day siege by the Israelites, and the city was burnt. Joshua cursed anyone who should try to rebuild the city. But the site was reinhabited (see 2 Samuel 10.5; 1 Kings 16.34 – Hiel rebuilt at a cost; 2 Kings 2.4–5 in the story of ELIJAH; and 2 Kings 2.18–22 where ELISHA purifies the water supply). The plentiful supply of water from nearby springs turned the site into a green oasis, which is described in 2 Chronicles 28.15 as 'the city of palm trees'.

Students of the ARCHAEOLOGY OF THE BIBLE have been frustrated by the lack of evidence discovered for the destruction by Joshua, for this would assist in confirming the date for the Israelite conquest of CANAAN. An earlier archaeologist, John Garstang, had found a ruined mudbrick wall and dated its destruction to c.1400 BCE, but Kathleen Kenyon's work showed that it was actually many centuries older than Joshua. No trace was found of any city walls from an appropriate date in the Late Bronze Age; it is possible that such remains would have been eroded and washed away in the lengthy period before Hiel's rebuilding.

In modern times Jericho became an important centre for the Palestinian Authority, but is now an impoverished and isolated Bedouin city beyond the Israeli checkpoints.

Jeroboam I Jeroboam was the first KING OF THE NORTHERN (DIVIDED) KINGDOM OF ISRAEL, and he reigned c.928–907 BCE. He came from Ephraim and his parents were Nebat and Zeruah. His stepping stone to political power came when SOLOMON appointed him as overseer of the forced labour in the tribal districts at EPHRAIM and MANASSEH (see 1 Kings 11.26–40). The prophet Ahijah of SHILOH had presented him with a symbolic demonstration of the division of the Davidic kingdom as a consequence of Solomon's disloyalty to YAHWEH. Jeroboam rebelled against Solomon, but was forced to escape to Egypt until the king was dead. Jeroboam's revolt succeeded only when the northern tribes withdrew support from Solomon's son and successor Rehoboam (who had refused to reduce the burdens placed upon them by his father – see 1 Kings 12.1–20).

As the Northern king, Jeroboam fortified SHECHEM, Penuel and TIRZAH. He set up golden bull images (*see* GOLDEN CALF) at BETHEL and DAN to assert the kingdom's religious independence from Jerusalem. His religious reforms, detailed in 1 Kings 12.26–33, were highly criticized by the writers of the books of KINGS, for whom he was the archetypal evil monarch. All subsequent kings of the North 'did what was evil in the sight of the Lord and walked in the way of Jeroboam'. Clearly the Jerusalem authorities were prejudiced in their religious and political viewpoint. Given the lack of evidence it is hard to assess any alternative view. But Jeroboam, as well as securing his political independence, may genuinely have sought to confirm traditional religious practices and revive older forms of worship (see Exodus 32.1–6). After all, Solomon's record in Jerusalem was hardly an example of purist policy.

Jeroboam II *See* AMOS, BOOK OF.

Jerome *See* VULGATE.

Jerubbaal *See* GIDEON.

Jerusalem Jerusalem may be the most excavated city in the world, with an average approaching an excavation a year in the last 150 years. But the results are not uniformly productive, for several reasons: some parts, like the TEMPLE Mount, are barred to archaeologists; some buildings lasted for centuries until the destructions of 586 BCE or 70 CE; unlike the superimposed layers of new building on existing mounds (tells) elsewhere in Israel, a new construction here needed to be founded on solid rock, so each time the site would be cleared, leaving few earlier traces.

The name of Jerusalem, in the form 'Salim', may appear in lists at EBLA c.2400 BCE; otherwise the earliest written reference comes in the Egyptian Execration Texts of the early 2nd millennium BCE, which mention two of its rulers. Then there are letters from Abdu-Hepa, king of 'Urusalim', in the EL-AMARNA archives of the 14th century. The name may refer originally to a deity named Salem, but Rabbinic and Christian interpretations of the name link it to the Hebrew word 'PEACE' (*shalom*). So the designation 'City of Peace' becomes popular after the Biblical period.

From the Biblical perspective, the story of Jerusalem does not start until just before the 10th century BCE (Iron Age II) when King DAVID conquers Jerusalem, after ruling in HEBRON for seven years. It was then a fortified city (ZION – see 2 Samuel 5.7), but in the time of David Jerusalem was confined to what is still called the City of David, that is the spur of land to the south of the Temple Mount bounded by the two valleys, the Kidron and the Tyropoeon. The results of the excavations in the early 1980s by Yigal Shiloh suggest that during the period of Israel's United Monarchy under David and SOLOMON this Jerusalem was well fortified, served by two complex water-supply systems associated with the Gihon spring, and inhabited by a socially stratified society, some living inside and some outside the city's fortification wall.

During the period of the divided monarchy, and until the fall of Judah in 587 BCE, the population of Jerusalem spread to include the western hill, and this too was fortified. Much of the defensive building, and the construction of a new water channel from the Gihon spring, was authorized by King HEZEKIAH (see 2 Kings 20.20). Later kings were not so optimistic in both practical and religious terms, and there were warnings of disaster (see Micah 3.12). Following the capture of the city by the BABYLONIANS, prophecies of disaster were fulfilled when the site was levelled in 587 BCE (see 2 Kings 25.10).

After the Babylonian EXILE, CYRUS of Persia permitted the exiles to return and rebuild the city. But the population was now a fraction of what it had been and was confined to part of the eastern spur. Walls and Temple were rebuilt (Ezra 3–6; Nehemiah 3, 7), but the belief in Jerusalem was less a matter of realism, more an apocalyptic dream (see Isaiah 2.1–4). During the HELLENISTIC PERIOD there was further tension caused by importing Greek cultural ideas and sporting practice. A fortress known as the Akra was apparently built for the control of the city by the Hellenists. After the revolt led by the MACCABEES, the HASMONEAN dynasty encouraged the expansion of the population, with housing and fortifications again on the western hill. The Romans under Pompey conquered the city in 63 BCE; an impressive rebuilding programme was instituted by HEROD THE GREAT affecting the Temple, palace and towers, including a fortress called the Antonia. The Jewish historian JOSEPHUS provides a detailed description of Jerusalem on the eve of the JEWISH WAR and its eventual destruction by the Roman legions in 70 CE (see *War*, book 5).

Jerusalem remained in ruins for the rest of the 1st century CE. After the revolt led by BAR KOKHBA in 130 CE, Emperor Hadrian had the city rebuilt as a Roman military camp named Aelia Capitolina; a temple to Jupiter was built on the site of the Temple Mount. But with the rise of Emperor Constantine in the 4th century the city became a Christian centre (*see* CHURCHES, CHRISTIAN). During the Byzantine period Jerusalem as a walled city reached its greatest extent.

Following the First Crusade, on 15 July 1099, after the holy city of Jerusalem had been captured from the Seljuk Turks, the Crusaders 'sobbing for excess of joy' offered up thanks in the Church of the Holy Sepulchre. But Jerusalem was surrendered again, to Saladin, in October 1187. The medieval maps of the world (*Mappae mundi*) habitually placed the city of Jerusalem at their centre, seen as the navel of the world. On such maps Jerusalem would be represented by the image of a small structure with a cupola, the Church of the Holy Sepulchre.

Jerusalem is not just an historic and holy city, but also a metaphor, an idea, a symbol, 'a mystic alternative to the real' (Amos Elon). In the poem by Yehuda Amichai, 'Jerusalem is a port city on the shore of eternity'. Earlier Jewish Zionists, considering a return to the HOLY LAND (*see also* DIASPORA and ALIYAH), had been deeply ambivalent about Jerusalem, associating the Old City with the reactionary past: 'We do not need the walls of Jerusalem, nor the Jerusalem temple, nor Jerusalem itself,' said Moshe Leib Lilienblum, a proto-Zionist, writing in 1882.

In the Christian tradition of ALLEGORY used for the interpretation of Biblical references to Jerusalem, the literal meaning of the text concerns the earthly city, while the moral sense identifies the place with the soul of each individual Christian, and the spiritual sense is equated with the Christian Church. In addition there is an eschatological meaning, a reference to the 'NEW JERUSALEM' as described in the book of REVELATION (see chapters 21 and 22). This idea picks up the threads of APOCALYPTIC hope about a future Jerusalem, noted during and after the Babylonian Exile.

In the words of Miri Rubin, 'Jerusalem is an affair of the mind, of the imagination: in the Jewish yearning for it in Exile; in the Muslim fostering of holy sites; in the Christian invocation of it in LITURGY. Jerusalem was made and recreated wherever it was remembered.' The Christian hymns which sing of 'Jerusalem the golden' and 'Glorious things of thee are spoken, Zion city of our God' are cases in point.

Jesse Jesse was the father of King DAVID. The GENEALOGY in the book of RUTH (4.17–22) claims that Jesse was the grandson of Boaz and Ruth. According to 1 Samuel 16 and 17 he was a prosperous farmer with a respected social position, an elder of the community. In the prophecy of ISAIAH (11.1, 10) concerned with the House of David, and subsequently applied to the MESSIAH, Jesse has a fundamental mention ('stump' and 'root'). Naturally he is also included in the New Testament genealogies of Jesus (Matthew 1.5–6; Luke 3.32). For this reason later artistic representations of the ancestry of Jesus are often referred to as a 'Jesse tree' or a 'Jesse window'.

Jesus The name Jesus, the Greek Iesous, is a version of the Hebrew/Aramaic name Joshua/Jeshua, which means 'God saves'. According to the stories of the birth of Jesus in the Gospels of MATTHEW and LUKE, this name is revealed in an angelic visitation (to Joseph or Mary, respectively); Matthew 1.21 explains the reason for the name, while the narratives in Luke refer repeatedly to the themes of 'saviour' and 'salvation'.

The questions about who Jesus actually was, and what he was like, have received a wide variety of responses since his time. In Richard Beard's words, 'I was finding it difficult to grasp the personality of Jesus … He could be anyone. He was a carpenter and King of the Jews, a peasant and heir to the royal line of David. He was a revolutionary, a prophet, a mystic, a teacher, a CHARISMATIC leader.' (See also TITLES OF JESUS.) Eduard Lohse qualifies this, 'When Jesus is called Rabbi by His disciples and others, this shows that He conducted Himself like the Jewish scribes.' Lesslie Newbigin adds the long-term historical perspective, 'It is simply a fact of history that Jesus has been and is portrayed in an amazing variety of portraits from the Byzantine Pantocrator through the medieval crucifix and the Jesus of the sacred heart, to the blue-eyed blond of American Protestantism and the Che Guevara freedom fighter of liberation theology.'

The older definition of 'Jesus' in *The Shorter Oxford English Dictionary* ran 'the name of the Founder of Christianity'. In the 1993 revision this was changed, on the advice of the Jewish scholar Geza Vermes, to: '(The name of) the central figure of the Christian faith, a Jewish preacher (c.5 BC–c.AD 30) regarded by his followers as the Son of God and God incarnate.' This change reflects the later stages of a scholarly 'quest for the HISTORICAL JESUS' and the recognition of the fact that Jesus was a Jew ('thoroughly Jewish in his role of teacher, exorcist and preacher, prophet and SON OF GOD'). In Vermes' words: 'The original catastrophe struck at 3 p.m. on Friday April 7th, AD 30, when the charismatic Galilean religious preacher, Jesus of Nazareth, expired on a Roman cross, wrongly sentenced to death as an insurgent by the governor of Judaea, PILATE, with the connivance of the local Jewish leaders. Within a few decades the followers of Jesus, by then largely non-Jews, recognized Jesus as Son of God, and finally as God.'

Gunther Bornkamm, a New Testament theologian, said: 'No one is any longer in a position to write a life of Jesus.' Such a negative assessment may be hotly contested. What can be said? A fairly cautious estimate of the dates of authorship for the four theological accounts (not biographies, by intention) of Jesus brings their composition within the lifetime of those who knew him, or knew his APOSTLES. There is as much or more evidence for Jesus' existence as for almost any other figure in the ancient world. If one may separate the existence of the man, the teacher and healer from later interpretation of him (see TITLES OF JESUS and SON OF GOD), this is what one might say.

Little is known of Jesus' early life (apart from the birth stories in Matthew and Luke, and Luke's story of a visit to Jerusalem at the age of 12 – see Luke 2.41–52) until at about the age of 30 he comes for BAPTISM by JOHN THE BAPTIST. He was known as the son of JOSEPH the carpenter, and had mother and siblings still alive. Apparently he originated from NAZARETH, but came to be connected with CAPERNAUM by the Sea of

GALILEE. Jesus was a pious Jew, regularly attending the SYNAGOGUE, where he read and preached from TORAH (see Luke 4.16), and was well versed in rabbinic exposition and debate, presumably derived from religious training as a young man.

Alignment with John's baptism brought about a radical career break; Jesus began an itinerant ministry after a period of reflection (*see* TEMPTATIONS). He gathered a group of followers (DISCIPLES), probably also would-be missionaries (*see* MISSION) or apostles; 12 in number, they would represent the New Israel (*see* NUMBER SYMBOLISM). As disciples they learnt from Jesus, committing his teaching to memory so as to pass it on. Teaching with authority was what marked Jesus out; he used rabbinic debating techniques, but also stories in the everyday language of farm and home, to appeal to ordinary people (*see* PARABLES).

Jesus was known as an effective healer (*see* MIRACLES). Because he did not respect the minutiae of the PHARISEES' rules, but healed to meet faith and human need whenever necessary, this set up a controversial relationship with the religious authorities (see Luke 14.1–6). They became increasingly hostile to him, so that a showdown was inevitable (Mark 3.6).

Jesus challenged his followers to draw conclusions about his true identity (see Mark 8.27). He then astounded them by denying the traditional baggage that went with the title they chose (*see* MESSIAH and TITLES OF JESUS). Jesus saw that it would entail suffering and death; PETER rejected such an idea, but was in turn rejected. The TRANSFIGURATION (see Mark 9.2–8) is the second of these two episodes on which the Gospel story is often said to pivot. Here God the Father confirms the Son's true status, and the presence of MOSES and ELIJAH underlines the continuity of the Biblical story of salvation. For Luke (9.31) there is an unavoidable link to Jesus' forthcoming death in Jerusalem.

Sooner or later Jesus made the journey to Jerusalem, entering the city on a donkey (as a Prince of PEACE), but with an acclaim that was indicative of a misunderstood messiahship, with nationalist palm leaves and royal trappings. By an action of CLEANSING THE TEMPLE, Jesus challenged the religious authorities. This led directly to the plot to kill him, because he was viewed as a liability. When attempts to catch him out with a public humiliation failed, the only way was to arrest him privately (with assistance from JUDAS ISCARIOT, who knew the Garden of GETHSEMANE where Jesus prayed). The trial before the HIGH PRIEST was a travesty; the charges were switched to that of a political threat to Caesar's authority. Jesus' execution was assured and took place at 3 p.m. on the day subsequently known as GOOD FRIDAY. Jesus had already instituted a memorial meal on the previous evening, to explain his sacrifice of body and blood (*see* EUCHARIST). More was to follow when his followers were shocked to discover evidence of his RESURRECTION (see Mark 16.6). They were convinced of the credibility of their experience (Luke 24.39–43 takes it further than most). For a short while afterwards appearances of the risen Jesus were reported by many witnesses (1 Corinthians 15.4–8), until his more final departure, known as the ASCENSION (see Luke 24.50–51).

Depending on one's interpretation of the evidence in the various Gospels, Jesus' active ministry of teaching and healing lasted between 18 months and three years, in fact a relatively small proportion of his earthly life, but one having a lasting impact to this day. *See also* JESUS, ACCORDING TO HIS OPPONENTS).

Jesus, according to his opponents There are some clues within the New Testament about how JESUS was regarded by his opponents. The reaction to a person may reveal important information about that person, and be of value in a quest for the HISTORICAL JESUS. The Gospel tradition may have preserved such traces because of a desire to defend Jesus against such criticism, personal jibes and formal complaints.

'Look, a glutton and a drunkard, a friend of tax collectors and sinners!' is cited in Matthew 11.19 and Luke 7.34 – probably a saying from Q (*see* Q (QUELLE) SOURCE) – see also Mark 2.16. This may well reflect the judgement of Deuteronomy 21.20 about a 'stubborn and rebellious' son who is 'a glutton and a drunkard'. The legal punishment prescribed is stoning to death, but this is not reflected in the TRIAL OF JESUS. In the Gospel saying from Q the criticism is countered by asserting that God's WISDOM is proved right by the deeds both of John and of Jesus.

A larger accusation is that of false prophecy on Jesus' part, based on the classic reference in Deuteronomy 13.1–5, identifying a deceiver who has led Israel astray. See Matthew 27.63 ('impostor'); Luke 23.2 ('perverting our nation'); John 7.12 ('deceiving the crowd'). It is arguable how big a part this accusation played in Jesus' trial, but it certainly figured in arguments between Jews and Christians (see Justin's *Dialogue with Trypho the Jew* 69, 108).

The discussion of the false prophet in Deuteronomy 13 refers briefly to the signs which he gives. Deuteronomy 18 goes on to attack those who work these signs as 'magicians' and 'sorcerers'. Justin's *Dialogue* 7.3 speaks of 'false prophets filled with the seducing and unclean spirit; they work MIRACLES to amaze men and give glory to the spirits of error and demons'. Demon possession is referred to in JOHN'S GOSPEL in accusations about Jesus in 7.20; 8.48; and 10.19. The source of Jesus' power is discussed in Mark 3. 21–27, and some attribute it to BEELZEBUL, the prince of demons (see also Matthew 12.24; Luke 11.15, probably from Q).

Such accusations appear early in the tradition, and figure largely in anti-Christian polemic. While the Gospels counter such charges by insisting on understanding Jesus in terms of his relationship to God, it is clear that others found Jesus' actions and teaching deeply offensive.

Jesus ben Sirach, Wisdom of *See* ECCLESIASTICUS.

Jesus boat, or Galilee boat When the water level of the Sea of GALILEE was significantly reduced in the mid 1980s, the outlines of a boat were identified in January 1986, buried in the mud where the shore was uncovered. The boat was raised and conserved and put on display in nearby Kibbutz Ginnosar. It measures 26 ft by 8 ft and was dated to the 1st century CE by its pots and lamps and by CARBON-14 tests on its planking. The boat is therefore from the time of Jesus and is of the type which would have been used for fishing or for crossing the lake.

Jethro *See* KENITES; MOSES.

Jewish-Christians, Judaeo-Christians The main historical studies of both ancient JUDAISM and early CHRISTIANITY have paid much less attention to Jewish-Christian groupings which are identifiable as falling between these major traditions. Their identities are not simply a compromise between the two.

Relevant subject matter includes the nature of the first Christian Church in Jerusalem; how the next generation regarded JAMES, BROTHER OF JESUS or Simon PETER; the evidence from early texts such as the DIDACHE and *1 Clement*; and the origin of the Ebionites.

The name Ebionite derives from the Hebrew word for 'poor', which can carry implications of righteous suffering (see Isaiah 61.1; Luke 6.20). The original Jerusalem Church was referred to as 'the poor' (Galatians 2.10). The Ebionites are a likely continuation of the Jerusalem Church, and a logical development from the Judaizers to whom PAUL referred critically in his letters. They held a possessionist Christology, that is, believing that Christ as a divine spirit entered Jesus the son of Joseph and Mary at his BAPTISM, and left him at the point of his PASSION. Such views may be reflected in the proclamation of 'another Jesus' attacked by Paul in 2 Corinthians 11.4, and in the group opposed in the first letter of John who deny the INCARNATION and refuse divine honour to Jesus (see 1 John 4.1–3; 5.5–8). The Ebionites did affirm that Joseph was the biological father of Jesus.

Jewish literature The Hebrew Bible (OLD TESTAMENT) is the best known collection of ancient Jewish writing. But much more was written in the centuries between the end of the Hebrew Bible – and within the period of the New Testament – up until the Mishnah in the 2nd century CE. Many of these writings have survived, and more have been discovered in the last century.

Scholars refer to these Jewish writings using a potentially confusing set of terms. There is the group of texts known to Protestant Christians as the APOCRYPHA. These are writings included in the Roman Catholic Bible but not in the Jewish Bible or the Protestant Old Testament: works such as Sirach (*see* ECCLESIASTICUS) and 1 & 2 MAC-CABEES. Another term, used for other writings, is the Jewish Pseudepigrapha. Originally this referred strictly to texts that were written under an assumed name (for example ENOCH or ADAM), but today it is often used more widely of Jewish texts written in the last centuries BCE or the 1st century CE. An English version of the Pseudepigrapha, edited by James Charlesworth, contains over 50 texts, including for example JUBILEES and the Testaments of the Twelve Patriarchs.

The DEAD SEA SCROLLS, discovered in the 20th century, represent a large group of new texts. As well as new versions of Biblical manuscripts, there are many texts relating to the beliefs and practices of what could be termed a sectarian or an ultra-orthodox Jewish community. These underline the variety of ideas which existed in ancient Judaism.

For an overview of ancient Jewish literature see the textbook by George W. E. Nickelsburg, *Jewish Literature between the Bible and the Mishnah: A Historical and Literary Introduction*, revised edition (Fortress, 2005).

Jewish War The Jewish revolt against Rome, as chronicled by the historian JOSE-PHUS, began in 66 CE. Although mainly concluded by 70, when JERUSALEM fell, it produced sporadic fighting until 73, when the Romans captured MASADA.

Jerusalem was razed to the ground by the Romans at the end of the Jewish revolt. The spoils from Jerusalem were taken to Rome; some of the Temple treasures are depicted on the ceremonial arch of Titus in the Forum of Rome. With even greater irony, the Roman emperor TITUS completed the construction of the Colosseum in Rome in 79 CE, making use of materials from Jerusalem.

Jezebel Jezebel, a princess from one of the PHOENICIAN royal houses in the 9th century BCE, is the wife of King AHAB of Israel and the opponent of the prophet ELIJAH (1 Kings 18–19). Her influence symbolizes the threat posed by the worship of the Canaanite deity BAʻAL. One particular example of her 'wickedness' is the way she contrives the murder of NABOTH, in order to acquire his vineyard for Ahab (1 Kings 21.1–16); she clearly believes in the absolute power of the ruler and has no concept of citizens' rights. This crime provokes Elijah to pronounce a divine curse upon Jezebel and Ahab (1 Kings 21.17–24). His prophecy of the death of Jezebel is fulfilled when she is assassinated by JEHU (2 Kings 9.30–37). The memory of this Old Testament tradition is recalled in REVELATION 2.20–23, when a prophetess who teaches false doctrine and apparently encourages immorality is referred to as 'Jezebel'.

Joab *See* ABSALOM; DAVID.

Job, book of This is an epic poem, framed with prose prologue and epilogue. The poem is in the WISDOM tradition, of the falling and rising again of a man who would not blame God. Job's wife, dragged down from riches to rags, looks at her husband, penniless and covered with boils, and tells him to 'curse God and die'. Imagine the modern psychiatrist asking, 'Tell me, Job, did you have anger-management problems when your children died and your roof fell in?' Job of Uz has three comforters, old friends who come to commiserate, and are full of eloquent platitudes. (A fourth figure, a younger man, Elihu, may belong to a separate literary tradition and represent an addition to the original poem.)

The root of Job's problems lies with the adversarial figure of SATAN, who has done a deal with God so that Job can be tried to the uttermost, short of being destroyed. Job wishes that he had not been born, but he does not attempt to kill himself. The happy ending, with Job's restoration, is the classic finish to a story; its celebration of the power and wisdom of God is theologically affirmative, but in terms of the problem of evil and of innocent suffering in the philosophy of religion this remains intellectually unsatisfying.

The setting of the book reflects that of the heroes of the Patriarchal period (*see* PATRIARCHS and Ezekiel 14.14) and their conditions of life. But the date of the book is almost impossible to decide, although there are a number of possible allusions in the text, and many scholars favour the late 6th or 5th century BCE. The development of the figure of Satan and several other theological ideas support a relatively late date. The tradition of the story is expanded in the *Testament of Job* so the Biblical text must have been in circulation by the 2nd century BCE. There is only one New Testament reference, in JAMES 5.11, to the 'patience/endurance of Job'. The book of Job has been open to many individualistic interpretations far from its Biblical roots; the most ambitious is probably Carl Gustav Jung's psychological reading in *Answer to Job* (1952). More directly apposite to the Biblical text are the words of James L. Crenshaw: 'If people will serve God without thought of the carrot or the stick, then religion [religious faith] will outlast any eventuality.'

TABULATION OF JOB

The story begins 1.1–2.13

1.1–12	God permits Satan to test a good man (Job) to destruction
1.13–2.10	Various calamities are inflicted on Job
2.11–13	Job is visited by his friends

The dialogue with his friends 3.1–31.40

3.1–26	Job curses the day he was born
4.1–14.22	Job's first discussion with Eliphaz, Bildad and Zophar
15.1–21.34	The second discussion of the group
22.1–27.23	The third discussion
28.1–28	Poem about where wisdom is to be found
29.1–30.31	Job sums up his defence
31.1–40	Job challenges God to disprove his innocence

Elihu's defence of God's justice 32.1–37.24

God's dialogue with Job 38.1–42.6

The story finishes happily ever after 42.7–17

Joel, book of Joel is the second of the group of texts known as the Minor Prophets in the Hebrew Bible (it comes later in the Greek SEPTUAGINT). The striking motif of the book is the LOCUST plague, which is used as a metaphor for the ultimate judgement of the 'day of the Lord'. Such characteristics involve elements of description which are reminiscent of later APOCALYPTIC texts (in DANIEL and ZECHARIAH). Only repentance and a return to God will produce a happy ending ('I will repay you for the years that the swarming locust has eaten', 2.25).

If the locusts represent invading armies, it is unclear whether the invaders are ASSYRIANS, BABYLONIANS or PERSIANS. This would affect the dating of the book, as these possibilities range from the 8th to 4th centuries BCE. Its literary and poetic character, and its more positive attitude to religious ritual, might favour a later date.

The identity of the prophet is unknown, as his patronymic (1.1) is not found elsewhere in the Bible. The two parts of his name ('Joel') have the same meaning as 'Elijah' but in reverse order = 'The Lord is My God'. PETER'S sermon at PENTECOST (Acts 2.17–21) quotes extensively from Joel 2.28–32 ('your sons and your daughters shall prophesy...') as part of a later call to repentance, interpreting the DEATH OF CHRIST as the cosmic turning-point.

John, apostle, son of Zebedee The sons of Zebedee, including his brother JAMES as well as John, were early followers of Jesus, who called them *Boanerges* (a Greek version of Aramaic/Hebrew apparently meaning 'Sons of Thunder' – Mark 3.17). Together with PETER they comprised an inner circle of the DISCIPLES. John (or Johanan) is a common Hebrew name, meaning 'God has been gracious' (1 Chronicles 26.3; Ezra 10.6). John's life as a Galilean fisherman, the events reported in the Gospels, his contacts in Jerusalem, the characterization as 'the BELOVED DISCIPLE' and the special relationship to MARY, Jesus' mother, his exile to PATMOS, and the writing of five books of the New Testament attributed to him (the Gospel, three letters and the book of REVELATION), all seem at the outset to be too much for one lifetime. If it is a problem, then one favoured academic solution is to think of a Johannine School, which shaped the traditions of and by John, and in which the apostle, and another John, an ELDER, had decisive influence. The Beloved Disciple then becomes a hagiographical memory of the school's founder, or an ideal role model of Christian discipleship. John 21.23 may indicate the problems created for the Johannine community, when a tradition that John would not die proved wrong.

There is little information about John in the ACTS OF THE APOSTLES (see chapters 3 and 4), and only one mention in the letters of PAUL (Galatians 2.9), but the book of Revelation locates John (if indeed it is the same John) on the island of Patmos, off the coast of Asia Minor. Later tradition, from Polycrates, bishop of Ephesus, c.190 CE, claims that John lived to a great age in EPHESUS. John may have been released from exile and allowed to return to his missionary charge in Asia (Eusebius, *HE* 3.20.9). The APOCRYPHAL *Acts of John* also have him based in Ephesus. In the Church calendar John's feast day is on 27 December, but there is also a commemoration of him 'Before the Latin Gate' on 6 May, which recalls the later tradition of an unsuccessful attempt to plunge the apostle into a pot of boiling oil outside one of the gates of Rome.

See also JOHN, GOSPEL ACCORDING TO; JOHN, LETTERS OF.

John, Gospel according to The fourth Gospel is the most poetic of all the Gospels, opening with one of the greatest passages of poetic prose in the language, rich with metaphor and dense with philosophical ideas. While the other three canonical Gospels are often studied together, to see their literary relationship, John's may seem to stand apart. Not only is it different in style, but it also contains a large amount of distinctive material; the ministry of Jesus is clearly set over a pattern of three years (PASSOVER occurs three times); and the activity is centred on JERUSALEM (mentioned frequently from chapter 2 onwards), rather than GALILEE. This raises questions about John's standpoint: did he set out to be independent, or to supplement or correct the other Gospels, and was he writing a spiritual Gospel rather than an historical narrative? Other scholars emphasize the historical tradition in John, and even its priority and earlier date, reflecting a strongly Jewish setting comparable with that of the DEAD SEA SCROLLS.

The John Rylands Library in Manchester possesses a fragment (P. Ryl. 457) of text from John 18 (parts of verses 31–33 and 37–38) which is probably the oldest piece of Christian writing to have survived, and certainly the oldest witness to this Gospel, as it dates from the first half of the 2nd century CE. If this Gospel was being used in

Egypt around 125 CE, it is argued that John's Gospel must have been written, probably in EPHESUS, before the end of the 1st century.

In GENESIS, at the beginning of the Bible, God is presented as bringing the CREATION into existence by the spoken word ('Let there be...'). In deliberate parallel to these opening words of Genesis, John presents God as now bringing salvation into existence by his spoken Word, in the person of Jesus, who is the WORD of God. (In *The Message* rendering of John 1.1: 'The Word was first, the Word present to God, God present to the Word. The Word was God, in readiness for God from day one.') The scene is set for the Gospel which is essentially 'following the One from Above' (*see also* ASCENSION). After this philosophical and poetic prologue (1.1–18), the Gospel can readily be analysed in the following parts: the narrative of the ministry of Jesus and the witnesses to him, up to the end of chapter 12; the Last Supper (*see* EUCHARIST) followed by an extended discourse between Jesus and his DISCIPLES (chapters 13–17); the account of the Passion and RESURRECTION of Jesus (chapters 18–20); and an epilogue in chapter 21, which may reveal something of the later expectations of the community whose Gospel this was.

Traditionally this Gospel was believed to be the work of JOHN THE APOSTLE, designated as the BELOVED DISCIPLE. Modern scholarship, also investigating John's letters (see next entry), while not tending to deny absolutely any link with John, often places the authorship within a Johannine school and therefore at one or two removes from the son of Zebedee.

TABULATION OF JOHN

Prologue 1.1–18	The eternal origins and relationships of Jesus set out with regard to his earthly ministry

The early ministry 1.19–6.71

1.19–34	The work of John the Baptist
1.35–51	Jesus gains his first disciples
2.1–12	The first sign at the Cana wedding
2.13–25	The cleansing of the Temple
3.1–21	The conversation with Nicodemus
3.22–36	The difference between Jesus and John the Baptist
4.1–42	Jesus in Samaria
4.43–54	The second sign – the cure of the official's son
5.1–47	The third sign – Jesus justifies the Sabbath cure of the cripple by the pool
6.1–71	The fourth sign – the feeding of the 5000 and the Eucharistic teaching; includes the fifth sign – the walking on the water 6.16–21

The growing controversy over Jesus' status 7.1–11.57

7.1–52	Trouble in Jerusalem
7.53–8.11	(The woman taken in adultery)
8.12–59	Jesus' origins are contested
9.1–41	The sixth sign – Jesus cures a blind man on the Sabbath, and causes a debate on true sight

10.1–42	Jesus teaches about the Good Shepherd and is charged with blasphemy
11.1–44	The seventh sign – the raising of Lazarus and teaching on the resurrection
11.45–57	The plot to kill Jesus

Holy Week 12.1–13.38

12.1–8	Mary anoints Jesus
12.9–11	The plot to kill Lazarus
12.12–26	The entry into Jerusalem
12.27–50	Jesus sums up his ministry and faces his death
13.1–38	The Last Supper and the foot-washing

The farewell discourses 14.1–16.33

14.1–14	Jesus is the way to the Father
14.15–31	The role of the Holy Spirit
15.1–16.4a	Jesus is the true Vine; persecution is to come
16.4b–33	Jesus' departure

Jesus' prayer 17.1–26

| 17.1–19 | Jesus prays for the unity and sanctity of the present disciples as he prepares himself for death |
| 17.20–26 | Jesus also prays for coming generations |

The Passion 18.1–19.16a

| 18.1–11 | Jesus is arrested |
| 18.12–19.16 | Jewish and Roman trials and Peter's denial |

The death and burial of Jesus 19.16b–42

| 19.16b–30 | The Crucifixion |
| 19.31–42 | The piercing and burial of Jesus |

The resurrection 20.1–21.25

20.1–18	The empty tomb and Jesus' appearance to Mary Magdalene
20.19–29	Jesus and the disciples meet in the house
20.30–31	The purpose of the Gospel is stated
21.1–25	Jesus in Galilee speaks to Peter about the future

John, letters of Strictly these three letters are anonymous, but there has never been a time when they were not claimed to be by John, even if the precise identity of 'John' was a matter of dispute. In theological terms, the first letter is by far the most significant, for its profound thought and simplicity of expression, and for the relationship with JOHN'S GOSPEL. The second letter has some parallels with the first, but claims to be by someone calling himself 'the ELDER'. The third letter is also from the Elder, but is primarily of interest because of the enigma it presents about early Church politics. All three letters have a definite bearing on the debate about orthodoxy and heresy in the early Church.

Modern thinking about authorship has tended to focus on the idea of a Johannine

School (*see* JOHN, APOSTLE) which leaves flexible the relationship of any of this material to the apostle. There are strong echoes between the Gospel and 1 John, but also a sense of dilution or lesser application of the great Gospel themes in the letter (see John 15.13 and 1 John 3.16–17). It would be possible to see 1 John as preceding the Gospel, and as the means by which apostolic input reaches the Gospel. But mostly the letter is seen as a sequel to the Gospel, giving a practical application, limited by the local context, to the Gospel's great themes.

1 John invites special comment for its beginning and ending, distinct from the usual letter formulae. The beginning has echoes of the prologue to John's Gospel, but some important differences: the Greek word *logos* now means 'message' about Christ, rather than a name ('WORD') for Christ himself. As time has elapsed in the Christian community, it seems important to stress the direct relationship to the original experience of Christ himself ('the HISTORICAL JESUS') on the part of the DISCIPLES. The final verse (5.21) is a puzzle, but presumably refers to the warning against the teaching of the author's opponents (the 'ANTICHRISTS'), as attacked in the body of this letter. 1 John contains memorable phrases of theological depth, which retain the reader's interest (2.1–2; 2.17; 4.8; 5.4); the reference to the TRINITY found in some manuscripts at 5.7 is not part of the original text.

In 2 John 'the elect Lady' is probably a metaphor for the CHURCH; opposition has clearly hardened, and even the normal custom of Christian HOSPITALITY is to be denied to the opponents. 3 John provides three particular names: Gaius the addressee; and Diotrephes and Demetrius who are on opposite sides of the argument. No more is known, outside this letter; it is possible that Diotrephes was the leader of the opponents attacked in the other letters. At this stage the labels 'orthodox' and 'heretic' might perhaps be applied to either side of the argument.

John the Baptist The traditional birthplace of John the Baptist is at Ain Karim ('the spring of the vineyard') on the western outskirts of Jerusalem.

According to JOSEPHUS (*Antiquities* 18.116–119) John was a down-to-earth Jewish prophet and baptizer, whom Josephus would naturally compare with the HELLENISTIC type of ethical teacher. His public message on SIN and repentance made him popular among his fellow Jews. He was executed as a potential threat to the local ruler Herod Antipas (*see* HERODIAN DYNASTY). The Gospels give a somewhat different picture: a man with a unique childhood (although the story is told in parallel with that of Jesus, his relative, in LUKE 1) and an ascetic lifestyle, who in adult life withdrew into the desert, dressed in animal skins and ate a subsistence diet. His mission was to prepare his followers for the coming of Jesus. He died at the whim of a female member of the Herodian household; he may have posed a personal rather than a political threat (see Mark 6.14–29). His accusations of royal adultery would support this.

John's action in baptizing Jesus raised some problems among early Christians (particularly those from a Jewish background), if Jesus was to be regarded as sinless by nature (see the discussion in MATTHEW 3.14–15). Gregory Thaumaturgus expressed John's problem at length: 'How shall I touch thy undefiled head? How shall I stretch out my right hand over thee who hast stretched out the heavens as a curtain and established the earth upon the waters? How shall I stretch out my servile fingers over thy divine head? How shall I wash the spotless and the sinless? How shall I enlighten the light?'

There is more than one site in the lower JORDAN valley associated with John's mission of repentance BAPTISM. This is unsurprising, given that the course of the Jordan altered widely in antiquity, that it is reasonable to assume that John baptized in more than one place, and that the SYNOPTIC Gospels, referring to the baptism of Jesus, do not say whether it was on the east or the west of the river. John's Gospel is more specific ('Bethany beyond Jordan' at 1.26–28 and 'Aenon near Salim' at 3.23). *See also* BETHABARA.

According to Josephus, John was taken to the palace of Herod Antipas at Machaerus (Mukawir) and was beheaded there. (Machaerus – on the Jordanian side of the Dead Sea – was originally built as a frontier fortress by Alexander Jannaeus.) The traditional site of his burial is again some distance away in the north, at Sebaste (SAMARIA/Sabastiyeh), where a tomb of the 1st century CE, a chapel, and later Byzantine and Crusader churches mark the spot, near the reputed tomb of ELISHA. (There is also a smaller ruined basilica built where a separate burial of a head was discovered.) As John the Baptist was often regarded in Christian tradition as ELIJAH the prophet, returning as the forerunner of the MESSIAH, it would have made theological sense for John to be buried, or be thought to have been buried, alongside Elisha his disciple and successor.

John Hyrcanus *See* HASMONEANS.

John Mark Mark was a common Latin name in the Roman world, so one must be careful with identifications. A certain John Mark is mentioned in Acts 12.12 as the son of the Mary to whose house PETER goes when released from prison, presumably because it was a meeting place of Christian believers. It is then said, in Acts 12.25, that John Mark accompanied PAUL (Saul) and BARNABAS on an early missionary journey; he was the cause of a dispute between Paul and Barnabas on a later journey. The last mention of John Mark in Acts is when he and Barnabas go off on an independent mission (Acts 15.36–40). There are other references to possibly the same Mark in Philemon 24; Colossians 4.10 (as the cousin of Barnabas); 2 Timothy 4.11; 1 Peter 5.13. Traditionally it has been assumed that these are all the same Mark; if so, there are possible consequences: firstly that he was later reconciled with Paul; and secondly that as an associate of Peter he was the author of MARK'S GOSPEL. But it is impossible to be sure.

Jonadab *See* RECHABITES.

Jonah, book of The fifth book in the collection of Minor Prophets is of a different order from the rest. It resembles RUTH in the Hebrew Bible or TOBIT in the APOCRYPHA in being a literary narrative with folk-tale characteristics. It is not a collection of oracles, but could be described as the story of 'Jonah the Moaner', a satirical account of a prophet's activities, or more particularly of his strenuous efforts to avoid doing his job. Jonah the prophet, son of Amittai, is otherwise mentioned at 2 Kings 14.25.

The prophet is called to go to the ASSYRIANS in NINEVEH, for historical reasons hardly Israel's favourite nation, as the book of NAHUM also reveals. Jonah is a com-

Jonah and the Whale Jonah 1–2

plex, very human figure, who first runs away from God, then shows great faith throughout his entombment in the whale; he confronts the Ninevites courageously and delivers a one-verse oracle (3.4) which is wonderfully successful. Finally he berates God for having the effrontery to forgive the Ninevites rather than inflicting upon them the terrible judgement that Jonah had prophesied.

God's question at 4.11 has wider implications for readers of the book. The purpose of such satire is to stimulate reaction on the issues raised by the book, notably the relationship between Jews and the GENTILE nations of the world, and the problem of undeserved forgiveness. For this reason it is an appropriate text to be read for reflection on the afternoon of YOM KIPPUR, the Day of Atonement.

The New Testament refers to the story of Jonah and the Ninevites at Matthew 12.38–41 and Luke 11.29–32. The echoing of the three-day period Jonah spent in the whale by the three days for Jesus between crucifixion and RESURRECTION suggests that Jonah is seen as a prototype of Christ's entombment and resurrection (*see also* NUMBER SYMBOLISM). In the Christian art of the catacombs Jonah often appears with a ship or a sea creature in this sense, as an Old Testament prototype figure who, like DANIEL in the lions' den, overcame certain death.

Jonathan (son of Mattathias) *See* KEDESH; MACCABEES.

Jonathan (son of Saul) Jonathan was the oldest son of King SAUL, and a close friend of DAVID. He first appears in 1 Samuel 14 when he has secured a victory over the PHILISTINES, but is condemned to die because he has disobeyed his father by taking food from a honeycomb. (The casting of the lots URIM AND THUMMIM reveal his guilt.) But the people intervene and ransom Jonathan.

In 1 Samuel 18 Jonathan makes a covenant of friendship with David. Some have interpreted this as perhaps indicating a relationship of HOMOSEXUALITY. In chapters 19 and 20 Jonathan keeps to the covenant, while risking his own life in defending David against King Saul. Jonathan and Saul both die in the battle against the Philistines on Mount Gilboa (1 Samuel 31); when David hears the news, his lament (in 2 Samuel 1.17–27) ranks as one of the Bible's earliest poems and one of the world's great and memorable dirges.

Joppa *See* TRADE.

Jordan (river; valley) The river Jordan (in Hebrew *ha-yarden*) flows from north to south, from the slopes of Hermon above the Sea of GALILEE and down to the DEAD SEA. It flows in the Palestinian section of the deep Rift Valley which extends from southern Turkey to south-east Africa. The Jordan is therefore flowing for the most part well below sea level and is fenced in by steep cliffs, particularly on the eastern side. One of its headwaters from Mount Hermon is the Banyasi which flows past the sacred cavern at Paneas, known in the New Testament as CAESAREA PHILIPPI (see Mark 8.27–29). The streams collect at Lake Huleh, a shallow lake slightly above sea level, which has now been drained. The road crossing south of Huleh was guarded by the Bronze Age city of HAZOR. South of Huleh the Jordan descends rapidly below sea level through a narrow gorge cut in the basalt to emerge at Galilee. Below Galilee the Jordan meanders for almost 200 miles in covering a straight-line distance of only 65 miles down to the Dead Sea.

Joseph (favourite son of Jacob) This Joseph is the Old Testament patriarch whose story fills the concluding chapters of Genesis. He was the favourite son of his father JACOB, by his second wife RACHEL. Jacob's other sons were roused to jealousy by this favouritism, and conspired to sell him into slavery. The tables were turned when Joseph rose to a prominent position under Pharaoh in EGYPT, and his brothers came to Egypt to beg for food during a critical famine, while Joseph was in charge of the administration of famine relief (one of the five key Egyptian offices, that of Overseer of the Granaries, corresponds to Genesis 41.48–49). Joseph and his brothers remain in Egypt, and Joseph dies and is embalmed there, according to the Egyptian custom. But the end of GENESIS sets the scene for the EXODUS or departure from Egypt and the return to the Promised Land. The highly literary character and construction of the Joseph narratives (literarily a 'romance') play an important role in the larger story of Israel. They contain fascinating scenes, such as the attempt by Potiphar's wife to seduce Joseph, and Joseph's skill in the interpretation of dreams (the dream motif is echoed in the experience of the later Joseph in Matthew's story of Jesus' birth – Matthew 1–2). This literary shape of the Joseph story has been translated into a new medium, with the musical *Joseph and the Amazing Technicolor Dreamcoat* by Tim Rice and Andrew Lloyd Webber that is still evolving, with increased popularity, from its earliest form in 1968.

Joseph (husband of Mary) Information about Joseph, the husband of MARY and the legal father of JESUS, is sparse and largely confined to the opening chapters of the Gospels of MATTHEW and LUKE. Both Gospels record that Joseph was a descendant of King DAVID, and confirm this by a detailed genealogical list. Matthew's Gospel tells the story of Jesus' birth from Joseph's perspective (while Luke's version is focused on Mary); there is a possible echo of the Old Testament patriarch Joseph (see previous entry) in the references to dreams. In Matthew 13.55 Joseph is described by the Greek word *tekton*, which has traditionally been understood as 'carpenter' or worker in wood; some popular paintings (e.g. by Blake or Holman Hunt) show Jesus as a young apprentice in a carpenter's workshop. It is more likely that the Greek word means 'craftsman' or 'builder', and it is plausible that Joseph in this line of business would have been involved in the construction of the new town of SEPPHORIS.

Joseph of Arimathea In the Gospel accounts it is Joseph of Arimathea, a wealthy member of the SANHEDRIN, who asks Pilate for Jesus' body after the CRUCIFIXION, so as to provide for it a proper burial. One can only speculate about his personal reasons for doing this. Matthew's Gospel (27.57–60) emphasizes that Joseph was a rich man; for the Evangelist this could be a fulfilment of the Old Testament prophecy of ISAIAH 53.9 (the association of the suffering servant with a rich man in his death). The most natural reason is that Joseph was an admirer, a secret follower and DISCIPLE of Jesus. But it has also been suggested that Joseph was a close male relative of Jesus, deputizing for his human father Joseph (see previous entry), if indeed it was the responsibility of a close relative to dispose of a crucified body under both Roman and Israelite law. (Burial was certainly mandatory in Judaism, as is still the case today in Israel with the search for body parts that are the remains of victims of suicide bombings.) Subsequently this Joseph figures as a persecuted Jew in several APOCRYPHAL texts, and in medieval literature he is said to have fled, or travelled as a merchant, to Britain and to Glastonbury, as the guardian of the Holy GRAIL.

Josephus, Flavius This significant Jewish historian was born 37/38 CE of a HASMO-NEAN family of Jewish priestly nobility and grew up within Palestinian JUDAISM. He was in Rome between 64 and 66 CE, then was the leader of the Jewish rebels in

Galilee at the start of the JEWISH WAR. He was taken prisoner by Vespasian in 67 and spared because he prophesied that Vespasian would become emperor. When this happened, Vespasian freed him and he joined TITUS' entourage at the capture of Jerusalem. Subsequently he was made a Roman citizen and granted a pension, writing his pro-Roman account of the Jewish War while living in Rome. He sought to commend Jewish history and culture 'with the thought that all the Greeks might perceive it to be worthy of serious attention' (1.5), retelling Biblical narratives for a wider readership in his *Antiquities of the Jews*. He died in Rome sometime after 100 CE.

Joshua Joshua, the son of Nun, was an Ephraimite (apparently renamed by Moses, according to Numbers 13.16; for his genealogy see 1 Chronicles 7.20–27). He became military leader of ancient Israel, and was primarily responsible for the conquest of the cities of the land of CANAAN, as recorded in the first half of the book of Joshua. He first appears on the scene at Exodus 17.9 leading the people against the Amalekites after the EXODUS from Egypt. He was assistant and then successor to MOSES; his faithfulness (as one of the spies sent to Canaan) allowed him to enter the Promised Land, when Moses was not able to do so (see Numbers 13–14). His military exploits included the exceptionally memorable occasions when he demolished the walls of JERICHO (Joshua 6) and when he commanded sun and moon to stand still over GIBEON, thus giving more time to achieve an Israelite victory (see Joshua 10.12–14). His leadership qualities as Moses' successor were also shown by his role in the ceremony of covenant renewal (see Joshua 24). His death and burial are recorded at Joshua 24.29–30 and Judges 2.8–9 in the territory allotted to EPHRAIM. See also next entry.

Joshua, book of It is sometimes thought that the PENTATEUCH (or the five books at the start of the Old Testament) should really be 'six books' with Joshua as the sixth. This would make sense because Joshua supplies a necessary climax to the opening narrative history with an account of the conquest of the Promised Land. Some scholars identify similar source materials in all six books, and point to Joshua 24 (the speech at the COVENANT ceremony at SHECHEM) as the climax which represents the overall pattern of these books in miniature. Alternatively the book of Joshua can be taken more closely with the following books of JUDGES, SAMUEL and KINGS, as part of a theologically motivated narrative of history, in which the ideology of DEUTERONOMY is worked out on the ground. The modern arrangement of Biblical books may allow readers to have the best of both worlds.

Chapters 6–12 describe the conquest of CANAAN (relatively few stories of actual warfare, inviting comparison with the account in Judges), while chapters 13–19 deal with the Settlement of the land, and its allocation by sacred lot to the Israelite tribes. Israel appears as a mighty army of twelve tribes, but the ultimate credit for the conquest rests with the enabling action of God. An archaeological dig on Mount Ebal has revealed what may be the altar stone, dedicated by Joshua to the true God (Joshua 8.30). Joseph W. Trigg says that, 'the Book of Joshua recounts the Hebrew conquest of Canaan as a war of extermination'. Yet the book offers a succinct account of how his people killed the king and taxed the natives, but 'did not utterly drive them out'. This altar stone may represent Israel's claim to territory, but no sooner had it been uncovered than a non-Jewish hand scrawled graffiti on it. For modern readers this will suggest those moral questions associated with JUST WAR theory and the problems of the Middle East peace.

Josiah Josiah may be reckoned as the most outstanding king of Judah, over which he reigned for 31 years in the latter half of the 7th century BCE (see 2 Kings 23.25; Jeremiah 22.15–16). He was made king at the age of eight in 639 BCE following the assassination of his father Amon. His was a reign of expansion and religious reform, the result firstly of the decline of the ASSYRIAN Empire, and secondly because of the reported discovery of 'the book of the law' in the TEMPLE at Jerusalem. His religious reform (c.621 BCE – see 2 Kings 23) sought to eliminate foreign worship and centralize the cult in Jerusalem (which suggests that the law book which set the agenda was probably a copy of DEUTERONOMY). Josiah was killed (or fatally injured) at Megiddo (*see* ARMAGEDDON) in 609 BCE in a political action in support of the BABYLONIANS against the invading EGYPTIAN Pharaoh Neco II, who was trying to bolster the power of Assyria.

jot and tittle This phrase comes from an older translation (KING JAMES VERSION) of the teaching of Jesus in the SERMON ON THE MOUNT. In the New RSV Matthew 5.18 reads: 'Until heaven and earth pass away, not one letter, not one stroke of a letter, will pass from the law [*see* TORAH] until all is accomplished.' (See also Luke 16.17.) The first letter referred to is the smallest letter of the HEBREW alphabet yodh (corresponding to the Greek iota – 'iott' in Tyndale's translation, hence 'jot'). The second reference is to a small stroke of the pen (a 'tittle' or diacritical mark), vital to distinguish between two Hebrew letters, beth and kaph.

Jubilee, year of Chapter 25 of LEVITICUS is concerned with ways of regulating the Israelites' proper use of the land, that is the land of CANAAN, 'promised' to them as a settled society. There are three distinct regulations: the SABBATH rest for the land (the fallow year); the occasion of the Jubilee and the restoration of the land to its original occupants; and, thirdly, procedures for the release of Israelites who were in debt-SLAVERY. At the heart of such discussion about land is the theological statement that the land belongs to God and is only gifted by him to the people.

According to Leviticus 25.8–55 there are special regulations after a period of 49 years (seven successive groups – sabbaths – of seven years). At the Day of Atonement (YOM KIPPUR), when the ram's horn is sounded, there will be a declaration of 'liberty throughout Israel', announcing the year of Jubilee. The land is to remain uncultivated for a second year (the 50th year) following the sabbatical year of the 49th year. Land that has been purchased at any time during the previous 50 years is then to revert to its original owners or settlers. And those who had been forced by POVERTY or bankruptcy to sell themselves into slavery were to gain their freedom.

These measures are clearly driven by a theological agenda. It is debatable to what extent they would ever have been observed. Apart from Numbers 36.4 (and just possibly Judges 3.11) the Bible does not mention the actual observance of the Jubilee regulations. Later JUDAISM argues that the rules only apply when all Jews live in the land in the original territories of their tribes, although ultra-Orthodox Jews today will still observe the pattern of the sabbatical year. Interest in the idea of the Jubilee has been reawakened more widely in recent times in the context of the international campaigns for debt relief.

Jubilees, book of *Jubilees* is one of the texts of the Pseudepigrapha (*see* JEWISH LITERATURE). It was composed originally in HEBREW, but now exists as a whole only in the later ETHIOPIC translation from the Greek. Some fragments are known in Greek and Hebrew, including significant fragments found at QUMRAN. These last may well point to an important link between the writer of *Jubilees* and the Qumran community, already suggested by a full reference to *Jubilees* in the Damascus Document.

The book is a midrashic exposition of the Biblical books of GENESIS and part of EXODUS (up to chapter 19), in the form of a secret revelation delivered to MOSES on Mount SINAI by an angel. The name of the book comes from its practice of dividing Israel's history into 'JUBILEE' periods, each of 49 years; these are then subdivided into seven units of seven weeks of years (*see* NUMBER SYMBOLISM). The precise date of the book is disputed, but is likely to be in the middle of the 2nd century BCE or possibly slightly earlier, at the time of the revolt of the MACCABEES.

Judaeo-Christians *See* JEWISH-CHRISTIANS.

Judah Judah is the fourth son of JACOB by his first wife LEAH (see Genesis 29.35). The blessing by Jacob, recorded in Genesis 49.9–12, makes Judah the ruler, so displacing the original priority of REUBEN. It is likely that it represents the later, enhanced situation in the time of King DAVID, when the tribe of Judah, seemingly named after its ancestor, Jacob's son, has become the kingdom or state of JUDAH, OR JUDAEA. David is ruling, initially from HEBRON as his capital, over a confederation of the southern tribes.

In the New Testament, Judah comes first in the list of the tribes that have been 'sealed' in REVELATION 7.5; *see also* LION, as in Revelation 5.5. According to the argument of HEBREWS 7.14, Jesus' descent from Judah is appropriate, because 'in connection with that tribe Moses said nothing about priests'.

Judah, or Judaea A geographical region, the highlands or mountains of Judah between Hebron and Jerusalem; it is debatable whether the tribal or the geographical name came first. The geographical name was applied to the independent country (or rump of the Davidic kingdom) which was left after the kingdom divided, with Israel in the north rebelling under JEROBOAM I; it also applied to those who returned from EXILE in the Persian period. 'Judaea' is the Greek and Latin version of the name, applicable in the Hellenistic and Roman periods.

Judaism The term Judaism refers to the life and religion of the Jews, and first came into use in the 2nd century BCE, during the time of the MACCABEES (see 2 Maccabees 2.21; 8.1; 14.38; and 4 Maccabees 4.26). Judaism enjoyed remarkable success, and the favour of the Roman rulers, in the Greco-Roman world (*see* DIASPORA). By contrast the common pagan attitude was incredulous, derogatory, and highly regrettable: 'How could one take seriously a people who adhered to silly superstitions, who would have no social or sexual intercourse with GENTILES, who wasted every seventh day in idleness, who did not eat ham or pork chops, and who mangled their genitals?'

The Jewish religion, seriously considered, has two basic axioms: there is a negative rule by which the one and only God may not be associated with other gods (everything associated with them is an abomination to God); and there is a positive rule whereby God is uniquely associated with his people, in that he made a COVENANT with Israel and gave the TORAH as a way of maintaining this covenant.

PAUL uses the term Judaism when referring to the religion in which he was brought up (Galatians 1.14); incidentally he never uses the term CHRISTIANITY. Subsequently 'Judaism' and 'Christianity' are used in contrast to one another by writers such as Ignatius, bishop of Antioch, at the beginning of the 2nd century CE. Judaism is essentially a religious identity, although at various times throughout history, and particularly in modern times since the establishment of the state of Israel, this identity can mutate into a national one, and Judaism become ZIONISM.

Judas the Galilean *See* GAMALIEL; ZEALOTS.

Judas Iscariot Judas is notorious in Christian tradition as the DISCIPLE who betrayed Jesus to the Jewish authorities, facilitating his arrest (see Mark 14; John 13, 18). In a modern treatment such as the musical *Jesus Christ Superstar* he has a prominent role as the anti-hero. The meaning of his cognomen (Iscariot) is not entirely certain: he could well be Judas, the 'man from Kerioth' (a town in Judaea in the south, while other disciples of Jesus came from GALILEE); alternatively it could be a version of the Latin *sicarius* (brigand or terrorist).

In the first three Gospels (Matthew 10.4; Mark 3.19; Luke 6.16), he comes last in the listing of disciples and is labelled as the betrayer. In John he is called a devil, and accused of pilfering from the common purse (6.70–71; 12.1–6; 13.29). All four Gospels tell how by agreement he led a party to arrest Jesus; while John has Jesus identifying himself, in the others Judas marks Jesus out by kissing him. Only Matthew mentions the 30 pieces of silver paid to Judas for his betrayal, and records his subsequent repentance and suicide (26.15; 27.3–8). Acts 1.16–20 also refers to Judas' death in what became known as *akeldama* or the 'field of blood'.

The reasons for Judas' betrayal are the subject of speculation: was it for financial gain, or out of impatience that Jesus was not fulfilling his expected messianic role? Did Judas hope to precipitate a climactic action by Jesus? Presumably Judas' advice was needed in order to identify for the authorities a quiet place where Jesus might be removed without disturbance, even at festival time. The kiss would have been an unusual action in public for Greco-Roman society (and so marking out Jesus for the soldiers), even if it might have been customary for Jews, as a way for disciples to greet a rabbi. Certainly early Christians continued to use the kiss as a greeting for fellow Christians (see Romans 16.16; 1 Peter 5.14).

A work called the *Gospel of Judas*, and linked to a GNOSTIC sect, was known to the 2nd-century Church Father Irenaeus, bishop of Lyon. A codex in COPTIC (Sahidic dialect) containing this and a mixture of other works (including for example *The First Apocalypse of James* and *The Epistle of Peter to Philip*, as well as some works in Greek) was discovered in an Egyptian tomb during the 1970s. It was acquired by a

Swiss foundation on the international art market, and they arranged for a translated section to be published in the April 2006 edition of *National Geographic* magazine. The work claims that Judas did what he did at Jesus' request, so enabling Christ's destiny to be fulfilled, and thus making Judas into a hero rather than the vilest of traitors. In Gnostic terms, by Judas' action Jesus was enabled to escape his physical body and enter heaven as pure spirit.

Judas Maccabeus Judas Maccabeus was the leader of the Jewish revolt against the Syrian king Antiochus IV Epiphanes, as recorded in 1 Maccabees 2–9 and 2 Maccabees 2–15 (*see also* MACCABEES). He was responsible for the recapture of JERUSALEM and the rededication of the TEMPLE (the Feast of Dedication is celebrated in the Jewish calendar as HANUKKAH). He was killed in battle in 161 BCE.

Jude (apostle) In the listing of the DISCIPLES of Jesus at Luke 6.16, Jude is referred to as 'Judas of James', and in John 14.22 he is called 'Judas, not Iscariot'. It may well be correct to identify him with THADDAEUS (or Lebbaeus), who is named in the same place in Matthew's and Mark's listings of disciples. Luke's reference to 'Judas of James' may naturally be taken as meaning 'son of James', but it could also mean 'brother of James', and, if so, possibly also the brother of Jesus (see Matthew 13.55 and JAMES, BROTHER OF JESUS), and so equally possibly the author of the letter of Jude (see next entry).

Jude, letter of Jude is termed a 'catholic' or 'general' epistle, because of its open designation of the intended recipients. It is possibly one of the earliest writings of the New Testament, and was certainly accepted early into the canon of the New Testament. Much of its material was adopted by the author of 2 PETER; the warning against false prophetic teachers was there reapplied in a more Hellenistic setting, compared with the early Palestinian context of Jude.

The letter claims to be written by the 'brother of James' and therefore one of the brothers of Jesus (according to Mark 6.3). Other identifications of the name Jude are 'Judas son of James' who appears in Luke's listing of Jesus' disciples (Luke 6.16; Acts 1.13); or Thomas, who is also called 'Judas Thomas' in the *Gospel of Thomas* (*see* THOMAS). At all events the letter's contents require a Palestinian JEWISH-CHRISTIAN author, which by no means excludes the claimed author (see 1 Corinthians 9.5).

The letter is written to confront a crisis where inspired prophets are relying on the AUTHORITY of visionary revelations to override any moral authority and behave in a liberated and indulgent manner. Jude insists on moral obedience, and the importance of living out the gospel in faith. His argument is based on Old Testament examples, expounded in an early Jewish midrashic manner; he also uses material from extracanonical tradition (which would have been in the Jewish public domain), quoting from *1 Enoch*, and a story about the burial of Moses, which probably came from the *Testament of Moses*.

Jude concludes with a magnificent commendation and doxology (24–25), which has been widely used in Christian liturgy.

Judges, book of The sources of this book are probably local histories of tribal conflicts, which have been fashioned into a national history of Israel following the death of JOSHUA. The stories concern 12 named figures who 'judged' Israel, hence the name of the book. But the term 'judge' can be misleading, since they were really military leaders, occasionally with a judicial function. Some are major leaders, whose exploits are described; others are minor figures, merely listed in 10.1–5 and 12.8–15. The stories may be arranged so that good examples of leadership (Othniel, DEBORAH, Jephthah) alternate with less good examples (Ehud, GIDEON, SAMSON). The story of Deborah is particularly interesting, not only as evidence of a woman leader, but also because it is documented in two parallel versions in prose and poetry (chapters 4 and 5). But the theological message of the book is that true leadership belongs to the universal Judge (11.27), who has the sole right to exercise kingly rule, and in whose spirit these charismatic tribal leaders operated. The final editing expresses these theological judgements (e.g. 2.11–16) and echoes the creed of covenant renewal (6.7–10; see also Joshua 24).

The impression given by the book of Joshua was of total conquest of CANAAN. Judges appears to provide a rather different perspective of local difficulties, continuing warfare with the Canaanites, and threats from other tribal groups, neighbouring states, and the presence of the PHILISTINES. This is also the situation in the following book, 1 SAMUEL, named after the prophet who was also a 'judge' and effectively established the monarchy by anointing SAUL and then DAVID.

Judith, book of The book of Judith is known only from Greek (SEPTUAGINT) versions and is regarded as an APOCRYPHAL or Deuterocanonical work in the Christian traditions. If there was a Hebrew or ARAMAIC original (as St Jerome claimed), it has disappeared. It is likely to have been the work of a Palestinian Jew in the HELLENISTIC PERIOD. The story contains historical references belonging to several different centuries. A principal character, Holofernes, belongs to the 4th century BCE campaigns of Artaxerxes III. The literary shape and style strongly suggest it was intended as didactic fiction.

The pious and beautiful heroine of the story, Judith, is responsible for relieving the siege of the city of Bethulia as it was on the point of capitulation to the ASSYRIANS. As a venture of faith she goes with her handmaid into the Assyrian camp. Here by her beauty she entices Holofernes, the army commander, to invite her into his tent. With two strokes she beheads the drunken Holofernes and conceals his head in her handmaid's sack. She flees to Bethulia, where the bloody trophy is seen as a symbol of divine deliverance. The next morning the Israelites attack and rout the Assyrians.

From later Jewish versions of the story some events are included in the liturgy for the festival of HANUKKAH. In the Christian tradition Judith is a favoured subject of art (see the works by Artemisia Gentileschi in Florence) and in literature; there is a modern poem by Vicki Feaver. Judith represents bravery, chastity, possibly revenge, and (like ESTHER) she symbolizes the Jewish people empowered by God.

Junia, Junias, or Julia PAUL, writing to ROME, sends greetings (at Romans 16.7) to someone variously named Junia, Junias, or even (by some) Julia. Junias is a masculine name (otherwise unattested) while Junia is a woman's name. She could be the wife of Andronicus, mentioned in the same verse. Clearly these two are numbered among Paul's co-workers, and were his companions in prison at some point. They were among the earliest followers of Christ, at least before Paul himself became a Christian. Most significantly they 'are prominent among the APOSTLES' (probably meaning that they were apostles). For this reason Junia, if it is she, is highly regarded today in the controversial area of the ordination of women to the priesthood and episcopacy.

just war 'Just war' is not itself a Biblical concept, but Christians have relied heavily on Biblical texts, mostly from the Old Testament, to justify it. *See also* WAR.

The Greek philosopher Aristotle wrote in the 4th century BCE that a war in self-defence was just. St Ambrose and St Augustine in the 4th/5th centuries CE taught that war to defend the Church against the opponents of the true faith was legitimate. This thinking permitted Christians to serve in the Roman army in order to defend the Roman Empire against the incursions of the barbarian hordes. St Thomas Aquinas in the 13th century CE taught that to be just a war must be properly authorized, and have a right cause and a just intention. Later scholars have added clauses regarding proportionality, a reasonable chance of success, and war as a last resort, as well as the immunity of non-military personnel from the effects of the fighting. So it will be seen that ethically there are two stages in the thinking about just war: when it is right to fight, and how to conduct the fighting – *ius ad bellum* and *ius in bello*.

justice One theme that runs throughout the different strands of writing in the Hebrew Bible – histories, prophecies and poetry (Psalms) – is that God is the supreme judge or arbiter of mankind, and will mete out his justice to his people (see 1 Samuel 2.10; Isaiah 3.13; Psalm 58.11). The New Testament stays with that belief; the final judgement became a standard feature of the End Time (see Matthew 25.31–46), rather than being confined to this present life. In many passages the function of judge is transferred to Jesus (see John 5.22). The divine right to judge humankind rests in God's supreme holiness and absolute truth. God judges in RIGHTEOUSNESS, but also, importantly, his characteristic of MERCY (or loving kindness) shines through (see some of the prophetic texts, such as Hosea 2.19, and LOVE).

The divine standard of justice is, or should be, the model for human justice. It holds a particular concern for the human rights of the oppressed and the poor, and it is a threat to those who abuse their positions of wealth and power (see Psalms 10.18; 72.4; Isaiah 11.4). Thus justice places great emphasis on what is fair and right. The prophet AMOS roundly condemned corruption in society (Amos 2.6–8) and spoke out against the perversion of human justice in the courts (Amos 5.10–12).

Human justice was held under the spotlight by the prophets and contrasted with divine justice. Nevertheless, short of perfection as the system undoubtedly was, in some periods more than others, a system did exist. In the period of the JUDGES – who were quasi-military leaders responding to crises, and not related to the legal system as recognized today – the avenging of perceived wrong was achieved by force of arms (see the matter of the Levite's concubine in Judges 19 and 20). Later in the Settlement period it appears that the elders of the community met regularly in the city gate, there to discuss the business of the day, and to judge questions and disputes brought to them (see Ruth 4.1–12). When there was a king, he became the final resource of the justice system, such that ABSALOM was able to attract support for his rebellion against

King DAVID by giving wistful accounts of what *he* would do (see 2 Samuel 15.4: 'If only I were judge in the land! Then all who had a suit or cause might come to me, and I would give them justice'). SOLOMON became famous for his WISDOM (1 Kings 3.16–28). The local system must have continued too.

During the period of the EXILE much work went into codifying the TORAH and its demands on God's people. Increasingly during the post-Exilic period civil administration and everyday justice was likely to be in the hands of the current superpower which governed Judaea, but the rules of the Torah, as the basis for justice, would still have been administered by religious personnel, first the PRIESTS and then later the RABBIS. This was certainly the case by New Testament times, as can be seen in the involvement of both Jews and Romans in the TRIAL OF JESUS.

K

Kabbalah This traditional system of Jewish mystical meditation became highly developed in the Middle Ages, as for example in the 13th-century Spanish Book of Zohar (Splendour). The study of Kabbalah was reserved for specialist scholars, until HASIDISM helped to widen access to its esoteric teachings from the 18th century onward; it now has a popular appeal, particularly in America, as a New Age movement, attracting the attention of celebrities including Madonna. One of the main themes of Kabbalah, as traditionally received, is meditation upon the 72 different names of God. Its extended interpretation of the CREATION of the world derives in part from the account at the beginning of GENESIS. Some traditional scholars trace the origins of Kabbalah to the action of ADAM in naming the animals in the Garden of Eden; such naming of the parts of Creation could be seen as providing an element of control.

Kabri Tel Kabri, in the western Galilee, only four miles from the Mediterranean Sea, was the centre of a prosperous CANAANITE kingdom in the 17th century BCE. It was a large city of 80 acres, defended by massive earthen ramparts. The royal palace was a labyrinth of rooms at least two storeys high. At its centre was a great hall, the floor of which was decorated with an elaborate fresco, probably painted by Minoan craftsmen from Crete. It seems that the palace suffered a sudden and total destruction, not unlike that which befell the island of Santorini.

Kadesh Barnea Kadesh Barnea was an oasis settlement in the northern part of the SINAI desert, identified with the present-day Ain el-Qudeirat. Its location is an important crossroads of the routes from EDOM to Egypt, and from Eilat to HEBRON. Following the EXODUS from Egypt the Hebrew tribes halted here for a time, because of its abundant water (Deuteronomy 1.46). Spies were sent to investigate the land of CANAAN, and there were bitter complaints against MOSES and AARON from the tribes (see Numbers 14); the waters became known as 'waters of bitterness' – Meribah – (Numbers 20.13; Psalm 95.8; see also Ezekiel 47.19). MIRIAM died at Kadesh (Numbers 20.1). Kadesh may have been used as a base for attacks against the Amalekites and the AMORITES (Numbers 14.40–45; Deuteronomy 1.44). The Hebrews left Kadesh for the plain of MOAB when they were not allowed passage by the inhabitants of Edom (Numbers 20.14–21).

Several Israelite fortresses were successively built on this site, dating from the 10th to the 6th centuries BCE, as administrative centre, outpost, or frontier post.

kashrut These are the regulations governing Jewish dietary or FOOD LAWS.

Kedesh 'Kedesh in Galilee, in the hill country of Naphtali' is about seven miles from the modern town of Kiryat Shemona, in the far north of Israel. It was one of the major CANAANITE cities which fought in the coalition led by Jabin of HAZOR that was conquered by the Israelites (JOSHUA 11). According to Joshua 20, Kedesh was made into a 'city of refuge', a place of sanctuary for anyone who kills a person 'without intent or by mistake'. In the PERSIAN and HELLENISTIC PERIODS (539–141 BCE) it seems to have been the administrative centre for the Galilee, and a place of special significance because of its close economic, political and social contact with the PHOENICIAN cities of the coast. Recent excavations have discovered in the corner of one building a cache of over 3000 Hellenistic seal impressions (*bullae*) – the largest number ever found in Israel – as well as the existence of another large building, probably an administrative centre with storerooms, and of a bath complex with frescoed walls. Kedesh was ultimately attacked by the MACCABEES under Jonathan in 144 BCE and never recovered, changing from an important centre to a rural outpost.

Kenites The Kenites were a group of people living in CANAAN before the Israelites, according to Genesis 15.19. They lived in the northern area of SINAI and the Negev, in an area well known for copper mining and smelting, which led to the theory that they were a tribe of nomadic metalworkers, whose name is related to the Hebrew word *qayin* meaning 'smith' (see Numbers 24.21–22). CAIN is also seen as their eponymous ancestor, not least because he is the ancestor of Tubal-cain (Genesis 4.22). Jethro, the father-in-law of MOSES, who was a 'priest of Midian' (Exodus 2.15–16; 3.1; 18.1), is also called a Kenite; there is confusion with the name Hobab in Judges 1.16, 4.11, who was probably Moses' 'son-in-law'. Because Moses first encountered YAHWEH when he was with Jethro, there is an unproved scholarly theory (called the Kenite hypothesis) that the religion of Yahweh originated with the Kenites. Subsequently Kenites are said to have accompanied the men of JUDAH to live in the Negev near ARAD (known as 'the Negev of the Kenites' – 1 Samuel 27.10). One Kenite family, Heber and his wife Jael, moved north to KEDESH; Jael later killed Israel's enemy Sisera in her tent (see Judges 4 and 5 and DEBORAH). According to 1 Chronicles 2.55 the Kenites were the forerunners of the RECHABITES; other versions say that they intermarried.

kerygma *Kerygma* is the Greek word for 'preaching', that is the element of proclamation in earliest Christianity, to be contrasted with the aspect of instruction (*see* DIDACHE). Particularly during the Biblical scholarship of the 20th century, this concept of 'kerygma' was emphasized as a vital clue to the understanding of how the first GOSPELS came about. Each Gospel was formulated within its own early Christian community, as that group made its own the first preaching of Jesus, within the context of that group's meeting for WORSHIP and its strategy for evangelism. But the shape of the written Gospel preserved the sense of directness of oral preaching (*see also* ORALITY).

In the words of Thomas Merton: 'for kerygma to take place there has to be a community and a sense of community. They are called together to hear the word of God proclaimed, and a proclamation is not the same as instruction. This idea of kerygmatic theology was worked out in the [nineteen] fifties to a great extent, and it is a very important idea because it involved the hearer as well as the speaker. It is the living word proclaimed in a community and received by that community with a consciousness that it is receiving the word of God.'

King James, or Authorised, Version of the Bible A new English translation of Holy Scripture was proposed at a conference of theologians and bishops at Hampton Court Palace in January 1604. Fifty-four scholars and Churchmen were allocated to six panels of translators: three for the Old Testament, two for the New, and one for the APOCRYPHA. They began work in 1606, meeting fairly regularly at Westminster Abbey, Oxford and Cambridge, with authorization to consult earlier translations (those of Tyndale, Coverdale and Whittingham's Geneva Bible). The Authorised Version appeared in 1611 but only gradually established its dominance as *the* translation in English. It had been created at the 'high noon' of the English language, of which the foremost constructs therefore were the plays of Shakespeare and the King James Version.

King of the Jews In the New Testament this term is double-edged. It appears as an ironic title in the mouth of Pontius PILATE at Mark 15.2; the charge at the CRUCIFIXION (Mark 15.26) implies sedition against Rome. In JOHN'S GOSPEL the irony is more acute: in the discussion at John 19.14–16; and in the inscription of the charge, with the chief priests' reaction, at John 19.19–22. John's version of the charge differs somewhat; in Latin it would be *Iesus Nazarenus Rex Iudaeorum* – the source of the acronym INRI seen in representations of the crucifixion. The three languages are appropriate for the different audiences: Latin for the Romans; Hebrew for the Jews; and Greek as a widely used administrative language (lingua franca). Pilate tends to ridicule Jewish kingship and underline the power of the Roman Empire as the occupying force.

But Pilate speaks more truly than he realizes in acknowledging (however ironically) the kingship of Christ. This theme is developed in John 18.33–37. Historically DAVID was the model of Israelite kingship, a model that later generations hoped to realize in the expectation of the MESSIAH. Before the Roman occupation, there had been a resurgence of kingship for the Jews under the HASMONEANS.

King's Highway *See* HIGHWAY OF THE KING.

Kingdom of God Mark 1.14–15 is the headline for Jesus' ministry: Jesus says, 'The time is fulfilled, and the kingdom of God has come near; repent, and believe in the good news.' Jesus had been baptized by JOHN THE BAPTIST and sorted out his ideas on Messiahship in the TEMPTATIONS (*see also* MESSIAH); now he was ready to start his preaching tour. But what precisely he was preaching about the Kingdom of God has exercised scholars greatly.

Jews of the 1st century CE thought that the Kingdom of God (or Kingdom of Heaven, as the more Jewish evangelist MATTHEW would have it) would involve the overthrow of the Romans by a powerful military leader or Messiah. They looked back wistfully to the great days of King DAVID, 1000 years previously, for the pattern of their ideal kingdom, and they hoped for a great political and national revival.

Jesus' ideas clashed with those of the Jews' military kingdom, and he tended to explain his version of the kingdom by telling stories (PARABLES) to get his point across. The Kingdom of God is like a man who sowed corn, or a man scattering seed, or a mustard seed, which grows to a great harvest with God's help – not by waging war (see Mark 4.1–34).

The phrase 'Kingdom of God' is better translated as kingly rule or reign, because it is not a political or geographical area like the United Kingdom or the United States of America. Instead God's kingdom is at work in the hearts of those who accept him as their king and do his will. Plainly not everyone yet accepts his rule, so God's kingdom is only partly here. Whereas it was seen as present in the life and work of Jesus and his followers, it is also claimed to be here in the lives and work of modern disciples. Yet it is still in the future as its final form (see ESCHATON), as is demonstrated in the LORD'S PRAYER: 'Your kingdom come' – Matthew 6.10. Jesus' beliefs about the Kingdom of God entail the understanding that it was imminent, but that it was non-political (see John 18.36). One needed to repent and enter it with the simplicity of a child (Mark 10.15). The rich and powerful would find it (almost?) impossible to enter (Mark 10.23), but Jesus thought that it was worth the sacrifice of home, FAMILY and possessions (Mark 10.29–31). To LOVE both God and the neighbour were the two commandments it was essential to keep (see TORAH), and then one would not be far from the Kingdom of God (Mark 12.29–34). These commandments formed the summary of the LAW. So to love God completely, to accept his kingly rule with obedience in one's life and heart, to turn from one's former bad ways in faith and simplicity, were all involved in Jesus' understanding of membership of the Kingdom of God.

The SYNOPTIC Gospels (Matthew, Mark and Luke) show Jesus at work in the kingdom. Jesus was in the kingdom as SON OF GOD, as the Messiah, doing the will of God. This is most clearly seen when he performs MIRACLES, especially of healing and EXORCISM (see Luke 11.20). It was also there in his call to repentance and preaching (Mark 1.14–15). Jesus had co-workers in the kingdom; he shared the work with special followers or DISCIPLES, both before his death and after his RESURRECTION. They carried his work on into the life of the CHURCH, which they believed then became the field for the Kingdom of God on earth, although still in its partial state. Jesus and his disciples seem to have believed that this was only a temporary arrangement, and that the complete coming of the kingdom in power was destined to happen fairly soon after his death. Certainly there seems to have been a belief that the End Time would come before the death of the original disciples (see Mark 9.1). Two thousand years on, the Christian Church still hopes for the kingdom, but more distantly.

Ironically, although Jesus was not interested in politics or nationalism, and did not intend to overthrow the Romans in a revolution, this is what his TRIAL and CRUCIFIXION were focused upon – was he a rebel seeking coronation (Mark 15.2)? JOHN'S GOSPEL debates the irony of this situation in a dramatic sequence between Pilate and Jesus (see John 18.33–19.22). The title on the cross, 'Jesus of Nazareth, the King of the Jews' (John 19.19) appears to show a complete and deliberate misunderstanding of what Jesus had actually said.

The Kingdom of God as a concept lived on in the Gospels, and was mentioned in the ACTS OF THE APOSTLES as the content of early preaching (see Acts 1.3; 8.12), but does not appear so frequently in the EPISTLES (see, for example, Romans 14.17: 'the kingdom of God is not food and drink but righteousness and peace and joy in the Holy Spirit'). The eschatological timing of the End Time naturally depended on the arrival of the kingdom, but that event was to be delayed, apparently beyond Jesus' expectations.

Kings, first and second books of These two books interpret the history of Israel, from the death of King DAVID and the accession of SOLOMON, through the division of the kingdom into two (Israel in the north and Judah in the south) following the revolt of JEROBOAM I, the fortunes of the respective kingdoms, culminating in the ASSYRIAN destruction of SAMARIA (the northern capital) and the eventual fall of Jerusalem and the EXILE of the southern leaders in BABYLON. This covers a timespan of four centuries from approximately 970 until 560 BCE. The last event recorded is the hopeful sign of the release of the exiled king of Judah, Jehoiachin, from prison in Babylon.

The interpretation of these events is theological, in accordance with the principles of the book of DEUTERONOMY (the blessings on obedience and the curses on disobedience set out in Deuteronomy 27–28). It seeks to offer an explanation of why Judah was exiled, despite the importance of the central presence of God in the TEMPLE at Jerusalem. The prayer of dedication of the Temple by King Solomon in 1 Kings 8 takes the fact of exile seriously (see verses 46–53). This interpretation during the time of exile presents a religious apologetic, a justification of God's action in judging his people, but also a message with some hope of a possible sequel to these events, if the religious lesson can be learnt.

In contrast to the hope for Judah, even while exiled in Babylon, there is no similar hope for Israel (the Northern Kingdom). The theological interpretation of events stresses with monotonous regularity the faithlessness of the northern kings. The basis of their offence is described as 'the sins of Jeroboam', namely the instruction to worship the GOLDEN CALVES (see 1 Kings 12.28 and 2 Kings 10.29) and to worship in BETHEL and DAN rather than Jerusalem, all of which is regarded by the Deuteronomistic historians as a repudiation of the COVENANT relationship with God.

kings of Israel (the United Kingdom)
The following were the kings in the earliest period, before the kingdom was divided, c.928 BCE. All suggested dates are approximate.

SAMUEL and SAUL   c.1020–1004 BCE
DAVID   c.1004–965 BCE
SOLOMON   c.965–928 BCE

The kingdom was divided at the death of Solomon.

kings of Judah (the Divided Kingdom)

The United Kingdom of Israel became divided after the death of SOLOMON *c.928 BCE.*
The following reigned in the Southern Kingdom of Judah; all suggested dates are
approximate.

Rehoboam	c.928–911 BCE
Abijah (Ahijam)	c.911–908 BCE
Asa	c.908–867 BCE
Jehoshaphat	c.867–846 BCE
Jehoram	c.846–843 BCE
Ahaziah	c.843–842 BCE
Athaliah	c.842–836 BCE
Joash (JEHOASH)	c.836–798 BCE
Amaziah	c.798–769 BCE
Uzziah (Azariah)	c.769–743 BCE
Jotham (regent)	c.758–743 BCE
Jotham (king)	c.743–735 BCE
Jehoahaz (Ahaz)	c.735–727 BCE
HEZEKIAH	c.727–698 BCE
MANASSEH	c.698–642 BCE
Amon	c.642–640 BCE
JOSIAH	639–609 BCE
Jehoahaz II (Shallum)	609 BCE
Jehoiakim (Eliakim)	609–598 BCE
Jehoiachin (Jeconiah)	598–597 BCE
ZEDEKIAH (Mattaniah)	596–586 BCE

The first deportation to Babylonia took place in 597 BCE, and the fall of Jerusalem and the
second deportation in 587/6 BCE.

kings of the Northern (Divided) Kingdom of Israel

The Northern Kingdom lasted from after the death of SOLOMON *c.928 BCE until the fall of*
SAMARIA *in 722/1 BCE. All suggested dates are approximate.*

JEROBOAM I	c.928–907 BCE
Nadab	c.907–906 BCE
Baasha	c.906–883 BCE
Elah	c.883–882 BCE
Zimri	c.882 BCE (7 days)
Timri	c.882–878 BCE
The dynasty of Omri	
Omri	c.882–871 BCE
AHAB	c.871–852 BCE
Ahaziah	c.852–851 BCE
Jehoram	c.851–842 BCE
The dynasty of Jehu	
JEHU	c.842–814 BCE
Joahaz	c.814–800 BCE

Jehoash*	c.800–784 BCE
Jeroboam II	c.784–748 BCE
Zechariah**	c.748–747 BCE
Shallum**	c.748–747 BCE
Menahem	c.747–737 BCE
Pekahiah	c.737–735 BCE
Pekah	c.735–733 BCE
Hoshea	c.733–724 BCE

*See KUNTILLET AJRUD. **Zechariah was the last of the Jehu dynasty; he was assassinated by Shallum, who proclaimed himself king but was himself assassinated a month later – 2 Kings 15.10–15.

Knights Templar See TEMPLARS.

Kuntillet Ajrud or Teman (Horvat) This is a site in north-east Sinai, 30 miles south of KADESH BARNEA, which seems to have functioned as a way station and religious centre for pilgrims on the route to Egypt. Its particular interest is in the ancient graffiti to be found on the plaster walls and on storage vessels in the main building. There are inscriptions in red and black ink, written in Hebrew in the PHOENICIAN script, as well as drawings of divine, human and animal figures. The motifs suggest links to Syria and Phoenicia, and to the Egyptian deity Bes. Inscriptions refer to 'YAHWEH of Teman and his ASHERAH' and to 'Yahweh of SAMARIA and his Asherah' (this latter inscription refers to Jehoash the king of Samaria (c.800–784 BCE; see 2 Kings 14.1, 8–16; 2 Chronicles 25.17–24).

Kursi See GADARA; GERGESA.

Laban *See* HOUSEHOLD DEITIES; LEAH.

Labourers in the Vineyard This is an eschatological PARABLE (Matthew 20.1–16). *See* THE ELEVENTH HOUR *at* ELEVEN.

Lachish The site of Lachish, Tel ed-Duweir, 25 miles south-west of Jerusalem, was first excavated in the 1930s by an English team led by James Starkey. Renewed excavations were carried out from 1973 to 1994 by David Ussishkin of Tel Aviv, and the full reports were published in 2004. Lachish was a large and prosperous CANAANITE royal city, mentioned in the EL-AMARNA letters. It was one of a coalition of cities defeated by JOSHUA (Joshua 10.5). During the Divided Monarchy (Iron Age II) the city was fortified by Rehoboam (2 Chronicles 11.9), and Amaziah of Judah was killed there after fleeing from Jerusalem (2 Kings 14.19). But Lachish is best known in relation to its siege and capture during the Palestinian campaign of the ASSYRIAN king SENNACHERIB in 701 BCE; there is evidence of an Assyrian siege ramp, and the capture is illustrated in the Lachish reliefs which came from the palace at NINEVEH, and are now in the British Museum. About a century later, with the end of the Southern Kingdom of Judah, Lachish was one of the last cities to fall (Jeremiah 34.7). These last few days are documented by a group of OSTRACA found by Starkey, which were probably sent to Lachish by the officer commanding a military outpost between Lachish and Azekah. 'We are waiting for the signal-fires of Lachish, according to all the signs which my lord gives, for we no longer see the signals of Azekah' (Letter IV in the Rockefeller Museum). The site of Lachish was abandoned until about 450 BCE, when it was resettled (Nehemiah 11.30).

lamb There is more than one word used in the New Testament for 'lamb' and several different strands of meaning in the symbolic use of the word. The lamb was a common animal in the ancient Near East, and was a natural simile for someone who was meek, obedient and in need of some protection.

The fact that the lamb was a common animal made it conveniently available for the rituals of sacrifice. In the Jerusalem TEMPLE there would be a sacrifice of a lamb twice a day, and for the FESTIVAL of PASSOVER each year every family would be expected to slaughter a Paschal lamb. When Jesus died on the cross at the time of Passover it was a natural extension of the symbolism of the feast to associate his death with that of the lamb (see John 19.33–37; 1 Corinthians 5.7). The Suffering

Servant in ISAIAH 53, who is compared with 'a lamb that is led to slaughter', is linked with these ideas of vicarious and expiatory sacrifice in the earliest Christian thought. But as Christ is also a SHEPHERD (John 10.11), so his followers can be a 'little flock' of sheep (Luke 12.32).

In the preaching of JOHN THE BAPTIST, according to John 1.29–34, he points to Jesus as the Lamb of God 'who takes away the sin of the world'. It is likely that underlying this theme is a mysterious APOCALYPTIC title for the conquering hero who will overcome evil and deliver the final victory for the chosen ones. To name as a lamb this victor over the evil beasts is clearly paradoxical (contrast LION). The same apocalyptic idea is developed in the book of REVELATION, where it is used 28 times to describe Christ as world ruler. But Revelation also describes the lamb as 'slaughtered', so combining in some way the idea of the death as redemptive or sacrificial (Revelation 5.6).

Lamentations, book of Traditionally Lamentations was ascribed to Jeremiah, which accounts for its position in English Bibles following JEREMIAH among the Prophetic Books. But in the Hebrew Bible it is found among the Writings (Ketuvim – the third section); it was one of the five FESTIVAL scrolls (Megilloth), associated in the Jewish calendar with the ninth day of the month Ab (a day of fasting for the destruction of the Jerusalem Temple). The link with Jeremiah is as late as the SEPTUAGINT translation and is disputed, but this anonymous author writes from Judaea during the period of the EXILE, vividly describing the situation after 586 BCE (compare 2 Kings 25; Jeremiah 41.5; Zechariah 7). This expression of grief (the first word in Hebrew is *ekha* – woe – and this is the book's name in the Hebrew Bible) can be seen as a theological acceptance of the predicted judgement on JERUSALEM, or even as a polemic against the pro-Babylonian attitude of Gedaliah (and Jeremiah?).

The book comprises five mournful poems, four of them highly structured as acrostics, in which lines or sections begin each with the next letter of the HEBREW alphabet. The prevailing metre of the poetry is known as *qinah* or lament, in which a longer line of three units is followed by a shorter line of two units, similar to a 'dying fall' (see, for example, Lamentations 5.14: 'The old men / have left / the city gate | the young men / their music'). See the account of word rhythm in Hebrew poetry under PSALMS.

The poet of Lamentations is 'the master of sorrow, the singer of loss, the pleader for divine attention. "Turn thou us unto thee, O Lord, and we shall be turned; renew our days as of old"' (Ronald Blythe).

In the Christian lectionary portions of Lamentations are read during Holy Week (Tenebrae), as much of the book was thought to be related to Christ and the Church (see how in Lamentations 3.30 and Matthew 5.39 the suffering of Christ and Christians is foreshadowed). There are frequent musical settings of the text, including Leonard Bernstein's 'Jeremiah' Symphony of 1942.

Laodikeia, or Laodicea Laodikeia is the seventh of the local Churches in Asia Minor to be addressed in chapters 2 and 3 of the book of REVELATION. The account in Revelation 3.14–22 serves as a particular example of all the unsatisfactory features in the Church situation. The description suggests an apparently resourceful, successful and perhaps rather self-satisfied community, which lacks spiritual depth. Laodikeia was a city in the fertile Lycus valley, a neighbour to both COLOSSAE and HIERAPOLIS. It was founded in the 3rd century BCE by the Seleucid king Antiochus II on the site of the earlier city of Diospolis and named after his wife (or sister) Laodike. Local features of the area are used in Revelation's text to point up the author's message. The quality of the local water supply was a famous joke; it travelled five miles through an aqueduct and was warmed by the sun. Colossae by contrast had cold pure water and Hierapolis was renowned for its hot medicinal springs. Laodikeia is actually criticized for its ineffectiveness (the water no use for anything) and not for being half-hearted, which is the usual sense in which the proverbial lukewarmness is understood today.

The city stood at a crossroads, controlling trade routes (hence the significance of the door or gate at Revelation 3.20). After an earthquake in 60 CE the city had embarked on an ostentatious building programme, including a monumental triple gate to the city. The city was a centre for banking and trade. A local speciality was the cloth woven from the raven-black wool of local sheep. There was also a medical school, renowned for its eye specialists, who would regularly use an eye salve made from alum (a 'Phrygian powder').

Last Judgement The Hebrew Bible gives many a solemn warning of the judgement of God not only on Israel's enemies, but also (much less welcome and even unexpected) on Israel herself because of her wickedness. See the prophetic descriptions of the 'Day of the Lord' in, for example, AMOS chapters 1–6. The later writers of APOCALYPTIC take up this prophetic tradition within their own projections of the signs of the End Time (see ESCHATON), with its sequence of judgements and woes, associated with their hope invested in the final triumph of God. The two main aspects of the Day of the Lord – the dreadful day of judgement and the dawn of the golden age of God's KINGDOM – are held together as essentially complementary, a vision of transformation from one extreme to the other. The Last Day is a cosmic phenomenon, depicted in the traditional mythology (see MYTH). The enemies of God are depicted in various ways, as dragons and other beasts, and as mysterious powers labelled with names such as GOG AND MAGOG. The final battle takes place at ARMAGEDDON, possibly Megiddo, the site of DEBORAH's historic victory. Other features of the End Time are the RESURRECTION of the dead, and the PAROUSIA of Christ.

The time of judgement is known only to God (see Matthew 24.36). It will happen like a thief in the night (see 1 Thessalonians 5.2–5). When the trumpet sounds, angels will gather humankind before the great white throne. The decision will be between unquenchable fire and brimstone for the wicked, and eternal life in the NEW JERUSALEM for those whose names are in the Book of Life. A new heaven and a new earth will replace the previous CREATION in its sinfulness. The scenario is described, not strictly chronologically, in chapters 20–22 of the book of REVELATION. From this basis a vast elaboration of ideas about the Last Judgement evolved in later apocalypses and in illuminated manuscripts and medieval art.

Last Supper *See* EUCHARIST.

Moses and the Law Exodus 19.16–25

law For Biblical and Jewish Law, *see also* TORAH.

A formal analysis of the codes of law in the Hebrew Bible reveals an interesting and significant distinction between two types of law found in ancient Israel. On the one hand there is case law (usually termed 'casuistic'), in which the pronouncements are conditional in form, dealing with a principal case and a number of subsidiary cases (see for example Exodus 21.20–21 concerning the death of a slave). Casuistic formulations are the normal form of legal provision throughout the ancient Near East, with abundant parallels of substance. In Israel this is probably a substantial survival of CANAANITE institutions, and reflects local jurisdiction carried out by tribunals of elders assembled in the village or the city gateway.

On the other hand there is a more distinctive type of law in Israel, presented in a series of single short clauses, either positive commands or negative prohibitions. This type, referred to as 'apodictic', is best illustrated by the DECALOGUE (Ten Commandments) in Exodus 20.2–17 and Deuteronomy 5.6–21. This unconditional form of law is often seen as unique to Israel and characteristic of religion focused on a deity with an implacable will ('the one and only God governed the whole of life by his will').

Lazarus The name Lazarus is applied to two persons in the New Testament: the beggar (derivation of the word 'lazar') outside the rich man's house, in the PARABLE told by Jesus to be found at LUKE 16.19–31; and Jesus' friend, the brother of Martha and Mary from BETHANY (JOHN 11 and 12; Luke 10.38–42). Both have to do with life after death. But Luke does not link the Lazarus of the parable with Martha and Mary. Only John's Gospel identifies their brother, in the course of telling the story, unique to John, of the RESURRECTION of Lazarus (John 11). Whether there is a literary relationship between parable and narrative is a subject of speculation. Even more speculative is the occasional suggestion that Lazarus was the BELOVED DISCIPLE, an important but anonymous and perhaps ideal figure in John (see 13.23).

The Raising of Lazarus, through the agency of Jesus, is a highly symbolic narrative in John, which anticipates Jesus' own resurrection (as well as being part cause of the hostility which leads to Jesus' death: John 11.47–53). The Lazarus event is the occasion for one of the SEVEN 'I AM' SAYINGS, the one about resurrection and life (11.25), while Martha, Lazarus' sister, is only groping towards a belief in the eschatological resurrection (11.24).

But there are also negative aspects to John's story, which may well be part of his thought-provoking and ironic style of narration. The key is provided by the ambiguous use of the word 'sleep' for death (11.11–14). Both sisters independently reproach Jesus for not coming sooner, when he could have performed a MIRACLE of healing (11.21, 32). It is a good question why Jesus delayed two days after hearing the news. There is also the issue of what happened subsequently to Lazarus: would he have had to face death again? There are frequent echoes, some very radical and sceptical, of the Lazarus story in English literature (for example in Robert Browning and Sylvia Plath). A current medical reference is the 'Lazarus drug', used to try to wake patients from a Permanent Vegetative State.

Leah The Hebrew name Leah may mean 'wild cow'! She was the elder daughter of Laban the Aramaean, and he deceived JACOB to make her his wife rather than the younger daughter RACHEL (see Genesis 29.25). She was the mother of REUBEN, SIMEON, LEVI, JUDAH, ISSACHAR, ZEBULUN and Dinah. Together with Rachel she is acclaimed as one of the builders of the House of Israel, according to RUTH 4.11. She was buried at Machpelah, in HEBRON.

Lebbaeus *See* THADDAEUS.

letters *See* EPISTLES; *see also* individual authors.

Levi Levi is the third son of JACOB by his first wife LEAH (see Genesis 29.34 and 49.5–7). Together with his brother SIMEON they massacred the men of Shechem, to avenge the rape of their sister Dinah (Genesis 34). He is told that as a consequence his descendants will be scattered. Levi is the ancestor of a tribe named after him, but they are not allocated any territory and consequently disappear from some later listings of tribes. In fact, as LEVITES, they are divinely chosen to serve as priests (see Deuteronomy 18.1; Joshua 18.7), and are given a number of towns to live in (Joshua 21).

Leviathan The Hebrew name possibly means 'coiled one', from a root meaning 'twist' or 'turn', and may well be identified with the seven-headed monster Lotan in the texts from UGARIT. This is a mythic monster, terrifying to humans but a plaything to God. It is a mixture of crocodile, sea-serpent and whale. The fullest description is in JOB 41; see also Job 3.8. In ISAIAH 27.1 the final destruction of Leviathan is seen in APOCALYPTIC terms. These parallel references show a virtual identification with a range of other sea monsters (dragon, serpent, Rahab, and in the background Tiamat, the monster of the BABYLONIAN creation myth); the corresponding land monster is

Behemoth. Thomas Hobbes entitled his treatise on political and ecclesiastical power *Leviathan* in a witty reference to the rule of an absolute monarch (Job 41.34).

levirate marriage When a married man dies without a son, there is an obligation (according to DEUTERONOMY 25.5–10) upon his brother to act as *levir* (the Latin word for the husband's brother) and marry the widow. The intentions were to resolve the anomaly of a young, childless widow within the social family, and for the living brother to perpetuate the name of the deceased brother. Clearly there would be a social stigma if the brother actually refused to conform. Two of the ancestors of King DAVID (according to the genealogies in Matthew's and Luke's Gospels) were born in ways that refer to this practice: Perez as the son of TAMAR (1) in Genesis 38; and Obed as the son of RUTH in Ruth 3–4. The practice apparently continued in Judaism into the medieval period. *See also* MARRIAGE.

Levites Although traditionally the Levites are members of the tribe of LEVI, the name seems to denote their role as PRIESTS and cultic personnel rather than any strictly tribal designation. In DEUTERONOMY they are priests whose functions include both sacrifice and the communication of TORAH. But when worship is centralized in Israel at Jerusalem they are reduced to a subordinate position in the cult, perhaps because of fears that they had become contaminated by CANAANITE practices (see Ezekiel 44.10–14). After the EXILE the distinction between priests and Levites is clearly maintained, the Levites being officials and servants of the TEMPLE; but the importance of their duties is enhanced, not least in the area of teaching the law (*see* 1 and 2 CHRONICLES).

The consecration of the Levites and their dedication to the service of God, through rituals of purification and SACRIFICE, is described in Numbers 8.5–26. For comparison, the anointing and ordination of the priests is described in Exodus 29 and Leviticus 8 (*see* UNCTION). Unlike the priests who served from the age of 30, the Levites were to begin their service five years earlier, completing it no later than the age of 50 (Numbers 8.24–25).

Leviticus, book of The name Leviticus means the Levitical book; it represents a solid block of legal material, so named because much has to do with the Israelite tribe of LEVI. The rabbis called it Torat Kohanim or the PRIESTS' Manual. It is important to recognize that in the Jewish tradition law and the function of priests encompass a wide field of teaching in theology and ethics, as well as social structure and ritual and liturgical observances. The ritual objects referred to in the book of EXODUS, such as the TABERNACLE and the priestly vestments, in Leviticus are taken up into descriptions of cult practice. The task of the priests is both to teach Israel how to avoid impurity and defilement, and also to purify the sanctuary when it is defiled. A section of particular interest, both historically and theologically, is that between chapters 17 and 26, known as the Holiness Code; this stands out from the rest with its own characteristic language and style. It is sometimes denoted by the letter 'H', while the rest of the material comes from strata labelled as 'P' according to PENTA-TEUCHAL CRITICISM.

Woody Guthrie's best-known song, 'This Land is Your Land', the anthem of radical America, alludes to Leviticus (see 25.2). Recently the campaign to reduce Third-World debt called on the idea of release in the year of JUBILEE (as in Leviticus 25).

life after death, or the afterlife For much of the Old Testament period death was indeed the end of life. God's blessing led to a promise of seeing one's grand-children around one in a prosperous old age. After that the best to hope for, whether peasant or prince, was a dusty dreary afterlife in SHEOL. Over the centuries the idea developed that God rewarded goodness and punished sin in this life, so justice had to be balanced out here and now. (It must be said that not all were convinced; the Psalmist (*see* PSALMS) railed against the prosperity of the wicked, and the book of JOB may have been written to counter such ideas.) The real problems in accepting such a life-view were sharply focused during the period of the revolt by the MACCABEES, when innocent and good people died in defence of their religious practices against a hostile Seleucid ruler. Where was the justice for them? Where was the reward for their piety?

It is thought that the answer to this problem was imported from religions further east. Where injustice had been meted out in this life, God would put it right in the next. The idea of the RESURRECTION was adopted into more progressive JUDAISM by the scholars of the PHARISEES, and well received by some sections of the population. The only unambiguous evidence in the Old Testament for the idea is in the (late) book of DANIEL: 'Many of those who sleep in the dust of the earth shall awake, some to everlasting life, and some to shame and everlasting contempt' (Daniel 12.2). Heb-rew man is widely held to be a unity of physical and psychological aspects. There-fore, in Richard Bauckham's words, 'the Jewish tradition of belief in life after death maintains the holistic view of the human person that is found in the Hebrew Scrip-tures … In the Jewish tradition human beings are a psychosomatic whole. Their bodiliness is intrinsic to their created nature.'

These ideas were in Jesus' inheritance from his people's teaching, and there are comparable passages in his own teaching (see Mark 10.34; 12.18–27). Resurrection to new life was a reasonable way for the early Christians to understand what happened to Jesus and to project what was in store for the believer too (see 1 Corinthians 15). These were, however, ideas with a very Jewish flavour, unlikely to win wide accept-ance in the GENTILE world, as the Gospel spread through the Mediterranean. Under Greek influence the Jewish world too became familiar with the concept of 'eternal life', and this is how JOHN'S GOSPEL in particular tends to refer to what Jesus has to offer. There is a new twist here, for believers: paradoxically the benefits of life after death/eternal life are already available in the here and now – in joy, PEACE and the gift of the holy SPIRIT (see John chapters 14–16).

PAUL, who bridged the Jewish and Greek thought worlds, was happy with both concepts; he worked with the notion of resurrection (as in 1 Corinthians 15), and with eternal life: 'the free gift of God is eternal life in Christ Jesus our Lord' (Romans 6.22). He married the two ideas together. The idea that resurrection should be the gateway to eternal life for the believer was rooted in the basic Hebrew concept that God was the Creator, the initial giver of life in CREATION: 'God … who gives life to the dead and calls into existence the things that do not exist' (Romans 4.17).

There is another concept of the afterlife which was adopted in Hellenistic JUDAISM, for example in the writings of PHILO. This is the immortality of the soul, an idea derived from Classical Greece and the writings of Plato. Given the example of Socrates, who was a martyr for his intellectual beliefs, such an idea of immortality is not totally separate from martyrdom (*see* MARTYR). But this was an intellectual belief that among Jews would be available only to those with a good Greek education, such as Philo or JOSEPHUS. The soul might be loosely associated with the Hebrew idea of *nephesh* as the life-breath which animated a human being (*see* HUMAN NATURE) but it had more to do with the Greek concept of *psyche*. Where the body was no longer regarded as valuable, but rather to be discarded at death, all that needed to be preserved in this intellectual belief was knowledge and the power of recollection or memory. The earliest Christians had nothing to do with such ideas of the soul's immortality, having no interest in preserving intellectual achievements after death. But as the APOCALYPTIC ideas about the End Time (the ESCHATON) lacked fulfilment, and Christianity spread more widely around the Roman Empire and through Roman society, so a synthesis began to take place between the ideas of bodily resurrection and the immortality of the soul.

Lilith The only time that Lilith is mentioned in the Hebrew Bible is at Isaiah 34.14, where she is a female demon associated with the night, one of a number of creatures inhabiting the ruins of EDOM. But in extra-Biblical Hebrew tradition Lilith is said to be the first wife of ADAM, created from the dust like Adam. She disliked the idea of being dominated by Adam, and so she escaped from the Garden of EDEN. Her replacement as Adam's partner was EVE, created by God out of Adam's rib. Lilith associated with demons and was accordingly punished by God. In origin Lilith was the SUMERIAN goddess of night. Her emblem was an owl, hence the translation 'screech owl' in the KING JAMES VERSION of the Bible at Isaiah 34.

lion During Old Testament times lions, as well as leopards, could be seen regularly, particularly in the wooded land around the river JORDAN (see Jeremiah 50.44). By the time of Jesus they were much less common, and they were certainly extinct in Palestine by the 14th century CE. Lions were regarded as a symbol of danger and of strength. In the empires of the ancient Near East the lion was hunted for sport, or kept in captivity. A lion hunt is depicted in relief at the ASSYRIAN palace at NINEVEH. Other representations of lions are in BABYLON, HAZOR, the SAMARIA ivories, and the NABATEAN tombs at PETRA.

An encounter with a lion is often fatal for the human being, but Biblical narratives record the survival of Benaiah (2 Samuel 23.20); DAVID (1 Samuel 17.34–36); SAMSON (Judges 14.6); and possibly PAUL (2 Timothy 4.17, if this is not metaphorical). DANIEL escapes without harm from the lions' den in Daniel 6.16–24. The predatory lion appears as a symbol for SATAN in 1 Peter 5.8. And aspects of the lion are characteristic of the beasts in REVELATION 9.17 and 13.2; but in Revelation 5 the 'Lion of the tribe of JUDAH', symbol of strength, appears paradoxically as a lamb. Sometimes guardian lions, in sculptured form, were placed in Jewish SYNAGOGUES to represent the 'Lion of Judah'.

See also ARIEL.

literary criticism There are two distinct kinds of literary criticism, the effects of which can be observed in Biblical scholarship. The differences between the older and newer varieties of criticism reflect the changes that have come over the methods for studying a literary text, in modern literature in English and other languages, just as much as in the study of the Bible. The changes came about in the last decades of the 20th century, when the focus of literary study shifted from the text, its historical growth and questions of authorship, onto the text as it is now encountered, the interraction with an audience, and questions about how a reader ideally or actually responds to the text. There is no longer anything definitive about an author's intention, but it is possible for any reader to react at will.

The older kind of literary criticism brought an expertise in the original languages to a study of the text as a given. HEBREW or GREEK would be mastered historically, so as to recognize changes in grammar and the meaning of words over their centuries of use. In this way a reliable report could be given of what a text was saying. Theological dictionaries were written for the Old and New Testaments to chart these developments and by etymology highlight the root meanings. When it is assumed that written documents are primary (contrast ORALITY), the intention was to analyse the existing text, establish the layers of earlier sources, and possibly reconstruct the original document. It was appropriate to identify the author/s and, if possible, the recipients, the date, and the purpose of writing. Many scholarly commentaries were produced with long introductions detailing these topics. The text's author could be identified by the style of writing and on the basis of preferences for particular vocabulary and grammatical constructions. With the advent of computer analysis using statistical data, it was hoped that the authorship of, for example, the genuine letters of PAUL could be confirmed scientifically.

Effectively such computerized analysis signalled a transition to a new kind of literary criticism based on a synchronic not a diachronic understanding of language. This means that it studies language in cross-section, showing a structure of interrelationships between words, rather than an historical study of language as an evolving, developing process. A major influence in this direction was the phenomenon of Structuralism (developed in French literary studies of the mid 20th century, based on the work of Ferdinand de Saussure, a Swiss professor of philology in the previous century). Studying a literary work in the light of the formal laws of language, the apparent meaning and aesthetic value of a text are placed in suspension, in order to disengage from the work the 'deep structure' which governed its operation. Subsequently a whole range of literary critical techniques have been applied in Biblical studies, following their success with other literatures. Because they operate 'in front of' the text, not historically 'behind' it as did the earlier criticism, they have much greater flexibility in the questions they ask and the directions that can be explored. These enquiries include the techniques of story-telling in narrative criticism; the reactions of modern readers, or of a reconstructed ideal original reader, to the text in reader-response criticism; and the ways in which an argument can be put across, using the historical methods of rhetoric as taught in the Greco-Roman world, or by means of a sociological construct, in rhetorical criticism. For examples, see John M. Court, *Reading the New Testament* (Routledge, 1997), chapters 2–5.

liturgy Liturgy is in origin a Greek word *leitourgia*, meaning literally 'work for the people'. In Classical Greece this referred to any kind of civic or public duty, such as financing the provision of the chorus for a performance of Greek tragedy at one of the dramatic festivals. In the SEPTUAGINT Greek translation of the Hebrew Bible it comes to refer to the services at the Jerusalem TEMPLE (see also Luke 1.23). PAUL uses the word more generally, both of EPAPHRODITUS' service to Paul's needs (Philippians 2.30), and of the sacrificial offering 'of your faith' (Philippians 2.17). In Christian tradition the English word 'liturgy' is used of all the structured 'services' of the Church, or with particular reference to the EUCHARIST as the chief act of public worship, or finally to denote the written texts for orders of service (as in the 'Liturgy of St John Chrysostom'). *See also* WORSHIP.

locusts Plagues of locusts were widely feared as pests and a threat to crops and food supplies in the Near East. The Desert Locust (*Schistocerca gregaria*) came from the savannas of the Sudan in spring and was devastating in its effects through Egypt, Palestine, and up to Anatolia. Such plagues affected Palestine roughly every 12 years. In a single day a swarm of 50 million locusts can consume enough food to feed 500 people for a year. Small wonder that such a natural plague can become a metaphor for eschatological judgement (as in JOEL 1–2 and REVELATION 9). In Exodus 10 locusts are the eighth of the PLAGUES in Egypt, symbolizing theological judgement, as well as a natural phenomenon. Biblical writers agree with present-day naturalists in describing the coordinated mass movement of locusts (Proverbs 30.27), their lethargy in cold weather (Nahum 3.17), their resemblance to an invading army (Judges 6.5), and the way the swarms blot out the sun (Joel 2.10). A BBC reporter described their sound as 'like the distant humming of an aeroplane'.

Locusts could be used as subsistence food (see Leviticus 11.22); there are reports that when fried they are a delicacy for desert dwellers. Locusts are indicated as a staple food of JOHN THE BAPTIST, although some commentators prefer to see him eating carob pods, the fruit of the locust tree. In the Biblical references to the locust plagues there is a single possibility offering some hope: Joel 2.25 speaks of God as restoring 'the years that the locust has eaten'.

logos *See* WORD.

Lord's Prayer Jesus, like many RABBIS of his time, taught his DISCIPLES a set PRAYER, which has remained the pattern prayer of Christians, as well as the daily prayer of private and public WORSHIP, ever since. There are two versions of this prayer in the New Testament (found only in Matthew 6.9–13 and Luke 11.2–4). MATTHEW sets the Lord's Prayer in the context of teaching about prayer within the SERMON ON THE MOUNT. Jesus spoke of the need for privacy when praying, and for brevity not garrulousness, on the grounds that God knows human needs anyway, before they are spoken. He emphasized the need for forgiveness to be a two-way process. On the other hand LUKE sets the scene with Jesus at prayer. His disciples then requested a model prayer, just like JOHN THE BAPTIST gave his followers. Jesus gave the Lord's Prayer and taught of the need for persistence in asking. Despite the different settings there is considerable agreement on the various elements of the prayer – worship, petition, confession – although Luke's version is briefer. Matthew's version is more Jewish in language and phrasing (see the use of 'heaven' in 6.9). It is largely these Jewish elements that are missing in Luke's crisper version. An ARAMAIC version of the prayer was successfully reconstructed by the German scholar Joachim Jeremias. (See a possible reconstruction of the original form in the article on FATHER.) Bernhard Lang suggested that the prayer originated in the circle around John the Baptist and was subsequently taken up by Jesus. He thought that the original context was highly political, and that 'your KINGDOM come' meant 'restore the independent Jewish kingdom'.

The prayer invokes GOD as father, in accordance with Jesus' sense of intimacy with God. God's name is to be revered; names were very powerful in ancient thought, and God's name was to be respected ever since the DECALOGUE (Exodus 20.7). The prayer begins by asking for the arrival of God's kingdom, which Matthew links to the fulfilment of God's plan ('your will be done'). The request is made for basic sustenance, material probably rather than spiritual, and sufficient just for today (this is a more correct understanding of the Greek word than the usual translation 'daily'). Forgiveness is at the heart of the Christian Gospel: that God should forgive Christian believers is conditional upon their forgiveness of others. There has been much discussion on the exact meaning of 'evil' – is it personal (the Devil) or impersonal? – and whether 'time of trial' should be preferred to 'temptation' and, if so, what it means; it seems to be asking that Christians should not falter or fail in the difficulties which are expected at the End Time (*see* ESCHATON). There is a balance established here: the first three sentences above are concerned with God in terms of divinity; the next three with human beings in terms of humanity.

Evelyn Underhill made some trenchant comments on the Lord's Prayer. Human beings 'have three wants which only God can satisfy. They need food, for they are weak and dependent. They need forgiveness, for they are sinful. They need guidance, for they are puzzled.' Over 2000 years Christians' individual interpretations of the Lord's Prayer have varied, down to the modern emphases as in liberation theology (see Leonardo Boff's *The Lord's Prayer*, Orbis, 1983), but the estimate of the text's importance has never varied. This was a reason for the addition of the doxology within some later manuscripts of Matthew's Gospel ('For the kingdom and the power and the glory are yours forever. Amen'). This concluding formula is used in worship, and is first found in the DIDACHE, where the text of the prayer is reproduced.

A possible and early allusion to the Lord's Prayer is found in an acrostic or word-square, composed before 79 CE, of which examples were found at Cirencester and Pompeii. It reads

```
R  O  T  A  S
O  P  E  R  A
T  E  N  E  T
A  R  E  P  O
S  A  T  O  R
```

The horizontal and vertical forms of the Latin word 'tenet' form a Christian cross. It is suggested that the 25 letters are an anagram (twice) of 'Pater noster' ('Our Father')

with the addition of ALPHA AND OMEGA, the first and last letters of the Greek alphabet. But other anagrams and explanations of the origin have been proposed.

Lord's Supper *See* EUCHARIST.

Lot Lot is ABRAHAM's nephew; according to GENESIS 19, he is living in SODOM when visited by two ANGELS. He offers them hospitality, but his house is surrounded by the men of Sodom who demand that he produce the guests 'that we may know them' (Genesis 19.5). Lot feels that his honour as a host is at stake, and so offers the townsmen his daughters instead. The divine visitors blind the townsmen outside and urge Lot and his family to escape before God unleashes his wrath on Sodom and its sister city, Gomorrah.

In the morning God annihilates Sodom and Gomorrah with 'brimstone and fire' (Genesis 19.24). Though warned by the angels to flee to the hills and not to look back upon the devastated cities, Lot's wife disobeys and is turned into a pillar of salt. But Lot and his daughters flee to Zoar and live in a cave in the hill country. Believing they are the last survivors, Lot's daughters plan to make their father drunk and in turn commit incest with him. Two sons are born, Moab and Ben-ammi, who become the ancestors of Biblical tribes to the east of the Jordan and the Dead Sea. In Christian tradition Lot came to be revered as a saint, and a Byzantine monastery was built at Deir 'Ain 'Abata in the area of the traditional cave. Lot was exonerated, either because not he but his daughters were to blame (and they had acted to regenerate the world) or because the real purpose of the story was to discredit the origins of the Israelites' traditional enemies to the east, the MOABITES and AMMONITES. In Islam Lot is described as a prophet (*Qur'an*, Sura 37.134) and his daughters named as Rubbah and Saghur.

Lotan *See* LEVIATHAN.

love In Biblical terms love is the expression of various kinds of relationship, both human and divine. It may be 'love at first sight' like that of JACOB with RACHEL in Genesis 29.18–20; or the sexual infatuation of Amnon for TAMAR (2) in 2 Samuel 13; or the relationship between two men such as DAVID and JONATHAN (see 1 Samuel 20.17). The Hebrew verb is *'ahab* and the noun *hesed* (*see* HOSEA). It could be said that human love is the analogy for the important theological sense of the expression of love to and from God; but the Biblical terms are used significantly more often in the divine than in the human context. *Hesed* as faithful, steadfast love is seen as a characteristic of God. God's love is expressed for individuals, for Jerusalem and Israel, and for ideals such as RIGHTEOUSNESS. Human love for God is summed up in the Hebrew confession of faith, called the SHEMA', in Deuteronomy 6.4–5: 'Love the Lord your God with all your heart and soul and strength.'

The commandment to love is taken up in the New Testament with the summary of the LAW offered by Jesus in Mark 12.28–31, combining the first line of the Shema' with the love for the neighbour (as in Leviticus 19.18; *see also* PAUL in Galatians 5.13–14). Greek has several words for 'love' and often preachers of sermons will exploit the difference between them. See, for example, in this Christmas sermon by Martin Luther King: 'There are three words for love in the Greek New Testament: *eros* is a romantic love; then *philia*, intimate love between friends. Then another word, *agape*, more than romantic love [and] friendship: an overflowing love that seeks nothing in return, the love of God operating in the human heart.'

It is true that *agape* and *agapao* have been given a depth of meaning in Christian thought, as self-giving and unconditional, that goes well beyond the general sense found in Classical Greek. But in a text such as John 21.15–17 it is open to debate whether the main point is in the use of two words for love, or the fact that Christ's question of PETER is repeated three times, in reminder of his threefold denial (John 18.17, 25, 27). JOHN'S GOSPEL has a primary focus on the theme of love; see for example John 3.16: 'For God so loved the world that he gave his only Son, so that everyone who believes in him may not perish but may have eternal life' (*see* LIFE AFTER DEATH) – where love is the divine motive for the INCARNATION and REDEMPTION, and Jesus' life and death are rooted in God's love for his world. See further examples at John 13.34; 14.21; 15.13. God's love spills over into a requirement to love one another (whether only within the Christian community reflected in this Gospel, or within the wider Christian society is not entirely clear). The first letter of John follows up this theme and provides the ultimate theological definition ('God is love') together with a fresh emphasis on the reciprocality of the loving relationship (1 John 4.8; 4.7, 9–12; 4.16; 5.2–3). The truth of the claim to love God, in response to his love in Christ, is entirely dependent upon the reality of the Christian's love for others.

Lucifer *See* SATAN.

Luke, Gospel according to Luke's work in the New Testament is divided into two parts, the Gospel and the ACTS of the Apostles. He directed both books to a single reader, 'the most excellent THEOPHILUS'. The language and style of Luke's GREEK, compared with the other canonical Gospels, indicates a more educated writer, with an awareness of secular literature, as in the Classical form of the Gospel's prologue (Luke 1.1–4). But there are also blocks of material, such as the birth narratives in the Gospel's opening chapters, and the speeches in Acts, which show a strong awareness of Semitic expression, and the traditions of the Old Testament such as SALVATION history.

Luke is rightly called the theologian of salvation history, but each word needs to be given weight. He is concerned with the details of history (see Luke 2.1–2; 3.1–2; 21.20); but these are important because of the salvation (through Israel in the Old Testament and through Christ in the New) that is realized in a scheme of history planned and guided by God. Luke refers to the plan or providence of God in the way that a classical Roman would speak of 'fate'. All of this is part of a theological interpretation of events by Luke: there are three significant stages in this history: the time of the Old Testament up to and including JOHN THE BAPTIST (Luke 16.16); the time of the ministry of Jesus who functions as a prophet (Luke 4.16–19); and the time of the SPIRIT-filled CHURCH, until Christ's PAROUSIA (as in Acts).

Luke's Gospel is probably best known for certain PARABLES in Jesus' teaching which are recorded only in this Gospel: notably those of the GOOD SAMARITAN (Luke 10.30–37) and of the Prodigal Son (Luke 15.11–31). It is possible that the Samaritan, as well as representing a person unpopular with Jews who performs a model act of charitable caring, may actually stand for Christ himself; the message is then about what the Church should do, until Christ comes again (10.35). The Prodigal Son is several parables in one: as well as the story of the wastrel but penitent son, it is also the story of the elder brother's jealousy, and above all the story of the FATHER who goes on loving and forgiving and does not count the cost. The reader is given a glimpse of the LOVE of God, and exhorted to 'follow the Heart of the Father'.

TABULATION OF LUKE

The setting of the Gospel 1.1–2.52

1.1–4	Dedication of the Gospel to Theophilus
1.5–2.40	Births of John the Baptist and Jesus
2.41–52	Jesus' youth

The Gospel begins 3.1–5.39

3.1–22	Preaching of John the Baptist and baptism of Jesus
3.23–38	Genealogy of Jesus, son of Adam, Son of God
4.1–13	The temptations
4.14–44	Jesus preaches and heals in Galilee, but is rejected in Nazareth
5.1–11	The call of the first apostles
5.12–26	Further healings
5.27–39	Call of Levi and the radical newness of the Gospel

The ministry develops in Galilee 6.1–9.50

6.1–11	Sabbath disagreements
6.12–16	The call of the 12 apostles
6.17–49	Sermon on the Plain
7.1–17	Jesus heals and raises the dead
7.18–35	The contrast between Jesus and John the Baptist
7.36–50	Jesus is anointed and forgives a woman
8.1–3	The women in Jesus' support group
8.4–56	Jesus teaches and works miracles
9.1–9	The news of the mission of the 12 astonishes Herod
9.10–17	The feeding of the 5000
9.18–36	Jesus' Messiahship is the way of suffering – confirmed by the Transfiguration
9.37–50	Jesus heals a demoniac and deals with the disciples

Jesus' journey to Jerusalem 9.51–18.34

9.51–62	Jesus on the road
10.1–24	Mission of the 70 and their return
10.25–37	The Good Samaritan
10.38–42	Jesus visits Mary and Martha
11.1–32	Jesus teaches on prayer and exorcism etc.
11.33–36	The light illuminates
11.37–12.12	Jesus is in conflict with legalistic religion, and so will the disciples be
12.13–21	The parable of the Rich Fool

12.22–59	Jesus warns against unnecessary ambition, and urges the disciples to be alert for the End Time
13.1–9	Warnings to repent
13.10–30	Jesus heals and preaches
13.31–35	Jesus laments over Jerusalem's fate
14.1–24	An eventful meal with a Pharisee
14.25–35	The cost of discipleship
15.1–32	3 'lost' parables, including the Prodigal Son
16.1–17.10	Further teaching including Dives and Lazarus
17.11–19	Jesus heals 10 Samaritan lepers
17.20–18.17	Teaching on the End Time and judgement in the kingdom
18.18–30	The would-be disciple and true discipleship
18.31–34	Jesus again predicts his Passion

Jesus' arrival at Jericho 18.35–19.27

18.35–43	Jesus is hailed by a blind beggar
19.1–9	Zacchaeus repents
19.11–27	Parable of the 10 pounds

Holy Week begins 19.28–21.38

19.28–44	Jesus enters Jerusalem and weeps over it
19.45–48	The cleansing of the Temple
20.1–47	Jesus' controversy with the authorities
21.1–4	A widow's offering
21.5–38	The destruction of the Temple and the Last Judgement

The Passion and death of Jesus 22.1–23.56

22.1–6	The plot against Jesus
22.7–38	The Last Supper
22.39–53	Jesus in Gethsemane and his arrest
22.54–23.25	Jesus' trials and Peter's denial
23.26–56	The crucifixion and burial

The resurrection 24.1–53

24.1–12	The women at the tomb
24.13–35	Jesus appears on the road to Emmaus
24.36–49	Jesus appears to the 11 and to other disciples, who are to be his witnesses
24.50–53	Ascension at Bethany

Luther, Martin Martin Luther was born at Eisleben in eastern Germany on St Martin's Day, 11 November 1483. He lived at the close of the Middle Ages, and changed the face of Europe. It is true that someone else would have released the revolutionary forces if he had not done so. But in fact Luther did it, within the particular circumstances of his life. He was a theologian, but also a master of language, a great musician and a poet. He was a friar for the first 20 years of his adult life, and a happily married man for the next 20 years.

To study Luther and his Bible involves the concentration on two aspects, in which Reformation theology and the understanding of the Bible text are intertwined. As a young professor at Wittenberg Luther lectured on the books of the Bible. He criticized the use of ALLEGORY in the interpretation of the text and demanded that the meaning of the text should be true to the actual words used. But he also emphasized the necessity of a deeper knowledge of scripture, reckoning that a purely historical approach was insufficient. He demanded a Christ-centred understanding of the Bible ('Die Christenheit und eine jede Christenseele ist in und durch das Wort Gottes geboren' – 'Christianity and every Christian soul is born in and through the WORD of God').

In 1545, a year before he died, Luther looked back on his earlier puzzlement as to what Biblical talk about divine RIGHTEOUSNESS meant, and the momentous impact of his discovery of the connection between those concepts of God and righteousness, in terms of his reading of PAUL's letters to the GALATIANS and the ROMANS. (Luther's reading is not now so central in much of modern scholarship on Paul and his letters.) What the Reformation discovered was a theological insight from the Bible.

The pressure to translate the Bible from Latin accompanied this insight. Luther's translation into German, made at the Wartburg in just 80 days, was the breakthrough which enabled widespread access to the Biblical text. Luther's German New Testament first appeared in September 1522, and the Old Testament in 1534. There were frequent reprints, for which Luther also made linguistic improvements, choosing the most apt expressions to render the Bible in modern speech. The linguistic power of Luther's translation in turn also shaped the expressive potential of German literature (as Herder, Goethe, Nietzsche and Brecht all acknowledged). Luther may never have produced the systematic version of his theology or of his interpretation of the Bible, but he continued to express his commitment to wider education by regular preaching and teaching on the texts which he had translated.

Lydia $\quad$ Lydia was patron of the early Church founded by Paul at Philippi (Acts 16.11–15). From this initial gathering grew one of the strongest and most generous of the early Churches (Philippians 4.15f.). Lydia was a businesswoman, originally from THYATIRA, and a dealer in the PURPLE dye and purple cloth which were highly valued in the Roman world. As a householder she may well have been a widow, but one of means, well able to extend hospitality to others (see Acts 16.15, 40; compare 1 Timothy 5.16). She had been a God-fearer, that is a GENTILE attracted to Judaism, one of many such in the SYNAGOGUES of the DIASPORA. Some scholars have argued that ACTS treats women as silent partners, and that it is Luke's intention to marginalize the status of women in the Jesus movement. In contrast the story of Lydia would seem to highlight the importance of this woman for the Christian mission. Compare this with JUNIA in Romans 16.7.

See also MINISTRY.

M

Maccabees The Maccabees were a strongly religious family who rebelled against the Greek rulers in the 2nd century BCE. The particular threat had been posed by Antiochus IV Epiphanes who strove to foster Hellenism in Judaea by suppressing Jewish practice. The leader of the Maccabee family, Mattathias, raised the banner of revolt against the Seleucids in 170 BCE at the ancient town of MODEIN, by killing a Jew who came to sacrifice at the royal altar. He and his five sons, John, Simon, Judas (see JUDAS MACCABEUS), Eleazar and Jonathan, took the revolt into the Judaean hills, where they were joined by many of the HASIDIM, in a programme of guerrilla warfare. The struggle was successful, under the leadership of Judas Maccabeus, and the Jerusalem TEMPLE was rededicated. This event is commemorated in the Jewish festival of HANUKKAH ('Dedication') on the eight days following 25 Kislev; lights are kindled in the Jewish home, one more on each evening. This 'festival of lights' is indicated as the setting of the narrative in JOHN'S GOSPEL 10.22.

After the successful revolt the family evolved into the HASMONEAN dynasty who ruled most of the area of present-day Israel as well as the West Bank and parts of Jordan, Syria and Lebanon. Some of the Hasmonean kings, combining the roles of king and High Priest, clearly had the ideals of the Davidic kingdom in mind, but others were worldly and tyrannical, the most grotesque of whom was probably Alexander Jannaeus. Above JERICHO, near the site of Herod's winter palace, are the remains of an elaborate Hasmonean palace of the 1st century BCE at Tulul Abu el-Alaiq, begun by Alexander Jannaeus (103–76 BCE). The Hasmoneans were finally defeated by the Romans in 36 BCE.

The first and second books of the Maccabees are alternative histories of the Maccabean revolt, to be found in the APOCRYPHA. 1 Maccabees celebrates the achievements of the Hasmoneans, legitimating them because of their success in liberating Judaea. 2 Maccabees honours Judas only as the leader of resistance, and focuses on the insult to the Jerusalem Temple by the Hellenizers.

Magi, or the Three Kings According to the story of Jesus' birth in MATTHEW 2, a number of magi (the Greek word for astrologers), wise men, or kings, journeyed as a result of their observation of the stars to greet the birth of a new 'king of the Jews'. They are sometimes seen as representatives of the Zoroastrian religion. Matthew's account does not say how many magi there were. The tradition of three kings, with the names of Gaspar (Caspar), Melchior, and Balthasar, is nowhere to be found in

Scripture, but is a later embellishment, perhaps based on the information about their particular gifts, from their treasure chests, of 'gold, frankincense, and myrrh'. The number three is first given by the Church Father Origen, and Tertullian is the first to call them kings. As the first Gentile believers, they were specially venerated in the Middle Ages. Their relics are splendidly enshrined in the cathedral at Cologne in Germany.

magic *See* WITCHCRAFT.

Magnificat *See* MARY, MOTHER OF JESUS.

makarism *See* BEATITUDES.

making many books, of / and much study Almost at the end of the book ECCLESIASTES, at 12.12, in contrast to the penetrating 'sayings of the wise' (*see* WISDOM), comes a reference to a further vanity, among those summarized in this Biblical text: 'Of making many books there is no end, and much study is a weariness of the flesh.' So be warned!

Malachi, book of Malachi is the last book in the collection of 12 Minor Prophets, and the last in the prophetic canon of the Hebrew Bible, but probably not the latest of the prophets in terms of date. The favoured theory is that it belongs in the period between 520 and 445 BCE, that is after the ministries of HAGGAI and ZECHARIAH, but before NEHEMIAH came to Jerusalem. It is likely that Malachi reflects the Deuteronomic law, rather than the Priestly code which EZRA later brought back from Babylon. The book is concerned with the fulfilment of the duties of the COVENANT relationship. An attractive suggestion is that the legal process recommended in DEUTERONOMY 17.8–13 (legal cases too difficult for decision at the JUSTICE tribunal in the town gates should be brought before the LEVITES or Levitical priests) is the key to the book. The form of the book with its questions and answers represents a court case in which the prophet plays the role of the priest. Israel brings charges against God, but God counters with accusations against the people. Malachi means 'my messenger' and may well not be a personal name; it is often said that the name is borrowed from Malachi 3.1, but it might be even better to link it with 2.7 where the priest is 'the messenger of the Lord of Hosts'.

The book ends on the eschatological note of chapter 4. In the Christian Bible this is followed immediately by the Gospel message of the birth of Jesus. For the earliest Christians of Mark's community, who knew the first Gospel, Mark, as the primary statement of the coming of Christ, there will have been the immediate juxtaposition: the prophetic book of Malachi is followed by the opening of MARK'S GOSPEL quoting Malachi 3.1 as the Old Testament prediction of JOHN THE BAPTIST, the forerunner of Christ.

Mamre *See* HEBRON.

Manasseh (king of Judah) Manasseh, the son of HEZEKIAH, succeeded him as king of Judah, reigning from c.698 to 642 BCE, politically a successful reign of nearly 50 years, the longest of any king of the House of DAVID. By contrast 2 Kings 21.1–18 returns a very negative verdict on Manasseh for reversing his father Hezekiah's reforms and encouraging foreign cults, in contravention of the TORAH. Accordingly he is held to blame for the ultimate destruction of Jerusalem and the EXILE of Judah. For much of his reign Manasseh had been a vassal to the ASSYRIANS, appointed by them to do as he was told; and the resulting pluralist society, from foreign contacts (including forced labour in building projects for the Assyrians), adequately explains his liberal policy on foreign cults. This must have been a reality, for otherwise the subsequent reforms of JOSIAH would not have been necessary. Compared with KINGS the judgement of CHRONICLES (2 Chronicles 33) is that Manasseh was evil, but ultimately penitent. Mention here of his prayer to God (33.13) provides the basis for the Prayer of Manasseh, to be found in the APOCRYPHA. This is thought to be a Greek work of the 1st century BCE, a penitential composition to fill an obvious gap.

Manasseh (son of Joseph) Manasseh is the elder son of JOSEPH born in Egypt by Asenath (Genesis 41.51: the meaning of the name is given as 'making to forget'). According to the narrative of Genesis 48, his younger brother EPHRAIM was blessed by his grandfather JACOB ahead of Manasseh. In part this echoes what happened in the previous generation with ISAAC's blessing of Jacob and ESAU; but it is also taken as prophetic of the future ascendancy of Ephraim as a tribe over the tribe of Manasseh (named after their ancestor).

Mandaeans The name 'Mandaeans' is given to a baptizing sect which still exists today on the borders of modern Iraq and Iran. Historically they produced a large sacred literature, written in an East ARAMAIC dialect, containing myths, liturgies, ritual commentaries, magical texts, and a book of astrology. When some of these works were being translated into German by the Semitic scholar Marc Lidzbarski, some New Testament scholars perceived a relationship between the poetic passages and some texts from JOHN'S GOSPEL. Rudolf Bultmann in particular argued that the Mandaean 'Book of John' and their stories about JOHN THE BAPTIST ('Yohannah') were important in discussing the sources of that Gospel. Followers of the Baptist might have converted to Jesus and brought their 'GNOSTIC'-sounding poetry with them. It is true that Mandaean means 'knowing one' in Aramaic and might seem to be the equivalent of the word 'Gnostic'. But the scholarly world in general is now sceptical of this simple equation; the Mandaean texts are reckoned to be much later (5th to 7th centuries CE at the earliest); both the link with the Baptist and the reconstruction of the background to John's Gospel ultimately failed to convince.

manna Manna literally means, in Hebrew, 'What is it?' The question asked by the Israelites also reflects the perplexity of modern scholars. The escapee slaves after the EXODUS did not find the wilderness diet based on this mysterious substance matched up to the tasty food of their captivity – 'If only we had meat to eat! We remember the fish we used to eat in Egypt for nothing, the cucumbers, the melons, the leeks, the onions and the garlic' (Numbers 11.4–5). Their grumbles precede a description of manna as 'like coriander seed, and its colour was like the colour of gum resin' (Numbers 11.7), and recipes for its use in Numbers 11.8–9. This is in addition to the account in Exodus 16.14 of how, when the dew had lifted, 'there on the surface of the wilderness was a fine flaky substance, as fine as frost on the ground'.

Speculation on what precisely this was seems to have settled on sugary flakes of a honey-like substance secreted by insects on the desert's tamarisk trees. This substance is much favoured by the nomadic inhabitants, and even sold to visitors by the natives who gather it early in the day before the ants consume it (which the Israelites apparently put down to its 'melting' – Exodus 16.21). The problems occur in combining the idea of honeyflakes with the recipes, and with the regulations for collecting a double portion on the sixth day, before its non-arrival on the seventh or Sabbath day (Exodus 16.4–5). This provision of manna taught obedience to God (Exodus 16.4), and dependence upon him: 'Man must not depend on bread alone to sustain him, but on everything the Lord says' (Deuteronomy 8.3).

The answer is probably to leave any precise identification as impossible. The story was after all told as a miraculous feeding, part of the salvation story of Israel's divine rescue and establishment as the People of God. And the story was probably written down so long after the event that the actual identification had not been remembered. This manna was understood by them as 'bread from heaven' (Exodus 16.4). This idea is picked up in the New Testament by JOHN'S GOSPEL. Jesus, in John 6.50–58, contrasted 'the bread which came down from heaven' eaten by the Israelites who died, with the 'bread of life' which conveys eternal life – the bread which is Jesus' own flesh, sacrificed on the cross (see SEVEN 'I AM' SAYINGS). The spiritual food given by Christ is referred to as 'the hidden manna' in Revelation 2.17.

maranatha This is an original ARAMAIC phrase, to be found in the New Testament at REVELATION 22.20 and 1 CORINTHIANS 16.22. As an Aramaic expression it is either a statement ('Our Lord comes') or an exclamation and plea ('Come, Lord!'). Among the earliest Christians it assumed great importance as an eschatological slogan and expression of hope in times of persecution; it was used in early days in the LITURGY – see DIDACHE 10.6. As a talismanic slogan it could be open to misunderstanding where Aramaic was unknown.

Marcion *See* CANON OF SCRIPTURE.

Mareshah One of the cities of Judah, as listed in Joshua 15.44 and 1 Chronicles 2.42, Mareshah lies on one of the main routes into the Judaean hills from the coastal plain. It was one of the towns fortified by Solomon's son Rehoboam (2 Chronicles 11.8) and also the home town of the prophet Eliezer (2 Chronicles 20.37). In the HELLENISTIC PERIOD it was called Marisa, and this area of southern Judah was known as Idumaea (indicating the spread of EDOMITE settlement). Its modern Arabic name is Sandahannah (referring to a 12th-century Crusader church of St Anne). At the beginning of the 20th century spectacular Hellenistic tomb paintings depicting animals, birds and mythological creatures were excavated here, representing the Hellenization against which the MACCABEES rebelled. An impression of the paintings can be gained from photographs preserved in the archives of the Palestine Exploration Fund.

Mari (Tell Hariri) Mari was a settlement (Tell Hariri) on the right (southern) bank of the Euphrates in south-eastern Syria, near the Iraqi border. Mari was inhabited from the 4th millennium BCE, and in the 3rd and 2nd millennia (until 1759 BCE) it became a prosperous commercial centre on the trade route between BABYLON and PALESTINE, and one of the largest cities in the area. Excavation began from 1933 when André Parrot discovered a grand AKKADIAN palace, with archives dating from the 18th century BCE, and spanning 500 years, containing 25,000 cuneiform tablets, mostly economic, legal and diplomatic documents, written in a West Semitic dialect, with links to the HEBREW language of the Old Testament (for example 'goy', meaning tribe or nation; *see also* GENTILE). A number of the texts refer to a group known as the HABIRU and a tribe of Benjaminites; these references have attracted some scholars to make links with the early 'Hebrews' and the tribe of BENJAMIN, but these interpretations are open to dispute. Also found on the site, within a sanctuary, is a LION measuring 30 cm high by 60 cm wide, made from 18 copper sheets, with eyes of limestone and slate.

Mariamne *See* HEROD THE GREAT.

Mark, Gospel according to Traditionally, according to Eusebius (*Ecclesiastical History* 3.39), Mark's Gospel was written in Rome to preserve PETER's reminiscences and his preaching. Mark, as Peter's interpreter, is sometimes identified with JOHN MARK, the cousin of BARNABAS, accompanying PAUL on the mission to Cyprus (Acts 12 and 13). But Mark was a common name in the 1st century CE. Modern scholars have suggested Galilee and Syria as alternatives to Rome as a place of composition for a Gospel written primarily for GENTILE Christians. Mark is widely thought to be the earliest of the four canonical Gospels, as the best explanation of the literary relationship between Mark, Matthew and Luke (*see* SYNOPTIC PROBLEM).

This Gospel starts not with the birth of Jesus but with his baptism by JOHN THE BAPTIST. It ends with a brief narrative of the RESURRECTION (16.1–8); the alternative and supplementary endings added in some manuscripts are not regarded as part of the original. A characteristic of this Gospel is its grouping together of short units (PARABLES, MIRACLES, conflicts and teaching), referred to as pericopes. A favourite word to introduce these units is 'immediately', which gives a sense of urgent movement to the text. A large proportion of the Gospel is concerned with the narrative of the Passion of Christ. Three predictions of Jesus' death (8.31, 9.31, 10.33) build up towards the CRUCIFIXION; the dark shadow of the cross falls over Mark's narrative for the disciples and later readers who are 'following the way of the cross'.

The difficulties of Christian discipleship represent one of the key themes of this Gospel; Jesus' own DISCIPLES – the twelve – are not idealized, but rather realistic role models. Another key theme, in the characterization of Jesus in this early Gospel, is what is known as the 'messianic secret'. In 1901 W. Wrede identified Gospel features where Jesus' identity is suppressed. His explanation was that the evangelist used messianic clues (and the revelation at CAESAREA PHILIPPI) to interpret the significance of Jesus, while Jesus himself had not thought of himself as MESSIAH.

TABULATION OF MARK

The Gospel of the Kingdom of God begins 1.1–20

1.1–13	John the Baptist's work and Jesus' baptism
1.14–20	Call of the first apostles

Jesus' ministry in Galilee 1.21–9.50

1.21–2.12	Jesus the teacher and healer
2.13–17	The call of Levi
2.18–3.6	Arguments with the Pharisees
3.7–12	Jesus the healer
3.13–19	The call of the 12 apostles
3.20–30	Jesus answers the charge of demon possession
3.31–35	Jesus' family
4.1–34	Jesus teaches in parables: the Sower etc.
4.35–41	Jesus calms a storm
5.1–20	Jesus the exorcist
5.21–43	Jesus heals and raises the dead
6.1–6a	Jesus' rejection in his home town
6.6b–13	The mission of the twelve
6.14–29	The execution of John the Baptist
6.30–52	Jesus the miracle-worker, the feeding of the 5000
6.53–6	Jesus the healer
7.1–23	Jesus and rule-keeping
7.24–37	Jesus the healer
8.1–21	The feeding of the 4000 and controversy with the Pharisees
8.22–26	Jesus the healer
8.27–9.1	Jesus' Messiahship revealed as the way of suffering
9.2–13	Jesus' transfiguration as God's Son
9.14–29	Jesus the exorcist
9.30–32	Jesus' way of suffering
9.33–50	True discipleship

Jesus' work in Judaea 10.1–52

10.1–16	Marriage and children
10.17–31	The would-be disciple
10.32–45	Discipleship as true service of others
10.46–52	Jesus the healer; blind Bartimaeus

Holy Week 11.1–14.52

11.1–11	Palm Sunday; Jesus enters Jerusalem
11.12–19	Monday
11.12–14	Curse of the fig tree
11.15–19	Cleansing of the Temple
11.20–13.37	Tuesday
11.20–26	Lesson about faith
11.27–33	Jesus' controversy with the authorities: True Authority

12.1–12	Parable of the Tenants
12.13–17	Paying taxes
12.18–27	The resurrection
12.28–34	The greatest commandment
12.35–37	The Messiah's status
12.38–40	Warning against teachers of the law
12.41–44	Widow's offering
13.1–37	The destruction of the Temple and the Last Judgement
14.1–11	Wednesday
14.1–2	The plot against Jesus
14.3–9	Jesus is anointed
14.10–11	Judas joins the plot
14.12–52	Maundy Thursday
14.12–31	The Last Supper
14.32–42	Jesus' prayer in Gethsemane
14.43–52	Jesus' betrayal and arrest

Jesus' trials 14.53–15.20

14.53–65	Jesus' trial before the Jewish Council
14.66–72	Peter's threefold denial
15.1–47	Good Friday
15.1–20	Jesus' trial before Pilate and mockery

The death and resurrection of Jesus 15.21 – 16.20

15.21–41	The crucifixion of Jesus
15.42–47	The burial
16.1–20	Easter Sunday
16.1–8	The visit of the women to the tomb
16.9–20	Various appearances of the risen Jesus, probably from other sources

Mark, Secret Gospel of The manuscript of this 'Gospel' as such does not exist. What evidence there is comes from an 18th-century copy of a letter ascribed to the 2nd-century Church Father Clement of Alexandria. This letter was found by the historian Morton Smith in 1958 in the library of the Orthodox monastery at Mar Saba in the Judaean wilderness. Clement's letter quotes two passages from a longer, 'more spiritual' edition of the Gospel of Mark, supposed to be produced for advanced believers in Alexandria. But Clement warns his correspondent Theodore that the text was further contaminated by the Carpocratian heretics. The Secret Gospel included, after Mark 10.34, an account of the raising of an unnamed young man from a tomb, which is reminiscent of the story of the Raising of LAZARUS in John 11. What follows is a rite of initiation of the young man, which has some HOMOSEXUAL implications. Many scholars doubt the authenticity of this material.

marriage In the earliest times reflected in the Hebrew Bible the PATRIARCHS appear to have followed the polygamous norms of the 2nd millennium BCE. The customs reported, for example of ABRAHAM taking the servant Hagar to supplement his childless wife Sarah in producing an heir, are paralleled in contemporary non-Biblical writing unearthed by archaeologists (such as the NUZI tablets of the Hurrians). See also the custom of LEVIRATE MARRIAGE, as in Genesis 38. At a considerably later date, c.1100 BCE, the prophet SAMUEL is born in a polygamous household. And during the period of the monarchy down to the EXILE the status of the king was proclaimed by the number of his wives and concubines.

The use of royal polygamy ran the danger of sealing international alliances by the acquisition of foreign wives. The Hebrew Bible is alert to the consequence in contaminating Israelite worship by the introduction of foreign deities. Increasing emphasis on the purity of the Jewish bloodline through the mother is well illustrated in NEHEMIAH's outburst to those returning from Exile (Nehemiah 13.23–27: notice the reference to SOLOMON some 500 years earlier in verse 26). (This attitude was not without its critics; it is often suggested that the point of the book of RUTH is to protest that King DAVID's own ancestor was devout, but foreign.) The exclusiveness of the marriage relationship (at least on the female side) was to safeguard the inheritance from bogus claimants, and was jealously protected. ADULTERY by either party was forbidden by the DECALOGUE (the Ten Commandments).

It is not known whether changing fashion or the economics of the Exilic period caused monogamy to evolve as the norm. By the time of Jesus monogamy appears to have been the usual pattern in JUDAISM, even if the fluidity of the debate on DIVORCE among the RABBIS may have permitted some men to enjoy serial monogamy (see Mark 10.11–12). Jesus' view appears to have been based on the CREATION story in Genesis, that an unbreakable lifelong bond is forged when a man unites with his wife (Mark 10.6–9). Any other sexual relationship, outside the marriage bed, was still forbidden by the commandment against adultery.

PAUL famously taught that, given the importance of spiritual preparation for the approaching End Time (*see* ESCHATON), marriage was a second-best option for those incapable of coping with CELIBACY (see 1 Corinthians 7.1, 7–9, 26, 32–34). Marriage was, however, preferable to immorality (7.2) and partners should satisfy one another, except for mutual abstinence for prayer (7.5). Paul quotes Jesus (7.10) that a wife should not leave her husband; if she does, she must remain single or be reconciled. Marriage to an unbeliever must have presented a tricky situation for a new convert; Paul's advice was to remain married, if this was acceptable to the pagan partner, as this might lead to the salvation of the partner (7.13–16).

When the pressure of imminent expectation of the End Time was eased, and the early Church had time to adjust to more uniform living, the later writings in the Pauline tradition (EPHESIANS, COLOSSIANS and the PASTORALS) offered more general advice to families. The marriage relationship for Christians appeared to be on the model of male domination and female submission (see Colossians 3.18). The theology justifying this polarity was worked out in Ephesians 5.22–33; the parallel was the headship of Christ over the CHURCH. The idea of female submission was seen in 1 Peter 3.1–6 as a means for winning an unbelieving husband's conversion. The gentle spirit of the devout wife was seen as her true beauty, earning the accolade of the daughters of SARAH. For modern readers the redeeming feature is that husbands should love their wives (Colossians 3.19). Ephesians 5.28–29 extends this: 'husbands should love their wives as they do their own bodies'. 1 Peter 3.7 requires an attitude of respect.

Marriage as an unequal partnership, with theological and Biblical warrant, was the norm for Christians, although the balance of power in the relationship may have been rather different for many GENTILE women. They could often be involved in business deals, and not totally immersed in domesticity like the Jewish housewife.

Martha and Mary of Bethany Martha and Mary were sisters, living at Bethany, whose brother LAZARUS was raised by Jesus from the dead (according to John 11). In this unique account, although Martha goes to meet Jesus while Mary stays at home, both sisters effectively rebuke Jesus for his delay in coming, and both express their belief in Jesus' power to intervene. Elsewhere in the Gospels, as in Luke 10.38–42, a contrast is drawn between Martha and Mary in the way they respond to Jesus. Here Martha seems preoccupied with concerns of domesticity and hospitality, while Mary is devoted to Jesus' teaching. In the Johannine account also (as narrated in chapter 12, but anticipated in 11.2) it is this Mary who anoints the feet of Jesus with expensive perfume; this action is elsewhere traditionally attributed to another Mary, MARY OF MAGDALA.

martyr The original meaning of the Greek word *martus* is 'witness', an idea which corresponds to the preaching activities of the first Christian APOSTLES (see Acts 1.8, 22; Revelation 11.3). These representatives of the faith 'are not called witnesses because they die, but they die because they are witnesses'. Facing up to death becomes a corollary of the definition: for the witness it is not only what you possess in faith, but also what you communicate and what you are prepared to give up.

The Greek word *martus* has a clear derivative in the English word 'martyr'. There is a question here about language: at what point did the Greek word move to a regular meaning of 'martyr' rather than 'witness'? From a study of early Christian history, as the context for the book of REVELATION, it can be concluded that 'the sphere in which the martyr concept developed was the Church in Asia Minor' and that 'the first clear steps taken towards such a development' are to be found in Revelation. By the end of the 1st century CE Clement of Rome is able to use the term to refer to the martyrdoms of the apostles PETER and PAUL (see *1 Clement* 5). The persecution of Christian scapegoats in Rome by Emperor Nero at the time of the fire of Rome (64–67 CE) will have helped to promote this sense.

Mary of Bethany *See* MARTHA AND MARY OF BETHANY.

Mary Magdalene, or Mary of Magdala Luke 8.2 mentions a number of women who were with Jesus, including 'Mary called Magdalene from whom seven demons had gone out'. After this EXORCISM she followed Jesus and provided for him. She was at the CRUCIFIXION (Matthew 27.56; Mark 15.40; John 19.25) and she watched JOSEPH OF ARIMATHEA bury Jesus' body (Mark 15.42–47). On Easter morning she came with other women to the tomb; they were met by angels who sent them to tell the disciples what had happened (Mark 16.1–8). John 20.11–18 has an account of a personal appearance to her by the risen Christ.

Mary was commonly regarded in Church tradition as a prostitute, and identified (without warrant) as the woman who is a penitent sinner in Luke 7.37. The word *M'gadd'la*, meaning 'hairdresser', was a common euphemism for a prostitute. (But Magdala was also the name of a city on the shores of the Sea of GALILEE, three miles north of Tiberias). In the early centuries there was often a 'collage', a conflation in both Jewish and Christian circles, of the various women who had been associated with Jesus, including MARY, MOTHER OF JESUS, because of the dubious reputation of the VIRGIN BIRTH. As an archetypal sinner, Mary Magdalene was thought to have been forgiven by Jesus (on another analogy, this time with the adulterous woman in John 8.11). Apparently because she is forgiven, she is traditionally regarded as a fit person to be commissioned to tell the news of the RESURRECTION (as in John 20.17).

The Church Father Origen promoted Mary Magdalene as the symbol of erotic asceticism, applying to her the language of the SONG OF SONGS. In the modern novel *The Last Temptation* by Nikos Kazantzakis she is the final test for Christ, as erotic love is 'the sweetest the world can offer'. Other modern interest in Mary Magdalene is from GNOSTIC or feminist perspectives. The Gnostic *Gospel of Mary* is an attack on 2nd-century orthodoxy: 'she is the Savior's beloved, possessed of [superior] knowledge'. This theme is exploited in Dan Brown's best-selling novel *The Da Vinci Code*.

Mary, mother of Jesus There is a contrast between the importance of Mary in Christian tradition as 'mother of my Lord', and the brevity of her modest cameo appearances in the narrative of the New Testament. Also, even today, there is debate about the precise nature of Jesus' birth (*see* VIRGIN BIRTH). Mary's appearances in the New Testament are, principally: the announcement of the birth by the archangel Gabriel (Luke 1.26–38); Mary's visit to her cousin Elizabeth (Luke 1.39–56); the journey to BETHLEHEM and the birth of Jesus (Luke 2.1–20); the presentation of Jesus at the Temple in Jerusalem, to SIMEON and ANNA (Luke 2.22–39); Mary's discovery of the 12-year-old Jesus discoursing with the elders (Luke 2.41–52); her intervention with Jesus about the wine at the CANA marriage (John 2.1–11); the visit of Mary with his brothers to Jesus (Mark 3.31–35); her place at the foot of the cross, together with the BELOVED DISCIPLE (John 19.26–27); and with the apostles at prayer (Acts 1.14). The text of Acts 2 does not say specifically that she was present at PENTECOST, although this is often assumed on the basis of 'all' in 2.1.

The ecumenical Church Council held at EPHESUS in 431 CE acknowledged Mary as *theotokos* ('the bearer of him who is God' or 'Mother of God'). The precise implications concerning Mary's place in the purposes of God are disputed between the various Christian traditions; the Reformation reacted against the devotion to Mary ('Our Lady') in the later Middle Ages, although Martin LUTHER was positive about her role as the Church's teacher of praise and thanksgiving: 'She leads the choir, and we should follow her with singing.' This idea is based on the song attributed to Mary (the Magnificat) in Luke 1.46–55: 'She sums up the way God rules, in one short text, a joyful song for all the lowly.'

The traditional house of the Virgin Mary, high up on the hillside overlooking Ephesus, was identified long distance in a sickbed vision by a German nun, Anne Catherine Emmerich. Given the association of John (as the Beloved Disciple) with Ephesus, and the instruction at the cross that he should look after Mary, it is at least logical that she should be associated with a particular site in or near Ephesus. But the huge bronze statue (on the pilgrim route) to Mary as Our Lady of Ephesus may owe something in her posture to the mother goddess Artemis, associated with Ephesus for even longer.

Masada Masada is a natural fortress covering 20 acres in the Judaean desert on the Dead Sea coast, 11 miles south of the oasis of Ein Gedi and 24 miles south of QUMRAN. Its diamond-shaped citadel rises to a height of 1500 feet above the surrounding area. Major excavations of the site were conducted between 1963 and 1965 by Yigael Yadin, Israel's most illustrious archaeologist. The Jewish historian JOSEPHUS chronicled the history of Masada, indicating that it was occupied by the HASMONEANS in the early 1st century BCE, but to date no archaeological evidence has been found for this period. When HEROD THE GREAT assumed the throne, with the help of the Romans, he rebuilt the fortress as part exotic palace, part defensive fortress. During the JEWISH WAR against Rome, between the years 66 and 74 CE, the site was occupied by Jewish rebels whom Josephus identified as *sicarii* (terrorists). But Yadin consistently referred to the occupants as ZEALOTS (or one of the Jewish parties particularly in favour of the war). The Zealots had fled to Masada with their families, where they maintained a religiously observant, family-orientated community, building a SYNAGOGUE and ritual baths. Some vessels found on site are made of earth or cattle dung, and used to store dry goods; apparently according to Jewish law such vessels made simply from natural materials, unlike those of fired pottery, cannot incur ritual impurity (*see also* PURITY). The Zealots held out until faced by the full deployment of the Roman Tenth Legion in 72 CE. Even then the Romans took time to evolve a successful plan of attack. The mountain was encircled by a wall two miles long; eight siege camps were constructed, and then finally a massive earth ramp on the western side for the deployment of battering rams. According to Josephus the Zealots finally committed suicide, rather than surrender to the Romans; food was left in view, to show that their supplies were not exhausted.

In modern Israel, not least as a result of Yadin's excavations, Masada has become a centre of youth pilgrimage, and a symbol of the indestructability of the Jewish people.

massebah *Massebah* is the Hebrew word for a stone set on end and standing upright, with possible associations of phallic symbolism. In the Hebrew Bible they are frequently mentioned, and criticized, in connection with the sanctuaries ('high places' or *bamoth*) – see for example 1 Kings 14.23 and 2 Kings 18.4. Here these stones or 'pillars' are mentioned in association with the ASHERAH, the wooden pole or sacred tree which symbolized the female deity. The massebah is not restricted to the sanctuary; see for example those at Tel DAN. It could certainly be used as a symbol of divine presence, as in the story of JACOB at Genesis 28.18. But other commemorative purposes are possible, as with the stone set up by JOSHUA in the sanctuary at SHECHEM (Joshua 24.26–27). In a cultic context it could represent the male deity, paired with the Asherah, but it could also stand as a memorial of the dead, or a reminder of an important idea. The purpose of particular examples, discovered by archaeologists, is often much debated.

Massoretes The Massoretes were Jewish scholars (grammarians) between the 6th and 10th centuries CE who were dedicated to preserving in the most accurate form the text of the Hebrew Bible. Working in centres such as Tiberias, they laid down conventions for the copying of manuscripts and established systems for representing the vowels in texts where only consonants were normally written down. When a living knowledge of HEBREW was either fading or being corrupted, the meaning of the consonantal text would be lost without the help of these systems of vocalic signs and accents, written either underneath or above the letters (Tiberian or Palestinian systems). The text these scholars promoted is known as the Massoretic text (Hebrew *massorah* = tradition); it was successful in ensuring accurate copying of scriptures over many centuries. Our knowledge of the Massoretes' work is largely due to the researches of Paul Kahle on a wealth of manuscripts discovered in the 19th century in the Cairo synagogue.

Mattathias 1 *See* MACCABEES; **2** *see* MATTHIAS.

Matthew (apostle) Matthew, a tax-collector called as a DISCIPLE of Jesus (according to Matthew 9.9), is traditionally the author of that Gospel. The Gospels of Mark (2.14) and Luke (5.27) refer to the tax-collector as Levi (son of Alphaeus); it is possible that he had both names as well as the patronymic. The Church Father Papias attributes to Matthew a collection of the sayings of Jesus in HEBREW.

Matthew, Gospel according to Matthew's Gospel was the most widely read and frequently used of any of the four Gospels in the formative years of the CHURCH. It provided the foundation for the lectionaries of Church readings, other Gospels being used to supplement. This probably explains why it occurs first in the canonical sequence of four, while most scholars now believe that MARK was the earliest Gospel. The prime position held by Matthew for 17 centuries must have been due to the initial support and advocacy of an important centre of early Christianity, such as ANTIOCH in Syria.

Matthew was especially significant for the local Church community for which it was originally composed. It has been suggested that it functioned as a handbook for Church teaching, administration, and discipline (see Matthew 18). The community emerges from a JEWISH-CHRISTIAN context and has to wrestle with the problem of its relationship to Judaism and particular Jewish teachers, the PHARISEES (see Matthew 23). In Matthew (27.25) the people of Israel strikingly declare their responsibility for the death of Christ. Only in this Gospel is the word *ekklesia* ('Church') used to define the community in relation to the authority of Peter and the power of excommunication (16.17–19; 18.17). The author himself may well have been trained as a rabbi (13.52).

This Gospel could be called 'the Torah of the New COVENANT' for it emphasizes law, practice and piety. The relationship with the Hebrew Scriptures is stressed by numerous formulaic proof texts, quoted from the Old Testament, and by the GENEALOGY (1.1–17). The genealogy also reveals an interest in NUMBER SYMBOLISM: 14 is actually the numerical value of the Hebrew letters in the name 'DAVID' (and thus of messianic significance); and 1.17 reveals that there are (or should be) three times 14 generations in Jesus' ancestry. The Gospel presents the teaching of Jesus arranged in five ser-mons/discourses (see the tabulation below) which are sometimes compared struc-turally with the PENTATEUCH, and theologically perhaps with the idea of Jesus as a new MOSES. What is advocated in these sermons is the active following up of the words of the Messiah. The most frequently quoted is the first of these discourses, the SERMON ON THE MOUNT (Matthew 5.1–7.27).

TABULATION OF MATTHEW

Note: Matthew may have thought of Jesus as the new Moses, the Lawgiver. He seems to have organized his material between Jesus' birth and Passion into five parts, perhaps mirroring the five books of the Law. Each part is rounded off with a conclusion – 7.28, 11.1, 13.53, 19.1, 26.1.

The Genealogy and Birth of Jesus 1.1–2.23

Part 1: The beginning of Jesus' ministry 3.1–7.29

3.1–17	The preaching of John the Baptist and the baptism of Jesus
4.1–11	The temptations of Jesus
4.12–25	Jesus preaches and heals in Galilee
5.1–7.29	The Sermon on the Mount
5.1–12	The Beatitudes
5.13–48	The new law
6.1–7.12	True religion and service to God
7.13–29	The challenge to accept Jesus' authoritative teaching

Part 2: Work in Galilee 8.1–11.1

8.1–9.38	Catalogue of healings
10.1–11.1	Call and mission of the 12; the nature and cost of discipleship

Part 3: The realm of God's Kingdom 11.2–13.53

11.2–19	John the Baptist reconsidered
11.20–12.50	Collection of teaching
13.1–53	Parables of growth and treasure related to the Kingdom

Part 4: The signs and wonders of the Kingdom and life in the 'Church' 13.54–19.2

13.54–58	The rejection of Jesus at Nazareth
14.1–12	Death of John the Baptist
14.13–16.12	Many miracles including the Great Feeding (of the 5000)
16.13–17.23	The nature of true Messiahship (including the Transfiguration)
17.24–27	Temple tax
18.1–35	Membership of the Kingdom
19.1–2	Galilee to Judaea

Part 5: The Kingdom and conflict 19.3–26.2

19.3–15	Marriage and children
19.16–20.16	Membership of the Kingdom
20.17–28	Jesus' death and the disciples' ambition

20.29–34	Cure of the blind
21.1–17	Entry into Jerusalem and cleansing of the Temple
21.18–22.46	Jesus' authority
23.1–39	Jesus pronounces against Jewish leaders
24.1–26.2	The signs of the End Time and the return of the Son of Man in judgement

The Passion and Death of Jesus 26.3–27.66

26.3–5, 14–16	The plot against Jesus and Judas' role
26.6–13	The anointing
26.17–35	The Last Supper
26.36–56	Jesus in Gethsemane and his arrest
26.57–27.26	Jesus' trial and Peter's denial
27.27–66	The crucifixion and burial

The Resurrection of Jesus 28.1–20

28.1–10	The appearance to the women
28.11–15	The guards cover their tracks
28.16–20	Jesus commands a worldwide mission

Matthias According to the narrative of Acts 1.15–26, Matthias (perhaps Mattathias) was selected by lot to take the place among the 12 DISCIPLES of Jesus that had been vacated by JUDAS ISCARIOT's betrayal. The suggestion is that he was a follower of Jesus from the early days of the mission, perhaps one of the SEVENTY, although there is no mention of him elsewhere in the New Testament. In more democratic days the selection by lot is sometimes distrusted, but the Biblical precedent would undoubtedly be the use of the sacred lot (URIM AND THUMMIM) by the HIGH PRIEST.

Megiddo *See* ARMAGEDDON.

Melchizedek Melchizedek is a shadowy priest figure, mentioned in the story of ABRAHAM at Genesis 14. His Hebrew name associates the ideas of kingship and righteousness. He was king of Salem (JERUSALEM?) and priest of 'GOD most high' (*'El Elyon'*); he came with bread and wine to meet Abram and pronounced a blessing upon him.

The combination of PRIEST/king is developed in the text of the enthronement psalm (Psalm 110.4), in which the Davidic king is declared to be 'a priest for ever after the order of Melchizedek'. In HEBREWS (5.6–10; 6.20–7.28) this particular line of priesthood is applied to Christ, to show his superiority over the regular Jewish (Aaronic) priesthood. There was widespread speculation about the significance of the Melchizedek figure in 1st century BCE Judaism; he could be historical, or an intermediary representing the WORD of God, or an ANGEL of the last days (see Qumran text 11QMelch).

mene, mene, tekel, and parsin According to the story of King BELSHAZZAR's Feast, in chapter 5 of the book of DANIEL, these are the words that appeared written on the wall by the fingers of a human hand, thereby striking terror into the king as he watched them. Daniel interprets the words in 5.26–28: 'God has numbered the days of your kingdom and brought it to an end; you have been weighed on the scales and found wanting; your kingdom is divided and given to the Medes and Persians.' The fact of the matter was that BABYLON was conquered by Cyrus of Persia in 539 BCE. The words written on the wall are actually ARAMAIC units of weight and COINAGE: the mina, the shekel, and the half mina, in diminishing order of value. So the simple meaning is that Babylon's worth is disappearing; the later interpretation in verses 26–28 is more complicated, and, by means of puns, creates Aramaic verbs from the names of the coins. For example, from *parsin* comes *prs* meaning 'divide' and, in addition, a further pun on the name 'PERSIAN'.

menorah This is the huge golden seven-branched candelabrum which stood in the First and Second TEMPLES in Jerusalem until Herod's Temple was sacked by the Romans in 70 CE. (Its prototype is described in Exodus 25.31–40, 37.17–24 and Num-

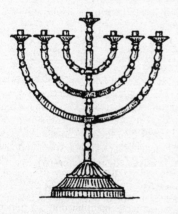

The Candelabrum

bers 8.2–4, as made for the desert TABER-NACLE in accordance with God's instructions to Moses. The books of MAC-CABEES describe how the Temple treasures were pillaged by Antiochus IV Epiphanes in 169 BCE, but the candelabrum and other altar furniture were purified and restored by JUDAS MACCABEUS in 164 BCE.) The Triumphal Arch of TITUS, which can still be seen in Rome on the site of the Forum, includes a relief depicting Roman legionaries bearing away the menorah in triumph with the other spoils of the campaign. JOSEPHUS' account of the *Jewish War* describes how a Jewish priest named Phineas handed over the sacred treasures and how they were carried in the Roman triumph ('a golden table and a menorah of gold, and a copy of the Jewish Law') and then stored in Vespasian's Temple of Peace. A persistent rumour suggested that the menorah was still kept in the Vatican, although the 18th-century historian Edward Gibbon believed that it was pillaged from Rome by Vandals and then lost in the Mediterranean following a shipwreck. Other suggestions are that it might be in Venice, or Constantinople, if not melted down long ago.

The menorah became a popular Jewish symbol and is the emblem of the state of Israel. The lamp for the feast of HANUKKAH is constructed on a similar pattern, but with eight or nine arms.

mercy Whereas the Hebrew Bible in picturing God frequently refers to his anger with his people (over APOSTASY and injustice, for example), it also often shows God as having overwhelming characteristics of mercy and compassion, that are usually completely undeserved by the recipient. So God's love for Israel, depicted in the life story of the unhappy prophet HOSEA and his faithless prostitute-wife GOMER, produces wider hope for the future with a renewal of their MARRIAGE vows (Hosea 2.19–20, where the keynote is the 'steadfast love and mercy' shown by God). The later prophecies in Isaiah 55.7 find hope for the future in God's nature to be merciful and quick to forgive. The dependability of God in response to prayer is also attributed to this quality of mercy: 'Gracious is the Lord and righteous; our God is merciful. The Lord protects the simple; when I was brought low, he saved me' (Psalm 116.5–6).

These aspects of mercy are shown in the New Testament too; here mercy is linked especially to SALVATION (see Romans 11.30; Titus 3.5; 1 Peter 2.10: 'Once you were not a people, but now you are God's people; once you had not received mercy, but now you have received mercy', quoting Hosea). Christians are to be merciful, as God is merciful (Luke 6.36). The BEATITUDES declare that God will be merciful to them in response to the mercy they show to others (Matthew 5.7). Mercy also becomes part of the prayer of Church leaders for their congregations in the later epistles, linked together with GRACE and PEACE (see 1 Timothy 1.2; 2 Timothy 1.2; 2 John 3; Jude 2).

Meribah See KADESH BARNEA.

Merkabah See CHERUBIM AND SERAPHIM; EZEKIEL, BOOK OF.

Merodach-baladan See BABYLONIANS.

Meshach See SHADRACH, MESHACH, AND ABEDNEGO.

Messiah The original Hebrew word refers to someone who is 'anointed'. The Greek word that is the proper name 'Christ' means the same. In the Old Testament both PRIESTS and kings were anointed for their tasks (see UNCTION). When kingship failed in Israel, largely after, and because of, the Babylonian EXILE, the ideas of a God-given ruler of his people were projected onto an ideal figure, a future king or Messiah. This figure would be associated with the tradition of the Son of DAVID, anointed as king and adopted as a SON OF GOD (the promise of the Davidic succession is contained in 2 Samuel 7.12–15 and further expressed in Psalms 2, 89, and 132, and in *Psalms of Solomon* 17). Actual expectations varied enormously at different times and places; the word itself occurs sparingly (see Daniel 9.25–26). JOSEPHUS (*Antiquities* 17) documents the existence of those who were viewed by their followers as messianic figures, basically rebels against the Romans and the Jewish ruling elite, before and after the death of HEROD THE GREAT (4 BCE). The prevalent powerlessness politically of the people had the effect of inspiring nationalism and messianic revolts.

For the wider view *see* TITLES OF JESUS.

messianic woes See TRIBULATION, GREAT.

Micah, book of In the Hebrew Bible, Micah is the sixth book of the Minor Prophets. It is attributed to an 8th-century BCE prophet, Micah of Moresheth-gath (south-west of Jerusalem in the Shephelah foothills) who was a younger contemporary of ISAIAH of Jerusalem. Some of Micah's words are quoted in JEREMIAH 26.18, to the rescue of the later prophet, in a context which suggests that Micah was one of the city elders of Judah; but other commentators describe Micah as a labourer, and his work as a rural protest movement against urban corruption.

In several respects Micah is similar to Isaiah as he faces the threat posed by ASSYRIA towards the Southern Kingdom of Judah. He did not believe that Jerusalem would be inviolable because of a reliance on the DAVID-ZION tradition. The book of Micah has three sections: chapters 1–3 contain the oracular preaching of judgement; chapters 4 and 5 are oracles of salvation which have the effect of softening the harshness of what has gone before; and finally chapters 6 and 7 are a mixture of critical reflections and cultic psalms. This last section contains the most quotable text from the book, the formulation of the divine demand for justice in 6.6–8: 'What does the Lord require of you, but to do justice, and to love kindness, and to walk humbly with your God?' Like AMOS, Micah is concerned with ethical issues, and attacks social and economic injustice.

The name Micah (a shortened form of MICAIAH) means 'Who is like the Lord!' which is an exclamation of the incomparability of Israel's God.

Micaiah The story of Micaiah, son of Imlah, as told in 1 Kings 22.6–28, provides an interesting contrast between types of PROPHECY in Israel. Micaiah is an independent prophet who refuses to be bullied into giving a prophecy favourable to the king, but suffers in consequence. He is in dispute with ZEDEKIAH, son of Chenaanah, who is the leader of a group of 400 court prophets, dedicated to giving the politically required answer. Religiously minded independence, that sees more clearly the fate King AHAB deserves, is ultimately commended in the traditions of Israelite prophecy.

Michael Michael is usually listed as the first of the archangels (chief ANGELS). In the visionary survey of past and future in DANIEL chapters 10–12, Michael appears as 'one of the chief princes' who offers assistance to the Jewish people (Daniel 10.13, 21). A prince in this sense is the patron angel of a people. This idea derives from ancient Near Eastern mythology in which a conflict between patron or guardian deities corresponds to actual warfare between their peoples. In the last days Michael will again appear as the prince of Israel who leads the good angels in the WAR IN HEAVEN (REVELATION 12). In Jewish traditions Michael is variously identified with the angel who wrestled with JACOB (Genesis 32) or who touched the prophet ISAIAH's lips with a live coal (Isaiah 6.6–7); when he contends with SATAN (or the devil Sammael) to preserve the body of Moses (JUDE 9), this also reflects a Jewish legend from the Talmud.

Michal Michal was the beautiful younger daughter of King SAUL, who was presented to DAVID in marriage as his first wife (see 1 Samuel 14.49; 18.20). But Saul was plotting to dispose of his popular rival and so set David the bride-price (*mohar*) of 100 PHIL-ISTINE foreskins. David produced double the number, which only increased Saul's anger. Michal, who loved David, helped him to escape from an ambush set for him by the king. Forced to lie by her father, Michal said that David had threatened her. Accordingly Saul gave her in marriage to Palti/Paltiel (see 1 Samuel 25.44). When David triumphed over Saul, he claimed his wife back, to legitimate his succession to the throne, and he dispatched his henchman Abner to fetch her. In a poignant moment (2 Samuel 3.16) Paltiel follows Michal, 'weeping as he walked behind her all the way to Bahurim', until Abner told him to go back. Later it is said that an embarrassed Michal rebuked David for dancing before the ARK OF THE COVENANT when it was brought to Jerusalem (see 2 Samuel 6.16; 6.20 suggests that the embarrassment was because the DANCE was performed naked – hardly proper for a man in mixed company, and certainly not for a king).

Midianites *See* GIDEON; POTIPHAR; SLAVERY.

Millennium, millenarianism The Millennium, literally the 1000-year reign on earth of Christ with his saints, is based on the expectation described in the book of REVELATION, chapter 20.1–7. It sounds like a long period, but it is conceived as an interim during which SATAN is imprisoned, and the saints who share Christ's RESURRECTION are vindicated. This Biblical prophecy became the basis of belief for a number of sectarian groups through the centuries, whose activities and ideas are often termed chiliastic, or millenarian.

Believers can be classified into two major categories, simply on the grounds of the decision they have made in the two related areas of chronology and psychology: which comes first, the LAST JUDGEMENT or the PAROUSIA or return of Christ; and is one at heart an optimist or a pessimist?

The *pre-millennialist* position operates with a quatrain of components: cataclysms – pessimism – doom – passivity. Such a believer typically would hold that the reign of Jesus Christ and the saints for 1000 years has not yet begun. When it is inaugurated, this will be a direct result of divine intervention; it will be accompanied by various cataclysmic happenings both in world affairs (affecting empires, governments, Churches) and in the natural realm (such as earthquakes, floods and fire). Christ will become the physical ruler of this world until the final ARMAGEDDON, when Satan is at last unbound, the final conflict takes place, the righteous are raised from the dead, and the Last Judgement occurs. (*See also* FUNDAMENTALISM.)

The corresponding position of the *post-millennialist* also works with a quatrain, only this time they are: reformism – optimism – progress – action. This believer also regards the millennium as a future event, but instead of direct divine intervention it is the work of God's human agents, the current Christian community in particular, which brings to realization the glorious future. The coming of the millennium will not be accompanied by a series of cataclysmic events; instead it develops and evolves through human history. The case has been argued to show that the medieval use of APOCALYPTIC concepts and utopian ideas itself became transformed into the modern, secular ideas of progress and EVOLUTION. So it could be claimed by E. L. Tuveson that 'the Enlightenment belief in progress was the spiritual heir of the prophetic vision of a perfect, future kingdom and thus had its roots in post-millennialism'.

miniature The word 'miniature' as a technical term refers to an illustration in an ancient manuscript of a Biblical book or commentary. Sometimes these can be described as 'large miniatures', for the word has nothing to do with a diminutive size. They are so called because these paintings make significant use of red lead, or *minium* in Latin.

ministry The New Testament period witnessed a number of different attempts by the fledgling Church to organize itself, with the result that many denominations today can legitimately claim New Testament precedent for their own distinctive form of ministry. There was no one blueprint to follow, in fact many Christians subscribe to the 'priesthood of all believers', rather than elevating a clerical class; this is on the basis of 1 PETER 2.9, with REVELATION 1.5–6 and 5.9–10.

Chronologically the first ministers were APOSTLES (DISCIPLES) chosen to be with Jesus, to preach and to exorcize (see EXORCISM), according to Mark 3.14–15. According to the ACTS OF THE APOSTLES, they became so busy in prayer and preaching during the post-RESURRECTION period, that they appointed assistants (deacons) to assist with the charitable distributions to the needy (see Acts 6.1–7). If this calling was the substance of their early ministry, their *curriculum vitae* had nevertheless required them to be 'full of the SPIRIT and WISDOM', and then they were marked out by an action of ordination in the laying on of hands (see Acts 6.3, 6). Two of these deacons in Acts became prominent for their preaching, and one of them, STEPHEN, died an exemplary MARTYR's death (see Acts 7.59–60).

Despite not being one of the original 12, PAUL claimed apostleship (Galatians 2.8). This great preacher founded Churches in the GENTILE world and recognized various categories of minister within them – 'God has appointed in the Church first apostles, second PROPHETS, third teachers' (1 Corinthians 12.28); various sorts of CHARISMATIC gifts and healing and leadership skills are also listed. All of these people worked together for, and within, the BODY OF CHRIST. Paul also notes freedom and flexibility within Church WORSHIP, particularly within the delivery of charismata; this does not seem to have been directed, or dominated, by any hierarchy (see 1 Corinthians 14, especially 14.26–33). Although Paul was anxious that the Lord's Supper (*see* EUCHARIST) be properly conducted (see 1 Corinthians 11), it is not obvious that this was the responsibility of a particular minister.

In accordance with Greek and Jewish traditions ELDERS were respected members of the community, and it may be in this sense that the elders in the Jerusalem Church are to be understood (see Acts 15.4). On the other hand, according to Acts 14.23, Paul and BARNABAS appointed officials – elders – to run their newly founded Churches after their own departures (this may have been on the model of the SYNAGOGUE). Then a generation later there are references to elders (presbyters) as leaders in the congregation, for example Titus 1.5–9, where the elder's conduct must be above reproach and monogamous, and 1 Timothy 3.1–7, where the elder must curb his drinking and control his own family before he can be entrusted with the care of a Church. (See also 1 Peter 5.1, and possibly 2 John 1; 3 John 1.) The same standard of upright personal behaviour is expected of Church helpers (1 Timothy 3.8–13) whose role is one of service (unspecified).

Nowhere is there mention of a class of PRIESTS, perhaps because for JEWISH-CHRISTIANS this would have recalled the staff of the Jerusalem TEMPLE, and for the Gentiles it bound them too closely with the cult at pagan shrines. Some would assume that the apostles were, however, the forerunners of the priests, and as the need for more managerial oversight across several Churches in an area became obvious, the prototype for bishops too. In the 2nd century CE, after the New Testament, we can trace the emergence of the proper episcopate as such, although the word for a bishop/overseer is already being used in 1 Timothy and Titus of the Church leader.

So far all of the above has assumed that ministers, of whatever title, were male, and much has been made in the past of Paul's injunction to women to remain silent in church (see 1 Corinthians 14.34–35) in the debate over the ordination of women. On the other side of the argument, Paul himself acknowledges the formidable ministry (diaconate) of Phoebe (Romans 16.1–2). PRISCILLA was the (leading?) partner of Aquila in their house church, first in Corinth (1 Corinthians 16.19) and then in Rome (Romans 16.3). Other women listed in the greetings in Romans are Mary (16.6); JUNIA (16.7); Tryphaena and Tryphosa (16.12); Julia and Nereus' sister (16.15). Even squabbling Euodia and Syntyche were acknowledged to have worked hard in spreading the Gospel (Philippians 4.2–3). Elsewhere older widows seem to have a valued role in pastoral and charitable duties (1 Timothy 5.10). The New Testament ministry certainly should not be seen as in any sense monochrome.

Minor Prophets, twelve See individual articles for the books of AMOS, HABAKKUK, HAGGAI, HOSEA, JOEL, JONAH, MALACHI, MICAH, NAHUM, OBADIAH, ZECHARIAH, and ZEPHANIAH.

miracles A miracle is an extraordinary happening, something not easily explained by existing frames of reference; as a result it is interpreted as directly caused by God or supernatural agencies. In some ages a miracle has been seen as proof of the divine and a justification for faith; at other times there is at least a reluctance to think that God would ever compel belief by 'knock-down' physical miracles that resemble a laser beam.

The miracles of the Hebrew Bible (such as creating a dry crossing of the Red Sea – Exodus 14), and more particularly the nature miracles, healings and resurrections recorded in the New Testament Gospels as the work of Jesus, and even the RESURRECTION of Jesus himself, have proved an embarrassment to many in modern times, as the result of rationalism and new scientific understanding, and also with the rise of BIBLICAL CRITICISM. The consequence may be agnosticism, secularism, or even atheism. Even in the time of Jesus there is some evidence of embarrassment, and of a tradition opposed to miracles, with which Jesus himself seems to sympathize (see Mark 8.12; John 4.48).

But the miracles have an important function in the New Testament which needs to be recognized, even in an age when such stories tend to be discarded as myths (in the basic sense, but *see* MYTH). They indicate a dimension of power that is outside normal human experience, a pointer to a cosmic dimension of existence, a breaking-in of the KINGDOM OF GOD into the realities of this world. In the imminent anticipation of the End Time, the order of CREATION comes to a future climax that will more than equal the impact of its first beginning. At the very least the best of the miracle tradition shows the respect that is due to the natural order, and this in modern terms might be translated into 'concern for the environment'.

The different kinds of miracle story in the New Testament are revelations – apocalypses – to their audience. The SYNOPTIC Gospels play on the dimension of 'wonder' and refer to them as 'powerful happenings' (*dunameis*). JOHN'S GOSPEL prefers to use

Jesus Heals a Leper Matthew 8.1–4

the language of SIGNS (*semeia*) and so point in a more intellectual or spiritual way to the deeper significance of these events.

Miriam Miriam was the sister of AARON and MOSES; she is probably mentioned in Exodus 2.1–10 as the woman who advised Pharaoh's daughter and so preserved the life of Moses (see the story of the BIRTH OF MOSES). The figure of Miriam appears in a fresco of the discovery of the child Moses at the 3rd-century synagogue at DURA EUROPOS. Because of this role she is celebrated as one of the great women of Israel. She functions as a prophetess (the first woman to be named in the Bible) as she leads the women of Israel in a song of victory, after the EXODUS from Egypt and the crossing of the Red Sea (see Exodus 15.20–21). According to the story in Numbers 12.1–15, she was specially afflicted with leprosy, when she (in fact together with

Aaron) questioned Moses' authority and objected to his marriage to an Ethiopian (a Cushite woman). Despite Moses' plea on her behalf, she was excluded from the camp (the normal practice for lepers), but her exclusion lasted only for a week.

Mishnah *See* HEBREW; JEWISH LITERATURE; SEPPHORIS; TALMUD.

mission A text like Luke 4.18 emphasizes how Jesus came to preach the good news (GOSPEL) to the poor; in their individual ways each of the canonical Gospels sets out post-resurrection instructions whereby the DISCIPLES are to carry on this work after Jesus' departure (see Matthew 28.19–20: 'Go therefore and make disciples of all nations, baptizing them in the name of the Father and of the Son and of the Holy Spirit, and teaching them to obey everything that I have commanded you.' See also Mark 16.15–18; Luke 24.47; John 20.19–23.) To this end Jesus appears to have given his disciples basic missionary training and a trial run (see Mark 6.7–13). The possibility of failure seems to be built in from the start (6.11); the later Church, reflecting on such problems, reinterpreted the parable of the SOWER to show the size of the harvest, despite the apparent wastage of seed sown in preaching (Mark 4.13–20).

The Acts of the Apostles speaks of the power to turn disciples into fully fledged and universal missionaries: 'you will receive power when the Holy Spirit has come upon you; and you will be my witnesses in Jerusalem, in all Judaea and Samaria, and to the ends of the earth' (Acts 1.8). This power is traced to their experience of the Holy SPIRIT at PENTECOST (Acts 2.1–4). The boldness of their missionary proclamation took their hearers by surprise (2.37–42) and the authorities off guard (4.1–2). The focus of Acts shifts from the original APOSTLES (disciples commissioned and 'sent') to other early Christians like STEPHEN (the deacon-martyr: 6.8–7.60) and PHILIP (who converted the Ethiopian eunuch: 8.4–40). PETER remains in the frame a little longer than most, but is supplanted by the newly converted Saul (Acts 9 – soon to be PAUL).

The story of Paul is that of taking the Gospel out beyond the confines of its parent JUDAISM, and working with GENTILE converts in communities which Paul helped to plant throughout the eastern Mediterranean world. The exponential growth of Christianity, throughout modern Lebanon to Turkey and Greece, is traced to his work. His letters in the New Testament – probably only a few surviving from a much larger body of correspondence – were treasured by the Churches which received them, as they usefully demonstrated his working through of ethical and theological problems, experienced by these early communities. Without doubt other apostles were hard at work elsewhere – for example Paul wrote of the Church in Rome as one not founded by himself – but his own work is best documented.

Within 50 years of Jesus' death, the missionary work of the early Church had succeeded in planting a good number of Churches in the Roman Empire, including in its capital. The mission work continued in the western Mediterranean and North Africa. Legend has THOMAS take Christianity to India, and JOSEPH OF ARIMATHEA to England; but there is little hard evidence to back the legends.

Christianity had waves of missionary zeal throughout history. But the linking of mission with empire building led to a subsequent withdrawal in other than the most enthusiastic circles. Subsequently mission combined with, or mutated into, more humanitarian projects in the Third World. By contrast Judaism is not usually regarded as a missionary faith, although it scrutinizes and accepts voluntary converts; hence the scarcity of reference in this article. There is some evidence for active quests for converts (PROSELYTES) during the Second TEMPLE period (see Matthew 23.15). But the later Roman Empire influenced by the rise of Christianity eventually declared conversion to Judaism a criminal act.

Mithraism Mithraism is the MYSTERY RELIGION associated with an earlier Persian and Indian deity, Mithras, a warrior figure linked to solar worship. As a result of the conquests of Alexander the Great this was one of the Eastern influences that spread into the Mediterranean world and became a popular cult. Originally favoured by the Parthians and the Cilician pirates, both of them problems for the Romans, the cult became widespread in the Roman army. It spread to the frontiers of the Empire (there was a temple of Mithras discovered on Hadrian's Wall in Northumbria), and was certainly known in Rome itself by the 1st century CE, if not earlier. The cult had striking similarities to Christianity in terms of initiation rites, group meals, and a high moral code. It is possible that the figure of Mithras is caricatured in the rider on the white horse at REVELATION 6.2; Mithraic initiation involving blood (of a sacrificed bull) may perhaps colour PAUL's language about BAPTISM and the DEATH OF CHRIST in Romans 6. And the MAGI in the story of Jesus' birth in MATTHEW'S GOSPEL may well be cult officials of Mithraism. It was not until the 4th century CE that Mithraism was substantially superseded by Christianity.

Moab The territory of Moab lay to the east of the DEAD SEA, in the southern part of the land on the far side of the JORDAN, bordered by the territories of EDOM and AMMON. The traditional ancestor of the Moabites was Moab the son of LOT, offspring of an incestuous relationship with Lot's elder daughter (Genesis 19.37). The Moabites were an agricultural people, mostly shepherds, who spoke a north-west Semitic dialect akin to Hebrew. Throughout history they were variously kinsmen, vassals or enemies of Israel. The Moabite Stone, a stele of black basalt found in 1868 at Dhiban (Biblical Dibon) in Jordan, has an inscription of major importance; it describes the achievements of Mesha king of Moab in the 9th century BCE and his defeat of the Israelite dynasty founded by King OMRI (see for comparison 2 Kings 3.4–27). The remains of the stone are in the Louvre in Paris. Chemosh, mentioned in the inscription, was the national deity of Moab. Current excavations at Khirbat al-Mudayna are investigating a fortified town on the Moabite/Israelite border.

See also the story of BALAAM.

Modein, or Modiim To the west of the modern city of Modiim are archaeological sites associated with the MACCABEES, the birth and burial places of the Maccabean family, whose story is told in the first book of the Maccabees in the Apocrypha (see for example 1 Maccabees 2.1). JOSEPHUS and Eusebius both refer to the monuments and mausolea of the Maccabees (which must have been similar to the tomb of ABSALOM in the Kidron valley at Jerusalem); no traces have survived, and the rock-cut tombs on the site, shown as the 'tombs of the Maccabees', actually date from the Byzantine period. A number of OSSUARIES (or bone boxes) were discovered nearby in 1995, with Jewish inscriptions, one of which bore the name *Hashmonaim*, the name of the HASMONEAN dynasty which developed from the Maccabean family.

Montanism Montanism was an ecstatic prophetic movement of the 2nd century CE with APOCALYPTIC emphases, developing and reanimating aspects of early Christian PROPHECY. This suggested a continuity of inspiration within the Church (*see also* CANON). The GOSPELS from the 1st century CE could not be regarded as the last word, or indeed as any final form of revelation. The movement spread quickly after 160 CE from Phrygia in Asia Minor to Rome and North Africa, being known as 'the Phrygian heresy'. The movement became strongly ascetic, which appealed to the Church Father Tertullian and others in Roman Africa. The name derived from an original prophet, Montanus, who was active between 150 and 175 CE, operating from the mountain village of Pepuza in Phrygia; two female acolytes or prophetic figures, Prisca and Maximilla, also played prominent parts in the movement. (Subsequent activity seems to have maintained the importance of such a ministry of female virgin prophets.) Montanism claimed that these three prophets were now receiving messages with ultimate authority, as being delivered in the names of the TRINITY in person. This was an essentially passive kind of verbal INSPIRATION. One of their prophecies concerned the imminent descent of a NEW JERUSALEM near Pepuza; possible links with the ideas in the letter to PHILADELPHIA in the book of REVELATION (see 3.12) suggest a recurrent enthusiasm for such apocalyptic ideas in this region of Asia Minor. There is also a tradition in Asia Minor of the daughters of PHILIP being regarded as prophetesses there.

Mordecai *See* ESTHER.

Moses Moses is probably the single most important figure in the Hebrew Scriptures, as the leader of the EXODUS from Egypt and the lawgiver who received the DECALOGUE (the Ten Commandments) in an encounter with God on Mount SINAI. Traditionally he was regarded as the author of the PENTATEUCH, the first five books of the Bible, often referred to as 'the five books of Moses'. In retrospect he was seen as a prophet, and was identified as one of the most significant anticipatory types of the Christ (see DEUTERONOMY 18.15 as the proof text).

Such a key figure becomes a magnet for a range of traditional features. There is a semi-miraculous story of the BIRTH OF MOSES and his preservation from death (as decreed by Pharaoh for Hebrew male children); other Near Eastern cultures know similar stories of great leaders. Moses was brought up in Pharaoh's court as a 'prince of Egypt'. As a young man he killed an Egyptian who was persecuting Hebrew slaves, and was forced to escape to Midian. Here Moses experienced the vision, and vocation to rescue the Israelites, associated with the burning bush (Exodus 3). Moses and his spokesman/brother AARON were unable to persuade Pharaoh directly to let the Israelites go, and so had recourse to inflicting a sequence of 10 PLAGUES. Finally Pharaoh let the people go, and Moses led them out of Egypt, guided by a God-given pillar of cloud by day and a pillar of fire by night (Exodus 13). Pharaoh's army pursued them, but was drowned in the act of following the Israelites across the Red Sea (Exodus 14). The Israelites survived for 40 years of wilderness wandering, probably supported by the land skills Moses would have acquired as Jethro's shepherd, as well as by the miracles of feeding which the Bible records (*see* MANNA and QUAILS). When Moses was given the Ten Commandments on Sinai, he came down to his people only to discover their idolatry, abetted by Aaron (*see* GOLDEN CALF). Moses was permitted to see the Promised Land of CANAAN (from the top of Mount NEBO) but was not allowed to enter it. He died at the age of 120 years; his body was 'hidden by God' and never found (Deuteronomy 34).

Biblical scholarship has often been occupied in a quest for the historical Moses, but the wealth of tradition probably renders that unachievable. It could be argued that a major world religion like Judaism requires a founder. But it is more important to recognize that the Hebrew scriptures see God himself as the principal actor, with Moses only as his agent.

music 'By the rivers of Babylon – there we sat down and there we wept when we remembered ZION. On the willows there we hung up our harps. For there our captors asked us for songs, and our tormentors asked us for mirth, saying, "Sing us one of the songs of Zion!"' Psalm 137.1–3 illustrates clearly the importance of music in the lives of the people of the Bible. Instrument-accompanied singing was the prevalent kind of music for centuries, in both the folk songs related to various occasions in life, happy or sad, and in the religious music – Psalm 137 is a hymn from the Second TEMPLE period. It also illustrates the type of poetry/song lyrics, no rhymes of course, but a gentle parallelism in the prose lines (*see* PSALMS).

Apart from this poignant reminiscence of the EXILE, when the love of music was turned into one of the torments of homesickness, there is plenty of evidence from earliest times of the part music played. According to Exodus 15 MOSES was concerned about making the songs of his people as well as their LAWS. JOSHUA used music to bring down the walls of JERICHO (Joshua 6). DEBORAH celebrated the victory over Sisera with a song (Judges 5). Instrumental music was used by the ecstatic prophets and this influenced SAUL (1 Samuel 10.5–6). It is thought that the oldest text in the Bible is a fragment of song led by MIRIAM and the women with tambourine and dance, to celebrate the defeat of the pursuing Pharaoh's forces in the Red Sea: 'Sing to the Lord, for he has triumphed gloriously; horse and rider he has thrown into the sea' (Exodus 15.21). Also the song of the well is paralleled in other ancient Near Eastern cultures – 'Spring up, O well! – Sing to it! – the well that the leaders sank, that the nobles of the people dug, with the sceptre, with the staff' (Numbers 21.17–18). One can imagine the excitement of the nomads approaching a water source in the dry desert conditions, whipped up further by the constant repetition of the refrain.

Originally, then, Israelite music was the song of the shepherd and of the nomad, but with the period of the Settlement the music became more sophisticated, and perhaps less spontaneous, in the grander settings of the monarch's court, and within the hierarchy's cultic worship in the Temple. Popular music would have continued to flourish among the common people, and may have supplied some tunes, for the Psalms, for example, as well as ideas and pastoral imagery: 'The Lord is my shepherd ...' Psalm 23.1. As we have seen with Miriam, or in 1 Samuel 18.6–7, women could participate in popular music, but from the building of the Temple onwards, cultic music was a male preserve. Musical influence from abroad would have been a natural consequence of royal marriages and international trading agreements in the period of the monarchy.

Although legend attributed responsibility for the gift and craft of music to one ancestor, Jubal (Genesis 4.21), the iconic figure as patron of Israelite music is of course King DAVID in both Jewish and Christian tradition. The story of David playing his harp to cheer the tormented Saul's melancholia (1 Samuel 16.23) has joined with his alleged authorship of all of the Psalms to swell his reputation. David's musical skills as the 'sweet psalmist of Israel' (2 Samuel 23.1) are reflected in some of the Psalms, even if we do not know exactly how they were originally sung (the word *selah* frequently found in headings of Psalms was probably some kind of performance indicator). According to the books of CHRONICLES David had provided the MUSICAL INSTRUMENTS for the ritual which surrounded his son SOLOMON's dedication of the Temple (2 Chronicles 7.6), and had appointed LEVITE musicians (1 Chronicles 15.16–24). This latter point tallies with the detailed account in the Mishnah of Levites playing in the Second Temple.

The return from the Exile was a great watershed in Jewish history, and was followed by such developments as the adoption of antiphonal singing in worship, which was indeed fashionable in other cultures at the time. One singer or choir was opposed by another group of singers, so that statements from the first met with a response from the second. The kind of liturgical song used was never written down (notation only exists from the 6–7th century CE) but it is thought that we can hear these melodies still in the music of the Yemenite Jews, and Jews from similar enclaves such as in North Africa.

The growth of the SYNAGOGUE movement, at first in parallel with Temple worship, and then as its survivor post 70 CE, also meant that Jewish musical traditions were preserved wherever the Jews were scattered. Unlike the professional musicians at the Temple, heard only during the three annual visits for FESTIVALS, the synagogue musicians were mostly lay, and the emphasis was on singing, not on instrumental music. The exponent became known as the chazzan or cantor, who needed a fine tenor or baritone voice and a formidable memory to commit all of the chants to heart. The traditional chanting of portions of scripture is called cantillation, and it is speculated that when Jesus read the lesson from Isaiah at the synagogue in Nazareth he would have cantillated it (Luke 4.16–21). Over the centuries the coloratura developed to the fine art it is today. Use of the voice does not bring the problem of SABBATH-breaking which the use of instruments does for Orthodox (but not Reform) Jews.

The early Church of the New Testament grew up within the familiar confines of synagogue WORSHIP and its music, which it probably carried across into its own emerging LITURGY. Responsive singing, modal melody and other features may still be heard in some Churches today, such as the Ethiopian Orthodox, and cantillation is still used extensively by the Eastern Orthodox Churches. The Jewish Psalms were shared by the Christians (see Ephesians 5.19) and despite minimal reference to music in the New Testament it may be assumed that it was an integral part of Christian worship: 'with gratitude in your hearts sing psalms, hymns, and spiritual songs to God' (Colossians 3.16). It was also projected that song was part of the heavenly worship too (see Revelation 5.9–14). There are fragments of hymns where the descriptions of singing in heaven may relate to music on earth (see Revelation 4.10–11; 7.15–17; 11.17–18). Luke preserves several songs in his birth narratives, including MARY's song (the Magnificat) in Luke 1.46–55, and other early Christian songs may include Philippians 2.5–11. This would certainly fit with the custom reported by the Roman Pliny the Younger in 111 CE that Christians sang hymns to Christ as to a god.

musical instruments It is not easy to identify the range of musical instruments used in Israel; largely one has to rely on literary descriptions (with ambiguity in some words), because only a few instruments survive for archaeology to discover, although there are numerous pictorial representations of music-making in the ancient Near East. The SUMERIANS trained bands of professional singers and provided pipes, horns, and percussion as accompaniment. Archaeologists have discovered the remains of lyre, harp, and lute in the remains of the royal palace at UR (birthplace of ABRAHAM). The Egyptians also trained bands of singers, and had orchestras; as time went by further instruments were invented or adopted (Psalm 150 mentions trumpets, harps, lutes, and tambourines). The instrument most frequently mentioned is the ram's horn (*shophar*), still used in the Jewish SYNAGOGUE. Its basic use was to sound a signal, such as in war. A metal trumpet of bronze or silver (*khatsotsrah*) was used by priests (see Numbers 10.2–10). The harp (*kinnor*) associated with DAVID was probably a lyre (a portable rectangular instrument with strings more equal in length than a harp's). There is also a *nebel* (a kind of harp), and a 'lute' with a sound-box shaped like a waterskin (Psalm 150.3). The main wind instrument was a *khalil*, a flute or pipe with twin reeds. For percussion there was the *toph*, a small tambourine (referred to as a 'timbrel', 'tabor', or 'tabret'); also used were small cymbals and castanets ('sistrums').

mustard seed *See* HERBS.

myrrh *See* PLANTS (RESINOUS); SMYRNA.

Mystery religions The Mysteries were secret religious cults with a popular appeal in the Mediterranean world during the Greco-Roman period. They were very different in character, reflecting the ethnic traditions or local preoccupations with fertility rituals that were their original context. Some came from ancient Greece, others from the Middle East in Asia Minor or Egypt. They include the cult of Isis from Egypt; of Adonis from Syria; and of Cybele from Phrygia in Asia Minor. For one particular example, of special relevance to early Christianity, *see* MITHRAISM, originating from the cult of a Persian god. Despite their differences they had in common a central motivation, focused on salvation for the individual, achieved by means of an initiation into a secret rite. It is argued that TARSUS in Cilicia was a significant centre for the Mysteries, and this was an influence on the thinking of the apostle PAUL, as reflected in his description of baptism into the death of Christ in Romans 6.

myth The English use of the word 'myth' is frequently negative and disparaging, the equivalent of 'nonsense'; but the Biblical context for the application of the Greek word *muthos* is by contrast highly positive, denoting a story (originally oral – *see* ORALITY) that is told about God or the gods. C. S. Lewis described a myth as a story whose power is independent of its telling. According to Alan Segal, 'Mythology is a narrative which attempts to get at the underlying assumptions of a society. It is not synonymous with fiction; indeed it is the opposite,' corresponding effectively to ultimate truth. In the words of Gerd Theissen, 'Myths explain in narrative form what fundamentally determines the world and life. Usually they tell of actions of various gods in a primal time or an end time which is remote from the present world in which people live.'

In the Biblical tradition a major modification took place here at a very early stage. The myth of the fundamental acts of God (as in CREATION) was extended through history to the present; it became a narrative of SALVATION history which also covered the present. This narrative concerns the dealings of the one and only GOD with his people Israel. In primitive Christianity this salvation history links with the concrete life-story of one particular individual from among the people of Israel, Jesus, who is at the centre of events.

The 'scandal of particularity', linking ultimate and necessary truths to the particular (and debatable) facts of history, became a philosophical problem which had taken on new life in the 18th century CE. In response it could be argued that to see revelation in identifiable and comparatively recent events was what separated Christianity from the 'fables' and 'myth-making' of the Classical Greeks and Romans. In 1835–6 a young German scholar in Tübingen, D. F. Strauss, caused uproar – and lost his academic teaching post – by writing a two-volume work that used the concept of myth as a literary and philosophical tool for the critical analysis of the life of Jesus as portrayed in the GOSPELS (*see* HISTORICAL JESUS). Its title was *The Life of Jesus Critically Examined* and it was translated into English by George Eliot and published in 1846. Strauss had challenged the historicity of the Gospels on the basis of contradictions between the four accounts and the impossibility of any supernatural or miraculous events (*see* MIRACLES). The Gospel material, he argued, was the product of early Christian consciousness and could be modelled on the stories of Old Testament figures such as ELIJAH and ELISHA. But for Strauss the mythical possessed a greater importance for religion than ever could be said for the historical.

Naaman Naaman was the commander of the army of Ben-Hadad, king of Aram (SYRIA). According to the narrative of 2 Kings 5, he was afflicted with leprosy and was persuaded by a captive Israelite girl, who was his wife's maid, to seek the assistance of the prophet ELISHA. Correspondence between the king of Aram and the king of Israel threatened to cause political complications; but Elisha intervened and instructed Naaman to wash seven times in the river JORDAN. Naaman was offended at the suggestion: 'Are not Abana and Pharpar, the rivers of Damascus, better than all the waters of Israel? Could I not wash in them and be clean?' (2 Kings 5.12). However, when his servants persuaded him to follow the prophet's instructions, he did so and was healed.

Naassenes *See* SERPENT.

Nabateans The Nabateans are first known in an historical record of 312 BCE when they are said to be using the rock shelters east of the JORDAN, in the former country of MOAB. The Greek word for 'rock' is *petra* and this may well be the place where the Nabateans built their impressive capital (*see* PETRA). They settled throughout Trans-jordan and developed many sites with impressive temples, but Petra is the best known. They left no historical documents of their own, but wrote their inscriptions in ARAMAIC, presumably because it was the lingua franca of the region. They are otherwise known from Greek and Roman sources. Their rulers are mentioned in the books of the MACCABEES (2 Maccabees 5.8; 1 Maccabees 5.25; 9.35). Subsequently relations with the HASMONEANS became less friendly as the Nabateans sought to expand into the fertile lands of southern SYRIA. Their king Aretas IV (9 BCE–40 CE) is mentioned as ruler of Damascus in 39 CE (see 2 Corinthians 11.32). From 62 BCE onwards the Nabateans had effectively been vassals of Rome.

Nabonidus *See* CYRUS.

Naboth Naboth was the vineyard owner evicted and killed by the scheming of JEZEBEL (see 1 Kings 21). The expression 'Naboth's vineyard' is a metaphorical way of referring to any coveted possession illegally sought.

Nag Hammadi Nag Hammadi is the town in Upper Egypt near which a collection of GNOSTIC texts was unearthed in 1945. They have been published as, and are frequently referred to as, the 'Nag Hammadi Gnostic Library' (although not all the texts are strictly Gnostic, nor is there any evidence that they actually constituted a library). Such texts, however, have proved very significant for their insights into early JUDAISM, as well as the roots of Christianity. In themselves they represent a multiplex religious outlook that can be regarded as a later but nonetheless a radically 'alternative scripture' to that of the New Testament.

Nahum This book of prophecy, seventh of the collection of 12 Minor Prophets, poses ethical challenges to the modern reader because of its apparently wanton celebration of violence. Its contents are oracles of judgement against NINEVEH, presumably delivered by an optimistic and nationalistic prophet before the city fell in 612 BCE. There is also an allusion, at Nahum 3.8–10, to the fall of Thebes which had taken place in 663 BCE. The position of Nahum after JONAH in the ordering of the Minor Prophets seems to be based on the assumption that Nahum is later than Jonah, and that Nineveh had relapsed into sinful ways after Jonah's mission. If the books were to be read in the reverse order, the compassion of Jonah might compensate for the vengefulness of Nahum.

God's judgement against ASSYRIA, and others who subvert his plan, is seen as a message of assurance and salvation to Judah, nearly a century after Assyria had destroyed the Northern Kingdom of Israel. Evil tyrants will be overthrown, for God is a safe refuge for his people. It may well be that an acrostic poem which can be detected in Nahum 1.2–8 is a later eschatological generalization of the original oracles. The QUMRAN community in turn saw the book as predicting ultimate disaster for their opponents (4Q169).

name of God *See also* GOD and YAHWEH.

One of the names of God, used in the Psalms, is 'the most high God' (Hebrew '*El Elyon*'). In the Greek translation, the SEPTUAGINT, this was translated as 'Theos Hypsistos' (see also Acts 7.48 and 16.17). In a context of POLYTHEISM this was a clear way for Jews to distinguish and assert their one and only God. The Greek expression is found in inscriptions within the SYNAGOGUE building on Delos.

Naomi *See* RUTH, BOOK OF.

Naphtali Naphtali is JACOB's second son by Bilhah, the handmaid of RACHEL (Genesis 30.7–8; 49.21). He was the ancestor of the tribe that bears his name; their territory lay to the east of that of ASHER and to the west of JORDAN and the Sea of GALILEE, and according to Judges 1.33 they 'lived among the Canaanites'. The territories of neighbouring ZEBULUN and of Naphtali are referred to in Isaiah 9.1–2, the text cited by MATTHEW at 4.15 in connection with Jesus' settling in CAPERNAUM.

nard *See* SPIKENARD.

Nathan Nathan is the prophet in the time of King DAVID who confronts David with the sins he has committed in the affair with BATHSHEBA and the death of Uriah the HITTITE. Nathan achieves this by means of a PARABLE about a rich man with many sheep who steals a poor man's single ewe lamb (2 Samuel 12.1–15). Earlier, in 2 Samuel 7, Nathan was commanded by God to deliver an oracle to David which was decidedly double-edged. David is promised by God that David's house (or the Davidic dynasty)

The Nativity Luke 2.1–20

will have a lasting rule over the kingdom. On the other hand, God refuses to grant David permission to build a TEMPLE as a permanent home for the ARK OF THE COVENANT, because of the essential mobility of God's presence. Further references to this theme of David's temple-building offer different reasons: in 1 Kings 5 it is because of David's preoccupation with war; and in 1 Chronicles 22 because his hands are blood-stained.

Nathanael Nathanael appears only in JOHN'S GOSPEL, where he is called a native of CANA (21.2). Through the agency of PHILIP he encounters Jesus (John 1.43–51); Nathanael's initial scepticism is overwhelmed by the impression Jesus makes. Although obviously an early follower of Jesus he is not listed among the 12 DISCIPLES, unless he is to be identified with BARTHOLOMEW, as has been quite widely accepted since the 9th century CE.

Nativity, or birth of Jesus The first Nativity play is believed to have been performed in a cave in 1223 by St Francis of Assisi, as a reminder to the local population that Jesus was not born into riches, but into a poor family like theirs. This is certainly the impression given by, for example, Luke 2.7.

See further at CHRISTMAS; INCARNATION; LUKE'S GOSPEL; MATTHEW'S GOSPEL.

Nazareth Modern Nazareth is a busy cosmopolitan tourist and pilgrimage centre, sprawling over the large area of the upper and lower cities, inhabited by Muslims, Jews and Christians, and dominated by the massive basilica of the ANNUNCIATION, next to which is the controversial site of a new mosque. The contrast between 1st and 21st century CE Nazareth could not be greater. In the time of Jesus Nazareth was an insignificant little Jewish country village. When NATHANAEL remarks, 'Can anything good come out of Nazareth?' (John 1.45–46) he is disparaging a place of which hardly anyone has heard. There is no mention of Nazareth in the Old Testament, although archaeology has revealed that it was an agricultural settlement in the Iron Age.

According to LUKE (1.26; 2.4–5), Mary and Joseph lived in Nazareth before the birth of Jesus, while MATTHEW (chapter 2) might seem to imply they lived in BETHLEHEM. At the time of Jesus' birth, Herod Antipas, the tetrarch of Galilee, was recruiting builders for his capital SEPPHORIS; it would have made good sense for JOSEPH to move his family northwards and settle near Sepphoris to obtain work, especially if Archelaus sustained the threat originally posed by his father HEROD THE GREAT down south (*see also* HERODIAN DYNASTY). There is an irony that, because of Jesus, Nazareth is now world famous, while Sepphoris is an insignificant village, apart from the archaeological discoveries.

The best impression of Nazareth in the time of Jesus is conveyed by the reconstructed Nazareth Village project, which shows agricultural conditions with terraced farming and watchtowers and small houses built on several levels. It is possible that the Grotto of the Annunciation, preserved in the basement of the modern basilica, accurately reflects the use of caves as living space at this period (*see also* HOUSES). It may have been used by JEWISH-CHRISTIANS as an early synagogue/church. But there is no way of confirming the traditional identification of this as MARY's house.

Nazirite The ascetic lifestyle of the Nazirite 'holy man' (see Numbers 6.1–21) involved taking a vow not to cut his hair, come into contact with a corpse, eat grapes or drink wine. The vow could be a temporary restriction or, like SAMSON's and SAMUEL's, lifelong (see Judges 13 and 16; 1 Samuel 1.11). It has been suggested that JOHN THE BAPTIST also took such a vow, but the evidence is meagre, restricted to Luke's Gospel (at 1.15; also 7.33 and parallel texts). References in the ACTS OF THE APOSTLES at 18.18 and 21.20–26 to a 'vow' may well indicate PAUL's continuity with Jewish practice, although it seems to be the reverse of the Nazirite vow, involving cutting of the hair rather than leaving it uncut.

Matthew's Gospel 2.23 has a proof text referring to Jesus which has not been identified among the Old Testament prophets; Matthew obviously refers to his residing in Nazareth, but the word used (Nazorean) is not the designation of an inhabitant. Some have suggested a link with 'Nazirite', but an allusion to the messianic branch (*netzer*) of Isaiah 11.1 is more probable.

Nebo Nebo is a mountain in MOAB (Jabal Nabo, or Jabal Musa). According to Deuteronomy 34, MOSES ascended the mountain in order to survey the Promised Land; he was able to see the area from this vantage point, but he was not able to go there and died shortly afterwards. Traditionally Moses is buried in this vicinity, but his grave was unmarked. Subsequently Christians in the 4th century CE identified an empy cave on Mount Nebo as Moses' final resting place. A church was built here and a community survived until the 9th century. In modern times it has been excavated by the Franciscans.

Nebuchadnezzar Nebuchadnezzar II, king of BABYLON, is particularly remembered for his conquest of the kingdom of Judah and the destruction of the Jerusalem TEMPLE (see 2 Kings 24–25). An inscribed cylinder (now in the Istanbul Archaeological Museum) shows another side of the picture. This records Nebuchadnezzar's temple construction projects in the first half of the 6th century BCE. There are temples for the deities Marduk, Nabu, Shamash and Ishtar in the cities of Borsippa, Larsa and Sippar as well as Babylon.

Nehemiah, book of For the literary and historical relationship between Nehemiah, Ezra and the narratives of Chronicles, see the article on EZRA, BOOK OF.

Nehemiah was a leading statesman and governor in the early post-Exilic period. The book which bears his name begins with chapters of a personal memoir (Nehemiah 1–5) which may be authentic, or a literary convention to enhance the narrative. The description of the night-time inspection of the ruined walls of Jerusalem is particularly graphic. The underlying motive in the decision to restore the walls is – like Ezra's legislation and commission on mixed MARRIAGE – TO DEFINE THE JEWISH IDENTITY AND MARK IT OFF FROM FOREIGN ELEMENTS.

The sequence of the work of Ezra and Nehemiah is puzzling, as it seems unlikely that they overlapped. It could make more sense if Nehemiah came first (rather than the traditional order of Ezra, Nehemiah). Nehemiah served King Artaxerxes I and could have come to Jerusalem on his orders in 445 BCE. This is either a decade later than Ezra, or, as H. H. Rowley suggested, nearly 50 years earlier, if Ezra's mission was under Artaxerxes II (not I).

After Nehemiah had enhanced the status of Jerusalem by rebuilding the walls, he remained as governor for 12 years. He resettled villagers in the capital, so enlarging the population. It seems that he returned for a second term as governor after 433 BCE (see Nehemiah 13).

Nero, Emperor *See* NUMBER SYMBOLISM; PERSECUTION OF CHRISTIANS; PETER; REVELATION, BOOK OF.

new heavens, new earth See 2 Peter 3.13: 'in accordance with his [God's] promise, we wait for new heavens and a new earth, where RIGHTEOUSNESS is at home'; also Revelation 21.1. *See* CREATION; ESCHATON; HEAVEN; and NEW JERUSALEM.

new Jerusalem The concluding vision in the book of REVELATION describes the present process of descent from HEAVEN of the 'holy city, new JERUSALEM' (Revelation 21.2). The comparison is with the advent (or arrival) of a bride for a wedding. The following verses (21.3–5) describe what this totally renewed presence (*see* PAROUSIA) of God will be like. God's presence is also compared with the concept of the TABERNACLE, for this is the word that lies behind the translations 'home' and 'dwell' (see also in John 1.14 speaking of the INCARNATION). The original orderly process of CREATION, now seen as corrupted and fallen, will be completely renewed. It seems as if the renewed holy city will be suspended over the earth, filling the earth with such radiance that the light of sun and moon will no longer be necessary (21.23). God's own presence also removes the necessity of a TEMPLE (21.22). The vision recalls some of the language found in the Old Testament prophecy of EZEKIEL (see 40.2–4; 48.35).

New Testament The New Testament is the collection of 27 books which comprises the second part of the Christian Bible, following on from the OLD TESTAMENT. The origin of the name is in the idea expressed in Jeremiah 31.31–34 of a 'new COVENANT', something which developed a special importance both within the QUMRAN community and also among the Christian Churches founded by PAUL (see for example 2 Corinthians 3).

The contents of the New Testament can be described in several ways. Classified by literary type they are the biographical and historical books (four GOSPELS and the ACTS); the letters (by Paul and others); and the APOCALYPTIC text of the book of REVELATION. In terms of contents, the Gospels relate to the Life of Jesus; the Acts, Revelation and Ephesians to the growth of the Church; and the variety of letters reflect the beginnings of Christian theology. The early Church Fathers had their own way of classifying the New Testament, namely in two broad categories: the Gospel (the four Gospels) and the Apostle (the rest).

On the growth of the New Testament consult the account in J. W. Rogerson and J. M. Lieu, *The Oxford Handbook of Biblical Studies* (Oxford University Press, 2006), pp. 518–543.

Nicodemus Nicodemus is a PHARISEE, known from JOHN'S GOSPEL, who comes to talk with Jesus at night (John 3). In Henry Vaughan's poem 'The Night' he refers to Nicodemus, who 'did at midnight speak with the Sun'. Nicodemus is clearly won over, for at a later point, according to John 7.50–52, he tries to intervene to prevent the Pharisees from censuring Jesus. Then finally he is involved together with another secret supporter, JOSEPH OF ARIMATHEA, in preparing the crucified body of Jesus for burial (John 19.38–42; *see also* DEPOSITION).

Nimrud Nimrud (in present-day Iraq) was a capital city of the ASSYRIAN Empire established by Assurnasirpal II (883–859 BCE), who was responsible for moving the capital from Assur to Nimrud and founding there an impressive city with large and lavish temples, palaces and fortifications. The Assyrian Empire stretched from western Iran to the Mediterranean; other capital cities were NINEVEH and Khorsabad. The site (a series of mounds along the east bank of the Tigris river in northern Iraq) has been excavated over a period of a century and a half, since the spectacular discoveries by Sir Henry Layard in the 1840s of the Assyrian bas-reliefs (which can be seen in the British Museum). A later excavator was Max Mallowan, with his wife Agatha Christie, the crime novelist, who photographed their finds. Particularly important is the range of Nimrud ivoryware, thousands of articles found during the 19th and 20th centuries. There are plaques, containers, flasks, and heads, pulled from wells in the domestic quarters. The royal archives, with original correspondence between Assyrian kings, were found in the north-west palace, and interpreted and edited by the eminent Assyriologist Harry Saggs as the Nimrud Letters.

Nimrod is the name of a warrior-hero in the area of Babylonia, famous as a hunter; Elgar used the reference to 'hunter' (German *Jaeger*), alluding to his champion at Novello's in the 12th of his 'Enigma Variations'. Nimrod was reputed to be the founder of Nineveh and of Nimrud, which therefore bears his name. He was the son of Cush and the grandson of Ham (*see* NOAH), and was responsible for building the city (and tower) of BABEL. According to the story about him in Genesis 10.8–11, Nimrud in Assyria is known as Calah.

Nineveh Nineveh was a capital of the ASSYRIAN Empire, located on the east bank of the river Tigris facing the modern Iraqi city of Mosul. Founded in the 3rd millennium BCE, it was destroyed in 612 BCE, as described in ZEPHANIAH 2.13–15. Islamic tradition holds that the grave of the prophet JONAH is now marked in this city by a mosque, where formerly there was a synagogue. The remains of Nineveh are covered by two mounds: Kouyunjik Tepe, containing the palace of Ashurbanipal with his great library of clay tablets (some of which can be seen in the British Museum); and Nebi Younis (the prophet Jonah), the site of the palace of SENNACHERIB, with its relief portraying the siege of LACHISH.

Nippur Nippur was a city of SUMERIAN foundation in central Babylonia. It was particularly important in the political and religious life of Mesopotamia in the mid 2nd millennium BCE. The city's deity was named Enlil. Again, in the 6th century BCE Nippur was an important centre for settlement of the EXILES from Judaea.

Early in the 20th century CE a library of early Babylonian tablets was unearthed at Nippur (these are now in the Museum of the University of Pennsylvania). One tablet relates a version of the story of the FLOOD, in which a gardener named Nuhu saves the world from disaster. There is also a story of the fall of humankind: the man ate from the tree of life and thereby lost eternal life. In this story the man is named NOAH not ADAM.

Noah Noah is the central character in two Old Testament stories. As a 'just man' he is preserved, with his family, from the FLOOD (Genesis 6.5–9.17). He builds an ark in accordance with divine directions and is thus spared the punishment which affects the rest of humanity. In the other story (Genesis 9.20–27) he is a cultural hero who discovers the art of making wine; his son Ham surprises him in a drunken state of nakedness. Noah curses Ham's son Canaan and blesses his own sons Shem and

The Flood

Japheth for respecting his shame. The genealogies of Noah's sons in Genesis 10 reveal distinctive racial stereotypes: Japheth's descendants are northern or European; the sons of Ham are African and also supposedly non-Semitic peoples of the Middle East; while the descendants of Shem are the Semites (as the name reveals). *See also* ANTI-SEMITISM.

In the Christian tradition Noah's drunkenness is criticized, excused or allegorized.

Noah himself is an example of obedience to God; the New Testament saw him as a preacher of righteousness (2 Peter 2.5) and an example of faith (Hebrews 11.7). See Norman Cohn's account of *Noah's Flood: the Genesis Story in Western Thought* (Yale University Press, 1996). Noah became a figure of special veneration at QUMRAN (e.g. 4Q Mess Ar). Later Jewish tradition held that he would live for ever, like Utnapishtim in the Mesopotamian epic of GILGAMESH.

Whatever one makes of the stories about Noah in Genesis 6–9, the traditions clearly contain memories of advanced shipbuilding and of the cultivation of vines, well before the Hebrew settlement in Palestine.

noli me tangere John's Gospel records the appearance of Jesus to MARY MAGDALENE in the garden after his RESURRECTION. She supposes that he is the gardener, but when Jesus speaks to her, she acknowledges him as 'teacher' and presumably reaches out to him. Jesus responds by saying, 'Do not touch me (or hold on to me), because I have not yet ascended to the Father' (John 20.17). The first four words of this quotation translate the Latin *noli me tangere*, which can be found as the title of numerous artistic representations of this incident, from Titian to Graham Sutherland.

number symbolism, or gematria In the traditions of Israel, numbers have always had the potential of a deeper symbolic significance, of which the readers of the Bible should at least be aware. When, as in HEBREW and GREEK, the letters of the alphabet are also employed as numbers, there is the additional possibility that the letters of a name, for example DAVID, should have significance as an arithmetical total. (*See also* GENEALOGY.) Gematria, or the symbolic exploitation of such numbers, was remarkably prevalent in many areas of the ancient world, long before the development of Jewish KABBALAH.

Firstly a brief survey of the significance that may be attached to simple numbers:

One expresses uniqueness or wholeness.

Two is the minimum number stipulated for legal witnesses to be relied upon.

Three – *see* TRINITY.

Three and a half is the number of days in half a week; in years it is half the complete period of seven years in God's plan, otherwise '42 months'.

Four represents the created world, with its four corners (or compass points) and four wind directions; so there are four horsemen of the Apocalypse. Much later it was to be argued that there had to be four GOSPELS for a universal MISSION, and that each Gospel was represented by one of the four 'living creatures' (humans, domestic animals, wild animals, creatures of sky and sea) – *see* REVELATION 4.

Five are the fingers of a hand, and so a handful.

Six represents incompleteness, as one short of the perfect number seven. So a sequence of six leaves one expecting a seventh, just as the days of CREATION required the SABBATH.

Seven is the perfect number of completeness, possibly as the sum of 3 and 4 (heaven and earth).

Eight is the day of RESURRECTION, or the first of a new sequence of seven days. This is parodied in Revelation 17.11 of Emperor Nero, one of the seven, who comes back again as the eighth.

Ten is an appropriately round number, as of the fingers of both hands. *See* DECALOGUE.

Twelve is the number of the tribes of Israel, and therefore the corresponding number of the DISCIPLES of Jesus. The figure 144,000 given in Revelation 7 and 14 is a symbolic multiple of 12.

Twenty-four is double 12. The 24 elders in Revelation 4.4 could represent Israel plus the Church.

Thirty was reckoned to be the optimum age of human vigour and maturity.

Forty denotes a limited period of time; 40 years corresponds to a generation.

Seventy is a further symbol of completeness. *See* SEPTUAGINT (the Greek version of the Hebrew Bible by 70 scholars).

There are several examples of gematria which can be found readily in the Bible, although their precise interpretation may remain controversial. Best known is the number of the Beast in Revelation 13.18: 'six hundred and sixty six'. The basic significance of such a number is clearly as a multiple symbol of incompleteness (six). But the Greek letters of the name and title 'Nero Caesar', transliterated into Hebrew as a coded reference, would also yield the arithmetical total of 666. In the context of Roman emperor-worship, of which Nero was an extreme example, this could well represent the tradition that Nero, who had committed suicide in 68 CE, was to return again with armies from the East to reconquer the Roman world. Such a symbol encapsulates the bestial threat posed by the extremes of the imperial cult, but also emphasizes its incompleteness and therefore its failure.

Another instance of what seems to be a significant number is in JOHN'S GOSPEL 21.11, where the spectacular catch is of 153 fish. Mathematicians find this number interesting, not least because it is the triangular number of 17 (the sum of all the numbers between 1 and 17). And 17 can be regarded as the sum of 7 and 10, both indicating comprehensiveness and completeness. It could represent the fullness of the Christian Church as a result of world mission, or, as the Syrian Orthodox suggest, these large fish are the great patriarchs of the Church.

Numbers, book of Numbers is the Greek title for the fourth book of the Bible, a descriptive name from the order of the march (or CENSUS) that is recorded in the opening chapter (see 1, and also 26). This serves as a reminder of the dynamic character of the Israelite camp in motion in the wilderness. The Hebrew name comes, as is the regular custom, from the opening words of the book: *Bemidhbar* ('in the wilderness') describes the setting exactly. The book spans the 40 years of wilderness wandering and finishes with the people poised for the conquest of CANAAN. The contents are a heterogeneous mixture of cultic legislation and epic narratives (including extracts from a collection known as the Book of Wars of YAHWEH). Several well-known Biblical themes are found in the book of Numbers: the NAZIRITE vow (6); the MANNA and QUAILS (11); the spies return from Canaan with the grapes (13); AARON's rod that budded (17); the red HEIFER (19); the brazen serpent (21); and BALAAM's oracles and the talking donkey (22–24).

The Priestly Benediction, from Numbers 6.24–26, is a famous prayer including the words, 'May the Lord cause his face to shine upon you and be gracious unto you.' This text is found etched on two silver scrolls, found in 1979 at Ketef Hinnom in sight of the Jerusalem city walls; from the 7th/6th century BCE, these are the earliest known artefacts documenting passages from the Hebrew Bible.

'There is nothing amusing about the Book of Numbers ... it inspired awe ... something to do with the absolute obedience these people's God demanded from the Israelites' (Ruth Rendell, *The Babes in the Wood*, Hutchinson, 2002, p. 239).

Nunc Dimittis These are the first two Latin words of the VULGATE translation of SIMEON's words, when he held the child Jesus in his arms, on the occasion when Mary and Joseph had brought Jesus to the Temple (see Luke 2.25–35). Simeon's hymn of prayer and thanksgiving has been used in Christian LITURGY from an early date, specially associated with evening prayer since the 4th century CE.

Nuzi Nuzi (modern Yoghlan Tepe) was an ancient city in the area that is now north-eastern Iraq. Several thousand tablets were discovered there, dating to the 15th century BCE. They are a primary source for information about the social customs and practices of the people known as the Hurrians. As the Hurrians also lived in the middle Euphrates valley at Haran and Nahor, in the original homeland of the Biblical PATRIARCHS, this information has been used to illuminate their cultural context too. This has been partly successful, particularly in the area of family law (for example in the actions of SARAH with her maid in Genesis 16.2 and of RACHEL with the household gods in Genesis 31), although there is disagreement as to whether the Nuzi tablets describe uniquely Hurrian institutions or common practice in Meso-potamia of the period.

O

Obadiah, book of The fourth book in the collection of Minor Prophets is also the shortest book in the Old Testament. The name Obadiah, meaning 'Servant of God', may be symbolic; but the actual name is borne by at least 12 men in the Hebrew Bible (e.g. King AHAB's steward in 1 Kings 18.3). Virtually nothing is known about the author. The book is now usually dated to the EXILE, or early in the post-Exilic period, on the assumption that verses 11–14 refer to the BABYLONIAN capture of Jerusalem in 587 BCE (with Edomite participation). The traditional grave of Obadiah is at SAMARIA, next to Elisha and John the Baptist (see Jerome, *Commentary on Obadiah* ch. 1).

The book has two parts: an oracle against EDOM (verses 1–14) and a prophecy of Israel's final triumph (verses 15–21), both expressions of retributive justice ('As you have done, it shall be done to you': verse 15). There are elements in common between Obadiah and Jeremiah 49.7–22. Obadiah 1 uses the technical HEBREW word (*hazah*) for a prophetic 'vision' as does Isaiah 1.1.

'Obadiah is of little theological interest and its presence in the canon can ... be explained as anti-Idumaean polemic' (J. A. Soggin). After Jerusalem's fall the Edomites moved into the area of the Negev which became known as Idumaea. Hostility against the Idumaeans was strong in the 1st century CE. Perhaps Obadiah's value can be slightly restored by its position within the Minor Prophets: on the 'Day of the Lord' it echoes AMOS and JOEL, while its xenophobic attitudes are set in contrasted relief by the positive theme of JONAH.

Og *See* BASHAN.

Old Testament The 'Old Testament' is a recognizably Christian way of referring to the Jewish Scriptures, or the Hebrew Bible. The epithet 'Old' compares this collection, perhaps unfavourably, to the heart of the Christian Bible, the New Testament. This collection of 39 separate books, comprising the English version of the Hebrew Bible, is grouped into three sections. In the Hebrew Bible the most important is the Law (TORAH) – the first five books of Moses – and the other two sections are the Prophets (the historical books and the books of the individual prophets) and the Writings (or Hagiographa). The whole collection is referred to as 'Tanak', which is an acronym of the names in Hebrew – Torah, Nebiim (Prophets) and Ketubim (Writings). The arrangement of the English Old Testament is somewhat different, being a broadly literary arrangement, firstly of prose works in law and history, then of poetical works, and finally of prophecy. The English arrangement derived from the Greek translation of the Hebrew Bible (*see* SEPTUAGINT). At the time of the Reformation, in Christian history, the English Bible had retained the order of the Greek version, but slimmed down the contents to include only the books of the original Hebrew Bible.

olives *See* CROPS; TREES.

Olives, Mount of The Mount of Olives lies to the east of Jerusalem, on the other side of the Kidron valley; its height is some 750 metres above sea level. It features in the apocalyptic battle described in Zechariah 14.4. According to 2 Samuel 15.30, 32 the Mount was a holy place of worship (see also Ezekiel 11.23, and the reference to SOLOMON's construction of sanctuaries there, which were destroyed by JOSIAH, in 2 Kings 23.13).

The Mount of Olives is venerated in the Christian tradition as the site of Christ's ASCENSION (see Acts 1.9–12, where it is said that the mount was 'a SABBATH day's journey' from the city). A church was built on the site in the 4th century CE, although the chapel which stands there today is from the Crusader period. Nearby was the Church of Eleona (*see* CHURCHES, CHRISTIAN), built by Emperor Constantine on the traditional site where Jesus foretold the destruction of Jerusalem (Mark 13.1–4; Matthew 24.1–3). The lower slopes of the Mount of Olives, facing the Temple Mount, are used as a Jewish burial ground.

Omri Ironically the historians writing 1 KINGS dismissed the important reign of Omri, KING OF THE NORTHERN KINGDOM OF ISRAEL (881–872 BCE), in very few verses (1 Kings 16.22–28). Because Omri did not fit the Davidic pattern of righteous rulers (who advocated centralized worship in Jerusalem) he was not regarded as important for a theology based on the book of DEUTERONOMY.

From the short text one may learn that Omri brought stability to Israel after a rapid turnover of monarchs through military coups. He established a centralizing capital city at SAMARIA and founded a dynasty (AHAB was his son). From archaeology there is confirmation of his settlement of Samaria, and the craftsmanship which was employed. In international diplomacy he became so well known that Israel was known as 'Omri's land' in ASSYRIAN documents, long after the extinction of his line. According to the Moabite Stone (*see* MOAB), Omri gained territory in Transjordan by peaceful acquisition.

Further Biblical evidence would suggest that, although a former army commander, Omri preferred the route of peace by negotiation to a military solution. Israel and Judah began anew to cooperate with each other; Omri will also have been the engineer behind an alliance with PHOENICIA, which led to the infamous marriage of Ahab with JEZEBEL, daughter of the king of Sidon. The trade concessions granted to DAMASCUS in the city of Samaria may have been forced upon him (1 Kings 20.34). His openness to other nations will have worsened the exposure of Israel to foreign religions, leading to more APOSTASY, and therefore more censure from the Deuteronomic historian.

one hundred and fifty-three 153 is the number given of the special catch of fish in JOHN'S GOSPEL 21.11. *See* NUMBER SYMBOLISM.

Onesimus *See* PHILEMON, LETTER OF PAUL TO; SLAVERY.

Ophites *See* SERPENT.

orality Oral traditions can survive without being written down, but only if they continue to be transmitted verbally. If the tradition is not maintained and exercised by word of mouth, it becomes lost for ever. The act of writing helps to preserve traditions, not only among those who would otherwise forget them, but also for the benefit of a wider audience. So it is that in the Bible there is a written record of the 'word of God' and related traditions which would otherwise have been lost irretrievably.

Stories are a powerful way of communicating. Not only are they entertaining, but they can be very efficient in effectuating social control. Stories are persuasive in ridiculing or praising people, criticizing contemporary norms or infusing specific codes of conduct. The Hebrew Bible is comprised of such stories. By chronicling the great events which constitute the past, these stories suggest what went wrong and what would have been a better way to proceed in the past. Its powerful role is suggested in these words: 'These stories which I give you are to be remembered and taken at heart. Repeat them to your children and speak of them indoors and outdoors, when you lie down and when you get up' (Deuteronomy 6.6–8).

The successful reception of the story presupposes the presence of an audience and a narrator sharing some mutual interests which are established before and sometimes during the narration. These interests differ from community to community and they are not explicit in the story. The context in which the story is told reflects those shared interests. For this reason the Old Testament provides more than one story about the same subject, for example two CREATION stories (Genesis 1 and Genesis 2–3), and two different accounts of the KINGS OF JUDAH in the books of SAMUEL and KINGS and in the books of CHRONICLES.

Orality attributes an important role to memory. Knowledge is not stored in abstract categories but in stories about people. Whenever and wherever they are told, the stories are a performance, as if the action is unfolding in the presence of the audience. But it is not the story alone that is important. Often the finer nuances of the story are underscored by the tone of voice, gestures, and general body language of the narrator, as in the actions of an African 'praise singer'. The performance also sheds some light on the power relationship within which the performance takes place.

The advent of writing and printing had a tremendous impact on orality. The ability to transmit a story via a text gave the story a permanence it never had before, but it also cut off any entrance to the finer nuances of the oral performance. Writing, as the systematic recording of the spoken language, marks the beginning of the historical period. Through writing one can access the past, but no text is without its prehistory, as if it has fallen out of the sky. Writing started as pictographic scripts that developed into CUNEIFORM (wedge-shaped) script or into hieroglyphic. The GEZER calendar (usually dated in the time of King SOLOMON) suggests that HEBREW writing developed from the cuneiform PHOENICIAN script.

In the early stages writing was a laborious and costly endeavour. Writing occurred on potsherds and clay tablets at first (*see* OSTRACA), and only much later on PAPYRI and parchments. It could only be afforded by people with political and economic power who used it for treaties and administrative purposes.

The time of the production of OLD TESTAMENT stories in text form is unknown, but at some stage after the EXILE several texts of the same stories existed. Texts were translated into other languages. After Christ's death, a struggle within JUDAISM saw the acceptance of only one text as officially representing the stories we now have in the Hebrew Bible. This process turned the ancient sacred story into a sacred text. Early Christianity never followed that textual tradition but another one which is represented by the SEPTUAGINT. During the Reformation the call to return to the original text resulted in the Hebrew Bible becoming the official text of the Old Testament within Protestant Christianity. The first recording of Hebrew manuscripts in book form was by Daniel Bomberg and of the Greek New Testament by Desiderius Erasmus.

The introduction of printing by Johannes Gutenberg in the 15th century made possible the popularizing of the Bible during the Reformation. Printing brought about a revolution in the human capacity for knowledge and learning. Within Christianity, it meant reading the sacred stories without the presence of a literate interpreter telling you what to believe.

The missionary zeal of the 19th century and the proliferation of print resulted in the industry of Bible translation worldwide. In South Africa it led to the translation of the Bible into African languages. Robert Moffat, a gardener from England who started to work as a missionary in Kuruman, finished his translation of the New Testament in Tswana in 1838. The translation was revered to such an extent that people exchanged sheep for a copy of it! The first completed translation of the Old and New Testament in Tswana was completed in 1857. The translation process is an ongoing one. In contrast to the hard and laborious achievements of the past, present-day technology allows for translation and comparison in many languages with the press of a key.

It is logical that a permanent text would soon receive the status of a sacred text, where nothing may be added or changed (*see also* CANON and AUTHORITY). People express their veneration of the text by linking its origins to a deity and not to human efforts, hence INSPIRATION. The sacredness of the transmitted text can be seen in words such as 'Holy Scripture' and maxims such as '*Sola Scriptura*', with the loss of the social embeddedness of the oral transmission. In the story of the Ten Commandments (*see* DECALOGUE), when MOSES descended from Mount SINAI, it is said that he carried the commandments of the Lord written on two clay tablets. In the story, the fact of writing ensured the permanence of God's laws for his people.

Today everything is text. To be without a text would be like an angel without wings. One is continuously informed by texts, and these influence the reading of the Bible. Just as stories were part of the oral context, texts are now part of a literate context. Whenever one speaks or writes, one imparts to others traces of other texts. The closure brought about by the printed text, especially in the case of ancient literature, obscures the social embeddedness within which these stories once orally originated – or were even later transmitted and eventually textualized. Nevertheless, the preacher, in preparing a sermon, follows the same process that the ancient writers or narrators followed when they wrote or told their stories.

[*This article is written with grateful acknowledgement to the presenters of an exhibition at the University of South Africa in the summer of 1999.*]

original sin The actual term 'original sin' is not Biblical, but first occurs in the writings of St Augustine of Hippo in North Africa, in connection with his controversy with Pelagius over the causes of SIN. Augustine quotes from the Bible to demonstrate the innate tendency of human beings to sin, as a consequence of the FALL, following the sin of ADAM. The seminal identity of humanity with Adam is understood from a particular, and hardly defensible, reading of Romans 5.12 ('in whom [i.e. in Adam] all have sinned' rather than 'in that [because] all have sinned' – this relative pronoun in Greek can be either masculine or neuter). Augustine supports this idea from Psalm 51.5 ('I was born guilty, a sinner when my mother conceived me') and from the VULGATE version of Job 14.4 ('no one is clean, not even if his life be only for a day').

ossuary Ossuary is the technical term for a bone casket, from the Latin word for 'bone'. In and around Jerusalem during the Second TEMPLE period, it was Jewish practice to rebury the bones of the deceased, once the flesh had rotted away. The bones were placed in ossuaries to wait for the physical RESURRECTION in the last days (in accordance with an interpretation of the prophecies of Isaiah 26.19 and Ezekiel 37.11–12). Although the SADDUCEES may not have accepted the reality of bodily resurrection (Mark 12.18; Acts 23.8), other Jews, including PHARISEES and the Essenes associated with QUMRAN, did so.

One of a number of ossuaries, found in a family tomb in Jerusalem in 1990, carries the inscription 'Joseph called Caiaphas'. This ossuary is now in the Israel Museum and is likely to be that of the HIGH PRIEST, CAIAPHAS of the Gospels. The age of the bones and the provenance of the family tomb make this a likely identification. Inscriptions were usually roughly scratched on the casket, not carved like a tombstone, which of course makes imitation relatively easy.

Highly controversial, by comparison, is the ossuary inscribed 'JAMES, son of Joseph, brother of Jesus' that was widely publicized in autumn 2002 as 'the first solid proof that Jesus ever existed'. This ossuary is now regarded by many scholars as a forgery, and is the subject of police investigation. The main problem is that it was not found *in situ*, but in the house of an antique dealer, and its provenance remains uncertain. It is also questionable whether a genuine casket would have been so labelled, while a later fake might well be.

ostraca An ostracon is a sherd of pottery with writing on it. Ostraca are of particular value to archaeologists, for the documentary evidence they provide. A good example is the collection of 18 Hebrew ostraca found in the guardroom at LACHISH, which allowed that site to be identified. These were written in the ancient (cursive) HEBREW script, not the later square script which is seen in printed Hebrew texts, and relate to the time of JEREMIAH and the BABYLONIAN capture of Jerusalem in 587 BCE. They were sent by Hosha'yahu, an officer in command of a military outpost, to Ya'ush the military commander of Lachish.

The English word 'ostracism' is derived from the Greek word 'ostraca' used for these pottery sherds; ostracism, or the expulsion of a named individual for a period of 10 years, was practised in Classical Greece, when the male citizens eligible to vote would write on a scrap of pottery the name of the preferred victim to be expelled from the city.

Oxyrhynchus Oxyrhynchus is now the desert site of a city of Middle Egypt, about 200 miles south of ALEXANDRIA. The name means 'sharp-nosed', referring to a species of fish in the Nile. Here were found the largest cache of PAPYRI ever discovered in Egypt, preserved in the rubbish dumps just outside the city. The mounds were first investigated in 1897 by two British archaeologists, Bernard Grenfell and Arthur Hunt; excavations continued until 1934, and many of the deciphered papyri have been published in a series by the Egypt Exploration Society.

The significance of the papyri is not just in their quantity but also in their range, including everyday papers, letters and lists, as well as official documents. Most of the texts are written in GREEK, because Oxyrhynchus was a Greek-speaking enclave, but other languages are also represented. The Greek papyri offer evidence for popular vocabulary and usage later than the Classical Greek texts and comparable with the language of the New Testament. There are literary works, such as poems by Callimachus and Sappho, and also fragments of the New and Old Testaments. P. Oxy LXVI 4499 is a 3rd- or 4th-century codex, published in 1999, which contains a significant amount of the text of the book of REVELATION, including some variant readings. Also among the papyri are hitherto unknown Greek gospel texts. In one example, P. Oxy.840, a Pharisaic chief priest charges 'the Saviour' with entering the Temple court unpurified, and asserts his own PURITY: 'I have bathed myself in the pool of David and have gone down by one stair and come up the other and have put on white and clean clothes.'

A collection of the Oxyrhynchus papyri is preserved in the Sackler Library in Oxford University.

paganism *See also* POLYTHEISM.

The word 'pagan' comes from the Latin *paganus* meaning a countryman or rustic. The modern sense of heathen or non-Christian may derive from the prejudice that heathen practices survived longer in the countryside, while Christianity was established in the towns. Also ancient Romans used the word contemptuously for civilians who were not serving in the army. When early Christians saw themselves as 'SOLDIERS OF CHRIST' they probably used the Roman term for those who were not of their number.

Some would argue that, in today's world, paganism is the fastest-growing spiritual orientation and might even constitute a world religion.

Palestine Palestine, as referred to in Biblical times, was a geographical area, rather than a nationally defined country; it formed a bridge of land between North Africa and the Near East of Asia, between Sinai and the Taurus mountains, a bridge which is sometimes found referred to technically as part of the FERTILE CRESCENT. Effectively (and often to its own disadvantage) it lay between the Egyptian kingdom of the Nile and the BABYLONIAN and ASSYRIAN empires which had developed in the valley of the two rivers, Tigris and Euphrates. The name Palestine derives originally from the coastal territory occupied by the PHILISTINES. In the 2nd century CE the Romans, under Emperor Hadrian, sought to obliterate references to the Jews, not only by rebuilding JERUSALEM as Aelia Capitolina, but also by abolishing the regional names of Judaea and Samaria and reviving the name Palestine.

palimpsest Palimpsest is a Greek work which literally means 'rubbed again'. It refers to a manuscript where the surface has been prepared for a second time so that it can be overwritten. Such recycling is an economical use of scarce writing material. The new writing may be at right angles to the original use of the manuscript; it is sometimes possible still to read the underwritten text, which may be of value as an earlier copy.

papyri Papyrus (*Cyperus papyrus*) grew in Egypt and Syria. It was exported from the Syrian port of Byblos (the name of which may be the origin of the Greek word for 'book' – *biblos*, *see* BIBLE). The word 'papyrus', from which comes the English 'paper', may be Egyptian in origin, meaning 'of Pharaoh'.

The stems of the reed plant are cut into thin ribbons; a double layer, with the strips set at right angles, is then beaten together and the surface polished smooth. Quality and thickness are naturally variable, but the maximum dimension is that of the usable height of the plant stalk (about 18 inches). Twenty sheets, slightly overlapped and pasted, produce a roll up to 20 feet long. The writing (with carbon-black or red-ochre ink, applied by a pen with a chiselled end made from rushes – *Juncus maritimis*) would be in columns, firstly on the side with the horizontal fibres (recto) and then parallel with the joins on the vertical fibres on the other side (verso). The end result could be rolled up with the horizontal fibres inside.

There was little development in the papyrus scroll from its origins in the mid 3rd millennium BCE. The material was naturally perishable, except under specially favourable conditions of climate and storage. A particularly exciting cache of papyri was found in the Egyptian desert sands at OXYRHYNCHUS.

parables In general, a parable is a piece of picturesque language, perhaps used as an analogy for a more abstract idea ('a short narrative fiction to reference a transcendent symbol'). The Biblical terms, in Old Testament Hebrew *mashal* and in New Testament Greek *parabole*, actually refer to a variety of sayings, such as riddles, proverbs and other WISDOM teaching, as well as the brief stories that are first thought of as parables. This wider perspective is important, even when modern scholars focus on the parables or stories which Jesus told. His stories were not just attractive anecdotes, instances of rural Palestinian local colour (although they certainly were that), but they were also ethical challenges, and riddles to make the hearers think. In C. H. Dodd's classic definition: 'At its simplest a parable is a metaphor or simile drawn from nature or common life, arresting the hearer by its vividness or strangeness, and leaving the mind in sufficient doubt about its precise application to tease it into active thought.'

Jesus' parables belong in a tradition from Old Testament stories (such as the trees in Judges 9.7–15, the poor man's lamb in 2 Samuel 12.1–14, and the vineyard in Isaiah 5.1–7) to the images used by Jewish rabbis. The phrasing and structure of the parables, whether long or short, made them easily memorable. It is often said, for this reason, that the parables recorded in the SYNOPTIC Gospels are the most reliable and authentic aspects of Jesus' teaching. The identification of the precise structure is however the subject of debate; some suggest it has a literary form in five sections, leading to a wisdom statement; others say that the form is that of traditional Hebrew poetry, a parallelism of ideas (*see* PSALMS). Perhaps Jesus composed his poetic parables during periods of quiet reflection in Galilee, around BETHSAIDA, or in Jerusalem, where he taught in the TEMPLE courtyards during the Jewish FESTIVALS. Scholars used to say that the authentic parable had a single point of comparison between the picture and the meaning, and that the more complex and coded multiple interpretations (or allegories) were introduced later in the Christian tradition. A parable such as that of the Wicked Tenants in Mark 12.1–12 calls into question such a simplistic ruling (*see* ALLEGORY). The allegorical tradition is a known factor before and after Jesus, so why not in his teaching too?

Paraclete The most developed theology of the Holy SPIRIT in the New Testament is to be found in the latter part of JOHN'S GOSPEL with the statements about the Paraclete or Comforter/Strengthener (see John 14.16–17, 26; 15.26–27; 16.5–15). The literal meaning of the Greek word *paracletos* is of someone 'called alongside in support', just as AARON was called to be MOSES' spokesman; perhaps the role of the best man alongside the bridegroom at a wedding might provide a good modern illustration. But the sequence of descriptions of the Spirit's role in these chapters of John's Gospel show that his work is infinitely wide-ranging, from the supportive to the judgemental. John 14.16 begins the sequence by showing that the Spirit is '*another* Advocate', that is an alternate to Jesus himself. Consequently the first LETTER OF JOHN, with a much restricted use of the 'Paraclete' language, can refer to Jesus Christ as 'an advocate with the Father' (1 John 2.1).

paradise The term 'paradise' derives from a Persian word (*pairidaeza*) meaning an area that is 'walled around', like a walled garden or circumscribed estate. The Hebrew word *pardes* is used in Nehemiah 2.8 for the Persian king's 'forest/park' (see also the 'enclosed garden' of Song of Songs 4.12; also Ecclesiastes 2.5). The Biblical concept also focuses on the Garden of EDEN, as the paradise that is lost in Genesis 3.23–24, and will one day be regained, as in the eschatological hopes for the end of time (see especially the book of REVELATION, 2.7 and chapter 22, and the poetry of John Milton). The Eden Project, circumscribed in a reclaimed china-clay quarry near St Austell in Cornwall, has as its aim to 'explore our place in nature and discover what the future could look like'.

parousia, or second coming *Parousia* is a Greek word, meaning variously 'presence', 'coming', or 'arrival'. In the Greek papyri it has a more specific sense of a royal visit, or a state visitation by an emperor or his representative. The word is also used by the Jewish writer JOSEPHUS to represent the holy cloud and mist surrounding the Israelite TABERNACLE in the wilderness (Exodus 33.10) and hence the *Shekhinah* or presence of God himself in a theophany. In early Christianity the word denotes the anticipated return (or second coming) of Jesus, coming in triumph and in judgement. According to Hebrews 9.28: 'Christ will appear a second time, not to deal with sin, but to save those who are eagerly waiting for him.' See also the references to the 'coming of the Son of Man' in Mark 8.38, Matthew 24.30, and the parables of Matthew 25 which illustrate the ideas in this eschatological context. Other New Testament references to the parousia are found at 1 Corinthians 15.23, 1 Thessalonians 2.19, James 5.7–8, 2 Peter 1 and 3, and 1 John 2.28.

As the first decades of the Christian movement extended towards a century or more, the problems posed by the delay in Christ's return became acute (see Matthew 16.28; John 21.22; 2 Thessalonians 2). Luke's Gospel in chapter 21 has a version of the APOCALYPTIC expectation, corresponding to Matthew 24 and Mark 13, but expressed in more historical terms (see Luke 21.20), which leaves room for an historical period of the Church's activity that will be covered by the Acts of the Apostles. This is at least part of a solution to the problem.

Passion Narrative This is the account of what happened to Jesus, from GETHSE-MANE to the grave. (See the accounts in Mark 14.1–15.47; Matthew 26.36–66; Luke 22.39–23.54; and John 18.1–19.42.) The story of Jesus' last hours was probably formulated very early in Christian history, as an explanation to the bereaved, as well as for preaching and apologetic purposes. Below are traced the common elements in all four Gospels, noting any major and significant variations.

- Gethsemane, the place of Jesus' prayer to the Father, is named in Matthew and Mark. In Luke it is the Mount of OLIVES, and in John a garden across the Kidron valley. There is no real difference other than of precision. For Jesus it was a prayer of some desperation, according to the SYNOPTIC Gospels; this is perhaps matched, in John, by an earlier question (see John 12.27); but it does not happen at this point in the story, where the prayer, in the Upper Room, for glorification has just finished (John 17).
- The arrest in all four Gospels is by a party of Jewish soldiers guided by JUDAS ISCARIOT; in John there is also a Roman presence; a scuffle took place in which a slave's ear was cut off, and Jesus healed it in Luke.
- PETER's denial of Jesus is differently placed, before (Luke), after (Matthew, Mark), or within (John), the narrative of the trial before the HIGH PRIEST.
- The High Priest's trial in the Synoptics condemned Jesus for BLASPHEMY (explicitly in Mark and Matthew); all three have Jesus effectively admitting to being the SON OF GOD, though naming himself the SON OF MAN. Despite irregularities (*see* TRIAL OF JESUS), the process goes to the next level, although John is bare of detail here. Matthew names the High Priest as CAIAPHAS; in John's account there is a previous interrogation by Annas (an earlier High Priest) before Jesus is sent to Caiaphas.
- Jesus then went to PILATE for trial and sentencing. There is some agreement that the charge had changed to one of being KING OF THE JEWS (to involve the political and military power in the affair and secure a conviction which would bring execution). Pilate was variously reluctant to pronounce the death sentence in three Gospels: he washed his hands of the responsibility in Matthew, postponed the moment by sending Jesus fruitlessly to HEROD in Luke, and debated the issue lengthily in John. Mark gives most impression of Pilate wishing to get on with things, and acceding to the crowd's pressure more quickly.
- The PASSOVER amnesty brought the release of the terrorist BARABBAS and not that of Jesus; this was done on the acclamation of a rent-a-crowd stirred up by the Jewish priests.
- Pilate bowed to public pressure and sentenced Jesus to death, preceded by the usual flogging, and mockery (with a royal flavour) from the soldiers – except in Luke where this mockery has already happened at the hands of Herod's men.
- Jesus was so weakened by this treatment that he could not manage the additional walk bearing the crossbeam of the cross to the place of execution, without assistance. The Synoptic Gospels have SIMON OF CYRENE compelled to help; in John, Jesus manages alone. Luke has Jesus address some women en route.
- All four Gospels agree that Jesus was crucified as 'King of the Jews'. John has the chief priests quibble, but Pilate, firm for once, sticks by what he has written.
- Jesus was variously crucified at GOLGOTHA, the place of the skull.
- He was placed between two other men in John; between two criminals, or bandits, in the Synoptics.

- Jesus was offered a drugged drink, which he tasted and rejected in Matthew, refused outright in Mark, or it was cheap wine or vinegar in Luke and John, which he drank in John. Either the drink was drugged to anaesthetize, or (far from a compassionate act) it was to torture a dying man (see Psalm 69.21).

- His clothes were divided up as perks by the soldiers; John adds a detail about a seamless robe, which was left intact and gambled for, rather than torn up.

- Present at the crucifixion were MARY MAGDALENE in Mark, Matthew and John; Mary the mother of James and Joseph in Matthew and Mark (was she the same as the wife of Clopas in John?); ZEBEDEE's wife in Matthew (was she called Salome in Mark?). Whereas Luke sums them up as the women who had followed Jesus from Galilee, John adds the story that Jesus handed his mother over to the care of the BELOVED DISCIPLE.

- Jesus was crucified at 9 a.m. in Mark; the timing is indefinite in the others. He died at 3 p.m. in the Synoptics, which ties in with the way John relates Jesus' death to the slaughter of the Paschal lambs in the TEMPLE precincts prior to the Passover.

- Once on the cross Jesus was taunted in the Synoptics, but not in John. A combination of the people, the chief priests and teachers of the law (called Jewish leaders in Luke) and those crucified with Jesus feature in each Gospel. Luke is partially different in adding the soldiers, and also in having the thieves debate the issue, with the penitent one being welcomed by the dying Jesus. The themes of mockery are a reproach based on the Temple saying, in Mark and Matthew, together with calls on Jesus to save himself, if he is indeed God's son, and an invitation to come down from the cross. The last two points are repeated by Luke, when the soldiers taunt him whether he was really King of the Jews.

- Jesus' last words from the cross were 'My God, My God, why have you forsaken me?' in Matthew and Mark, which in the ARAMAIC Jesus spoke was misunderstood by bystanders as a call for Elijah. This was followed by a loud cry prior to expiry. The mood is quite different in Luke. The events of the CRUCIFIXION are told by Luke with a slant towards forgiveness to the squad of soldiers and the penitent thief. There Jesus calls out, 'Father forgive them; for they do not know what they are doing'; he then responds to the penitent thief, 'Truly I tell you, today you will be with me in Paradise'. Finally, on expiry the mood is more serene with 'Father, into your hands I commend my spirit' being the substance of the loud cry. John's words are radically different. 'Woman here is your son,' and 'Here is your mother,' are the instructions to MARY and the Beloved Disciple. Later Jesus cried, 'I am thirsty'; and when all was complete, 'It is finished.'

- The moment of Jesus' death was followed by the acclamation of him as Son of God by the officer present, in Mark and Matthew; in Luke, the centurion declared that Jesus was innocent. In John, the test of piercing Jesus' side, to assess the reality of his death, replaces the breaking of the legs for the other criminals. This allows John to draw further on the symbolism of the Passover lamb.

- The Temple curtain was split from top to bottom, and, according to Matthew, there was an earthquake and a general RESURRECTION.

- Jesus' body was removed from the cross and buried by JOSEPH OF ARIMATHEA, accompanied by NICODEMUS in John, as well as by the women who are to rediscover the tomb as empty on the first EASTER Sunday morning.

- The burial was hasty because of the approaching SABBATH, and although Joseph and Nicodemus are reported to have lavishly anointed the body in John, the Synoptics think that the real preparation was left to the women to achieve, after the Sabbath was over.

- Matthew alone speaks of a guard being mounted at the tomb, to prevent robbery by the disciples.

Passover, feast of While the Jerusalem TEMPLE was still standing, the Passover lambs were slaughtered in the afternoon of the day in the Jewish CALENDAR known as 14 Nisan; the blood was poured out and the intestines sacrificed on the Temple altar, in readiness for the roasted meat of the lamb to be eaten at the evening meal (the Passover Seder) which was held to celebrate the EXODUS from Egypt. After the final destruction of the Temple by the Romans in 70 CE, the Seder has been observed regularly as a family meal, in a symbolic recollection of the original sacrifice. Quite frequently non-Jews are invited to join a Passover observance, especially in Israel (see Numbers 9.14).

Jesus made arrangements to eat the Passover meal with his disciples, on the prescribed day, or perhaps in anticipation of it, or in accordance with an alternative sectarian calendar in use at QUMRAN; this happened on the evening prior to his arrest, and the subsequent trial leading to his death. Jesus' actions and blessings at the meal (see especially the account in Luke's Gospel, chapter 22) echo the practice and symbolism of Passover. Matthew, Mark and Luke all suggest that the Last Supper (*see* EUCHARIST) was a Passover meal, while John 18.28 clearly indicates that Jesus was arrested before the official Passover.

Cups of wine and unleavened bread (*matzah*) are essential parts of the Passover meal, consumed after appropriate blessings. There are four cups: first, for the sanctification (*kiddush*) of the day; second, to follow the narration (*haggada*) of the Exodus story; third, for thanksgiving and grace after the meal; and fourth, to accompany the singing of the Hallel psalms (Psalms 113–118, 136). That the bread is unleavened recalls the eating of the meal in haste at the time of the Exodus.

The original Passover circumstances are described in Exodus 12–13. On the first anniversary, the first celebration of Passover took place, 'according to all its statutes and all its regulations' (see the account in Numbers 9). Numbers 9.6–12 indicates how a problem of ritual PURITY might emerge, if people are unclean through touching a corpse, or are otherwise unable to participate because they are absent on a journey. In such circumstances it is permitted to celebrate the 'alternative/second Passover' exactly a month later.

Pastoral Epistles These three New Testament letters were written in the name of Paul to two of his co-workers in the Christian mission, TIMOTHY and TITUS. The contents suggest that they were not the personal letters they might appear to be: Thomas Aquinas described 1 Timothy as 'virtually a pastoral rule'. They have been known as the Pastoral Epistles since the 18th century, because of their concern with matters of leadership, office, and pastoral care.

It is widely held that Paul was not their author, because of differences in style, vocabulary, and the treatment of key Pauline themes, compared with the authenticated letters of Paul. To identify their historical settings within Paul's career is problematic, for it would require speculating about a release from imprisonment in Rome (*see* ACTS 28 and 2 Timothy 1.8). Alternatively, if someone else wrote the Pastorals towards the end of the 1st century CE (or early in the 2nd), then it is also probable that the addressees were not still living, but were rather intended as symbolic representative figures. In the New Testament these three letters are arranged in order of length, but may well not have been written in this sequence; Titus or 2 Timothy may have been written first. The author seeks to recall and cherish the memory of Paul (2 Timothy is close to the literary pattern of the 'testament' – farewell or memorial speech – of that period), and then to reinterpret the teaching of Paul, in terms of the changing circumstances within the HELLENISTIC culture and later JUDAISM by the end of the century. References to false teachers have become rather formal denunciations, compared with the intense argument of Paul's own writing. Key topics such as Church order, Christian conduct in the world, and the role of women, recur in these letters. Modern thinking often finds the subordinationist language about women (e.g. 1 Timothy 2.8–15) difficult to accept.

Patmos Patmos (now Patino) is a small Greek island – one of the chain known as the Sporades – in the Aegean Sea off the west coast of Asia Minor. It is approximately 30 miles in circumference. Historically it was one of the uninviting places used for the banishment of political exiles during the period of the Roman Empire; it was garrisoned by the city of Miletus on the mainland, for which these islands functioned as outlying fortresses. The author of the book of REVELATION says that he was on Patmos 'because of the word of God and the testimony of [to] Jesus' (Revelation 1.9). It is highly likely that John was exiled because of his prophecies with their distinctly political overtones. Presumably he then experienced some of his visions on the island, and put the prophecies in writing in order to communicate with (at least) the SEVEN CHURCHES named in the second and third chapters of the book of Revelation. There is no reason to think, as some have suggested, that he was no longer on the island at the time of writing. Eusebius (in *Ecclesiastical History* 3.20.8–9) says that John was recalled from Patmos as part of an amnesty following the death of Emperor Domitian by whom he had been banished. If so, John would have returned to EPHESUS some 50 miles away.

The APOCRYPHAL *Acts of John* record several miracles performed by John on Patmos. The important Monastery of St John on the island was founded in the 11th century CE. Patmos today is a popular site for pilgrims and tourists from cruise ships; a hillside grotto is pointed out as the claimed site of John's visions. One visitor I know was disconcerted to receive a landing card numbered SIX HUNDRED AND SIXTY-SIX!

Patriarchs ABRAHAM, ISAAC, JACOB and JOSEPH, the Biblical Patriarchs of the book of GENESIS, are seen as the 'founding fathers' of what was to become ISRAEL. There are no archaeological traces of their existence as individual persons, but many of the customs reflected in the narratives correspond to what is known archaeologically about societies of the period 2500–1550 BCE. Traditionally Abraham is supposed to have travelled from UR 'of the Chaldees' to CANAAN by way of HARAN (in Turkey). Certainly long-distance caravan traffic of a bedouin type was well established by the 3rd millennium. It is therefore plausible that the Patriarchs could have entered PALESTINE during the 3rd or early 2nd millennium. However, the stories of the Patriarchs would not have been put into their final written form until the 7th to 5th centuries BCE.

Traditions relating to the Patriarchs can be found also in the New Testament: see, for example, John 4, where Christ comes to the Samaritan town of Sychar and to the well associated with Jacob and Joseph.

Paul According to the ACTS OF THE APOSTLES, Paul was a citizen both of Rome and of TARSUS. There is some dispute about the Roman citizenship, because Paul's letters do not mention it; Luke probably refers to it (see Acts 16.38) because such status would have been important to THEOPHILUS, to whom he wrote. By trade Paul was a tentmaker, working in leather or linen or goat's hair compressed like felt; he may have belonged to an inner circle of privileged craftsmen/citizens, although his trade may have counted against him at Tarsus.

Again according to Acts, the name 'Paul' (a Roman one) is adopted in place of the Semitic 'Saul' (13.9). This happens immediately after his meeting at Salamis on Cyprus with the Roman proconsul Sergius Paulus, and a confrontation with the sorcerer Elymas. It is suggested that the governor became a believer (13.12); Paul's change of name may commemorate this occasion (as St Jerome suggested) by adopting the name of a significant Roman official who was both sympathizer and convert.

The story of Paul's life, from his childhood in Tarsus and years as a student in Jerusalem, to the successes and failures of his subsequent ministry, is set against the background of the Greco-Roman world, which provides several fixed points for his biography. Traditionally the Acts have provided a framework, such as the structure of three missionary journeys in chapters 13–20, but although this is accurate in many details, it can mislead both because of Luke's theological intentions, and also because of variations in narrative pace, sometimes giving equal space to days and months. Paul's own writings provide a primary source for his life, but, although they do relate to specific situations, their concern is with the Churches' needs rather than with the biography of the author. Paul is in prison when he writes some letters (as PHILIPPIANS), but it is less clear whether his prison is in EPHESUS, CAESAREA (MARITIMA), or ROME.

Paul was educated as an orthodox Jew, studying in Jerusalem under GAMALIEL. He became involved in actions against the new Christian believers and was implicated in the death of STEPHEN (see Acts 8.1). In pursuit of similar measures against Christians in Damascus, Paul was brought up short by a vision (variously interpreted as a conversion experience or a prophetic call to a new direction of activity – see Acts 9 and Galatians 1). Paul goes to Jerusalem to visit the Christian leaders, and subsequently he is active in the Christian MISSION in Syria and Cilicia. His second visit to Jerusalem is for charitable purposes of famine relief (see Acts 11.30); this was the famine in the reign of Emperor Claudius, referred to by JOSEPHUS and dated to 46 CE.

What is traditionally known, from the Acts account, as Paul's first missionary journey begins from ANTIOCH and goes to Cyprus, Pamphylia and South Galatia in the years 47–48 CE. Paul returns to Jerusalem for the Council (variously described in

Paul in Prison Philippians 1.12–14

Acts 15 and Galatians 2) late in 48 CE. The so-called second missionary journey begins from Antioch early in 49 CE and goes through North Galatia to TROAS, Philippi, Thessalonica, Beroea and Athens. Late in that year Paul arrives in Corinth, where he meets Aquila and PRISCILLA; they had come from Rome, and the date corresponds to the edict of Emperor Claudius in 49 CE, expelling Jews from Rome. Paul was to remain in Corinth for 18 months, during which time he wrote his earliest surviving letter, 1 THESSALONIANS. Corinth in 51 CE provides the pivotal point for the chronology of Paul's life: Gallio was proconsul of Achaea then, as we know from an inscription found at Delphi, and Paul appeared before him (Acts 18.12).

Paul

In 52 CE Paul makes an expedition from Antioch to Galatia and Phrygia, and overland to EPHESUS. He may well have been imprisoned in Ephesus during 55 CE, but in 56 he leaves for Macedonia, and then returns to Corinth for the winter. During these years Paul writes letters to the GALATIANS, 1 CORINTHIANS, probably PHILIPPIANS and PHILEMON, and two separate letters that now form 2 Corinthians. In 57 CE he returns to Jerusalem (Acts 21) with the charitable COLLECTION from the Churches. Now Paul is imprisoned in Caesarea, while Felix is Roman procurator of Judaea; Paul writes to the Church at Rome, anticipating his journey there, and introducing himself to a readership that does not know him personally. ROMANS is the latest of Paul's letters, and the closest to (but by no means identical with) a systematic theology. Probably in 59 CE Felix is succeeded as procurator by Porcius Festus. Paul appears before Festus and Agrippa (see HERODIAN DYNASTY), and as a Roman citizen appeals to Caesar. On the journey to Rome, Paul is shipwrecked and spends the winter in Malta. In 60 CE Paul arrives in Rome and is imprisoned there. The possibility of a further journey to Spain (alluded to in Romans 15.28) is only speculative on the basis of available evidence. Paul was probably executed in Rome sometime between 62 and 64 CE; the evidence from 1 Clement 5.7 certainly suggests a MARTYR's death in Rome.

Paul identifies himself as an APOSTLE, one 'sent' by Jesus Christ. There were various ways in which Paul conceived his apostolic role: as prophet (see Galatians 1.15 for a prophetic vocation like that of Jeremiah 1.5); moral philosopher (1 Thessalonians 2.3–12, expressed in the language of pastoral care related to the Cynic philosophy of the times); preacher; pastor; and spiritual guide. The exact nature of the relationship between Paul and JESUS has always been controversial: Paul is variously described as a faithful follower of Jesus, or as the real founder of Christianity. There is less straightforward continuity between the Gospel accounts of Jesus and Paul's writings than might initially be expected. But then the circumstances of a wandering CHARISMATIC in Galilee and an urban missionary in the Roman Empire would be rather different.

From a Jewish perspective, Paul has been described as the main promoter of a group of rogue messianic Jews who set up a new standard for JUDAISM, using the SEPTUAGINT and APOCALYPTIC fervour, to open up the Abrahamic covenant to the GENTILES and abandon the observances of TORAH. His letters, especially that to the Romans, might be regarded as 'fundamental messianic texts', concentrating on the 'time that remains' (see Romans 13.11–12), concerned with transforming Jewish law in an apocalyptic-revolutionary mode rather than with establishing a new religion. It could be said that Paul is 'the bearer of a universal truth that simultaneously shatters the strictures of Judaic Law and the conventions of the Greek *Logos* [Reason]'.

In Christian terms Paul was a missionary and a theologian. But because his theology was developed in relation to the needs of the moment in local Churches of the Mediterranean world, he cannot be regarded as a systematic theologian, even if his letter to the Romans seeks to summarize some of his main arguments. One question endlessly discussed by students of the New Testament is, 'What is the heart of Paul's Gospel?' At the time of the Reformation the favoured answer was 'justification by faith' (see RIGHTEOUSNESS), and this has remained prominent, especially in Lutheran thought. But this terminology is largely restricted to Romans and Galatians, and may well be more sympathetic, and less adversarial, to Jewish thought than was assumed in the past (see the critical works of E. P. Sanders). In contrast, Albert Schweitzer proposed that the real centre of Paul's religion was the believer's union with Christ (as expressed repeatedly in the phrases 'in Christ' and 'in the Lord', or in ideas like that of Galatians 2.19: 'I am crucified with Christ'). Apocalyptic mysticism of this kind has found new favour with some Pauline scholars; Paul looks to a real climax and end of history (see 1 Corinthians 10.11 and ESCHATON), with the ultimate triumph of God.

DATING PAUL'S LIFE AND TIMES

Externally fixed points	Reconstruction of events in Paul's life	Approximate dates of widely accepted letters by Paul
	Born at Tarsus, a cosmopolitan city	
	Educated as an Orthodox Jew	
	Studied in Jerusalem under Gamaliel	
30 Crucifixion of Jesus	Involved in actions against Christians and in the death of Stephen	
	33 Call/conversion of Saul	
	35 First journey to Jerusalem (Acts 9.26–30; Galatians 1.18)	
	Activity in Syria and Cilicia	
46 Famine in the reign of Emperor Claudius (Josephus *Antiquities* 20.101)	46 Second journey to Jerusalem – famine relief (Acts 11.30)	
	46–47 Expedition from Antioch to Cyprus, Pamphylia and South Galatia (first missionary journey)	
	48? Council of Jerusalem (Acts 15; Galatians 2.1)	
	49 Expedition from Antioch through North Galatia to Troas, Philippi, Thessalonica, Beroea, Athens (second missionary journey)	
49 Edict of Emperor Claudius expelling Jews from Rome	late 49 Arrival in Corinth	
	Meeting with Priscilla and Aquila	
	18-month stay in Corinth	
51 Gallio proconsul of Achaea (Delphi inscription)	Hearing before Gallio (Acts 18.12)	50 1 Thessalonians
52 Felix as procurator of Judaea	52 Expedition from Antioch to Galatia and Phrygia, overland to Ephesus	53 Galatians

	55 Ephesus (imprisonment)	54 1 Corinthians
		55 Philippians
		55 Philemon
		55? 2 Corinthians 10–13
	56 Macedonia	56? 2 Corinthians 1–9
	Winter in Corinth	
	57 Return to Jerusalem (Acts 21)	57 Romans
	Imprisonment in Caesarea under Felix	
		58? Colossians
60 Porcius Festus succeeds Felix as procurator of Judaea	60 Hearing before P. Festus and Agrippa	
	Journey to Rome	
	Shipwreck (winter in Malta)	
	61 Arrival and imprisonment in Rome	
	62–64 Execution at some point in Rome	

Dates are CE, approximate and may vary within a year or two. Adapted from J. M. and K. M. Court, *The New Testament World* (Cambridge University Press, 1990).

peace In the Hebrew Bible peace is SHALOM, the future fulfilment of the pastoral idyll ('they shall all sit under their own vines and under their own fig trees' – MICAH 4.4). In a society which (unlike ours) did not see any tension between war and what was evil in God's sight, in fact the reverse – that God might command the war anyway – peace was for them a goal only periodically attained, however much desired.

In the New Testament there is the spiritualization of peace as an eschatological gift (see John 14.27), but also the distinct possibility that Jesus saw peace as a realizable goal in the present life too. Despite the nationalism of many of his own Jewish people, and the oppressive militarism of the Roman occupation, it is possible to see the Jesus of Matthew's Gospel standing out against this worldview and in favour of pacifism. 'All who take the sword will perish by the sword' (Matthew 26.52). 'Blessed are the peacemakers' (Matthew 5.9; see also 5.24; 5.43–45).

It is frequently maintained that early Christianity was pacifist, until the over-whelming need of the Roman Empire to survive led St Augustine of Hippo to sanction the JUST WAR (*see also* WAR, HOLY WAR). This pacifist teaching disappeared until revived by the 'Peace Churches' (e.g. Anabaptists and Quakers) from the Reformation onwards. Pacifism became more widespread in the 20th century, and Christians used the Bible passages cited above to justify their stance as conscientious objectors in world wars, and as a protest against nuclear weapons more recently.

The interpretation of these texts in a pacifist way is disputed by other Christians who take Jesus' teaching to relate to individual, personal conduct in relationships, and therefore regard it as irrelevant to international affairs as viewed by the state. They rely on the teaching of PAUL for society's resistance to evil, and for a clear indication of the passive approach in matters for the individual (see Romans

12.19–20). Jesus' CLEANSING OF THE TEMPLE (Mark 11.15–16) can be used as an argument to bolster direct action by Christians.

pelican The Psalmist in his affliction described his state as being 'like a pelican of the wilderness' (Psalm 102.6 in the KING JAMES VERSION); the simile might express the

loneliness and isolation of a naturally gregarious bird. It is possible that the pelican is also listed in Leviticus 11.18 and Deuteronomy 14.17, although the translation 'desert owl' may be more appropriate (as in other versions of Psalm 102). In medieval theology the pelican was thought to possess mystical properties, and so it figured in art as a symbol of the compassion of Christ (sometimes perched on Christ's cross), and therefore also of Christian charity. The female pelican was said to feed its young by pecking its own breast and drawing blood; it could then symbolize the nourishment of Christians by the EUCHARIST.

The Pelican

Pella *See* DECAPOLIS.

Pentateuch Pentateuch and TORAH are both used to denote the first five books of the Hebrew Scriptures (Old Testament). *See* PENTATEUCHAL CRITICISM. As Peter Ackroyd wrote: 'The literary status of these [five] books [of the Jewish Law] has been the subject of endless debate. Their origins are obscure and their chronology tentative, although the best guess seems to be that the four principal "strands" were written between the 8th and 6th centuries [BCE] before being brought together as a single narrative in the late 6th [or 5th] century. But what kind of narrative is it? It is comprised of individual stories, cultic regulations, patriarchal tales, lists of tribes, historical accounts and so many other varieties of prose that it seems almost to resist definition. It is in a sense The Book, the source and origin of all the narratives of the world. The story of Adam and Eve in the Garden of Eden, and their temptation by the serpent, is one of the shaping myths of the human imagination. The myth is perpetual because it corresponds very deeply to some need or belief of humankind.'

TABULATION OF THE PENTATEUCH

Genesis
Israel's prehistory 1.1–11.32

1.1–3.24	Creation and Fall
4.1–5.32	Adam's family
6.1–10.32	Noah and family
11.1–9	The tower of Babel
11.10–32	The origins of Abram's family in Babylon

Israel's early history 12.1–50.26

12.1–35.29	The Patriarchs – Abraham, Isaac, and Jacob
36.1–43	Esau's family
37.1–45.28	Joseph's family and adventures
46.1–50.26	Israel in Egypt

Exodus

Israel's slavery in Egypt and escape 1.1–15.21

1.1–22	Slavery conditions
2.1–4.31	The boy Moses
5.1–11.10	Moses' challenge to Pharaoh
12.1–15.21	Passover and escape

After the Exodus 15.22–40.38

15.22–18.27	Journey to Sinai
19.1–24.18	The giving of the Torah (Law) on Sinai (this includes the Ten Commandments 20.1–17)
25.1–40.38	Instructions for worship

Leviticus

Cultic holiness 1.1–27.34

1.1–7.38	Rules about sacrifices
8.1–10.20	Rules about priesthood
11.1–15.33	Rules about being clean
16.1–34	The Day of Atonement
17.1–27.34	Rules about being holy

Numbers

Departure from Sinai 1.1–9.23

1.1–4.49	Census of people, priests and Levites with numbers of Israelites
5.1–8.26	Regulations
9.1–23	Passover is kept

From Sinai to the Promised Land 10.1–33.49

10.1–21.35	Journey and conquest en route
22.1–33.49	The Moab story
22.1–24.25	Balaam blesses Israel
25.1–17	Idolatry at Peor
26.1–27.11	Census and property
27.12–23	Joshua as successor to Moses
28.1–31.54	Offerings and arrangements
32.1–42	Some tribes settle east of Jordan
33.1–49	Summary of journey from Egypt to Moab

Instructions ready to cross the Jordan 33.50–36.13

Deuteronomy

Moses' religious instructions to Israel before entering the Promised Land 1.1–34.12

1.1–4.49	Moses' first sermon
5.1–26.19	Moses' second sermon (includes the Ten Commandments 5.6–21)

27.1–28.68   Obedience brings blessings
29.1–30.20   The covenant and the choice between life and death
31.1–34.12   Moses' eulogy and death

pentateuchal criticism The Pentateuch, or 'five scrolls' (so named by the Church Father Origen in the 3rd century CE), denotes the first five books of the Old Testament; this is what the Jews call the TORAH (Law) – the first section of the Hebrew Bible. The traditional belief that these five books were written by Moses is not supported anywhere in the Pentateuch, although it was assumed in the New Testament period. Critical questioning began early, and the Jewish philosopher Spinoza wondered how Moses could have written an account of his own death.

An essential point of Biblical criticism is the identification of multiple source traditions which underlay the Pentateuch. There are four principal strands, commonly called J, E, D, and P, in the classical critical theory developed in the second half of the 19th century. A long period of oral tradition was assumed, out of which emerged these four, more literary, strands: J from Judah in the 9th century BCE (uses YAHWEH for the name of God, SINAI for the mountain of God, and CANAANITES (*see* CANAAN) for the inhabitants of Palestine); E from the Northern Kingdom in the 8th century (uses Elohim for GOD, Horeb for the mountain, and AMORITES for the population); D the law-book of King JOSIAH's reform (621 BCE – see 2 Kings 22.3–13); and P from a 5th-century date, during or just after the EXILE, with an interest in priestly matters. The climax was a process of redaction in which all these strands were tied together.

The issues can be illustrated by one of many examples concerned with the sanctuaries and places of sacrifice mentioned in these books. The PATRIARCHS sacrificed in many places (e.g. Genesis 28.10–22), but not in a single religious centre such as Jerusalem. They planted trees and set up pillars in total contradiction to the law stated in Deuteronomy 16.21–22. Jerusalem is not explicitly mentioned in these five books. BETHEL is described as 'none other than the house of God, and this is the gate of heaven'. According to Exodus 12, the PASSOVER festival offering can be sacrificed anywhere; but in the time of the later monarchy this law was abolished (2 Kings 23.21–23).

Scholars agree that the Deuteronomistic History (Deuteronomy, Joshua, Judges, Samuel, and Kings) was a work compiled in the late 7th century BCE, and driven by the programme of the book of Josiah's reform. The idea of a centralization of sacrifice at a single sanctuary was a creation of this period, superimposed on the text in this theological interpretation. Other source materials widely used in the History and the Pentateuch derive from earlier times and reflect earlier attitudes and different practices. So, for instance, in the J source Abraham builds altars at every place he visits in Canaan. These divergent attitudes offer clues to the reader about the origins of these source materials. The Pentateuch is not a single agenda, but a richly accumulating set of traditions.

Pentecost The Jewish FESTIVAL of Pentecost (Shavuot) originated as a harvest festival, but became the occasion to celebrate the receiving of the Law (TORAH) on

Pentecost Acts 2.1–13

Mount SINAI. Biblical tradition states that Israel in the wilderness was far from prepared to receive the Torah. Accordingly there is now a Jewish custom to stay awake through the night of Shavuot, studying Torah in the Bet Midrash, so as to be more worthy of its acceptance. The Hebrew term for this practice is *tikun layl Shavuot*, or 'restoring the night of Shavuot'. At dawn there is a gathering for morning prayers; at that time one can find the plaza at the Western Wall in Jerusalem thronged with people at their devotions.

The significance of Pentecost for Christianity is documented in the narrative of the ACTS OF THE APOSTLES, chapter 2. Following the religious experience described here, PETER stands up and explains, by means of a quotation from the Old Testament prophet JOEL (2.28–32), what was happening on Pentecost to the Christians in Jerusalem: the Holy SPIRIT of God was falling upon them and affecting their behaviour.

Peraea The geographical term Peraea comes from the Greek word meaning 'beyond'. It is used to indicate the area to the east of the river Jordan, 'beyond the Jordan' from the Israelite/Jewish point of view (as in Transjordan). Contrast this with the reference to 'the WAY OF THE SEA, the land beyond Jordan' in Isaiah 9.1 which is looking from east to west.

The actual term Peraea does not occur in the Bible (except in Luke 6.17 in a few manuscripts). But the equivalent expressions 'across/beyond the Jordan' are common (see Matthew 4.25; 19.1; Mark 3.8; 10.1; John 1.28; 3.26; 10.40 – *see also* JOHN THE BAPTIST). The word Peraea occurs frequently in the writings of JOSEPHUS.

Pergamon Pergamon is one of the seven Churches addressed in chapters 2 and 3 of the book of REVELATION. The city, now called Bergama in modern Turkey, is located in the fertile river valley of the Caicus in the west of Asia Minor, within the area historically called Mysia, which formed part of the Roman province of Asia. In the previous centuries Pergamon had been the centre of the Hellenistic kingdom of the Attalids, but when Attalos III died in 133 BCE he bequeathed the kingdom to the Romans, who transformed it into their Asian province.

A central feature of the old city was the acropolis, a higher and steeper elevation than the well-known acropolis of Athens. In the 1st century CE, when Revelation was written, most people lived to the south of the acropolis, with their northern horizon dominated by the Great Altar of Pergamon, and the temples of Athena and Zeus. What little remains of the dedicatory inscription of the Great Altar suggests that it was erected in honour of Attalos III. The Great Altar of Pergamon has been reconstructed in the Pergamon Museum of the Staatliche Museen in Berlin. It may be referred to in Revelation 2.13 as 'the throne of Satan'. A bust of Emperor Augustus was found at Pergamon (it is now in the Istanbul Archaeological Museum), which may suggest in addition an association with the cult of the emperor. The city was also the site of one of the great libraries of the ancient world, comparable to that in Alexandria. The city's association with book production is recalled in the modern term 'parchment' (made originally from the thinnest skins of certain animals), which is derived from the name 'Pergamon'.

persecution of Christians During the period when the majority of the New Testament books were composed, it has often been argued that the early Christians were formally persecuted by the Romans, as well as experiencing hostility from their Jewish neighbours. The evidence for official persecution is very hard to establish, and it is necessary to recognize the possibilities of varying degrees of discrimination against the Christians. Within the Roman Empire, apart from formal persecution based upon legal edicts, there also existed the possibility of unofficial social and economic sanctions, verbal and physical abuse, harassment and maltreatment; it is unlikely that much of this would ever have been recorded.

As a general principle, during the 1st century CE, it would seem that Roman officials tolerated any believers in Jesus as MESSIAH, so long as they could be reckoned as Jews. Jews were expected to honour the emperor and pray for his welfare and that of the Empire. But because it was understood that Jews believed in only one God, they would not be expected to worship the emperor as divine, in the way that most Greeks and Hellenized provincials will have done with varying degrees of enthusiasm. However, the action taken by Emperor Nero against the Christians of Rome after the fire in 64 CE may well have set a precedent, such that Christians were marked out from Jews and could be executed merely for being Christians. As a consequence, in the time of Emperor Trajan (98–117 CE), Christians who refused to curse the name of Christ, and to worship the emperor together with the official gods of Rome, were liable to be executed as stubborn adherents of a 'superstition'. The action of Christians, like that of Christ himself, could be construed as treasonable opposition to the good government of Rome.

Official and Empire-wide persecutions of Christians are known from the later centuries. Before this any formal and legal actions are likely to have been local and sporadic (although none the less serious for those accused). There is evidence, in a letter of Pliny the Younger to Emperor Trajan, early in the 2nd century CE, of some prosecution before a provincial governor, if there was an accusation brought and a denunciation of the offender, possibly by some neighbours who were resentful. Earlier there is evidence that some Jews were expelled from Rome by Emperor Claudius in 49–50 CE (see, for example, PRISCILLA); according to the writer Suetonius this was a consequence of tumults instigated by someone called 'Chrestus' (a possible misunderstanding of the name 'Christ', or a more general reference to a common slave). Notoriously, as recorded by the Roman historian Tacitus, Emperor Nero made the Christians scapegoats for the fire of Rome in 64 CE. At this point it is highly probable that both PETER and PAUL were killed. In the final decade of the 1st century CE Emperor Domitian may have been the second persecutor of Christians after Nero. But the evidence is patchy and may be heightened by prejudice, and a text like PETER'S FIRST LETTER is variously interpreted. There are some references in the early Christian writing *1 Clement*, as well as the internal evidence of conflict between Church and state in the book of REVELATION. The strong and explicit language of the visions in this book may, it is true, reflect an apprehension of what is to happen sooner or later, rather than being direct evidence of persecutions in Asia Minor that can be dated to the reign of Domitian or earlier.

See also MARTYR.

Persians In the Biblical world the Persian period lasted approximately from 539 until 332 BCE. Descendants of Jews who had been deported to BABYLON were allowed to return during the reign of CYRUS (549–530 BCE), who also contributed to the cost of rebuilding the TEMPLE. Cyrus was a Persian ruler who had taken over the Babylonian Empire following the defeat of Nabonidus in 539 BCE. A clay cylinder (now in the British Museum) records these events, to be compared with the narratives of the Biblical books of EZRA and NEHEMIAH. It is suggested that Cyrus' general intention was to flatter his subject peoples and confirm their dependence; he 'felt free to claim the favour of a whole multitude of gods precisely because he believed in none of them' (Tom Holland). The Persians actually left little permanent trace in Palestine. Cultural influences in the coastal regions were already Greek, transmitted by PHOENICIAN and Greek colonists, even before the conquest by Alexander the Great. The vast empire of the Persians throughout Asia crumbled and fell to Alexander following the battle of Issus in 332 BCE.

Peshitta *See* SYRIAC.

Peter (apostle) Peter, the Galilean fisherman, became regarded as the classic apostolic figure of the Christian Church, the 'rock-like' leader providing stability in his teaching and missionary work. Originally Simon or Simeon, son of Jonah, he

The Call of Peter Luke 5.1–11

has the Aramaic nickname 'Kephas', which means 'rock'; this translates into Greek as *petra*. This feminine noun (Latin neuter *petrum*) is the basis of the punning association which Jesus apparently made with the common personal name Petros (Latin *petrus*) or Peter (see John 1.42; Matthew 16.17–19). This second text is also the basis for the special calling of Peter to leadership among the disciples after Jesus' death, which, in the tradition following Matthew's specific wording (referring to 'Church'), became the foundation of the Roman Catholic papacy traced back to Peter. Two letters in the New Testament are ascribed to Peter (see next two entries), but their authorship is disputed. There is also a tradition which associates him with Mark's Gospel as embodying his reminiscences.

According to John's Gospel, Peter's birthplace was BETHSAIDA, but he also had a house in CAPERNAUM (possibly as a consequence of his marriage – see Mark 1.30). Among the DISCIPLES of Jesus, Peter belongs to the inner circle of three (Mark 5.37). He is impulsively devoted to Jesus and impetuous in his actions. His impetuosity might be illustrated by John 18.10, where he is named as the one with Jesus at the arrest in Gethsemane who drew a sword and cut off the right ear of the High Priest's slave. (A 9th-century German version of the story, influenced by the idea of the warrior saint, has Peter vowing to fight to the death.) The Gospel narratives represent also his human fallibility and weaknesses (most obviously in the threefold denial of Jesus); but it is possible that these traditions emphasize his failings in order to encourage other later followers to believe that one can still serve Christ. A typical episode which shows both sides of Peter occurs at CAESAREA PHILIPPI (Mark 8.27–33), when Peter confesses that Jesus is MESSIAH, but is criticized by Jesus for failing to understand that this will involve suffering.

After Jesus' death and ASCENSION, and the spiritual experience of the disciples at PENTECOST, Peter becomes the spokesman of the new community and preaches a powerful sermon (Acts 2). The reference to Peter and John as 'unlearned and ignor- ant' (Acts 4.13) should not perhaps be taken too literally; but Peter will not have been trained as a rabbi. Acts 11 indicates his initiative in opening the Christian community to GENTILES, in the person of Cornelius. But GALATIANS 2.11 reveals a difference of opinion with Paul on a question of table-fellowship. Peter appears at the Jerusalem Council in Acts 15, but is not found again in the New Testament record (unless the two witnesses in REVELATION 11 are to be identified as Peter and Paul). The epilogue to John's Gospel (chapter 21) refers to a post-resurrection appearance to Peter, in which he is questioned three times (corresponding to his threefold denial of Jesus before the crucifixion); this narrative may indicate a rivalry between the Christian com- munities allied to Peter and to John. Later sources, and the APOCRYPHAL *Acts* (of *Peter* and *Peter and Paul*), speak of the joint work of Peter and Paul in the Church at Rome, and of their martyrdom. Traditionally Peter was crucified upside down, around 64 CE, at the time of a pogrom by Emperor Nero against Roman Christians (Tacitus *Annals* 15).

Peter's life and death have featured in novels and films of the 20th century such as Henry Sienkewicz's *Quo Vadis* and Lloyd C. Douglas's *The Robe* and *The Big Fisher- man*. Morris West wrote a novel about the papacy entitled *The Shoes of the Fisherman*.

Peter, first letter of 1 Peter is classified, like JAMES, as a 'general' or 'catholic' epistle because it is addressed to Christians over a large area of northern Asia Minor, effectively to five Roman provinces. It is a letter of warm pastoral care for Christians suffering hardship and expecting a future that will be worse. Variously it is described as 'a microcosm of Christian faith and duty, the model of a pastoral charge' and as a 'gallant and high-hearted exhortation which breathes a spirit of undaunted courage and exhibits as noble a type of piety as can be found in any writing of the New Testament outside the Gospels'. The traditional view is that the letter was written to JEWISH-CHRISTIANS (the 'dispersion' in 1.1; see Galatians 2.9) by the apostle Peter who was in Rome (referred to in 5.13 as 'Babylon') before his martyrdom in 64 CE. Some anxieties about the traditional view are due to the letter's literary character (more than might be expected from a Galilean fisherman, unless he used a secretary, such as Silvanus, mentioned in 5.12), and the similarity in argument to writings of Paul. It has been seen as a later composition, designed to harmonize relations between the Petrine and Pauline traditions.

1 Peter is concerned with the nature of the elect, that is Christians, as the people of God. This identity is derived from the Old Testament understanding of Israel, and provides the basis for the author's ethical exhortations (parenesis). 'For the exodus, desert wandering and promised land motifs from the PENTATEUCH have been taken over and imaginatively reapplied to the conversion of GENTILES in Christ. If that desert experience made the slave tribes from Egypt into a people, God's people, so has the Christian conversion made the Gentiles who were once no people into God's people' (R. E. Brown). The readers are seen also as 'aliens and exiles' (2.11), which has suggested that the community felt itself marginalized because of its faith. BAPTISM is a key theme (see 3.21) as the identifying mark of Christian initiation; some scholars have suggested that the letter originated as a sermon in the context of a baptism, or even as a liturgy for baptism.

Peter, second letter of 2 Peter is closely related to the letter of JUDE, and both of them are termed 'catholic' or 'general' epistles, because they seem to be addressed to a very broad audience (although it is likely that they have unnamed but specific target readerships in mind). Most scholars now agree that the author of 2 Peter was dependent on Jude, adapting material for his own purpose (see especially 2 Peter 2.1–18 and 3.1–3). 2 Peter is written as a letter but presents what is termed the 'testament' of Peter, that is a kind of 'deathbed' recollection of one's teaching with advice for the future. Such a farewell speech was quite a popular form in Jewish writing; it became a convention to attribute such a testament to a great figure of the past. So although it might have been written by Peter from Rome before his martyrdom in 64 CE, it is more likely to have been written by another at a later point, using the method to restate Peter's teaching for a later crisis.

2 Peter is directed against specific objections to Christian teaching, and probably against particular teachers. The issues of belief defended by the writer are the strictness of the Christian moral code, and the relevance of an eschatological belief in the LAST JUDGEMENT. Scepticism arising from the delayed PAROUSIA will prove to be the undoing of the false teachers (who probably maintained a libertine position influenced by pagan HELLENISM). 'The condemnation pronounced on them long ago is not idle' (2.3); Old Testament examples such as the angels of Genesis 6, NOAH and the flood, and the destruction of SODOM and Gomorrah, show that judgement is no idle threat. Thomas Hardy made dramatic use of this text early in his novel *Tess of the D'Urbevilles*, with the words of judgement in vermilion paint on a country stile.

2 Peter was rejected by John Calvin, but Martin LUTHER, who had a high regard for 1 Peter, may have allowed 2 Peter to stay in the canon by association. Luther believed that Jude copied 2 Peter, the opposite view of the relationship to that held by most modern scholarship.

Petra The ruins of the 'rose-red city' of Petra (the colour from the sandstone cliffs) are located in south-west Jordan. The area was occupied by the Edomites as early as the 7th century BCE. Some authorities also identify the site of Petra with the Biblical Sela, in EDOM (Judges 1.36; 2 Kings 14.7). Petra became the royal capital of the NABATEANS, who settled there in the 3rd century BCE, establishing a flourishing caravan city. The site was central to Near Eastern trade routes and so the Nabatean merchants prospered through trade in perfumes and spices. The easily defended site protected them against aggressive rivals, and the buildings reflected the wealth of the occupants. Petra was visited by Pompey and his Roman troops in 65 BCE, but was not annexed and integrated into the Roman Empire until 106 CE; the site of the city was eventually abandoned sometime after 592 CE. The site was rediscovered and identified by the Swiss explorer Johann Ludwig Burckhardt in 1812.

Petrie, Sir Flinders Flinders Petrie was born in London in 1853 and died in Jerusalem in 1942. He became a pioneer in the archaeology of ancient Egypt, beginning his work with a project to measure accurately the great pyramid at Gizeh. The initial impetus was a beautiful theory in a book by Piazzi Smyth that there was a correlation between the dimensions of the pyramid and the Biblical history of the world. The measurement proved the theory false by 71 inches. The experience transformed Petrie into a scientific archaeologist, first in Egypt and then in Palestine, and earned him a reputation as a founder of Biblical ARCHAEOLOGY.

The twin bases of the scientific archaeological method which he established were stratification and the typology of pottery. In work in Israel at Tel el-Hesi in 1890 he investigated the structure of the large mound (tel) which resulted from frequent rebuilding of settlements on the same site. It was possible to identify the different strata of occupation of the site, and then to date the layers by the nature of the pottery sherds found within them. From such excavations, and comparison with Egyptian evidence, Petrie was able to construct something closer to an absolute chronology based on the variations in types of pottery. Tel el-Hesi may be the site of Biblical Eglon.

Pharisees JOSEPHUS refers to three main schools of religious thought prior to 70 CE, describing them by the Greek word 'philosophy': Pharisees, SADDUCEES, and ESSENES. 'The Pharisees are considered the most accurate interpreters of the laws, and hold the position of the leading sect.' They were meticulous advocates of the oral law, validated as an exposition of Mosaic law from Sinai, and were consequently open to more modern ideas (such as RESURRECTION) compared with the Sadducees. Their name probably comes from an ARAMAIC word meaning 'the separated ones'; this relates to their concern for the observance of PURITY. Nevertheless, because of their interest in education, they cultivated good relations with the ordinary people of the land. Their traditions survived the fall of Jerusalem in 70 CE and contributed substantially to the reconstitution of JUDAISM after that date. They probably do not deserve, as a whole, the pejorative judgement upon them in the New Testament narratives.

Philadelphia 1 Philadelphia is the sixth of seven Churches of Asia Minor to receive messages in chapters 2 and 3 of the book of REVELATION. The site of the ancient city is now occupied by Alasehir in modern Turkey. Philadelphia was originally founded by Attalos II, king of PERGAMON, possibly as a centre for the spread of Greek ideas (hence its Greek name). It occupied a strategic position, linking communications between SARDIS and Pergamon to the west, and LAODIKEIA and HIERAPOLIS to the east. Its 'open door' (Revelation 3.8) for trade communications was equally a missionary opportunity for the Christian Church. The modern town of Alasehir has a strikingly square and symmetrical plan, at least suggesting the possibility of a link with prophecies of NEW JERUSALEM (see Revelation 3.12 and chapter 21). There is evidence that the 2nd-century CE movement known as MONTANISM, for whom the actualization of new Jerusalem was an important belief, originated in the area of Philadelphia.

2 *See* DECAPOLIS.

Philemon, letter of Paul to At first sight this is a short and straightforward letter from Paul to a Christian living in COLOSSAE (*see also* COLOSSIANS). But of course we only know Paul's side of the story, and we would like to know more of the circumstances and what happened next. It appears that Philemon's slave, Onesimus (whose name means 'useful' – see pun in verse 11) had run away, possibly after a theft. Somehow he had found Paul in prison, been of help to him there, and was converted (or re-converted) to Christianity by him. Paul would like Onesimus to stay, but decides to send him back to his master together with the judicious and skilful arguments of this letter.

An alternative scenario suggests that it is not a personal letter to an individual, but is written to a Church congregation of which Philemon and Apphia are the leaders. Onesimus is with Paul during his imprisonment because he was sent there by Archippus on behalf of the Church at Colossae. Paul is writing formally (in quite technical language) to request that Onesimus be released from his obligations in Colossae, so that he might stay with Paul and work in the Christian ministry. There is a separate request that Onesimus be released from his status as slave (manumitted).

The historical circumstances of the case may not be straightforward. Other aspects of the letter may be equally important. There is a relevance to the debate on the abolition of SLAVERY; it may be strange to note that in 1864, prior to the Civil War, an American defence of slavery as an institution was based on the letter to Philemon. And there are social features to this text which are more timeless: not only the question whether the word describing Paul in verse 9 should be translated 'old man' or 'ambassador', but also the wide range of social categories mentioned (brother, father, child, slave, master, prisoner, freeman, host, patron, partner) and their compatibility within a newly formed Christian network. The Church Father Ignatius knew a bishop of Ephesus called Onesimus, but such a link with this slave is only an interesting speculation.

The name Philemon is also known in Greek mythology (see also Gluck's opera *Bauci e Filemone*). He was a countryman in Phrygia, living with his wife Baucis; uniquely they responded with hospitality when Zeus and Hermes visited in disguise, to test human piety. As a reward they were permitted to die at the same moment, so as to avoid the pain of bereavement. They were honoured as priests of the religious cult, or seen as symbolized by trees. Any link therefore with the New Testament text is unlikely.

Philip The name of two distinct figures in early Christianity, who are frequently confused. Philip, the deacon, was appointed to assist the twelve APOSTLES (Acts 6.1–6), proved a highly successful evangelist in Samaria, enlightened the Ethiopian on the Gaza road, and settled in Caesarea (Maritima). Philip the apostle was a DISCIPLE of Jesus who came from BETHSAIDA in Galilee (John 1.44); only this Gospel supplies any details about him, such as how he persuaded NATHANAEL to come to Jesus (see John 1. 43–51; see also 6.5–7; 12.21; 14.8). According to tradition he worked in Phrygia in Asia Minor. He is said to have settled in HIERAPOLIS, where the cult of the goddess Cybele originated, and where MONTANISM (the Christian sect of ecstatic prophecy) took root. Luke took trouble to distinguish the apostle from the evangelist (see Acts 21.9). It is the evangelist, in Caesarea, who has four unmarried daughters with prophetic gifts. But Church tradition, including the historian Eusebius in *Ecclesiastical History* 3.31, increased the confusion, by crediting the other Philip with four prophetic daughters in HIERAPOLIS.

Philippians, letter of Paul to Philippi was a Roman colony in Macedonia, which Paul had visited on his second missionary journey (according to Acts 16). Paul writes to the Church he had founded then (c.49/50 CE – his first converts in Europe), and with which he seems to have had a special relationship (Philippians 4.10–20). Here he accepted hospitality and financial support, while elsewhere he earned his keep (see 1 Corinthians 9.18). Paul writes from prison (1.7, 13); the traditional view is that he was in ROME towards the end of his life. But there are practical difficulties with this view, because of the distance between Rome and Philippi, and the number of communications back and forth which the letter suggests. It would be better to think of Paul imprisoned in EPHESUS (only a week away by sea), and so writing c.55 CE. References to the 'imperial guard' (1.13) and 'Caesar's household' (4.22) make as good sense for Ephesus, as Rome's local administrative centre, as they would for Rome itself.

Through the centuries most of the interest of interpreters has centred on the hymn to be found at 2.5–11. These verses are widely seen as an existing hymn (probably known to his readers) which Paul has used to support his plea for humility. He seems to have made changes to the hymn itself, transforming a view of Christ as a divine hero (a kind of Prometheus figure who climbed to heaven to capture fire) into a higher understanding of Christ as pre-existent in heaven, from where he 'emptied himself' to take on an earthly incarnation. This represents an early but high Christology, comparable with that of JOHN'S GOSPEL (*see also* ASCENSION).

A keynote of the letter is 'joy' : the word occurs 16 times. It is possible that there is more below the surface of this simple impression and that Paul is using this sense of harmony to bring additional moral pressure upon the Philippians, just as his use of the technical language of economics might reflect a serious financial concern. But the really jarring note comes in chapter 3 – so abrupt a change to a harsh tone of invective in 3.2–4.3 that some scholars argue this is a separate letter. But as with other Churches founded by Paul (*see* GALATIANS), subsequently a clear threat may have arisen from other missionaries, perhaps JEWISH-CHRISTIANS (as 3.2 is a scathing reference to physical circumcision), whom Paul denounces here as 'dogs', 'workers of evil', and 'enemies of the cross of Christ'. This is a warning of urgent danger which Paul must couple with his general exhortations.

Philistines During the reign of Rameses III (1198–1166 BCE) Egypt was attacked by a league of invaders known as the 'Sea Peoples'. They came from the Aegean or southern Anatolia, and the Philistines were among them (called 'Peleset' on the Medinet Habu reliefs). Following these invasions the Egyptian Empire fell apart; by c.1150 BCE Egypt no longer controlled CANAAN and the Philistines moved to settle its southern coastal plain, while the Israelites were living in the more barren interior to the east. As the Philistines became more threatening, this is the context of the stories about SAMSON and GOLIATH. The semi-independent communities of Israelites drew together to become a single national force, and then established a kingdom ruled first by SAUL and then by DAVID. This is the historical context for the sustained contest over territory between Israelites and Philistines. Anachronistically they are written back into an earlier context in GENESIS (see chapter 26), where the PATRI-ARCHS are in rivalry for land with the neighbouring tribes. At the other end of the time-scale, in the future projections of the book of ZECHARIAH (see chapter 9), those who survive in the Philistine cities will be treated as 'a remnant for God ... like a clan in Judah' (9.7); this may be preferable to extermination. In fact the Philistines disappeared at the time of the BABYLONIAN conquest and were not heard of again.

The Philistines had developed five cities in the coastal plain (ASHDOD, ASHKELON, and GATH; also Ekron and Gaza). An early Philistine inscription has been found recently at Gath, which may shed light on the origins of the Philistine language; although written in Semitic letters it may be related to ancient GREEK.

Philo of Alexandria Philo was born c.15–20 BCE into a prominent Jewish family in ALEXANDRIA, Egypt, where he received a broad Greek education. He was a man of two worlds: a philosopher and ethicist, while remaining a deeply committed Jew. 'He lived all his life in the double context of the Jewish community and the Alexandrian Greek community. Philosophy was Philo's life interest' (Peder Borgen). His particular method of interpreting the Bible depended on ALLEGORY. For him scripture was the source of all ideas of value and of the moral good.

In 39/40 CE Philo led a Jewish delegation to Emperor Gaius (Caligula) in Rome, to ask for exemption from the duty of worshipping the emperor. This proved unsuccessful, leading to a deterioration in relations with Rome, and prompted Caligula's idea of installing a statue of himself in the Jerusalem TEMPLE.

Phinehas 1 The first mentioned, and probably most significant, of Old Testament characters named Phinehas was the grandson of AARON (see Exodus 6.25), and an ancestor of Gershom who accompanied EZRA (see Ezra 8.2). During Israel's wilderness wanderings he earned a reputation for zeal (*see* ZEALOT); observing an Israelite man, Zimri, having intercourse with Cozbi, a Midianite woman, he killed them both with a single thrust of a spear (see Numbers 25). This episode can be seen as a decisive move against mixed MARRIAGE, or as a protest against ADULTERY in the context of sacral prostitution, part of the rites of the Canaanite deity BA'AL. Either way it prevented a plague on Israel, symbolizing God's wrath, and earned for Phinehas and his descendants an eternal priesthood (see also Psalm 106.30–31).

2 *See* ELI.

Phoenicia, Phoenicians These are the classical names for the coastal land of Lebanon and northern Palestine and its inhabitants (see Mark 7.26). At its greatest, the region extended from DOR in the south to UGARIT in the north. In Old Testament times the Hebrews included this territory within the land of Canaan. In the New Testament the name Phoenicia occurs in the ACTS OF THE APOSTLES in connection with the aftermath of STEPHEN's death (Acts 11) and with the journeys of PAUL (Acts 15 and 21). The area was often referred to by the names of its principal cities, TYRE AND SIDON. The Phoenicians remained in the area until Roman and early Christian times.

The Phoenicians were a navigating and trading people who may have penetrated the western Mediterranean as early as the 11th century BCE from their bases at Tyre and Sidon. The Canaanites of this area had become known as Phoenicians (or 'the purple-dye people', because they were principal producers and traders in the PURPLE dye made from murex shells). Certainly by the 8th century the Phoenicians had established trading settlements as far afield as Sicily, Sardinia, Iberia, and North Africa. The tree of life (*see* ASHERAH) was a popular motif in Phoenician art and architecture.

Phrygia *See* MONTANISM; MYSTERY RELIGIONS.

phylacteries Phylacteries (in Hebrew *tephillin*) are small black leather boxes containing texts from the PENTATEUCH written on parchment. A pair of these boxes is worn by male Jews for morning prayer, fastened to the body by black leather straps, one to the forehead, the other to the upper left arm. This practice is specified in Exodus 13.9, 16; Deuteronomy 6.8; 11.18. These references point to the passages of text which are placed in the phylacteries.

Pilate, Pontius Pilate is named in the creeds of Christianity and features in the New Testament accounts of the TRIAL OF JESUS (Mark 15.1–15; Matthew 27.19, 24–26; Luke 23.1–5, 11–25; John 18.28–19.16). Dante may refer to Pilate among the 'neutrals' in the third canto of *Inferno*, as one who made the *gran rifiuto* (the great refusal) – the most terrible act of neutrality in Christian history – by neither authorizing nor stopping the CRUCIFIXION of Christ. But the New Testament is quite definite that he did authorize it, although Matthew allows for doubt and vacillation, or yielding to the pressure of the crowd. A more detailed account of his dealings as Roman procurator of Judaea is recorded by the Jewish historian JOSEPHUS (see *Jewish War* 2.9.169–177). Little is known about him before 26 CE (appointed governor), or after 36 CE (recalled to Rome in disgrace).

Emperor Tiberius sent him to rule a notoriously difficult province; the accounts imply that he set out to offend the Jews, e.g. by putting Roman religious emblems on coins he minted, and setting up images of Caesar in the Jerusalem Temple, but these accounts may well be politically biased. His coinage, including a sacred staff and the ladle for drink-offerings, may have sought to integrate Roman and Jewish culture, rather than upset the Jews. A dedicatory inscription to Tiberius was discovered in the Roman theatre at CAESAREA (MARITIMA) in 1961; it had been re-used upside down in a 4th-century CE renovation of the theatre; here Pilate is described as praefectus (prefect), not procurator. (The title seems to have been changed when direct Roman rule was restored after the death of Agrippa in 44 CE.) In 36 CE Tiberius recalled him, but the emperor died before Pilate reached Rome. According to Eusebius, Caligula forced Pilate to commit suicide; alternatively he died in banishment at Vienne in Gaul. The *Acts* and the *Letter of Pontius Pilate* are apocryphal. The Greek Orthodox Church canonized him as a Christian convert (feast day 25 June).

pilgrimage Pilgrimage is a feature of the Biblical religions of Judaism and Christianity, just as it is of other major world faiths. Among the earliest were ancient Egyptian pilgrims who travelled regularly to the tomb of Osiris, honoured as Ruler of the Dead. A typical definition of pilgrimage is that of a journey to a place of religious importance, for the fulfilment of a religious purpose involving prayer and worship. MOSES conveyed God's command that all men of Israel should come together three times a year, to sacrifice and to declare their identity. In the Judaeo-Christian traditions JERUSALEM has been a special focus for pilgrimage for almost three millennia, ever since King DAVID brought the ARK OF THE COVENANT there. The Israelites would make pilgrimage to the central sanctuary for rites of cleansing and the fulfilment of vows. A good example is the story of HANNAH in 1 Samuel 1–2. According to the PENTATEUCH it is a religious duty for a male Israelite to visit Jerusalem three times a year, for the festivals of PASSOVER (Pesach), Weeks (Shavuot or in Greek PENTECOST), and TABERNACLES (Succoth – Deuteronomy 16.16).

Subsequently even observant Jews, in the Second TEMPLE period, would have been content with an annual visit. When the majority of Jews actually lived outside the country, in the DIASPORA, even an annual visit might be impractical, and the original laws would not apply outside Israel. Within the book of PSALMS there is a collection of 15 psalms (120–134) all entitled 'A Song of Ascents'. It is widely thought that these are pilgrimage songs for the journey to Jerusalem and the ascent of Mount ZION.

Jesus of Nazareth was himself an observant Jew, and observed the pilgrimage festivals. According to JOHN'S GOSPEL, the length of his earthly ministry can be measured over three years by the references to the journeys to Jerusalem at Passover (see John 2.13ff.; 6.4; 12.12ff.). After the RESURRECTION, pilgrimage gradually became a central part of Christian experience, not least because of the powerful attraction of walking where Jesus had walked.

Christian pilgrimage, to the sites of Jerusalem and elsewhere in the Holy Land, became a major activity as a result of Emperor Constantine and his mother Helena. Constantine founded basilicas in the 4th century (*see* CHURCHES, CHRISTIAN). Actual journeys, often perilous, in the early centuries and the Middle Ages, may now be translated into tourist visits to the Holy Land. There has also been, through the Christian centuries, a pervasive idea of spiritual pilgrimage: the Christian faith is seen as a journey, from earth to heaven, from curse to blessing, from judgement to

SALVATION, from the earthly city to the city of God. A key text for this is in Hebrews 12.22: 'You have come to Mount Zion and to the city of the living God, the heavenly Jerusalem.' In the Middle Ages the west–east axis of churches was exploited to provide a pilgrimage route from world (west) to heaven (east).

plagues of Egypt According to the narrative of EXODUS, the following are the 10 plagues inflicted upon Egypt through the agency of MOSES:

1. Nile waters turned to blood (7.14–25)
2. Swarms of frogs (8.1–15)
3. Lice, gnats, or mosquitoes (8.16–19)
4. Swarms of flies (8.20–32)
5. Plague on the Egyptians' cattle (?anthrax) (9.1–7)
6. Skin plague of festering boils (9.8–12)
7. Heavy hail with thunder, lightning and rain (9.13–35)
8. Locust plague (10.1–20)
9. Darkness from *khamsin* dust-storm (10.21–29)
10. Death of the firstborn (11.1–10; 12.12–14, 21–36)

There is a poetic version of the narrative to be found in Psalm 105.26–36. These Egyptian plagues also feature in the Seder (order) for the feast of PASSOVER; there is here a ritual involving the flicking of wine, which shows that the cup of joy is not full. Other sequences of plagues, echoing this Egyptian pattern, can be found in the book of REVELATION (the trumpet and bowl sequences from 8.6 and 16.1 respectively).

plants

FLOWERS Exact identification can sometimes be difficult for all flowers. It is usually asserted that the 'lilies of the field' (Matthew 6.28) were the wild anemones or poppies around the shores of GALILEE, whereas the 'lilies' of the Song of Solomon could be hyacinths or Madonna lilies (for example Song of Songs 2.1; 4.5). When English translations of the Bible offer 'rose' this could be the oleander or the 'rose of Jericho' (e.g. Ecclesiasticus 24.14; 39.13), but historically it could never be the rose familiar to English gardeners. For other references tulips, narcissi and crocuses have all been suggested as a more accurate rendering than rose.

Even if exact identification is enigmatic, the flowers of the day were valued. This is shown by the substitution of the sweet-scented myrtle with its pink and white blossoms for the desert thorns and briars in Isaiah 41.19 and 55.13.

RESINOUS PLANTS Resinous plants were highly prized in the ancient world and Israel's use was of imported products and not of home-grown species. The aromatic myrrh was produced from shrubs – either secreted naturally or extracted artificially. It may have been one of the expensive ingredients of priestly anointing oil in Exodus 30.23 (*see* UNCTION), as well as of a luxury perfume sachet in Song of Songs 1.13. It was also an ingredient in the embalming process (see John 19.39). The background ideas provided are of sacerdotalism, richness, or accompaniment to death; any of these may have contributed to the understanding of the significance of the MAGI's gift to the baby Jesus in Matthew 2.11. The association of myrrh with death is also picked up in Mark 15.23 where Jesus refused a drink infused with myrrh prior to the crucifixion, which would have alleviated his pain. Later herbalists used myrrh as a potent antiseptic and for oral hygiene.

Another expensive import was frankincense (*boswellia carteri*), referred to in Isaiah 60.6; this was used by the priests in oil for anointing and as incense (Exodus 30.34). For the incense the spices were mixed with another imported resin, galbanum, which was made from the juice yielded by the stem of a member of the carrot family (Exodus 30.34). Later herbalists used frankincense as an antiseptic and a decongestant, as well as for incense.

WEEDS Canterbury Cathedral has a stained-glass window depicting a miserable Adam delving with his spade. The predicament of man after the FALL is to toil for his food, knowing that 'cursed is the ground because of you' … 'thorns and thistles it shall bring forth for you' (Genesis 3.17–18). Gardeners and farmers of today can identify with this picture. Neglect and desolation in the Bible are depicted by the ready growth of thorns, nettles and thistles, e.g. Isaiah 34.13; Hosea 9.6. It is possible that both the milk and Syrian thistles stifling the young corn at the edges of the field were the 'thorns' of the parable of the SOWER (Matthew 13.7). The weeds that grew among the wheat in the parable of Matthew 13.24–30 have been identified as darnel or tares. Darnel establishes a network of underground roots very rapidly, and in its early stages the leaves resemble those of wheat. When the ears appear it is all too obvious – and too late; it can no longer be removed without uprooting the precious wheat too. Darnel grass must, however, be separated at the harvest or the resulting mixed flour would be dangerous to eat. This sorting out at the end clearly provides the clue to indicate the LAST JUDGEMENT.

Platonism Strictly, Platonism refers to the teaching of the idealist Greek philosopher Plato (427–347 BCE). He believed in two worlds: that the one in which we live is an illusory shadow of the true and real world constituted by ideas. This principle is explained most vividly in the celebrated image of the cave in book 7 of Plato's dialogue *The Republic*. Later developments of Plato's thought, in the period of the New Testament and subsequently, are often referred to generally as Middle- and Neo-Platonism.

politics and political language The Old Testament prophets (*see* PROPHECY) proclaimed JUSTICE and RIGHTEOUSNESS in contrast to a religion of careful cultic observance – which left other matters to the will of the individual and permitted cruelty and injustice. Human beings understood how to bend the LAW, which should be obeyed and served, to their own service instead. Jesus did not set out to create a better law, but showed how the will of God makes claims upon humanity, beyond the requirement of the law.

Rudolf Bultmann wrote:

Jesus' attitude toward property cannot be explained from social ideals or from any socialistic and proletarian instincts and motives. It is true that the poor [*see* POVERTY] and hungry are blessed, because the KINGDOM OF GOD will end their need, but the Kingdom is no ideal social order. Subversive ideas and revolutionary utterances are lacking in Jesus' preaching. There were splendid buildings erected under HEROD and his successors in Jerusalem and other Jewish cities – palaces, theatres, hippodromes – but no mention of them occurs in the Gospel record; from the Gospels we learn nothing at all about the economic situation in Palestine, except that there were peasants and fishermen, hand workers and merchants, rich and poor – and all this only incidentally, mostly from the PARABLES. Then we see clearly that all these things played no role in the thought of Jesus and his community, that they did not look with envious and longing eyes toward worldly splendour. Jesus' imagination did not concern itself with pictures of the overthrow of wealth or with hopes of achieving still greater splendour.

Some interpreters have argued that the historical Jesus was more involved in the nationalist politics of his day than such a picture of the apolitical Jesus would suggest. Does the fact that the *titulus*, the charge affixed to the cross, refers to 'the KING OF THE JEWS' argue for a greater political activity that the Romans would have seen as seditious? (But *see* TRIAL OF JESUS.) Jesus' preferred response might well have been as indicated in JOHN'S GOSPEL 18.36: 'My kingdom is not from this world.'

Elsewhere in the New Testament political metaphors are encountered in the language of statehood. See, for example, 1 Peter 2.9–10: 'chosen race, royal priesthood, holy nation, God's own people'; Ephesians 2.19: 'no longer strangers and aliens, but you are citizens with the saints and also members of the household of God'; Philippians 1.27: the technical Greek expression used can be translated literally as 'life-style as a citizen'; 1 Corinthians 6.1–6: 'the saints will judge the world'; compare *Letter to Diognetus* 5: 'constitution of their own citizenship'.

polytheism The majority of people in the Roman world of the New Testament period were polytheistic, that is they believed in the existence of many gods and goddesses. Images of the deities as objects of worship could be found everywhere, even in Palestine. This multiple belief, either casually or seriously undertaken, was what distinguished the religions of the Greco-Roman world from both JUDAISM and CHRISTIANITY. The Jewish historian JOSEPHUS is typical in representing the attitude of religious Jews towards polytheism: Greeks present the gods as being 'as many as they want, even born from one another and in all kinds of ways, and they assign them to different places and various ways of living, just like the species of animals, some under the earth and some in the sea' (*Contra Apionem* 2.33). PAGANISM, he claimed, attributes illicit sexual relationships and erotic unions to both sexes of the deities. Even Zeus, the chief of the gods, seduced women, made them pregnant, and then abandoned them. As a general attitude polytheism was more prevalent than the MYSTERY RELIGIONS and could lead to an indifference to morality.

Porcius Festus (Roman procurator) *See* PAUL; PROCURATORS, ROMAN.

porphyry *See* PURPLE.

Potiphar Potiphar was an Egyptian officer in Pharaoh's service, who acted as a key person in the unfolding saga of Jacob's son JOSEPH. He purchased Joseph as a slave from Midianite/Ishmaelite traders (Genesis 37.36 or 39.1), and eventually promoted him to be steward of his household, where he excelled. Potiphar was nevertheless swift to punish him with imprisonment, because his wife accused Joseph of attempted rape when her seductive moves were rebuffed (Genesis 39.7–20). Joseph in prison was then available to assist in the interpretation of Pharaoh's dreams and aid his own rise to power. The incident with Potiphar's wife is alluded to in JUBILEES 39 and in the *Testament of Joseph* (*see* TESTAMENTS OF THE TWELVE PATRIARCHS); in these extra-canonical texts it becomes the basis of an extensive exhortation to chastity.

poverty Despite the expectation of 'milk and honey' associated with the Promised Land, the Hebrew Bible recognized that there would be endemic poverty in Israelite society. It also classified the groups most at risk (see Deuteronomy 14.29). These were LEVITES, foreigners, orphans and widows; their condition was to be alleviated by the giving of TITHES. It is clear that the TORAH's call for economic justice was being widely ignored by the 8th century BCE, and the prophets were strongly reminding the rich of their obligations. By this stage debt was also endemic, and had led to SLAVERY, as well as the kind of injustice seen in not returning a man's warm cloak for his nightly protection after he had been driven to pawn it (see Exodus 22.26–27; Amos 2.6–8). Later war and the dislocations of EXILE must have added to the poverty of the people.

By the time of Jesus there were many poor among the 'people of the land' in Judaea and Galilee, but inevitably there were also some who had taken advantage of the Roman occupation in order to feather their own nests (see Luke 19.1–9). Jesus was clearly on the side of the poor people (an attitude comparable to the 'bias to the poor' of modern Liberation Theology). Jesus commended the simplicity of the poor (Luke 6.20; Matthew 5.3 has a more spiritual interpretation in the reading of 'poor in spirit'). See also the adapted quotation from Isaiah 61.1 in Jesus' synagogue sermon in Luke 4.18. Jesus highlighted the example of the poor woman who, in contributing the two smallest coins available (*see* COINAGE) to the Temple treasury, had given more than the rich visitors donating from their loose change (Mark 12.41–44).

For the teaching by Jesus, and the other New Testament teaching, on the obligations of the rich to the poor, *see* WEALTH. In economic terms Christians would be an underclass in the Roman Empire, whether their backgrounds were as slave or free man, for some centuries to come.

prayer Prayer has been described as 'communion with God, whether in silence, song or shouting, whether alone or in a group' (Anthony Gittins). Books of prayers and examples of people at prayer can be inspirational instruments to that end, although needed by some more than others, who pray on their own initiative. The Bible became a tremendous source of inspiration in prayer to later generations. So the Jewish people have used their Bible as a source of prayer for three millennia.

Prayer, as the mode of human communication with God and the building of a relationship (through talking and listening) with him, is frequently mentioned in the Bible. Prayer was seen as accessing God in heaven (see 1 Kings 8.43; Lamentations 3.41; Matthew 6.9). Main characters in the Bible, from Moses to Jesus, are found in the act of prayer (see Exodus 5.22; Luke 6.12; Hebrews 5.7). Prayer took various forms according to circumstances, whether praising (Isaiah 38.10–20), or laying out troubles before God (1 Samuel 1.9–13), confessing wrongdoing (Psalm 51.1–5), or giving thanks (Luke 22.19). Asking for a blessing (1 Kings 8.14), or for something more tangible (1 Kings 8.25) was also common. Prayer was clearly an essential part of the life of faith, although the idea of prayer as a set routine (three times a day) was not a command from the Hebrew Bible but had become formalized in JUDAISM very late in the post-Exilic period by the Great Synagogue. The FAITH accompanying the act of asking came to be seen as helping to bring about the desired object of prayer (see Mark 11.24; James 1.6: 'But ask in faith, never doubting, for the one who doubts is like a wave of the sea, driven and tossed by the wind'). Prayer had always been seen as needing to be done earnestly (Jonah 3.8; Colossians 4.2) to be effective. Prayer could be individual and private (Mark 6.46–47), or open and public (Nehemiah 9.6–37 – where the whole congregation confesses their sins). Jesus practised both kinds of prayer, but was concerned that the real relationship with God occurred behind closed doors (Matthew 6.5–6). The Bible presents examples of representative individuals engaged in a formal kind of prayer, such as SOLOMON dedicating the Jerusalem TEMPLE in 1 Kings 8, or Jesus at prayer at the Last Supper (*see* EUCHARIST) in John 17.

New Testament writers came to realize that God himself as the SPIRIT would aid prayer (see Romans 8.26; Jude 20: 'Build yourself up on your most holy faith; pray in the Holy Spirit'). The emphasis on prayer to the FATHER is a New Testament custom (see 1 Peter 1.17: 'If you invoke as Father the one who judges all people impartially according to their deeds ...'); this follows Jesus' own precedent, both in GETHSEMANE (Mark 14.36) and in his teaching (Matthew 6.9; *see* LORD'S PRAYER). Prayer is also commanded to be done in Jesus' name (John 14.13–14). Christians are required to make what seem to be paradoxical requests, for forgiveness to be given to others (Matthew 6.12); prayers should also be offered for enemies and persecutors (Matthew 5.44).

See also SPIRITUALITY.

priest In the earliest nomadic days the PATRIARCH acted for his family and household in relation to the deity. After the Settlement in CANAAN, like most of her settled neighbouring states, Israel quickly developed a worship based on cultic sanctuaries which were manned by professional personnel. Sanctuaries were established from DAN to BEER-SHEBA. The priests (designated by the Hebrew word *cohen*) were Levitical in descent (*see* LEVI), and had to follow strict codes of holiness to qualify for the role, for example they could only marry a virgin of Israel (latterly also a priest's widow) and they must not be contaminated by the corpses of other than the closest family members (*see also* LEVITES). The priests of Aaronic descent (*see* AARON) were the highest rank; they were themselves anointed for office, and alone held the right to anoint with sacred oil (Exodus 28.41; 29.7 – *see* UNCTION). From their number the HIGH PRIEST was chosen.

As the result of King JOSIAH's reforms the local countrywide shrines were closed down, the contamination by pagan deities was purged from the Jerusalem TEMPLE and the nation's worship was centralized there (2 Kings 23.8). The priests from the local sanctuaries were compelled to come to the capital's Temple to work there in subsidiary roles. After the EXILE the people returned and set to building a new, if inferior, Temple and the priesthood was reinstated. There were now too many priests for an impoverished nation to support financially, and so divisions of priests were set up. This meant that a rota of divisions could be imposed, and when the priest had served his allotted span at the Temple, he could return home and work to support his family until his next turn.

Some priests became wealthy and influential. From their aristocracy were some who became wide open to Greek cultural influences during the HELLENISTIC PERIOD. In a religious sense the aristocracy were conservative; politically they became very powerful, leading the SADDUCEES and the SANHEDRIN. Their leader was the High Priest. Their accommodations to the various external empires who ruled them, and their conservatism, seem to have led to alienation from the common people. By Jesus' day the spiritual leaders were more likely to seem to be the PHARISEES. The decisive destruction of the Jerusalem Temple by the Romans in 70 CE ended their real political and religious roles.

The main task of the priests was to serve God as attendants, particularly in 'feeding' the deity with various animal and other SACRIFICES; some of the meat thus obtained would be burnt whole, other parts depending on the occasion could be cooked and consumed by the priests and sometimes the worshippers. The priests naturally were responsible for the care of the sanctuary (see 2 Kings 12.6). They also taught the LAW (Deuteronomy 33.10), judged (Deuteronomy 17.9), and discerned infectious cases for public health (Leviticus 13).

In the New Testament priesthood belongs to CHRISTIANS generally (see 1 Peter 2.5). 'You are a chosen race, a royal priesthood' (1 Peter 2.9). APOSTLES and ELDERS function in CHURCH life, but the role of the Christian priest has not yet recognizably emerged (*see also* MINISTRY). Instead, the role of priest is assigned to CHRIST and not to Christian clergy. Christ replaced the sacrificial cult with his own death on the cross, acting as both victim and as High Priest in offering his sacrifice to God. He acts as mediator between God and man (Hebrews 5.1–6; 7.26–27).

Priscilla, or Prisca Priscilla is perhaps the best known of a number of prominent women in the early Christian Church. In the ACTS OF THE APOSTLES she is referred to by the name Priscilla, while PAUL in his letters calls her Prisca. Her husband was Aquila and the two are usually named together, although she is mentioned first (which would not be customary in Roman society, unless she was of higher status socially; but it might simply mean that she was more influential in the Christian movement). Aquila was a leather-worker by trade. The couple lived in ROME, but were forced to move to Corinth when the edict of the Emperor Claudius in 49 CE expelled Jews (and those that seemed to the Romans to be Jews) from the capital city. In Corinth they encountered Paul and subsequently moved with him to EPHESUS. See Acts 18.2–28; Romans 16.3; 1 CORINTHIANS 16.19; 2 Timothy 4.19.

procurators, Roman The procurator of the Roman emperor was originally a financial agent, recruited from the classes of knights (*equites*) or freedmen, essentially responsible for the imperial finances within the district or province. Procurator was also the title used of the governor of a minor Roman province, such as Thrace or Judaea. These belonged to the emperor, but contained no important garrison. Here the governor would not be restricted to financial matters, and also held the power of life and death; he would operate either directly or through an arrangement with a client-king (such as those of the HERODIAN DYNASTY).

Pontius PILATE is the best-known example of these procurators. However, in the inscription referring to him at CAESAREA (MARITIMA) Pilate is described as praefectus (prefect) and not as procurator. The title seems to have been changed when direct Roman rule was restored after the death of Agrippa in 44 CE.

The list of known procurators for Judaea is as follows:

Coponius	c.6–9 CE
Marcus Ambibulus	9–12 CE
Annius Rufus	12–15 CE
Valerius Gratus	15–26 CE
Pontius Pilatus	26–36 CE
Marcellus	36–37 CE
Cuspius Fadus	44–46 CE
Tiberius Alexander	46–48 CE
Ventidius Cumanus	48–52 CE
Antonius Felix	52–60 CE
Porcius Festus	60–62 CE
Albinus	62–64 CE
Gessius Florus	64–66 CE

Prodigal Son This is one of the best known of Jesus' PARABLES, but it is found only in the Gospel of LUKE, at 15.11–32. The Prodigal Son is several parables in one: as well as the story of the 'prodigal' younger son, who wastes his inheritance but finally comes to his senses, it is also the story of the elder brother's jealousy, and above all the story of the Father who goes on loving and forgiving and does not count the cost. The reader of this story is given a glimpse of the love of God, and exhorted to 'follow the Heart of the Father'.

progressive revelation Christian attitudes towards the Old Testament tended to be modified or radically changed in the 19th century, for a variety of reasons. Developments in critical methods of approach to the text, in historical and literary terms, and an attitude of rationalism following the Enlightenment, had a profound effect on the way the Old Testament was viewed. No longer was it seen as a 'once-for-all' presentation, with a firm foundation of LAW going back to MOSES, and the rest built upon this. Critical attitudes produced a realization of a composite form of text that was the consequence and record of centuries of development. Theological conclusions tended to be drawn from this historical picture of evolution in the text: here was a religion of the progressive revelation of God's nature, beginning from a primitive level, and ascending through the prophets to a moral monotheism. This was thought to prepare the way for the New Testament GOSPELS and the doctrine of the INCARNATION. However much historical truth there is in this view, it represents a value judgement formulated from the material. A view of progressive revelation might suggest that the earliest stages of the process could be redundant – some comfort for Christians who found the Old Testament difficult.

There are warnings to be raised about the view of progressive revelation. It may only be a partial truth. Not all would agree that ethical monotheism, as taught by the prophets, is the crown of Hebrew religion; some would say that it neglects, for example, the dynamic view of the divine conveyed by much of the Old Testament's historical narratives. The theory of progressive revelation represents a neat pattern of advance which may be misleading insofar as it is simply a transfer to the field of theology of those scientific ideas formulated by Charles Darwin in the quite distinct biological and zoological fields of the theory of EVOLUTION.

prophecy The word is from a Greek root which can mean to speak in advance, to forecast or predict, as well as to be a spokesman on behalf of someone. The origins of the Hebrew equivalent *nabhi'* are controversial: it may denote someone who has a message to proclaim, perhaps by ecstatic means, and therefore a messenger of God's word. In the Old Testament context the functional relation of MOSES to AARON is described as that of God to his prophet (Exodus 7.1), and the prophet JEREMIAH (1.9) is the mouthpiece of God.

The Hebrew Bible knows at least four kinds of prophet: the seer (such as SAMUEL, who reveals hidden knowledge); the ecstatic prophet, with characteristics as described in 1 Samuel 10.5–6, of whom ELIJAH is a climactic and individual example; the cultic prophet, or member of a prophetic guild (such as the company around ELISHA in 2 Kings 4.38–41, and the later Levitical groups associated with the sanctuary as in 2 Chronicles 20); and the major and minor writing prophets, the tradition of whose teaching is collected in the Biblical books which bear their names. The term 'prophet' is also applied to earlier figures such as ABRAHAM and MOSES, but this is the judgement of a later generation who saw them as interpreters of God's actions in historical events, on analogy with the canonical prophets. The Jewish tradition regards prophecy as coming to an end after the EXILE, with figures such as HAGGAI and ZECHARIAH, although for some the apocalyptists continued the tradition of interpreting historical events. The Christian tradition adopts the APOCALYPTIC perspective as its own, and sees a rebirth of prophecy in the New Testament period and beyond.

The phenomenon of prophecy, in its varied manifestations, achieves acceptability, usually with the benefit of hindsight, when its predictions and interpretations are seen as true. The Bible is acutely aware of the tensions between true and false prophecy, as can be seen in the story of MICAIAH ben Imlah in 1 Kings 22, and in the analysis of Jeremiah 23. It used to be claimed that there was a rigid divide between prophecy and the cult in Israel's religion, and this was even linked with the Reformation divide in Christianity between Protestantism and Catholicism. The evidence of the Hebrew Bible scarcely supports this: denunciations of the sacrificial system in Micah 6 and Amos 5 are balanced by what is known of the cultic prophets, and the association of prophets and the sanctuary in Isaiah and Ezekiel, for example. Prophecy is a critical instrument applied in order to reform religious activities of all kinds. In a classic work on prayer, the Protestant theologian Friedrich Heiler distinguished between prophetic prayer (that is a dynamic and Biblical view oriented on time and history, which sees SALVATION at work in history) and contemplative prayer (thought to be more static and concerned with the presence of God here and now).

Prophetic materials are found in a variety of literary and non-literary forms, from the signs of oral tradition in slogans and oracular utterances to the polished textual form of Second Isaiah. There are important connections between prophecy and later apocalyptic (e.g. Isaiah 27 and the latter chapters of Zechariah) which suggest that some continuity should be recognized. It is also vital to see the prophetic import-ance of symbolic activities (*see* SIGNS) and direct political action (shown in its most extreme form in EZEKIEL). Prophetic word and action lay claim to the efficacy of divine power.

The New Testament provides some clues as to the continuation of prophetic activity among the earliest Christians. How it functioned, or ought to function, within Christian congregations is described graphically in 1 Corinthians 12 and 14. Twelve prophets and prophetesses are named specifically in the ACTS OF THE APOSTLES; the word *prophetes* is used 19 times in the New Testament of early Christian figures, and a further 21 times in the writings of the Apostolic Fathers. The Eleventh Mandate of the work known as the *Shepherd of Hermas*, dated around 130 CE, presents a picture of early 2nd-century prophecy. Shortly after this a major prophetic move-ment within Christianity, called MONTANISM, began in the 2nd century CE in Asia Minor and spread widely.

proselyte This is a religious term to describe a convert to JUDAISM. It was a Greek word used in the SEPTUAGINT to translate the Hebrew *ger* – a word which in the Hebrew Bible referred to a 'resident alien' or 'sojourner'. The Greek word, essentially 'newcomer' or 'incomer', developed alongside the later Hebrew to have a religious rather than an ethnic or social meaning. The word is used four times in the New Testament in the sense of 'convert' at Matthew 23.15 (*see* MISSION); and Acts 2.10; 6.5; 13.43. It is likely that there were two classes of convert in Judaism, the full proselyte who accepted the full laws and rituals, and the half-proselyte (possibly known as 'god-fearer' in the more technical sense) who undertook only some basic principles. From at least the 1st century CE a full convert was required to take a ritual bath (or 'proselyte BAPTISM') and CIRCUMCISION (for men). It is possible that the baptizing activity of JOHN THE BAPTIST bears some relation to this proselyte baptism.

Proverbs, book of One way of looking at Proverbs is as 'the wisdom of many'; everyday proverbial wisdom crystallizes past experience to benefit the present. But there are also indications of WISDOM in Israel as a significant theological concept, so that books of wisdom, such as Proverbs, could represent the height of philosophical theology. Ultimately both are true: Proverbs rests on popular culture, but the author/editor has taken popular sayings of his time, given them the status of a universal ethic, and developed his philosophy by an interaction with and assess-ment of that culture.

The contents of Proverbs have a long history; it is certainly not the composition of a single author, but a compilation of snatches of Wisdom from Israel and beyond. The traditional ascription to SOLOMON is associated with his fabled wisdom (1 Kings

3–4). One section of Proverbs (22.17–24.22) is known to be Egyptian in origin, derived from the *Instruction of Amenemope*. The latest section of the book is the introductory nine chapters which see Wisdom as the fundamental order of God running throughout the entire CREATION; by observing the ways of the world one can discover that order and the deepest possible knowledge in the 'fear of the Lord'. Wisdom is equated with life, and death (the underworld of SHEOL) with foolishness (see 9.18). The final editing of the book is post-Exilic, in the 6th century BCE or later.

The recent re-awakening of interest in the Wisdom tradition is due, in part, to the striking personification of Wisdom as a female figure in chapters 1–9 and 31 (the poem on the Woman of Worth in 31.10–31 is a sophisticated acrostic, in which each new line begins with the next letter of the HEBREW alphabet). Notice especially the role in creation in Proverbs 8. The source of these ideas is disputed: it may derive from observing the role of the Israelite woman in running the home, or it may be a survival of the concept of goddess, officially resisted as an object of worship in Israel; the simplest explanation may be that Wisdom in Hebrew is a feminine noun. Such thoughts have contributed greatly to developments in modern Feminist Theology.

Proverbs 9.1 provided T. E. Lawrence (Lawrence of Arabia) with the title *Seven Pillars of Wisdom* for a book he wrote in 1913 about adventures in seven cities of the Middle East; he subsequently re-used the title for his famous book on the Arab Revolt.

Psalms, book of The compilation of the Psalter in its present form was one of the creative achievements of the post-Exilic period of JUDAISM. Studies of the collection have revealed not only the pattern of its liturgical use in the Second TEMPLE but also indications of the earlier origins of individual psalms in cultic worship. The evidence is found in ideas expressed in the Psalms and also in the titles which contain instructions to choirmasters, and the external 'glosses' which may well be stage directions. The Hebrew title of the whole collection is *Tehillim*, meaning 'cultic songs of praise'.

The Psalms are arranged in five books, perhaps in deliberate parallel to the books of the Law (TORAH). But there is evidence of earlier groupings, based on function and use, or by association with named musicians, not necessarily indicating authorship. So there are Psalms of Korah and Asaph, as well as a large number traditionally associated with DAVID. The Davidic collection appears to end with book two (72.20), but other 'Davidic' Psalms occur later as well. There are PILGRIMAGE Psalms ('Songs of Ascent') for the occasion of 'going up' to Jerusalem at festival time; Royal Psalms associated with the theology of kingship in Israel; and the Hallel Psalms of praise, linked to occasions such as PASSOVER (and probably used by Jesus and his disciples – see Mark 14.26).

Different literary types are to be identified within the Psalm collection. There are hymns of praise and thanksgiving, prayers for divine assistance, and lamentations which may embody threats and curses. Some of the Psalms are clearly appropriate for individual expression of religious ideas, and others are collective statements of the worshipping community. Above all the Psalms are concerned with the mysterious power of evil and the act of seeking deliverance from this. To understand the Psalms it is also desirable to have some idea of the nature of Hebrew poetry, found in these texts but also extensively elsewhere in the Hebrew Bible. The underlying principle is of a parallelism of ideas, an echoing or a development of thought between the two or three parts of a numbered verse. The rhythm set up by the grouping of words in Hebrew readily expresses a rising mood of celebration or a falling tone of grief. Such ideas are lost in translation into languages where other ideas of poetry prevail.

pseudepigrapha *See* JEWISH LITERATURE.

psychology *See* HUMAN NATURE.

Ptolemais *See* ACCO.

publicans Publicans are not to be confused with innkeepers, for the Latin word *publicani*, echoed in the KING JAMES VERSION, actually refers to businessmen who are contracted to collect taxes in a particular region, as well as possibly trading in war captives and plunder, or supplying the Roman army or administration with food and equipment. The Roman treasury was to be paid a set sum for the right to collect these taxes, so naturally the *publicani* collected a sum that was substantially higher than this from the provincials, in order to make their profit. This could readily provoke grievance among those who had to pay. The taxes included customs duties on produce (such as fish from GALILEE) when exported to another part of the country.

ZACCHAEUS (1) was a chief tax-collector in JERICHO (Luke 19.2). The Gospel narratives bracket together 'tax-collectors and sinners' (see Matthew 9.11; 11.19; Luke 15.1), which reflects not only social prejudice but also the view of the Jewish leaders that such operators are ritually unclean, either because they are GENTILES, or more likely have direct contact with Gentiles. Jesus reverses this attitude, by paying attention to such people, and by calling one of them, MATTHEW, to be a DISCIPLE. In Matthew 21.31 Jesus tells the Jewish leaders that 'the tax-collectors and the prostitutes are going into the KINGDOM OF GOD ahead of you'.

punishment The LAW codifications (TORAH) of the Hebrew Bible set out a penal code for certain specific offences (see, for example, the casuistic law concerning a quarrel which results in injury but not death – Exodus 21.18–19). Some clearly relate to criminal law, and others are concerned with matters of ritual cleanliness (see Leviticus 7.26–27 on the eating of blood); both religion and society are involved. Old Testament ideas of punishment are largely concerned either with retributive justice (see Exodus 21.23–24: 'life for life, eye for eye, tooth for tooth …') or with restorative justice (see Exodus 22.5, which envisages a man making good the loss of crops consumed by his own straying animals). Punishment as a deterrent is *not* a Biblical concept. Capital punishment was used for serious offences, such as murder, from earliest times, to judge from the terms of the covenant with NOAH (see Genesis 9.6: 'Whoever sheds the blood of a human, by a human shall that person's blood be shed'). The reason given for this rule is that a human being is made like God (*see* IMAGO DEI).

Naturally there is not a parallel set of regulations in the New Testament to order Christian society. Paul clearly felt that Roman justice was to be respected in civil society (ROMANS 13.1–7), although the book of REVELATION might suggest that this view was not held by all. Jesus does not give any direct advice on criminal justice, but Christians have drawn conclusions from the general tenor of his teaching. Jesus set aside the concept of retribution in personal relationships, so 'an eye for an eye' becomes 'turn the other cheek' (Matthew 5.38–40). Restoration as such is not discussed, but this Matthaean text continues with the advice to give one's coat as well to someone demanding one's shirt. Forgiveness is at the very heart of the Gospel (see Matthew 6.12; 18.21–35; Luke 23.34, 43; John 20.23; 21.15–19; Acts 7.60) and this has influenced the Christian debate on punishment.

The example of Jesus as a teacher who forgave his own executioners (Luke 23.34), and who came to save sinners (1 Timothy 1.15; 1 John 2.2), has led many modern Christians to take Jesus' view of justice as expressing a wider need for reformation and a fresh start, rather than for retribution. But other Christians, who have interpreted Jesus' teaching as being in terms of the individual rather than society, may then fall back on Old Testament teaching to justify their hardline stance on societal issues such as capital punishment ('a life for a life').

purgatory According to the traditions of Roman Catholic theology, purgatory is the sequel to death, when faithful souls experience a process of purification, prior to the state of blessedness. These ideas are not defined anywhere in the Bible, but might possibly be inferred from certain texts. The text most frequently quoted is from the APOCRYPHA (Deuterocanonical books) at 2 Maccabees 12.39–45, where JUDAS MACCA-BEUS 'made ATONEMENT for the dead, so that they might be delivered from their sin'. The image of testing by fire as at the LAST JUDGEMENT (see 1 Corinthians 3.12–15) is often used to colour up the picture of purgatory in later Christian APOCALYPTIC texts.

Purim The Jewish FESTIVAL of Purim is a celebration of the deliverance of the Jews. The book of ESTHER is set as the text for that day, to be read publicly in the synagogue from a special scroll.

purity At the end of the Second TEMPLE period, ritual purity came to play an increasing role in Jewish society. Purity laws were expanded and sources of impurity avoided by many. The main areas of concern were leprosy (and other skin disease), genital discharges, and contamination from contact with corpses. Jesus' attitude to these matters of impurity can be construed as indifference, and his behaviour clashed on occasion with current purity regulations (see the Gospel accounts of conflict with the PHARISEES). It could be said that Jesus is responding to regional problems in Galilee, but more significantly that he is challenging the paradigms of purity as part of an eschatological struggle against demonic evil.

purple The colour purple was particularly valued in Roman society, especially during the Empire. The purple dye (Hebrew *tekhelet*) was extracted from the shells of Murex (*M. brandaris* or *trunculus*), a marine mollusc; apparently some 12,000 shells were needed to produce $1\frac{1}{2}$ grams of the dye. Pliny advocated the use of a vegetable alternative, but this tended to wash out with use. Some beach tanks (pans) near DOR may well have been for the use of the purple dye industry. (This was in the area of the ancient PHOENICIANS who had produced and traded in purple centuries before.) In the Acts of the Apostles LYDIA is mentioned as a trader in purple.

Porphyry is a purple-coloured marble which was only found high up in the eastern deserts of Egypt, five days' journey from the Nile. The Roman emperors fell in love with porphyry and required it to be quarried in vast quantities. These quarries have recently been identified; on site were found potsherds (OSTRACA) on which were recorded details of everyday life in the eastern desert; they reveal that the quarries were worked not by slaves but by free men.

Q

Q (Quelle) source Scholars argue that there may be a source document behind the New Testament GOSPELS, which was largely devoted to the sayings of Jesus. This reconstructed, but theoretical, source is usually referred to as 'Q', the initial letter of the German word *Quelle*, meaning 'source'. The idea first arose as part of the critical investigation, known as the SYNOPTIC PROBLEM, of the relationship between the first three Gospels, and in particular of an apparent literary relationship between MATTHEW and LUKE. In the words of Richard Valantasis: 'Q is actually not a real document. It does not exist on its own. Rather, Q is a scholarly reconstruction of a supposed source used by Matthew and Luke to supplement their revisions of the Gospel of Mark.' The scholarly debates are far from being resolved about a reconstructed document known as Q, or the alternative possibility of a collection of sayings made in the oral tradition (*see* ORALITY).

But evidence bearing on this process of collecting Jesus' individual sayings seems to have become more substantial in recent years. There are two main reasons for this. One is the consolidation of academic reconstructions of the Synoptic Sayings Source (Q). Earlier reconstructions were highly subjective and impressionistic. Later versions, while still reconstructions and often reflecting individual preferences, have achieved a measure of academic collaboration and agreement, resulting in the critical edition produced by Robinson, Hoffmann and Kloppenborg (2000). Another reason is the recognition of possibly analogous collections of sayings in extant manuscripts which can demonstrate what a collection, alternative to the Synoptic Gospels, actually looked like. The *Gospel of Thomas* (*see at* THOMAS), significant in other ways as a GNOSTIC text, has grown in importance as representing such an organized collection of sayings. The early Christian work the DIDACHE, or Teaching of the Twelve Apostles, can also demonstrate the development of the process of a collection of sayings, in the further stages of interpretation and application to the needs of a religious group.

Qaisariyeh *See* CAESAREA (MARITIMA).

Qalat es-Salihiya *See* DURA EUROPOS.

Qoheleth *Qoheleth* in Hebrew means 'the Teacher' or 'the Preacher'. *See* ECCLESIASTES.

quails The grumbling Israelites in the wilderness after the EXODUS missed their meat (Numbers 11.4), and remembered sitting 'by the fleshpots' of Egypt (Exodus 16.3); their need was satisfied by the miraculous arrival of flocks of these small game birds (Exodus 16.13). The SINAI desert is the stopover point for exhausted birds to rest on their annual springtime migration from Africa to Europe. They are apparently so tired that it is possible to pick them up off the sand.

Quirinius *See* CENSUS.

Qumran Khirbet ('the ruins of') Qumran is a much-publicized archaeological site close to the western shore of the DEAD SEA. Although there was some earlier occupation in the area, most interest is now focused on the resettlement in the HELLENISTIC PERIOD, which survived until its destruction by the Romans in 68 CE. The archaeological excavation of the well-preserved site was conducted following the Second World War by Fr. Roland de Vaux, one of the best excavators of his time, although his death in 1971 left to others the task of completing his reports for publication. De Vaux was responsible for the influential theory that the establishment at Qumran was something like a monastery. The complex of buildings covers a terrace area about 90 metres east to west, and 110 metres north to south. There is an elaborate water system to supply the site, channelled into storage cisterns and ritual baths. The discoveries since 1947 in nearby caves of a large number of scrolls (*see* DEAD SEA SCROLLS) naturally led to a close association of site and scrolls (although no scrolls were actually found on the Qumran site itself), and the widespread theory that here was a community of ESSENES, or a similar ultra-orthodox group within JUDAISM, who were perhaps religious refugees from Jerusalem. This theory has been questioned from time to time, drawing attention to the differences between Essenes and the supposedly monastic group at Qumran. There is some external evidence that Essenes lived in this area; but the scrolls themselves refer to a Jewish group, perhaps called *Yahad* ('togetherness'). The cemetery eastwards between the site and the Dead Sea became a focus of interest, to see the nature of the burials, which differ from usual Jewish custom. It is also the case that there are female as well as male graves in the area adjacent to the main cemetery. Other interpretations of the site have seen it not as a religious centre, but as a reservoir of water for a plantation nearby at Ein Feshkha, or as a trading base, or a country estate (a manor house whose owner facilitated the storage of scrolls from Jerusalem in anticipation of the Roman siege), or a HASMONEAN fortress to control the area. But the original insights into Qumran's religious importance are still maintained by many scholars.

rabbi The title 'rabbi' means 'my teacher' or 'my master'. A variant Aramaic form, 'rabbouni', is found, addressed to Jesus, on two occasions in the New Testament (Mark 10.51 and John 20.16). The term came to be applied during the 1st century CE as a way of addressing authoritative teachers who were members of the SANHEDRIN. The DISCIPLES both of JOHN THE BAPTIST and of Jesus adopted the same convention for their respective teachers (see John 3.26 of John the Baptist; Matthew 26.25, 49, Mark 9.5, 11.21, 14.45 of Jesus). In JUDAISM from the 1st to the 5th centuries CE the title was used only in PALESTINE, while in BABYLONIA the corresponding title was *Rav*.

Rachel Rachel was an ARAMAEAN woman, the younger daughter of Laban, and the second – also the favourite – wife of JACOB. She was the mother of his younger sons, JOSEPH and BENJAMIN. After a long period of childlessness, during which her hand-maid bore Jacob's children (see the NUZI texts for this convention), Rachel gave birth to Joseph. Jacob and Rachel then sought to return to PALESTINE; Rachel's deviousness is shown by her theft (Genesis 31.34) of her father's household gods (*teraphim*), either to symbolize new independence from Laban, with the inheritance of his wealth (again see the Hurrian custom in the Nuzi tablets), or to secure religious protection for the long journey. According to Genesis 35, she died giving birth to Benjamin. She was buried on the journey between BETHEL and BETHLEHEM. The actual site is unknown, although Jacob is said to have marked it with a pillar; it may have been at Ramah, 5 miles north of Jerusalem, but there is also a strong traditional association with Bethlehem itself (RUTH 4.11; the idea then reinforced by the massacre of the innocents by King HEROD – Matthew 2.16–18 and the prophecy in Jeremiah 31.15). Rachel is sometimes identified as the Great Mother, with special reference to the sufferings of women in childbirth. Her name in Hebrew means 'ewe' or female sheep.

radiocarbon dating *See* CARBON-14 DATING.

Rahab 1 There was a widespread idea in the ancient Near East of a monster of chaos from primordial times, who had to be conquered so that CREATION and order could be imposed. In BABYLONIAN creation mythology the monster was called Tiamat. In the Bible the monster is variously LEVIATHAN or Rahab (meaning pride), and is connected with the sea. In Job the monster opposes the divine ruler at creation (Job 26.12), and in the imagery of the Psalms, for example Psalm 89.10, God smites the monster in his control of the Red Sea, aiding the EXODUS. The image of Rahab could also be used pejoratively of enemy nations, for example of Egypt in Psalm 87.4 and Isaiah 30.7.

2 Rahab was a prostitute who sheltered Joshua's spies when they reconnoitred JERICHO during the conquest of CANAAN. The spies were nearly caught, but she hid them under flax on the roof and misdirected their pursuers. Fortunately her house was by the city wall, and she enabled the spies to escape to safety, negotiating safe passage for herself and her household when the Israelite army subsequently took the city (see Joshua 2). When Jericho fell to the invaders she joined the Israelites, and received honourable mention both then and subsequently, when she was listed in Matthew's GENEALOGY of Jesus (Matthew 1.5) and also in the catalogue of those who acted by faith in Hebrews 11.31. James 2.25 also looked back to her as an example of one who was justified by her works.

rainbow The rainbow is seen as the sign of the COVENANT which God makes with NOAH and his family after the FLOOD (see Genesis 9.8–17). God promises that he will never repeat such destruction, and sets the rainbow in the clouds as a reminder.

Ramat Rachel Ramat Rachel is on the southern outskirts of Jerusalem, approximately halfway to BETHLEHEM. It is the site of a royal palace and citadel from the First TEMPLE period (8th–7th centuries BCE), where a number of seal impressions (*bullae*) have been found, dating to the reign of King HEZEKIAH. There is also evidence, including seals, from the Persian period, as well as a Jewish rock-cut tomb, a Roman villa and bath-house, and a Byzantine church. A Christian tradition of the 6th century CE claims that MARY and JOSEPH rested here at the well on the way to Bethlehem.

Raphael Raphael is one of the seven archangels of God (*see* TOBIT 12.15; ANGEL). His name means 'God heals'. In the story of Tobit, Raphael is disguised as a young man, Azarias (a name which means 'God helps'), who accompanies Tobit's son, Tobias, on a perilous expedition to recover the family fortune, arranges Tobias' marriage to a bride who is freed from the demon Asmodeus, and teaches Tobias how to cure his father's blindness. Raphael also appears in a number of the pseudepigrapha (*see* JEWISH LITERATURE), such as *1 Enoch* 40.9, where he is 'set over all disease and every wound'.

Ras Shamra *See* UGARIT.

Rebekah, or Rebecca Rebekah was the wife of ISAAC, and the daughter of ABRAHAM's nephew Bethuel. She was selected for marriage to Isaac by Abraham's chief steward, who returned to HARAN to find her. For the first 20 years of her marriage she was infertile, but then bore twin sons, JACOB and ESAU, with an oracle foretelling their different destinies (Genesis 25.20–26). Rebekah favoured Jacob and planned the deception for him to receive Isaac's blessing; she also helped him subsequently to escape from Esau. She and Isaac were buried at HEBRON (Genesis 49.31).

Rechabites The Rechabites were a pietistic religious sect, founded during the reign of JEHU (842–815 BCE), by Jonadab the son of Rechab, after whom they were named.

Jonadab assisted Jehu in destroying the altars to BA'AL erected by King AHAB (see 2 Kings 10.15–23). The Rechabites are described and commended in JEREMIAH 35. They lived in tents as nomads, did not practise agriculture and abstained from wine (this last requirement is akin to the vow of the NAZIRITES). 1 Chronicles 2.55 suggests a link with the KENITES. A certain Malchiah, 'son of Rechab', is named in Nehemiah 3.14 as one of those engaged in rebuilding Jerusalem after the EXILE.

redemption, redeemer The English use of the term 'redemption' currently means to release someone or something by making a payment. The Biblical understanding covers a broader range of actions (although the release of a debtor by another person paying the debt remains one of them); the meaning is often more theological, and this is particularly true of the person who acts as 'redeemer'.

In the Old Testament several Hebrew roots are used, but the most frequent is the verb *ga'al*, meaning to act on behalf of someone who is unable to act for themselves. This can be to discharge a family obligation (see for example Ruth 4.1–6). Another term, *pada*, translated as 'ransom', is used in a related sense of the redemption of a life (see Exodus 21.30; Psalm 49.7–8). The fullest theological sense applies when God himself acts to restore or reestablish the relationship with Israel as the chosen people (see Psalm 130.8; Job 19.25; compare Luke 1.68).

The New Testament employs the Greek root *lutron* (as in Mark 10.45), together with its cognate verbs, to refer to the DEATH OF CHRIST as an act of redemption. This goes beyond the underlying metaphor of a financial transaction, in a 'once for all' action which gives to humanity the forgiveness and restoration which only God could bestow (see Romans 3.21–26; 1 Corinthians 1.30).

Rehoboam *See* JEROBOAM I.

religion Religion is a topic which defies adequate and satisfactory definition, often revealing the particular affiliation or prejudice of the person defining it. Broadly it denotes a community or personal system which is likely to combine the following ingredients: belief (which may or may not depend upon scriptural texts or other AUTHORITY); the public or private practice and expression of WORSHIP; and consequent rules or principles governing conduct. A recent definition of a more academic and sociological kind was offered by Gerd Theissen, defining religion as 'a socio-cultural sign system or language, which promises an improvement or intensification in life, by corresponding to an ultimate reality that is believed in'.

Rephaim *See* ZAMZUMMIM.

resin *See* PLANTS (RESINOUS).

resurrection Alan F. Segal in 2004 wrote about the origin of the concept of resurrection within JUDAISM at the time of the MARTYRS among the MACCABEES, when they were experiencing suffering and oppression and facing death at the hands of foreigners: 'a new notion of afterlife was born – resurrection of the body. Under the pressure of martyrdom, the death of the faithful for their faith became a public drama that overcame the evil of the oppressor ... God will restore the bodies of the martyrs which the oppressors so cruelly destroyed.' Although the SADDUCEES

The Resurrection John 20.11–18

may not have accepted the reality of bodily resurrection (see Mark 12.18; Acts 23.8), other Jews, including PHARISEES and ESSENES, certainly did so. Jesus himself is recorded as having restored individuals to life on three occasions (see Luke 7.11–17; 8.49–56; John 11 – notably, this chapter offers contrasting declarations of resurrection belief). Against this background, in modern times, some dialogue between Jews and Christians has become possible on a partly shared concept of resurrection.

PAUL expressed the essential importance of belief in the Resurrection of Christ at the heart of the Christian faith. See 1 Corinthians 15.13–14: 'If there is no resurrection of the dead, then Christ has not been raised; and if Christ has not been raised, then our proclamation has been in vain and your faith has been in vain.' Allowing for the particularities of Paul's controversy here with the CORINTHIANS, the basic emphasis is plain. At the start of chapter 15 he sets out the traditional Christian preaching, as well as the argument from the post-resurrection appearances of Christ to certain groups and named individuals. To some readers at least it may be a puzzle that Paul offers no account of the empty tomb, to correspond with the references in the Gospels (see Matthew 28.1–10; Mark 16.1–8 – the Gospel's original ending; Luke 24.1–12; John 20.1–18). Apart from Mark, the other Gospels do also contain narratives of post-resurrection appearances (which scholars attempt to co-ordinate with Paul's list). Certainly the traditions of Christ's resurrection are of more than one kind.

Reuben Reuben is the first-born son of JACOB by his first wife LEAH (see Genesis 49.2–3). Not unnaturally he favours his mother's cause when his father transfers his affections to RACHEL; two episodes in Genesis 30.14–15 and 35.22 demonstrate his plans to bring Jacob back, when he gathers aphrodisiac mandrakes for his mother, and when, in a rebellious spoiling act, he has sex with Bilhah (Rachel's handmaid and his father's concubine). He is the ancestor of the tribe that bears his name.

Revelation, book of, or the Apocalypse of John The book of Revelation is the only complete APOCALYPTIC book in the New Testament. It is most helpful to understand it in relation to DANIEL in the Old Testament and other apocalypses outside the canon. Sometimes it can be referred to as Christian prophecy, but this tends to understate its literary visions and coded symbolism, as well as the concluding threats against tampering with the text (22.18–19). But the literary genre of a letter (like the EPISTLES in the New Testament collection) should also be noticed: this apocalypse begins and ends like a letter (1.4–5; 22.21) and contains seven short letters in chapters 2 and 3. The human author is named as 'John' (but which John is uncertain, *see* JOHN, APOSTLE), and he seems to write from banishment on PATMOS (1.9). His authorization is impressive, by direct link to God himself (1.1–2: a passage which invites comparison with the original AUTHORITY of the eyewitnesses at the start of the first of JOHN'S LETTERS). But John does not seem to claim apostolic authority in the technical sense; instead he refers to the APOSTLES as figures of the past (21.14).

Old Testament themes are prominent in the book, particularly from EZEKIEL, DANIEL, JOEL, and the PLAGUES of the EXODUS. This reinforces the sense of a Jewish background and invites comparison with inter-testamental Jewish apocalypses where traditional ideas are updated and developed. The author's historical context is as the pastor of the SEVEN CHURCHES in Asia Minor, named at 1.11. It is noteworthy how little these 'Johannine' Churches overlap with those associated with PAUL. The context of Christian WORSHIP 'on the Lord's day' is mentioned at 1.10 (*see* SUNDAY), which prepares the reader for the hymns and phrases throughout the book that sound liturgical. The influence is probably from Revelation to LITURGY, for it is too early for the formal Christian liturgies. The book's larger context is that of the Roman Empire, with its various pagan cults, especially the worship of the emperor as divine; the administrative centre for the Roman province of Asia was at EPHESUS. While the earliest Jewish apocalypses attacked the domination of the Seleucid successors of Alexander the Great, later apocalypses, including Revelation, regard the particular threats of religious, political, and economic kinds as deriving from Rome. Such threats may include organized persecution of Christians, such as that by Emperor Nero in Rome, or perhaps with the later Emperor Domitian (regarded by

Vision of the Woman and the Dragon Revelation 12.1–5

some as 'Nero come back again'); or they may be projections of fears expected to be realized soon. Although there are plenty of allusions to possible historical events, these are not precise enough to date the book without question: suggestions range from 60 to 90 CE (emperors Nero, Titus, or Domitian), and it is possible that the book grew in stages.

TABULATION OF REVELATION

1.1–8	Introduction to apocalypse and to letter
1.9–20	John's heavenly vision of Christ as the Son of Man
2.1–3.22	John's letters to seven particular Churches of Asia Minor
4.1–5.14	John's vision of worship in the royal throne-room of heaven
	Christ as the Lamb receives the sealed book of prophecy

6.1–17	Christ breaks open the first six of seven seals: present realities and recent history
7.1–17	Heavenly interlude, including the sealing of those to be spared
8.1–9.21	The opening of the seventh seal; silence, trumpets and disaster
10.1–11	The mighty angel gives John the scroll to eat; he has a message of doom for mankind
11.1–19	The contents of the scroll revealed and the blast of the seventh trumpet The fall of Jerusalem and the model of apostolic witness
12.1–13.18	The woman clothed in the sun, who has a child; the dragon, war in heaven, and the two beasts
14.1–20	The saints in heaven, three angels and the harvest and winepress of the earth
15.1–8	The angels with the bowls containing the last plagues
16.1–21	The bowls of God's wrath are poured out (like the plagues of Egypt)
17.1–18.24	The Roman Empire (Babylon the great whore) is to be destroyed; lament of the merchants and clients who are affected by Rome's fall
19.1–21	Song of triumph in heaven; the Lamb is to be married; and Christ the white rider goes out to the last battle; the beast is defeated and thrown into the lake
20.1–15	The true Millennium, the defeat of Satan, and the Last Judgement
21.1–22.5	The vision of the heavenly new Jerusalem, and the new created order of paradise
22.6–20	Final guarantees, solemn apocalyptic warnings, Christ's Parousia is imminent
22.21	Ending appropriate to a letter (see beginning, 1.4–8)

righteousness The Hebrew word *tsedaqah* in the Old Testament and the Greek equivalent *dikaiosune* in the New Testament are both pre-eminently concerned with a characteristic of God, expressed in quasi-legal, juridical terms. It expresses the belief that absolute justice, fair play and truth are found uniquely here. God is a reliable judge, and he will act in accordance with his power in CREATION and his fidelity to the COVENANT.

The problem for an English translation is how to sum up the whole complex of the Hebrew and Greek ideas in a single word. 'Faithfulness' hardly carries the sense of justice and of restoring things to rights. 'Righteousness' too readily sounds like an upright ethical stance; and 'justification' often carries with it the Reformation doctrine of imputing to the faithful a status which is not innately theirs. 'JUSTICE' comes from the same root, but may be closer to an expression of the obligation of putting the world to rights, on the grounds of a commitment to the created order and the covenant people.

In the Hebrew Bible high standards of righteousness are expected among God's people; they are condemned when injustice and oppression are found instead (see Amos 5.10–24: 'Let justice roll down like waters, and righteousness like an everflowing stream'). The righteous people and qualities are particularly close to God (see

Psalms 1.6; 85.13). In this sense Matthew's Gospel also speaks of the 'way to fulfill all righteousness' (Matthew 3.15). In later JUDAISM the 'righteous' became synonymous with the obedient and observant 'orthodox' (*see* QUMRAN and the DEAD SEA SCROLLS), and with their representative leader, called the 'Teacher of Righteousness'.

In a human context righteousness can be applied (by extension from the divine principle) to human beings as being found 'not guilty'/ 'innocent' in the setting of God's final court of law (despite all evidence to the contrary – see Romans 3.20). Developed by PAUL in the New Testament, this amazing verdict is achieved by the supreme act of SALVATION (the DEATH OF CHRIST on the cross), an act which justifies by GRACE through FAITH (see Romans 3.22–26).

rites and rituals 'Rites are patterns of behaviour which repeat themselves, patterns with which people break up their everyday actions in order to depict the [underlying] other reality that is indicated in MYTHS' (Gerd Theissen). Such rituals are traditionally analysed into the following three components: the words of interpretation (a concentrated form of the myth); the actions (originally blood sacrifices, but replaced in Judaism and Christianity by new – bloodless – rites); and the objects, those affected by the ritual actions (identifiable persons, places and things that are as a result characterized by HOLINESS, identifications which are often replaced in later stages by symbolic equivalents). It has been suggested that an investigation of ritual issues might more helpfully begin, not with such an analysis of the ritual's form and content, but rather with an identification of the situation which creates the need for the ritual performance. Rituals are understood as human reactions to various causes (events in nature or culture). They may be seen as having differing functions, as an act of legitimizing, or of defining, or of marking-out. It may also be possible to distinguish levels of interpretation in the 'meaning' of symbols and rituals. There are three possible levels: the level of ideology, the level of use, and the level of structure. A single ritual may well have different interpretations on different levels. For example the ritual of FOOT-WASHING can have the deepest meaning in terms of the imitation of Christ in discipleship (as shown in John 13.14–17); at the level of use in a civilized society it represents the conventions of hospitality (compare Luke 7.44); and as a basic formality it denotes the needs of cleanliness in a hot and dusty climate.

Romans, letter of Paul to The reader of Romans hears a conversation between Paul and an audience in Rome, about whom he has been informed, though he has not yet visited them. He is also in conversation with the Hebrew scriptures, realigning them in order to understand his own situation and that of Israel. He is also responding to his critics, those critical voices Paul has heard. So any readers of Romans, before they are able to join in the conversation and to understand the letter for what it is, have to reckon with these four participants in the dialogue, each with their own profound concerns about God and human experience.

Romans has a number of key themes which raise fundamental questions for interpreters. Should believers keep the LAW of MOSES? What is the relationship between natural law and Mosaic law? Does God specifically choose certain individuals for SALVATION, and by implication condemn others eternally? Should secular government always be obeyed? Although answers are offered, they may in themselves be provocative; so Paul's letter may provide more openings than conclusions for doing theology.

Paul's letter to the Romans has exercised a major role in Christian history, as a centre of theological controversy; it had an inspirational influence on key figures such as Augustine, Luther, Calvin, Wesley, Barth and Bultmann. For Augustine a primary concern was the doctrine of original SIN; his reading of Romans 5.12 was central to this, and his exegesis is highly debatable, in that it depends on the Latin rather than the Greek. Another major theme for Augustine, which was also central to controversies at the Reformation, was the idea of the 'RIGHTEOUSNESS of God' (as in Romans 1.17). This is not simply a descriptive attribute of God, but an active process of declaring people righteous, or even transforming people to make sinners righteous. Here is the root idea of 'justification by faith' (as in Romans 3.21–26), which is often regarded (mistakenly) as the situation of Christians, over against JUDAISM's justification by works. This is to misunderstand Judaism, and to forget that Paul himself was an educated Jew.

A third centre of controversy, encountered in modern ANTI-SEMITISM, is Paul's view of the Chosen People: is there an ultimate future in God's plan for his original Chosen People? The central section of the letter (Romans 9–12) offers some indications (e.g. 9.3–5; 11.17–24).

TABULATION OF ROMANS

1.1–17	Paul introduces himself and states his purpose in his proposed visit to Rome
1.18–3.20	God's ways were plain to Jews learning from the Law or to Gentiles learning from the world around them. Man's refusal to live accordingly means judgement for all is inevitable
3.21–31	God has enabled people to be right with him through faith in Jesus – sins are forgiven. Law is irrelevant
4.1–25	Abraham is given as an example of a man who was right with God because he had faith
5.1–6.23	What Christ has done for mankind is to make believers God's friends and free from sin; they also have the gift of eternal life Paul works out the contrast with Adam
7.1–25	The role of the Law with regard to sin
8.1–30	Life with the Spirit of God
8.31–39	Nothing can separate the believer from God's love
9.1–11.36	Salvation and God's people – the position of the Jews is explored
12.1–21	Advice on Christian living
13.1–14	Christian duties to the state and to one another
14.1–15.13	Criticism of one another's religious practices is to stop; instead believers should try to please one another
15.14–33	Paul's credentials and his travel plans – to Jerusalem, to Rome and then to Spain
16.1–27	Greetings and final prayer of dedication

Rome The city of Rome was traditionally founded in 753 BCE by Romulus and Remus. This was year one in a calendar which calculated the years 'from the foundation of the city' (*AUC*). Rome is situated in an area with seven hills on the plain beside the river Tiber. Initially it was ruled by legendary Etruscan kings, the last of whom – Tarquin the Proud – was expelled in 509 BCE, and a Roman Republic established. The authority of Rome was signified by the initials SPQR, which stand for *Senatus Populusque Romanus* (the Senate and the People of Rome). Rome dominated the Mediterranean world, rivalled only by the PHOENICIAN colony at Carthage. Carthage was destroyed in 146 BCE at the end of the Punic Wars. Rome had also defeated the Seleucids (one of the HELLENISTIC kingdoms that were the successors of Alexander the Great) and later came to control the eastern Mediterranean, following an expedition by Pompey, who conquered Jerusalem in 63 BCE.

Eventually the city of Rome became the centre of the Roman Empire. By the close of the 1st century BCE the city's population may have been around a million. Initially Pompey, Julius Caesar, and Crassus had formed a triumvirate; but Caesar emerged from a period of civil war as dictator, only to be assassinated in 44 BCE. Mark Antony assumed command, associating himself with Cleopatra, the last of the Ptolemies (the other Hellenistic kingdom) in EGYPT. Octavian was, however, designated as Caesar's heir and he defeated Antony in the naval battle of Actium in 31 BCE. In 27 BCE the Roman Senate conferred the title Augustus upon the victorious Octavian. Augustus then ruled from Rome as the first Roman emperor until 14 CE. He was succeeded by Tiberius (14–37 CE), Gaius or Caligula (37–41 CE), Claudius (41–54 CE) and Nero (54–68 CE). PAUL arrived in Rome during the reign of Emperor Nero; he had never been to Rome until he was imprisoned and executed there (it is only his two-year stay that is actually recorded in Acts 28.16–31; *see also* SPAIN). One could draw a contrast between the perspectives of Paul and the Roman Empire. Paul's was still looking towards the east, towards Jerusalem, as the focus of Judaism and even more as the location of Christ's death and the origins of the Christian movement; while Rome had generated an enormous cultural outreach from Italy, in all directions. In 20 BCE Emperor Augustus had set up the Golden Milestone in the Roman Forum; this was the starting point of all the imperial roads built by the Romans, and it recorded the distances to all the Empire's major cities.

It is likely that both Jews in the DIASPORA and Christians engaged in MISSION would be drawn eventually to Rome, although details and actual dates are unknown. Emperor Claudius is said to have issued an edict expelling Jews (and Christians as well, because it would be hard to differentiate at this stage) from Rome in 49 CE, although the historian Cassius Dio said that Jews were instructed, 'while continuing their traditional mode of life, not to hold meetings'. By the time of Nero at any event they are likely to have returned to Rome. Certainly Nero is said to have blamed the Christians, or held them as scapegoats, for the fire of Rome in 64 CE. There is an early tradition of the martyrdom of both PETER and Paul in Rome at this time.

Royal Road *See* HIGHWAY OF THE KING.

Ruth, book of In Christian Bibles the book of Ruth is to be found after Judges and before 1 Samuel in what is principally a chronological arrangement, for the story is set in this period and involves a Moabite in BETHLEHEM. In Jewish Bibles Ruth is found in the third section of the Bible (the Writings) among the Five Scrolls which are associated with significant days in the Jewish CALENDAR; its position here is therefore liturgical.

The story tells of the sad journey of Naomi and her daughter-in-law Ruth from MOAB to JUDAH after the death of Ruth's husband. But the story has a happy ending, because Ruth is allowed to forage for grain at harvest time and ends up married to Boaz, who is a wealthy landowner and a distant kinsman of Naomi. So Ruth is accepted into the community and restores her mother-in-law to honour among her own people. A modern parallel to the story would be to see Ruth and Naomi as archetypes of women refugees displaced by politics or history.

Ruth is a short pastoral narrative (a story loved by Thomas Hardy), set at the time of the barley harvest, a beautiful piece of sophisticated writing that is perhaps best seen as a theological and literary development of a folk-tale. Written after the time of DAVID, and perhaps as late as the EXILE (as a critique of EZRA's campaign for racial purity), the story shows how God directs even domestic human affairs in the choice of an ancestor for the royal line (see 4.18–22, where the GENEALOGY states that Ruth is the great-grandmother of David). The New Testament interest in Ruth is also genea-logical (see Matthew 1.5): in the ancestry of Jesus she is symbolically a Gentile with an irregular marital status, matching the roles of TAMAR (1) and RAHAB (2).

In an age when Judaism was renowned for seeking converts (see Matthew 23.15), the book of Ruth was selected to be read in SYNAGOGUE at the FESTIVAL of Weeks (*see* PENTECOST). This festival celebrates the revelation of the LAW on Mount SINAI; the inclusion of the book of Ruth on this occasion would underline the fact that con-verts to Judaism (Ruth 1.16) are as valued as those who are Jews from birth. One Jewish rabbi said that the book was written 'to teach you of a magnificent reward to those who practise and dispense love'.

S

Saba *See* SHEBA.

Sabbath The importance of a distinctive day of the week, set apart for rest (Hebrew *shavat* means 'rest') and worship, dates from the Ten Commandments (DECALOGUE): 'Remember the sabbath day, and keep it holy ...' (Exodus 20.8–11). Even domestic fire-laying was forbidden (Exodus 35.2–3). The ban on working was complete, for family, slaves, and animals, even foreigners resident in Israel, but the motive was not humanitarian. The day was to be kept holy; it may have been only later thought that attributed the rationale to an imitation of God's rest on the seventh day of CREATION (Genesis 2.1–3); the version in Deuteronomy 5.12–15 gives as the reason God's rescuing them from slavery in Egypt (*see* EXODUS). Sabbath observance was taken so seriously that death was to be the punishment for non-observance (Exodus 31.14), and not even agricultural peak-time demands of ploughing and harvest were to override the prohibition (Exodus 34.21).

The Sabbath became of even greater importance as a distinctive mark of JUDAISM in the EXILE and post-Exilic period; the evidence is in the majority of references to Sabbath to be found in writing of this later period (see 1 Chronicles 9.32; Isaiah 58.13; Ezekiel 20.20). Ezekiel in Exile in BABYLON reminded the Jews of their ancestors' sins in profaning the Sabbath, and claimed its origin and authority, not in connection with Creation or Exodus, but as a sign of God's COVENANT with Israel. NEHEMIAH on return from Exile was much exercised by poor Sabbath practice; he organized the signing of an agreement not to trade with foreigners on the Sabbath (Nehemiah 10.31), and reprimanded attempts to bring goods to market (13.15–18); finally, he resorted to barring the gates of Jerusalem to prevent the despoiling of the Sabbath (13.19–22).

Increasing formalization and codification of Sabbath-keeping continued for centuries; many rules were made to interpret exactly what 'do no work' meant, and what could override the commandment in emergencies. Later Judaism listed the 39 categories of prohibited work (TALMUD *Shabbath* 7.1). There are glimpses of the process in the Gospel healings, when Jesus' cures breached the 'life or death crisis' rules for the Sabbath. Controversies with the PHARISEES were particularly pointed on the need for compassion to win out over rule-keeping (*see* LUKE 13.15 – loosing an animal to water it on the Sabbath; Luke 14.5 – rescuing a son or an ox fallen in a well). In JOHN'S GOSPEL the cure of the man born blind produced the Pharisaic comment that Jesus did not come from God, as he broke Sabbath TORAH. Jesus does not enter the debate, but the rejoinder from others was to ask how Jesus, as a sinner, could work MIRACLES (John 9.13–16). The story of the DISCIPLES' snacking on hand-rubbed grain from a Sabbath cornfield provoked from Jesus the most theological of rebuffs to criticism (Mark 2.23–27). Jesus argued from DAVID's precedent in breaking religious rules to meet human need; the conclusion was that the Sabbath was made for the benefit of man, not vice versa; 'so the SON OF MAN is lord even of the Sabbath' (Mark 2.28). The implications of this would take time for the Church to work through.

In contrast to Judaism's observance of the Sabbath on Saturday (commencing on Friday evening), most Christian traditions came to associate the Sabbath with SUN-DAY, although whether modern Christians 'rest' on Sundays (as observant Jews still do on Saturdays) is open to debate. Can a Christian practice of observing the Lord's Day (see Revelation 1.10) be regarded as keeping the fourth of the Ten Command-ments? The Christian argument developed in the Middle Ages, by St Thomas Aqui-nas for example, justifies the change to Sunday while fulfilling the intent of the commandment in rest and worship on one day out of the seven (the first day of the week as the day of RESURRECTION, rather than the seventh day). The change to Sun-day happened in some Christian circles much earlier, as a result of Emperor Hadrian's anti-Jewish legislation in 135 CE, outlawing the practices of the Jewish religion including Sabbath-keeping. Gentile Christians were encouraged to adopt the Day of the Sun rather than the Sabbath, to show separation from the Jews and identification with Roman society.

Orthodox Judaism today is still exercised over the problems of Sabbath observance in modern society. The Institute for Science and Halacha in Jerusalem advises on various solutions to the problem using electronics and other technology. The first Israeli astronaut, Ilan Roman, who died in the loss of the American space-shuttle *Columbia* in 2003, asked before the launch when he should observe Sabbath in circumstances when sunrise and sunset occurred every 90 minutes.

For Sabbath as a sequence of seven (seven days = a week) and of seven times seven, *see* JUBILEE.

sacraments St Thomas Aquinas defined the sacrament as 'the sign of a sacred thing in so far as it sanctifies human beings'. Its solemn seriousness is reflected in the use of a Latin word *sacramentum*, which originally meant an 'oath' or 'pledge' (such as the oath of allegiance made by a soldier). In the Latin translation of the New Testament *sacramentum* was used to translate the Greek *musterion*, meaning 'mystery' or 'secret' (and thus conveying a sense of hiddenness).

In the Catholic tradition of Christendom there are said to be seven sacraments (seven being a theologically complete number) formally defined in the 12th century CE; they are identified as Baptism, Confirmation, Eucharist, Penance, Extreme Unc-tion, Orders, and Matrimony, all of which, the Council of Trent claimed, were instituted by Christ. In some other Christian traditions, as in Article 25 of the Church of England, two of the sacraments (Baptism and Eucharist) are identified as the 'two ordained of Christ' as distinct from the other five 'lesser sacraments'. For these five there are disagreements as to the occasion when they were instituted by Christ.

See BAPTISM; CONFIRMATION; EUCHARIST; MARRIAGE; UNCTION.

sacrifice In the Bible this word usually refers to the sacrificial offerings made in Old Testament Judaism, in which an animal such as a lamb or a kid, or a pair of doves, might be sacrificed in order to propitiate God and to atone for human sin and guilt. In the New Testament it is transferred to relate to the PASSION and DEATH OF CHRIST, regarded as the ultimate atoning sacrifice (*see* ATONEMENT). God takes the initiative and Christ takes the place of humanity. Christians 'may have ceased to sacrifice animals, but in their interpretations they reactivated a form of sacrifice which was already long obsolete, namely human sacrifice – as the atoning sacrifice of Jesus' (Gerd Theissen).

Animal sacrifice features in the story of CAIN AND ABEL, and also with NOAH and the PATRIARCHS. It is likely that the CANAANITES offered human sacrifice, but one important aspect of the story of ABRAHAM and the binding of Isaac (the AKEDAH) is to indicate God's rejection of human sacrifice. In the course of the Hebrew Bible, the offering of sacrifices becomes focused on the central, and single, sanctuary of the Jerusalem TEMPLE. (An independent tradition is maintained by the SAMARITANS at their northern sanctuary on Mount Gerizim.) A variety of RITES was carried out in the Temple, not only the sacrifice of animals, including the 'peace offering' (*shelamim*) and the PASSOVER lamb, but also of meal and incense, and other guilt offerings, and the daily burnt offering (HOLOCAUST) which was performed by the priests. Some sacrifices were congregational offerings, others offered on behalf of an individual. The sacrifices are listed systematically in LEVITICUS chapters 1–7. All sacrifice ceased after the destruction of the Temple by the Romans in 70 CE, and the pattern of SYNAGOGUE prayer was regarded as a substitute. In modern Judaism the ultra-orthodox pray for the restitution of the sacrificial system.

Sadducees The dominant groupings in Jewish society were the Sadducees and the PHARISEES. The Sadducee families were the ruling aristocracy, people of fortune and position within the TEMPLE and the SANHEDRIN. During the New Testament period all Sadducees would be officiating PRIESTS at the Jerusalem TEMPLE (within the 24 priestly courses that are indicated in Luke 1.8), but not all priests were Sadducees.

saints PAUL addresses members of his congregations as 'holy ones' (*hagioi*) or 'saints' (*see also* HOLINESS). He uses this as his particular form of address for the recipients of his letters (although not in Galatians) – see, for example, 1 Corinthians 1.2; Romans 1.7. The earliest use is probably in 1 Thessalonians 3.13, although here the reference is to the PAROUSIA or return of Christ, accompanied by the believers who had already died (see 1 Thessalonians 4.13–18). The background idea is probably ZECHARIAH 14.5: 'Then the Lord my God will come, and all the *holy ones* with him.' A comparable idea is found in the only occurrence of the term in the Gospels, at Matthew 27.52: 'The tombs also were opened, and many bodies of the saints who had fallen asleep were raised.' But when Paul comes to write to the Corinthians he has anticipated the eschatological time scale and is clearly referring to the living members of his assembly. Paul can therefore think of the community at Corinth (and elsewhere) as a group destined as holy people, who should be able to settle disputes among themselves rather than needing to be judged by the outsiders or the unrighteous. See 1 Corinthians 6.1–2: 'Do you not know that the holy ones will judge the world?'

Within the later traditions of the Christian Church, 'saints' have been variously defined as those with lives of heroic virtue; those who die for the faith (witnesses to the ultimate point of death, or 'MARTYRS'); and, in the Russian Orthodox Church, Passion Bearers.

Salome Salome was the daughter of Herodias and the stepdaughter of Herod Antipas (*see* HERODIAN DYNASTY). On Herod's birthday she danced before him, leading him to offer her whatever she wanted. Influenced by her mother she asked for the head of JOHN THE BAPTIST (currently imprisoned for denouncing the marriage of Herodias and Antipas). The story is found in Mark 6.21–28 and Matthew 14.6–11. The New Testament does not call her by name, but JOSEPHUS (*Antiquities* 18.5.4) identifies the 'daughter of Herodias' as Salome.

salt Until modern times salt was very valuable as a flavour enhancer (see Job 6.6), as well as a means of preserving food. In this latter way it came to be associated with the cereal offerings of the TEMPLE (see Leviticus 2.13; Ezekiel 43.24) as representing the bond of the COVENANT between Israel and God. Salt was also used in the treatment of animal hides, and in the pickling of fish caught in the Sea of GALILEE.

Israel had a ready supply of salt on the shores of the DEAD SEA, and in the rock salt of the nearby hill of Salt (Mount SODOM). The curious shapes of fossil salt can explain the derivation of the myth of LOT's wife. Rock salt was of variable quality, owing to decomposition, and this may explain Jesus' comparison of useless disciples with salt that had lost its savour (see Matthew 5.13). Salt was also obtained by running seawater into pits and allowing the water to evaporate. Salt was a valuable commodity in international trade.

Salt on the soil was recognized as rendering it useless for agriculture, and this was even used as an action against enemies, in making their land barren by sowing it with salt; in this way Abimelech was revenged on SHECHEM (see Judges 9.45).

Salt Sea *See* DEAD SEA.

salvation; saviour Both the Hebrew and the Greek words which are often translated as 'salvation' in the English Bible were used originally in a strongly secular way, either in the military sense of 'victory' (such as those of GIDEON, SAMSON, and DAVID), or in the sense of 'rescue' from danger or distress (see, for example, the unusual case in Deuteronomy 22.27).

But clearly the Old and New Testaments also offer a more theological sense, in which God is seen as the ultimate source of victory or deliverance (see Psalm 91.14–16; Ezekiel 34.22; Isaiah 49.6–8). Such salvation can be seen as the practical hope in the restoration of the nation of Israel to its own land.

Many instances in the New Testament are concerned with the more ultimate and spiritual salvation of the believer through faith in Christ. Examples include the MIRACLES of healing, and teaching about the KINGDOM OF GOD. The link between Old Testament language and the New Testament focus on ultimate salvation is provided, for example, in the prophetic words of ZECHARIAH, the father of JOHN THE BAPTIST in Luke 1.68–79. In JOHN'S GOSPEL Jesus is identified as 'saviour' (see

John 4.42), a theme which is already indicated in the name Jesus/Jeshua, meaning 'God saves'.

Samaria, Sebaste Originally this was an important city of the Iron Age, called Shomron. Samaria was founded in 876 BCE as the capital of the Northern Kingdom of Israel (see 1 Kings 16.24, where the hill is purchased by King OMRI from a man called Shemer – the popular origin of the name; the hill of Shamir is also mentioned at Judges 10.1–2, the seat of a judge named Tola from the tribe of ISSACHAR. Omri was also from the tribe of Issachar which may explain his choice of this site for his new capital.) In Samaria was the elaborate palace of King AHAB and his Phoenician wife JEZEBEL; here also were the 'houses of ivory' of King Jeroboam II, denounced by the prophet AMOS (see 1 Kings 22.39; Amos 6.4 – some 500 ivory pieces were found in Samaria); and the house of OSTRACA where 103 examples were found, giving evidence of a widespread literacy in the 8th century BCE. Samaria was to withstand the ASSYRIAN siege for three years (725–722 BCE) but was eventually captured, and its citizens deported (2 Kings 17.6). It became the centre of the Assyrian province of Samerina, with new settlers being imported.

Alexander the Great captured Samaria in 332 BCE and his Macedonian veterans were settled there. During the HELLENISTIC PERIOD it was a flourishing urban centre, home to pagan culture. As a result the HASMONEANS destroyed it completely in 108–107 BCE. It was reconstructed as a Roman town after 63 BCE when Pompey annexed Samaria to the Roman province of Syria. Emperor Augustus gave it to HEROD THE GREAT, who renamed it Sebaste in honour of his benefactor (*sebastos* is the Greek version of 'Augustus'). Herod married Mariamne there in 37 BCE and subsequently poured money into an elaborate rebuilding programme (see JOSEPHUS *Antiquities* 15.296–298). Sebaste was a pagan city at the time of Jesus, but both Jews and Samaritans were permitted. The SAMARITAN presence was strong in the surrounding area. Here PHILIP probably clashed with the pagan miracle-worker SIMON MAGUS (Acts 8.5). Later there was a notable Christian presence with a bishop of Sebaste. A cathedral was built to focus attention on the traditional site of the burials of JOHN THE BAPTIST, ELISHA, and OBADIAH.

See also SANBALLAT.

Samaritans Their name is possibly preserved in the village of West Galilee, al-Sumayriyya (the site of the Kibbutz, Lohamei ha-Getaot), which was conquered and destroyed by the Israelis in 1948. The Samaritan community had survived thereabouts until the 18th century. Today some 650 Samaritans still survive, in two communities: Neve Marqeh in Holon, near TEL AVIV (educated in Hebrew); and Kiryat Luza on their holy mountain Gerizim (ar-Garizein) near Nablus (educated in Arabic). Numbers are seriously diminishing because of strict rules against the girls marrying out. As representatives of an alternative covenant community of Israel, the Samaritans trace their Mosaic religious tradition back 3600 years; the focus is in an annual feast of PASSOVER at which 18 young rams are sacrificed by men and boys dressed in white (*see* SACRIFICE). The Samaritan version of the Ten Commandments (*see* COVENANT and DECALOGUE) has a distinctive and additional tenth commandment concerned with building an altar at the true sanctuary on Mount Gerizim. Compared

Samson and the Lion Judges 14.5–19

with the Jewish tradition, the total of 10 commandments is preserved by not count-ing the introductory formula 'I am the Lord your God' as a commandment. (See www.mystae.com/samaritans.html.)

Samson Tins of Lyle's Golden Syrup carry the motto 'Out of the strong came forth sweetness'. The reference is to the story of the Israelite strong-man Samson in Judges 14. On a visit to TIMNAH he had become engaged to a PHILISTINE woman, but on the way he had torn apart a young lion who roared at him. Returning, he observed that a swarm of bees had occupied the lion's carcase, producing honey, some of which he ate. Samson, inspired by this experience, put a riddle to the guests at the wedding: 'Out of the eater came forth meat, and out of the strong came forth sweetness.' Solving the riddle would earn the Philistines 30 sets of clothes; failure would cost them the same. Frustrated, the Philistines persuaded Samson's bride to use her wiles to find the solution. Samson realized the trick: 'If you had not ploughed with my heifer, you would not have found out my riddle.' So he went and killed 30 men in ASHKELON to provide the clothes for the wager, and he gave away his wife to the best man.

Four chapters of the book of Judges represent a mosaic of events involving Samson. Judges 14 and 15 depict Samson's heroic exploits as strong-man in a very secular mode. His birth, as prophesied to a previously childless couple, and his NAZIRITE vow, in chapter 13, and the uprooting of the city gates of Gaza and the ultimate destruction of the pagan temple of Dagon in chapter 16, provide the religious envelope which contains these heroic sagas. He appears as a promising leader whose leadership fails; but he is also chosen of God, destined to save the Israelites from Philistine oppression, although he ultimately dies with the Philistines. So he can be included in the list of those who 'through faith conquered kingdoms' in HEBREWS 11.32–33. Today he might be termed a terrorist, killing innocent civilians for political ends, essentially as a suicide killer, while his supporters would call him a freedom fighter. The Israeli novelist David Grossman agrees that Samson could be seen as the world's first suicide bomber, taking 3000 Philistines with him when he killed himself; for Grossman he is an exile in the world, tortured and lonely. Much earlier, John Milton glorified Samson's actions in *Samson Agonistes*:

> O dearly-bought revenge, yet glorious!
> Living or dying thou hast fulfill'd
> The work for which thou wast foretold
> To Israel […] self-killed
> Not willingly, but tangled in the fold
> Of dire necessity.

Samuel Samuel combines the functions of prophet and priest in ancient Israel. He plays an important role in the first of the books named after him (see next entry), although he was not himself its author. Samuel was also a 'judge' or leader of Israel, responsible for the purifying of worship from that of the CANAANITE deities, and for the expulsion of the PHILISTINES (1 Samuel 7). He effectively established the monarchy in Israel, by anointing first SAUL and then DAVID. He was not only a kingmaker but he also revoked Saul's kingship (see 1 Samuel 15.28; 28.17). The traditions about Samuel reveal more than one religious attitude towards the idea of kingship in Israel: is it by popular demand and with God's assent, or is it a rejection of Samuel's leadership and, more importantly, a treasonable reaction to the ultimate rule of God himself?

Samuel was the son of HANNAH and Elkanah, a God-given birth in response to a vow. His mother's celebratory song in 1 Samuel 2 invites comparison with the song of MARY, MOTHER OF JESUS in LUKE 1.46–55. Samuel was brought to serve ELI the priest at the sanctuary of SHILOH; here he received a divine revelation (1 Samuel 3) that he would succeed Eli, because his priestly line would cease.

Samuel is celebrated as one of the 'famous men' in ECCLESIASTICUS 46.13–20 and is included among the heroes of faith in HEBREWS 11.32.

Samuel, first and second books of The situation described in the book of JUDGES, of political unrest and conflict on all sides for the Israelite tribes, is also the situation in the following book, 1 Samuel, which is named after the prophet/priest SAMUEL. He plays an important role in the book, but was not himself its author.

Samuel was also a 'judge' and effectively established the monarchy by anointing first SAUL and then DAVID. The inauguration of kingship in Israel could be said to be the central theme of the two books of Samuel. 1 Samuel 8 reveals a theological perspective that warns against the dangers of kingship.

The source material used by these historical books is diverse: sanctuary legends such as that of SHILOH (1 Samuel 3); the story of the ARK and its capture by the PHILISTINES (1 Samuel 4–7); tribal legends and histories, focused on Saul (1 Samuel 11) or on Samuel (1 Samuel 9–10, see 1 Chronicles 29.29); and possibly near-contemporary writing about David, the history of his court, the revolt of his son ABSALOM (2 Samuel 15–18), and other problems in ensuring the dynastic succession to David. The Hebrew text of these books is defective and so translators rely on the Greek text of the SEPTUAGINT and on three fragmentary manuscripts from QUMRAN (4QSam).

1 and 2 Samuel form part of a theological interpretation of Israel's history (known as the Deuteronomistic History, because of its basis in the theology of the book DEUTERONOMY). From this viewpoint David and his approved descendants have a special relationship with God (see the oracle of NATHAN in 2 Samuel 7). David is the only ideal king, the standard by which other kings are to be judged and condemned. By contrast, Judges showed an earlier view – that kings are usurpers of the sole right of God to rule – and the royal theology in the later book of PSALMS holds a generally favourable attitude to kings as the adopted agents of God.

Sanballat NEHEMIAH found considerable opposition to his plans to rebuild Jerusalem and the TORAH community on the return from EXILE. Sanballat was one of his principal opponents, and as governor of SAMARIA he was well placed to interfere. Why he did so is not so clear; although his name was Babylonian he called his sons by names indicating that he worshipped YAHWEH, and he married his daughter into alliance with the HIGH PRIEST's family in Jerusalem. Nehemiah would have found Samaria's attempts to extend its political influence into Judah as galling as the syncretism of SAMARITAN worship.

The ELEPHANTINE papyri name him as governor of Samaria in 407 BCE, and this is part of the puzzle in dating Nehemiah's work, for Nehemiah appears to have returned in 445 BCE. JOSEPHUS adds to the confusion by naming Sanballat as the builder of the Samaritan temple under Darius III a century or so later; but this may well have been a subsequent Sanballat.

Sanhedrin The name Sanhedrin is a Hebraic version of a Greek word *sunedrion* meaning 'a sitting together'. It refers to the supreme legislative assembly of 70 (or 71) members which gathered in the 'chamber of hewn stone' in Jerusalem, until the TEMPLE was destroyed in 70 CE. It continued to meet after that in other places until the 5th century CE. There is some discrepancy between Jewish Rabbinic accounts (Mishnah tractate *Sanhedrin*) and the New Testament references, for example in the TRIAL OF JESUS. In the former the *Nasi* ('Prince') presides; in the latter it is the HIGH PRIEST. The emphasis of the institution tilts between the political and the religious.

Sarah, or Sarai 1 Sarah was the principal wife of ABRAHAM, and also his half-sister. On more than one occasion she posed as Abraham's sister (Genesis 12 and 20).

Because of her infertility, she offered her servant Hagar to her husband as his concubine, producing the child Ishmael (Genesis 16). Subsequently when God promised a son to Sarah and Abraham in their old age, the response was incredulity and laughter (Genesis 17.17; 18.12). But such laughter was turned to an expression of joy with the birth of her own son ISAAC (Genesis 21.6; the name 'Isaac' is explained as meaning 'he laughs' – Genesis 17.19). Sarah thereafter asked for the expulsion of Hagar and Ishmael (Genesis 21.10). When Sarah died at the age of 127, Abraham had her buried in the cave of Machpelah, at HEBRON.

2 See TOBIT, BOOK OF.

Sardis Sardis is the fifth of the seven Churches of Asia Minor to receive a message in chapters 2 and 3 of the book of REVELATION. It was the capital of the kingdom of Lydia, the extent and wealth of which was legendary in the 6th century BCE, particularly under Croesus. But Croesus rashly challenged the power of the PERSIAN Empire and was defeated. Much later, in Roman times, Sardis was the centre of the cult of the Roman emperor for this region. The Jewish historian JOSEPHUS speaks of a significant Jewish community here; there is substantial archaeological evidence, in the form of a 3rd-century CE synagogue, for a large body of Jews, at least at a later date.

Satan The Greek word for devil (*diabolos*) relates to an underlying verb *diaballo*, which means either to carry across or to divide and set at variance. The thought must have developed along these lines: from separation and setting in opposition, to the making of accusations (not so much judicial as complaints, reproaches and denunciations) and then to the theme of slander and misrepresentation, and therefore deception. It may all depend on one's point of view as to whether the devil is accuser, seducer, adversary, or enemy. There is a reference in Plutarch where the abstract noun means 'to see oneself in a mirror as one is'.

Satan in the Hebrew Bible is initially seen as a figure within the divine council, with particular tasks. In JOB (chapters 1–2) he is the accuser of the righteous in a role similar to that of the later Devil's Advocate in the Roman Catholic process of canonization. See also 1 Chronicles 21.1 and Zechariah 3.1–2. Later traditions, between the Old and New Testaments, identified the serpent in the Garden of EDEN and Lucifer in Isaiah 14.12–15 with the devil and Satan. Satan's role becomes much more extensive in the New Testament, with both personal and impersonal influences. Christ is tested in the wilderness by Satan (Matthew 4 and Luke 4 – *see also* TEMPTATIONS OF CHRIST). If Christ had performed MIRACLES and exorcisms by the power of Satan, this would have amounted to civil war in Satan's domain (see Matthew 12.26). Revelation 12.7–12 depicts the ultimate fall of Satan from any heavenly influence.

The Yezidi, who live on the borders of Turkey and Iraq, pray to the fallen angel, whom Christians and Muslims call Satan, but they call Malek Tawwus or the Peacock King. Their belief is that, after the creation of man, God ordered the angels to pray for Adam, but that one angel refused. Instead of becoming the fallen Satan, this recalcitrant angel was forgiven by God.

Saul 1 Saul was the first king of Israel, whose story is told in the first book of SAMUEL. He came from the tribe of BENJAMIN and was anointed king by the priest/prophet

Samuel. He was a valiant leader, but disobeyed the command of God by sparing the life of the defeated Amalekite king Agag (*see* WAR). As a result his kingship and dynasty were called in question; Samuel disowned him in favour of DAVID (see 1 Samuel 28.17). The rivalry between Saul and David, given David's popularity after defeating the PHILISTINE champion GOLIATH (1 Samuel 17), reduced Saul to acute depression. After Samuel's death, Saul consulted the witch of Endor (*see* WITCHCRAFT) for advice from Samuel's ghost (1 Samuel 28). Unable to escape from the finality of divine judgement, Saul was wounded in battle against the Philistines and committed suicide (1 Samuel 31.4).

2 The original Semitic name of the apostle PAUL.

saviour *See* SALVATION; TITLES OF JESUS.

scapegoat On the Day of Atonement (YOM KIPPUR), according to the ritual prescribed in Leviticus 16.1–34, lots are cast over two goats, one to be sacrificed, and the other, the scapegoat, or goat for Azazel (chief of the evil angels, according to traditions outside the canon), is presented live before the Lord. The HIGH PRIEST then places his hands on the head of the live goat and transfers to it all the sins confessed by Israel. Then this goat is taken out into the wilderness and released there. Later the rite is developed according to the Mishnah (c.200 CE; see also *Epistle of Barnabas* 7.11): a crimson thread is divided into two; one part is tied to the goat's horns, and the other to a rock; also the goat is to be pushed over a precipice, not simply released in the wilderness.

The translation 'scapegoat' in Leviticus 16.8 originated with Tyndale and was then used in the KING JAMES VERSION. It might be more accurately rendered as the name 'Azazel' (demon of the wilderness). The New English Bible translates as 'the goat for the precipice'. The controversial painting by William Holman Hunt, *The Scapegoat* (1854–5, 1858), was executed with Pre-Raphaelite realism on the shores of the DEAD SEA, and finished in Jerusalem. It is accurate to Leviticus, apart from the age of the goat (presumably dictated by available models); it also shows the later tradition of the crimson thread around the horns; the mountains of MOAB are in the background of the painting; however, there is no precipice for the goat to be pushed over.

There might be a slight parallel to this Jewish practice in Roman religion, when in March each year, at the procession of the Argei, the Vestals threw wicker effigies into the river Tiber as a sacrifice of purification.

scribes Scribes are also known as teachers of the LAW; their expertise in teaching, expounding and ruling on matters of the TORAH dates from after the EXILE. They had schools of disciples and considerable power. They considered the application of the written law, by a plethora of orally transmitted rules, extremely important. Because of their debating style, which depended upon an assemblage of various eminent scholars' views, the ordinary people commented that Jesus' way of teaching with authority – 'But I say to you' – was impressive in contrast. This did not endear Jesus to the scribes, and they were among his strongest opponents. SYNAGOGUE worship may well have originated with them, and in many ways their views coincided with those of the PHARISEES, whose party counted most of them as members.

With the destruction of the Jerusalem TEMPLE and the loss of the cultic system of worship in 70 CE, the scribes' teaching was found to provide the way forward for JUDAISM. *See also* RABBIS.

Scythopolis *See* BETH-SHEAN.

sea *See* SHIPS AND THE SEA.

Sebaste *See* SAMARIA.

second coming *See* PAROUSIA.

Sennacherib Sennacherib was the king of Assyria (from 705 to 681 BCE) who invaded Judah in 701 BCE, during the reign of King HEZEKIAH of Judah. The account of the invasion is found in the Hebrew Bible at 2 Kings 18 and at 2 Chronicles 32; there is also an ASSYRIAN account in a CUNEIFORM text known as Sennacherib's Prism. Here he boasts, 'Hezekiah the Jew did not submit to my yoke. I laid siege to 46 of his strong cities … and conquered them … [Hezekiah] himself I made a prisoner in Jerusalem his royal residence, like a bird in a cage.' A famous relief depicts Sennacherib high on his throne at the conquest of LACHISH in Judah in 701. JERUSALEM was certainly besieged in this year but Sennacherib did not succeed in capturing it. His own version does not explain why he lifted the siege and withdrew, whether for military or political reasons; the Biblical account ascribes Jerusalem's escape to a divine miracle.

Sepphoris Sepphoris, now Zippori, was an important administrative and rabbinic centre in Roman Galilee; it is now a green hill-top site, four miles north-west of NAZARETH. Its past importance may date from the devolution of power to it (and four other councils) in Gabinius' organization of the government of Judaea after 57 BCE. In the 1st century CE it became the capital of the Roman district of Galilee. Herod Antipas (*see* HERODIAN DYNASTY) effectively urbanized Galilee by his building projects here (as well as at Tiberias). Flavius JOSEPHUS, the Jewish historian, called it 'the ornament of all Galilee'. A Christian tradition claims it as the birthplace of MARY, MOTHER OF JESUS. It later became the seat of the Jewish SANHEDRIN and was the home of Rabbi Judah (the Prince), who compiled the Mishnah there about 200 CE (the foundational document for later collections of rabbinic materials, the Babylonian TALMUD – ultimately authoritative for JUDAISM – and the Palestinian Talmud).

Extensive archaeology (still continuing) in this national park has rediscovered a city of high culture. There are many beautiful mosaics (including the 'Mona Lisa of Galilee'), a large Roman villa, a theatre, a civic basilica, an aqueduct, baths, synagogues and a row of shops along a colonnaded street (the *decumanus* or main east–west Roman road). It has been suggested that Mary's husband JOSEPH (and Jesus) could have been employed as builders there. If Jesus had visited Sepphoris from nearby Nazareth, he would certainly have been exposed to a more cosmopolitan environment. It is interesting to speculate on the impact of Antipas' kingdom building here; did he merely apply a Greco-Roman architectural veneer to the life of the Jewish population? In fact Sepphoris did not join the JEWISH WAR against Rome; it wavered, but then issued coins describing itself as 'the city of peace'.

Septuagint With the dispersal of Jewish communities throughout the HELLENISTIC world, translation of the Hebrew Bible into GREEK became imperative. The story goes that Ptolemy II Philadelphus (285–246 BCE) ordered that 70 (or 72) elders of Israel should translate the scriptures into Greek in ALEXANDRIA in 70 (or 72) days. Certainly the Septuagint translation, the name of which mirrors the legend of The SEVENTY, was composed in the 3rd century BCE for the Greek-speaking Jewish communities of Egypt. The John Rylands Library in Manchester possesses probably the oldest texts from the Greek Bible, six tiny fragments of the Septuagint text of DEUTERONOMY, copied in the 2nd century BCE and so obviously Jewish and, remarkably, copied within a century of the original. In due course this translation from the Hebrew Scriptures was adopted by the Christians, especially in quotations to demonstrate the fulfilment of the Old Testament in the New. After the 1st century CE Jews tended to avoid the Septuagint, because of its Christian use, and favoured other Greek versions (those by Aquila and Theodotion).

seraphim *See* CHERUBIM AND SERAPHIM.

Sergius Paulus *See* PAUL.

Sermon on the Mount, Sermon in the Plain The particular arrangement of the teaching of Jesus known as the Sermon on the Mount is found only in MATTHEW'S GOSPEL in chapters 5 to 7 (see also the tabulation of that Gospel). Related material but in a different arrangement is found in LUKE'S GOSPEL (Luke 6.20–49), sometimes referred to as the Sermon in the Plain.

Matthew's and Luke's Gospels both offer versions of a collection of Jesus' sayings and there are considerable overlaps. It is widely disputed whether either is (or both are) transcribed from an actual sermon. Following the pattern of a RABBI's students, Jesus' DISCIPLES may well have learned collections of his sayings by heart, so that the present 'sermon' formats owe much to unseen editorial hands, or particularly to those of the evangelist himself.

Matthew's Gospel shaped the teaching of Jesus into five distinct blocks, interspersed with narrated activities, such as healings. The Sermon on the Mount is the first of these blocks; its delivery on a hill is taken as a deliberate analogy to MOSES on Mount SINAI. There seems to be a positive recollection of the revelation to Moses on Sinai (see Exodus 19–24), so that it is part of the portrayal of Jesus as the giver of the new TORAH. These five blocks replace the PENTATEUCH (the five books of the old Torah) for the new believer.

Luke apparently was not so systematic in his approach, nor did he need to promote such an image of Jesus for his largely GENTILE readership. So Jesus had just come down from a hill, and was engaged in healing the crowds, when he launched into this teaching. Luke's presentation is far briefer than Matthew's – 29 verses compared with three chapters.

Both sermons begin with the BEATITUDES with some variations: Luke (6.20) with his interest in the materially poor (*see* POVERTY) has Jesus declare them (paradoxically) happy, whereas Matthew commends the spiritually poor. Luke 6.27–36 continues with teaching to love one's enemies and avoid revenge. Matthew only reaches that point once Jesus has described the outstanding nature of discipleship to resemble salt and light (Matthew 5.13–16). He then has a controversial passage about keeping the Torah faithfully (5.17–20), but straightaway launches into Jesus' restatement of the Torah on murder (no anger – 5.21–26), ADULTERY (avoid lust – 5.27–30), DIVORCE (5.31–32), oaths and promises (5.33–37), before reaching revenge ('turn the other cheek') and loving one's enemies (5.38–47). This section concludes with the startling challenge to be perfect, as God is (Matthew 5.48).

In Matthew 6 the advice on avoiding a show of piety (in charity – 6.1–4; PRAYER – 6.5–15, *see also* LORD'S PRAYER; and FASTING – 6.16–18) is followed mainly by teaching against materialism (6.19–21, 24–34) but also with the advice to be full of light (6.22–23). Luke includes the teaching on prayer, and the text of the Lord's Prayer, not here in the sermon, but later in 11.2–4; Luke also explores the idea of shunning display in prayer in the PARABLE of the PHARISEE and the Tax-Collector (*see* PUBLICAN; 18.10–14). Luke will also give an expanded version of Matthew 7.7–12, on asking in prayer, in Luke 11.5–13.

Both sermons then unite by including teaching against judging others, with the vivid picture of the man blinded by a log (Matthew 7.1–5) who foolishly attempts to remove a speck from his brother's eye (Luke 6.41–42). Luke's inclusion of the other picture of the two blind men tumbling into the ditch (Luke 6.39) is told by Matthew elsewhere (Matthew 15.14) and more pointedly – against the Pharisees. The judgement of the false prophets, in parallel with judging a tree by its fruits (Matthew 7.15–20; Luke 6.43–45), must reflect a common problem for Matthew's and Luke's communities. Both Gospels conclude the sermon with the story of the two housebuilders (Matthew 7.24–27; Luke 6.47–49) – doubtless perceived as a summons to build lives on the sure foundations of teaching such as has just been given. But first Matthew injects warnings to enter by the narrow gate (7.13–14), and that not everyone addressing Jesus as Lord in lip-service will gain entry to the Kingdom of Heaven (7.21–23). Luke's treatment of the latter saying differs (Luke 6.46: 'Why do you call me "Lord, Lord," and do not do what I tell you?').

No audience reaction to the sermon is recorded in Luke; Jesus just departs for CAPERNAUM (Luke 7.1). But there is a significant comment from the crowd in Matthew 7.29: they 'were astounded at his teaching, for he taught them as one having authority, and not as their scribes'.

serpent The serpent, as a reptile, otherwise a snake, is regarded with suspicion and distrust in the Bible; it was assumed to be poisonous and therefore dangerous to humanity. The older account of the CREATION (Genesis 2.4–3.24), with its explanation of the FALL and human sinfulness (*see* SIN), establishes the serpent as the villain of the story, persuading the woman to persuade the man to eat the forbidden fruit. Notice that the serpent is not identified with SATAN until much later in the tradition (as for example in Revelation 12.9). The only redeeming feature seems to be the serpent's crafty cunning and wisdom (see Genesis 3.1 and Matthew 10.16).

In other ancient cultures the serpent was more highly regarded, being associated with healing (as in the Greek tradition of Asclepius); a similar idea may lie behind the brazen serpent set up by MOSES in the WILDERNESS, to offer healing for those suffering snake-bites by a kind of sympathetic magic (see Numbers 21.8–9). Another ancient association is with fertility (as in the Canaanite religion of BA'AL and ASHERAH, who

The Serpent

are depicted with a serpent). In Mesopotamian mythology, however, the great sea-serpent was seen as the symbol of chaos, the enemy of the gods. Old Testament references to figures such as LEVIATHAN and RAHAB (1) are echoes of this theme, subordinated to the power of YAHWEH.

King HEZEKIAH destroyed Nehushtan, the brazen serpent of the Moses tradition, because it had become an object of worship (see 2 Kings 18.4). At a much later date it is interesting to note that groups of GNOSTICS, known as Ophites (from the Greek word for serpent), or Naassenes (from the Hebrew equivalent), had produced a kind of mirror-image or negative version of the Genesis account of creation, and were venerating the serpent as a medium of revelation.

Seth Seth was the son born to ADAM and Eve to replace Abel, after he was murdered by his brother CAIN. Seth was an ancestor of NOAH. See Genesis 4.25; 5.3–4, 29. Thus he also features in Luke's GENEALOGY of Jesus (Luke 3.38).

Settlement of Canaan *See* CANAAN.

seven Churches of Asia Seven is a symbolic number for theological completeness. Therefore the seven Churches, listed in the book of REVELATION 1.11, to whom messages are directed in chapters 2 and 3, must be a significant and representative grouping of those Churches in Asia Minor that are responsive to John as pastor and missioner. It is noticeable that there is little overlap with those Churches associated with the mission of PAUL, as recipients of his letters, or as described in the narrative of the ACTS OF THE APOSTLES.

John's Churches are EPHESUS (2.1–7), SMYRNA (2.8–11), PERGAMON (2.12–17), THYATIRA (2.18–29), SARDIS (3.1–6), PHILADELPHIA (3.7–13), and LAODIKEIA (3.14–21).

seven 'I Am' sayings These significant theological sayings are distinctive of JOHN'S GOSPEL. The closest parallel to them in the other Gospels is the authoritative 'But I say to you', or the absolute claim 'I am' by Jesus at his TRIAL. There are also two absolute 'I Am' sayings in John (see John 8.24, 58). Although they are brief declarations, almost to the point of ellipsis, they bear an ultimate theological significance because the formula 'I Am' (*ego eimi*) echoes the Hebrew name of God in EXODUS 3.14 : 'I am who I am' (compare with Genesis 17.1; Isaiah 41.4). The grouping of the seven extended sayings in John is probably intentional, because of the symbolism of the number seven representing completeness.

The seven declarations, in Gospel order, are all couched in the form of potent symbols, through which Jesus reveals his divine nature:

I AM	The Bread of Life	(6.35)
	The Light of the World	(8.12)
	The Gate for the Sheep	(10.7, 9)
	The Good Shepherd	(10.11, 14)
	The Resurrection and the Life	(11.25)
	The Way, and the Truth, and the Life	(14.6)
	The True Vine	(15.1, 5)

Bread of life: In the context of the great feeding John gives the EUCHARISTIC teaching one might otherwise have expected to be part of the Last Supper. The Old Testament background includes the episode of the MANNA in the wilderness (Numbers 11) and the idea of the messianic banquet at the end of time. The basic understanding, that Jesus' death on the cross is instrumental in bringing about this feeding, is widely accepted; but the degree of sacramentalism to be drawn from John 6.51–58 has been disputed across the centuries (*see* SACRAMENT).

Light of the world: In the context of the feast of TABERNACLES, when the TEMPLE was brilliantly illuminated by night, Jesus claimed controversially to provide the ultimate illumination to his followers. In the next chapter John illustrates this with the cure of the blind man and the ensuing debate. Although light is linked to CREATION and to ideas of dualism (conflict of light and darkness) in other ancient Near Eastern religions, the more immediate understanding comes from the Old Testament view of the inspiration of God's teaching. 'Your word is a lamp to my feet and a light to my path' (Psalm 119.105).

Gate for the sheep/Good Shepherd: Israel's pastoral economy provided abundant imagery for God as their good leader, and evil rulers as bad shepherds, within the Old Testament (contrast Psalm 23.1 and Ezekiel 34). There is evidence from the other Gospels too that Jesus saw his role as modelled on a SHEPHERD (see Mark 6.34). In John, Jesus' double claims are to be the means of entry to SALVATION and that, unlike mere employees, he is prepared to die in the service of his flock.

Resurrection and life: The Old Testament gives very limited support for the idea of RESURRECTION (as a poetic symbol for the revival of Israel after the EXILE in Ezekiel 37, and as a belief to cheer those dying in the revolt of the MACCABEES of 167 BCE in Daniel 12.2–3). By Jesus' day the idea had caught on – at least for those in the PHARISEES' modernizing ranks, for the SADDUCEES were scornfully sceptical (Mark 12.18–27) – and Jesus asserted his belief in it. In John he goes further, stating that he has the power of God to raise the dead (in this case LAZARUS). The raisings of the ministry depicted in the SYNOPTIC Gospels are surpassed here, because the whole story points to the forthcoming death and resurrection of Jesus himself (*see* DEATH OF CHRIST).

The way, the truth and the life: Although John has been accused of using GNOSTIC language here, his phraseology is completely understandable from within contemporary JUDAISM. Both the Rabbis and the QUMRAN community spoke of correct ethical conduct as 'the Way' to God. Development of teaching from the TORAH, to apply to everyday life, was called *halakah* (literally 'walking'). The early Church, prior to the invention of the term 'Christian', called itself 'the Way', presumably for the same reason. 'Truth' is one of John's favourite words; *aletheia* conveys something closer to 'reality' than the English translation suggests. Life is naturally enough a vital Biblical concept. God gave life at CREATION (Genesis 1–2) and alone could restore life to the dead (Ezekiel 37).

The true vine: Again the background to the symbol is the Old Testament, with Israel symbolized as God's VINE or vineyard on numerous occasions (for example, Isaiah 5.1–7). Note that God has the power to sit in judgement over his vine and to punish it. Here in the context of the Last Supper and the (unmentioned) words over the wine cup, Jesus' claim is linked to his integral unity with his DISCIPLES. The unity of Christ and believer is, however, conditioned by LOVE and the keeping of the commandments.

seven last words These are the seven final utterances of Jesus from the cross, as recorded in the four Gospels. They have been set to music on many occasions, on their own as well as part of a setting of the entire Passion; for example, Haydn's *Seven Last Words* was published in 1802. For the detail on the sayings, *see* PASSION NARRATIVE.

seven pillars of wisdom *Seven Pillars of Wisdom* is familiar as the title of a book by T. E. Lawrence (Lawrence of Arabia), first published in 1926. In fact Lawrence chose this title for an early book he had written about seven cities, which he decided not to publish, but instead he transferred the title to his book on Arabia. The phrase is a quotation from Proverbs 9.1: 'Wisdom has built her house, she has hewn her seven pillars'. It is part of a poem, in 9.1–6, about the woman who personifies the principle of WISDOM and whose work is central to good society, contrasted with the picture of the woman of folly in 9.13–18. The reference to 'seven pillars' is probably intended to recall the mythic picture of the act of CREATION, laying the foundations of the earth, in which wisdom has a part with God himself (see Proverbs 8.22–31).

seventh heaven The idea of separate levels of heaven, of which the seventh is highest, may derive from the Mesopotamian ZIGGURAT (a stepped tower or staircase to heaven) that is echoed in the Tower of BABEL (Genesis 11). Biblical references to such thoughts about heaven are found in the phrase 'heaven of heavens' (Deuteronomy 10.14; Psalm 148.4; Nehemiah 9.6) and possibly in Job 28.24, if translated as 'through all the heavens'.

Inter-testamental Jewish thought reflects the idea of several spheres of heaven, one above the other, which may number three or seven. PAUL refers to a visionary experience of the third heaven in 2 Corinthians 12.2. Within the Pseudepigrapha (*see* JEWISH LITERATURE), for example, *The Martyrdom of Isaiah* 6.13 speaks of seven heavens, above which stands the divine throne (cf. *Testament of Levi* 2.7–10; 3.1–4; *Ascension of Isaiah* 7–9). In the Jewish TALMUD the 'SHEKINAH' or GLORY of God is in the seventh heaven, while the lowest heaven is the one that is visible from earth.

A similar idea might be expressed in modern terms in the poem by J. G. Magee, following his high-altitude flying test in 1941: 'I've trod / the high untrespassed sanctity of space, / put out my hand, and touched the face of God.'

Seventy, The According to the Gospel of LUKE, the mission of the 12 DISCIPLES of Jesus is succeeded by a larger-scale mission involving a wider grouping of 70 followers (Luke 9.1–10 and 10.1–24). The choice of this number is variously explained: it could correspond to the 70 nations of Genesis 10 (the SEPTUAGINT Greek translation reads 72, as do some texts of Luke); or it could match the 70 elders chosen by MOSES from the twelve tribes of Israel (Exodus 24.1, 9; Numbers 11.16, 24).

Shadrach, Meshach, and Abednego These are the Babylonian names given to Hananiah, Mishael, and Azariah, the three companions of DANIEL (see Daniel 1.6–7). They are the heroes of the episode in Daniel 3, when they are rescued from the fiery furnace to which they had been condemned by King NEBUCHADNEZZAR. In the APOC-RYPHA there is an extended version of the story, with added features of the narrative and the songs of Azariah and of the three young men. There is a splendid illustration of the three men in the burning fiery furnace in a 3rd-century CE fresco within the catacombs of Priscilla in Rome.

Shalmaneser III *See* AHAB; ASSYRIANS; JEHU.

shalom This Hebrew word for peace occurs more than 250 times in the Bible. Its use ranges from a polite greeting to a reflective ideal of well-being and completeness. In its fullest sense it is a description of God, who is the source of the gracious gift of peace to his people. Such ideas from the Hebrew Bible are reflected in the theological greeting with which PAUL opens some of his letters (e.g. 'Grace to you and peace' in 1 Thessalonians 1.1). In the world of Greece and Rome peace (*eirene* and *pax*) is more likely to be defined as the absence of war and conflict, as when the doors of the temple of Janus in Rome are ceremonially closed. But even here it is not a passive or static quality, but a dynamic idea that requires activity and vigilance to preserve it. The ideology of peace in the Roman Empire is well represented by the sculpture which decorated the Altar of the Augustan Peace (*Ara Pacis Augustae*) in Rome.

See further at PEACE.

Shaphan This is the name of a family of Judaeans who in several generations played important roles in the royal court. In the time of King JOSIAH (639–609 BCE) Shaphan was the secretary who relayed the discovery of the law book, found in the TEMPLE, from Hilkiah the High Priest to the king (see 2 Kings 22.3–20). In the life of the prophet JEREMIAH, a descendant of Shaphan named Ahikam prevented the prophet's being put to death (Jeremiah 26.24); another son, Elasah, relayed Jeremiah's letter to the exiles in Babylon (Jeremiah 29.3); and another, Gemariah, provided the venue for BARUCH to read Jeremiah's dictated scroll (Jeremiah 36.10–12). It was this Gemariah (Gemaryahu) – clearly an important official – whose inscribed seal has been found in Jerusalem, in the City of David.

Sheba, queen of The reputation of King SOLOMON had spread far and wide, according to the narrative of 1 Kings 10 (see also 2 Chronicles 9), and attracted the attention of this powerful 'queen of the south'. The story of her visit to Jerusalem is probably symbolic in that it attests to Solomon's fabled WISDOM. But it is plausible that she came for the practical purpose of negotiating a trade agreement. Sheba (or perhaps better Saba) controlled extensive trade routes from Arabia; in Solomon's time the Sabaeans may have been based in the east of modern Yemen, but their contacts extended to East Africa and India. Trading caravans dealing in spices, gold and precious stones (see 1 Kings 10.3, 10) travelled to the markets of DAMASCUS and Gaza by way of oases such as Mecca and Medina. In the New Testament MATTHEW 12.42 compares the 'queen of the south' favourably to the SCRIBES and PHARISEES. Ethiopian legends commemorate this queen as ruler of Ethiopia, and her son by Solomon as the first king of Ethiopia (Menelik I). She is unnamed in the Bible but Arabian legends call her Bilqis or Balkis.

Shechem Ancient Shechem (Tel Balatah) lies a mile and a half to the east of the modern West Bank city of Nablus, on a crossroads between Mount Ebal and Mount Gerizim (see SAMARITANS) in the hill country of Ephraim, 41 miles north of Jerusalem. It was an influential centre of commerce from the Middle Bronze Age to the late HELLENISTIC PERIOD (c.1900–100 BCE) and is mentioned frequently in Egyptian annals and in the Bible. Albrecht Alt called it the 'uncrowned queen of Palestine'. ABRAHAM passed through the city on his way to CANAAN (Genesis 12.6); JACOB bought a plot of land there (Genesis 33.19); it was the scene of the rape of Jacob's daughter Dinah by the eponymous Shechem in Genesis 34; Jacob's sons pastured flocks nearby (Genesis 37.12–14); and it is the traditional site of JOSEPH's burial place (Joshua 24.32). Judges 9 refers to the temple of 'BA'AL-berith' (Lord of the COVENANT) on the mountain overlooking Shechem, and describes the massacre conducted there by Abimelech (son of the judge GIDEON, or Jerubbaal) in seizing control of the city.

The city was destroyed by the ASSYRIANS in 722 BCE, but a Samaritan settlement was erected on the site 400 years later. That city was razed to the ground in 197 BCE by John Hyrcanus, the HASMONEAN ruler of Jerusalem, and it was never rebuilt. Archaeology, on that part of the site which has not been encroached upon by Nablus, has revealed city wall and gates, temples, houses, and a granary. Today the site, where mud-brick buildings are exposed, is in desperate need of conservation, being listed in the 2004 Watch List of the 100 most endangered archaeological sites in the world. Shechem should be distinguished from Sychar (the traditional site of Jacob's well) which lies just opposite, at the modern Al-Askar.

sheep, and the parable of the Sheep and the Goats Apparently there are more than 500 references to sheep in the Bible, a clear indication of the animal's economic importance (for food, milk, wool, and skins) as well as its symbolic significance (docile, easily led, and gregarious). The lamb is the sacrificial victim, literally as in the PASSOVER lamb, but then as a developed metaphor (most strikingly in Isaiah 53.6–7, and in the application of such ideas to the CRUCIFIXION of Christ – see Acts 8.32; 1 Peter 1.19). Jesus is 'the Lamb of God who takes away the sin of the world' (John 1.29; compare similar thought, but different words, in Revelation 5). Associated imagery is found in references to the lost sheep and the Good SHEPHERD (see also the SEVEN 'I AM' SAYINGS).

The PARABLE of the Sheep and the Goats in Matthew 25.31–46 is a representation of the LAST JUDGEMENT, when the SON OF MAN, in the manner of a shepherd, will separate the sheep from the goats; the sheep are placed on his right and the goats on his left (see Ezekiel 34.17–22; DIDACHE 12; compare 1 Kings 22.19). Those on the right share the inheritance of the KINGDOM OF GOD; those on the left the fate of eternal fire. The text has taken on the character of an APOCALYPTIC discourse or warning, rather than simply a parable. The original intention of the parable relates to a judgement on the basis of charitable deeds, and how active the believer has been. But Matthew's Gospel, with its awareness of the problems of a mission to the GENTILES ('nations'), suggests rather a judgement on the basis of how the Christian missionaries and their gospel have been received (compare Matthew 10.16–33).

Wilfred Thesiger, a celebrated explorer, described his experience of the annual migration of the Bakhtiari nomads from the Zagros mountains in Iran: 'the narrow track was choked for miles with a continuously moving string of beasts and people. Flocks of sheep and goats, the sheep white and the goats black, each in their separate herds.'

shekel *See* COINAGE; TEMPLE (for Temple tax).

shekinah This Hebrew word means a 'dwelling'; it comes from the same root as the word for TABERNACLE (or the temporary tented dwelling of God). In JUDAISM it is used as a reverential way of referring to the divine presence. During the period of the WILDERNESS wanderings, the Israelite tribes believed themselves to be accompanied by the divine presence, in the symbolic forms of cloud and fire. What was then an aura or sense of presence subsequently became almost personified as a distinct divine entity.

See further at GLORY.

shema' The Hebrew word *shema'* means 'Hear!' and is the opening word of Deuteronomy 6.4 ('Hear, O Israel: the Lord is our God, the Lord alone'). Deuteronomy 6.4–5 functions in Jewish PRAYER at morning and evening as a regular expression of belief, a kind of creed. It is used in the teaching of Jesus as part of a two-point summary of TORAH (the commandments of the LAW) based on LOVE (see Matthew 22.34–40; Mark 12.28–34).

Sheol The Hebrew word Sheol (*se'ol*) is used frequently (66 times) in the Old Testament for the ultimate place of the dead. In Numbers 16.30–33 the earth swallows whole the rebels from the company of Korah, who 'go down alive into Sheol'. Like the Greek 'Hades' it was not in itself a place of reward or punishment, merely the final destination of the dead. It is variously described as dark and disordered, a land of silence, a grimly gated city, and far from God's presence. When in later Hebrew thought ideas of heaven and hell were developed, Sheol remained as a kind of waiting-room. The original meaning of the word is uncertain, but it is possible to link it to the name of SAUL, his enquiry from the witch of Endor in 1 Samuel 28, and a Hebrew root *s'l* meaning 'ask'.

shepherd The natural, pastoralist image of shepherd and sheep is arguably the oldest metaphor for leadership in the Biblical world, applied to rulers both divine and human. The ideal shepherd is just and faithful; the metaphor signals prosperity, protection, and the provision of social order and justice. In the WILDERNESS wanderings God is the shepherd of his people, through the agency of MOSES and AARON (Psalm 77.20). The ideal king of Israel, and shepherd of God's people, was DAVID (2 Samuel 5.2; but compare NATHAN's parable in 2 Samuel 12.1–6). Later God will give judgement against the false shepherds and intervene personally to appoint a righteous Davidic shepherd (Jeremiah 23; Ezekiel 34). The New Testament develops this image with reference to Jesus (Mark 6.34): in Mark 6 Jesus is contrasted with HEROD as King of the Jews; Luke 15 tells the story of the lost sheep, and John 10 declares that Jesus is the good shepherd and the sheep gate (*see* SEVEN 'I AM' SAYINGS); in Revelation 7.17 Jesus is both slain lamb and reigning shepherd. Hebrews 13.20 invokes 'the God of PEACE, who brought back from the dead our Lord Jesus, the great shepherd of the sheep' and 1 Peter 2.25 says, 'You were going astray like sheep, but now you have returned to the shepherd and guardian of your souls.' The responsibility passes to the disciples and the Church leaders: see especially John 21.15–17 and 1 Peter 5.1–4.

shibboleth Shibboleth variously denotes a test case, a catchword, or an outdated (but none the less strongly held) principle. The origin of the expression is in the story of Judges 12: at verse 6 Jephthah and the Gileadites use it as a password. Their EPHRAIMITE enemies, when challenged at the ford of the river JORDAN, cannot pronounce the word (meaning 'ear of wheat' or 'stream') with the initial 'sh'; they can only manage to say 'sibboleth' and so betray themselves.

Shiloh Shiloh was an administrative and religious centre for the Israelite tribes within the period of the Judges (the last centuries of the 2nd millennium BCE). It was located in the territory of the tribe EPHRAIM. The ARK OF THE COVENANT rested here for several decades, until it was captured by the PHILISTINES.

In Genesis 49, within JACOB's blessing of his 12 sons (the ancestors of the twelve tribes of Israel) there is a puzzling reference to Shiloh at verse 10, within the blessing of JUDAH. There are various readings, including 'until Shiloh comes', which would suggest either a reference to the coming of MESSIAH or to a later hope in Judah that they would regain control over the Northern Kingdom. The gnomic phrase of Genesis 49.10 seems to be echoed in Ezekiel 21.27.

ships and the sea Although Israel was close to the Mediterranean Sea, the Israelites were not seafarers. In the Bible ships usually belonged to foreigners; CANAANITES, PHILISTINES and especially the PHOENICIANS made good use of the sea ('ships of Tarshish' – which *may* be Tartessus in Spain – see Ezekiel 27.25). By contrast Israel's attitude tended to be negative and distrustful (see Deuteronomy 28.68; Judges 5.17; Isaiah 33.21; Proverbs 30.19), with the exception of some trading during the time of SOLOMON.

While Israel is negative and fearful, it is Yahweh, the God of Israel, who created the waters and exercises power over the sea and its demons (Psalm 104.25–26; Isaiah 27.1). In the same way Jesus calms the storm on Galilee that terrifies his disciples (Mark 6.47–52). The Ark, which NOAH constructed on the God-given plan, was a refuge from the worst that the FLOOD could do. It should be no surprise that in the final book of the Bible, in the vision of a new heaven and earth, 'the sea was no more' (Revelation 21.1).

shophar The Hebrew *shophar* is a TRUMPET made from the horn of a ram (see Joshua 6.4), to be blown on ceremonial occasions. Originally it was sounded at the New Year Festival (Rosh Hashanah – see Leviticus 23.23–25) and on the Day of Atonement (YOM KIPPUR) and to herald the year of JUBILEE. It is now used more widely in the SYNA-GOGUE on SABBATH and feast days. *See also* CALENDAR and MUSICAL INSTRUMENTS.

showbread, or bread of the presence The offering of 'showbread' (also 'shew-bread') was to be found in the TABERNACLE and later in the TEMPLE, arranged on a table in the sanctuary in two rows, with six loaves in each row. New bread was provided at weekly intervals (see Leviticus 24.8); it was to be made of the choicest flour and topped with frankincense. Only the priests were permitted to eat it, according to Leviticus 24.5–9. There had to be special reasons for allowing DAVID and his men to eat it (1 Samuel 21.1–6); and this action was cited as a precedent for Jesus and his disciples (see Mark 2.23–28).

Shunammite woman, the *See* ELISHA.

Sidon *See* TYRE AND SIDON.

signs The importance of any sign lies not in itself, but in the thing or reality signified. In the Old Testament there are many signs of various types and the correct interpretation is vital – for example the rainbow after the FLOOD is a sign of God's everlasting COVENANT (Genesis 9.13). God's presence with his chosen people during the period of the EXODUS was marked with signs (as in signs and wonders), e.g. Exodus 4.28, where the PLAGUES to afflict EGYPT are in view. Many prophets marked out their ministry with signs and symbolic actions; for example JEREMIAH bought a field at Anathoth when land prices were at an all-time low, with the country besieged by the BABYLONIANS (Jeremiah 32.1–15). Madness at the time, but a reassuring sign that the current situation would not last for ever: 'For thus says the Lord of hosts, the God of Israel: Houses and fields and vineyards shall again be bought in this land' (Jeremiah 32.15). The most extreme, in giving signs to validate and reinforce his message, was EZEKIEL, who on one occasion had to lie on his side for a lengthy period, enduring a restricted diet to show the realities of life and despair awaiting the people of JERUSALEM under siege (Ezekiel 4.1–17).

The New Testament apparently displays ambivalence towards signs. Plenty of MIRACLES are recorded of Jesus in the SYNOPTIC Gospels – healings, EXORCISMS and nature miracles of great power; these showed his status. 'Jesus of Nazareth, a man attested to you by God with deeds of power, wonders, and signs that God did through him among you, as you yourselves know' (Acts 2.22). Such activity is also recorded of the APOSTLES in the early Church (Acts 4.30, 5.12). Indeed, PAUL claimed through Christ to have won the obedience of his GENTILE converts, not just by his preaching, but also 'by the power of signs and wonders'. On the other hand: 'This generation is an evil generation; it asks for a sign, but no sign will be given to it except the sign of JONAH' (Luke 11.29). This disparagement of the desire for a sign validating Jesus' messiahship or real status is typical of the other side of the New Testament's attitude to signs. The people's desire for the spectacular with no understanding of what is really being shown about Jesus is firmly rejected. This may lie behind the story of the TEMPTATIONS, where Jesus sternly rejects the headlong fall from the TEMPLE tower and an ensuing angelic rescue mission (see Matthew 4.5–6); observers would have been won over superficially, but without comprehension and commitment.

The word 'sign' is distinctively and deliberately used for the miracles of Jesus in JOHN'S GOSPEL. This sharpens the ambivalence towards signs by deliberately focusing on a small number of miracles, calling a selection of them signs, and making theological points or explanatory narratives with them, and then abandoning the wealth of other miracles that were probably available to him in the tradition (see John 2.23; 21.25).

Traditionally scholars have maintained that there are seven signs in the Fourth Gospel, to match the SEVEN 'I AM' SAYINGS, and for this reason the tabulation of the contents of the Gospel of John indicates them as they occur. In fact one might argue that things are not so clear-cut.

Sign 1: the turning of water into wine at the wedding at CANA in Galilee, 2.1–11.
Sign 2: the healing of the official's son, 4.46–54.
Sign 3: the healing on the SABBATH, 5.1–18.
Sign 4: the feeding of the 5000, 6.1–15.
Sign 5: the walking on the water, 6.16–24.
Sign 6: the cure of the blind man, 9.1–12.
Sign 7: the raising of LAZARUS, 11.1–44.

There is a developed debate, dialogue, or teaching attached to signs 3, 4, 6, and 7. 'I am' sayings are embedded in the stories of signs 4, 6, and 7. Nothing is developed of the potential symbolism in signs 1, 2, and 5. If the focus was not so strongly on the number seven, one might wish to consider also including other incidents within the category of signs, as being acted out prophetic symbols: the CLEANSING OF THE TEMPLE early in Jesus' ministry (2.13–22), and the FOOT-WASHING at the Last Supper (*see* EUCHARIST) (13.1–15). Interestingly Jesus' actions provoke a demand from the Jews for a sign validating his right to cleanse the Temple (2.18) and they are offered a coded sign of the Temple – destroyed and rebuilt – that is, the DEATH OF CHRIST and his RESURRECTION on the third day. In John this is the supreme thing signified, together with the reality that Jesus must be the SON OF GOD in order to accomplish it. This is also represented in the sign of Jonah, the only sign offered in Luke 11.29, because Jonah emerged from the whale on the third day.

Silas Silas was a member of the Jerusalem Church, well equipped to work in a wider MISSION field. He had prophetic gifts, and was able to work with the mixed Jewish/ GENTILE Church in ANTIOCH when he took to them the decree from the Council of Jerusalem (Acts 15). Later he became a staunch companion of PAUL on his later missionary journeys, after Paul's rift with BARNABAS over the role of JOHN MARK. Like Paul he was a Roman citizen, which proved useful when travelling ever westwards, in the European part of the Roman Empire (Acts 16). He is mentioned not only in Acts but also, if he is to be identified with Silvanus, in several of the epistles. He may also have acted as an assistant to Peter in writing PETER'S FIRST LETTER.

Siloam, Pool of HEZEKIAH, king of Judah, anticipating the siege of JERUSALEM by the Assyrian SENNACHERIB, arranged for the construction of a tunnel from the spring Gihon to bring a supply of water within the city of David. This was a major project of engineering, with two teams of tunnellers working from opposite ends and meeting in the middle; the Siloam Inscription is a plaque celebrating the feat, which is now in the museum at Istanbul. Water flowed through the 1750-foot length of what is still known as Hezekiah's Tunnel from Gihon to the Pool of Siloam.

The prophet ISAIAH, contemporary with Hezekiah, refers to 'the gently flowing waters of Siloam' (8.6). After the Babylonian EXILE, according to NEHEMIAH 3.15, a certain Shallun rebuilt 'the wall of the Pool of Shiloah by the King's Garden'. In the time of Jesus the Pool of Siloam is the setting for the cure of the man who had been blind from birth (JOHN 9.1–7). Finally, in the Byzantine period, Empress Eudocia (c.400–460 CE) built a church and a pool where the water emerges from Hezekiah's Tunnel, to commemorate the miraculous healing of the blind man.

Early in the 20th century archaeologists discovered the remains of the Byzantine church, now under a mosque. But as a result of the latest discoveries, it is now thought that the pool in the time of Jesus was in a different place, just to the south-east, adjacent to the area known as the King's Garden and on land owned by the Greek Orthodox Church. Here an area with sets of steps, and coins dating the construction to the 1st century BCE, were found by archaeologists in June 2004. The earlier pools may still lie underneath.

Silvanus *See* PETER, FIRST LETTER OF; SILAS.

Simeon 1 Simeon is the second son of JACOB by his first wife LEAH (see Genesis 49.5–7). Together with his brother LEVI, Simeon massacred the men of SHECHEM, to avenge the rape of their sister Dinah (Genesis 34). He is told that as a consequence his descendants will be scattered. He is the ancestor of the tribe of Simeon, which was initially allocated land in the territory of JUDAH.

2 Simeon is a 'righteous and devout' man in Jerusalem (see Luke 2.25–35). It is often claimed that he was an elderly priest, but Luke does not say so explicitly. He is said to have been 'looking forward to the consolation of Israel'; in other words, he was expecting the coming of MESSIAH. Along with the prophetess ANNA, he recognized the child Jesus as the Messiah, when Jesus' parents presented him in the TEMPLE. As he held Jesus in his arms, according to Luke's account, he uttered the words of praise, well known from their subsequent use in the LITURGY, that are called the NUNC DIMITTIS (from the Latin translation, the VULGATE; see Luke 2.29–32).

For Simeon Niger *see* SIMON OF CYRENE.

Simon the Cananaean, or Simon the Zealot or 'Patriot' Simon occupies one of the penultimate places in the listing of the DISCIPLES of Jesus, just before JUDAS ISCARIOT. In Mark 3.18 he is called 'Simon the Cananaean' while in Luke 6.15 he is known as 'Simon who is called the Zealot'. The two terms are identical, because

'Cananaean' comes from an ARAMAIC root word meaning someone with religious zeal (and nothing to do with Canaan). Nothing is known of Simon beyond the assumption that he must have belonged to the ZEALOT party among the Jews. There is an apocryphal text, *The Passion of Simon and Jude*, which relates their mission and martyrdom in Persia. In the Churches of the West, Simon and JUDE are usually coupled together, with the same feast day on 28 October.

Simon of Cyrene The name Simon is a later form of the Old Testament name Simeon. As a common name there is much scope for confusion, or erroneous equations, between characters in the Bible with this name. Simon of Cyrene is the man who was compelled to carry the cross for Christ (according to Mark 15.21). Mark identifies Simon as the father of Alexander and Rufus, presumably because they were known in the Roman Church (if that is where MARK'S GOSPEL was published). For Rufus ('red') see Romans 16.13. It is possible that Simon of Cyrene is identical with the Simeon (Niger) at Antioch in Acts 13.1.

Simon Magus Simon/Simeon is a common name, but this particular Simon appears in Acts 8.9–24. He was a charlatan who practised sorcery and had gained a reputation in SAMARIA as 'the power of God that is called Great'. He had been converted and baptized during the ministry of PHILIP; he was so impressed by the miracles worked by the APOSTLES that he offered them money for a share in the power of the Holy SPIRIT (hence the term 'simony' for trying to buy spiritual powers). He was severely reprimanded by PETER.

Simon later appears (in 2nd-century texts) as Simon Magus (Simon the magician – *see* MAGI), an early heretic who is also regarded as the father of GNOSTICISM. There are probably two distinct traditions here. The magician appears in the apocryphal *Acts of Peter*, where he is fatally injured by a fall during a conjuring trick before Emperor Nero. The Gnostic teacher is also Simon, from Gitta in Samaria, who supposedly came to Rome in the time of the earlier Emperor Claudius. This Simon may actually be a figure of the 2nd century CE, part of a Simonian movement opposed by Irenaeus; their ideas focused on Simon's companion, Helen, who was primary 'Thought', creator of the lower world, but trapped in the body of a prostitute.

Simon Peter *see* PETER.

sin Sin is a Biblical concept for anything that lies outside the proper relationship between humanity and GOD (see Romans 14.23). An action or attitude that is in opposition to God's purpose (as expressed in CREATION, ongoing care, COVENANT and LAW) is regarded as sin, as an offence or a rebellion against God. Human guilt is seen as constituted by such a wilful stance against God.

The basic Greek word for 'sin', as used in the New Testament, is *hamartia*; this occurs in the plural for a number of offences or sins, or in the singular, often as the collective concept of sin. The fundamental meaning of this word was to miss the target or to fall short of it. So what might be a military (or sporting) metaphor comes to denote a failure to meet God's demands. In the Hebrew Bible there is a very similar idea in the Hebrew word *hata'*, which also indicates failure to reach a target, and then the violation of God's law. Another Hebrew word used in this context is *pasa'* which begins from the idea of rebellion (which may be an action against the king or against God). Both Hebrew roots are found together in Job 34.37: 'he adds rebellion to his sin; he claps his hands among us, and multiplies his words against God' (see also Isaiah 43.27). A third Hebrew word, *'awon*, introduces an explicit reference to human guilt in addition to the idea of error and offence.

There are parallels to all three of these component ideas from the Hebrew in the letters of PAUL: firstly, in Romans 3.23 – 'since all have sinned and fall short of the glory of God'; secondly, in 1 Corinthians 8.12 – 'when you thus sin against members of your family ... you sin against Christ'; and thirdly, in Romans 8.3 – 'God ... condemned sin in the flesh'. In the LORD'S PRAYER (Matthew 6 and Luke 11) the fifth petition associates God's forgiveness of human sins with human forgiveness of others; this reflects a Jewish tradition that sin is a kind of debt to be paid. Other New Testament words used in the context of sin include *anomia* (lawlessness) and *asebeia* (impiety).

See also HUMAN NATURE.

Sinai, or Horeb Mount Sinai is the traditional mountain site for the giving of the law to MOSES and Israel (*see* DECALOGUE). Here God made a COVENANT with the Hebrews whom Moses had led out of captivity in Egypt. The mountain can also be referred to as Horeb; this is either an alternative name in another tribal tradition, or it could denote the wider mountainous area in the Sinai desert, of which Sinai, 'the mountain of God', is a specific peak.

Another reference to Horeb, much later than the context of the giving of the Mosaic law, concerns ELIJAH's journey to 'the mountain of God' in 1 Kings 19.8.

There is some doubt about the precise location of Mount Sinai. Early Christian tradition identified it with Jebel Musa ('the Mount of Moses'), in the valley below which sits the monastery dedicated to St Catherine of Alexandria in 527 CE. The monastery was built on the orders of the Roman Emperor Justinian, to replace a fortified church associated with St Helena on her Holy Land pilgrimage in 326 CE. The Mount of Moses rises to some 7500 feet, and 2700 rocky steps lead from the monastery to the summit. One problem with this identification is the length of detour through the rough southern terrain which the Israelites would have made in order to reach it. Accordingly some scholars have preferred an identification with a more northerly site, Jebel Hillal. *See* EXODUS and accompanying map.

Sinaiticus Sinaiticus is a codex (manuscript in book form) of the Bible in GREEK, written in the middle of the 4th century CE, the earliest manuscript of the complete NEW TESTAMENT, as well as an important witness to approximately half of the books of the OLD TESTAMENT; it also contains two early extra-canonical Christian texts, the *Epistle of Barnabas* and the *Shepherd of Hermas*. It is named after the Greek Orthodox monastery of St Catherine, near the foot of Mount Sinai in Egypt, where the codex was discovered by the German Biblical scholar Constantine Tischendorf in 1859. The monks believed that Tischendorf was borrowing the codex for copying. He did indeed publish the text, but he took 43 leaves to Germany, which are in the University of Leipzig, and gave 347 leaves to Tsar Aleksandr II of Russia, which were placed in the Imperial Library. These were sold by the Soviet Government in 1933 to raise money, and were bought by the British Library, after a public appeal, for what was at the time a record sale price for a manuscript of £100,000.

Sirach, the Wisdom of Jesus ben Sirach *See* ECCLESIASTICUS.

Sisera Sisera was a military commander from CANAAN who was defeated by the Israelite forces of DEBORAH and Barak, when battle was joined 'by the waters of Megiddo' (ARMAGEDDON; see Judges 4–5). His name is not a Semitic one, and perhaps should be linked to the PHILISTINES. He was subsequently lured into her tent and murdered by a KENITE woman, Jael the wife of Heber (see Judges 4.17–22).

six hundred and sixty-six 666 is the number of the Beast in REVELATION 13.18 (*see* NUMBER SYMBOLISM). The alternative reading of 616 is not well supported; it may be a creation of copyists seeking to solve the puzzle of this coded number.

slavery Slavery was an accepted part of the socio-economic world of both the Old Testament and the New Testament, from the earliest to Roman times. So ABRAHAM took slaves with him as part of his WEALTH when he began his epic journey from HARAN (Genesis 12.5). Slaves were used for domestic and farming purposes, and also to breed children (*see* MARRIAGE). Some were born into slavery, some were sold into it, to escape debt and destitution, while some chose slavery voluntarily (see Deuteronomy 15.12–17). The experience of JOSEPH (in Genesis 37.25–28; 39.1), involving Ishmaelites (or Midianites) and POTIPHAR in Egypt, illustrates the widespread practice of slavery.

The LAW codes of the Hebrew Bible (*see* TORAH) were very fair in how a slave should be treated, and respected the rights of female slaves used for sexual relations. Regulations existed for the freeing of slaves in the seventh year of their slavery (see Exodus 21.2; Leviticus 25.40). It is unclear how far these were wishful thinking. The fact that laws exist which envisage a slave being beaten to death also suggests that such cruelty did happen (see Exodus 21.20–21).

In the New Testament Christians came into contact with the practice of slavery in the Roman Empire, largely in the GENTILE lands away from Judaea. Slaves converted to Christianity in considerable numbers, but there was no question of their new religion exciting them either to rebel or to pursue a quest for freedom. In fact a common reading of the letter to PHILEMON is that it concerns a runaway slave, Onesimus; Paul would return him to his rightful owner, although he would have liked to keep him. The household codes recommended for Christians take the fact of slavery for granted (see Colossians 3.22–25; Ephesians 6.5–8). The institution of slavery, and the injustice of it to modern eyes, is never questioned in the Bible. Modern revulsion at the notion is datable to the 18th-century evangelical Christians who applied other Biblical principles of LOVE and JUSTICE to make a critique of this age-old institution.

Smyrna Smyrna is the second of the seven Churches of Asia Minor addressed in the second and third chapters of the book of REVELATION. Today it is the busy city of Izmir in modern Turkey, situated 40 miles north of EPHESUS, but even in ancient times it was a large city and port on the gulf into which flowed the river Hermus. It was a

Greek city which became part of the Ionian League. Traditionally, according to the orator Aristides, it was founded at least three times, most recently by Alexander the Great; its destruction and rising again like a phoenix from the ashes may be echoed in Revelation 2.8.

The name Smyrna may be related to the Greek word for 'myrrh' (*smurna*) and 'the symbolism of weeping, burial and resurrection attached to myrrh may have been reflected in the portrayal of a city of suffering' (Colin Hemer). Traditionally the poet Homer is associated with Smyrna; a further possibility, therefore, is the echo of the Niobe theme ('like Niobe all tears') from Homer's *Iliad* 24.602–617. Here 'ten days' (see Revelation 2.10) is stipulated as a period for mourning. And there is a local association of a Hittite carving (Tas Suret), nearby on Mount Sipylus, which has been identified as Niobe.

Smyrna became an important Christian centre early in the 2nd century CE. Ignatius of Antioch, travelling to martyrdom in Rome, stopped here and wrote to four other Churches in the region, as well as writing to Smyrna, and its bishop Polycarp, from TROAS. The *Acts of Paul* and the *Acts of John* record visits to Smyrna of their respective apostles.

Sodom Sodom is one of the 'cities of the Plain' (Genesis 19), in the area of the DEAD SEA, but its exact location is unknown. The story of Sodom (the origin of the verb 'sodomize') is often used especially by Christian religious leaders as an argument against HOMOSEXUAL relationships, together with the proof text from LEVITICUS 18.22 ('You shall not lie with a male as with a woman; it is an abomination'). But an Orthodox Jewish rabbi, Steven Greenberg, in *Wrestling with God and Men* (Eurospan, 2004) argues that the prohibition in Leviticus is more accurately interpreted as banning acts of sexual domination ('You shall not sexually penetrate a male to humiliate; it is an abomination'). The point was to prevent violent and destructive sexual relationships, rather than to prohibit loving sexual relationships of equality; the 'reading offers gay people a way to reconnect to God, Torah and the Jewish people'.

soldiers of Christ This designation of early Christians derives from PAUL's description of his co-workers (see Philippians 2.25; Philemon 2; also 2 Timothy 2.3–4). In the context such military language is figurative, borrowed from the familiar image of the Roman legionary, and does not prejudge the issue about engaging in literal warfare or maintaining pacifism (*see* WAR and PEACE). The classic study of the subject is Adolf Harnack's *Militia Christi* (1905).

Solomon Solomon was the second child of BATHSHEBA by King DAVID (2 Samuel 12); at the time of David's death, Bathsheba organized the succession of Solomon to become the third king of Israel, with the help of the prophet NATHAN (see 1 Kings 1). According to 1 Kings 4.21, 'he was sovereign over all the kingdoms from the Euphrates to the land of the PHILISTINES, even to the border of Egypt'. Solomon instituted an extensive building programme, including the TEMPLE in Jerusalem, and fortified cities throughout his empire. In financial terms, although he negotiated many trade agreements with other nations, he was also responsible for dispersing the nation's resources by his lavish expenditure, and was compelled to unpopular measures of punitive taxation and conscripted labour. His international alliances were sealed by the polygamous acquisition of foreign wives (*see* MARRIAGE) with the consequence of religious SYNCRETISM (see 1 Kings 11). He was renowned for his expertise in WISDOM, represented by proverbs and riddles as well as decisions of JUSTICE. His wisdom apparently attracted the attention of the Queen of SHEBA (see 1 Kings 10.1–13). But the association with the Wisdom literature that bears his name is only the result of later tradition based on his reputation. *See also* SONG OF SONGS.

Son of God In the Gospel of Mark the title 'Son of God' is used at strategic points throughout the narrative:

- The divine voice at the BAPTISM of Jesus and the TRANSFIGURATION (1.11; 9.7)
- How Jesus is recognized by demons or 'unclean spirits' (3.11; 5.7)
- Jesus' answer – 'I am' – to the High Priest's question (14.61)
- The acknowledgement by the centurion at the time of Jesus' death (15.39).

Scholars are divided as to whether this title occurred in the original version of the Gospel's opening verse (as part of the book's title). 'Son of God' is not simply a synonym for the Davidic MESSIAH ('the Christ'), so, if the text refers to 'Christ, the Son of God' (1.1), it is claiming that Jesus is not only the coming Jewish king but also represents a participation in the lordship of God.

For the wider view *see* TITLES OF JESUS.

Son of Man The Gospel sayings about the 'Son of Man' fall into three distinct categories:

1. Sayings concerned with the present, earthly situation of Jesus
2. Sayings concerned with the PASSION (suffering) of Jesus
3. Sayings that relate to a future coming of the 'Son of Man' and the triumph of an eschatological figure.

See further on the TITLES OF JESUS.

Song of Songs, Song of Solomon, or Canticles In recent times, the focus of interest in this text has been its literary character, possibly derived from Egyptian love poetry, and its potential as a feminist Biblical text, which gives at least equal weight to the woman's point of view as to the man's. Historically it ranked as one of the most important texts for Christian devotion, as a powerful allegorical statement of Christ's love for his Church, expressed through the individual believer or the religious community. It had finally been accepted in Jewish scriptures, following the fervent advocacy of Rabbi Akiva (who called it the 'Holy of Holies' of scripture), also as an ALLEGORY, of the relationship of God to Israel.

At heart it is a rich, sensual, indeed erotic, love song, which may have originated in the preparations for, or the LITURGY of, a MARRIAGE celebration. Its structure has been analysed in a variety of ways, either as a collection (an anthology) of separate poems or a single drama; in the latter case its plot-line is not explicit and needs to be supplied by a reconstructed story. The attribution to SOLOMON can only be traditional; in its present form the composition seems to date from the 4th or 3rd century BCE. As a literary text it repays close study, both in comparison with other love poetry of the ancient Near East, and in its use of imagery from the GEOGRAPHY, flora and fauna of Israel, as well as allusions to the story of the Garden of EDEN in Genesis.

Sons of Thunder JAMES and JOHN, the sons of ZEBEDEE, are given an additional name by Jesus, when he appoints his DISCIPLES (see Mark 3.17). This name is 'Boanerges' which Mark translates here as 'Sons of Thunder'. It is usually interpreted as referring to a psychological trait, that is hot-tempered; but the actual meaning of the term is obscure.

sophist The Greek word means a wise man, someone knowledgeable about religion and such matters, a professional teacher of WISDOM and the art of rhetoric (public speaking in the law-court or the political Assembly). In popular usage it comes to denote, rather less flatteringly, an 'alternative' philosopher whose art is to ask awkward questions, inspire others, and rely on the innate skills of human wisdom, supported by rational evidence. He is essentially freelance, perhaps slightly disreputable, and maybe someone who teaches on street corners (or the equivalent of a soap-box at Hyde Park's Speakers' Corner), but certainly charges a considerable fee. He would teach virtue, but be less concerned with truth. Socrates in Classical Athens of the 5th century BCE would not have been entitled to call himself a sophist; in fact he regarded them with scorn and ironic contempt, although some would say that he behaved rather in the way the later sophists did.

What would ordinary citizens of a Hellenistic city have been likely to think if they came across Christian missionaries like PHILIP, BARNABAS, or PAUL preaching at a street corner or in a marketplace (*see* MISSION)? The answer is that it would be nothing unusual. They might even have gone out into the street to hear such preaching. What Acts 17 says about the Athenians was true of the people of the Mediterranean world in general: 'All the Athenians and the foreigners living there would spend their time in nothing but telling or hearing something new' (17.21). This task was met by many wandering preachers propagating their various schemes of salvation in the streets and markets of the cities and also at the staging posts on the great highways. For those interested in ideas there were alternatives to the sophists in the marketplace: there were Cynic philosophers in the schoolroom; the possibility of a teacher–student relationship in a private home, with the help of a patron; or a range of voluntary associations to join.

Sower, parable of the Jesus' PARABLE of the Sower is to be found in each of the SYNOPTIC gospels (Matthew 13.3–8; Mark 4.3–8; Luke 8.4–8) as well as in a simpler version in the gospel of THOMAS (sayings 8–9). The basic story is drawn from contemporary agricultural practice, where the seed is sown broadcast and some falls on the path, or among rocks or thorns, and only a proportion produces a harvest from good soil. This way of sowing may seem to be an uneconomic procedure, but it happened because in Palestine sowing preceded ploughing. The sower 'took the risk of broadcasting seed high in the air so that it landed where it could not flourish, or the birds might gobble it, or it might yield a hundredfold. He was not a nervous, edgy character; he did not narrowcast, concerned only with the purity of the few' (Lavinia Byrne). The story thus presents a challenge, with preaching and teaching (*see* MISSION) represented as the sowing of seed, with a view to gathering the harvest, that is the coming KINGDOM OF GOD, in the End Time (*see* ESCHATON). Christ's ministry reveals the secret of this kingdom to the DISCIPLES (Mark 4.11).

The story is followed by an interpretation (see, for example, Mark 4.13–20) which develops the explanation in more sophisticated terms that verge on ALLEGORY. This fits the context of the early Christian Church, where the rocks and thorns become the circumstances of PERSECUTION and worldliness that threaten the success of the mission. The message of the parable becomes a psychological exhortation to test the genuineness of conversion. The interpretation is not strictly consistent but blends two themes, of the seed identified as the Word of God, and of the crop composed of various types of people.

Spain The last days of PAUL, and his ultimate fate in ROME (or possibly elsewhere) are topics that are not recorded specifically in the New Testament. The evidence for a conjectured journey to Spain is based firstly on the hope expressed by Paul in ROMANS 15.24, 28 that he might travel as planned from Jerusalem to Rome and then on to Spain, and secondly on the complete silence of the documents as to whether he ever carried out the last stage of these plans. The narrative of the ACTS OF THE APOSTLES, which charts Paul's other journeys and his shipwreck on the way to Rome, finishes on the triumphant note that he was preaching unhindered in the capital city and heart of the Roman Empire (Acts 28.30–31). It remains possible that he was able to travel in the western Mediterranean before his (traditional) martyrdom in Rome at the time of Emperor Nero (*see* MARTYR). But the New Testament does not tell us, and later writers (*1 Clement*; the *Muratorian Canon*; and the *Acts of Peter*) seem to have no more hard evidence than we do. If the PASTORAL EPISTLES are late but authentic writings of Paul, then they might suggest a further stage of journeying, but this is the *eastern* rather than the *western* Mediterranean, after the end of the Acts of the Apostles (see 2 Timothy 4).

spikenard An aromatic herb with a pungent root, spikenard or nard (*Nardostachys jatamansi*) is related to valerian. It was used by the ancient Egyptians as an aromatic and is mentioned in the SONG OF SONGS (chs. 1 and 4). It was the perfume used by the woman in Mark 14 (and by Mary of Bethany in John 12) to anoint Jesus shortly before his death. Roman perfumiers used it in the preparation of *nardinum*, a celebrated scented oil.

Spirit, Holy Spirit In the Hebrew Bible the original idea of a 'spirit' was as a creative life-force, such as 'a wind from God' in Genesis 1.2. There are comparatively few references to the specific idea of a Holy Spirit from God (but see Isaiah 32.15–17; 63.10; Ezekiel 36.26–27; Psalms 51.10–12; 143.10). This is found more frequently in the QUMRAN scrolls and in other inter-testamental Jewish texts. Because of the developed Israelite belief in one GOD (monotheism) the definition of the Spirit as belonging to God is essential; but when in the latter part of the Old Testament period the otherness and distance of God was dominant in their experience, so the importance grew of mediating figures, such as agents and spirits of God.

In the New Testament the Spirit plays an essential part in the BIRTH OF JESUS (see Matthew 1.18; Luke 1.35). The visible descent of the dove at the time of Jesus' BAPTISM is interpreted as an empowerment by the Spirit (see Mark 1.10; John 1.32; Acts 10.38). JOHN THE BAPTIST predicts that Jesus will baptize with the Spirit (see Mark 1.8). It is

also the Spirit that drives Jesus out into the wilderness for a period of testing (see Matthew 4.1; Mark 1.12; and TEMPTA-TIONS). But John 7.39 explains why dur-ing the MINISTRY of Jesus the Spirit was not made more widely available: 'as yet there was no Spirit, because Jesus was not yet glorified'.

The Dove

According to the ACTS OF THE APOSTLES (2.1–21) the beginnings of what became the Christian Church took place on the feast of PENTECOST with the outpouring of the Holy Spirit upon Jesus' followers, in fulfilment of the prediction of the prophet JOEL (Joel 2.28–32). Subsequent expansion of the believing community is often attributed by New Testament writers to the action of the Spirit. The activity of the Spirit was experienced in a variety of ways, as PAUL indicates in 1 Corinthians 12.4–11; this was not always unproblematic, as Paul shows when discussing Spirit-inspired speaking with tongues in 1 Corinthians 14; 1 John 4 also illustrates the problem of discrimin-ating between true and false spirits. The most developed theology of the Holy Spirit in the New Testament is to be found in the latter part of JOHN'S GOSPEL with the statements about the PARACLETE or Comforter/Strengthener (see John 14.16–17, 26; 15.26–27; 16.5–15).

spirituality, Biblical basis for The term 'spirituality' refers to people's personal and most intimate convictions and motivations; it is a source of energy generating a sense of purpose and a recognition of values in social life. Traditionally spirituality stands for a life of PRAYER and contemplation, for LITURGY and the attitude of waiting on God, most marked in the discipline of the monastic community. The Benedictine watchword 'Pray and work' (*Ora et labora*) indicates a parallel between prayer and action. In the era of Liberation Theology, the Vancouver Assembly of the World Council of Churches (1983) affirmed that 'the spiritual struggle of the Church must involve it in the struggle of the poor, the oppressed, the alienated and the exiled. The Spirit is among struggling people.' In the words of Nikolai Berdiaev, rice for myself alone may be unspiritual, but rice for my hungry sister and brother is spiritual.

The Bible is full of evidence for a publicly engaged spirituality, including acts of non-violent resistance. In particular the Hebrew prophets are examples of a spiritu-ality which challenges the structures of injustice and unmasks the misuse of power. The same is true of the Gospel accounts of Jesus' proclamation and action. The story of Jesus' TEMPTATIONS can be seen as a model for the spirituality of resistance. PAUL uses the imagery of struggle to describe the Christian spiritual life, a struggle not against flesh and blood, but against the cosmic powers and evil forces of this present darkness (see Ephesians 6.10–17).

Star of David The modern Jewish symbol, commonly called the 'Star of David' or properly the *magen* or shield of DAVID, is the national symbol of the state of Israel. It is a hexagram or six-pointed star, assembled from two equilateral triangles pointing up and down. It probably originated as a symbol representing fire and water, perhaps with magical properties as a shield against evil powers. There are various associations with JUDAISM from the Middle Ages: Jewish amulets from the 12th century; a specific Jewish symbol from the 17th century; then adopted as a ZIONIST symbol; and in 1948 incorporated in the flag of Israel. The connection with David is unclear; it does not appear to have any basis in Rabbinic texts. But there is a possible link with the prophecy of BALAAM in Numbers 24.17: 'I see the nation of Israel. A king, like a bright star, will arise in that nation.'

stations of the cross These are 14 traditional representations, often in the form of paintings or carvings, of stages in the last journey of Christ from PILATE's house to CALVARY and the tomb. They may be identified in a sequence for an act of PILGRIMAGE, or arranged around the walls of a church for devotional purposes. Many of them correspond to aspects of the PASSION NARRATIVE (or account of the suffering of Jesus, as harmonized from the texts of the four Gospels), but some of them come from later traditions or are embellishments of the story. The practice of observing the stations in devotion probably dates back to early Christian pilgrims who would follow the route in Jerusalem, particularly on the night of Holy Thursday or on Good Friday; but it became a much more widespread practice in the Middle Ages, being popularized by the Franciscan friars in the 14th century.

These are the incidents commemorated:

1. Christ is condemned to death
2. Christ receives the cross
3. He falls for the first time
4. He meets MARY his mother
5. SIMON OF CYRENE is made to carry the cross
6. Christ's face is wiped by VERONICA
7. He falls for the second time
8. He meets the women of Jerusalem
9. He falls for the third time
10. Christ is stripped of his garments
11. He is nailed to the cross
12. Christ dies on the cross
13. His body is taken down from the cross (DEPOSITION)
14. His body is placed in the tomb.

In JERUSALEM today the Way of the Cross, the Way of Sorrows or Via Dolorosa, 'is defined by faith not history'; the route 'has little chance of corresponding to historical reality' (Jerome Murphy-O'Connor). It is most likely that Pilate will have condemned Jesus to death on the other side of the city, at the Palace of HEROD, the

Citadel. The likely route to execution will have been 'east on David Street, north on the Triple Suk, and then west to GOLGOTHA'.

The 14 stations of the traditional route stretch between the Muslim and Christian quarters of Jerusalem, the first nine in the Muslim quarter and the last five within the Church of the Holy Sepulchre itself (*see* CHURCHES, CHRISTIAN), on the site where tradition claims that Helena, mother of the Roman Emperor Constantine, found a fragment of the True Cross. The earlier stations in the Muslim quarter are identified as follows:

1. Monastery of the Flagellation, within the Mamluk college Madrasa el-Omariyya
2. Outside the Franciscan complex of the Monastery of the Flagellation
3. A small chapel
4. The Armenian Church of Our Lady of the Spasm, built over a Crusader church
5. A Franciscan oratory
6. Chapel of St Veronica
7. A Franciscan chapel
8. A cross on the wall of a Greek Orthodox monastery
9. An Ethiopian monastery.

Stephen Stephen is traditionally regarded as the first Christian MARTYR; his death is recorded in the Acts of the Apostles (7.58–8.1). He is one of seven men appointed by the apostles to assist with problems, including food distribution. The seven are known as 'Hellenists', probably because their native language was GREEK (they all have Greek names – *stephanos* means 'crown') while being JEWISH-CHRISTIANS from the DIASPORA. Stephen's work was impressive, but provoked jealousy and argument, leading to his arrest on charges similar to those brought against Jesus. The HIGH PRIEST and elders listen to a speech/sermon (rather than a response to the charges, it is a sample of early Christian preaching which Luke gives in Acts 7) and then order him to be taken out to suffer the death penalty by stoning. There are two notable details in this death: one is Stephen's vision of Jesus as the SON OF MAN seen standing ready for intervention, rather than traditionally seated beside God (7.55–56); the other is the fact that Saul (PAUL) is implicated in the death (8.1).

stigmata In origin the stigmata are the wounds of Christ's CRUCIFIXION, as revealed for THOMAS to see and touch, that is the wound of the spear in his side and the marks of the nails in his hands (see John 20.25–29). They may also include wounds on the feet, marks on the head made by the CROWN OF THORNS, and scarring on the shoulders and back, from the scourging and from carrying the cross. In Christian tradition some saints (in particular St Francis of Assisi in 1224) have claimed to have the marks of these wounds reproduced on their own bodies, perhaps because of the intensity of their identification with the sufferings of Christ.

Stoic A Stoic was a follower of the school of moral philosophy founded by Zeno at the beginning of the 3rd century BCE. Stoics believed that the duty of human beings was to follow reason and the natural law, and to suppress emotion. A belief of head rather than heart, Stoicism advocated the virtues of humanity and tolerance, as well as the appropriateness of suicide as a last resort. A number of the eminent figures of

Stoning of Stephen Acts 7.54–60

Roman society, such as the writer and teacher Seneca in the 1st century CE, were committed Stoics.

stoning This was the routine method of execution for Jews from earliest times. So Achan, with his family and animals, was stoned in retribution for disobeying the laws of holy WAR by removing loot for his own use from what should have been dedicated to God and destroyed (Joshua 7). The punishment was specified in the TORAH as appropriate for those approaching the holy mountain (Exodus 19.13), and for those inciting to IDOLATRY (Deuteronomy 13.9). The method of throwing stones meant that the executioners did not touch the victim.

Jesus was invited to rule on the case of the woman taken in ADULTERY, which legally would/could have resulted in her being stoned to death; but his method of dealing with the problem saved her life (John 8.7). STEPHEN, the first Christian MARTYR, died in this way (Acts 7), despite the evidence that in Jesus' execution the Jews apparently lacked jurisdiction, and had to defer to the Romans (*see* TRIAL OF JESUS); perhaps this suggests that in Stephen's case this was more the action of a lynch-mob.

The Mishnah tractate *Sanhedrin*, which sets out judicial rules, later than the New Testament period, but possibly applicable to it, gives directions for stoning procedures (6.1–4), and also maintains that the appropriate sentence for BLASPHEMY is hanging. Elsewhere the Talmudic tractate *Sanhedrin* 43a claims, in contrast to the Gospel accounts, that Jesus was preceded by a herald, inviting help with his defence, for 40 days before execution by stoning; although it then goes on to say that he was in fact hanged. The Romans are in no way involved in Jesus' death in this version of events, which may be the result of special pleading.

Succoth *See* TABERNACLES, FEAST OF.

Sumerians The Sumerians were the earliest known inhabitants of Mesopotamia, at the end of the 4th millennium BCE. They were organized in a series of city-states, of which UR, Kish, Lagash and Erech were the chief. Their culture was the basis of later BABYLONIAN civilization; there were Sumerian myths of CREATION and the FLOOD.

Sumerian was an ancient agglutinative language written in CUNEIFORM (wedge-shaped letters). Cuneiform was used by several Middle Eastern cultures (AKKADIANS, BABYLONIANS, ELAMITES, HITTITES and ASSYRIANS as well as Sumerians) to write letters, record their taxes and remember their myths. Economic texts in the Umma archive held in the British Museum provide detailed information on irrigation and canal systems, work assignments and wages, male and female workers, clothing production, gathering of reeds and barley, government food rations, and beer production.

The city of NIPPUR, 100 miles south of Baghdad, yielded a large store of clay tablets in Sumerian. Because Sumerian seems unrelated to any other language, its decipherment has depended on parallel texts in Akkadian, a younger Mesopotamian language distantly related to Arabic. The initial success was due to the work of Sir Henry Rawlinson in 1835 on the parallel inscriptions found on a cliff-face in south-western Iran. Now the University of Pennsylvania is building an electronic dictionary on the Internet to share research and bring understanding of the language closer to completion.

Sunday The English name of the first day of the week means literally the 'day of the sun'. This pagan name, with its dedication to the sun, was given a Christian reinterpretation, referring to Jesus Christ, making use of the Old Testament theme of 'Sun of Righteousness' (Malachi 4.2). According to Revelation 1.10 this day of the week was known as 'the Day of the Lord'. For Christians it began to take over from the Jewish SABBATH (Saturday) as a commemoration of the RESURRECTION of Christ on the 'first day of the week' (John 20.1), a day of rejoicing, free of fasting. See the indications of earliest Christian practice in Acts 20.7 and 1 Corinthians 16.2.

superscription This word is sometimes used technically to refer to the placard displayed over Jesus' head on the cross. It was Roman practice to make the victim wear the charge around his/her neck on the way to the gallows, and then to fasten it to the upright beam. In church crucifixes the initials 'INRI' are usually shown. These are from the Latin 'Jesus of Nazareth, King of the Jews', which is the version of the charge given in John 19.19. *See* KING OF THE JEWS.

Susanna This 'courtroom drama', of the righteous heroine, wife of a Babylonian Jew, falsely accused in a Jewish court, occurs as an additional chapter in the Greek version of DANIEL. Daniel himself as a young boy is the detective/advocate who saves her from being stoned. This novella must have been written between the 3rd and 1st centuries BCE. Considering its brevity, the story has exercised an enormous influence in subsequent literature and art.

Sussita, or Hippos Sussita is a Greek city, one of the 10 cities of the DECAPOLIS, situated on the heights overlooking the Sea of GALILEE from the east, and about a mile distant from the shore. It was conquered by the HASMONEAN Alexander Jannaeus early in the 1st century BCE, then freed by Pompey in 63 BCE and made a member of the group of Decapolis cities. The Hebrew word *sus* means 'horse' and is translated into Greek as *hippos*. The city had been founded in the HELLENISTIC PERIOD by the Seleucids or the Ptolemies, and clearly became important in the Roman era. Recent excavations have revealed temples, bathhouses, marketplaces, and the main east–west street (*decumanus maximus*) of the city. Merchandise was brought across Galilee from TIBERIAS to Sussita, for onward transit to DAMASCUS. The city was never resettled after a violent earthquake in 749 CE, although in modern times it became a frontier post for the Israel Defence Forces facing the Syrian border.

swords Swords come in many shapes and sizes, depending on their function, for example stabbing and slashing; they may be straight or curved, and with a single or double cutting edge. In the New Testament period, two types are mentioned particularly: the *machaira* or the Roman legionary's *gladius*, a straight double-edged sword about 60 cm long; and the *rhomphaia*, a much larger broadsword, such as that used by the Thracians. The *rhomphaia* is used as a vivid image in the book of REVELATION of the sword of judgement from the mouth of Christ (see 1.16; 2.16; 19.15–21); it also occurs at Luke 2.35 of the sword that will pierce the soul of MARY, MOTHER OF JESUS. *Machaira* is used of the spiritual sword 'which is the word of God', the only offensive weapon in the catalogue of the Christian's armoury (closely modelled on that of the Roman legionary) in Ephesians 6.17. It is also used of the penetrating, dividing sword in Hebrews 4.12. God-given armour is also symbolized by the golden sword of JUDAS MACCABEUS, given to him in a vision by Jeremiah (see 2 Maccabees 15.15–16; Jeremiah 50.35–37).

In the face of the power politics and military might that colours the whole period of the Bible, there is an expression of prophetic hope for an age of PEACE, which will eliminate the need for swords. This is expressed in Isaiah 2.4 and Micah 4.3 in terms of beating 'swords into ploughshares', although the reverse action is still contemplated in Joel 3.10.

Sychar Sychar (modern Al-Askar) lies adjacent to SHECHEM at the eastern end of the valley between Mounts Ebal and Gerizim (*see* SAMARITANS). This is close to the site of the plot of land bought by JACOB at Shechem and also the traditional location of Jacob's well, where Jesus encountered the Samaritan woman, according to the narrative of John 4.5–6.

symbolism *See* IMAGE AND SYMBOL.

synagogue 'Synagogue' comes from a Greek word meaning 'a gathering (of people)'. It is used of a congregation of Jews, coming together to pray and to read the appointed Scriptures, or of the place where they assemble, which provides a focus for teaching. Compare the word 'Church', which equally can apply to a congregation of people or a designated building. What remains unclear is the time at which synagogues began. There are plausible theories associating the rise of the synagogue with the loss of the TEMPLE during the Babylonian EXILE (see Ezekiel 11.16; 14.1), or alternatively as a focus of traditional Jewish belief and practice in the 2nd century BCE, in the face of the pressures of Hellenism to force conformity to Greek customs and culture (see 1 Maccabees 3.48). There is clear evidence from the New Testament Gospels for synagogues in Palestine in the 1st century CE, where Jesus preached (see, for example, Luke 4.16–28).

Remains of synagogues from the New Testament period survive at MASADA, Herodium, Gamla, and probably in the earlier basalt building underlying the famous 4th-century CE synagogue at CAPERNAUM. There were probably hundreds of synagogues in Jerusalem before the destruction of the city by the Romans under their general TITUS in 70 CE. One of these synagogues housed a slab of limestone, known as the Theodotus Inscription, now to be seen in the Rockefeller Museum in Jerusalem. In beautifully carved Greek letters it commemorates Theodotus as ruler of the synagogue (*archisynagogos* – see Mark 5.22; Acts 18.8). It reads: 'Theodotus, son of Vettenus, priest and synagogue leader, son of a synagogue leader, grandson of a synagogue leader, rebuilt this synagogue for the reading of the LAW and the teaching of the commandments, and the hostelry, rooms and baths, for the lodging of those who have need from abroad'. The language of the inscription, in GREEK not Hebrew, and the reference to 'those ... from abroad', suggest that it might have been a synagogue used by Jews from the DIASPORA, accommodating a significant number of pilgrims. Alternatively it has been identified with the Synagogue of the Freedmen (former slaves in the Roman Empire) that is mentioned in Acts 6.9.

The Greek word for a 'minister' is *hyperetes*, which in turn can translate the Hebrew *hazzan*. This refers to the paid employee of a synagogue. The head of the synagogue had an adjutant, the *hazzan*, undoubtedly the *hyperetes* of Luke 4.20, who acted as executive officer in the practical details of running the synagogue. Officers with similar functions had been attached to the Temple.

syncretism Syncretism refers to the fusion or blending together of religious traditions, in the attempt to reconcile different systems of belief. It is not necessarily a simplistic or accommodating approach which refuses to recognize the differences. It can be a creative attempt at fusion, for rational purposes of comparison, in teaching or apologetic. The work of PHILO in presenting the traditions of JUDAISM in terms of Greek philosophy could be a good example, as is the parallel development and integration in early Christianity of the traditions of Hebraic, Palestinian, and Greek cultures. It has been said that syncretism is a beneficial term in religious studies, provided that it allows for tension and IRONY, which may lead to controversy, rather than simply the preservation of traditions. Plutarch analysed syncretism and offered an etymology of the term which was not intended seriously: from *syn-Kretoi*, because Cretans (*Kretoi*) would always be quarrelsome with each other, but when faced with an outside foe they would immediately band together (*syn*).

Synoptic Problem The term 'Synopsis' is used in Biblical scholarship in the technical sense of an analytical tool which allows a detailed comparison of three of the New Testament Gospels, Matthew, Mark, and Luke. The texts are here set out on the printed page in three parallel columns, allowing them to be 'seen together' (the basic meaning of the Greek word *synopsis*). The earliest such critical synopsis was produced by J. J. Griesbach in 1776. There have been many refinements since, in both Greek and English editions, including the possibility of incorporating comparisons with the Gospel of John and other gospel traditions. But the basic comparison is between the first three Gospels, which are therefore known collectively as the Synoptic Gospels.

According to most scholars, these have some kind of literary relationship, probably depending upon Mark as the primary source, but with contributions from other sources, either documentary or oral. The basic relationship is seen in terms of the subject matter, in the arrangement and order of events, and in the choice of particular vocabulary and the use of certain grammatical constructions. There is a conspicuous amount of agreement in these terms between the Gospels, but there are also significant disagreements which complicate the investigation of any 'borrowing' relationship (what today might even be called 'plagiarism'!). Determining just what the relationship between these Gospels might be is what is known as the Synoptic Problem.

The solution to the Synoptic Problem that is most widely accepted is known as the Two Source theory. Matthew and Luke both used Mark (or an earlier version of Mark) as their major source. But since there are other agreements (but of less precise kinds) between Matthew and Luke apart from the Marcan material, a case is also made for a second source, referred to as 'Q' (see further at Q (QUELLE) SOURCE). Unlike Mark this is a hypothetical and reconstructed text; some would argue that sources from oral tradition would be an equally adequate explanation (*see* ORALITY). Apart from the Two Source theory there is some renewal of interest in the explanation first offered in scientific terms by J. J. Griesbach, namely that Matthew was written first, and used by Luke; Mark was a third composition, essentially conflating the accounts of Matthew and Luke. To experience the nature of the problem, two samples of text that would repay examination are Mark 2.1–12 (the healing of the paralysed man) and Mark 3.22–27 (the BEELZEBUL controversy), together with their Matthaean and Lucan parallels.

Syria The name Syria is originally Greek, probably derived from ASSYRIA (as Herodotus explained). Older names for the area included Aram, after the ARAMAEAN population. Mesopotamia was known as the 'Aram of the two rivers'; southern Syria as 'Aram of Damascus' (see 2 Samuel 8.6); and northern Syria as 'Aram of Zobah [Aleppo]' (see 2 Samuel 10.8). Historically ancient Syria existed as a political entity only during the period of the HELLENISTIC monarchy of the Seleucids. They ruled over a kingdom stretching from east Asia Minor to Persia and the borders of India, following the conquests of Alexander the Great. Antiochus III in 198 BCE added Palestine, which was taken over from the Ptolemies of Egypt. After 129 BCE the realm shrank drastically; eventually even the geographical area of Syria itself (from the Taurus mountains to the western bend of the river Euphrates, then bordering the Arabian desert down towards the Dead Sea, and then across to the Mediterranean) was annexed by Pompey in 64 BCE, to become the Roman province of Syria.

In some English versions of the Old Testament 'Syrians' is used loosely for Aramaeans. In the New Testament the term 'Syrophoenician' (see Mark 7.26) is used for an inhabitant of PHOENICIA (TYRE AND SIDON), which formed part of the Roman province of Syria.

Syriac Syriac is a Semitic language, a dialect of ARAMAIC. Its immediate predecessors were the languages used in Palmyra in SYRIA and Hatra in Iraq. Syriac is mostly a Christian language, used for the communication of Christian literature and liturgy, derived from the dialect of Edessa (modern Urfa in southern Turkey). It is important as a witness to the earliest Eastern traditions in Christianity, probably from the end of the 2nd century CE. One of the early writers contributing to the vast literature in Syriac was Ephraem the Syrian. Syriac is still used colloquially in isolated Christian communities as well as in LITURGY, for example in India, but it declined as a theological language with the ascendancy of Arabic in the 13th century CE. Jews may have translated the TORAH into Syriac for their community in Edessa, but the translation of the whole of scripture was a Christian responsibility. The earliest Syriac translations of the Gospels are in the Old Syriac of the Curetonian and Sinaitic manuscripts. The most common translation of the Bible is the Peshitta ('current' or 'simple' version), probably completed in the 5th century, which became the authorized version of the ancient Syriac Church; the book of Revelation and the lesser Catholic epistles were omitted from this translation. A later and literal Syriac translation, the Harklean, named after a bishop of Hierapolis, is said to have been completed in 616 CE.

tabernacle The tabernacle was a portable sanctuary, housed in a tent, that was made in obedience to the commands of God during the Israelites' wanderings in the wilderness (see the account in EXODUS chapter 25 onwards). It was superseded by the Jerusalem TEMPLE constructed by SOLOMON.

Tabernacles, feast of Tabernacles (Succoth) is the third and last of the great FESTIVALS of PILGRIMAGE in the Hebrew Bible. It recalls the 40 years of Hebrew wanderings in the desert, when they lived in booths or temporary shacks, and so it is known as the Feast of Booths. It is also the celebration of harvest (known as the Feast of the Ingathering), in particular the harvest after the arrival in the Promised Land, and a celebration of the coming of the winter rains (see Exodus 23.16; 34.22). The eight-day festival in the month of Tishri is a statement that God provides in all ways for his people. No work is permitted on the first and last days of the festival. It is a time of rejoicing and inclusiveness, when historically the Jews were to welcome Gentiles to Jerusalem ('the place that the Lord will choose'; indeed as Deuteronomy 16.13–15 says, originally to celebrate with everybody in 'your towns'). The vision of the future, as in ZECHARIAH 14.16–17 (read at the festival), sees this as an occasion for the ingathering of the nations, when multitudes of Gentiles will come to worship God in Jerusalem at Succoth. So today even the ultra-Orthodox Jews welcome visitors during Tabernacles.

According to the regulations of Leviticus 23.42, a temporary booth (*succah*) is set up as a centre of hospitality for the duration of the festival, and the family will eat all meals there alfresco. The roof is covered with cut vegetation and must be open to the sky. The four species (palm, myrtle, willow and citrus fruit – see Leviticus 23.40) are held during family prayers, and at the conclusion they are waved in all four directions. They are also carried in procession around the synagogue.

On the last day of Tabernacles, in Second TEMPLE times a day for water drawing and libation, and which is now known as Simchat TORAH (Joy in the Giving of the Law), JOHN'S GOSPEL records that Jesus stood up in the Temple and shouted, 'Let anyone who is thirsty come to me, and let the one who believes in me drink. As the Scripture has said, "Out of the believer's heart shall flow rivers of living water"' (7.37–38; see Isaiah 44.3; Zechariah 14.8).

Tabgha Tabgha is to be found on the north-west shore of the Sea of GALILEE and is the site of a church dating back to the Byzantine period which is dedicated to Jesus' miracle of the loaves and fishes, the feeding of the 5000 (see Matthew 14.13–21; Mark 6.32–44; Luke 9.10–17; John 6.1–13). The church has exquisite mosaic floors, with representations of loaves and fishes, that are often used as Biblical illustrations, echoing as they do the Christian EUCHARIST and the stories of ELIJAH and ELISHA (see 1 Kings 17.8–16; 2 Kings 4.42–44). Other chapels on the site, of similar date, seem to be dedicated to the SERMON ON THE MOUNT, and the post-RESURRECTION appearance of Jesus to PETER, as in John 21.

Tabor Mount Tabor is a hill, some 1750 feet above sea level, in the Jezreel valley, at the southern limits of Lower Galilee. It was the place where, in the time of DEBORAH, Barak gathered his army before defeating the CANAANITE forces of Sisera (see Judges 4). According to Hosea 5.1 it was a place of worship with a shrine to BA'AL from ancient times, and it was on the boundary between the tribes of ZEBULUN, ISSACHAR, and NAPHTALI (see Joshua 19.12, 22, 34). In early Christian tradition Mount Tabor was the scene of the TRANSFIGURATION of Jesus (see Matthew 17.1–8; Mark 9.2–8; Luke 9.28–36). In the Byzantine period three churches were built to commemorate the three tabernacles for Moses, Elijah, and Jesus.

Talmud Talmud, meaning 'learning', is the comprehensive term for the compilation of teaching and commentary concerning the Bible by centuries of Jewish RABBIS. It includes the Mishnah, compiled at the end of the 2nd century CE, together with the two great commentaries (Gemara) which are known respectively as the Palestinian (or Jerusalem) Talmud – dating from c.400 CE – and the Babylonian Talmud – c.500 CE. The main language of the Talmud is ARAMAIC. The work became the source of reference for Jewish LAW, and its study forms the basis of orthodox Jewish life.

Tamar 1 The daughter-in-law of JUDAH, who bore him two sons, Perez and Zerah, as a result of offering herself to her father-in-law in the guise of a prostitute (Genesis 38.1–30). This action allowed the fulfilment of the laws of LEVIRATE MARRIAGE.

2 A daughter of King DAVID and a sister of ABSALOM. She was raped by her half-brother Amnon (2 Samuel 13.1–32). This case of incest provoked Absalom her brother to kill Amnon in revenge, and ultimately was the cause of Absalom's revolt. The story is graphically retold in a modern novel by Dan Jacobson, *The Rape of Tamar*.

3 *See* TAMARA.

Tamara, or Tamar A town on the southern borders of the land of Israel (as mentioned in Ezekiel 47.19; 48.28) in the area otherwise referred to as the 'wilderness of Zin'. Some 30 miles south of the DEAD SEA, it was one of the main cities of the spice trade. Excavations have discovered many objects from the First TEMPLE up to the early Arab period, including a pit with EDOMITE cultic figures, Iron Age walls, gates and an altar, as well as a Roman fort.

Tanak, or Tanakh This is the conventional Jewish name for the Hebrew Bible which Christians tend to call the OLD TESTAMENT. The Jewish name is made up from the initial letters of the names of the three sections of the Bible: TORAH, Nebiim, and Kethubim (PENTATEUCH, Prophets, and Writings or Hagiographa).

targums, targumim The targums (Hebrew *targumim* = 'translations') are the ARAMAIC translations of the Hebrew Bible (see TEXTUAL CRITICISM). During the Second TEMPLE period, after the EXILE, an Aramaic simultaneous translation would be added, verse by verse, in the course of public readings of the Bible, so that the sense would be comprehensible to listeners who knew spoken Aramaic rather than classical Hebrew. The substance of these translations was committed to writing eventually. There are several extant targums of the PENTATEUCH, including *Targum Onkelos* and *Targum Jonathan*, while the targum to the Former and Latter Prophets is called *Targum Pseudo-Jonathan*.

Tarshish *See* TRADE; SHIPS AND THE SEA.

Tarsus Tarsus was an important commercial centre, some 10 miles from the Mediterranean, on the south-eastern coast of Asia Minor, at the foothills of the Taurus mountains. The city controlled the trade routes to Asia Minor and Syria, and was also created the capital of the Roman province of Cilicia by Pompey in 67 BCE. It was apparently the birthplace of PAUL (Saul), who commended it, and himself, by his claim to be 'a citizen of an important city' (Acts 21.39), although only Acts says that Paul was from Tarsus. There is evidence that citizenship in Tarsus was awarded on merit. Dio Chrysostom (34th Discourse) instances a man who is not rated as a citizen 'through poverty or the decision of some keeper of the rolls', even though he and his father and forefathers had been born in Tarsus. It was not right that a 'linen-worker' (or a 'tent-maker' or worker in leather, like Paul, according to Acts 18.3) should be reviled for his occupation, and regarded as inferior to neighbours who were dyers, cobblers, or carpenters. Luke says that Paul was a citizen of Tarsus as well as being a Roman citizen; such dual affiliation was permissible.

Tarsus was also renowned as a centre of STOIC philosophy. So, in relation to Paul, one needs to think of an upbringing in the Jewish DIASPORA (dispersion), in a cosmopolitan context, with strong influences from Hellenistic philosophy, as well as from the MYSTERY RELIGIONS (also held to be significant here). 'Its Greek orientation had to struggle with a strong Eastern spirit.'

Tatian One of the great puzzles in the study of early Christianity is how to recover the history of the Biblical text during the period before the earliest surviving copies were produced. Quotations in the Church Fathers provide hints, and fragments of scriptural texts indicate a greater variety than we have access to currently. It is understandable if there is a popular yearning for great manuscript discoveries (to rival the DEAD SEA SCROLLS or the NAG HAMMADI texts); meanwhile scholars must seek to find out more from the resource materials to hand.

An especially interesting figure for the study of the early Christian movement is Tatian (c.120–c.185 CE). This is partly because he crosses the boundaries separating different language groupings. His only extant writing survives in GREEK (in which language it was produced), but it is clear that he was also a native speaker of SYRIAC (see Ephraim Syrus' commentary on the *Diatessaron*). In addition it is known that Tatian travelled to Rome, where he studied with Justin Martyr. This means that he could well have had access to much of the entire range of scriptural texts that were used by Christians during his lifetime. He produced the *Diatessaron* – a gospel harmony for use by Christians – although the original text has not survived. A 2001 study of Tatian's work by R. F. Shedinger presents a good case for the existence of a broader array of textual options in the early centuries of the Church's life than survive today. It is a powerful stimulus for the interest in Christian community life prior to the existence of fixed texts.

tax-collectors *See* PUBLICANS.

Tekoa Tekoa is a town in Judah, mentioned several times in the Bible, although not in the list of places conquered by JOSHUA during the Settlement (except in a SEPTUA-GINT addition at Joshua 15.59). Tekoa – identified with Khirbet Tequa – stands on a ridge about five miles south of Bethlehem. It is likely to have been the birthplace of the prophet AMOS (see Amos 1.1).

Tekoa was the home of some of DAVID's thirty warriors (2 Samuel 23.26). In 2 Samuel 14 a 'wise woman' of Tekoa was sent to David by Joab, to plead for ABSALOM's return to the court. It was one of the cities which Rehoboam fortified (see 2 Chronicles 11.6). Much later, after the Babylonian EXILE, people from Tekoa assisted in the rebuilding of the walls of Jerusalem, although their nobles did not co-operate (see Nehemiah 3.5, 27). JOSEPHUS reports that during the JEWISH WAR he was sent by TITUS to prospect the site for a camp at Tekoa; it was also the scene of battles during this war.

Tel Aviv This modern Israeli commercial centre grew out of the Arab town of Jaffa. Its name means 'hill of spring'. Extensive building operations for the modern city have revealed some 20 archaeological sites, dating from Neolithic to Roman times. Probably of greatest interest are fortifications ascribed to the HASMONEAN king Alexander Jannaeus, described by JOSEPHUS in *Jewish War* 1.99. In the Bible, Tel Abib on the river Chebar in Mesopotamia was a place of Jewish exile (see Ezekiel 3.15).

Teman *See* KUNTILLET AJRUD.

Templars, or Knights Templar The Templars were soldier monks belonging to an order that was founded in Jerusalem, after the success of the First Crusade, on the site of the TEMPLE built by King SOLOMON. Their mission was to protect PILGRIMS as they travelled to and from the HOLY LAND. In order to recruit men and raise money, they also built temples/monasteries in the capital cities of Europe, including that surrounding the Temple Church in London. Their churches were built according to a circular plan, as a reminder of the round domed Church of the Holy Sepulchre in Jerusalem (see CHURCHES, CHRISTIAN).

Temple at Jerusalem The Temple Mount (*Haram al-Sharif*) in Jerusalem is the site of SOLOMON's Temple. The building and dedication of the original Temple is described in detail in 1 Kings 5.1–9.9. The account, including its fittings, is so detailed that it may well have drawn in part from the Temple archives. 1 Kings 8 narrates the depositing of the ARK OF THE COVENANT and the dedication of the Temple; the building is seen to be both the central shrine, because of the Ark, and at the same time a royal sanctuary. The prayer of dedication, from 1 Kings 8.22 onwards, is a key passage

A model of Herod's Temple in Jerusalem

for later beliefs about the Temple (seen as even being accessed from a remote distance during the EXILE). As 1 Kings 5.5 states, it is a house for the 'name' of the Lord God, signifying an actual divine presence, or a reflection of God's personality, or a location where a 'rendezvous with God' might take place.

After this Temple was destroyed by the BABYLONIANS in 586 BCE (the event commemorated in the Jewish CALENDAR on the ninth day of Ab), a Second Temple, more modest than the first, was built by the exiles returning from Babylon later in the 6th century BCE. Then, just before the end of the millennium, HEROD THE GREAT rebuilt this structure. Herod's Temple Mount compound was very extensive, likened by some to the area of 24 football pitches. The Jewish historian JOSEPHUS wrote about Herod's Temple of gold and marble: 'to approaching strangers the Temple appeared from a distance like a snow-clad mountain; for all that was not overlaid with gold was of purest white'.

The Temple of Herod was destroyed by the Romans in 70 CE. Josephus reported that the Temple was burnt in defiance of the orders, and despite the efforts to prevent it, of the Roman commander TITUS. The spoils of the Temple were carried in triumph in Rome; they included the golden table for the SHOWBREAD, the seven-branched candelabrum (see MENORAH), incense cups, TRUMPETS, and the 'Book of the Court' (a copy of the Hebrew Bible read on festal occasions, and from which Biblical scrolls were corrected). Titus left the Roman Tenth Legion to garrison the city; part of a column which they had erected was rediscovered and used as the base of a street lamp in Jerusalem.

Much later, in the 7th century CE, Jerusalem was conquered by the Muslims and the Temple Mount was adorned with the gleaming Dome of the Rock. But in the intervening years, firstly in 130 CE, 60 years after the destruction of Herod's Temple, the Roman Emperor Hadrian founded a pagan Roman city on the site, Aelia Capitolina, and built a temple to Jupiter on the Temple Mount. Jews were forbidden on pain of death to enter the Roman city, with the occasional exception of Jewish pilgrims mourning the destruction of their city and Temple on 9 Ab. By the 4th century CE the city had become Christian, and various Byzantine churches, monasteries, shops and houses were constructed in the area to the south of the Temple Mount. The main Christian site was the Church of the Holy Sepulchre, founded by Emperor Constantine in 325 CE further to the north (see CHURCHES, CHRISTIAN).

While the Temple still stood, a tax of a half-shekel was levied annually on adult males to support the sacrificial system in the Temple (see Matthew 17.24–27). The rabbis prescribed that it should be paid in Tyrian silver (PHOENICIAN coins minted in Tyre) because of the purity (95% silver) of this COINAGE. From 18 BCE to 66 CE these Tyrian shekels became lumpier and less regular; it is thought that the minting was moved to Jerusalem, because the authorities needed the coins for the tax, after Tyre had discontinued minting in 19 BCE. These Jerusalemite coins bear the letters 'KP' (possibly meaning 'by the authority of the Roman constitution'). After the destruction of the Temple in 70 CE, Rome still exacted the tax in favour of the temple of Jupiter Capitolinus in Rome.

Readers of Dan Brown's *Da Vinci Code* may like to know that Isaac Newton, in 17th-century England, 'spent endless hours studying the floor plan of the lost Temple of King Solomon in Jerusalem (teaching himself Hebrew in the process, the better to scan original texts) in the belief that it held mathematical clues to the dates of the Second Coming of Christ and the end of the world' (according to Bill Bryson's *A Short History of Nearly Everything*, Doubleday, 2005). *See also* PAROUSIA and ESCHATON.

temptations of Christ The temptations, or perhaps better the testing, of Christ, are identified in the threefold structure of Matthew 4.1–11 and also (with interesting variation in order) of Luke 4.1–13. A brief summary of the episode is given in Mark 1.12–13 ('in the wilderness forty days, tempted by Satan'). The process of testing is seen as a necessary sequel to the public (or semi-public) acknowledgement of Jesus' identity at the time of his BAPTISM by JOHN THE BAPTIST. This is what being SON OF GOD entails. The three 'temptations' can be summarized (in Luke's order) as firstly, food without effort; secondly as sensation without sacrifice; and thirdly as crown without cross (see the further testing in the AGONY IN THE GARDEN). Jesus resists these temptations and perseveres in his God-given mission.

Ten Commandments *See* DECALOGUE.

teraphim *See* HOUSEHOLD DEITIES.

Testaments of the Twelve Patriarchs The *Testaments of the Twelve Patriarchs* (*see* PATRIARCHS) are Jewish works of the 2nd century BCE (with some interpolation from Christian sources perhaps early in the 2nd century CE). They stand within the Old Testament tradition, claiming to be the final utterances of the 12 sons of JACOB, and they are modelled on Jacob's own last words in Genesis chapter 49. The pattern of the testament presupposes the family gathered around the bedside of the dying patriarch. He reflects on his life, confesses his misdeeds, and urges his relatives to avoid his SINS and to pursue virtue, perhaps accompanying this with blessings and curses. The testament may well conclude with some description of the nation's future, as revealed to him in an APOCALYPTIC vision. The first manuscript of the *Testaments* was brought to England by Robert Grosseteste, the great 13th-century Oxford master, probably in 1241, and was translated by him from Greek into Latin.

The 'testament' form occurs elsewhere, although it is not a very precisely defined literary genre. It can be seen, for example, in the APOCRYPHA in TOBIT 4.1–19, and in the New Testament, possibly at John 17 and 2 Peter.

tetragrammaton *See* YAHWEH.

textual criticism Textual criticism is a fundamental kind of BIBLICAL CRITICISM, concerned as it is with the actual text of the Bible as it stands before the reader, translator, or interpreter. A variety of methods are used to analyse the text, and all available evidence in support of that text, seeking to discover its original form (the one that would have stood at the beginning of the process of written transmission – *see also* ORALITY) and to determine that form as exactly as possible. This reconstruction serves as a starting point with which it is possible to compare the vast number of texts, versions, and quotations that appear in the course of the text's transmission, and by that comparison seek to understand the reasons for variations.

For the Hebrew Bible the major 'witnesses' (evidence for different forms of the text) include the Hebrew texts from QUMRAN, the Greek translation known as the SEPTUAGINT, the vocalized form of the Hebrew authenticated by the MASSORETES, and a range of translations and interpretative commentaries including those in ARAMAIC, SYRIAC, and the Latin version of the VULGATE. For the New Testament the witnesses range from early papyrus fragments (very fragmentary of parts of texts) to later minuscules, the major codices (such as SINAITICUS), quotations in the Church Fathers, and translations into Syriac, COPTIC, ARMENIAN, Georgian, ETHIOPIC, Latin, Gothic, Slavonic, and Anglo-Saxon.

Scribes copy the text that lies in front of them, as they have been instructed to do. In this process they may, quite naturally, make mistakes that are casual errors, negligences in copying that are revealed in various quite unsystematic ways. But some changes may be unconscious, half-conscious, or deliberate interpretations which come from the mind of the copyist, such as theological additions enhancing reverence, or harmonizations between, for example, the four Gospels. The Biblical CANON also exercises an influence on the reproduction of the text, a scriptural concern which demands exact copying, even of apparent mistakes in the text in front of the scribe, simply because this preserves the text as it stands and erects a barrier against heretical falsifications. The history of text transmission thus reveals a tension between two driving concerns: the scriptural desire to preserve and the contemporary concern to clarify and interpret.

Thaddaeus, or Lebbaeus The name Thaddaeus occurs in the listing of the DIS-CIPLES of Jesus at Matthew 10.3 and Mark 3.18; its position in these lists corresponds to that of 'Judas of James' in Luke 6.16 (*see* JUDE). At Matthew 10.3 there is an alternative reading 'Lebbaeus' or 'Lebbaeus surnamed Thaddaeus'; it is possible that these are explanations or alternative versions of the same name (*tad* = breast, from the ARAMAIC, and *leb* = heart, from the Hebrew).

Theodotus *See* SYNAGOGUE.

Theophilus Theophilus in Greek means 'lover/friend of God'. He is the person, otherwise unknown, to whom LUKE addressed both his Gospel and the ACTS OF THE APOSTLES (see Luke 1.3; Acts 1.1). It is a plausible theory that both works were dedicated to Theophilus as a patron or benefactor, as would be a custom in Hellenistic writings. The flattering title 'most excellent' or 'your excellency' lends support to this theory, and might indicate a government official of high rank. Certainly it is one of Luke's intentions to commend the Christian movement to the existing political authorities.

Thessalonians, first and second letters to Thessalonica is a port on the northern shore of the Aegean Sea. The city was founded by one of Alexander the Great's generals in 316 BCE. When Macedonia became a Roman province in 146 BCE, Thessalonica became its capital, being well placed on a Roman road, the Egnatian Way. The city was involved, fortunately on the winning side, in the Roman Civil War that led to Octavian's (Augustus') triumph in 42 BCE. Thus began a new era of prosperity, as the coinage shows; during Augustus' reign a temple was founded to the imperial cult of Julius Caesar as divine.

1 Thessalonians is probably the earliest document in the New Testament. In it PAUL 'made the mistake of thinking that Jesus would return to earth in judgement within one generation' (*see* PAROUSIA). This first letter is warmly pastoral but also highly emotive, in autobiographical terms; Paul uses both Jewish and Greek traditions to build something new out of his readers' conventional expectations. Without systematic excavation, no trace of a Jewish SYNAGOGUE has been found; but it is highly likely that a Jewish community would have regarded Paul's message as a direct assault on the social and religious position of the synagogue.

2 Thessalonians is 'full of APOCALYPTIC fire, and yet chillingly cold'. The letter seems more concerned with divine revenge on the 'wicked' enemies of Christianity than with developing religious thought. Whether Paul was the author is hotly debated. The real puzzle with these two letters is their closeness in wording, compared with their distance in thought. If Paul wrote both letters close together, and quoted from memory, why had he changed his views so much on the future and on the Thessalonians? If a later author wrote the second letter, he could have quoted extensively from Paul to authenticate his own work. Did Paul put himself straight about the expectation of Jesus' return, or did other teachers do it for him (see 2 PETER 3.3–16)?

Through the centuries (and even today) certain groups of Christians have been particularly concerned with expectations of the End Time, and have relied on texts from the Thessalonian letters. The idea of the Rapture is found in 1 Thessalonians 4.15–17. And 2 Thessalonians 2.3, 6 speaks of the 'lawless one' who is being restrained for a time. JOHN'S LETTERS refer to this figure uniquely as 'Antichrist', while REVELA-TION 12–13 speaks of the Beast and the false prophet, aided by the power of SATAN.

Theudas *See* GAMALIEL.

third day According to 1 Corinthians 15.4, Jesus, following his death and burial, 'was raised on the third day in accordance with the scriptures'. The reference here may well be to the Old Testament tradition according to which some decisive act will take place on the third day; this may well be the day on which God intervenes and rescues his people. Among possible echoes from the Old Testament are: Genesis 40.20, when JOSEPH's interpretation of the dreams of the cupbearer and the baker is fulfilled; Exodus 19.11, as MOSES is told that God will come down on Mount SINAI; 2 Kings 20.5, in God's answer to HEZEKIAH's prayer for healing; ESTHER 4.15–5.1, when Esther takes decisive action to deliver the Jews in Persia; perhaps most significantly in HOSEA 6.2, prophesying the day on which God 'will raise us up'; and JONAH 1.17, of the three days and nights spent in the whale's belly. The ancient world regularly counted inclusively: today is day one, so the third day is reckoned as the day after tomorrow. See also RESURRECTION.

thirty pieces of silver This was the amount of the bribe offered by the Jewish leaders, and accepted by JUDAS ISCARIOT, to betray Jesus' whereabouts, according to Matthew 26.14–16 (the amount is not specified in the other Gospels). This is the value placed on a slave injured by an ox in Exodus 21.32, but in Matthew it is likely to be a deliberate allusion to ZECHARIAH 11.12–13. It is in accord with this 'prophecy' that afterwards Judas in remorse throws down the silver coins in the Temple (Matthew 27.9). The priests refuse to restore it to the treasury, calling it 'blood money', and so they use it to purchase the 'potter's field', as a burial place for foreigners. The text of Matthew 27.5 inaccurately attributes the prophecy to JEREMIAH, not Zechariah; the reference to Jeremiah may have been suggested by his purchase of land at Anathoth (Jeremiah 32.6–15) and his visits to the potter's in Jeremiah 18 and 19. According to the Acts of the Apostles 1.18, Judas himself bought the field in which to commit suicide.

See also COINAGE.

Thomas Thomas is mentioned in all four Gospels as a DISCIPLE of Jesus. Thomas is not actually a proper name, but an ARAMAIC word meaning 'twin' (as in the Greek form Didymus, used in JOHN'S GOSPEL, where he appears three times, in 11.16; 14.5; and most significantly in 20.24–28). In Church tradition the name is Judas Thomas, but more than one of Jesus' disciples bore the name Judas, and whose twin he was is a further question. In Luke's list (6.16) 'Judas the brother/son of James' replaces Thaddaeus (Matthew 10.3; Mark 3.18), but Thomas is also listed in Luke 6.15. The confusion may well be due to attempts to harmonize the lists. It is possible that Judas Thomas is directly related to JAMES, BROTHER OF JESUS and is the 'twin' of Jesus, thus giving additional authority to APOCRYPHAL texts such as the *Gospel of Thomas* (see next entry).

Thomas, gospel of The *Gospel of Thomas* is a collection of sayings, 114 in total, described as the 'secret teachings' of Jesus, written down by Judas THOMAS, known as Didymus. In terms of the GOSPELS, as defined by the New Testament examples, this fails the definition by its lack of any narratives such as MIRACLE stories or an account of the DEATH OF CHRIST. It is closer to a 'sayings source', comparable to the theoretical source Q (QUELLE) for its emphasis on teaching. Some of the sayings in the *Gospel of Thomas* are very similar to sayings of Jesus recorded in the New Testament. It is argued that the version of the SOWER parable (*Thomas* 9) is closer to the original form, as taught by Jesus, than the interpreted text of the New Testament. Other sayings in the *Gospel of Thomas* are quite different, appearing strange to ears attuned to the Bible, and reflecting a later perspective that sounds GNOSTIC. See, from saying 114: 'every woman who makes herself male will enter the Kingdom of Heaven'. The *Gospel* may be a collection, originally in ARAMAIC, which has developed and evolved into later versions in the first few centuries CE. A full COPTIC text of the Gospel was found at NAG HAMMADI; previously three Greek manuscript fragments (datable to the 3rd century CE) were known from OXYRHYNCHUS, but were only identified as parts of the Gospel following the appearance of the full Coptic version. In themselves they provide evidence of how this gospel was handled in the early period.

thorn in the flesh This reference to a limiting personal weakness, or disability, originates with PAUL, in 2 Corinthians 12.7. The precise nature of Paul's 'thorn' is a mystery, although various post-mortem diagnoses have been attempted – migraine, leprosy, epilepsy, malaria, and ME have all had proponents – as well as the suggestion that Paul found possession of the STIGMATA debilitating. In the 2 Corinthians text Paul attributes the gift of pain from this ailment to a need to keep him from being conceited, and claims that he had prayed to have it removed, but had been reassured that Christ's power is made perfect in weakness.

thorns, crown of *See* CROWN OF THORNS.

Three Kings, Three Wise Men *See* MAGI.

Thyatira Thyatira is the fourth of seven cities of Asia Minor, addressed in chapters 2 and 3 of the book of REVELATION. The modern town on the site is Akhisar in Turkey, lying some 55 miles north-east of Izmir (SMYRNA). Thyatira is situated on the road which runs between PERGAMON and SARDIS and this sequence is followed by the messages in Revelation. The ancient city's organization was based on trade guilds, for industrial, commercial, and military purposes. One example was the trade in PURPLE and dyed goods, of which LYDIA was an entrepreneur, according to Acts 16. The letter to Thyatira in Revelation 2.18–29 is the longest of the seven letters, and includes the unique word *chalkolibanos* as a trade term in metalwork for an alloy of copper or bronze with zinc, as well as a reference to the work of potters. The text also refers to a local figure, known as JEZEBEL (2.20), who is seen as an advocate of practices condemned by the Apostolic Decree of Acts 15.20; there may also be an allusion to the appearance and attributes of a local deity, Tyrimnus, who resembles Apollo (2.18).

Tiamat *See* RAHAB (1).

Tiberias Tiberias was – and still is – the most important harbour on the Sea of GALILEE (referred to in John 21.1 as the Sea of Tiberias), situated on the south-west shore. It was the capital of Herod Antipas (*see* HERODIAN DYNASTY), and subsequently became an important cultural centre during the Roman and Byzantine periods. Following the Roman destruction of Jerusalem in 70 CE, Tiberias grew as a centre of Jewish life, and the seat of the SANHEDRIN, and in the 3rd century CE it became the seat of Jewish political, religious, and cultural activity. During the Roman period many important Jewish leaders resided here; the Palestinian TALMUD was compiled and edited in Tiberias; and Jewish institutions thrived there until the 10th century. It was also a major centre of Christian PILGRIMAGE. Recent and ongoing archaeological excavations have uncovered the *cardo* (the main street in Roman times), shops and a covered bazaar, a theatre, a BASILICA of the 4th century CE, and a large bathhouse with a polychrome mosaic floor dating from the 6th century CE.

Tiberius, Emperor *See* COINAGE; PILATE, PONTIUS.

Tiglath-Pileser III *See* ASSYRIANS; HAZOR.

Timnah The Hebrew word *timnah* means 'allotted portion' and so is a natural choice for a place-name in the HOLY LAND. Not surprisingly the name occurs in several locations. Timnah is important in the story of SAMSON (see Judges 14), where the woman seems to be as 'allotted' as the place, in Samson's eyes. The town of Timnah is on the northern border of the territory of Judah, and has been identified with Khirbet Tibnah or, perhaps more likely, with Tel Batash, 4 miles north of Beth-shemesh ('the house/temple of the Sun god'). Another town, in the hill-country of Judah, is mentioned in Joshua 15.57, but has not been identified. Also called Timnah is the valley of that name, some 15 miles north of the Gulf of Elath (Eilat), enclosed on all but the east side by a mountain range, Zuqe Timnah. This is the area where archaeologists discovered the remains of copper mines and smelting operations, called 'King Solomon's Mines' by Nelson Glueck in 1940. Subsequently systematic investigations by Tel Aviv University and others have revealed several sites for smelting, developed at different times, from the Chalcolithic to the Roman and Byzantine periods. An Egyptian temple, dedicated to the goddess Hathor, was found at the centre of this mining area. It is now certain that the major mining operation was overseen by Egyptian pharaohs of the 14th to 12th centuries BCE (rather than the kings of Israel and Judah of the 10th to 6th centuries), with the aid of indigenous peoples such as the KENITES.

Timothy Timothy is the best known of Paul's companions, having worked with him in Asia, Greece, and Macedonia. He is mentioned in Paul's correspondence to Thessalonica, Corinth, and Rome, as well as in Colossians, Philippians, and Philemon. In the two PASTORAL EPISTLES addressed to him, Timothy is identified with the Churches of Asia Minor, and particularly with Ephesus, the provincial capital (1 Timothy 1.3). Timothy had been born in Lystra, of a Jewish mother and Greek father (Acts 16.1).

Tirzah Tirzah is one of the city-states of CANAAN conquered by JOSHUA (according to Joshua 12.24). It is identified with the present Tell el-Farah, six miles to the north of Nablus. It is not mentioned in the lists of places which the Israelites inhabited; however, the name appears in Numbers (26.33; 27.1) as the name of a daughter of Zelophehad, and scholars have assumed that these 'daughters' are actually towns inhabited by the families of MANASSEH (SON OF JOSEPH).

In the later period Tirzah was the capital of the kings of Israel until the time of OMRI (see 1 Kings 14–16). Omri reigned at Tirzah until he built his new capital at SAMARIA (1 Kings 16.23–24). Tirzah is mentioned in Song of Songs 6.4 as a symbol of beauty, perhaps of beautiful decoration. Excavations at the site of Tirzah revealed significant social changes which took place between the 10th and 8th centuries BCE, changes from a broadly egalitarian society with houses of similar size to a developing class society in which rich and poor were segregated to different parts of the town.

tithe A tithe (Hebrew *maaser*) is literally one tenth of one's annual income, dedicated for religious purposes, such as the support of a sanctuary. Tithing seems to have been a widespread practice in the ancient Near East. There is some evidence that it could be used as a system of taxation, for more secular purposes (see 1 Samuel 8.15, 17; 1 Maccabees 10.31; 11.35).

In the PATRIARCHAL traditions the tithe appears as a freewill offering made at the sanctuary, as when ABRAHAM gives a tenth of his war-booty to MELCHIZEDEK of Salem, following his blessing (Genesis 14.20), and when JACOB vows a tithe to God after his dream at BETHEL (Genesis 28.22). The subsequent legal regulations for tithes are quite specific and complex (see Leviticus 27.30–33; Numbers 18.21–32; Deuteronomy 14.22–29). Tithes applied to a wide range of produce and livestock, and involved a meal eaten at the temple; transportation to the sanctuary might then pose a problem, but the tithe could be converted to cash (with a surcharge); replacement food must still be bought for the temple meal. After the Babylonian EXILE, the tithe is seen as a tax collected at the Jerusalem TEMPLE to support the PRIESTS and LEVITES (see Nehemiah 10.37–38). Malachi 3.8, 10 shows that there could be cheating in the practice.

The tithe was still maintained in later JUDAISM with the stipulation that all things used for food, which were watched, or which grew from the earth, should be tithed (see the boast of the PHARISEE at Luke 18.12). The Mishnah adopted two tithes (to clarify the discrepancies in the PENTATEUCHAL texts above): the first for the Levites, and the second to be eaten by the people. In two of the years of the Jewish seven-year cycle, the second tithe was replaced by a tithe for the poor. SABBATH regulations insist that food intended for the Sabbath had to be tithed before the Sabbath began. Jesus does not seem to have condemned the practice of tithing as such, though he was critical of those who tithed even their HERBS but neglected more important religious and ethical demands (see Matthew 23.23). It is possible that PAUL alludes to tithing in 1 Corinthians 9.7. Very much later a system of tithing was revived under English Church law, at some time before the 9th century CE, affecting all produce of land, for the benefit of the parochial system.

titles of Jesus Jesus is known by many different titles in the New Testament. Some have roots in the Hebrew Bible and JUDAISM and would have been meaningful to early believers from that background (for example MESSIAH). Other titles were imported from the GENTILE/PAGAN world, to make more sense to readers from that milieu (for example, Saviour – *see* SALVATION). Christians were trying to make sense of what appeared to them as the unique Christ-experience, and seized on whatever gave them some hold on the situation. But this meant that no individual title was felt to be sufficient by itself, to sum up all that Christians believed about Jesus. Titles alone may not have been adequate, so the fuller impression was also given by narrating stories about his actions (including MIRACLES).

Jesus' DISCIPLES (and others too) might call him 'Teacher/Master' or RABBI (see Mark 12.32). But some scholars argue that, if Jesus himself preferred any title, it was the mysterious SON OF MAN which was borrowed from the Hebrew Bible (Daniel 7.13 – 'one like a human being'; Ezekiel 2.1 – 'mortal') and developed with its own new content. It could be seen primarily as a challenge to Jesus' listeners to think and to draw their own conclusions about him. This would have gone with a refusal to work with other people's preconceptions of Jesus' role.

The most obvious preconceived role that could have been waiting for Jesus to adopt with its title was that of the Jewish nationalist 'anointed' leader or Messiah. Accompanying Messiah (or 'Christ' in Greek) was a group of others: Son of DAVID, SON OF GOD and King. Son of David (Mark 10.47) acknowledged Jesus as a descendant of Israel's favourite king, 1000 years before. Son of God was a title which was used by Israel's monarch in time past; it did not represent a claim to be descended from a deity (unlike in the pagan world), but a job description and status to which God had appointed him. 'King' was a role which others certainly wished upon Jesus (see John 6.15). The Roman occupation of Jewish land was much hated; to seize a military advantage and expel the enemy was an aspiration of the people which Jesus could have capitalized upon, but did not. (*See also* ZEALOTS.)

Of these titles, Messiah and Son of David were foreign to the Greek-speaking world, which is why Messiah in its Greek form of 'Christ' became a proper name and not a title. Son of God was recognized, but as an affirmation of divine parentage; this provided a strong line of development. King was instantly available, but as a political threat and so not so popular.

Metaphors ultimately derived from the Hebrew Bible could be applied to Jesus, and universal concepts such as 'image' (see Hebrews 1.3) or philosophical ideas such as *logos* ('WORD/rational principle') – see John 1.1. But the overwhelming popularity was ascribed to 'Lord' (Hebrew *Adonai*, Greek *Kurios*). A practice of calling Jesus 'Lord' had grown up during his ministry, at which point it may just have been a respectful 'Sir', but in the later New Testament usage it moved towards an open acknowledgement of divinity (see Philippians 2.11).

Titus In the PASTORAL EPISTLE addressed to him, Titus is PAUL's representative on the Mediterranean island of Crete (Titus 1.5). There is no reference elsewhere in the New Testament to a mission to Crete. Eusebius in his *Church History* (3.4.6), however, describes him as bishop of Crete until his old age. Titus is not mentioned in Acts, but is documented in Galatians and 2 Corinthians, where he is one of Paul's co-workers. In the controversy over whether GENTILE Christians should be circumcised (see CIRCUMCISION), Titus provided a test-case (Galatians 2.3), having accompanied Paul to Jerusalem; and was a diplomatic agent of Paul and administrator in the city of Corinth, dealing with matters such as the COLLECTION for Jerusalem (2 Corinthians, chapter 8; see also 2.13; 7.6; 12.18).

Titus, Emperor It is claimed (although JOSEPHUS attempts to exonerate him) that Titus, the son of Emperor Vespasian, following his capture of JERUSALEM in 70 CE, was responsible for the despoliation of the TEMPLE. He is said to have stormed the Temple, slaughtered captives, defiled the Temple court with a ritual Roman sacrifice, and then burned the city to the ground. The triumphal Arch of Titus was erected in the Roman forum, where it still stands, to celebrate these events and to depict the Temple spoils, including the MENORAH, being carried in procession. In consequence Titus became a much-hated figure in Jewish and JEWISH-CHRISTIAN tradition. It is possible that Titus should be identified as the sixth head, now reigning, of the seven-headed beast in REVELATION 17.10. Titus acceded to the throne in 79 CE, on the death of his father, but died just two years later. Jewish tradition ascribed an agonizing end to the destroyer of their Temple; rabbinic traditions speak of an insect which devoured his brain (*Genesis Rabbah* 10.7), while other texts speak of his sword drawing blood from the TORAH scroll or the Temple curtain.

Tobias *See* RAPHAEL; TOBIT, BOOK OF.

Tobit, book of This book of the Old Testament APOCRYPHA was composed in HEBREW or ARAMAIC, probably during the 2nd century BCE; a range of ancient and medieval versions exist, including five DEAD SEA SCROLL fragments. It is a piece of historical fiction, possibly combining Jewish teaching with material from ancient folklore, and its purpose is as a moral tale, concerned with the efforts of a Jewish family to remain faithful while living, separated from the HOLY LAND, in the DIASPORA. The details of the story should not be regarded as accurate, historically or geographically. As a WISDOM text, like JOB, it offers an explanation of the problem of suffering.

Tobit is a blind man, a devout Jew living in exile in NINEVEH. He sends his young son, Tobias, on a long journey to Media to recover a debt. His travelling companion is none other than the angel RAPHAEL who undertakes to guide him and help with the challenges of the trip, revealing magic formulae for healing and EXORCISM. In Media a demon-possessed kinswoman, Sarah, is rescued and subsequently marries Tobias. On Tobias' return, Tobit is cured of his blindness and told to write down everything. His book becomes an account of the woes of one generation being redressed in the next, essentially a vindication of the long-term JUSTICE of God.

The book's themes are popular in later art and literature. Among the most recent examples is a novel by Salley Vickers, *Miss Garnet's Angel*.

topheth This is in origin an ARAMAIC word meaning 'fireplace' or 'hearth' which was adopted as a name for the site of child sacrifice such as in the valley of Ben-Hinnom near Jerusalem. Accordingly the name was pronounced with the vowels of the Hebrew word for 'shame', as such practice ('sacrifices to Moloch') was condemned as a PAGAN and foreign import into the religious practice of Israel in the times of Isaiah and Jeremiah (see Isaiah 30.33; Jeremiah 7.31; 32.35; 2 Kings 16.3; 23.10; 2 Chronicles 28.3). Ahaz and MANASSEH among the KINGS OF JUDAH are said to have been involved in the practice, while JOSIAH tried to put a stop to it.

Torah, or Law The Hebrew word *torah* means 'teaching'. In the Hebrew Bible this teaching consists of the first five books of Scripture, Genesis to Deuteronomy, known as the 'PENTATEUCH' (*see also* PENTATEUCHAL CRITICISM), traditionally regarded as being written by MOSES after his meeting with God on Mount SINAI. These texts of the 'written law' are supplemented for JUDAISM by a verbal exposition (known as the 'oral law'). Taken together, and with the fullest Rabbinic interpretation (*see* RABBI), Torah comes to mean the sum total of Jewish Law, a comprehensive system of guidance for both religious and social life, that was believed to have been given by divine revelation. The expression 'Torah scroll' can also be used of a single scroll of the law books. *See also* LAW; SCRIBES.

In the Christian tradition the DECALOGUE (Ten Commandments) has often been highlighted as the focus of the Law, but Rabbinic exegesis does not seem to have privileged it in this way. (An exception would be the work of PHILO, who used the Decalogue as a series of headings in his attempt to relate Biblical law to Greek philosophy.) The rabbis debated extensively about the first principles of the Law (see Mark 12.28). Jesus' response to such questioning, in terms of a summary of the Law, a definition of the two great commandments, or the two commandments of LOVE, is essentially an exposition of Deuteronomy 6.4–5. In the Jewish LITURGY this text is known as the SHEMA' (from its opening Hebrew word meaning 'hear'), a text which is to be recited twice a day.

trade Israel in Old Testament times benefited from its geographical position as a land bridge linking Egypt to Asia Minor and to Mesopotamia (see FERTILE CRESCENT). Israel had ready access to the main travel routes, the WAY OF THE SEA, and the HIGHWAY OF THE KING which ran east of the JORDAN. Commercial traffic flowed through Israel as well as to it; in times of political and military power the imposition of taxation on the through traffic must have been lucrative. In good times, therefore, the country prospered. Its best trading alliance was with PHOENICIA, with an exchange of the oil, grain and wine that Israel produced for the manufactured goods and crafts in which Phoenicia specialized. At the height of its trading powers under SOLOMON the opulent goods to furnish the TEMPLE arrived this way too. According to 1 Kings 10–12 Solomon obtained quantities of gold from various sources, as well as silver, ivory and amusing novelties such as apes and baboons (even peacocks from India, if this translation of 10.22 is preferred, and Tarshish is located in that direction). Oil, grain and wine also were exported elsewhere, together with wool from Israel's flocks. Whereas King Ben-Hadad of Aram (Syria) and King OMRI had clearly made an agreement to hold markets in each other's capitals, this was not such a longstanding working relationship, for it foundered when hostilities broke out. The PHILISTINES moved into the Iron Age quicker than their neighbours and Israel later benefited from the resultant trade, especially with Egypt. Life domestically was made sweeter by the import of spices, incense, and perfumes from afar, and during the early years of the monarchy trade came from Arabia, Africa, and possibly further afield, for instance India. The Queen of SHEBA visited Solomon with many gifts of gold, jewels, and spices, doubtless in ratification of this kind of commerce. About this period the camel caravans came to be used to traverse the deserts, which must have increased the volume of trade.

Although sea travel (*see* SHIPS AND THE SEA) was not something the Israelites embraced, and their own coastline lacked natural harbours to facilitate this, their neighbours in Philistia and Phoenicia were adept sailors and this brought another possibility of Mediterranean trade. The major ports were at Joppa, DOR and ACCO. The richness of seaborne trade may be seen in Ezekiel's funeral lament for the Phoenician city of TYRE (see Ezekiel 27) and this some 400 years after the time of King Solomon mentioned above.

At the end of this period COINAGE came to be employed widely in trading, and the Jews acquired expertise in banking, which was itself an exportable skill and led to the formation of expatriate communities of specialists in ALEXANDRIA and throughout Asia Minor (accounting for the SYNAGOGUES awaiting PAUL's visits).

In New Testament times Judaea did not see financial benefits so directly from trade, because everything was tightly controlled – and taxed – by the Romans. Prosperity came more from collaboration with the occupying power and sharing in the farming of taxes or collecting of tolls. Trading operated by the NABATEANS, with their camel trains from Arabia and the East, still flowed through southern Palestine to the ports at Gaza and to the south; this continued until the rise of Palmyra in the 2nd century CE diverted the trade to other routes. There are incidental references in Acts, such as to LYDIA's prosperous trade in PURPLE, and to the threat posed, by the success of Paul's preaching, to the silversmiths of EPHESUS, whose votive figures of Diana saw a downturn in sales figures. The letters to the SEVEN CHURCHES in the book of REVELATION are full of local knowledge, and include several references to local trades and guilds. Revelation 18 (in a lament with parallels to Ezekiel 27) illustrates vividly the way the merchants and entrepreneurs are disastrously implicated in the anticipated fall of Rome (Babylon). But by and large issues of trade are not a major New Testament concern.

Trajan, Emperor *See* PERSECUTION OF CHRISTIANS.

Transfiguration of Christ Narrative accounts of the Transfiguration of Jesus can be found (with slight variations) in Matthew 17.1–13, Mark 9.2–13, and Luke 9.28–36; it is also referred to in 2 Peter 1.16–18. Jesus is accompanied by the inner group of three DISCIPLES (PETER, JAMES, and JOHN) as witnesses; they climb a mountain (traditionally identified as Mount TABOR), where Jesus meets and talks with MOSES and ELIJAH in a scene of glorious brilliance. The event is highly symbolic, uniting the LAW and the prophets of the Old Testament with representative figures of the New Testament Church. 'Was it a vision? Or did we see that day the unseeable one GLORY of the everlasting world?' (Edwin Muir).

The Transfiguration Matthew 17.1–8

trees There are abundant references to trees in the Bible, both real and symbolic (see Judges 9.8–15 for a parable of trees, and also Ezekiel 31.3–18). Israel's own arboreal culture meant that important crops were gathered from the olive (oil for cooking, lighting and personal use, as well as fruit as a relish for a meal), the fig, and the VINE. So important were they that the vision of PEACE was in these terms: 'they shall all sit under their own vines and under their own fig trees, and no one shall make them afraid' (Micah 4.4). There are commands expressly against destroying fruit trees in warfare (Deuteronomy 20.19), because trees were not their enemies. Should this also apply to the Israeli government today, when bulldozing Palestinian olive orchards? People were well aware of the uses of the wood, once the tree was past its productive life (Ezekiel 15.3). Other woods were imported for specific purposes (see 1 Kings 5.6).

Both the vine and the olive became symbols for Israel as a nation (see Isaiah 5.1–7; Ezekiel 19.10; Romans 11.17). Further symbols were removed from contact with actual species, such as the tree of life (a motif shared with many other cultures). The tree of life grows in the heavenly city, and its leaves are for the healing of the nations (Ezekiel 47.12; Revelation 22.2). The 'family tree' of Jesus was said by early Christians to originate from JESSE (interpreting Isaiah 11.1); this verse explains the design of the 'Jesse tree' in church carvings and stained-glass windows.

trial of Jesus There are four accounts of the trial of Jesus of Nazareth, given in the Gospel texts known as PASSION NARRATIVES (see outline of contents there). Two of the accounts (Mark and Matthew) are broadly similar, although Matthew lays special emphasis on Jewish blood-guilt. Luke has an extra scene of a trial before the Roman client-king, Herod Antipas, while John offers an extended political discussion between Jesus and Pontius PILATE, the Roman PROCURATOR, in the course of the trial.

In Mark the mood is dark and sombre; by contrast John seems triumphalist, with Jesus ultimately in charge. Luke has modified the accusation against Jesus (23.2) in a way which may recall the trial of Socrates in Athens. He also suggests a parallel between the trial of Christ and the subsequent trials of Christians, such as PAUL in the ACTS OF THE APOSTLES. Within a conventional date-order of composition (Mark, Matthew, Luke, John), it is possible to argue for a progressive attempt to lighten the responsibility of the Romans for the CRUCIFIXION of Jesus, and correspondingly to increase the responsibility of the Jews. Ultimately and tragically the Christian belief that the Jews killed Jesus resulted in intensifying ANTI-SEMITIC attitudes, up to the HOLOCAUST enacted by the Nazis in 20th-century Europe.

On what charge, by whose instigation, did Jesus of Nazareth die? It is clear that he underwent processes more formal than those of a lynch-mob, and was sentenced to die by crucifixion. So much does most extant documentation from Roman, Jewish, and Christian authors attest. But the sources desert us in the details, because the fullest sources of the Gospels were not written to guide historians.

For centuries the Christian Church followed Paul (1 Thessalonians 2.15), saying that 'the Jews killed both the Lord Jesus and the prophets'. But no Jew ever crucified anyone; unlike stoning, crucifixion was not a Jewish punishment (any more than the electric chair was ever the death penalty in the UK). The Mishnah tractate *Sanhedrin* 7.1 stipulates: 'The Court had power to inflict four kinds of death penalty: stoning, burning, beheading and strangling.' This sounds clear-cut, but the ordinances of the Mishnah were not codified until well after the time of Jesus, although much of the material is retrospective (not new legislation) and so might well be valid already in the time of Jesus. But there is no certainty whether the Jewish authorities possessed the right to pass the death sentence, or to carry it out without reference to the Roman military governor, during the time of Jesus. A key text here is John 18.31: 'It is not lawful for us to put any man to death.' This is corroborated by the Jerusalem TALMUD which says that 'forty years before the destruction of the TEMPLE [70 CE] the right to inflict the death penalty was taken away from Israel'. Neither of these statements is incontrovertible; both may be only partial accounts.

Whatever the competence of Jewish authorities during the time of Jesus, it remains indisputable that crucifixion was a Roman penalty. Jesus was therefore executed in the Roman manner, as prescribed by Roman law. The punishment was normally restricted to certain lower classes of society (to which Jesus belonged) and to certain categories of crime (including the charge against Jesus). This makes it inevitable that the court was Roman. We know that crucifixion was a penalty for slaves, or for rebels against the state (according to *Sentenzia Pauli* V.xxii, *De Seditiosis* 1). In the JEWISH WAR against Rome, nearly 40 years after Jesus' death, the Romans crucified many of the prisoners they took; as JOSEPHUS describes (*Jewish War* 5.451), 'so great was their number that space could not be found for the crosses, nor crosses for the bodies'.

Is it necessary to conclude, from the fact that Jesus was crucified, that he must have led an armed revolt against Rome? Some have argued this, but the evidence is sparse: it might include the titulus 'KING OF THE JEWS' on the cross (Mark 15.26) and the references in all four Gospels to a sword and its use in the garden of GETHSEMANE (Matthew 26.51; Mark 14.47; Luke 22.35–38; John 18.10). Concentration on Jesus as political revolutionary does not accord well with Gospel evidence, but it remains possible that Jesus was mistakenly regarded as a political rebel by the authorities. Under the Roman *lex Julia*, to claim to be king of a province ruled by Rome, without being appointed or recognized by the emperor, constituted the capital crime of *laesa maiestatis*, for which crucifixion was a prescribed penalty.

In Gospel accounts of the Jewish trial (see Mark 14.61–64) Jesus is judged guilty of the crime of BLASPHEMY and would therefore be liable to capital punishment under religious law. But there are two difficulties here: if Jesus was guilty of blasphemy he should have suffered the traditional punishment of stoning (not crucifixion), for Jewish law is quite specific. Secondly there is the technical question whether Jesus was guilty of blasphemy; according to the Mishnah (*Sanhedrin* 7.5), '"the blasphemer" is not culpable unless he pronounces the Name itself'. The reference is to the sacred tetragrammaton, the four original Hebrew letters of God's proper name, only uttered by the HIGH PRIEST once a year, and otherwise paraphrased out of reverence as 'my Lord' (*Adonai*). According to the Gospel accounts of the trial, Jesus had not actually used this proper name; he had not even employed the word 'God', but instead had spoken in a periphrasis of 'the Power'. To claim to be MESSIAH (if that is what 'SON OF MAN' is taken to mean) was not in itself blasphemous, and therefore not an offence under Jewish law.

One might conclude that 'the Roman court had to define sedition that was not strictly sedition' while 'the Jewish court had to define blasphemy that was not technically blasphemy' (C. K. Barrett). The death of Jesus was a complex event, made up of mixed motives and cross-purposes. On the legal issues, it is reasonable to state that up to a date around 30 CE there appear to have been two systems of criminal law in force in Judaea. Offences against Roman law would be tried by the military governor who, exercising the delegated jurisdiction of the emperor, would sit *in camera* in his Praetorium or headquarters. His sentences could only be executed by the troops under his direct command. Normally only a single individual could appear as prosecutor, but an accused's confession of guilt would be sufficient to convict. Offences that were purely against Jewish law, on the other hand, were left to the jurisdiction of the native Jewish courts, the Great or the Small SANHEDRIN. These could properly sit as criminal courts in the daytime, in the precincts of the Temple (not in the High Priest's palace), and not on FESTIVAL days (possibly not also on the eve of a festival). Their sentences had to be executed by their own officials, in strict accordance with Jewish law. Confessions of guilt were not in themselves admissible, but the sworn evidence of at least two witnesses would be necessary to convict. The question remains incompletely answered as to who – or, perhaps better, what – crucified Jesus.

The historical timing of Jesus' arrest and trial also deserves discussion, not only because of implications of Jewish irregularities in a hurried night-time trial. The Gospel traditions associate the trial and DEATH OF CHRIST with the Jewish feast of PASSOVER, but they are by no means agreed on the exact chronology. Passover lasts for several days, but the key event, then as now, is the meal taken on the first evening (Jewish days are measured from dusk, not dawn). There is evidence that more than one religious CALENDAR was in operation in the 1st century CE. Just as now Passover is celebrated a day earlier in Jerusalem than in the Jewish Diaspora, so then the Temple priests or the monastic community at QUMRAN might well have started the festival up to three days before the rest of the population.

Why could this be significant? Firstly because if Jesus had been arrested on Tuesday evening (Wednesday) rather than Thursday evening (Friday), there would have been more time for proper procedures in the trials, instead of a summary lack of justice. And secondly it provides a chance to resolve the drastic inconsistencies between the Gospels on the all-important association with Passover. According to Mark, Matthew, and Luke it is fairly clear that Jesus and his disciples left the Passover supper to go to his arrest in Gethsemane. But in John's version (18.28, 19.14, supported by Paul in 1 Corinthians 5.7), Jesus dies on the cross at the time when the Passover lambs are being offered in the Temple, so that Jesus was already dead by the time the Jews in general were eating their Passover. Both these schedules could be true historically, if two different calendars were in operation. Beyond this, there is clearly theological significance both in the sacrificial nature of Christ's death, and also in the Passover character of the Last Supper, now commemorated by Christians in the EUCHARIST. There is also a link with the charges brought at the Jewish trial, for there is a Jewish tradition that the Messiah would come and bring deliverance on Passover night ('a night in which one watches for the Lord' – interpreting Exodus 12.42).

tribulation, great, or messianic woes Early Jewish thought among the RABBIS, and subsequently Christian ideas, anticipated a final time of suffering and trial, which would be a feature of the End Time (*see* APOCALYPTIC and ESCHATON). A good example of such thinking in the New Testament is to be found in the 'Little Apocalypse' of Mark 13. The great tribulation or trial is sometimes envisaged in terms of the pains of childbirth. The use of the term 'messianic' was widespread in earlier scholarship, but should only be applied when the figure of the MESSIAH is directly implicated.

Mark Dubis has defined well the expectation of the messianic woes: 'a tumultuous period of eschatological distress. Characteristic features include apostasy, war, earthquakes, drought, famine, pestilence, familial strife and betrayal, cosmic signs, increasing wickedness, and scarcity of truth and wisdom. Known as the "birth pangs of the Messiah" these woes lead inexorably to the birth of the final state of blessedness.'

tribute money *See* COINAGE.

Trinity In Christian theology the Trinity represents a major doctrinal theme, exploring the relationship between the three persons of the Godhead: God the FATHER, Jesus Christ the SON OF GOD, and God the Holy SPIRIT. However, no precise term for the Trinity is to be found in the Bible, nor does the New Testament contain any exactly equivalent term to the later credal formulations of Christian doctrine, expressing a threefold equal partnership.

The New Testament writers do focus on the individual persons (Father, Son and Spirit) and JOHN'S GOSPEL in particular discusses the relationship between Father and Son (see 1.1; 10.30) and the role of the Spirit as PARACLETE. The earliest New Testament use of a formula bringing together the three persons is found at 2 Corinthians 13.13 ('the grace of the Lord Jesus, the love of God, and the communion of the Holy Spirit'), although this may be an addition to the text, from Christian WORSHIP. Similarly MATTHEW'S GOSPEL, at 28.19, contains a threefold commission to teach and to baptize 'in the name of the Father and of the Son and of the Holy Spirit'; this probably reflects a growing understanding of BAPTISM in the Church. In the earliest days of Christianity there is a wealth of reflection on the ideas in Jesus' teaching and a development in worship practice, giving rise to a variety of phrases, hymns, and prayers that anticipate in a provisional way some aspects of the later credal declarations.

In the development of later Christian IMAGERY, for example for the icons that were used by Orthodox theologians, time was spent in looking for anticipatory glimpses within the Old Testament of the Holy Trinity. One example, used in icons from the 6th century CE, and most famously by Andrei Rublev in 1422, is the episode in Genesis 18 concerning ABRAHAM's hospitality to three visiting ANGELS (identified in Christian theology as the One and Triune Godhead). Similar efforts are made to assemble a Trinitarian reference in the story of CREATION in Genesis 1 involving God, his creative WORD, and the wind from God over the face of the waters. Others have suggested that the threefold formula ('Holy, holy, holy') of the TRISAGION implies a reference to the Trinity.

Trisagion The Trisagion, a Greek expression meaning 'thrice holy', refers to the chant of praise which begins 'Holy, holy, holy', as sung by the seraphim above the altar in the TEMPLE in Isaiah 6.3, and by the four living creatures around the throne of God in heaven in Revelation 4.8. Later this formula becomes a regular feature of Christian LITURGIES first in the East and then in the Western Roman rite.

See also HOLINESS.

triumphal entry As the name traditionally given to Jesus' arrival in Jerusalem on the first Palm Sunday this term is in fact deeply ironic. Jesus appears to have signalled something quite different from triumphalism in any form by his choice of a humble workaday donkey as his mount. He may have been planning to fulfil the Zechariah

9.9 quotation, as a clear indication that his perception of being the MESSIAH involved PEACE, and not the imminent overthrow of the Roman occupation. That the welcoming, and/or accompanying, crowds perceived it differently is apparent by their cheers and actions. That it was thus seen by the Jewish authorities as a provocative act is made clear in the Gospels. All four Gospels carry this story: Matthew 21.1–11; Mark 11.1–11; Luke 19.28–40; John 12.12–19. This indicates the importance which was ascribed to it.

According to the SYNOPTIC Gospels Jesus had planned this event in advance, with arrangements in place to borrow the donkey (two animals for Matthew, because of his literal adherence to the prophetic text, ignoring Hebrew parallelism). Security was also in place to protect it, with an agreed formula or password to achieve the loan of the beast. In contrast John's Gospel reports a more *ad hoc* adopting of a donkey. The disciples draped the animal with cloaks, imitating royal trappings, in the Synoptics, and the crowd responded by throwing down cloaks as a makeshift red carpet, which is augmented by freshly cut branches in Matthew and Mark. John makes the crowd cut palm branches (Israel's national plant, like the rose for England) and carry them – perhaps to wave. The exact words shouted by the people differ slightly from Gospel to Gospel, but the inclusion of a messianic welcome formula, and the mention of 'King' and 'David', are universal, and would have sounded threatening to those in power.

In Matthew the crowd accompanies Jesus into the city, and would appear to be largely Galilean pilgrims, who have to explain Jesus' identity to the inhabitants; the crowd is with Jesus in Mark too, and is identified as Jesus' disciples in Luke. On the other hand John's (more local) crowd associates Jesus with the man who cured LAZARUS, and comes out to welcome him in, hoping for another miracle. This leads the PHARISEES to despair at Jesus' ever-growing popularity. Luke also involves the Pharisees at this point, but as telling Jesus to rebuke his disciples for their noise, which he refuses to do.

What happens next is the CLEANSING OF THE TEMPLE in the Synoptics, straightaway in Matthew, deferred until the following day in Mark, and after Jesus has wept over Jerusalem in Luke. John's rather briefer account leads into the story of the Greeks coming to Jesus, because he has told the story of the cleansing at the start of Jesus' ministry.

Troas Troas was a major seaport constructed in Asia Minor on the north-west coast facing Macedonia and about 12 miles from ancient Troy. An earlier name was Alexandria, but it was called Troas (after Troy) to distinguish it from other cities named after Alexander the Great. It was an important link in Roman communications and became one for the early Christians too. The land route to ROME was reached by sailing across the Aegean Sea from Troas to Neapolis in Macedonia. According to Acts 16.9 it was here that PAUL received his VISION of a man requesting his help in Macedonia, which led to the gospel being taken to Europe. It is argued that Luke was also with Paul in Troas, for it is from here (Acts 16.10) that the so-called 'we' passages (the use of the first person plural in narrative in Acts) begins. It was in Troas also that Eutychus fell from a third-floor window (having fallen asleep during Paul's lengthy sermon) and was revived by Paul (see Acts 20.7–12). The Church there saw much coming and going of missionaries (*see* MISSION), and there are incidental references in the epistles; 2 Timothy 4.13 represents Paul as desperate to be reunited with the coat and books he left there.

trumpets According to the narrative of Numbers chapter 10, two silver trumpets are to be made for use during the period of the people's WILDERNESS wanderings. These are to be blown by the priests, and their use is almost entirely for sacred rather than secular purposes. They were to symbolize the gathering and assembly of the people; the break-up of the camp and the continuation of the journey from SINAI; the sounding of an alarm; a battle-cry or call to WAR; and at FESTIVALS as a celebration of well-being over the offerings and SACRIFICES. JOSEPHUS subsequently stated that these were slender trumpets, about a foot long, with a wide mouth; such trumpets are also depicted on later coins.

The Hebrew language has several words for trumpets. Other important examples are made from animal horns, such as the ram's horn (*shofar*) which is sounded at the New Year or on the Day of Atonement (YOM KIPPUR). See Leviticus 23.23–25 and Numbers 29.1–6. The Feast of Trumpets, or the 'day of horn-blasts', occurs on the first day of the month of Tishri in the Hebrew CALENDAR. It is possible to use any horn of a clean animal, except for a cow's horn (because Israel once worshipped the GOLDEN CALF). But the horn of a ram is preferred for symbolic reasons as it echoes the substitution of a ram for the sacrifice of ISAAC in the AKEDAH (see Genesis 22.13).

In the book of REVELATION (see chapters 8–9; 10.7; 11.15) the sequence of seven trumpet blasts, blown by ANGELS, introduces divine judgements (echoing the tradition of the PLAGUES OF EGYPT). Trumpets may signal the beginning of the End Time (see Isaiah 27.13; Joel 2.1; Matthew 24.31; 1 Corinthians 15.52; 1 Thessalonians 4.16; *Didache* 16.6; *see also* ESCHATON).

typology A distinction needs to be maintained in methods of Biblical interpretation between ALLEGORY and typology. While allegory claims that the real meaning of a text has no continuity either with the historical situation of the author or with the apparent surface meaning of the text, typology argues that there is an essential continuity between the two situations, and a correspondence which is to be recognized within the plan of God. In this method of interpretation the Old Testament can supply a prefiguration of what God is to fulfil in the New Testament. A standard example of such typological exegesis is to be found in the correspondence which PAUL draws, in 1 Corinthians 15.22 and Romans 5.14, between ADAM and CHRIST. Strictly speaking, Paul's 'allegories' are typological interpretations, being very conscious of the various prefigurations provided in the Hebrew Bible. The actual word for prefiguration/antitype first occurs in 1 Peter 3.21, in a comparison between NOAH's Ark and BAPTISM.

Tyre and Sidon These two cities on the Mediterranean coast of Israel/Palestine were important trading centres for the PHOENICIANS. Tyre was originally built on the coastal strip and extended onto a fortified island about half a mile offshore. It was the source of skills and materials for the building of the Jerusalem TEMPLE by King

SOLOMON (see 1 Kings 9–10). Tyre was frequently denounced by the prophets; see, for examples, Ezekiel 26–28 (28.13 indicates the riches of the place in the Babylonian period) and Zechariah 9.1–4. The island city was besieged and demolished by Alexander the Great c.332 BCE.

Sidon was one of the most ancient Phoenician cities, situated to the north on the fertile coastal plain. It was fortified with a strong wall and had twin harbours, protected by small islands and a breakwater. Ships from Sidon ventured onto the open seas, and it is said that they could navigate by night using the stars. Sidon was destroyed by Artaxerxes III following a rebellion against the Persians in 352 BCE. Twenty years later it opened its gates to Alexander the Great, and as a consequence benefited greatly from its rival's fall.

U

Ugarit, or Ras Shamra Ugarit is an ancient town in northern Syria which has been identified as Ras Shamra. It was inhabited as early as the Neolithic period, and later provides evidence of Hyksos, Horite and HITTITE occupation. Probably its greatest importance is for its CANAANITE evidence. There is a large temple dedicated to BA'AL, and a store of documents showing the development of religious epics and an alphabetic script with some relationship to Biblical HEBREW.

unction, extreme unction The word 'unction' refers to the act of anointing with oil in a context where this has religious significance. Originally in the Hebrew Bible it would refer to the special anointing of a priest or the coronation of a king (at 1 Samuel 16.13 DAVID is anointed as king of Israel; *see also* MESSIAH – the Hebrew word means 'anointed one'). Holy objects such as the TABERNACLE, its altar and furnishings could also be anointed. Anointing is a sign of consecration, as when Moses is instructed to anoint and consecrate the tabernacle (see Exodus 40.9–16). In the Christian tradition the rite of unction is sometimes used at BAPTISM and CONFIRMATION, as part of the process of initiation. There is an enigmatic reference to 'anointing' in 1 John 2.27 which may well refer to the particular act of initiation and its consequences. But the word 'unction' is most frequently used in the Christian tradition of the SACRAMENTAL act of anointing the sick. This corresponds to New Testament instances of such anointing (see Mark 6.13; James 5.14) in the context of ritual actions in the healing of the sick (*see* MIRACLES). Extreme unction usually refers to the giving of the last rites, when someone is on the point of death; the use of the word 'extreme' is contested, and it may simply refer to the last of three sacramental rites involving the use of oil.

Underworld *See* SHEOL.

Ur (Ur of the Chaldees) The original home of ABRAHAM is identified in the Bible (Genesis 11.31) as the city of Ur, which is now in modern Iraq. But some scholars have questioned this identification, on the grounds that the next place mentioned in Abraham's travels, HARAN, is over 1000 miles away; for this reason some prefer to locate Ur at Ura or Urfa nearby, within the boundaries of modern Turkey.

At the time of Abraham, c.1900 BCE, Ur in Mesopotamia was a wealthy and cosmopolitan city, originally founded c.5000 BCE by the Ubaids, but absorbing both Semites and SUMERIANS, the latter becoming dominant. Sumerian records chronicle three royal dynasties at Ur, the third of which flourished, and the cultural life of the city with it, in the century before Abraham. Much of the knowledge about Ur comes from the archaeological work of Sir Leonard Woolley, who excavated there between 1922 and 1934, and who claimed mistakenly to have found evidence for the great FLOOD.

Ur is referred to as 'Ur of the Chaldees' for a later reason, being named after the particular and powerful dynasty which settled there and fought against the ASSYRIAN Empire c.900 BCE.

Uriah the Hittite *See* BATHSHEBA; NATHAN.

Urim and Thummim EXODUS 28.15–30 indicates that these are appendages to the special breastplate worn by the HIGH PRIEST, and that they were used for purposes of divination throughout the Old Testament period and into the Second TEMPLE period. 'In the breastpiece of judgement you shall place the Urim and the Thummim, and they shall be on AARON's heart when he goes in before the Lord.' The breastplate had rows of precious stones, totalling 12, one for each of the tribes of Israel. Urim and Thummim were two stones kept in a pouch inside the breastplate, giving a yes/no answer to questions put to them. Their names denote the 'revelation and truth' (literally 'lights and perfections') associated with this oracular power. The precise way in which they worked is unclear: some suggest they were light and dark stones, the latter being the equivalent of a black ball; JOSEPHUS (*Antiquities* 3.215–216) says they were sardonyxes, and one of the two would shine out with an unnaturally bright splendour when God was present at, and so approving of, a SACRIFICE. Three fragments from the DEAD SEA SCROLLS (1Q29, 4Q376, 4Q408) refer to MOSES' tongues of fire in this same context of the oracular properties of light/fire in the High Priest's breastplate. The shield of the University of Yale carries the Hebrew words 'Urim and Thummim', reflecting 18th-century Puritan theology which emphasized the Old Testament and linked the oracular will of God to the person of Christ.

Utnapishtim *See* FLOOD; GILGAMESH.

Uzziah Uzziah (otherwise known as Azariah – see 2 Kings 14 and 15) was an 8th-century BCE KING OF JUDAH, the son of Amaziah, whom he succeeded at the age of 16, when his father was driven from office. Uzziah proved a popular king, both in military matters, by victories and equipping the army (see 2 Chronicles 26), and also in improvements for agriculture and the cultivation of the VINE. As an older man he contracted leprosy; this was seen as a divine judgement, and Uzziah was compelled to abdicate in favour of his son Jotham. The prophets AMOS and HOSEA were both active during his reign, and ISAIAH's temple vision (Isaiah 6.1–13) happened in the year that Uzziah died.

V

vanity of vanities The origin of this phrase is ECCLESIASTES 1.2: 'Vanity of vanities, says the Teacher, ... all is vanity.' They are words which seem to sum up the pessimistic theme of this book, or at least the problem with which the author grappled. The word translated as 'vanity' – in Hebrew *hebel* – is being used metaphorically from its meaning of 'breath' or 'breeze'. The parallelism which is characteristic of Hebrew poetry (*see* PSALMS) often balances this idea with 'chasing after wind' (as in 1.14).

Vashti, Queen *See* ESTHER, BOOK OF.

Veronica Veronica is the name of the woman who, according to Christian tradition (probably from the 14th century), wiped Jesus' brow at the point of the sixth of the STATIONS OF THE CROSS. Her cloth was said to bear the imprint of Jesus' face. The name Veronica actually means 'true image'. In tradition (in a late version of the *Acts of Pilate* 7) she is identified as the woman with an issue of blood who was healed as she touched the hem of Jesus' garment (Mark 5.25–34; Matthew 9.20–22; Luke 8.43–48). Saint Veronica's feast day is 12 July.

Via Dolorosa *See* STATIONS OF THE CROSS.

Via Maris *See* WAY OF THE SEA.

vine, vineyard This central image of Mediterranean cultures is richly developed in the Bible. The vine was one of the blessings of the Promised Land (Genesis 49.11; Deuteronomy 6.11). While the Israelites previously had been nomadic, the Settlement of CANAAN made it possible for everyone to sit 'under his vine and under his fig tree' (1 Kings 4.25). Symbolically it becomes a description of the nation Israel, as precious to their God, YAHWEH (Psalm 80.8–14; cf. Isaiah 5.1–7). But in some of the prophetic writings and in the WISDOM traditions this vine is regarded as degenerate. In the New Testament the metaphor is transferred to apply to the KINGDOM OF GOD (Matthew 21.33–43); the significant difference is that this vine will bear lasting fruit. Jesus is identified as the true vine (*see* SEVEN 'I AM' SAYINGS) into which is incorporated his DISCIPLES and his CHURCH as they carry on his work (John 15). Revelation 14.18–20 applies the image to the LAST JUDGEMENT: the vintage is of 'the grapes ... of the wrath of God'. (Compare Isaiah 63.1–6; the American words of Julia Ward Howe's 'Battle Hymn of the Republic'; and the title of John Steinbeck's novel *The Grapes of Wrath*.)

virgin birth The BIRTH OF JESUS from the virgin MARY is important in Christian creeds and doctrine, but is only mentioned in a small number of texts in the New Testament (Matthew 1, Luke 1, but not Galatians 4.4). The Hebrew word of Isaiah 7.14, translated as 'virgin', can be used to refer less restrictedly to any young woman or girl; but it is clear from Matthew's emphasis that he understood Mary to have been a virgin.

Parthenogenesis (literally, from the Greek 'virgin birth') is the technical term in genetics for the situation where there is no mixture of parental genes, but all the genes come from one parental organism. As a natural process of cloning it is known to happen occasionally in plants and animals.

Stories of other human virgin births do exist in ancient and modern times. Some great men, such as Alexander, are said to be born without human father. A young woman was injured on the streets during Allied bombing of Hanover in 1944; she claimed she had not had sex, but gave birth to a daughter, identical to the mother, nine months later. This formed the inspiration for a piece of music-theatre by James MacMillan, *Parthenogenesis*, first performed in 2002.

virginity *See* CELIBACY; VIRGIN BIRTH.

vision Most known categories of visions and auditions can find examples in Scripture as well as in the lives of saints. The borderline between vision and dream is very hard to achieve in classifying a religious experience. The heightened awareness, and the perception of the message or purpose of the divine, are both critical, and the combination of ecstatic experience with the acquisition of revealed knowledge is an important characteristic.

The Old Testament acknowledges the role of seers when in an ecstatic state (*see* PROPHECY); ISAIAH and EZEKIEL would fit this category, as well as others. Both recorded visions that involved God in heavenly splendour. Some prophets' visions were much simpler than the elaborate mythological detail with which Ezekiel records the call he received to prophesy, while in EXILE in Babylon. The importance of the vision lies not so much in the detail of what is seen, fascinating though this is, but in the response of the prophet in accepting the message and then undertaking the task of relaying it. Sometimes the vision was disarmingly simple and relied on wordplay to convey its meaning, as with JEREMIAH's branch of 'almond blossom' which sounded so like the word for 'watching' (see Jeremiah 1.11–12). The role of the prophet was tied up with the particular history of God's people, not only understanding and expounding the divine plan of SALVATION history but also giving shrewd political advice. Isaiah is frequently perceived as a statesman as well as a prophet, for example. Forthcoming disaster on the international scene was interpreted as a chance to amend the ways of APOSTASY, or to change political allegiance away from dangerous allies. The nearer disaster loomed, the more possible it was to explain that this or that foe was about to wreak punishment, divinely ordained, on God's people, because of their failure to respond to the previous warnings:

After the main Old Testament era of classical prophecy was over the use of elaborate visions, redolent with symbolic meanings, became the preferred method of teaching of apocalyptists such as DANIEL. Later APOCALYPTIC texts developed the scope of visions experienced as a heavenly journey (see *1 Enoch* 12–36; 83–90; compare PAUL in 2 Corinthians 12.2–4; and *see* SEVENTH HEAVEN).

New Testament stories about visions show that it was a phenomenon that resurfaced with the new religious era; PETER'S PENTECOST sermon claimed this was the fulfilment of JOEL's eschatological prophecy (see Acts 2.14–36). At the close of the New Testament is the book of REVELATION recounting numerous visions which are again classified as apocalyptic.

Adela Yarbro Collins wrote: 'Vision accounts ... grasp the imagination and evoke feelings in ways that ordinary language cannot. Like poetry they present an interpretation of reality and invite the reader or listener to share it.' In this way she suggests that a vision from an original and quite specific context may have a symbolic application way beyond this in time and space.

vows A vow represents a sacred and binding commitment, an undertaking to give, or dedicate, something or someone – perhaps produce, or money, or the life of a child – to God. Jephthah's vow, resulting unintentionally in the sacrifice of his beloved daughter, belongs to this last category (see Judges 11). There are classical Greek parallels to this in the sacrifice of Iphigenia. Another good example is that of the child SAMUEL, who was left at the shrine at SHILOH in the care of the priest ELI, to fulfil HANNAH's VOW. NAZIRITES were vowed to God, and as a mark of this wore their hair uncut (*see* SAMSON) and drank no alcohol. In Acts 21 PAUL is persuaded by the Jerusalem Church to accompany four men to the Temple and help them finish their vow, ceremonially, and also to pay their expenses. This would demonstrate Paul's good faith to JUDAISM, as well as enabling the men to finish their vow by shaving their heads (not then a Nazirite vow). It ended disastrously, however, with Paul's arrest.

A meaningless or a mean-spirited vow was, of course, not tolerated; Mark 7.9–13 has Jesus condemning the hypocrisy which pronounced Corban (dedicated to God) goods which could have been used to assist aged parents.

Vulgate The earliest translations of the Bible into Latin exist in 3rd-century CE fragments. But the Latin version most widely used (*editio vulgata*) in Western Christianity was compiled by Jerome at the request of Pope Damasus in 382 CE. This was the version in which the Scriptures were read by Western Christians throughout the Middle Ages. The Gospels were finished first, followed by the rest of the New Testament, and the whole Bible was completed around 404 CE. For the Old Testament Jerome had begun with the SEPTUAGINT version, but then turned directly to the original HEBREW. As a translator his approach was radical and somewhat brutal. But the result was a Bible which largely replaced the Septuagint in the Christian Church. It was Jerome's Vulgate which Gutenberg printed in the Mazarin Bible of 1456, and Jerome's interpretations which Erasmus amended in his 1516 edition of the Greek New Testament.

See also TEXTUAL CRITICISM.

W

Wandering Jew The legend of the Wandering Jew is not Biblical; it probably originated in medieval folk traditions. An early account in 1228 refers to a Jew who represented himself as the doorkeeper to Pontius PILATE, and claimed that he himself had struck Jesus before the CRUCIFIXION in an incident something like that of John 18.22. The Jew has different names in different traditions: sometimes Cartaphilus, Joseph, Samuel, or even Malchus (the HIGH PRIEST's servant – see John 18.10).

war, holy war It is possible to perceive a split between Old and New Testament approaches to war. In the Hebrew Bible war may be interpreted as a religious duty, to forward the progress of God's state (especially during the period of the conquest of CANAAN, when war was viewed as 'holy war'). It became increasingly necessary for political aggrandizement under the early monarchy, and then to protect status (even to survive at all) during the international developments of the later monarchy. This would also involve the use of foreign mercenaries.

God was viewed as the instigator of the early wars; to settle in Canaan at all, the defeat of the indigenous peoples, and the ethnic cleansing entailed in the Settlement, were justified in this way. War was a religious activity, with the army preceded by priests bearing the ARK OF THE COVENANT. Participants had to follow strict rules of conduct, especially in the dedication of all booty and the lives of the enemy to the avenging God of battles. Individuals who disobeyed were punished, as a deterrent to all Israel: Achan and his family and livestock were executed because he appropriated goods to himself (Joshua 7). The prophet SAMUEL executed Agag, king of Amalek, when SAUL had failed to do this following the defeat of the Amalekites; Saul was effectively deprived of establishing a dynasty ('And the Lord was sorry that he had made Saul king over Israel' – 1 Samuel 15).

As today, Israel's ordinary male citizens were liable to be conscripted into the army to cope with eventualities. Exceptions were made for weakness, and recently married men were given a chance to establish a family (Deuteronomy 24.5). There was never a suggestion that 'You shall not murder' (Exodus 20.13) had anything to say about activities in wartime. Love and forgiveness are not Old Testament teachings in relation to war; the principle of revenge is paramount. Peace was a desirable goal, but the route to achieving it was governed by pragmatism.

The New Testament era was one of Roman military domination. Apart from the ZEALOTS there was little or no appetite for opposition. War in the normal sense is not a topic discussed by Jesus or the apostles. PAUL has been interpreted as indirectly sanctioning Christians to fight for the state by his admonitions to obey the authorities (Romans 13.1–2). Military metaphors are used (see Romans 13.12; 2 Corinthians 10.3–4; Ephesians 6.11–17; 1 Thessalonians 5.8; 2 Timothy 2.3–4) for the war against spiritual evil; and war was to be one of the preliminary events of the End Time (see Luke 21.9–10; Revelation 6.4). A Christian's active participation in these eschatological events is unclear, and whether Jesus did or did not sanction Christians' fighting is an area of considerable debate (*see* PEACE).

It would seem that Augustine of Hippo in the early 5th century brought an end to a period of apparent pacifism for Christians, in response to the emergencies facing the Roman Empire. He began the traditional definition of the JUST WAR which has been developed by saints and scholars subsequently, and relied upon by politicians to this day. Augustine was responsible for a flexible merging of holy war and just war; strictly a just war was a legal category (with secular application) while a holy war was a religious act with spiritual rewards; a just war was not necessarily a holy war, while a holy war was a just war in the eyes of its adherents. Indeed in today's Western world, zeal for a holy war may be seen as the behaviour of a fanatical minority. By contrast, to the people of medieval Europe, the Crusades were seen as a mainstream activity, promoted by the Church and endorsed by society through the active participation of everybody from monarchs to peasants.

war in heaven This heavenly battle is described (uniquely in Jewish and early Christian writings) in the book of REVELATION 12.7–9. The conflict is between the archangel MICHAEL and the 'great dragon' or SATAN. The outcome is the expulsion of Satan from heaven, which gives him greater scope to create problems on earth. For this idea compare Luke 10.18 and Isaiah 14.12–15; notice also John 12.31.

Watchers These are the 'fallen angels' in the ancient myth based on Genesis 6.1–4, about the 'sons of God' or 'nephilim' who consort with the daughters of human beings. In the section of the extra-canonical book *1 Enoch*, known as the 'Book of Watchers', these astral figures are the instigators of evil who bear responsibility for the judgement of the earth by the FLOOD. As the cosmic myth develops, these become the evil enemies who contaminate the earth and will ultimately be condemned in the LAST JUDGEMENT.

Way of the Cross *See* STATIONS OF THE CROSS.

Way of the Sea, or Via Maris The Via Maris was an historic route of north/south communication through the FERTILE CRESCENT along the coast of Palestine but bending inland at the Carmel range. *See also* HIGHWAY OF THE KING. The Via Maris may be referred to specifically in Isaiah 9.1, as quoted in Matthew 4.15.

Way of Sorrows *See* STATIONS OF THE CROSS.

wealth In the nomadic period of the PATRIARCHS wealth was primarily measured in the size of one's flocks of sheep and goats (see Genesis 13.2). In the later period of the Settlement and conquest of CANAAN the economic situation summed up in the familiar description of a 'land flowing with milk and honey' is usually taken still to reflect pastoral simplicity and not vast wealth. The period of the monarchy was to see rich entrepreneurs amassing wealth and creating an imbalance in society. Among the 8th-century BCE prophets AMOS condemned their attitude in furnishing extravagant lifestyles (4.1) and luxurious homes (3.15). He saw clearly the injustice to the poor and the creation of debt-SLAVERY (2.6) which shored up the security of the affluent (see also POVERTY).

Possession of wealth brought an obligation to TITHE, and to care for the poor (see Deuteronomy 26.12), but this could, of course, be ignored. If it was respected, then there was apparently no shame in being rich, and it became commonplace to regard wealth and longevity as God's reward for righteous behaviour (see Psalm 128.1–6). This view, and its converse – that the stripping of wealth was God's punishment for those in disfavour because of SIN – is subjected to criticism in the book of JOB.

Jesus' attitude to wealth appears to have been that its possession could endanger a person's chances of gaining eternal life, or entry to the KINGDOM OF GOD (Mark 10.25: 'It is easier for a camel to go through the eye of a needle than for someone who is rich to enter the kingdom of God'). According to Matthew and Luke, Jesus recommended that disciples should store up riches in heaven (Matthew 6.20; Luke 12.33), and those who hoarded on earth were in particular danger if they did not share. Extra barns full of goods would not save the rich fool (Luke 12.18–20), and the rich man (Dives) was to pay dearly for not even sharing his table scraps with the homeless beggar at his gate (Luke 16.21; see also LAZARUS). While Luke 16 explores the theme of wealth, some tension and uncertainty is raised by the commendation of the example of the dishonest manager in Luke 16.8–9 ('make friends for yourselves by means of dishonest wealth [mammon] so that when it is gone, they may welcome you into the eternal homes [tents]'). This seems to be at odds with Luke 16.13 – 'You cannot serve God and wealth [mammon]' (see also Matthew 6.24).

Following Jesus' example the early Christians clearly saw their role as including charitable giving to the poor (1 John 3.17); and PAUL encouraged believers to make a COLLECTION for the Jerusalem relief programme (2 Corinthians 9.1–14). In the later Pauline tradition, 1 Timothy 6.10 memorably declares that 'the love of money is a root of all kinds of evil'.

wedding feast The wedding feast is a significant image in the Bible, when one takes account of the participants including bride and BRIDEGROOM, and of the customs of a wedding celebration. A royal wedding, such as that of King SOLOMON, is reflected in Song of Songs 3.6–11, and the imagery spills over into the rest of the love poem. Similarly a royal wedding is the setting for Psalm 45. The COVENANT between God and his people is depicted by the metaphor of a marriage (see Isaiah 54.5–6; 62.4; Ezekiel 16; Hosea 2). And the Jewish rabbis interpreted both the Song of Songs and Psalm 45 as an ALLEGORY of God's betrothal to Israel. Ultimately the book of REVELATION focuses on the 'marriage supper of the Lamb' (19.9), which is the APOCALYPTIC banquet of the MESSIAH, celebrating the marriage of Christ (the Lamb) and his bride (the Church, or the NEW JERUSALEM – see 21.2).

Within the Gospels, the wedding feast is a recurrent theme. JOHN'S GOSPEL describes the sign at the wedding feast at CANA as the first occasion for the demonstration of Christ's power (see John 2.11). Jesus' parable of the Marriage Feast (in Matthew 22.1–14; see also Luke 14.16–24, where it is simply a banquet) illustrates the point that 'many are called but few are chosen' for the Kingdom of Heaven (*see* KINGDOM OF GOD); this affects not only those who refuse the invitation, but also those who are unprepared (*see* WEDDING ROBE). A wedding is the context for the parable of the Wise and Foolish Virgins in Matthew 25.1–13. In his teaching, Jesus alludes to himself as the bridegroom (Mark 2.19–20) and speaks of the apocalyptic banquet which involves the whole world (see Matthew 8.11; compare also Luke 14.15, which sets the scene for the banquet parable already mentioned).

See also MARRIAGE.

wedding robe, or garment MATTHEW'S GOSPEL 22.1–10 (see also Luke 14.16–24 and *Gospel of Thomas* 64) has a PARABLE told by Jesus about a wedding banquet. The wedding guests refuse their invitations and the king is understandably angry; he sends his slaves to gather substitute guests from the streets. This parable is frequently regarded as an ALLEGORY, warning of the rejection of Israel's established religious leaders and the opening of the KINGDOM OF GOD to a different group of people. (The point is similar to that of the previous parable, the Wicked Tenants, in Matthew 21.33–46.)

Matthew alone has added a supplementary aspect to the story of the wedding banquet. In 22.11–14 when the king visits the wedding hall he finds one of the replacement guests who is not wearing a wedding robe. To modern readers this sounds most unfair; how can someone brought in off the streets be expected to find special clothes for the occasion? But for Matthew the point is that those of the kingdom's new membership are required to have a sense of belonging, and a commitment to such a new way of life. This individual stands out as a 'non-conformist'. A verse such as this from the prophet ZEPHANIAH may well be in mind: 'I will punish … all who dress themselves in foreign attire' (1.8) – because they are alien and uncommitted. Clothes indicate identity and strange apparel denies this participation. Could there be echoes in the modern controversies over the Islamic veil? 'Do not dress like the infidels lest you become like them.'

weeds *See* PLANTS.

weights and measures For a system of measurement to work effectively a prerequisite is political stability, so as to authorize the application of official standards to local practice. Such a situation of relative stability existed in Mesopotamia (BABYLON) and EGYPT, where the most ancient standards of weights and measures are found, as well as later in the Greco-Roman world. There is a wide range of references to measurement to be found in the Biblical texts; some are distinctive to Israel/ Palestine, but many correspond to the systems of neighbouring lands. The Babylonian system of units (based on astronomical calculations) was widely used in the ancient Near East. The Hebrews basically used the Babylonian system, but modified it in the light of Egyptian practice; other changes were made as a result of PHOENICIAN and later PERSIAN influences.

Measurement of length was originally based on the limbs of the human body, ranging from finger width (0·7 or 0·9 inches/17 or 22 mm) and hand (four fingers) to span and CUBIT. Six cubits made a 'rope' measuring 9 or 10 feet (3 metres). There was a difference with the sacred/long cubit (as Ezekiel 40.5), which was a hand longer than the ordinary cubit. 1 Kings 6.2 gives the measurements of Solomon's TEMPLE as 60 cubits long, 20 cubits wide, and 30 cubits high (= 90 ft × 30 ft × 45 ft).

To measure distances in the Greco-Roman world was complicated by variation in the values ascribed to a foot, from the Olympic and the Alexandrian (about one third of a metre) to the Delphic (just below one fifth of a metre). Alexandrian and Delphic stadia accordingly differed in length by almost 10 metres. The Roman mile was standardized at 1480 metres.

There is no particular terminology for the measurement of area to be found in the Old Testament. 1 Samuel 14.14 refers to a 'yoke', which is presumably the area which a pair of oxen could cover in a day's ploughing (this could be an 'acre'; although the VULGATE translates this by *jugerum*, or five-eighths of an acre). When ELIJAH digs a trench around his altar on Mount CARMEL (1 Kings 18.32) this is expressed in terms of what could be planted with 'two measures [*seah*] of seed' (almost 6 gallons/27 litres in volume).

Measures of volume and liquid in Israel were based on the Babylonian system, and ranged from the 'log' (= a pint or half a litre; see Leviticus 14.10) through 'qab', 'omer', 'hin', 'seah', 'ephah' or 'bath', 'leteck', to 'homer' or 'kor' (720 logs or 86.5 gallons/390 litres).

Measurement of weight seems to have been the most complex of the systems. The weights were made of stone, and goods were weighed on scales (a balance consisting of two equal sized bowls suspended by strings from a horizontal cane). Weights representing the same unit could vary considerably, as archaeologists have discovered; perhaps different values were in use for different commodities, as happens in some societies today. Cheating, by using small weights for selling and heavier ones for buying, was condemned in the Bible (see Deuteronomy 25.13–16). The weight most often mentioned is the 'shekel', but it existed in lighter and heavier versions; the average would be 11.5 grams. Units below the shekel are the 'gerah' (one twentieth of a shekel), and a 'beqa' or half-shekel. The 'maneh' or 'mina' weighed 50 shekels, and the 'kikkar' or 'talent' (used for a quantity of silver) equalled at least 3000 shekels (sometimes 3600).

whited sepulchre, or whitewashed tomb The origin of this metaphorical expression for hypocrisy is to be found in Matthew 23.27–28, in a denunciation of the SCRIBES and PHARISEES. The contrast in MATTHEW is between the highly ornamented exterior and the interior containing the corpse or bones, contact with which is to be avoided according to Jewish rules of PURITY. The corresponding image in Luke's Gospel, at 11.44, refers to 'unmarked graves'. At times of festival pilgrimage to Jerusalem, it was the practice to whitewash graves so that pilgrims should not incur impurity (thus preventing their participation at the festival) by walking on them unawares. PAUL's comment about Ananias in Acts 23.3 ('whitewashed wall') may refer, like Matthew, to hypocrisy; but in the light of Ezekiel 13.10–12 it may denote weakness, where the whitewash (or plaster) does not really increase the limited strength of the wall.

widow's mite This expression denotes the valued contribution of the poor widow who puts two small copper coins into the treasury (see Mark 12.42; Luke 21.2). Jesus recognizes the costliness of her gift ('all she had to live on') compared with the gifts of others who could afford much more. *See also* COINAGE.

wilderness, or desert The term 'wilderness', originally translating the Hebrew word *midbar*, refers to what is 'deserted' or 'beyond' the limits of any settlement. For Israel the primary experience was probably that of the EXODUS from Egypt and the subsequent wanderings through the SINAI desert (see for example Exodus 16). But in both Old and New Testaments the reference could be more general, that is to any uncultivated land, so including steppe and even forest, in accord with the modern socio-anthropological distinction between 'the desert and the sown'. It could refer to the area around DAMASCUS (1 Kings 19.15), or to Lebanon (see Isaiah 29.17; 32.15). JOHN THE BAPTIST preached his baptism of repentance in the wilderness – but near the river JORDAN (Mark 1.4). Jesus was driven out into the wilderness for a period of testing by SATAN (Mark 1.12–13). And Jesus fed the hungry crowd who had followed him into the desert (Mark 8.4).

In the modern territories of Israel and Palestine, where claims are made of 'making the desert bloom', the term 'wilderness' might now be taken to apply to the southern areas, represented by the Negev and the Arabah. Elsewhere both Israelis and Palestinians seek to cultivate the land, but in different ways, with different priorities. *See also* GEOGRAPHY OF THE BIBLE.

wisdom Wisdom is one of the key themes in the Bible, reflected specifically in the literary category of the WISDOM BOOKS in the Hebrew Bible. The intention of these wisdom discourses is to establish and summarize the facts of experience, to pose questions, and to make ethical admonitions. It presupposes that there is an identifiable order at the heart of God's Creation, a natural theology there to be discovered.

Wisdom is represented in Hebrew by the word *hokmah*, and in Greek by *sophia*. After the EXILE wisdom tends to be personified as an intermediary of the divine (see Job 28). Because the word for wisdom happens to be feminine in gender, it is a natural development to see the person of Wisdom as a woman (see Proverbs 8). She is associated with the process of CREATION. After the time of the New Testament the Greek word 'Sophia' represents the woman or female principle of creation in the GNOSTIC systems (with their rationalization of knowledge of SALVATION). This theme is often taken up in modern theology with a feminist orientation.

Wisdom Books Wisdom is a special category in the thought of the Hebrew Bible, comparable to law, history and prophecy. The intention of the wisdom discourse is to establish and summarize the facts of experience, to pose questions, and to make ethical admonitions. There is an identifiable order at the heart of God's creation, a natural theology which is there to discover. The 'wise man' is a professional, like the priest and the prophet, who gives advice ('counsel' – see Jeremiah 18.18). The wisdom saying is a proverb (*mashal*); the Hebrew word can also be translated as 'maxim', 'riddle', or 'figure of speech'.

In the Old Testament the canonical books of wisdom are JOB, PROVERBS, and ECCLESIASTES; other wisdom poetry is to be found in the PSALMS. The principal wisdom texts in the APOCRYPHA are WISDOM OF SOLOMON, ECCLESIASTICUS and TOBIT. Comparable wisdom traditions have survived from Egypt and Mesopotamia. It is argued that such texts also served an educational purpose in training for professions such as the civil service. In the 3rd century CE in Palestine a leading member of the rabbinic movement put together what was to be a highly popular wisdom treatise entitled *Pirke Avot* (TALMUD tractate *Wisdom of the Fathers*). This reflects ideas of wisdom both in the local Jewish context and as applied to the Greco-Roman Near East.

Wisdom of Solomon The Old Testament APOCRYPHAL book of the Wisdom of Solomon was written originally in GREEK; Jerome said it is 'redolent of Greek eloquence'. The author was probably a Jew of ALEXANDRIA and wrote during the early period of the Roman Empire, possibly during the reign of Gaius Caligula (37–41 CE). The APOCALYPTIC vision of chapter 5 bears comparison with the Little Apocalypse of Mark's Gospel (chapter 13), which may have been formulated about the same time. Just as the Gospel text may be resisting the Roman threat to install a statue of Jupiter in the Jerusalem TEMPLE, so Wisdom identifies a threat to the Jewish community of Alexandria from Egyptians and Greeks. Alexandria saw anti-Jewish riots in 38 CE.

Wisdom 7.22–8.4 represents a climax in the personification of the female figure of Wisdom, with her 21 attributes. She is an emanation from God, pervading everywhere, making 'holy souls' into 'friends of God'. Wisdom 8.19 contains what may be the earliest mention of the idea of the pre-existent soul in Jewish writing.

witchcraft, magic The Hebrew Bible censures the practice of a wide range of magical arts, including witchcraft, sorcery, the casting of spells and charms, enchanting, divination, the calling up of the dead (necromancy), and astrology. See the list of evil practices in, for example, Deuteronomy 18.9–12, and the episode about the witch of Endor in 1 Samuel 28. The New Testament mentions such matters less frequently, but sees them as incompatible with faith in Christ (see, for example, Galatians 5.20 and Revelation 22.15, where the Greek word *pharmakeia* is used). It may be that the Christian converts in EPHESUS at Acts 19.17–20 had previously been practitioners of magical arts. *See also* SIMON MAGUS. Modern criticism (especially by some Christians) of the use of this kind of subject matter in children's books (and films) such as those by J. K. Rowling (the Harry Potter series) and Philip Pullman (*His Dark Materials*) may be based on these Biblical texts.

witness *See* MARTYR.

word, the Word 'In the beginning was the Word, and the Word was with God, and the Word was God.' These words may be familiar as the opening of JOHN'S GOSPEL, in the reading for CHRISTMAS, explaining the belief in the divine origins of the baby born in BETHLEHEM, but they may also present something of a puzzle. John has reached into the teaching of some Greek philosophy, namely that the universe originates from, and continues to be organized and run by, a *logos*. This Greek term is usually translated into English as 'word', but could equally well be rendered as 'thought', or 'rational principle', to try and capture further nuances of its meaning for the first Christian believers in the educated GREEK-speaking world of the 1st century CE. Anyone familiar with ideas from the Old Testament about WISDOM or other intermediaries to the one God, or who had encountered the writing of PHILO presenting Jewish ideas in terms of Greek philosophy, would find these a help in understanding John's thinking about *Logos*.

It was a daring use of the idea by this evangelist, to link into his readers' thought world, but certainly no Greek philosopher would have dared to go so far as to say that 'the Word became flesh and lived among us, and we have seen his glory, the glory as of the FATHER'S only son, full of grace and truth' (John 1.14). This was not a term which found widespread use, compared with some other TITLES OF JESUS, although it was favoured by some early Church Fathers working in Greek philosophy. John's own Church may well have continued to use it, but the first letter of John (1.1) may suggest a more restricted sense – the gospel message of Jesus rather than Jesus himself – when writing of the 'word of life'. Even John's Gospel does not return to it overtly, but as the Word – the Communication – Jesus does put across clues to his divine status in the SEVEN 'I AM' SAYINGS within the Gospel. The major 20th-century scholar Rudolf Bultmann called the Jesus of John's Gospel 'the Revealer' as a result.

A further background to these ideas can of course be seen in the Old Testament, in the more general (as well as theological) understanding of the concept of word and speech. The HEBREW language seemed to delight in the physical ways of expressing deeper truths; as in the Psalmist's prayer, 'O Lord, open my lips, and my mouth will declare your praise' (Psalm 51.15). The creative word was an essential aspect of the nature of God, as underlined by the repetition in the account of CREATION in Genesis 1: 'And God said … and it was so.' The prophets also recognized the ways in which God spoke to them directly. See, for example, the experience of ELIJAH (in 1 Kings 19) after the contest with the prophets of BA'AL on Mount CARMEL. He escaped to Beersheba from the threat posed by JEZEBEL. Sitting under a solitary broom tree, feeling sorry for himself, he wanted to quit and die. But he was contacted by an angel and provided with food to make it to Mount Horeb (*see* SINAI). There God spoke to him, not with the wind or earthquake or fire of the traditional theophany, but in a still, small voice within the sound of silence. The Hebrew term often used for such a revelatory voice of God is *bath qol* ('daughter of the voice'), perhaps a quiet, more feminine whisper, or maybe an echo. Rabbinic writings frequently mention this idea of the divine voice. It resembles the 'voice from heaven' which is heard at Jesus' BAPTISM (see Mark 1.11).

wormwood *See* HERBS.

worship The original meaning of the English word 'worship' is the 'recognition of worth/worthiness'. God as creator and redeemer of the world is presented in the Bible as expecting worship from human beings. The first commandment of the 10 in the DECALOGUE is to worship the Lord God alone. The summary of the TORAH in the formula of the SHEMA' (Deuteronomy 6.5; see also Mark 12.30) provides the content of worship: 'You shall love the Lord your God with all your heart, soul and might.' In the Hebrew Bible formal worship is structured within a system of SACRIFICE, with offerings to God as gifts to maintain the relationship between God and humanity. The prophets envisage the orientation of the whole world in worship at the holy mount of God and his TEMPLE. Ultimately, according to the book of REVELATION (22.3), worship will take place in the heavenly city of NEW JERUSALEM, where there is no temple apart from the Lord God and the Lamb. Meanwhile, according to the Acts of the Apostles, the earliest Christian believers continued to worship in the Jerusalem Temple. But the Christian traditions evolved with their own patterns of worship, focused on BAPTISM and the EUCHARIST. The New Testament offers some examples of hymns (continuing the function of the PSALMS in Israel). It may also offer some clues as to orders (patterns) for worship; some scholars have identified the shape of LITURGIES within the chapters of the book of Revelation (but for fully formed Christian liturgies it is necessary to wait several centuries). And the New Testament, as well as what Christians called the Old Testament, began to provide the material for public readings in services analogous to the practice in the Jewish SYNAGOGUE.

writing *See* ORALITY; OSTRACA.

writing on the wall *See* MENE, MENE, TEKEL, AND PARSIN.

X

xenophobia The TORAH was very specific that the pious Israelites were to care for the foreigners within their community, for example Deuteronomy 26.12. It is perhaps not surprising that experiences of foreigners introducing the worship of alien gods, and the SYNCRETISM which emerged from the EXILE, should have resulted in a movement to purify JUDAISM and purge out all that related to foreigners and foreign ways in the returned community. Certainly NEHEMIAH was a zealot in this cause, enclosing Jerusalem with a wall, and purging foreign elements from the community (see Nehemiah 13). EZRA in turn insists on separation from non-Jews, including foreign wives (see Ezra 9–10). It may be that in protest against this narrow attitude the books of RUTH and JONAH came to be written as propaganda for a more universally caring God – even the inhabitants of NINEVEH could be preached to and spared upon their repentance; and even the great hero King DAVID was descended from a heathen great-grandmother.

Y

Yahweh, or Jehovah, name of God Yahweh (or strictly the four consonants YHWH, which form the sacred tetragrammaton) is the particular name of Israel's GOD. There are different theories as to which was the local context in which the name originated; one possibility is that Yahweh was the name of a tribal deity of the KENITES (Midianites) and MOSES learnt the name when he took refuge in Midian (Exodus 2–3). It could be argued that Yahweh would not have existed without the particular worship of a group of people. But in the course of the Old Testament Yahweh is established as the single God of a universal monotheism.

Jewish reverence required that the name of G*d should not be uttered (except by the HIGH PRIEST on the Day of Atonement – *see* YOM KIPPUR). To overcome the difficulty in regular usage, when reading the text aloud, the conson-

The Name of God

ants of the name were given the vowels of a different HEBREW word meaning 'Lord'. The form 'Jehovah' is a Christian misunderstanding of this convention, which appears in Bible translations from the 16th century CE (Tyndale and the KING JAMES OR AUTHORISED, VERSION).

Bernhard Lang has argued for the evolution of the Hebrew idea of God, from the worship of a small community to the monotheism of the Western tradition, under five images: lord of WISDOM, lord of WAR, lord of the animals, lord of the individual and the lord of harvest, showing how the rule of God extends to the whole of life.

Yom Kippur, or Day of Atonement The Hebrew name Yom Kippur (Day of Covering) denotes the day which is holiest in the Jewish CALENDAR, even up to the present; it is a day of fasting which concludes the 10 days of repentance which began on the Jewish New Year's Day (Rosh Hashanah). This day of prayer begins in the evening, continuing through the night and the following day. 'May it therefore be Your will, Lord our God, and God of our Fathers, to forgive us all our SINS.' The best known prayer, Kol Nidrei (All the Vows), became famous through the music of Max Bruch; it declares that all oaths and vows which one has made unthinkingly before God are null and void. The main prayers are a confession, in alphabetical order, of all the sins one has committed; after each sin one beats oneself on the chest with the right hand. Repentance opens the way of return to the COVENANT; reconciliation restores the relationship, and atonement covers the sin.

The original covering was that of the ARK OF THE COVENANT which the HIGH PRIEST sprinkled with blood in the Jerusalem TEMPLE liturgy, after he had SACRIFICED two animals and sent a third – a SCAPEGOAT – into the desert. This was the only day in the year that the High Priest entered the HOLY OF HOLIES in the Temple, and was able to pronounce aloud the name of GOD (*see* YAHWEH).

The Jewish SYNAGOGUE services contain readings from Leviticus 16 and Numbers 29, which gave the original instructions about Yom Kippur. Also read are passages from Isaiah 57 and 58, Leviticus 18, and the story of the book of JONAH. The New Testament refers to these ideas about the Day of Atonement in the letter to the HEBREWS (relating the blood to the DEATH OF CHRIST, for example in Hebrews 10.19–22, 29), and in PAUL's letter to the Romans 3.25.

Z

Zacchaeus 1 Zacchaeus was the chief tax-collector in JERICHO, where he encountered Jesus (see Luke 19.1–10). Jesus was passing by, but Zacchaeus was unable to see him because of the crowd and his own small build, and so he climbed a sycamore tree to gain a vantage point. Jesus calls him down and wishes to stay at his house. Zacchaeus as a tax-collector (*see* PUBLICAN) would have been very unpopular as an effective collaborator with the Roman administration. He responds to the popular reaction with penitent humility, offering to give half his riches to the poor and make fourfold restitution to anyone he has defrauded. In Luke's narrative, Jesus is near the end of his final journey to Jerusalem; his meeting with Zacchaeus clearly had a transforming effect on that man's life.

2 Zacchaeus is also the name of an officer in the army of JUDAS MACCABEUS (see 2 Maccabees 10.19).

Zacharias Zacharias (otherwise Zechariah) was a PRIEST, the father of JOHN THE BAPTIST and the husband of Elizabeth (see the narrative of Luke 1). Although his wife was elderly, an ANGEL (Gabriel) promised that they would have a child who would be the herald of the MESSIAH. Zacharias asked for a confirmatory sign and was struck dumb. He regained the power of speech at the time of the CIRCUMCISION and naming of his son. According to Luke's account (1.67–79) Zacharias is then inspired to utter a prophetic prayer of blessing to God for what he has done (this is traditionally referred to, in subsequent liturgical use, as the Benedictus). Such poetic texts, very much in the style of Hebrew Psalms, are a characteristic feature of LUKE's opening chapters (*see also* SIMEON (2) and MARY, MOTHER OF JESUS).

Zadok Zadok was a PRIEST in the time of King DAVID and had supported him during ABSALOM's revolt (see 2 Samuel 15). After the death of David, Zadok supported SOLOMON in the struggle for the succession (see 1 Kings 1.8, 32, 39–45; and compare ABIATHAR). Therefore Zadok as sole priest anointed Solomon (*see* UNCTION).

The descendants of Zadok served as HIGH PRIESTS, as a family controlling the Jerusalem priesthood from the time of Solomon until the 2nd century BCE, when the office passed to the HASMONEANS. For a partial list see 1 Chronicles 6.8–15. At the time of the EXILE it is specified that only Zadokite priests would minister in the Jerusalem TEMPLE when rebuilt. Subsequently the DEAD SEA SCROLLS stress the sole legitimacy of the Zadokite priests, who are clearly associated with QUMRAN, after the Hasmonean takeover of the Jerusalem priesthood.

Zamzummim According to Deuteronomy 2.20–21, the name Zamzummim (possibly meaning 'mumblers') was given by the AMMONITES to the ancient race of giants who were thought to be the original inhabitants of the land east of JORDAN, occupied later by Ammon and MOAB. These may be referred to as the Zuzim in Genesis 14.5, while the usual Israelite name for the race of giants is Rephaim.

Zarephath *See* ELIJAH.

Zealots JOSEPHUS traces the origins of the Zealot movement to the uprising in 6 CE when a certain Judas from Gamla in Gaulanitis (the Golan) started a revolt by claiming that it was high treason against God (the true ruler of Israel) to pay tribute to the empire of an occupying power (see Acts 5.37). Certainly the descendants of Judas continued to shape the activity of the Zealot movement during the lifetime of Jesus, with their fervent hope for a victorious MESSIAH to defeat the Romans. Gamla again became their major stronghold, until it was overcome by the Romans in 67 CE, and 9000 defenders died. The Zealots' last stand was at MASADA, which fell at the end of the JEWISH WAR in 73/4 CE.

One of Jesus' disciples is called Simon the Zealot in Luke 6.15. Mark 3.18 and Matthew 10.4 refer to him as 'SIMON THE CANANAEAN'; this term derives from the HEBREW *qanna'i* or ARAMAIC *qan'ana*, words which are the equivalent of the GREEK *zelotes* (zealot). Adherents of this strongly religious and nationalistic party probably would have traced their roots back to the MACCABEAN revolt (see 1 Maccabees 2.27). But the underlying idea of 'zeal' (see Philippians 3.6) is the attitude of a religious vigilante who takes personal and individual responsibility, following the example of PHINEHAS in Numbers 25.6–8 who slew the Israelite man and the Midianite woman he had married. The Jewish philosopher PHILO states that such religious zeal allows anyone 'to exact the penalties offhand and with no delay, without bringing the offender before jury or council or any kind of magistrate' (*The Special Laws*).

Zebedee Zebedee was a fisherman, the father of JAMES and JOHN, the disciples of Jesus (see Mark 1.19–20). The fact that he had 'hired servants' is a reminder that fishing on GALILEE was a substantial business, as indicated also by the discoveries in the fishermen's houses at BETHSAIDA. It is possible that Zebedee's wife was named Salome (by a comparison of the lists of women followers in Mark 15.40 and Matthew 27.56). See Matthew 20.20 for the way that she pressed Jesus on favours for her sons.

Zebulun Zebulun is the sixth son of JACOB by his first wife LEAH (see Genesis 30.19–20; 49.13). This blessing suggests that the tribe of Zebulun, named after their ancestor, would live near the Mediterranean coast and be in contact with the PHOENICIANS (see also Deuteronomy 33.18–19). According to Joshua 19.10–16 the tribe's allocated territory was in south-central Galilee, from Mount CARMEL to Mount TABOR. NAZARETH, the hometown of Jesus, was then in the heart of the territory of Zebulun (see Isaiah 9.1; Matthew 4.15).

Zechariah, book of Zechariah is the penultimate book in the collection of 12 Minor Prophets. The historical ministry of the prophet Zechariah overlapped with that of HAGGAI, but lasted longer (specifically from 520 to 518 BCE) during the reign of the PERSIAN king Darius I (Hystaspis), that is after the Babylonian EXILE. The promised restoration is to be accomplished solely by the power of God; the new age will be characterized by the rebuilding of the Jerusalem TEMPLE, and this will be among the responsibilities of the new ruler, a royal figure of the DAVIDIC line (see 4.6–10 and 6.9–15). Zechariah's prophetic credentials will be validated by this outcome, as the king mediates new life and well-being, and the Temple guarantees the right relationship with God.

Chapters 1–8 reflect this historical ministry of Zechariah. The remaining chapters, 9–14, are quite different in tone and later in date, reflecting a progressive disillusionment with the cultic establishment. There is a growing sense of APOCALYPTIC urgency about the Day of the Lord in this second section that is full of messianic allusions. How this part was compiled has been much debated, and the final chapter may belong to the late 5th century BCE. The suggestion of a prophetic school of thought may be needed to account for such continuities as do exist between the two parts. Second Zechariah was particularly open to later allegorical interpretation, as can be seen in the commentaries of the Church Fathers Didymus the Blind and Theodore of Mopsuestia (*see* ALLEGORY). The book has certainly exerted an influence disproportionate to its length, ever since the original nucleus of its oracles was assembled.

This Zechariah is not to be confused with the much later father of JOHN THE BAPTIST (Luke 1) – *see* ZACHARIAS. In Matthew 23.35 there is a confusion between this prophet Zechariah, who *was* son of Barachiah (Zechariah 1.1), and the earlier Zechariah, son of Jehoiada the priest, who was killed in the Temple, according to 2 Chronicles 24.20–22. Matthew's reference is strictly to all the blood spilt in the course of the Hebrew Bible, from beginning to end (in the Hebrew Bible, 2 Chronicles is at the end of the third and final section, the Writings, while the book of Zechariah comes among the Prophets in the second section). According to the *Protevangelium of James* (2nd century CE; *see* JAMES, PROTEVANGELIUM OF) John the Baptist's father Zechariah was also slaughtered in the Temple courtyard by the soldiers of HEROD searching for John.

Zedekiah This Hebrew name, meaning 'YAHWEH is righteousness', occurs several times in the Old Testament. Among these is the false prophet opposed by MICAIAH ben Imlah in 1 Kings 22. But the most significant is Zedekiah, the last of the KINGS OF JUDAH, appointed by NEBUCHADNEZZAR as a puppet ruler, after his conquest of JERUSALEM in 597 BCE. Despite the warnings of the prophet JEREMIAH, Zedekiah rebelled against BABYLON; Jerusalem was recaptured by the Babylonians in 586 BCE; and Zedekiah was taken to Babylon in chains.

Zephaniah, book of Zephaniah is the ninth of the collection of 12 books known as the Minor Prophets. The prophet's name is a double attestation of Israel's God, referring to Zaphon as the mountain in the far north (see Isaiah 14.13). Zephaniah's oracles belong to the earlier years of King JOSIAH of Judah (640–609 BCE), before the religious reforms that took place around 623 BCE. His radical message of the great Day of the Lord follows some 60 or more years after the prophecies of ISAIAH and MICAH. The book should come just after Micah, but its later position is due to a misidentification of Hezekiah in 1.1 as the later King HEZEKIAH. The Greek historian Herodotus refers to a menace from the Scythians about 626 BCE; it is possible that it could be the unnamed physical menace referred to in Zephaniah.

The book has three sections: judgement on Judah (1.2–2.3); oracles against foreign nations (2.4–3.8); promises of redemption (3.9–20). Despite these divisions there is an organic wholeness in the way the book is assembled, with connecting verbal links and related images between the sections. The dominant theme is undoubtedly the Day of the Lord, in terms which anticipate the medieval hymn the Dies Irae. The book was adopted at QUMRAN (commentary fragments 1Q15 and 4Q170). The *Apocalypse of Zephaniah*, a work of the 1st century BCE or CE, recognizes the prophet as an APOCA-LYPTIC visionary. Jesus' triumphal entry into Jerusalem, according to the account of John 12.13–15, correlates the prophecies of Zephaniah 3.14–15 and ZECHARIAH 9.9.

Zerubbabel The Hebrew name Zerubbabel means 'shoot of BABYLON'. Together with Joshua the HIGH PRIEST he is called upon by HAGGAI to rebuild the Jerusalem TEMPLE (see Haggai 1.1; 2.2, 20–23; also ZECHARIAH 4.6–10; and probably 2.10 and 6.12). The narrative about Joshua and Zerubbabel appears in EZRA chapters 3 and 4. 1 ESDRAS 3.1–5.3 contains a story of a contest of wits at the court of Darius, in which Zerubbabel is the winner and as a result is allowed to rebuild Jerusalem and the Temple.

ziggurat Ziggurat comes from an AKKADIAN word meaning 'temple tower'. These were stepped temple buildings, on a square or rectangular base, erected in Mesopotamia. The basic concept seems to have been that of a staircase towards the heavens, perhaps used for astrological purposes. The stars were called 'the silent writing of the heavens' and optimistic astrologers strove to communicate its meaning. A parallel theme might be suggested by the Hebrew poet in Psalm 19.1–4: 'The heavens are telling the glory of God ... There is no speech, nor are there words; ... yet their voice goes out through all the earth.' (This image is reapplied to the Christian MISSION by Paul in Romans 10.18.) The story of the Tower of BABEL (see Genesis 11.1–9) is likely to represent a similar idea to that of the Mesopotamian ziggurat.

Zion, Zionism The Hebrew word *zion* possibly means 'citadel' or 'fortress', or just 'dry place', but it comes to represent a deep and significant ideology, focused spe-cifically on JERUSALEM. 2 Samuel 5.6–10 describes how Jerusalem was captured from the Jebusites by DAVID; his men climbed up a water shaft from the outside and were then able to open the city gate from the inside. The name Zion is particularly applied to this captured stronghold, which, according to archaeologists, at that date covered only the south-eastern ridge of Jerusalem. Subsequently the designation Zion was enlarged, as the city was enlarged, and in particular was focused on the TEMPLE Mount to the north, where SOLOMON's temple was built. Many of the PSALMS cele-brate Zion in relation to the Temple (see, for example, 2.6; 78.68–69; compare 46.4 on 'the city of God'). A great variety of pictorial language is used as the symbolism is enhanced with reference to the HOLY LAND.

In the New Testament Zion can refer metaphorically to the Church and the heav-enly Jerusalem (*see further at* NEW JERUSALEM). The imagery extends further in ideo-logical and political directions, as with the movement of Zionism in modern times.

In the Jewish tradition Zionism is a movement committed to the return of the Jewish people to the land of Israel (*see* ALIYAH). As an ideology, Zionism was opposed by substantial numbers of Orthodox Jews who believed that human action should not be allowed to usurp God's prerogative to intervene in his own time and place.

There are also some movements of Christian Zionism, particularly from the United States of America, who believe in the ideology of a 'Greater Israel', and therefore that the return of the Jews to the Holy Land, and the establishment of the state of Israel in 1948, were in accordance with those Biblical prophecies. 'Christian believers are instructed by Scripture to acknowledge the Hebraic roots of their faith and to actively assist and participate in the plan of God for the Ingathering of the Jewish People and the restoration of the nation of Israel in our day' (from the Proclamation of the 1996 Christian Zionist Congress in Jerusalem). Such movements may recognize that, by Christian support for the policies of Israel, a version of ARMAGEDDON could well be precipitated; the *Left Behind* series of novels by Tim LaHaye and Jerry B. Jenkins boosted popular interest, with their focus on the prophetic role of Israel in the APOCALYPTIC End Time.

In a letter from the Archbishops of Canterbury and York written to Tony Blair on 25 June 2004, critical of government policies in Iraq and the Middle East, a guarded reference was made to the growing influence of the Christian Zionist movement in the United States: 'Within the wider Christian community we also have theological work to do to counter those interpretations of Scripture, from outside the mainstream of the tradition, which appear to have become increasingly influential in fostering an uncritical and one-sided approach to the future of the Holy Land.'

See also the volume edited by Naim Ateek, Cedar Duaybis and Maurine Tobin, *Challenging Christian Zionism* (Melisende, 2005).

Zipporah Zipporah was the wife of MOSES (see Exodus 2.15–22). She came from Midian, and was the daughter of the Midianite priest Jethro. It seems that she too may have exercised priestly functions, circumcising their son Gershom (Exodus 4.24) and possibly Moses as well (Exodus 4.25). Zipporah, with Gershom and their second son Eliezer, remained in Midian with Jethro, while Moses returned to Egypt to lead the EXODUS (see Exodus 18.2–5). According to Judges 1.16; 4.11, Moses was said to have a KENITE father-in-law. Only in Numbers 12.1 is Moses' wife said to have come from Ethiopia (a Cushite), and this, as a foreign marriage with risk of cultic impurity, is objected to by MIRIAM (the sister of Moses and Aaron), who then suffers for her outspoken criticism. The Numbers tradition may be comparatively late, and not unconnected with later controversies about foreign marriages at the time of EZRA. It is also possible that Moses had more than one wife, even more than one foreign wife.

Zippori *See* SEPPHORIS.

Zoar Zoar was one of the five cities of the plain (see Genesis 14.1–12); the others were SODOM, Gomorrah, Admah, and Zeboiim. LOT was allowed to flee to Zoar before Sodom was destroyed (see Genesis 19.18–23). It is also mentioned, with reference to the destruction of MOAB, in Isaiah 15.5 and Jeremiah 48.34. But its exact location is unknown.

Old Testament Texts Quoted in the New Testament

OT	OT Ref.	Version	NT	NT Ref.
Genesis	1.26		James	3.9
Genesis	1.27		Matthew	19.4
Genesis	1.27		Mark	10.6
Genesis	2.2		Hebrews	4.4
Genesis	2.7		1 Corinthians	15.45
Genesis	2.24		Matthew	19.5
Genesis	2.24		Mark	10.7–8
Genesis	2.24		1 Corinthians	6.16
Genesis	2.24		Ephesians	5.31
Genesis	5.2		Matthew	19.4
Genesis	5.2		Mark	10.6
Genesis	5.24	LXX	Hebrews	11.5
Genesis	12.1		Acts	7.3
Genesis	12.3		Acts	3.25
Genesis	12.3		Galatians	3.8
Genesis	12.7		Galatians	3.16
Genesis	13.15		Galatians	3.16
Genesis	14.17–20		Hebrews	7.1–2
Genesis	15.5		Romans	4.18
Genesis	15.5		Hebrews	11.12
Genesis	15.6		Romans	4.3, 9, 22
Genesis	15.6		Galatians	3.6
Genesis	15.6		James	2.23
Genesis	15.13–14		Acts	7.6–7
Genesis	17.5		Romans	4.17, 18
Genesis	17.7		Galatians	3.16
Genesis	17.8		Acts	7.5
Genesis	17.8		Galatians	3.16
Genesis	18.10, 14		Romans	9.9
Genesis	18.18		Acts	3.25
Genesis	18.18		Galatians	3.8
Genesis	21.10		Galatians	4.30

OT	OT Ref.	Version	NT	NT Ref.
Genesis	21.12		Romans	9.7
Genesis	21.12		Hebrews	11.18
Genesis	22.9		James	2.21
Genesis	22.16–17		Hebrews	6.13–14
Genesis	22.17		Hebrews	11.12
Genesis	22.18		Acts	3.25
Genesis	22.18		Galatians	3.8, 16
Genesis	25.23		Romans	9.12
Genesis	26.3–4		Acts	3.25
Genesis	26.3–4		Galatians	3.8, 16
Genesis	28.12		John	1.51
Genesis	28.13–14		Acts	3.25
Genesis	28.13–14		Galatians	3.8
Genesis	47.31	LXX	Hebrews	11.21
Genesis	48.4		Acts	7.5
Exodus	1.8		Acts	7.18
Exodus	2.11–15		Acts	7.23–29
Exodus	2.14		Acts	7.27–28, 35
Exodus	3.2		Acts	7.3
Exodus	3.5–10		Acts	7.32–34
Exodus	3.6		Matthew	22.32
Exodus	3.6		Mark	12.26
Exodus	3.6		Luke	20.37
Exodus	3.6		Acts	3.13
Exodus	3.6		Acts	7.32
Exodus	3.12		Acts	7.7
Exodus	3.15		Matthew	22.32
Exodus	3.15		Mark	12.26
Exodus	3.15		Luke	20.37
Exodus	3.15		Acts	3.13, 7.32
Exodus	9.16	LXX	Romans	9.17
Exodus	12.46		John	19.36
Exodus	13.2		Luke	2.23
Exodus	13.12		Luke	2.23
Exodus	13.15		Luke	2.32
Exodus	16.4		John	6.31
Exodus	16.18		2 Corinthians	8.15
Exodus	19.5–6	LXX	1 Peter	2.9
Exodus	19.12–13		Hebrews	12.20
Exodus	20.12		Matthew	15.4
Exodus	20.12		Mark	7.10
Exodus	20.12		Ephesians	6.2–3

OT	OT Ref.	Version	NT	NT Ref.
Exodus	20.12–16		Matthew	19.18–19
Exodus	20.12–16		Mark	10.19
Exodus	20.12–16		Luke	18.30
Exodus	20.13		Matthew	5.21
Exodus	20.13–14		James	2.11
Exodus	20.13–15, 17		Romans	13.9
Exodus	20.14		Matthew	5.27
Exodus	20.17		Romans	7.7
Exodus	21.17		Matthew	15.4
Exodus	21.17		Mark	7.10
Exodus	21.24		Matthew	5.38
Exodus	22.28		Acts	23.5
Exodus	24.8		Hebrews	9.20
Exodus	25.40		Hebrews	8.5
Exodus	32.1		Acts	7.40
Exodus	32.6		1 Corinthians	10.7
Exodus	32.23		Acts	7.40
Exodus	33.19		Romans	9.15
Exodus	34.30		2 Corinthians	3.7
Exodus	34.33, 35		2 Corinthians	3.13
Exodus	34.34		2 Corinthians	3.16
Leviticus	2.13		Mark	9.49
Leviticus	11.44–45		1 Peter	1.16
Leviticus	12.6–8		Luke	2.24
Leviticus	16.27		Hebrews	13.11
Leviticus	18.5		Romans	10.5
Leviticus	18.5		Galatians	3.12
Leviticus	19.2		1 Peter	1.16
Leviticus	19.12		Matthew	5.33
Leviticus	19.18		Matthew	5.43
Leviticus	19.18		Matthew	19.19
Leviticus	19.18		Matthew	22.39
Leviticus	19.18		Mark	12.31, 33
Leviticus	19.18		Luke	10.27
Leviticus	19.18		Romans	13.9
Leviticus	19.18		Galatians	5.14
Leviticus	19.18		James	2.8
Leviticus	24.20		Matthew	5.38
Leviticus	26.12		2 Corinthians	6.16
Numbers	9.12		John	19.36
Numbers	12.7		Hebrews	3.2, 5

OT	OT Ref.	Version	NT	NT Ref.
Numbers	16.5		2 Timothy	2.19
Numbers	27.17		Matthew	9.36
Numbers	27.17		Mark	6.34
Numbers	30.2		Matthew	5.33
Deuteronomy	4.24		Hebrews	12.29
Deuteronomy	4.35		Mark	12.32
Deuteronomy	5.16		Matthew	15.4
Deuteronomy	5.16		Mark	7.10
Deuteronomy	5.16		Ephesians	6.2–3
Deuteronomy	5.16–20		Matthew	19.18–19
Deuteronomy	5.16–20		Mark	10.19
Deuteronomy	5.16–20		Luke	18.20
Deuteronomy	5.17		Matthew	5.21
Deuteronomy	5.17–18		James	2.11
Deuteronomy	5.17–19, 21		Romans	13.9
Deuteronomy	5.18		Matthew	5.27
Deuteronomy	5.21		Romans	7.7
Deuteronomy	6.4–5		Mark	12.29–30
Deuteronomy	6.4–5		Mark	12.32–33
Deuteronomy	6.5		Matthew	22.37
Deuteronomy	6.5		Luke	10.27
Deuteronomy	6.13		Matthew	4.10
Deuteronomy	6.13		Luke	4.8
Deuteronomy	6.16		Matthew	4.7
Deuteronomy	6.16		Luke	4.12
Deuteronomy	8.3		Matthew	4.4
Deuteronomy	8.3		Luke	4.4
Deuteronomy	9.4		Romans	10.6
Deuteronomy	9.19		Hebrews	12.21
Deuteronomy	17.6		Hebrews	10.28
Deuteronomy	17.7	LXX	1 Corinthians	5.13
Deuteronomy	18.15		Acts	7.37
Deuteronomy	18.15–19		Acts	3.22–23
Deuteronomy	19.15		Matthew	18.16
Deuteronomy	19.15		John	8.17
Deuteronomy	19.15		2 Corinthians	13.1
Deuteronomy	19.15		1 Timothy	5.19
Deuteronomy	19.19		1 Corinthians	5.13
Deuteronomy	19.21		Matthew	5.38
Deuteronomy	21.23		Galatians	3.13
Deuteronomy	22.21, 24		1 Corinthians	5.13
Deuteronomy	24.1		Matthew	5.31

OT	OT Ref.	Version	NT	NT Ref.
Deuteronomy	24.1		Matthew	19.7
Deuteronomy	24.1, 3		Mark	10.4
Deuteronomy	24.7		1 Corinthians	5.13
Deuteronomy	25.4		1 Corinthians	9.9
Deuteronomy	25.4		1 Timothy	5.18
Deuteronomy	25.5		Matthew	22.24
Deuteronomy	25.5		Mark	12.19
Deuteronomy	25.5		Luke	20.28
Deuteronomy	27.26	LXX	Galatians	3.10
Deuteronomy	29.4		Romans	11.8
Deuteronomy	29.18		Hebrews	12.15
Deuteronomy	30.12–14		Romans	10.6–8
Deuteronomy	31.6, 8		Hebrews	13.5
Deuteronomy	32.17		1 Corinthians	10.20
Deuteronomy	32.21		Romans	10.19
Deuteronomy	32.21		1 Corinthians	10.22
Deuteronomy	32.35		Romans	12.19
Deuteronomy	32.35		Hebrews	10.30
Deuteronomy	32.36		Hebrews	10.30
Deuteronomy	32.43		Romans	15.10
Deuteronomy	32.43	LXX	Hebrews	1.6
Joshua	1.5		Hebrews	13.5
1 Samuel	2.1		Luke	1.46–47
1 Samuel	2.26		Luke	2.52
1 Samuel	13.14		Acts	13.22
2 Samuel	7.8, 14		2 Corinthians	6.18
2 Samuel	7.12–13		Acts	2.3
2 Samuel	7.14		Hebrews	1.5
2 Samuel	22.5		Romans	15.9
1 Kings	19.10, 14		Romans	11.3
1 Kings	19.18		Romans	11.4
1 Kings	22.17		Matthew	9.36
1 Kings	22.17		Mark	6.34
2 Kings	1.10, 12		Luke	9.54
2 Chronicles	18.16		Matthew	9.36
2 Chronicles	18.16		Mark	6.34

OT	OT Ref.	Version	NT	NT Ref.
Nehemiah	9.15		John	6.31
Job	5.13		1 Corinthians	3.19
Job	41.11		Romans	11.35
Psalms	2.1–2	LXX	Acts	4.25–26
Psalms	2.7		Acts	13.33
Psalms	2.7		Hebrews	1.5
Psalms	2.7		Hebrews	5.5
Psalms	2.7		Luke	3.22
Psalms	2.7		Mark	1.11
Psalms	2.8–9		Revelation	2.26–27
Psalms	4.4	LXX	Ephesians	4.26
Psalms	5.9	LXX	Romans	3.13
Psalms	8.3	LXX	Matthew	21.26
Psalms	8.4–6	LXX	Hebrews	2.6–8
Psalms	8.6		1 Corinthians	15.27
Psalms	8.6		Ephesians	1.22
Psalms	10.7	LXX	Romans	3.14
Psalms	14.1–3		Romans	3.10–12
Psalms	16.8–11	LXX	Acts	2.25–28
Psalms	16.10		Acts	2.31
Psalms	16.10	LXX	Acts	13.35
Psalms	18.49		Romans	15.9
Psalms	19.4	LXX	Romans	10.18
Psalms	22.1		Mark	15.34
Psalms	22.1		Matthew	27.46
Psalms	22.7		Luke	23.35
Psalms	22.7		Mark	15.29
Psalms	22.7		Matthew	27.39
Psalms	22.8		Matthew	27.43
Psalms	22.18		Matthew	27.35
Psalms	22.18		Mark	15.24
Psalms	22.18		Luke	23.34
Psalms	22.18		John	19.24
Psalms	22.22		Hebrews	2.12
Psalms	24.1		1 Corinthians	10.26
Psalms	31.5		Luke	23.46
Psalms	32.1–2		Romans	4.7–8
Psalms	34.8		1 Peter	2.3
Psalms	34.12–16		1 Peter	3.10–12
Psalms	34.20		John	19.36
Psalms	35.19		John	15.25

OT	OT Ref.	Version	NT	NT Ref.
Psalms	36.1		Romans	3.18
Psalms	37.11		Matthew	5.5
Psalms	40.6–8		Hebrews	10.5–7
Psalms	41.9		John	13.18
Psalms	44.22		Romans	8.36
Psalms	45.6–7		Hebrews	1.8–9
Psalms	48.2		Matthew	5.35
Psalms	51.4	LXX	Romans	3.4
Psalms	53.1–3		Romans	3.10–12
Psalms	68.18		Ephesians	4.8
Psalms	69.4		John	15.25
Psalms	69.9		John	2.17
Psalms	69.9		Romans	15.3
Psalms	69.21		Matthew	27.48
Psalms	69.21		Mark	15.36
Psalms	69.21		John	19.28–29
Psalms	69.22–23	LXX	Romans	11.9–10
Psalms	69.25		Acts	1.20
Psalms	78.2		Matthew	13.35
Psalms	78.24		John	6.31
Psalms	82.6		John	10.34
Psalms	90.4		2 Peter	3.8
Psalms	91.11–12		Matthew	4.6
Psalms	91.11–12		Luke	4.10–11
Psalms	94.11		1 Corinthians	3.20
Psalms	94.14		Romans	11.2
Psalms	95.7–8	LXX	Hebrews	3.15
Psalms	95.7–8		Hebrews	4.7
Psalms	95.7–11		Hebrews	3.7–11
Psalms	95.11		Hebrews	3.18
Psalms	95.11		Hebrews	4.3, 5, 10
Psalms	102.25–27	LXX	Hebrews	1.10–12
Psalms	103.8		James	5.11
Psalms	103.17		Luke	1.50
Psalms	104.4	LXX	Hebrews	1.7
Psalms	109.8		Acts	1.20
Psalms	110.1		Matthew	22.44
Psalms	110.1		Matthew	26.64
Psalms	110.1		Mark	12.36
Psalms	110.1		Mark	14.62
Psalms	110.1		Mark	16.19
Psalms	110.1		Luke	22.69
Psalms	110.1		Luke	20.42–43

Old Testament Texts Quoted in the New Testament

OT	OT Ref.	Version	NT	NT Ref.
Psalms	110.1		Acts	2.34–35
Psalms	110.1		1 Corinthians	15.25
Psalms	110.1		Colossians	3.1
Psalms	110.1		Ephesians	1.2
Psalms	110.1		Hebrews	8.1
Psalms	110.1		Hebrews	12.2
Psalms	110.1		Hebrews	1.3, 13
Psalms	110.1		Hebrews	10.12–13
Psalms	110.4		Hebrews	5.6
Psalms	110.4		Hebrews	7.17, 21
Psalms	112.9		2 Corinthians	9.9
Psalms	116.10	LXX	2 Corinthians	4.13
Psalms	117.1		Romans	15.11
Psalms	118.6	LXX	Hebrews	13.6
Psalms	118.22		Acts	4.11
Psalms	118.22		1 Peter	2.7
Psalms	118.22–23		Matthew	21.42
Psalms	118.22–23		Mark	12.10–11
Psalms	118.22–23		Luke	20.17
Psalms	118.25–26		Matthew	21.9
Psalms	118.25–26		Mark	11.9
Psalms	118.25–26		John	12.13
Psalms	118.26		Matthew	23.39
Psalms	118.26		Luke	13.35
Psalms	118.26		Luke	19.38
Psalms	132.11		Acts	2.30
Psalms	135.14		Hebrews	10.30
Psalms	140.3	LXX	Romans	3.13
Psalms	143.2		Romans	3.20
Proverbs	3.4		2 Corinthians	8.21
Proverbs	3.11–12	LXX	Hebrews	12.5–6
Proverbs	3.12		Revelation	3.19
Proverbs	3.34	LXX	James	4.6
Proverbs	3.34		1 Peter	5.5
Proverbs	4.26		Hebrews	12.13
Proverbs	10.12		1 Peter	4.8
Proverbs	11.31	LXX	1 Peter	4.18
Proverbs	22.9		2 Corinthians	9.7
Proverbs	25.21–22	LXX	Romans	12.20
Proverbs	26.11		2 Peter	2.22
Isaiah	1.9	LXX	Romans	9.29

OT	OT Ref.	Version	NT	NT Ref.
Isaiah	5.1–2		Matthew	21.33
Isaiah	5.1–2		Mark	12.1
Isaiah	6.3		Revelation	4.8
Isaiah	6.9	LXX	Luke	8.10
Isaiah	6.9–10	LXX	Matthew	13.14–15
Isaiah	6.9–10	LXX	Mark	4.12
Isaiah	6.9–10	LXX	Acts	28.26–27
Isaiah	6.10	LXX	John	12.40
Isaiah	7.14	LXX	Matthew	1.23
Isaiah	8.8, 10	LXX	Matthew	1.23
Isaiah	8.12–13		1 Peter	3.14–15
Isaiah	8.14		Romans	9.33
Isaiah	8.14		1 Peter	2.8
Isaiah	8.17	LXX	Hebrews	2.13
Isaiah	8.18		Hebrews	2.13
Isaiah	9.1–2		Matthew	4.15–16
Isaiah	10.22–23	LXX	Romans	9.27–28
Isaiah	11.4		2 Thessalonians	2.8
Isaiah	11.5		Ephesians	6.14
Isaiah	11.10	LXX	Romans	15.12
Isaiah	14.13, 15		Matthew	11.23
Isaiah	14.13, 15		Luke	10.15
Isaiah	22.13		1 Corinthians	15.32
Isaiah	22.22		Revelation	3.7
Isaiah	24.17		Luke	21.35
Isaiah	25.8		1 Corinthians	15.54
Isaiah	27.9	LXX	Romans	11.27
Isaiah	28.11–12		1 Corinthians	14.21
Isaiah	28.16	LXX	Romans	9.33
Isaiah	28.16		Romans	10.11
Isaiah	28.16		1 Peter	2.6
Isaiah	29.10		Romans	11.8
Isaiah	29.13	LXX	Matthew	15.8–9
Isaiah	29.13		Mark	7.6–7
Isaiah	29.13		Colossians	2.22
Isaiah	29.14	LXX	1 Corinthians	1.19
Isaiah	29.16		Romans	9.20
Isaiah	35.3		Hebrews	12.12
Isaiah	35.5–6		Matthew	11.5
Isaiah	35.5–6		Luke	7.22
Isaiah	40.3	LXX	Matthew	3.3
Isaiah	40.3		Mark	1.3
Isaiah	40.3		John	1.23

OT	OT Ref.	Version	NT	NT Ref.
Isaiah	40.3–5	LXX	Luke	3.4–6
Isaiah	40.6–8		1 Peter	1.24–25
Isaiah	40.13	LXX	Romans	11.34
Isaiah	40.13		1 Corinthians	2.16
Isaiah	41.8		James	2.23
Isaiah	42.1		Matthew	3.17
Isaiah	42.1		Matthew	17.5
Isaiah	42.1		Mark	1.11
Isaiah	42.1		Luke	3.22
Isaiah	42.1		Luke	9.35
Isaiah	42.1		2 Peter	1.17
Isaiah	42.1–3		Matthew	12.18–20
Isaiah	42.4	LXX	Matthew	12.21
Isaiah	43.20–21	LXX	1 Peter	2.9
Isaiah	45.9		Romans	9.20
Isaiah	45.21		Mark	12.32
Isaiah	45.23	LXX	Romans	14.11
Isaiah	45.23		Philippians	2.10–11
Isaiah	49.1		Galatians	1.15
Isaiah	49.6		Acts	13.47
Isaiah	49.8		2 Corinthians	6.2
Isaiah	49.18		Romans	14.11
Isaiah	52.5	LXX	Romans	2.24
Isaiah	52.7		Romans	10.15
Isaiah	52.7		Ephesians	6.15
Isaiah	52.11		2 Corinthians	6.17
Isaiah	52.15	LXX	Romans	15.21
Isaiah	53.1	LXX	John	12.38
Isaiah	53.1		Romans	10.16
Isaiah	53.4		Matthew	8.17
Isaiah	53.4–6		1 Peter	2.24–25
Isaiah	53.7–8	LXX	Acts	8.32–33
Isaiah	53.9		1 Peter	2.22
Isaiah	53.12		Luke	22.37
Isaiah	53.12		Hebrews	9.28
Isaiah	53.12		1 Peter	2.24
Isaiah	54.1		Galatians	4.27
Isaiah	54.13		John	6.45
Isaiah	55.3	LXX	Acts	13.34
Isaiah	56.7		Matthew	21.13
Isaiah	56.7		Mark	11.17
Isaiah	56.7		Luke	19.46
Isaiah	57.19		Ephesians	2.17

OT	OT Ref.	Version	NT	NT Ref.
Isaiah	59.7–8		Romans	3.15–17
Isaiah	59.17		Ephesians	6.14, 17
Isaiah	59.17		1 Thessalonians	5.8
Isaiah	59.20–21	LXX	Romans	11.26–27
Isaiah	61.1		Matthew	11.5
Isaiah	61.1–2	LXX	Luke	4.18–19
Isaiah	61.1		Luke	7.22
Isaiah	62.11		Matthew	21.5
Isaiah	64.4		1 Corinthians	2.9
Isaiah	65.1–2	LXX	Romans	10.20–21
Isaiah	65.17		2 Peter	3.13
Isaiah	65.17		Revelation	21.2
Isaiah	66.1		Matthew	5.34–35
Isaiah	66.1–2		Acts	7.49–50
Isaiah	66.15		2 Thessalonians	1.8
Isaiah	66.24		Mark	9.48
Jeremiah	1.5		Galatians	1.15–16
Jeremiah	5.21		Mark	8.18
Jeremiah	7.11		Matthew	21.13
Jeremiah	7.11		Mark	11.17
Jeremiah	7.11		Luke	19.46
Jeremiah	9.24		1 Corinthians	1.31
Jeremiah	9.24		2 Corinthians	10.17
Jeremiah	16.16		Mark	1.17
Jeremiah	18.6		Romans	9.21
Jeremiah	22.5		Matthew	23.38
Jeremiah	22.5		Luke	13.35
Jeremiah	31.15		Matthew	2.18
Jeremiah	31.31–34		Hebrews	8.8–12
Jeremiah	31.33–34		Romans	11.27
Jeremiah	31.33–34		Hebrews	10.16–17
Ezekiel	12.2		Mark	8.18
Ezekiel	20.34, 41		2 Corinthians	6.17
Ezekiel	34.5		Matthew	9.36
Ezekiel	34.5		Mark	6.34
Ezekiel	37.27		2 Corinthians	6.16
Daniel	5.23		Revelation	9.20
Daniel	7.2–7		Revelation	13.1–2
Daniel	7.13		Matthew	24.30
Daniel	7.13		Matthew	26.64

OT	OT Ref.	Version	NT	NT Ref.
Daniel	7.13		Mark	13.26
Daniel	7.13		Mark	14.62
Daniel	7.13		Luke	21.27
Daniel	7.13		Revelation	1.7
Daniel	7.21		Revelation	13.7
Daniel	7.25		Revelation	12.14
Daniel	11.31		Matthew	24.15
Daniel	11.31		Mark	13.14
Daniel	11.36		2 Thessalonians	2.4
Daniel	12.7		Revelation	12.14
Daniel	12.11		Matthew	24.15
Daniel	12.11		Mark	13.14
Hosea	1.10		Romans	9.26
Hosea	2.23		Romans	9.25
Hosea	2.23		1 Peter	2.10
Hosea	6.6		Matthew	9.13
Hosea	6.6		Matthew	12.7
Hosea	10.8		Luke	23.30
Hosea	10.8		Revelation	6.16
Hosea	11.1		Matthew	2.15
Hosea	13.14	LXX	1 Corinthians	15.55
Joel	2.28–32	LXX	Acts	2.17–21
Joel	2.32		Romans	10.13
Amos	5.25–27	LXX	Acts	7.42–43
Amos	9.11–12		Acts	15.16–17
Jonah	1.17		Matthew	12.40
Micah	5.2		Matthew	2.6
Micah	5.2		John	7.42
Micah	7.6		Matthew	10.35–36
Micah	7.6		Luke	12.53
Nahum	1.15		Ephesians	6.15
Habakkuk	1.5	LXX	Acts	13.41
Habakkuk	2.3–4	LXX	Hebrews	10.37–38
Habakkuk	2.4		Romans	1.17
Habakkuk	2.4		Galatians	3.11

OT	OT Ref.	Version	NT	NT Ref.
Haggai	2.6	LXX	Hebrews	12.26
Zechariah	8.16		Ephesians	4.25
Zechariah	9.9		Matthew	21.5
Zechariah	9.9		John	12.15
Zechariah	10.2		Matthew	9.36
Zechariah	10.2		Mark	6.34
Zechariah	11.12		Matthew	26.15
Zechariah	11.12–13		Matthew	27.9–10
Zechariah	12.10		John	19.37
Zechariah	12.10		Revelation	1.7
Zechariah	13.7		Matthew	26.31
Zechariah	13.7		Mark	14.27
Malachi	1.2–3		Romans	9.13
Malachi	3.1		Matthew	11.10
Malachi	3.1		Mark	1.2
Malachi	3.1		Luke	1.76
Malachi	3.1		Luke	7.27
Malachi	4.5–6		Matthew	17.10–11
Malachi	4.5–6		Mark	9.11–12
Malachi	4.5–6		Luke	1.17

Old Testament Sources of Quotations in the New Testament

NT	NT Ref.	OT	OT Ref.	Version
Matthew	1.23	Isaiah	7.14	LXX
Matthew	1.23	Isaiah	8.8, 10	LXX
Matthew	2.6	Micah	5.2	
Matthew	2.15	Hosea	11.1	
Matthew	2.18	Jeremiah	31.15	
Matthew	3.3	Isaiah	40.3	LXX
Matthew	3.17	Isaiah	42.1	
Matthew	4.4	Deuteronomy	8.3	
Matthew	4.6	Psalms	91.11–12	
Matthew	4.7	Deuteronomy	6.16	
Matthew	4.10	Deuteronomy	6.13	
Matthew	4.15–16	Isaiah	9.1–2	
Matthew	5.5	Psalms	37.11	
Matthew	5.21	Exodus	20.13	
Matthew	5.21	Deuteronomy	5.17	
Matthew	5.27	Exodus	20.14	
Matthew	5.27	Deuteronomy	5.18	
Matthew	5.31	Deuteronomy	24.1	
Matthew	5.33	Leviticus	19.12	
Matthew	5.33	Numbers	30.2	
Matthew	5.34–35	Isaiah	66.1	
Matthew	5.35	Psalms	48.2	
Matthew	5.38	Exodus	21.24	
Matthew	5.38	Leviticus	24.20	
Matthew	5.38	Deuteronomy	19.21	
Matthew	5.43	Leviticus	19.18	
Matthew	8.17	Isaiah	53.4	
Matthew	9.13	Hosea	6.6	
Matthew	9.36	Numbers	27.17	
Matthew	9.36	1 Kings	22.17	
Matthew	9.36	2 Chronicles	18.16	
Matthew	9.36	Ezekiel	34.5	

NT	NT Ref.	OT	OT Ref.	Version
Matthew	9.36	Zechariah	10.2	
Matthew	10.35–36	Micah	7.6	
Matthew	11.5	Isaiah	35.5–6	
Matthew	11.5	Isaiah	61.1	
Matthew	11.10	Malachi	3.1	
Matthew	11.23	Isaiah	14.13, 15	
Matthew	12.7	Hosea	6.6	
Matthew	12.18–20	Isaiah	42.1–3	
Matthew	12.21	Isaiah	42.4	LXX
Matthew	12.40	Jonah	1.17	
Matthew	13.14–15	Isaiah	6.9–10	LXX
Matthew	13.35	Psalms	78.2	
Matthew	15.4	Exodus	20.12	
Matthew	15.4	Exodus	21.17	
Matthew	15.4	Deuteronomy	5.16	
Matthew	15.8–9	Isaiah	29.13	LXX
Matthew	17.5	Isaiah	42.1	
Matthew	17.10–11	Malachi	4.5–6	
Matthew	18.16	Deuteronomy	19.15	
Matthew	19.4	Genesis	1.27	
Matthew	19.4	Genesis	5.2	
Matthew	19.5	Genesis	2.24	
Matthew	19.7	Deuteronomy	24.1	
Matthew	19.18–19	Exodus	20.12–16	
Matthew	19.18–19	Deuteronomy	5.16–20	
Matthew	19.19	Leviticus	19.18	
Matthew	21.5	Isaiah	62.11	
Matthew	21.5	Zechariah	9.9	
Matthew	21.9	Psalms	118.25–26	
Matthew	21.13	Isaiah	56.7	
Matthew	21.13	Jeremiah	7.11	
Matthew	21.26	Psalms	8.3	LXX
Matthew	21.33	Isaiah	5.1–2	
Matthew	21.42	Psalms	118.22–23	
Matthew	22.24	Deuteronomy	25.5	
Matthew	22.32	Exodus	3.6	
Matthew	22.32	Exodus	3.15	
Matthew	22.37	Deuteronomy	6.5	
Matthew	22.39	Leviticus	19.18	
Matthew	22.44	Psalms	110.1	
Matthew	23.38	Jeremiah	22.5	
Matthew	23.39	Psalms	118.26	
Matthew	24.15	Daniel	11.31	

NT	NT Ref.	OT	OT Ref.	Version
Matthew	24.15	Daniel	12.11	
Matthew	24.30	Daniel	7.13	
Matthew	26.15	Zechariah	11.12	
Matthew	26.31	Zechariah	13.7	
Matthew	26.64	Psalms	110.1	
Matthew	26.64	Daniel	7.13	
Matthew	27.9–10	Zechariah	11.12–13	
Matthew	27.35	Psalms	22.18	
Matthew	27.39	Psalms	22.7	
Matthew	27.43	Psalms	22.8	
Matthew	27.46	Psalms	22.1	
Matthew	27.48	Psalms	69.21	
Mark	1.2	Malachi	3.1	
Mark	1.3	Isaiah	40.3	
Mark	1.11	Psalms	2.7	
Mark	1.11	Isaiah	42.1	
Mark	1.17	Jeremiah	16.16	
Mark	4.12	Isaiah	6.9–10	LXX
Mark	6.34	Numbers	27.17	
Mark	6.34	1 Kings	22.17	
Mark	6.34	2 Chronicles	18.16	
Mark	6.34	Ezekiel	34.5	
Mark	6.34	Zechariah	10.2	
Mark	7.6–7	Isaiah	29.13	
Mark	7.10	Exodus	20.12	
Mark	7.10	Exodus	21.17	
Mark	7.10	Deuteronomy	5.16	
Mark	8.18	Jeremiah	5.21	
Mark	8.18	Ezekiel	12.2	
Mark	9.11–12	Malachi	4.5–6	
Mark	9.48	Isaiah	66.24	
Mark	9.49	Leviticus	2.13	
Mark	10.4	Deuteronomy	24.1, 3	
Mark	10.6	Genesis	1.27	
Mark	10.6	Genesis	5.2	
Mark	10.7–8	Genesis	2.24	
Mark	10.19	Exodus	20.12–16	
Mark	10.19	Deuteronomy	5.16–20	
Mark	11.9	Psalms	118.25–26	
Mark	11.17	Isaiah	56.7	
Mark	11.17	Jeremiah	7.11	
Mark	12.1	Isaiah	5.1–2	

NT	NT Ref.	OT	OT Ref.	Version
Mark	12.10–11	Psalms	118.22–23	
Mark	12.19	Deuteronomy	25.5	
Mark	12.26	Exodus	3.6	
Mark	12.26	Exodus	3.15	
Mark	12.29–30	Deuteronomy	6.4–5	
Mark	12.31, 33	Leviticus	19.18	
Mark	12.32	Deuteronomy	4.35	
Mark	12.32	Isaiah	45.21	
Mark	12.32–33	Deuteronomy	6.4–5	
Mark	12.36	Psalms	110.1	
Mark	13.14	Daniel	11.31	
Mark	13.14	Daniel	12.11	
Mark	13.26	Daniel	7.13	
Mark	14.27	Zechariah	13.7	
Mark	14.62	Psalms	110.1	
Mark	14.62	Daniel	7.13	
Mark	15.24	Psalms	22.18	
Mark	15.29	Psalms	22.7	
Mark	15.34	Psalms	22.1	
Mark	15.36	Psalms	69.21	
Mark	16.19	Psalms	110.1	
Luke	1.17	Malachi	4.5–6	
Luke	1.46–47	1 Samuel	2.1	
Luke	1.50	Psalms	103.17	
Luke	1.76	Malachi	3.1	
Luke	2.23	Exodus	13.2	
Luke	2.23	Exodus	13.12	
Luke	2.24	Leviticus	12.6–8	
Luke	2.32	Exodus	13.15	
Luke	2.52	1 Samuel	2.26	
Luke	3.4–6	Isaiah	40.3–5	LXX
Luke	3.22	Psalms	2.7	
Luke	3.22	Isaiah	42.1	
Luke	4.4	Deuteronomy	8.3	
Luke	4.8	Deuteronomy	6.13	
Luke	4.10–11	Psalms	91.11–12	
Luke	4.12	Deuteronomy	6.16	
Luke	4.18–19	Isaiah	61.1–2	LXX
Luke	7.22	Isaiah	35.5–6	
Luke	7.22	Isaiah	61.1	
Luke	7.27	Malachi	3.1	
Luke	8.10	Isaiah	6.9	LXX

NT	NT Ref.	OT	OT Ref.	Version
Luke	9.35	Isaiah	42.1	
Luke	9.54	2 Kings	1.10, 12	
Luke	10.15	Isaiah	14.13, 15	
Luke	10.27	Leviticus	19.18	
Luke	10.27	Deuteronomy	6.5	
Luke	12.53	Micah	7.6	
Luke	13.35	Psalms	118.26	
Luke	13.35	Jeremiah	22.5	
Luke	18.20	Deuteronomy	5.16–20	
Luke	18.30	Exodus	20.12–16	
Luke	19.38	Psalms	118.26	
Luke	19.46	Isaiah	56.7	
Luke	19.46	Jeremiah	7.11	
Luke	20.17	Psalms	118.22–23	
Luke	20.28	Deuteronomy	25.5	
Luke	20.37	Exodus	3.6	
Luke	20.37	Exodus	3.15	
Luke	20.42–43	Psalms	110.1	
Luke	21.27	Daniel	7.13	
Luke	21.35	Isaiah	24.17	
Luke	22.37	Isaiah	53.12	
Luke	22.69	Psalms	110.1	
Luke	23.30	Hosea	10.8	
Luke	23.34	Psalms	22.18	
Luke	23.35	Psalms	22.7	
Luke	23.46	Psalms	31.5	
John	1.23	Isaiah	40.3	
John	2.17	Psalms	69.9	
John	6.31	Exodus	16.4	
John	6.31	Nehemiah	9.15	
John	6.31	Psalms	78.24	
John	6.45	Isaiah	54.13	
John	7.42	Micah	5.2	
John	8.17	Deuteronomy	19.15	
John	10.34	Psalms	82.6	
John	12.13	Psalms	118.25–26	
John	12.15	Zechariah	9.9	
John	12.38	Isaiah	53.1	LXX
John	12.40	Isaiah	6.10	LXX
John	13.18	Psalms	41.9	
John	15.25	Psalms	35.19	
John	15.25	Psalms	69.4	

NT	NT Ref.	OT	OT Ref.	Version
John	19.24	Psalms	22.18	
John	19.28–29	Psalms	69.21	
John	19.36	Exodus	12.46	
John	19.36	Numbers	9.12	
John	19.36	Psalms	34.20	
John	19.37	Zechariah	12.10	
Acts	1.20	Psalms	69.25	
Acts	1.20	Psalms	109.8	
Acts	2.3	2 Samuel	7.12–13	
Acts	2.17–21	Joel	2.28–32	LXX
Acts	2.25–28	Psalms	16.8–11	LXX
Acts	2.30	Psalms	132.11	
Acts	2.31	Psalms	16.10	
Acts	2.34–35	Psalms	110.1	
Acts	3.13	Exodus	3.6	
Acts	3.13, 7.32	Exodus	3.15	
Acts	3.22–23	Deuteronomy	18.15–19	
Acts	3.25	Genesis	22.18	
Acts	3.25	Genesis	26.4	
Acts	4.11	Psalms	118.22	
Acts	4.25–26	Psalms	2.1–2	LXX
Acts	7.3	Genesis	12.1	
Acts	7.3	Exodus	3.2	
Acts	7.5	Genesis	17.8	
Acts	7.5	Genesis	48.4	
Acts	7.6–7	Genesis	15.13–14	
Acts	7.7	Exodus	3.12	
Acts	7.18	Exodus	1.8	
Acts	7.23–29	Exodus	2.11–15	
Acts	7.27–28, 35	Exodus	2.14	
Acts	7.32	Exodus	3.6	
Acts	7.32–34	Exodus	3.5–10	
Acts	7.37	Deuteronomy	18.15	
Acts	7.40	Exodus	32.1	
Acts	7.40	Exodus	32.23	
Acts	7.42–43	Amos	5.25–27	LXX
Acts	7.49–50	Isaiah	66.1–2	
Acts	8.32–33	Isaiah	53.7–8	LXX
Acts	13.22	1 Samuel	13.14	
Acts	13.33	Psalms	2.7	
Acts	13.34	Isaiah	55.3	LXX
Acts	13.35	Psalms	16.10	LXX

NT	NT Ref.	OT	OT Ref.	Version
Acts	13.41	Habakkuk	1.5	LXX
Acts	13.47	Isaiah	49.6	
Acts	15.16–17	Amos	9.11–12	
Acts	23.5	Exodus	22.28	
Acts	28.26–27	Isaiah	6.9–10	LXX
Romans	1.17	Habakkuk	2.4	
Romans	2.24	Isaiah	52.5	LXX
Romans	3.4	Psalms	51.4	LXX
Romans	3.10–12	Psalms	14.1–3	
Romans	3.10–12	Psalms	53.1–3	
Romans	3.13	Psalms	5.9	LXX
Romans	3.13	Psalms	140.3	LXX
Romans	3.14	Psalms	10.7	LXX
Romans	3.15–17	Isaiah	59.7–8	
Romans	3.18	Psalms	36.1	
Romans	3.20	Psalms	143.2	
Romans	4.3, 9, 22	Genesis	15.6	
Romans	4.7–8	Psalms	32.1–2	
Romans	4.17, 18	Genesis	17.5	
Romans	4.18	Genesis	15.5	
Romans	7.7	Exodus	20.17	
Romans	7.7	Deuteronomy	5.21	
Romans	8.36	Psalms	44.22	
Romans	9.7	Genesis	21.12	
Romans	9.9	Genesis	18.10	
Romans	9.9	Genesis	18.14	
Romans	9.12	Genesis	25.23	
Romans	9.13	Malachi	1.2–3	
Romans	9.15	Exodus	33.19	
Romans	9.17	Exodus	9.16	LXX
Romans	9.20	Isaiah	29.16	
Romans	9.20	Isaiah	45.9	
Romans	9.21	Jeremiah	18.6	
Romans	9.25	Hosea	2.23	
Romans	9.26	Hosea	1.10	
Romans	9.27–28	Isaiah	10.22–23	LXX
Romans	9.29	Isaiah	1.9	LXX
Romans	9.33	Isaiah	8.14	
Romans	9.33	Isaiah	28.16	LXX
Romans	10.5	Leviticus	18.5	
Romans	10.6	Deuteronomy	9.4	
Romans	10.6–8	Deuteronomy	30.12–14	

NT	NT Ref.	OT	OT Ref.	Version
Romans	10.11	Isaiah	28.16	
Romans	10.13	Joel	2.32	
Romans	10.15	Isaiah	52.7	
Romans	10.16	Isaiah	53.1	
Romans	10.18	Psalms	19.4	LXX
Romans	10.19	Deuteronomy	32.21	
Romans	10.20–21	Isaiah	65.1–2	LXX
Romans	11.2	Psalms	94.14	
Romans	11.3	1 Kings	19.10, 14	
Romans	11.4	1 Kings	19.18	
Romans	11.8	Deuteronomy	29.4	
Romans	11.8	Isaiah	29.10	
Romans	11.9–10	Psalms	69.22–23	LXX
Romans	11.26–27	Isaiah	59.20–21	LXX
Romans	11.27	Isaiah	27.9	LXX
Romans	11.27	Jeremiah	31.33–34	
Romans	11.34	Isaiah	40.13	LXX
Romans	11.35	Job	41.11	
Romans	12.19	Deuteronomy	32.35	
Romans	12.20	Proverbs	25.21–22	LXX
Romans	13.9	Exodus	20.13–15, 17	
Romans	13.9	Leviticus	19.18	
Romans	13.9	Deuteronomy	5.17–19, 21	
Romans	14.11	Isaiah	45.23	LXX
Romans	14.11	Isaiah	49.18	
Romans	15.3	Psalms	69.9	
Romans	15.9	2 Samuel	22.5	
Romans	15.9	Psalms	18.49	
Romans	15.10	Deuteronomy	32.43	
Romans	15.11	Psalms	117.1	
Romans	15.12	Isaiah	11.10	LXX
Romans	15.21	Isaiah	52.15	LXX
1 Corinthians	1.19	Isaiah	29.14	LXX
1 Corinthians	1.31	Jeremiah	9.24	
1 Corinthians	2.9	Isaiah	64.4	
1 Corinthians	2.16	Isaiah	40.13	
1 Corinthians	3.19	Job	5.13	
1 Corinthians	3.20	Psalms	94.11	
1 Corinthians	5.13	Deuteronomy	17.7	LXX
1 Corinthians	5.13	Deuteronomy	19.19	
1 Corinthians	5.13	Deuteronomy	22.21, 24	
1 Corinthians	5.13	Deuteronomy	24.7	

NT	NT Ref.	OT	OT Ref.	Version
1 Corinthians	6.16	Genesis	2.24	
1 Corinthians	9.9	Deuteronomy	25.4	
1 Corinthians	10.7	Exodus	32.6	
1 Corinthians	10.20	Deuteronomy	32.17	
1 Corinthians	10.22	Deuteronomy	32.21	
1 Corinthians	10.26	Psalms	24.1	
1 Corinthians	14.21	Isaiah	28.11–12	
1 Corinthians	15.25	Psalms	110.1	
1 Corinthians	15.27	Psalms	8.6	
1 Corinthians	15.32	Isaiah	22.13	
1 Corinthians	15.45	Genesis	2.7	
1 Corinthians	15.54	Isaiah	25.8	
1 Corinthians	15.55	Hosea	13.14	LXX
2 Corinthians	3.7	Exodus	34.30	
2 Corinthians	3.13	Exodus	34.33, 35	
2 Corinthians	3.16	Exodus	34.34	
2 Corinthians	4.13	Psalms	116.10	LXX
2 Corinthians	6.2	Isaiah	49.8	
2 Corinthians	6.16	Leviticus	26.12	
2 Corinthians	6.16	Ezekiel	37.27	
2 Corinthians	6.17	Isaiah	52.11	
2 Corinthians	6.17	Ezekiel	20.34, 41	
2 Corinthians	6.18	2 Samuel	7.8, 14	
2 Corinthians	8.15	Exodus	16.18	
2 Corinthians	8.21	Proverbs	3.4	
2 Corinthians	9.7	Proverbs	22.9	
2 Corinthians	9.9	Psalms	112.9	
2 Corinthians	10.17	Jeremiah	9.24	
2 Corinthians	13.1	Deuteronomy	19.15	
Galatians	1.15	Isaiah	49.1	
Galatians	1.15–16	Jeremiah	1.5	
Galatians	3.6	Genesis	15.6	
Galatians	3.8	Genesis	12.3	
Galatians	3.8	Genesis	18.18	
Galatians	3.10	Deuteronomy	27.26	LXX
Galatians	3.11	Habakkuk	2.4	
Galatians	3.12	Leviticus	18.5	
Galatians	3.13	Deuteronomy	21.23	
Galatians	3.16	Genesis	12.7	
Galatians	4.27	Isaiah	54.1	
Galatians	4.30	Genesis	21.10	

NT	NT Ref.	OT	OT Ref.	Version
Galatians	5.14	Leviticus	19.18	
Ephesians	1.2	Psalms	110.1	
Ephesians	1.22	Psalms	8.6	
Ephesians	2.17	Isaiah	57.19	
Ephesians	4.8	Psalms	68.18	
Ephesians	4.25	Zechariah	8.16	
Ephesians	4.26	Psalms	4.4	LXX
Ephesians	5.31	Genesis	2.24	
Ephesians	6.2–3	Exodus	20.12	
Ephesians	6.2–3	Deuteronomy	5.16	
Ephesians	6.14	Isaiah	11.5	
Ephesians	6.14, 17	Isaiah	59.17	
Ephesians	6.15	Isaiah	52.7	
Ephesians	6.15	Nahum	1.15	
Philippians	2.10–11	Isaiah	45.23	
Colossians	2.22	Isaiah	29.13	
Colossians	3.1	Psalms	110.1	
1 Thessalonians	5.8	Isaiah	59.17	
2 Thessalonians	1.8	Isaiah	66.15	
2 Thessalonians	2.4	Daniel	11.36	
2 Thessalonians	2.8	Isaiah	11.4	
1 Timothy	5.18	Deuteronomy	25.4	
1 Timothy	5.19	Deuteronomy	19.15	
2 Timothy	2.19	Numbers	16.5	
Hebrews	1.3, 13	Psalms	110.1	
Hebrews	1.5	2 Samuel	7.14	
Hebrews	1.5	Psalms	2.7	
Hebrews	1.6	Deuteronomy	32.43	LXX
Hebrews	1.7	Psalms	104.4	LXX
Hebrews	1.8–9	Psalms	45.6–7	
Hebrews	1.10–12	Psalms	102.25–27	LXX
Hebrews	2.6–8	Psalms	8.4–6	LXX
Hebrews	2.12	Psalms	22.22	
Hebrews	2.13	Isaiah	8.17	LXX
Hebrews	2.13	Isaiah	8.18	
Hebrews	3.2, 5	Numbers	12.7	

NT	NT Ref.	OT	OT Ref.	Version
Hebrews	3.7–11	Psalms	95.7–11	
Hebrews	3.15	Psalms	95.7–8	LXX
Hebrews	3.18	Psalms	95.11	
Hebrews	4.3, 5, 10	Psalms	95.11	
Hebrews	4.4	Genesis	2.2	
Hebrews	4.7	Psalms	95.7–8	
Hebrews	5.5	Psalms	2.7	
Hebrews	5.6	Psalms	110.4	
Hebrews	6.13–14	Genesis	22.16–17	
Hebrews	7.1–2	Genesis	14.17–20	
Hebrews	7.17, 21	Psalms	110.4	
Hebrews	8.1	Psalms	110.1	
Hebrews	8.5	Exodus	25.40	
Hebrews	8.8–12	Jeremiah	31.31–34	
Hebrews	9.20	Exodus	24.8	
Hebrews	9.28	Isaiah	53.12	
Hebrews	10.5–7	Psalms	40.6–8	
Hebrews	10.12–13	Psalms	110.1	
Hebrews	10.16–17	Jeremiah	31.33–34	
Hebrews	10.28	Deuteronomy	17.6	
Hebrews	10.30	Deuteronomy	32.35	
Hebrews	10.30	Deuteronomy	32.36	
Hebrews	10.30	Psalms	135.14	
Hebrews	10.37–38	Habakkuk	2.3–4	LXX
Hebrews	11.5	Genesis	5.24	LXX
Hebrews	11.18	Genesis	21.12	
Hebrews	11.21	Genesis	47.31	LXX
Hebrews	12.2	Psalms	110.1	
Hebrews	12.5–6	Proverbs	3.11–12	LXX
Hebrews	12.12	Isaiah	35.3	
Hebrews	12.13	Proverbs	4.26	
Hebrews	12.15	Deuteronomy	29.18	
Hebrews	12.20	Exodus	19.12–13	
Hebrews	12.21	Deuteronomy	9.19	
Hebrews	12.26	Haggai	2.6	LXX
Hebrews	12.29	Deuteronomy	4.24	
Hebrews	13.5	Deuteronomy	31.6, 8	
Hebrews	13.5	Joshua	1.5	
Hebrews	13.6	Psalms	118.6	LXX
Hebrews	13.11	Leviticus	16.27	
James	2.8	Leviticus	19.18	
James	2.11	Exodus	20.13–14	

NT	NT Ref.	OT	OT Ref.	Version
James	2.11	Deuteronomy	5.17–18	
James	2.23	Genesis	15.6	
James	2.23	Isaiah	41.8	
James	4.6	Proverbs	3.34	LXX
James	5.11	Psalms	103.8	
1 Peter	1.16	Leviticus	11.44–45	
1 Peter	1.16	Leviticus	19.2	
1 Peter	1.24–25	Isaiah	40.6–8	
1 Peter	2.3	Psalms	34.8	
1 Peter	2.6	Isaiah	28.16	
1 Peter	2.7	Psalms	118.22	
1 Peter	2.8	Isaiah	8.14	
1 Peter	2.9	Exodus	19.5–6	LXX
1 Peter	2.9	Isaiah	43.20–21	LXX
1 Peter	2.10	Hosea	2.23	
1 Peter	2.22	Isaiah	53.9	
1 Peter	2.24	Isaiah	53.12	
1 Peter	2.24–25	Isaiah	53.4–6	
1 Peter	3.10–12	Psalms	34.12–16	
1 Peter	3.14–15	Isaiah	8.12–13	
1 Peter	4.8	Proverbs	10.12	
1 Peter	4.18	Proverbs	11.31	LXX
1 Peter	5.5	Proverbs	3.34	
2 Peter	1.17	Isaiah	42.1	
2 Peter	2.22	Proverbs	26.11	
2 Peter	3.8	Psalms	90.4	
2 Peter	3.13	Isaiah	65.17	
Revelation	1.7	Daniel	7.13	
Revelation	1.7	Zechariah	12.10	
Revelation	2.26–27	Psalms	2.8–9	
Revelation	3.7	Isaiah	22.22	
Revelation	3.19	Proverbs	3.12	
Revelation	4.8	Isaiah	6.3	
Revelation	6.16	Hosea	10.8	
Revelation	9.20	Daniel	5.23	
Revelation	12.14	Daniel	7.25	
Revelation	12.14	Daniel	12.7	
Revelation	13.1–2	Daniel	7.2–7	
Revelation	13.7	Daniel	7.21	
Revelation	21.2	Isaiah	65.17